Reading Church Latin

Techniques and Commentary for Comprehension

Robert Schoenstene

Hillenbrand Books

Chicago / Mundelein, Illinois

READING CHURCH LATIN: TECHNIQUES AND COMMENTARY FOR COMPREHENSION © 2016 Archdiocese of Chicago: Liturgy Training Publications, 3949 South Racine Avenue, Chicago, IL 60609; 800-933-1800; fax: 800-933-7094; email: orders@ltp.org; website: www.ltp.org. All rights reserved.

Hillenbrand Books is an imprint of Liturgy Training Publications (LTP) and the Liturgical Institute at the University of St. Mary of the Lake (USML). The imprint is focused on contemporary and classical theological thought concerning the liturgy of the Catholic Church. Available at bookstores everywhere, through LTP by calling 800-933-1800, or visiting www.LTP.org.

Cover image © The Crosiers/Gene Plaisted, osc.

Printed in the United States of America

26 25 24 23 22   2 3 4 5 6

Library of Congress Control Number: 2016932975

ISBN: 978-1-59525-042-1

HRCL

To the memory of Fr. Joseph Przysucha, CR, who in his teaching of
Latin and Greek at Weber High School in Chicago, somehow turned
the burden of learning dead languages into a love for what
they could communicate.

Contents

Preface

"Latin is a dead tongue, as dead as it can be, first it killed the Romans, and now it's killing me." This jingle was something that many high school students of Latin would have heard fifty years ago, when Latin was a common topic of secondary education. Latin is now a rarity in high school, and often comes as an unpleasant necessity for students of theology or philosophy. Students of these disciplines may need to know the basics of reading Church Latin texts, or of comparing them to translations, but do not wish to take up the burden of becoming scholars of Latin.

This little book will teach you what you need to know; also, I hope it may foster an interest in learning and reading more of the ancient texts that continue to influence students today. At the very least it will help you develop a reading knowledge of Latin.

This book is intended to provide students of theology, philosophy, or Scripture with an introduction to the art of reading texts written in ecclesiastical Latin. The goal is to provide beginners in Latin with the tools to be able to deal with texts encountered in theological, philosophical, historical, or scriptural research. A student who completes the lessons and exercises should be able to deal competently with, or at least to understand the gist of, an untranslated Latin text, and certainly to have the ability to compare a translated text to its original.

This book can be used either as a class text or for independent study. In each lesson the grammar and syntax encountered in a Latin text are explained and exercises drilling points of grammar, syntax, and vocabulary are included. Since the aim is the reading of Latin, I won't waste your time by requiring you to translate exercises from English to Latin. I have supplied some guides to the pronunciation of ecclesiastical Latin because sometime in your career, you may need to use a Latin phrase in conversation and I want to help you out. Accent and pronunciation are not stressed. I hope to help you to be able to read and understand a Latin text, not to be able to speak Latin (which is very rarely done!). For example, a sentence such as *Caesar exercitum ducit* could be pronounced as *Kaisar exerkitum dukit, Chāsar exerchitum duchit* or *Sesar exersitum dusit.* Since Latin is no longer a spoken language, the pronunciation is rather less important than knowing that it means *Caesar is leading the army.*

To simplify matters, long vowels are only marked as such in cases where a confusion of form could occur. In first declension nouns, for example, the ablative singular will be marked with a long ā to avoid confusion with the short a of the nominative. Similarly, verbs of the second conjugation will have a long ē marked in the infinitive to avoid confusion with the short e of the third conjugation. For anyone interested in the length of vowels in the inflection of nouns, adjectives, and verbs, there is an appendix of morphology in which all the long vowels are marked with a macron.

ORGANIZATION OF THE BOOK

In the study of each lesson, the student should read through the Latin text at least three times, along with its translation. The commentary following the translation will point out the grammar and syntax, but it is in the close comparison of text and translation that the student should be able to gain insights into the working of Latin theological literature. The texts are taken from prayers, liturgical, biblical, patristic, and medieval theological and hymn texts. Each lesson has a vocabulary list of new (and sometime of already seen) words. The drills provide a way to exercise the grammar, syntax, and vocabulary of each lesson.

In the later lessons there are additional readings supplied, which have fewer notes and no translation. These will prepare students for the reading of texts on their own. A glossary of the Latin words that appear in the texts and lessons is supplied.

The study of Latin can be a difficult affair. It is hoped that this book will make the acquisition of a basic reading knowledge of ecclesiastical Latin a bit easier and a bit more interesting than it might otherwise have been. For most students, the lessons in this book may be their only occasion of studying Latin. For those who may wish to learn more, it should provide a good foundation.

An answer key for the exercises is provided principally for students who are using this book for self-study. There is a temptation in working through the exercises to give up if a sentence or phrase seems to be impenetrable and to look for the answer in the back of the book. Don't do this. Struggling with an exercise is the best way to learn to read Latin. Look to the key only after you have come up with your own translation of the exercise. Another danger of becoming dependent on the key is that there may be several ways to translate a sentence or phrase, and the key will give only one. The key is there simply as a guide for you to check to see if your translation is on the right track.

This book began as an experiment in teaching Latin for one year to seminarians in pretheology at University of St. Mary of the Lake / Mundelein Seminary. It originally took the shape of loose leaf handouts. Thanks are due to Kevin Thornton of Hillenbrand Books™ who saw the possibilities of a book in those handouts. Thanks also to Christian Rocha, the copyeditor who offered many and valuable suggestions, and to Robin Hilliard who took time from teaching and raising her children to read the proofs. The designer, Juan Alberto Castillo, and production artist, Luis Leal, gave a beautiful form to those odd assortments of handouts. Thanks also to Christopher Magnus, who kept everything on schedule. These lessons began riddled with errors; most of them have been caught and corrected by the above-mentioned sharp-eyed readers. If any remain, they are my fault, not theirs.

Schola Prima
The First Lesson

Lectio

We begin the first lesson with the Sign of the Cross in Latin. This short prayer is of course a prayer we say every day—the Sign of the Cross. These words first appear in Matthew 28. Let's examine this simple statement of our Faith .

In nomine Patris, et Filii, et Spiritūs Sancti.

Translatio

In the name of the Father, and of the Son, and of the Holy Spirit.

Pronuntiatio

Unlike the pronunciation of written English, the pronunciation of Latin is quite regular. There are, however, various ways of pronouncing the language. In the United States, Church Latin is generally pronounced following the rules of Italian.

The word *in* is pronounced as the last syllable of *machine*. The *i* in *nomine, Patris, Filii, Spiritūs,* and *Sancti* follows the same pronunciation. The word *nomine* is pronounced with a long *o*, as in *boat*. The final *e* is pronounced as the *ey* in *they*. The accent falls on the first syllable: *no'mine*. The accent of *Patris* is also on the first syllable. All of the *i*'s in *Filii* are pronounced, with the accent on the first syllable: *Fi'li-i*. The *u* in *Spiritūs* is pronounced as a long *u* in *rude*. The accent also falls on the first syllable, as does the accent of *Sancti*.

Grammatica

Notice that in the English translation, the words *Father, Son, Holy Spirit* are all preceded by the preposition *of* and the definite article *the*. In Latin the article, definite (the) or indefinite (a, an), does not exist. The word *pater*, for example, can mean *father, a father,* or *the father*. An English translation must consider the context into which a noun is being translated, and supply or not supply a form of the English articles.

There are two ways of indicating possession in English. One is to use the preposition *of* followed by a noun or pronoun, as in the Sign of the Cross above. Another way is to use the possessive case form of a noun. The case ending for the possessive in English is usually an *s* preceded by an apostrophe, which indicates a vowel which is no longer pronounced: *the Father's name, the boy's book, the teachers' lounge.* In the last instance, *teachers* is plural, and the apostrophe follows rather than precedes the *s* because the form is a contraction of *teacherses.*

All three of the nouns *Patris, Filii,* and *Spiritūs* are in their possessive forms. In Latin, this case is regularly called the *genitive.* It indicates possession, and other things that will eventually be encountered. Latin does not indicate possession by using an equivalent of the English *of,* it indicates it by placing a noun or pronoun in the genitive case.

English has retained three cases, the forms of which show up more readily in pronouns than in nouns:

1. Nominative (the subject of a sentence): he, she, who, tree, book, they
2. Possessive (the owner of a thing): his, her, whose, tree's, book's, their
3. Objective (the object of a verb or preposition): him, her, whom, tree, book, them

Latin nouns are arranged in five groups, each group having similar endings and patterns in forming the cases. Each of these groups is called a *declension.* Latin nouns (and adjectives) have the following possibilities of case:

1. Nominative: as in English, the case of the subject of a sentence
2. Genitive: the case of the possessive and other specialized uses
3. Dative: the case of the indirect object, to or for whom something is done
4. Accusative: case of the direct object of a verb or of a preposition indicating motion
5. Ablative: the case of many prepositions, an indication of agency, and a number of other specialized uses
6. Vocative: the case of direct address (in English this is sometimes indicated by the particle O, as in prayers, O God . . .)

7.   Locative: a fairly rare case indicating place where, usually only used with names of cities or countries

In grammar books, generally only five of the seven cases are given in declensions, since for all but the second declension, the vocative is the same as the nominative, and the locative is rare.

When a noun is listed in a glossary, dictionary, or vocabulary list, it is usually given in the nominative case, along with the genitive ending. By knowing both the nominative and genitive, the declension of a noun can be easily known. Nouns must always be memorized with both the nominative and genitive forms. For example, the word for *lesson* is *schola*. This word is actually a loan word from Greek, in which the word originally meant *leisure*. (The *ch* in the word is from the Greek letter *chi*, and is pronounced as a *k*). In a vocabulary list, it would be given as *schola, scholae* or as *schola, -ae*. (The *ae* is pronounced in Church Latin just like the long *a* sound, as found in *they*.) The nominative and genitive endings provide enough information to understand that this noun belongs to the first declension. When translating, you will need to look at the endings of the nouns to be able to tell the case of the word, and its role in the sentence. You will eventually and gradually learn to recognize the five declensions.

English nouns do not have grammatical gender, other than in a few archaic instances. People and animals can be male or female, generally inanimate things are regarded as neuter. The pronouns *he, she,* and *it* indicate these genders. In Latin, individuals have natural gender, but even inanimate things may have grammatical gender. For example, *pater* (*father*) is masculine, as is *filius* (*son*). *Spiritus* (*wind, breath, spirit*) is also masculine, but *schola* (*class, lesson*) is feminine. A word such as *tabula* (*board, plank*) is also feminine. *Liber* (*book*) is masculine, while *nomen* (*name*) is neuter, as is *bellum* (*war*).

The gender of a noun must be learned along with its nominative and genitive forms, since both adjectives and pronouns must agree in gender and number with the nouns they are modifying or describing. Adjectives will also have the same case as the nouns they modify. *Number* grammatically means either singular (one) or plural (many). All of the nouns in the text for this lesson (*schola*) are singular.

Let us look again at the possessive forms *Patris, Filii,* and *Spiritūs: of the Father, of the Son,* and *of the Spirit* (or *Father's, Son's,*

Spirit's). The nominative forms of these three nouns are *Pater, Filius,* and *Spiritus.* In a vocabulary list, they would appear as follows:

pater, patris (or **pater, -tris**), *m.,* father
filius, filii (or **filius, -i**), *m.,* son
spiritus, spiritus (or **spiritus, -ūs**), *m.,* wind, breath, spirit

Notice that the nominative forms of *filius* and of *spiritus* look the same. The nominative ending for both is *-us.* However, the genitive of each noun is different. That of *filius* is *filii,* and that of *spiritus* is *spiritūs.* These nouns belong to different declensions. *Filius, -i* is a noun of the *second declension.* Most of the nouns of this declension are masculine in gender. These nouns have a nominative case ending in *-us* and a genitive case ending in *-i* in the singular. *Spiritus, -ūs* is a noun of the *fourth declension.* Most of these nouns are also masculine in gender; they are known by having their nominative singular end in *-us,* and their genitive singular in *-ūs.* (Notice that the genitive has a long *u,* which is here marked as *ū.* Long and short *u* in Church Latin have the same pronunciation. In the classical tongue, the long vowels would have had a longer pronunciation in time than the short vowels.)

The noun *pater, -tris* (*father*) is a noun of the *third declension.* This declension contains nouns in all three genders. *Pater* (*father*) is masculine by nature. The nominative of a third declension noun does not have a particular ending. The stem of the noun (that is, the form used for forming the various cases) is derived from the genitive case form, *patris.* The genitive ending is *-is.* If the ending is dropped, the stem appears as *patr-.* This type of formation is common in the third declension. For example, the word *mater, -tris* means *mother.* (Of course, the gender is feminine.) *Frater, -tris* is *brother,* and *soror, sororis* is *sister.*

The word *nomine* is also a third declension noun. Its nominative is *nomen,* the genitive is *nominis,* its gender is neuter, and the meaning is *name.* The form *nomine* should indicate to you that this is neither the genitive nor the nominative case form. It is, in fact, the ablative case. *Nomen* is in its ablative case form, *nomine,* because it follows the preposition *in,* which takes the ablative case. In the third declension, the ablative singular ending is *-e.* If one were to say *in the father,* the Latin would appear as *in patre.* Similarly, *in matre, in fratre, in sorore.*

Second declension nouns such as *filius* have their ablative in -*o*. *In the son* would be *in filio*. The word *servus, -i* means *servant, slave*. *In the servant* would be *in servo*. Similarly, *liber, libri* is a second declension noun meaning *book*. *In libro* means *in a book* or *in the book*.

The fourth declension noun *spiritus, -ūs* has its ablative as *spiritu*. The ablative ending of the fourth declension is -*u*. The first declension noun *schola, -ae* has its ablative as *scholā*. The ablative ending of the first declension is an -*ā*. Notice the ending of the ablative is long, while the nominative has a short *a*. Often, but not always, texts will mark the ablative of the first declension or the genitive of the fourth declension with a macron, or long mark (as we have done above).

Table 1.1 shows the endings for the nominative, genitive, and ablative singular nouns of the first through fourth declensions.

Table 1.1

	First	Second	Third	Fourth
Nominative	-a	-us	-	-us
Genitive	-ae	-i	-is	-ūs
Ablative	-ā	-o	-e	-u

Finally, since there is a modifier or an adjective in our sample sentence, we need to discuss how modifiers work in the Latin language. Nouns are name words. They are described, or modified, by adjectives. In English, the adjective usually precedes the noun it is modifying, as in *the green grass, the Holy Spirit, the famous name*. Note that the article *the* is an adjective, as are *green, holy*, and *famous*. In Latin, the adjective will often follow the noun it is modifying, or at times it may precede it. There are also times when the adjective may be some distance away from its noun in the sentence. The noun and adjective in Latin are tied together by their case endings. *An adjective will always have the same number, gender, and case as the noun it is modifying.* In the text, for example, *Spiritūs Sancti* means *of the Holy Spirit*. Both noun and adjective are masculine, singular, and in the genitive case.

If they are both in the genitive case, why are the endings different? *Spiritus* is, as you remember, a noun that belongs to the fourth declension. The adjective *sanctus* (*holy*) has the endings of the second declension when it is modifying a masculine noun. In the nominative case this adjective appears as *sanctus* when the noun is masculine and as *sancta* when the noun is feminine. This adjective will only have endings of the first and second declensions. The nominative singular neuter ending is *-um*. This is the regular nominative ending of neuter nouns and adjectives of the second declension. Masculine nouns of the second declension end in *-us* in the nominative, but neuter nouns of this declension are marked by *-um*. The other singular case endings of the second declension are shared in common by masculine and neuter nouns.

When an adjective appears in a dictionary or glossary entry, it will always be given with its three nominative endings, one for each gender, in the order of masculine, feminine, and neuter. *Sanctus*, for example, will appear as *sanctus, -a, -um*. The adjective modifying *schola* at the begining of this lesson is *prima*. *Primus, -a, -um* means *first*. So we have *schola prima* (*the first lesson*), but *frater primus* (*the first brother*), and *nomen primum* (*the first name*). Note how the number, gender, and case agree in *mater prima* (*the first mother*) and *matris primae* (*of the first mother*), or in *nominis primi* (*of the first name*), or in *in nomine sancto* (*in the holy name*).

Table 1.2 shows noun and adjective endings which will include the neuter endings of the second declension.

Table 1.2

	First	Second		Third	Fourth
		Masculine	**Neuter**		
Nominative	-a	-us	-um	–	-us
Genitive	-ae	-i	-i	-is	-ūs
Ablative	-ā	-o	-o	-e	-u

Vocabula

First Declension Nouns
schola, -ae, *f.,* lesson, class, school
gloria, -ae, *f.,* glory

Second Declension Nouns
filius, -i, *m.,* son
servus, -i, *m.,* slave, servant

Third Declension Nouns
frater, fratris, *m.,* brother
mater, matris, *f.,* mother
pater, patris, *m.,* father
nomen, nominis, *n.,* name
soror, sororis, *f.,* sister

Fourth Declension Nouns
spiritus, spiritūs, *m.,* spirit

Adjectives
primus, -a, -um, first
sanctus, -a, -um, holy, sacred

Prepositions
cum, *followed by the ablative case,* with
in, *followed by the ablative case,* in, on
sine, *followed by the ablative case,* without

Conjunctions
et, and
et . . . et, both . . . and

Exercitia

Translate the following.
1. in nomine sancto
2. in nomine sancto Patris
3. in nomine sancto Patris sancti
4. in nomine Spiritūs
5. in nomine sancto Spiritūs
6. in nomine sancto Spiritūs sancti
7. in scholā primā
8. in scholā primā sororis
9. in scholā primā sororis primae
10. nomen sanctum patris
11. nomen sanctum patris primi
12. nomen sanctum fratris primi
13. cum nomine matris primae

14. cum scholā primā fratris primi
15. sine nomine sancto filii
16. sine nomine sancto filii sancti
17. sine scholā primā sororis patris
18. sine patre sancto primo
19. sine matre sanctā
20. cum sorore primā
21. cum fratre primo
22. cum fratre primo filii
23. cum filio primo fratris primi
24. cum sorore primā matris
25. cum sorore primā matris primae
26. sine fratre sancto patris primi
27. et gloria et nomen matris
28. et gloria et nomen filii primi
29. et gloria nominis et gloria patris
30. nomen sanctum gloriae primae
31. cum gloriā patris et nomine filii
32. sine nomine matris et sororis

Schola Secunda
The Second Lesson

Lectio

The second lesson looks at the prayer often called the lesser Doxology. The greater Doxology is also called the Gloria. The lesser doxology is prayed alone and at the end of psalms in the Liturgy of the Hours in the traditions of both the Western and Eastern Churches.

Gloria Patri, et Filio, et Spiritui Sancto. Sicut erat in principio, et nunc et semper, et in saecula saeculorum.

Translatio

Glory to the Father, and to the Son, and to the Holy Spirit. As it was in the beginning, is now and always, unto ages of ages.

Pronuntiatio

In classical Latin pronunciation, the letter *c* is always a hard sound, as in *cow*. In the Italianate Church pronunciation, the letter *c* is hard when it is followed by the vowels *a*, *o*, or *u*, or when it is followed by another consonant. When the letter *c* is followed by the vowels *e* or *i*, it is pronounced as the *ch* in *church*. In the text, the word *principio* is pronounced with the soft sound of *ch*: *preen-chée-pee-o*. The "double vowel," or diphthong *ae* is pronounced in Church Latin as the *ey* in *they*, or as the long a in *bake*. In classical pronunciation, it sounds like the ai of *aisle*.

Grammatica

There are some familiar words here, but the case endings are different than those already learned. Note that in the translation, the preposition *to* occurs before the Father, the Son, and the Holy Spirit. In English, the preposition *to* before a noun indicates that something is being done for someone or something, or that something is being given to someone or something. In the sentence *I gave the soup to the beggar*, *I* is the subject (nominative case), *soup* is the direct object of the verb (accusative case), and *the beggar* is the indirect object. In Latin, the dative case is used to express the indirect object, that is, the person or thing to or for whom something is done.

Table 2.1 illustrates the singular forms of the first four declensions, now including the dative case.

Table 2.1

| | First | Second | | Third | Fourth |
		Masculine	Neuter		
Nominative	-a	-us	-um	-	-us
Genitive	-ae	-i	-i	-is	-ūs
Dative	-ae	-o	-o	-i	-ui
Ablative	-ā	-o	-o	-e	-u

Notice that once again the adjective *sanctus* is following the forms of the case endings of the second declension, even though it is modifying a fourth declension noun, *spiritus. Spiritui* is in the dative case singular, as is *Sancto.* The dative case of *mater* is *matri. To the first mother* is *matri primae.* Similarly, *to the first son* is expressed as *filio primo.* Note also that both masculine and neuter nouns of the second declension differ only in the nominative case ending.

This phrase is often rendered into English as *Glory be to the Father . . .* , but in Latin there is no verb expressed. Latin often omits forms of the verb *to be,* particularly in the present tense. The present tense of a verb indicates something occurring at the present time, such as *he eats, she reads, it is.* These three English examples are also in the indicative mood. The indicative mood simply states an action or existence. But notice also that the phrase is usually not rendered into English as *Glory is to the Father, and to the Son, and to the Holy Spirit.* The verb of *Glory be to the Father . . .* is not in the indicative mood, but the subjunctive. The subjunctive mood indicates a possibility, a hope, or a wish. Sometimes it appears in English as *may be,* as in *may he be forgiven.* If one were to express the verb *to be* in this phrase, it would appear as either the indicative *est* or the subjunctive *sit.*

Est means *he, she,* or *it is.* Notice that the Latin verb contains a pronoun within it. If a noun is not indicated as the subject of a verb, then the subject is probably a pronoun. If the subject of a verb is *he, she,* or *it,* the verb is said to be in the third person singular. (The first person is *I*, the second person is *you*.) But the translations of the phrase indicate that the verb which is unexpressed, but understood to be there, is probably a subjunctive form. In Latin, this would be *sit*, meaning *may he, she*, or *it be*. Distinguish carefully between *est* (he, she, or it *is*) and *sit* (may he, she, or it *be*).

We have seen that the genitive case expresses possession, as in *pater filii* (*the father of the son* or *the son's father*). Ownership can also be expressed in Latin by the proper form of the verb *to be* and the dative case. This idiom can be translated into English with forms of the verb *to have* or *to own*. For example, *the father has a son* would appear in Latin as *filius patri est*. Literally translated, this reads as *a son is to the father*. Another example: *Matri filia est* (*to the mother is a daughter* or better *the mother has a daughter*). Idioms are proper to each language. They are the usual ways in which thoughts are conveyed, but at times the idioms of various languages are at odds with each other. The art of translation demands the rendering of thoughts from one language into another, in an idiomatic manner.

Est can also be used to express the English idiom *there is*, as in *there is a book on the table*. In Latin, the adverb *there* is never used in such a way. The verb *est* can mean *there is* or *he is, she is, it is*. One can decide from the context how to translate the verb into English. Similarly, the subjunctive form *sit* can be translated as *he, she, it may be* or as *there may be*, as in *there may be ships on the ocean*. Here is another example, this time in Latin: *pax est in terrā*. This may be translated as *peace is on earth* or as *there is peace on earth*. When the verb is subjunctive, the sentence appears as *pax sit in terrā* (*may there be peace on earth* or *may peace be on earth*).

The second phrase of the Doxology in the lectio begins *sicut erat in principio*. *Sicut* is an adverb meaning *as*. *Principium* is a neuter noun meaning *beginning*. Here it is in the ablative case following the preposition *in*, which can mean *in* or, as we saw in the paragraph above, *on*, as in *pax in terrā* (*peace on earth*). The word *erat* is the past tense of *est*. In English it is expressed as *was*. *Erat* is the third person singular indicative form of the verb *to be* in the *imperfect* or *past tense*. As with *est*, *erat* can mean *he, she*, or *it was*, or *there was*.

As with *est* and the dative case, *erat* can also indicate ownership in the past, as in *filia matri erat* (*a daughter was to the mother* or *the mother had a daughter*). Distinguish this carefully from *filiae mater erat* (*the daughter had a mother*). This idiom can become confusing because English expresses an owner by the nominative case and the verb to have or to own, but Latin often expresses ownership by the dative case for the owner and the nominative case as that which is owned or possessed. (There is also a verb meaning *have, hold, own* that will eventually appear.)

Let's continue with the rest of the doxology. *Et nunc et semper, et in saecula saeculorum*. Both *nunc* and *semper* are adverbs, *nunc* means *now*, and *semper* means *always*. Adverbs modify verbs or adjectives, as adjectives modify nouns. Adverbs do not change their forms.

The phrase *in saecula saeculorum* is particularly difficult to render into English. It is the translation of a Greek phrase, which is itself translating a Hebrew or Aramaic idiom. In Latin, Greek, and Hebrew or Aramaic there is a word which indicated the world in the extent of time or in the extent of space. In Latin, that word is *saeculum*, from which English has borrowed the word *secular*. *Saeculum*, like *principium*, is a neuter noun of the second declension. Here, however, we are dealing with plural forms of the word. *Saecula* is both the nominative and accusative plural form of second declension neuter nouns. *Saecula* can be rendered as *worlds* or as *ages*.

The accusative case is the case of the direct object. A verb is called *transitive* if it takes a direct object, as in *the dog chases the ball*. In this sentence, *dog* is the subject, the performer of the action, and *ball* is the direct object, the receiver of the action. English nouns do not change their forms in the nominative or objective case. The direct object form can be seen more clearly in the sentence *whom do you seek?* In this case, *you* is the subject and *whom* is the direct object. In Latin, the direct object of a verb is in the accusative case, and the indirect object (for whom something is done) is in the dative case.

We have seen that the preposition *in* takes the ablative case when it means *in* or *on*. It can also mean *into* or *unto*. These prepositions indicate motion or direction. When *in* means *into* or *unto* it is followed by the accusative case. This is true of all prepositions indicating motion. Prepositions which are "static" will be followed by the ablative, prepositions indicating motion will be followed by the accusative. *In saecula* means *unto ages* or *unto worlds*.

It is followed by *saeculorum*. You can probably guess that this is another case of *saeculum*. This is the genitive plural. The nominative

and accusative plural of neuter nouns of the second declension end in
-*a*, the genitive plural ends in -*orum*. The phrase *in saecula saeculorum*
can be translated as *unto ages of ages, unto worlds of worlds, for worlds of
worlds*, or *for ages of ages*. The usual English rendering is *world without
end*, which tries to capture the meaning of the Latin *saeculum* as the
extent of both space and time.

Table 2.2 shows the case endings of neuter nouns of the
second declension.

Table 2.2

Singular		
Nominative	-um	(principium, saeculum)
Genitive	-i	(principii, saeculi)
Dative	-o	(principio, saeculo)
Accusative	-um	(principium, saeculum)
Ablative	-o	(principio, saeculo)
Plural		
Nominative	-a	(principia, saecula)
Genitive	-orum	(principiorum, saeculorum)
Accusative	-a	(principia, saecula)

Note that in both the singular and plural, the nominative and
accusative endings are the same, -*um* in the singular and -*a* in the plural.

Vocabula

Verbs
est, *3rd person singular indicative active,* he, she, it is; there is; is
sit, *3rd person singular subjunctive active,* may he, she, it be
erat, *3rd person singular indicative imperfect,* he, she, it was;
there was; was

First Declension Nouns
terra, -ae, *f.,* earth, land
gloria, -ae, *f.,* glory
filia, -ae, *f.,* daughter

Second Declension Nouns
dominus, -i, *m.,* lord, master
Deus, -i, *m.,* God
principium, -i, *n.,* beginning, start, origin
bellum, -i, *n.,* war
saeculum, -i, *n.,* age, world

Third Declension Nouns
pax, pacis, *f.,* peace

Adjectives
bonus, -a, -um, good
secundus, -a, -um, second, following

Adverbs
sicut, as, just as
nunc, now
semper, always

Conjunctions
aut, or
aut . . . aut, either . . . or

Exercitia

Translate the following.
1. et bellum et pax
2. aut bellum aut pax
3. et nunc et semper
4. aut nunc aut semper
5. Principium bello est.
6. Principium bello erat.
7. Principium paci est.
8. Principium paci sit.
9. Filia est matri bonae.
10. Filia sit matri bonae.
11. Filia erat matri bonae.
12. Filius est patri bono.
13. Filius erat patri bono.

14.   Filius sit patri bono.
15.   Gloria pacis in terrā est.
16.   Gloria pacis in terrā erat.
17.   Gloria pacis in terrā sit.
18.   Gloria Deo in terrā sit.
19.   Gloria Domino Deo in terrā sit.
20.   Gloria Spiritui Sancto sit.
21.   Gloria Spiritui Sancto in pace sit.
22.   In pace gloria Deo bono est.
23.   Gloria Deo in saecula sit.
24.   Gloria Domino in saecula.
25.   aut gloria aut nomen
26.   et gloria et nomen
27.   Gloria Domino Deo bono sit in pace et in bello in saecula.
28.   Gloria Domino Deo bono sit in pace et in bello in saecula saeculorum.
29.   Deo Domino bono sit nomen bonum in saecula saeculorum.
30.   Matri primus filius et secundus.
31.   Patri filia prima et secunda.
32.   In scholā primā principium bonum fratri est.
33.   In scholā secundā principium bonum sorori erat.
34.   In scholā secundā principium bonum filiae sit.
35.   In scholā primā principium bonum filio secundo sit.

Schola Tertia
The Third Lesson

Lectio

In this lesson, we begin looking at the Hail Mary. The Hail Mary is a prayer made up of a paraphrase of Luke 1:28, the words of Gabriel, followed by Elizabeth's greeting to Mary in Luke 1:42. The prayer then concludes by asking Mary to pray for us and all sinners.

Ave Maria, gratiā plena, Dominus tecum.

Translatio

Hail Mary, full of grace, the Lord is with you.

Pronuntiatio

In Church Latin, the combination of letters *ti* before a vowel (unless the *ti* is preceded by *s*, *t*, or *x*) is pronounced as if there were the letter *s* between them. *Gratia* is pronounced *grá-tsee-a*. *Tertius* is pronounced *tér-tsee-us*.

Grammatica

The word *ave* is a verb. Its basic meaning is *be well* or *fare well*. The form of it in this sentence is a second person singular active imperative. The imperative form of the verb is usually used for giving commands. Here it serves as a greeting. The verb *ave* (*hail, be well*) is found only in the imperative. There is also a plural form of the verb, *avete*, used for greeting two or more people. *Ave* or *avete* is used upon meeting someone. For leave taking or farewells, the verb *salve*, *salvete* is generally used. This verb also means *be well* or *fare well*. *Salve* can also be used as an initial greeting, as is found in the hymn *Salve Regina* (*Hail [Holy] Queen*).

     Maria is in the vocative case, the case of direct address. For all declensions except the second, the vocative has the same form as the nominative. *Maria* (*Mary*) is a noun of the first declension. As a name, it is sometimes referred to as a proper noun.

The vocative case of the second declension replaces the *-us* ending of the nominative with an *-e*. *Dominus* (*Lord*) becomes *Domine* in the vocative. Two other nouns of the second declension which have been encountered, *Deus* (*God*) and *filius* (*son*), are irregular in that they form their vocatives as *Deus* and *fili*. Most other second declension masculine nouns will have their vocative singular in *-e*.

Plenus, -a, -um is an adjective meaning *full*. In English, that which fills someone or something is expressed using the prepositions *with* or *of*, as in *full of grace* or *filled with joy*. The Latin idiom is expressed by a noun in the ablative case, as above, *gratiā plena*. So, a man full of peace would be described as *plenus pace*, or a land filled with war would be *terra bello plena*.

The word *tecum* is made of two words, *cum* (*with*) and *te* (*you*). *Te* is the ablative singular form of the pronoun *tu* (*you*, *thou*). English no longer differentiates between the singular and plural of the second person pronoun, although the archaic forms *thou* and *thee* for the second person singular can be found. The compounding of a pronoun in the ablative case and the preposition *cum* is another Latin idiom. This occurs only with the personal pronouns of the first and second persons. Nouns are not combined with *cum* in this way. *Tecum* and the plural *vobiscum* are the usual way of expressing *with you*.

Table 3.1 indicates the declension of the second person pronoun in the singular.

Table 3.1

Nominative	tu	(you)
Genitive	tui	(usually replaced by the adjective tuus, -a, -um)
Dative	tibi	(to/for you)
Accusative	te	(you)
Ablative	te	(by/with/from you)
Vocative	tu	(O you)

Note that the ablative and accusative forms are exactly alike, as are the nominative and vocative forms. The genitive form *tui* is often replaced by the adjective *tuus, -a, -um* which agrees with its noun in number, gender and case. Note that the number, gender, and case of *tuus, -a, -um* will agree with the noun it is modifying, not with the person it is replacing. For example, if one were saying to a woman, "This is

your war," *your war* would be *bellum tuum*. Similarly, if one were saying
to a man, "This is your land," *your land* is *terra tua*.

Table 3.2 presents the declension of the second person pronoun
in the plural.

Table 3.2

Nominative	vos	(you)
Genitive	vestri, vestrum	(usually replaced by the adjective vester, vestra, vestrum)
Dative	vobis	(to/for you)
Accusative	vos	(you)
Ablative	vobis	(by/with/from you)
Vocative	vos	(O you)

Note that *vos* is the form for the nominative, accusative, and
vocative plural forms of *you*, and that the dative and ablative forms
are both *vobis*. The adjective *vester, vestra, vestrum* often replaces the
genitive case of the pronoun. Note the masculine form *vester*. Unlike
masculine nouns or adjectives of the second declension encountered
to this point, the nominative ending is not -*us*. This is true of a number
of nouns and adjectives of the second declension. *Vester* forms its other
cases on the stem *vestr-*. The genitive masculine is *vestri*, the dative
vestro. It is only unusual in its masculine singular nominative form.

There are also a number of nouns of the second declension
which form their singular nominatives in -*er* rather than in -*us*.
Two of these are *puer, pueri* (*boy, servant*) and *ager, agri* (*field*).

Table 3.3 compares the singular declensions of -*us* and -*er*
nouns of the second declension (including the accusative).

Table 3.3

Nominative	dominus	(master)	puer	(servant)
Genitive	domini	(of a master)	pueri	(of a servant)
Dative	domino	(to/for a master)	puero	(to/for a servant)
Accusative	dominum	(master)	puerum	(servant)
Ablative	domino	(by/with/from a master)	puero	(by/with/from a servant)
Vocative	domine	(O master)	puer	(O servant)

Note that the vocative of -*er* nouns is the same as the nominative, and that the accusative singular looks like the nominative and accusative ending of neuter nouns. The accusative singular of most nouns end in an *m*. For first declension nouns, the accusative is -*am*, for third declension masculine and feminine nouns, -*em* (neuter nouns have the same form in the accusative as in the nominative), and for fourth declension nouns, -*um*.

Vocabula

Verbs
ave (*plural* **avete**), Hail! Hello! Greetings!
salve (*plural* **salvete**), *as above or* Farewell! Good-bye!

First Declension Nouns
gratia, -ae, *f.*, grace, favor
regina, -ae, *f.*, queen

Second Declension Nouns
ager, agri, *m.*, field
puer, pueri, *m.*, boy, lad, servant, child
magister, magistri, *m.*, teacher, master
caelum, -i, *n.*, heaven, sky

Adjectives
dignus, -a, -um, worthy, worthy of *(followed by the ablative case)*
plenus, -a, -um, full (of), filled (with) *(followed by the ablative case)*
tertius, -a,-um, third
tuus, -a, -um, your, yours *(referring to a singular person)*
vester, vestra, vestrum, your, yours *(referring to a plural group)*

Pronouns
tu, you *(singular)*
vos, you *(plural)*

Exercitia

Translate the following.
1. Ave filia.
2. Ave fili.

3. Ave mater.
4. Ave pater.
5. Ave magister.
6. Ave domine.
7. Avete filia et fili.
8. Avete mater et pater.
9. Ave Regina caeli.
10. Salve Regina caeli.
11. Regina tua in caelo est.
12. Regina vestra in caelo est.
13. Regina vestra in caelo erat.
14. Bellum tuum in terrā sit.
15. Ave regina gratiā plena.
16. Deus Dominus gloriā dignus est.
17. Terra pace digna sit.
18. Terra regina digna sit.
19. Terra tua pace digna sit.
20. Terra tua regina digna sit.
21. Terra vestra regina bonā digna sit.
22. In terrā vestrum pax sit.
23. In terrā tui pax sit, sicut in caelo.
24. Terra tui pace plena sit.
25. Dominus vobiscum sit.
26. Dominus tecum est.
27. Pax vobiscum sit.
28. Pax tecum sit nunc et semper.
29. Puer tui te dignus erat.
30. Filia tua te digna est.
31. Mater vestrum gloriā plena sit.
32. Pater vestrum gloriā plenus sit.
33. Principium tuum gloriā plenum sit.
34. Principium tui gloriā dignum est.
35. Nomen tuum gloriā dignum sit.
36. Nomen tui te dignum semper sit.
37. Caelum Domini pace plenum nunc est.
38. Caelum Dei pace plenum sit.

39. Caelum Dei pace et gloriā plenum nunc et semper et in saecula sit.
40. Ager Domini vestri bello plenus est.
41. Salve, magister pacis!
42. In agro bellum est.
43. In agro gloriā pleno bellum est.
44. Magister agri dominus bonus est.
45. Tibi, magister, gloria sit!
46. Tibi, mater, pax sit!
47. Tecum pax sit, magister.
48. Vobiscum pax sit, filia et fili!
49. Tecum Dominus sit, regina!
50. In scholā tertiā vobiscum magister est.
51. Schola tertia gloriā plena est.
52. Dominus tecum.
53. Dominus tecum est.
54. Dominus tecum sit.
55. Dominus tecum erat.
56. Dominus vobiscum.
57. Dominus vobiscum est.
58. Dominus vobiscum sit.
59. Dominus vobiscum erat.

Schola Quarta
The Fourth Lesson

Lectio

Let's continue with the Hail Mary.

Benedicta tu in mulieribus, et benedictus fructus ventris tui, Jesus.

Translatio

Blessed are you among women, and blessed is the fruit of your womb, Jesus.

Grammatica

The adjective *benedictus, -a, -um* means *blessed*. It is derived from a verb, *benedico*, which means *I bless*. The form *benedictus* is called a participle, or verbal adjective. Participles can be active or passive, this form is the passive participle, as is the English equivalent, *blessed*. In English, the active participle appears as *blessing*, as in *the priest is blessing the people*.

    Benedicta is feminine, because it is modifying *tu*, which refers to Mary. In the second clause, *benedictus* is masculine, since it is modifying the word *fructus*. *Fructus* is a fourth declension noun meaning *fruit*.

    Notice that both clauses are lacking some form of the verb *to be*. In the second clause the third person singular present tense verb *est* needs to be understood, and in English needs to be expressed, as in the translation *blessed is the fruit of your womb*. (*Venter, ventris* is a third declension masculine noun meaning *womb*.) In the first clause, the second person singular present tense of the verb *to be* needs to be supplied. In Latin, the *tu* is sufficient, in English the verb *are* has to be expressed. The Latin form of *you are* (singular) is *es*. This is the indicative form. If one wished to say *may you be blessed*, the verb would be *sis*. The indicative mood indicates that something exists, or occurs. The subjunctive mood indicates a wish or hope that something may be or may occur, not something that will occur.

    Table 4.1 shows the four singular forms of the second and third persons of the verb *to be* in the present tense.

Table 4.1

	Indicative Mood		Subjunctive Mood	
2nd Person	es	(you are)	sis	(may you be)
3rd Person	est	(he, she, it is)	sit	(may he, she, it be)

The present tense singular can be completed by adding the first person form of the verb, namely, *I am*, which is *sum*, and the subjunctive *may I be*, which is *sim*. Table 4.2 illustrates the singular forms of the present tense of the verb *to be*.

Table 4.2

	Indicative Mood		Subjunctive Mood	
1st Person	sum	(I am)	sim	(may I be)
2nd Person	es	(you are)	sis	(may you be)
3rd Person	est	(he, she, it is)	sit	(may he, she, it be)

Notice that in both the indicative and subjunctive moods, the verb forms end with the same letter in each person. In the first person, *sum* and *sim* both end in *-m*, in the second person, *es* and *sis* both end in *-s*, and in the third person, *est* and *sit* both end in *-t*. It will be helpful to memorize these personal endings, since they will be common to all singular verbs in the present, imperfect, and future tenses:

• 1st person *-m* (or *-o*)
• 2nd person *-s*
• 3rd person *-t*

Similarly, here are singular forms of the imperfect, or simple past tense, of *to be*:

• 1st person: *eram* (*I was*)
• 2nd person: *eras* (*you were*)
• 3rd person: *erat* (*he, she, it was*)

Note that each of the forms of the imperfect singular consists of *era* -+ the personal endings *-m*, *-s*, and *-t*.

We can conclude the notes on the text with the phrase *in mulieribus*. The preposition *in*, when followed by the ablative case, can mean *in* or *on*. It can also be translated into English as *among*.

A *mulier* is a *woman*. It is a third declension noun which is feminine in gender. The genitive of *mulier* is *mulieris*. The dative and ablative plural ending for third decelension nouns is *-ibus*. Table 4.3 shows the (as yet) incomplete declension of *mulier*.

Table 4.3

	Singular	Plural
Nominative	mulier	
Genitive	mulieris	
Dative	mulieri	mulieribus
Accusative	mulierem	
Ablative	muliere	mulieribus

The dative and ablative plural will be the same for all other third declension nouns, giving phrases such as *cum nominibus* (*with the names*), *cum fratribus* (*with the brothers*), *in sororibus* (*among the sisters*), and so on.

The name *Jesus* is borrowed through Greek from Hebrew and Aramaic. In other places, the same name is usually rendered as *Joshua*. In Hebrew it is *Yehoshua*, in Palestinian Aramaic *Yeshua*, in Greek *Iesous*, and in Latin *Jesus* or *Iesus*. The letter *j* is a medieval version of the Latin letter *i*. It arose in the middle ages to differentiate between *i* as a vowel and *i* used as a consonant (which has the sound of the *y* in *yes*). The name Jesus can appear in Latin texts as either *Jesus* or *Iesus*. The declension of *Jesus* is unique:

- Nominative: *Jesus*
- Genitive, Dative, Ablative, and Vocative: *Jesu*
- Accusative: *Jesum*

(These same forms are used when the name *Joshua* appears).

In the clause *benedictus fructus ventris tui, Jesus*, *Jesus* is described as being in apposition to *fructus*. That is, *fructus* is the subject of the sentence, and the *fructus*, the fruit of Mary's womb, is (*est*) *Jesus*. The verb *to be* is active but intransitive. Intransitive means it cannot take a direct object in the accusative case, since it does not show action or motion. The replacement for the direct object is a noun in the nominative case which is in apposition to the subject of the sentence.

Vocabula

Verbs

The additional forms of the verb *to be*, present indicative singular, all three persons:

sum, I am
es, you are
est, he, she, it is

To be, present subjunctive singular, all three persons:

sim, I may be
sis, you may be
sit, he, she, it may be

To be, imperfect indicative singular, all three persons:

eram, I was
eras, you were
erat, he, she, it was

Third Declension Nouns

dolor, -is, *m.*, pain, sadness, sorrow
venter, ventris, *m.*, womb
mulier, -is, *f.*, woman

Fourth Declension Nouns

fructus, -ūs, *m.*, fruit

Adjectives

benedictus, -a, -um, blessed
quartus, -a, -um, fourth

Exercitia

Translate the following.

1. Benedictus sum.
2. Benedictus sim.
3. Benedictus eram.
4. Benedictus es.
5. Benedictus sis.
6. Benedictus eras.
7. Benedictus est.
8. Benedictus sit.
9. Benedictus erat.
10. Sancta sum.
11. Sancta sim.
12. Sancta eram.
13. Sancta es.
14. Sancta sis.
15. Sancta eras.
16. Sancta est.

17. Sancta sit.
18. Sancta erat.
19. Ave filia.
20. Ave nomen sanctum.
21. Ave fili sancte.
22. Salve regina sancta.
23. Salve nomen Dei.
24. Ave Deus sancte.
25. Salve Domine.
26. Avete filia et fili.
27. Avete mater et pater.
28. Gloria patri sit.
29. Gloria filio sit.
30. Gloria spiritui sit.
31. Nomen matri erat.
32. Nomen sorori erat.
33. Nomen fratri erat.
34. Nomen matri sit.
35. Nomen filiae sit.
36. Nomen filio sit.
37. In principio gloria Deo erat.
38. In principio benedictus eras.
39. In nomine Jesu tu sis benedictus.
40. In nomine Jesu sim benedictus.
41. Maria dolore plena erat.
42. Filius dolore plenus est.
43. Pater dolore plenus erat.
44. Es dolore plena.
45. Benedictus sit venter Mariae.
46. Benedictum erat nomen Mariae
47. Benedictus es, Domine sancte.
48. Benedictus sis, Fili sancte.
49. Benedictum sit nomen sanctum Domini, nunc et in saecula saeculorum.
50. Benedictus sit fructus ventris Mariae.
51. Fructus Domini gratiā plenus est.

Schola Quinta
The Fifth Lesson

Lectio

In this lesson, we'll complete the Hail Mary.

Sancta Maria, mater Dei, ora pro nobis peccatoribus, nunc et in horā mortis nostrae.

Translatio

Holy Mary, mother of God, pray for us sinners, now and at the hour of our death.

Grammatica

Ora is the second person singular active imperative form of the verb *oro*. *Oro* means *I pray.* The imperative mood has appeared before in *ave, avete* and *salve, salvete.* The plural of *ora* (*pray!*) is *orate.* The verb *oro* belongs to the first conjugation. As nouns fall into different declensions, so verbs are also classed according to conjugations. There are four conjugations in Latin, which provide models for the formation of verbs according to person, number, tense, mood, and voice.

When verbs appear in a vocabulary list or dictionary, they will be given with principal parts. English verbs generally have three principle parts, consisting of the present tense, the past tense, and the past participle, as in *pray, prayed, prayed* or *sink, sank, sunk.* Latin verbs generally have four principle parts. These parts are:

1. The first person singular present active indicative
2. The active infinitive
3. The first person singular perfect active indicative
4. The passive participle

For a verb such as *oro,* the four principal parts appear as *oro, orare, oravi, oratus.* Most verbs of the first conjugation will look quite like this. Another example is the verb *to praise: laudo, laudare, laudavi, laudatus.* For the present, we will be dealing mainly with the first and second principal parts. The second principal part is the verb as an idea, or in the abstract. This is called the infinitive (meaning *unbounded*) form of the verb, as in *to pray, orare,* or *to praise, laudare.* The infinitive form *to be* has already been mentioned; in Latin it is *esse.* The first two principle parts of the verb *to be* in Latin are *sum, esse.*

The imperative is formed by taking the first principal part, for example, *oro.* The final *-o* of the first principal part is the present tense ending indicating the first person singular, *I.* If this is dropped off, the stem of the verb remains, namely *or-.* For first conjugation verbs, the vowel *-a* is added to the stem, giving the imperative form *ora* (*pray!*). Similarly, for the verb *laudo,* the singular imperative is *lauda* (*praise!*). The plural forms of each are *orate* and *laudate.*

We have seen the present tense of the singular forms of the verb *esse* (*to be*): *sum* (*I am*), *es* (*you are*), *est* (*he, she, it is*). We have also seen the personal endings of verbs, namely *-m/-o* for the first person (*I*), *-s* for the second person(you), and *-t* for the third person (*he, she,* or *it*). The present tense singular active indicative forms of *oro* and *laudo* (and all other verbs of the first conjugation) are formed by taking the stem, and for the second and third persons adding an *-a-,* and then the personal endings. Table 5.1 lists the singular forms of the present tense of these verbs.

Table 5.1

1st	oro	(I pray)	laudo	(I praise)
2nd	oras	(you pray)	laudas	(you praise)
3rd	orat	(he, she, it prays)	laudat	(he, she, it, praises)

This formation for the present tense will be true for all four of the conjugations, the difference will be in the connecting vowel. Remember that the first conjugation is marked by the vowel *-a-,* as in *oro, orare, orāvi, orātus.*

The verbs *oro* and *laudo* are active verbs that take a direct object, as in *ora Dominum* (*pray [to] the Lord*) or *laudo Deum* (*I praise God*). In English, one prays *to* another, but in Latin the preposition *to* need not be used. The object of an active transitive verb is always in the accusative case. The usual sign of the accusative singular is an *-m,* except in the neuter, where the nominative and accusative are the same.

Table 5.2 reviews the singular forms of nouns in the nominative and accusative cases.

Table 5.2

Declension	Nominative	Accusative
First	hora	horam
Second Masculine	filius	filium
Second Neuter	bellum	bellum
Third Masculine	venter	ventrem
Third Feminine	pax	pacem
Third Neuter	nomen	nomen
Fourth	fructus	fructum

The preposition *pro* means *on behalf of, for, instead of,* or *before.* It is followed by the ablative case. The word *nobis* is the ablative plural of the first person pronoun *nos* (*we*). Table 5.3 illustrates the plural forms of the second personal pronoun *vos* (*you,* which has already appeared) and *nos* (*we*).

Table 5.3

	Second Person Plural		First Person Plural	
Nominative	vos	(you)	nos	(we)
Genitive	vestri, vestrum	(your, yours)	nostri, nostrum	(our, ours)
Dative	vobis	(to/for you)	nobis	(to/for us)
Accusative	vos	(you)	nos	(us)
Ablative	vobis	(by/with/ from you)	nobis	(by/with/ from us)

Note that both genitive forms of the pronouns are usually replaced by the adjectives *vester, vestra, vestrum* (*your, yours*) and *noster, nostra, nostrum* (*our, ours*). The first person possessive adjective appears in the phrase *in hora mortis nostrae. Mors, mortis* is a feminine noun of the third declension meaning *death. Mors nostra* is *our death; mortis nostrae* is *of our death. Hora* is a first declension noun meaning *hour* or *season.*

Nobis is further explained by the noun *peccatoribus.* A *peccator* is a sinner. It is a third declension noun whose genitive is *peccatoris. Peccatoribus* is the ablative plural form, following the preposition *pro.*

There is also a first conjugation verb formed from this root, which means *to sin, to make a mistake*, namely *pecco, peccare, peccavi, peccatus*. Do you see a similarity in the formation of the principle parts of *pecco* to those of *oro* and *laudo*? The similarity should be a help in memorizing the parts of these verbs.

Vocabula

Verbs

laudo, laudare, laudavi, laudatus, I praise, to praise, I have praised, having been praised

oro, orare, oravi, oratus, I pray, to pray, I have prayed, having been prayed

pecco, peccare, peccavi, peccatus, I sin (err, make a mistake), to sin, I have sinned, having been sinned (but the passive participle generally appears only as the neuter noun peccatum, sin, mistake.)

sunt, *3rd person plural indicative present of* **sum,** they are

sint, *3rd person plural subjunctive present of* **sum,** they may be

First Declension Nouns

hora, -ae, *f.,* hour, season

Second Declension Nouns

caelum, -i, *m.,* heaven, sky

Third Declension Nouns

peccator, -is, *m.,* sinner

mors, mortis, *f.,* death

Pronouns

nos (nostrum/nostri, nobis, nos, nobis), we, us

Adjectives

noster, nostra, nostrum, our, ours

quintus, -a, -um, fifth

Prepositions

pro, *followed by the ablative case,* for, on behalf of, before, in place of

Adverbs

non, not

Exercitia

Translate the following.

1. Ora pro nobis.
2. Orate pro nobis.
3. Lauda Deum.
4. Laudate Dominum.
5. Laudate reginam.
6. Lauda Deum caeli.
7. Non te laudo.
8. Non vos laudo.
9. Deum laudas.
10. Mariam laudas.
11. Matrem Dei laudas.
12. Filium Dei oras.
13. Non laudo mortem.
14. Non laudas mortem.
15. Non laudat mortem.
16. Pro vobis orat.
17. Pro nobis oras.
18. Pro mulieribus ora.
19. Regina nostra pro nobis orat.
20. Regina nostra in horā mortis nostrae pro nobis orat.
21. Deus sancte, te laudo.
22. Deus sancte, filius tuus te laudat.
23. Quartus filius matris quintae Deum laudat.
24. Quinta filia sororis nostrae benedicta est.
25. Tertia filia matris tuae benedicta sit.
26. Frater tuus Dominum nostrum laudat.
27. Soror tuae matris in horā mortis pro peccatoribus orat.
28. Mater peccatoris non peccat, pro peccatoribus orat.
29. Fili Dei, pater Mariae te in horā mortis laudat.
30. Filia tua nos laudat.
31. Filius tuus gratiā plenus est, ave sancta mater.
32. Filii tui dolore pleni sunt, gloriā pleni nunc sint.

SCHOLA SEXTA
THE SIXTH LESSON

Lectio

In the next two lessons, we will look at the Our Father. Also referred to as the Lord's Prayer, it was taught by Jesus in Matthew 6:9–13. An alternate form appears in Luke 11:2-4.

Pater noster, qui es in caelis, sanctificetur nomen tuum.
Adveniat regnum tuum. Fiat voluntas tua, sicut in caelo, et in terrā.

Translatio

Our Father, (you) who are in the heavens, may your name be hallowed. May your kingdom come. May your will be done, as in heaven, also on earth.

Grammatica

The word *qui* is a relative pronoun. A relative pronoun refers to an earlier, or antecedent, noun. The relative pronoun ties its antecedent to a new sentence or clause. Relative clauses often act in an adjectival or descriptive way. In the text, notice that the verb following *qui* is *es*, the second person singular *you are*. Note that an older form of English had a way of expressing *you are* which did not need a pronoun, *art*, as in the familiar translation *Our Father, who art in heaven*. *Qui* (*who*) is the masculine singular nominative relative pronoun. The feminine form is *quae* (*who*) and the neuter form is *quod* (*that, which*).

The word for *heaven* is *caelum, -i*, a neuter noun of the second declension. This word is peculiar in that in the singular it is neuter, but in the plural it is treated as a masculine noun of the second declension. In the phrase *in caelis*, the noun is in the ablative plural. We have seen the ablative (and dative) plural of third declension nouns which end in *-ibus*. Both masculine and neuter nouns of the second declension have their dative and ablative plurals end in *-is*. The same is also true of first declension nouns. Table 6.1 shows the dative and ablative plural endings of the four declensions we have seen.

Table 6.1

	First	Second	Third	Fourth
Dative	-is	-is	-ibus	-ibus
Ablative	-is	-is	-ibus	-ibus

Adjectives of the first and second declensions have their dative and ablative plurals in *-is*, as do the nouns of these declensions. *In the high heavens* would be *in caelis altis*; *with the blessed names* would be *cum nominibus benedictis*, and so on.

The nominative plural masculine ending of the second declension is *-i*. The plural of *caelum* in the nominative is (irregularly, since it is neuter in the singular) *caeli*. Similarly, the plural nominative of *filius* (*son*) is *filii* (often appearing as *fili*). The plural nominative ending of neuter nouns of the second and third declension is *-a*. These endings are true of adjectives as well. Table 6.2 presents the plural endings that have been encountered to this point.

Table 6.2

	First	Second Masculine	Neuter	Third Neuter	Fourth
Nominative		-i	-a	-a	
Genitive			-orum		
Dative	-is	-is	-is	-ibus	-ibus
Accusative				-a	
Ablative	-is	-is	-is	-ibus	-ibus

The three verbs that we will examine below will form the core of the grammatical interest of this lesson. These verbs are: *sanctificetur*, *adveniat*, and *fiat*. All three of these verbs are in the present tense and in the subjunctive mood. One of the verbs, *sanctificetur*, is in the passive voice, the other two are in the active voice. They are all in the third person singular.

If we take the two active verbs, *adveniat* and *fiat*, the third person singular ending should be obvious in the *-t* which concludes each word. *Adveniat* is from the verb *advenio, advenire, adveni, adventus*. The base verb for it is *venio, venire, veni, ventus*, which means *to come*. The preposition *ad* has been added to it. *Ad* means *to* or *toward* as a function of motion. As a preposition it takes the accusative case. Here, combined with *venio*, it becomes *advenio*, meaning *to arrive, come*. The word *Advent* is derived from this root. *Advenio* is a verb of the fourth conjugation. Its indicative third person present active form is *advenit*, which means *he arrives, he comes*. Compare the indicative and subjunctive forms of this verb in table 6.3

Table 6.3

Indicative		Subjunctive	
advenit	(he arrives)	adveniat	(may he arrive)

Notice that the indicative form connects the personal ending with an *-i-*, and the subjunctive with *-ia-*. In table 6.4 is the complete singular present active conjugation of the verb *advenio, advenire, adveni, adventus*.

Table 6.4

	Indicative		Subjunctive	
1st	advenio	(I arrive)	adveniam	(may I arrive)
2nd	advenis	(you arrive)	advenias	(may you arrive)
3rd	advenit	(he, she, it arrives)	adveniat	(may he, she, it arrive)

The verb *fio* means *to become, come about, to be done*. It is a bit unusual in the formation of its principal parts, so we will concern ourselves only with the present tense of it. While it is active in form in the present, it can have a passive meaning *to be made, to be done*, as well as an active meaning, *to happen, come about*. In table 6.5 is the conjugation of *fio* in the present singular indicative and subjunctive.

Table 6.5

	Indicative		Subjunctive	
1st	fio	(I become, I am made)	fiam	(may I become)
2nd	fis	(you become, you come about)	fias	(may you become)
3rd	fit	(he, she, it becomes, it happens)	fiat	(may it happen, come about)

Once again, notice that the indicative has an *-i-* before the personal ending, and the subjunctive has *-ia-*. Notice also in both verbs that the first person indicative ends in -*o*, and the subjunctive in -*m*. This will be consistent in all the conjugations for the present tense.

The verb *sanctifico, sanctificare, sanctificavi, sanctificatus* means *to hallow* or *to sanctify*. It is made up of two roots, *sanct-* (*holy*) and *facio* (*to do* or *to make*). *Sanctifico* is a verb of the first conjugation. In the text, it is a passive verb, but in table 6.6, we can see its present active conjugation, in both the indicative and subjunctive forms.

Table 6.6

	Indicative		Subjunctive	
1st	sanctifico	(I make holy)	sanctificem	(may I make holy)
2nd	sanctificas	(you make holy)	sanctifices	(may you make holy)
3rd	sanctificat	(he, she, it makes holy)	sanctificet	(may he, she, it make holy)

Table 6.7 shows the third person singular indicative and subjunctive passive forms.

Table 6.7

	Indicative		Subjunctive	
3rd	sanctificatur	(he, she, it is hallowed)	sanctificetur	(may he, she, it be hallowed)

Notice the difference between the active third person singular ending -*t* and the passive -*tur*. Notice also the difference between the active connecting vowel -*a*- and the subjunctive -*e*- in the first conjugation. Let's consider another first conjugation verb, *laudo, laudare* (*to praise*). The third person present indicative active form is *laudat* (*he praises*). The passive form is *laudatur* (*he is being praised*). In the subjunctive, the forms are *laudet* (*let him praise*) and *laudetur* (*may he be praised*). There is a big difference between praising and being praised.

To the singular personal active verb endings of -*o/-m* (first person), -*s* (second person), and -*t* (third person), the third person singular passive ending -*tur* can be added.

Vocabula

Nouns
regnum, -i, *n.,* kingdom, rule, reign
caelum, -i, *n.,* sky, heaven; *in the plural, it becomes masculine,* **caeli**
voluntas, voluntatis, *f.,* will, desire

Pronouns
qui, quae, quod, *relative pronoun,* who, which, that

Verbs
sanctifico, sanctificare, sanctificavi, sanctificatus, *1st conjugation,* to hallow, sanctify
fio, fieri, factus sum, *3rd conjugation,* to become, be made, happen
venio, venire, veni, ventus, *4th conjugation,* to come, arrive
advenio, advenire, adveni, adventus, *4th conjugation,* to come, arrive

Adjectives
sextus, a, um, sixth

Adverbs
sicut, as

Exercitia

Translate the following.

1. Fiat voluntas tua.
2. Fiat voluntas Dei.
3. Fiat voluntas Spiritūs.
4. Adveniat regnum tuum.
5. Adveniat regnum Dei.
6. Adveniat regnum Filii.
7. Advenit regnum tuum.
8. Advenit regnum Dei.
9. Advenit regnum Filii.
10. Venit regnum tuum.
11. Venit regnum Dei.
12. Venit regnum Filii.
13. Veniat regnum caeli.
14. Veniat voluntas caeli.
15. Veniat nomen Dei.
16. Veniat nomen Jesu.
17. Venit nomen Mariae.
18. Venit nomen Filii.
19. Sanctificat nomen Spiritūs.
20. Sanctificat nomen Dei.
21. Sanctificat nomen Jesu.
22. Sanctificet nomen Spiritūs Dei.
23. Sanctificet nomen Jesu in caelo.
24. Sanctificet regnum Dei in caelo.
25. Voluntas tua sanctificatur.

26. Voluntas tua sanctificetur.
27. Regnum tuum sanctificatur.
28. Regnum tuum sanctificetur.
29. Regnum tuum in caelis
    sanctificatur.
30. Regnum tuum in caelis
    sanctificetur.
31. Regnum tuum in terrā
    sanctificatur.
32. Regnum tuum in terris
    sanctificetur.
33. Voluntas Dei in terrā
    sanctificatur.
34. Voluntas Dei in terris
    sanctificetur.
35. Regnum voluntatis tuae in
    terrā et in caelo sanctificatur.
36. Regnum voluntatis tuae in
    terrā et in caelo sanctificetur.
37. Regnum voluntatis tuae in
    terris et in caelis sanctificatur.
38. Regnum voluntatis tuae in
    terris et in caelis sanctificetur.
39. Regnum voluntatis tuae in
    terrā et in caelo fiat.
40. Regnum voluntatis tuae in
    terris et in caelis fiat.
41. Regnum voluntatis Filii in
    terris et in caelis fit.
42. Regnum nominis Filii Dei
    in terrā et in caelo adveniat
    et fiat.
43. Regnum nominis tui in ter-
    ris et in caelis advenit et fit.
44. Nomen filii sexti in scholā
    quintā laudatur.
45. Nomen filii sexti in scholā
    quintā laudetur.
46. Tu es in caelis.
47. Tu qui es in caelis.
48. Tu quae es in terrā.
49. Tu qui es filius Mariae.
50. Tu quae es filia Mariae.
51. Tu qui es benedictus.
52. Tu quae es benedicta.
53. Tu quod es benedictum.
54. Tu quod es quartum.
55. Tu qui es benedictus in terrā
    sicut in caelis.

Schola Septima
The Seventh Lesson

Lectio

Here is the conclusion of the Our Father.

Panem nostrum cotidianum da nobis hodie. Et dimitte nobis debita nostra, sicut et nos dimittimus debitoribus nostris. Et ne nos inducas in tentationem. Sed libera nos a malo.

Translatio

Give to us today our daily bread. And forgive us our obligations, as we also forgive our debtors. And do not lead us into temptation. But deliver us from evil.

Grammatica

There are two verbs in the imperative singular in the first line of the text, namely *da* and *dimitte*. *Da* is from the verb *do, dare, dedi, datus*, meaning *to give* or *to place*. Recall that the plural second person form of *da* would be *date*. *Dimitte* is the second person singular imperative of *dimitto, dimittere, dimisi, dimissus* (*to forgive*). The root verb here is *mitto, mittere, misi, missus* (*to send*).

The direct object of *da* is *panem*. The nominative of *panem* is *panis*. The genitive of this third declension noun is also *panis*. Nouns of the third declension whose nominative and genitive singular have the same number of syllables are termed *parisyllabic*. *Panis* is a masculine noun. There are two adjectives modifying *panem*, *nostrum* and *cotidianum*. *Cotidianus, -a, -um* means *daily* or *of the day*. (It can sometimes be found spelled *quotidianus* or *cottidianus*). Both adjectives are here in the masculine singular accusative, modifying *panem*.

The direct object of *dimitte* (*forgive*) is *debita*. The nominative singular form is *debitum* (*debt, obligation, something owed*). *Debitum* is treated as a neuter noun of the second declension. Its origin is as the participle of the second conjugation verb *debeo, debēre, debui, debitus*. *Debeo* means *to owe, ought*. Notice the infinitive of *debeo*. It has a long *ē, debēre*. The infinitive, or second principal part, can tell you to which conjugation a verb belongs. Verbs of the second conjugation have a long *ē* before the *-re* infinitive ending. Verbs of the third conjugation also have an *e* in the infinitive, but it is short. Verbs of the first and fourth conjugations have an *a* and *i* before the *-re* infinitive ending respectively.

Following both *da* and *dimitte* is the dative plural pronoun *nobis* (*us, to us, for us*). *Nobis* serves as the indirect object for both verbs. The indirect object indicates to or for whom or what something is done, and is always in the dative case.

We have seen the singular personal endings for verbs: first person, *-o/-m*; second person *-s*; third person *-t*. *Dimittimus* is in the first person plural. To the singular endings we can now add the first person plural ending *-mus*. In the first conjugation, the vowel *-a-* connects the ending to the stem, as in *oramus* (*we pray*). In the second conjugation, an *-ē-* is used, as in *debēmus* (*we owe*). *Dimittimus* is in the third conjugation, with the connecting vowel *-i-*, as with the fourth conjugation *venimus* (*we come*). The first person plural of the verb *sum* (*I am*) is *sumus* (*we are*). Table 7.1 shows the personal endings of the present active verbs that have been encountered to this point.

Table 7.1

	Singular	Plural
1st	-o/-m	-mus
2nd	-s	
3rd	-t	

The last line contains another imperative form, *libera*, from the first conjugation verb *libero, liberare, liberavi, liberatus* (*to free, deliver*). There is also a negative command, *ne inducas*. To form negative commands in Latin, the particle *ne* (*not*) is placed before the subjunctive. *Inducas* is a third conjugation subjunctive verb. The principle parts are *induco, inducere, induxi, inductus* (*to lead into*). *Inducas* is the second person singular active subjunctive of the present tense. The indicative form is *inducis* (*you are leading into*). Table 7.2 compares the present indicative and subjunctive active present tense of the third conjugation.

Table 7.2

	Indicative		Subjunctive	
Singular				
1st	induco	(I lead)	inducam	(may I lead)
2nd	inducis	(you lead)	inducas	(may you lead)
3rd	inducit	(he leads)	inducat	(may he lead)
Plural				
1st	inducimus	(we lead)	inducamus	(may we lead)

The negative particle *ne* is used with the subjunctive. To make in indicative verb negative, *non* is used. For example, *induco* (*I lead into*), *non induco* (*I do not lead into*). In the subjunctive, the examples become *inducam* (*may I lead into*) and *ne inducam* (*may I not lead into*).

The direct object of *ne inducas* and *libera* is *nos. Nos* is the accusative plural of the first person pronoun. Its nominative and accusative plural forms are both *nos* (*we, us*). The dative plural form (which is also the ablative plural form) has already appeared as *nobis*.

The preposition *a* means *from*. It is followed by the ablative case. Before a word beginning with a vowel, it appears as *ab. Malus, -a, -um* is an adjective meaning *evil, bad*. It can be used in the neuter to mean evil in general. The ablative *malo* is ambiguous, it can be understood as either being the neuter or the masculine. The translation *evil one* could be argued, as well as the more general *evil*.

Vocabula

Nouns
debitor, -is, *m.*, debtor, ower
debitum, -i, *n.*, debt, obligation
panis, -is, *m.*, bread
tentatio, tentationis, *f.*, temptation

Verbs
do, dare, dedi, datus, *1st conjugation,* to give, put, place
dimitto, dimittere, dimisi, dimissus, *3rd conjugation,* to send away, forgive
induco, inducere, induxi, inductus, *3rd conjugation,* to lead into

libero, liberare, liberavi, liberatus, *1st conjugation,* to free, deliver, liberate

Adjectives
cot(t)idianus, -a, -um, daily, of the day
malus, -a, -um, evil, bad
septimus, -a, -um, seventh

Adverbs
hodie, today
non, *with indicative,* not
ne, *with subjunctive,* not
sicut, as

Prepositions
ab, a, *with ablative,* from, away from

Exercitia

Translate the following.

1. Induco.
2. Non induco.
3. Inducam.
4. Ne inducam.
5. Inducis.
6. Non inducis.
7. Inducas.
8. Ne inducas.
9. Inducit.
10. Non inducit.
11. Inducat.
12. Ne inducat.
13. Inducimus.
14. Non inducimus.
15. Inducamus.
16. Ne inducamus.
17. Dimitto.
18. Non dimitto.
19. Dimittam.
20. Ne dimittam.
21. Dimittis.
22. Non dimittis.
23. Dimittas.
24. Ne dimittas.
25. Dimittit.
26. Non dimittit.
27. Dimittat.
28. Ne dimittat.
29. Dimitte.
30. Dimittite.
31. Libera.
32. Liberate.
33. Da.
34. Date.
35. Induce.
36. Inducite.

37. Ne dimittas.
38. Ne inducas.
39. Ne liberes.
40. Ne des.
41. panis noster
42. Pater noster
43. tentatio nostra
44. debitum nostrum
45. Libera nos a malo.
46. Liberate nos a malis.
47. Ne liberes nos a gratiā.

48. Induce nos in gratiam.
49. Ne inducas nos in malum.
50. Da nobis panem bonum.
51. Ne des nobis panem malum.
52. Debitor debitum debet.
53. Debitor debitum non debet.
54. Debitum patri debeo.
55. Debitum matri debes.
56. Debitum fratri debet.
57. Debitum sorori debemus.

SCHOLA OCTAVA
THE EIGHTH LESSON

Lectio

In this lesson, we begin to look at the Gloria from the Mass. The Gloria was an early hymn, originally in Greek. It was brought into the Latin rite liturgy along with the Te Deum Laudamus in the fourth century. It opens with the song of the angelic choirs at the birth of Jesus, taken from Luke 3:14.

Gloria in excelsis Deo, et in terrā pax hominibus bonae voluntatis. Laudamus te. Benedicimus te. Adoramus te. Glorificamus te. Gratias agimus tibi propter magnam gloriam tuam. Domine Deus, Rex caelestis, Deus Pater omnipotens.

Translatio

Glory to God in the heights, and on earth peace to men of good will. We praise you. We bless you. We adore you. We glorify you. We give thanks to you because of your great glory. Lord God, heavenly King, God the almighty Father.

Grammatica

Excelsus, -a, -um is an adjective meaning *high, lofty, exalted*. Here it is in the ablative plural, and probably in the neuter gender. It is being used as a noun. This is called the substantive use of adjectives. We have seen it before with *malum* (*evil*). The phrase *in excelsis* (*in the heights*) is usually translated into English as *in the highest*. It is paralleled in the second clause by *in terrā*. *In excelsis* and *in terrā* as a pair state that the heavens (highest places) and the earth are both filled with God's glory. *Hominibus* is the dative plural of the noun *homo, hominis* (*human being, man*). *Bonae voluntatis* is, of course, in the genitive case. This use of the genitive is called the genitive of description, *to men of good will*.

The second line contains four verbs, all in the first person plural present active indicative, followed by the accusative *te* (*you*). A new verb here is *adoramus*, a first conjugation verb. Its principal parts are *adoro, adorare, adoravi, adoratus*. It is composed of the root verb *oro, orare* plus the preposition *ad* (*to* or *toward*). All of the verbs except *benedicimus* belong to the first conjugation. Table 8.1 presents the indicative present active forms of the first conjugation, now including the second and third persons plural.

Table 8.1

	Singular		Plural	
1st	adoro	(I adore)	adoramus	(we adore)
2nd	adoras	(you adore)	adoratis	(you adore)
3rd	adorat	(he, she, it adores)	adorant	(they adore)

Note that the personal ending of the second plural is -*tis*, and that of the third plural is -*nt*. Like the other personal endings, these will be the same in all four conjugations for the active forms of the present, imperfect, and future indicative and subjunctive.

Compare the subjunctive forms of the first conjugation present tense to the indicative. Note in table 8.2 that the connecting vowel changes from -*a*- to -*e*- in the subjunctive.

Table 8.2

	Singular		Plural	
1st	adorem	(may I adore)	adoremus	(may we adore)
2nd	adores	(may you adore)	adoretis	(may you adore)
3rd	adoret	(may he, she, it adore)	adorent	(may they adore)

Table 8.3 shows the present active indicative and subjunctive forms of the second conjugation. Note that the strong *ē* of the second conjugation persists in the subjunctive forms, along with the connecting vowel -*a*-. The verb we will use is *sedeo, sedēre, sedi, sessus* (*to sit*).

Table 8.3

	Singular		Plural	
	Indicative			
1st	sedeō	(I sit)	sedēmus	(we sit)
2nd	sedēs	(you sit)	sedētis	(you sit)
3rd	sedet	(he, she, it sits)	sedent	(they sit)
	Subjunctive			
1st	sedeam	(may I sit)	sedeāmus	(may we sit)
2nd	sedeās	(may you sit)	sedeātis	(may you sit)
3rd	sedeat	(may he, she, it sit)	sedeant	(may they sit)

Although the long vowels are marked in this model conjugation, ordinarily in this text they will not be. The long mark (the macron) will be used only to distinguish the long $\bar{e}$ of the second conjugation infinitives from the short e of the third.

Table 8.4 shows the third conjugation verb *benedico, benedicere, benedixi, benedictus* (*to bless*). Note that in the third plural, the connecting vowel changes from *i* to *u*.

Table 8.4

	Singular	Plural
Indicative		
1st	benedico	benedicimus
2nd	benedicis	benedicitis
3rd	benedicit	benedicunt
Subjunctive		
1st	benedicam	benedicamus
2nd	benedicas	benedicatis
3rd	benedicat	benedicant

Table 8.5 illustrates the fourth conjugation present tense. The verb used is *advenio, advenire, adveni, adventus* (*to arrive*).

Table 8.5

	Singular	Plural
Indicative		
1st	advenio	advenimus
2nd	advenis	advenitis
3rd	advenit	adveniunt
Subjunctive		
1st	adveniam	adveniamus
2nd	advenias	adveniatis
3rd	adveniat	adveniant

There is an idiom in the third line, *gratias agimus. Gratias* is the accusative plural of *gratia.* The verb *agimus* is the first person plural present active indicative of *ago, agere, egi, actus.* This verb has a multiplicity of meanings such as *to do, drive, act, treat,* and so on. *Ago gratias*

means *I give thanks. Let us give thanks* is, similarly, *gratias agamus.*
The indirect object of *gratias agimus* is *tibi*, the dative of *tu* (*you*). The
accusative *te* appeared in the second line. Table 8.6 reviews the second
person pronoun, singular *tu* and plural *vos*.

Table 8.6

	Singular	Plural
Nominative	tu	vos
Genitive	tui	vestrum, vestri
Dative	tibi	vobis
Accusative	te	vos
Ablative	te	vobis

Remember that the genitive forms are usually replaced by the
use of the possessive adjectives, *tuus, -a, -um* in the singular and *vester,
vestra, vestrum* in the plural. The singular form *tuam* occurs at the end
of the line, modifying the accusative *gloriam*. The noun is also modified
by *magnus, -a, -um* (*great*). The preposition *propter* means *on account of,
because of* and is followed by the accusative.

The fourth line contains a number of nouns in the vocative
case. Remember that, for most nouns, the vocative looks like the nominative. The second declension alone has a particular vocative ending *-e*.
However, *Deus* is an exception. Its vocative, even though it is a second
declension noun, is the same as the nominative. *Rex, regis* is a third
declension noun meaning *king*.

Caelestis is a third declension adjective meaning *heavenly, of
heaven*. In the nominative singular, *caelestis* is the form for both the
masculine and feminine , and *caeleste* is the neuter. It is termed a third
declension adjective in two endings. *Omnipotens* is a third declension
adjective in one ending, that is, the nominative singular has the same
form for all three genders. Adjectives of the third declension vary a bit
from nouns in that the ablative singular ends in *-i* rather than *-e*. Table
8.7 shows the singular declension of *omnipotens* in all three genders.

Table 8.7

Nominative	omnipotens
Genitive	omnipotentis
Dative	omnipotenti
Accusative	omnipotentem (but neuter: omnipotens)
Ablative	omnipotenti

Table 8.8 shows the singular declension of *caelestis* in all three genders:

Table 8.8

	Masculine & Feminine	Neuter
Nominative	caelestis	caeleste
Genitive	caelestis	caelestis
Dative	caelesti	caelesti
Accusative	caelestem	caeleste
Ablative	caelesti	caelesti

Compare the declension of *rex caelestis* and *nomen caeleste* in table 8.9.

Table 8.9

Nominative	rex caelestis	nomen caeleste
Genitive	regis caelestis	nominis caelestis
Dative	regi caelesti	nomini caelesti
Accusative	regem caelestem	nomen caeleste
Ablative	rege caelesti	nomine caelesti

Compare the declension of *rex omnipotens* and *nomen omnipotens* in table 8.10.

Table 8.10

Nominative	rex omnipotens	nomen omnipotens
Genitive	regis omnipotentis	nominis omnipotentis
Dative	regi omnipotenti	nomini omnipotenti
Accusative	regem omnipotentem	nomen omnipotens
Ablative	rege omnipotenti	nomine omnipotenti

Vocabula

Nouns
homo, hominis, *m.,* human being, man
rex, regis, *m.,* king
pax, pacis, *f.,* peace

Adjectives
excelsus, -a, -um, high, lofty, exalted
caelestis, -e, *3rd declension in two endings,* heavenly, of heaven
omnipotens, *3rd declension in one ending,* all-powerful
omnis, -e, *3rd declension in two endings,* all, every
suus, -a, -um, one's own, his own, her own, its own, their own

Verbs
adoro, adorare, adoravi, adoratus, to adore
glorifico, glorificare, glorificavi, glorificatus, to glorify
sedeo, sedēre, sedi, sessus, to sit
ago, agere, egi, actus, to do, drive, act, treat (*with* **gratias,** to give thanks)

Exercitia

Translate the following.
1. Ago tibi gratias.
2. Agis Patri gratias.
3. Agit matri gratias.
4. Agimus vobis gratias
5. Agamus vobis gratias.
6. Agam tibi gratias.
7. Agis Patri omnipotenti gratias.
8. Agas Patri omnipotenti gratias.
9. Agit Patri caelesti gratias.
10. Agat Patri caelesti gratias.
11. Agimus Deo omnipotenti gratias.
12. Agamus Deo nostro gratias.
13. Agimus Deo magno gratias propter magnam gloriam suam.
14. Agamus Deo magno gratias propter magnam gloriam suam.
15. Agunt Deo caelesti gratias magnas propter gloriam nominis sui.

16. Agant Deo caelesti gratias magnas propter gloriam nominis sui magni.

17. Agis Deo caelesti gratias magnas propter magnam gloriam nominis sui magni.

18. Agas Deo caelesti gratias magnas propter magnam gloriam nominis sui magni.

19. Agitis Deo caelesti gratias magnas propter magnam gloriam nominis sui sancti.

20. Agatis Deo omnipotenti gratias propter magnam gloriam regni sui.

21. Agimus Patri sancto gratias propter magnam gloriam regni sui.

22. Agamus Filio omnipotenti gratias propter magnam gloriam regni sui.

23. Agamus Spiritui Sancto gratias propter gratiam magnam suam.

24. Glorificamus Deum omnipotentem propter Filium suum sanctum.

25. Glorificemus Deum omnipotentem propter nomen suum caeleste.

26. Laudamus te, Deus omnipotens, propter nomen tuum caeleste.

27. Laudemus te, Deus omnipotens, propter nomen caeleste Filii tui.

28. Adoramus te, Deus bone, propter nomen caeleste Filii tui.

29. Adoremus te, bone Jesu, propter gloriam nominis Patris tui.

30. Benedicamus Domino propter magnam gloriam suam.

31. Omnis gloria sit tibi.

32. Omnis gloria est tibi.

33. omnis gloria in omni terrā

34. omnis gloria in omnibus terris

35. Gloria Dei est sua.

36. Nomen Dei est suum.

37. Filius Dei est suus.

38. Filius Mariae est suus.

39. Filia Mariae est sua.

40. Nomen Mariae est suum.

41. Ago Deo gratias.

42. Agam Spiritui Sancto gratias.

43. Jesus in caelo sedet.

44. Maria in caelo sedeat.

45. Tu in terrā sedes.

46. Tu in terrā tuā sedeas.

47. Sedeo in omni terrā.
48. Sedeam in omni terrā.
49. Sedemus in caelis.
50. Sedeamus in caelis.
51. Sedetis in terrā sanctā.
52. Sedeatis in terrā sanctā.
53. Sedent in terrā suā.
54. Sedeant in terrā suā.
55. Adoratis Deum in excelsis.
56. Adoretis Deum in excelsis.
57. Adoramus Deum in excelsis.
58. Adoremus Deum in excelsis.
59. Adorant Deum in excelsis.
60. Adorent Deum in excelsis.

Schola Nona
The Ninth Lesson

Lectio

In this lesson, we conclude our look at the Gloria.

Domine Fili unigenite, Jesu Christe, Domine Deus, Agnus Dei, Filius Patris. Qui tollis peccata mundi, miserere nobis. Qui tollis peccata mundi, suscipe deprecationem nostram. Qui sedes ad dexteram Patris, miserere nobis. Quoniam tu solus sanctus, tu solus Dominus, tu solus Altissimus, Jesu Christe, cum Sancto Spiritu in gloria Dei Patris.

Translatio

Lord, only begotten Son, Jesus Christ, Lord God, Lamb of God, Son of the Father. You who take the sins of the world, have mercy on us. You who take away the sins of the world, receive our prayer. You who sit at the right (hand) of the Father, have mercy on us. For you alone are holy, you alone are Lord, you alone are the Most High, Jesus Christ, with the Holy Spirit in the glory of God the Father.

Pronuntiatio

The combination *sc* before an *i* or an *e* is pronounced as the *sh* in *fish*, so *suscipe* is pronounced su-shee-pe, with the accent on the first syllable. (In classical pronunciation, *sc* would be pronounced as *sk*.)

Grammatica

Note the number of vocatives in this section of the Gloria. *Unigenite* is from the adjective *unigenitus, -a, -um* meaning *only begotten*. It is made from two words, *genitus* (*begotten*) and *unus* (*one*). *Agnus, -i* is a *lamb*. It is irregular in that its vocative is the same as the nominative, even though it is a second declension noun.

The verb *tollo, tollere, sustuli, sublatus* means *to take away, lift up*. The principal parts are somewhat irregular, but it is a verb that needs to be learned, since it occurs in both liturgical and theological texts. It belongs to the third conjugation, as can be noted by the short *e* of the infinitive. A *peccatum* is a *sin* or a *mistake* or *error*. It is a neuter noun of the second declension. Note the accusative plural *peccata* (which is the same form as the nominative plural). *Mundus, -i* is the *world*.

Suscipio, suscipere, suscepi, susceptus is another third conjugation verb meaning *to take, receive*. Here, as *suscipe*, it is the second person singular imperative. A *deprecatio, -onis* is a *prayer* or *request*. It is a feminine noun of the third declension.

We have seen the relative pronoun *qui* before. *Qui* is the masculine singular nominative meaning *who*. Table 9.1 shows the declension of *qui, quae, quod* in the singular.

Table 9.1

	Masculine	Feminine	Neuter
Nominative	qui	quae	quod
Genitive	cujus	cujus	cujus
Dative	cui	cui	cui
Accusative	quem	quam	quod
Ablative	quo	qua	quo

Note that, in the genitive and dative, the *q* has been replaced by *c*. Note also the endings of these two cases, *-jus* (which can be written as *-ius*) and *-i*. There are a small number of adjectives of the first and second declensions which also have these genitive and dative endings, as well as some other pronouns that will be encountered eventually. One of those adjectives is *solus, -a, -um* (*sole, only, alone*). Table 9.2 illustrates the singular declension of *solus*.

Table 9.2

	Masculine	Feminine	Neuter
Nominative	solus	sola	solum
Genitive	solíus	solíus	solíus
Dative	soli	soli	soli
Accusative	solum	solam	solum
Ablative	solo	solā	solo

Note the accent of the genitive. The endings -ius and -jus differ in that in *cujus*, the letter *j* is a consonant, and in *solíus*, it is a vowel. The ancient Romans did not distinguish these usages, they used the same letter *i* for both of them. In the middle ages, scribes began to distinguish the use of *i* for the vowel and *j* for the consonant sound.

We have seen the ordinal number adjective *primus, -a, -um* (*first*). The number *one* also is treated as an adjective in Latin. Only the first three cardinal numbers are declined in Latin, the numbers from four on are indeclinable. Table 9.3 shows the declension of *unus, -a, -um* (*one*).

Table 9.3

	Masculine	Feminine	Neuter
Nominative	unus	una	unum
Genitive	uníus	uníus	uníus
Dative	uni	uni	uni
Accusative	unum	unam	unum
Ablative	uno	unā	uno

Note the similarity of this declension to that of *solus* and *qui*. These adjectives and pronouns have the normal endings of the first and second declension in the singular nominative, vocative, accusative, and ablative, but the genitive and dative are particular to them. (The plural endings will be the same as the first and second declension in all cases.)

Let us return to the text, in particular to *Qui sedes ad dexteram Patris, miserere nobis*. The adjective *dexter, dextera, dexterum* means *right* (as opposed to *left*). Here it is in the feminine accusative following the preposition *ad*, meaning *at, to*, or *toward*. Since it implies motion, *ad* takes the accusative. There is an implied noun here, namely *manum* (*hand*). *Manus, -ūs* is a fourth declension noun which is feminine in gender.

The verb *miserere* is of particular interest. It is an imperative singular of the verb *misereor* (*to have mercy*). The principal parts of this verb are *misereor, miseréri, misertus sum*. You have probably noticed that the principal parts of this verb do not look at all like a verb such as *sedeo, sedēre, sedi, sessus* (*to sit*). Both of these verbs are of the second conjugation, but *misereor* is of the class called "deponent verbs." A deponent verb has its forms in the passive, but is active in meaning.

We have seen a passive form in the Our Father in the verb *sanctificetur*, which is the third person singular present passive sub-junctive (remember that the indicative of this verb is *sanctificatur*). The third person singular passive ending is *-tur*. Similarly, the second person singular passive ending is *-ris* or *-re*. In the second person singular imperative, the ending is only *-re*. So, for example, the singular imperative of *sedeo* is *sede* (*sit!*). The passive form is *sedere* (*be seated!*). Note the letter *r* appears quite often in the passive personal endings, as in *misereor* (*I have mercy*). Table 9.4 shows the personal endings of verbs in the present, imperfect, and future tenses.

Table 9.4

	Singular	Plural
1st	-r	-mur
2nd	-ris/-re	-mini
3rd	-tur	-ntur

With this introduction to the passive forms, we will say no more at this point. Passive verbs will, of course, return. For now, know that the form *miserere* is the passive form of the second person singular imperative of *misereor*, a second conjugation deponent verb. *Misereor* takes its object in either the genitive or, as here, the dative case.

There is one final grammatical point to be made. The adjective *altissimus* means *most high*, *highest*, or *deepest*. It is the superlative form of *altus, -a, -um* (*high, deep*). In English the superlative form of adjectives is formed either by adding an adverb, such as *most* to an adjective, as in *most high*, or by adding the ending *-est*, as in *highest*. Latin forms its superlative form by adding *-issimus, -a, -um* to the stem of an adjective. So, *altus* becomes *altissimus*, and *sanctus* becomes *sanctissimus*. As in English *good, better, best*, there are some irregular superlative forms in Latin, but they will not concern us here.

Vocabula

Nouns
agnus, -i, *m.,* lamb (*vocative is the same as the nominative*)
peccatum, -i, *n.,* sin, error
deprecatio, -onis, *f.,* prayer, supplication

mundus, -i, *m.,* world
manus, -ūs, *f.,* hand

Adjectives
unigenitus, -a, -um, only begotten
dexter, dextera, dexterum, right
sinister, sinistra, sinistrum, left
altus, -a, -um, high, deep (*superlative form* **altissimus, -a, -um,** highest, deepest)
solus, -a, -um, *gen.* **-íus,** *dat.* **-i,** sole, only, alone
unus, -a, -um, *gen.* **-íus,** *dat.* **-i,** one
nonus, -a, -um, ninth

Verbs
misereor, miserēri, misertus sum, to have mercy, + *gen. or dat.*
tollo, tollere, sustuli, sublatus, to take away
suscipio, suscipere, suscepi, susceptus (sub + capio), to receive, take

Conjunctions
quoniam, because, for

Exercitia

Translate the following.

1. qui tollis peccata
2. qui tollit peccata
3. qui tollo peccata
4. quae tollis panem
5. quae tollit panem
6. quae tollo panem
7. quod tollis
8. quod tollit
9. quod tollo
10. cujus peccata tollis
11. cujus peccata tollit
12. cujus peccata tollo
13. quem tollis
14. quam tollit
15. quod tollo
16. Sedeo ad dexteram manum.
17. Sedeo ad sinistram manum.
18. Sedes ad dexteram manum.
19. Sedes ad sinistram manum.
20. Sedet ad dexteram manum.
21. Sedet ad sinistram manum.
22. Sedemus ad dexteram manum.
23. Sedemus ad sinistram manum.
24. Sedetis ad dexteram manum.
25. Sedetis ad sinistram manum.
26. Sedent ad dexteram manum.
27. Sedent ad sinistram manum.
28. Es altissimus.

29. Sum altissimus.
30. Est altissimus.
31. Es sanctissima.
32. Sum sanctissima.
33. Est sanctissima.
34. Suscipe deprecationem nostram.
35. Suscipe deprecationem meam.
36. Suscipio deprecationem nostram.
37. Suscipis deprecationem nostram.
38. Suscipit deprecationem meam.
39. Suscipimus deprecationem tuam.
40. Suscipitis deprecationem meam.
41. Suscipiunt deprecationem tuam.
42. Miserere nobis.
43. Miserere filiae.
44. Miserere matri.
45. Misereor filiae.
46. Misereor filio.
47. Misereor matri.
48. Miserere mundo.
49. Miserere peccato.
50. Miserere filiae.
51. Filius solus Patris solíus.
52. Filia sola matris solíus.
53. Unigenitus filius Patris uníus.
54. Filia una matris uníus.
55. Gloria sit unigenito Filio.
56. Gloria sit uni Filio.
57. Gloria sit uni Patri.
58. Gloria sit uni Spiritui Sancto.
59. In nomine uníus Patris.
60. In nomine uníus Spiritūs Sancti.

Additional Reading

Translate these prayers from the Mass. Unfamiliar words are defined below.

Agnus Dei, qui tollis peccata mundi, miserere nobis.
Agnus Dei, qui tollis peccata mundi, miserere nobis.
Agnus Dei, qui tollis peccata mundi, dona nobis pacem.

Sanctus, sanctus, sanctus Dominus Deus *Sabaoth*.
Pleni sunt caeli et terra gloriā tuā. Hosanna in excelsis.
Benedictus qui venit in nomine Domini.
Hosanna in excelsis.

dono, donare, donavi, donatus, to give, grant
Sabaoth is a plural Hebrew word that was picked up and used in Latin. It means hosts, armies and is not declined. In this context, assume it is in the genitive case.

Schola Decima
The Tenth Lesson

Lectio

The tenth lesson begins a series of excerpts from Latin Vulgate translation of the Bible. First, we will be reading from Exodus 20:2–3, where God begins to give the Ten Commandments.

Ego sum Dominus Deus tuus, qui eduxi te de terrā Aegypti, de domo servitutis. (verse 2)
Non habebis deos alienos coram me. (verse 3)

Translatio

I am the Lord your God, who led you out from the land of Egypt, from the house of slavery. (verse 2)
You shall not have strange gods before me. (verse 3)

Grammatica

The Perfect Tense

All of the verbs that we have seen until now have used the same set of endings in the active voice, which are shown in table 10.1.

Table 10.1

	Singular	Plural
1st	-o/-m	-mus
2nd	-s	-tis
3rd	-t	-nt

      The verb *eduxi* is the first person singular perfect active indicative. The perfect tense indicates an action that has been completed in the past. In English, *eduxi* can be translated as *I led out* or *I have led out*. The perfect indicates a completed past act, the imperfect tense a continuing past act. The verb is a combination of *duco, ducere, duxi, ductus* (*to lead*) and the preposition *e* (*ex* before a vowel—see below for an explanation), meaning *out (of)*, *from*.

      Notice the principal parts of both *duco* (above) and *educo, educere, eduxi, eductus*. If you look closely, you will see that the third principal part is the same form of the verb appearing in Exodus 20:2, *eduxi*. The third principal part is the perfect form of the verb in the first person singular active indicative. *Educo*, like *duco*, is a third conjugation verb. However, the personal endings of the perfect tense will be the same for all four conjugations. Table 10.2 shows the conjugation of the perfect active indicative of verbs from all four conjugations.

Table 10.2

	First	Second	Third	Fourth
			Singular	
1st	oravi	sedi	duxi	veni
	I (have) prayed	I (have) sat	I (have) led	I have come, I came
2nd	oravisti	sedisti	duxisti	venisti
3rd	oravit	sedit	duxit	venit
			Plural	
1st	oravimus	sedimus	duximus	venimus
2nd	oravistis	sedistis	duxistis	venistis
3rd	oraverunt	sederunt	duxerunt	venerunt

Table 10.3 indicates the perfect tense active personal endings.

Table 10.3

	Singular	Plural
1st	-i	-imus
2nd	-isti	-istis
3rd	-it	-erunt

Notice that the first plural ends in *-mus*, as in the present system endings. The second person adds an *-s* to the singular ending *-isti* (*-istis*). The third singular ends in a *-t* as does the present system, and the third plural also has the final *-nt*, like in the present system. The perfect tense is easily formed, but the principal parts of each verb have to be memorized in order to form it.

The Simple Future Tense

In our *lectio*, the verb *habebis* allows us to discuss the simple future. The simple future uses the same personal endings as the present tense.

In the first and second conjugations, the future is formed by taking the present stem, adding a connecting vowel (-*a*- for the first conjugation, -*e*- for the second), and then the tense sign -*b(i)*- plus the personal ending. The future tense sign -*bi*- is related to the English word *be*. It loses the *i* in the first person singular, and the *i* becomes a *u* in the third plural. Table 10.4 shows the future conjugation of the first conjugation verb *oro, orare, oravi, oratus* (*to pray*) and the second conjugation verb *habeo, habēre, habui, habitus* (*to have, hold*).

Table 10.4

	Singular			
1st	orabo	(I will/shall pray)	habebo	(I will/shall have)
2nd	orabis	(you will/shall pray)	habebis	(you will/shall have)
3rd	orabit	(he, she, it etc.)	habebit	(he, she, it etc.)
	Plural			
1st	orabimus	(we will/shall pray)	habebimus	(we will/shall have)
2nd	orabitis	(you will/shall pray)	habebitis	(you will/shall have)
3rd	orabunt	(they will/shall pray)	habebunt	(they will/shall have)

Prepositions

The preposition *de* takes the ablative case. It can mean *from, down from, about*, or *concerning*. It often appears in the titles of essays or books, as in St. Augustine's *De doctrinā christiānā*.

The preposition *e* means *out of* or *from*. It is followed by the ablative case. Before a word beginning with a vowel it appears as *ex*, just as the preposition *a* (*away from, by, by means of*) appears before a word beginning with a vowel as *ab* or *abs*.

The preposition *coram* also takes the ablative. It means *in front of, before* (in a spatial, not temporal sense).

The Relative Pronoun

Please be sure to note that the verb used with the relative pronoun *qui, quae, quod* is in the same person and number as the verb of the main clause. *Ego sum . . . qui eduxi.* This follows the Hebrew usage. The Latin of the Vulgate has been affected by the grammar of the text it is translating.

The Accusative Plural of the Second Declension

Masculine (and the few feminine) nouns of the second declension have their accusative plural in -*os*, as in *deos*. Masculine adjectives of the second declension also have their accusatives in -*os*. (Neuter nouns have their accusative and nominative plurals in -*a*.)

The First Person Pronoun

The verb *sum* means *I am*. In verse two it is preceded by the first person singular nominative pronoun *ego*, meaning *I*. The use of the pronoun with the verb is added for emphasis. Table 10.5 gives the declension of the first person pronoun. It should be noted that these genitives, like those of the other personal pronouns, are rarely used for possession. Instead, the possessive pronouns are used.

Table 10.5

	Singular	Plural
Nominative	ego	nos
Genitive	mei (meus, -a, -um)	nostri/nostrum (noster, -a, -um)
Dative	mihi	nobis
Accusative	me	nos
Ablative	me	nobis

Vocabula

Nouns

Aegyptus, -i, *f.,* Egypt (*the names of countries are generally feminine in gender*)

domus, -i, *f.,* house

servitus, servitutis, *f.,* slavery

servus, -i, *m.,* slave, servant

doctrina, -ae, *f.,* teaching, instruction

lex, legis, *f.,* law

Moyses, Moysis, *m.,* Moses (acc. Moysen)

Pronouns

ego, I

Adjectives
alienus, -a, -um, foreign, strange, alien
decimus, -a, -um, tenth

Verbs
educo, educere, eduxi, eductus, to lead out
habeo, habēre, habui, habitus, to have, hold
doceo, docēre, docui, doctus, to teach

Prepositions
de, + *ablative,* from, down from, about, concerning
e, ex, + *ablative,* out of, from
coram, + *ablative,* before, in front of

Exercitia

Translate the following.

1. coram me
2. coram te
3. coram Deo
4. ex Aegypto
5. ex Aegypto altissimā
6. de domo
7. de domo altā
8. e domo meā
9. e domo tuā
10. Ego sum qui eduxi te.
11. Tu es qui eduxisti me.
12. Moyses est qui eduxit nos.
13. Nos sumus qui eduximus vos.
14. Vos estis qui eduxistis nos.
15. Eduxerunt nos de terrā Aegypti.
16. Moyses doctrinam et legem docet.
17. Moyses doctrinam et legem docuit.
18. Moyses doctrinam et legem docebit.
19. Moyses in domo nostrā sedet.
20. Moyses in domo nostrā sedebit.
21. Moyses in domo nostrā sedit.
22. Servus legem alienam habet.
23. Servus legem alienam habuit.
24. Servus legem alienam habebit.
25. Habeo doctrinam bonam.
26. Habebo doctrinam bonam.
27. Habui doctrinam bonam.
28. Venio de domo servitutis.
29. Venis de domo servitutis.
30. Venit de domo servitutis.
31. Venimus de domo servitutis.
32. Venitis de domo servitutis.

33. Veniunt de domo servitutis.
34. Veni de terrā sanctissimā.
35. Venisti de terrā sanctissimā.
36. Venit de terrā sanctissimā.
37. Venimus de terrā sanctissimā.
38. Venistis de terrā sanctissimā.
39. Venerunt de terrā
    sanctissimā.
40. Laudo fructum Aegypti.
41. Laudas fructum Aegypti.
42. Laudat fructum Aegypti.
43. Laudamus fructum Aegypti.
44. Laudatis fructum Aegypti.
45. Laudant fructum Aegypti.
46. Laudabo legem decimam.
47. Laudabis legem nonam.
48. Laudabit legem octavam.
49. Laudabimus legem sextam.
50. Laudabitis legem quintam.
51. Laudabunt legem quartam.
52. Moyses legem tertiam
    docebit.
53. Legem secundam docebis.

54. Legem primam docebo.
55. Docebunt doctrinam servo.
56. Docebitis doctrinam servo.
57. Docebimus doctrinam servo.
58. Docui legem in terrā.
59. Docuisti legem in terrā.
60. Docuit legem in domo.
61. Docuimus legem in domo.
62. Docuistis doctrinam
    in Aegypto.
63. Docuerunt doctrinam
    in Aegypto.
64. Gratias ago Domino Deo.
65. Gratias agam Domino Deo.
66. Gratias egi Domino Deo.
67. Gratias agimus
    Domino Deo.
68. Gratias agamus
    Domino Deo.
69. Gratias egimus
    Domino Deo.
70. Gratias agunt Domino Deo.
71. Gratias agant Domino Deo.

Schola Undecima
The Eleventh Lesson

Lectio

Here we continue with the First Commandment as given in Exodus 20:4–6.

Non facies tibi sculptile, neque omnem similitudinem quae est in caelo desuper, et quae in terrā deorsum, nec eorum quae sunt in aquis sub terrā. (v. 4)
Non adorabis ea, neque coles: ego sum Dominus Deus tuus fortis, zelotes, visitans iniquitatem patrum in filios, in tertiam et quartam generationem eorum qui oderunt me: (v. 5)
et faciens misericordiam in millia his qui diligunt me, et custodiunt praecepta mea. (v. 6)

Translatio

You shall not make for yourself a carved image, nor any likeness which is in the heaven above, and which (is) in the earth below, nor of them that are in the waters below the earth. (v. 4)
You shall not adore them, nor cherish (them): I am the Lord your God, strong, jealous, visiting the iniquity of the fathers upon the sons, to the third and fourth generation of those who hate me: (v. 5)
and making mercy unto thousands to those who love me, and keep my commandments. (v.6)

Grammatica

The Future Tense of the Third and Fourth Conjugations

We have seen that the formation of the future tense of the first and second conjugations entails the addition of *-ab-* (first) or *-eb-* (second) plus a connecting vowel (*-i*, except for first singular and third plural) and the personal endings. The third and fourth conjugations form their future tenses by taking the present stem of the verb and adding a connecting vowel, which is *a* in the first person singular, and *e* in all the other persons, then adding the personal endings. In the fourth conjugation, the *i* remains, as it also does in *-io* verbs of the third conjugation (as explained below). Table 11.1 illustrates the third conjugation present and future indicative active.

Table 11.1

	Present	Future	-io Present	-io Future
		Singular		
1st	duco	ducam	suscipio	suscipiam
2nd	ducis	duces	suscipis	suscipies
3rd	ducit	ducet	suscipit	suscipiet
		Plural		
1st	ducimus	ducemus	suscipimus	suscipiemus
2nd	ducitis	ducetis	suscipitis	suscipietis
3rd	ducunt	ducent	suscipiunt	suscipient

Table 11.2 shows the fourth conjugation present and future indicative active.

Table 11.2

	Present	Future
	Singular	
1st	venio	veniam
2nd	venis	venies
3rd	venit	veniet
	Plural	
1st	venimus	veniemus
2nd	venitis	venietis
3rd	veniunt	venient

Notice the future tense of *facio, facere, feci, factus* (*to make*) in verse 4. *Facio* is a verb of the third conjugation. It is termed an *-io verb* of the third conjugation because its present form has the ending *-io*, similar to verbs of the fourth conjugation. The infinitive *facere*, which has a short *e*, signifies that this verb is third conjugation. In verse 5, there is a future verb of the first conjugation, *adorabis*. Both verbs are second person singular.

The Third Person Pronoun

We have seen the first and second person pronouns. The third person pronoun varies with gender, as does *he*, *she*, and *it* in English. In Latin, these forms are *is* (*he*), *ea* (*she*), and *id* (*it*). Table 11.3 shows us the declension of these pronouns. Note the formation of the genitive and dative singular.

Table 11.3

	Masculine		Feminine		Neuter	
			Singular			
Nominative	is	(he)	ea	(she)	id	(it)
Genitive	ejus	(his)	ejus	(hers)	ejus	(its)
Dative	ei	(to him)	ei	(to her)	ei	(to it)
Accusative	eum	(him)	eam	(her)	id	(it)
Ablative	eo	(by/with/ from him)	eā	(... her)	eo	(... it)
			Plural			
Nominative	ei, ii	(they)	eae	(they)	ea	(they)
Genitive	eorum	(their)	earum	(their)	eorum	(their)
Dative	eis	(to them)	eis	(to them)	eis	(to them)
Accusative	eos	(them)	eas	(them)	ea	(them)
Ablative	eis	(... them)	eis	(... them)	eis	(... them)

The endings, except for the genitive and dative singular, which follow adjectives such as *solus* and *unus* (genitive: *solíus, uníus*; dative: *soli, uni*) are generally the endings of the first and second declension attached to an *e-*. The neuter follows the usual pattern of having the same form for the nominative and accusative. To review the endings of nouns and adjectives of the first two declensions, see table 11.4, which shows the endings of the nouns *filius* (*son*), *filia* (*daughter*), and *templum* (*temple*).

Table 11.4

	Singular			Plural		
Nominative	fili-us	fili-a	templ-um	fili-i	fili-ae	templ-a
Genitive	fili-i	fili-ae	templ-i	fili-orum	fili-arum	templ-orum
Dative	fili-o	fili-ae	templ-o	fili-is	fili-is	templ-is
Accusative	fili-um	fili-am	templ-um	fili-os	fili-as	templ-a
Ablative	fili-o	fili- ā	templ-o	fili-is	fili-is	templ-is

The Vulgate text is a rather literal rendering of the Hebrew text into Latin. There are a number of influences from Hebrew grammar and usage that make the Latin a bit difficult at times. For example, the *quae* of verse 4 is the feminine nominative singular relative pronoun. It is referring to *similitudinem* (*likeness*), which is feminine, but also to *sculptile* (*carving, statue*), which is here a neuter noun of the third declension. One would expect something like *or of any of the things that are in the heavens above* but there is no genitive plural here, because the Hebrew does not use it. If it were to be supplied, it could perhaps come from the *eorum quae sunt* (*of the things that are*) in the second part of verse 4, which could be made to serve double duty for both of the relative pronouns which occur. The first *quae* is feminine singular, since it is followed by the verb *est*, while the second *quae* is the neuter plural nominative, followed by *sunt*.

In verse 5, the pronoun *ea* is neuter plural accusative, the object of the two future verbs *adorabis* (*you shall not adore*) and *coles* (*nor shall you cherish*). Verse 5 also contains the masculine genitive plural *eorum* (*of them*) followed by the masculine plural nominative *qui*. Note that the relative pronoun has the nominative singular forms *qui* (m.), *quae* (f.), *quod* (n.) and the plural forms *qui* (m.), *quae* (f.), *quae* (n.).

The Demonstrative Adjective

In verse 6, the Latin word *his* occurs. This is the dative masculine plural of the demonstrative adjective *hic, haec, hoc* (*this* or *he, she, it*). A demonstrative points to something. If it is near, in English, *this* or *these* is used; if it is far, *that* or *those* is generally used. The two can be used in contrast, as in *I prefer these cakes to those.*

In Latin, *hic, haec, hoc* is usually used to mean *this* or *these*, but it can serve at times as a third person pronoun. Here, the English idiom demands *his* be translated as *to those who love me.* Table 11.5 shows us the declension of *hic.*

Table 11.5

	Singular			Plural		
Nominative	hic	haec	hoc	hi	hae	haec
Genitive	hujus	hujus	hujus	horum	harum	horum
Dative	huic	huic	huic	his	his	his
Accusative	hunc	hanc	hoc	hos	has	haec
Ablative	hoc	hac	hoc	his	his	his

Participles

A participle is an adjective derived from a verb. The active participle is formed in English by adding -*ing* to a verb stem, such as *seeing* or *sitting*. In Latin, the active participle is treated as an adjective of the third declension in one ending, that is, the nominative singular of all three genders ends in -*ns*. The participle is formed by taking the present stem (drop the -*o* of the first principal part to get the stem), add a connecting vowel (1st -a, 2nd -e, 3rd -e or ie, 4th -ie), and then the ending -ns. For example, one participle in the *lectio* is *visit-a-ns*, from the first conjugation verb *visito, visitare, visitavi, visitatus* (*to visit*).

The participle is then declined for the other cases with -*nt*- coming before the case endings. (The *t* of the nominative was absorbed by the nominative ending -*s*.) For example, in table 11.6, the second participle in the passage, *faciens*, from *facio, facere, feci, factus* (*to make, do*), is partially declined in the singular.

Table 11.6

Nominative	faciens	faciens	faciens
Genitive	facientis	facientis	facientis
Accusative	facientem	facientem	faciens

Vocabula

Nouns
sculptile, -is, *n.*, carving, graven image, statue
similitudo, similitudinis, *f.*, likeness
aqua, -ae, *f.*, water
iniquitas, iniquitatis, *f.*, iniquity, evil
generatio, -onis, *f.*, generation

misericordia, -ae, *f.,* mercy
praeceptum, -i, *n.,* commandment, precept
zelotes, zelotae, *m.,* a jealous person, one who loves zealously
(*borrowed from Greek*)
vir, viri, *m.,* man, male
mille, *n., 3rd declension, pl.* **milia** *or* **millia,** a thousand

Adjectives
omnis, omne, *3rd in two endings,* all, every, *(in this passage)* any
fortis, forte, *3rd in two endings,* strong, mighty
undecimus, -a, -um, eleventh
hic, haec, hoc, this, these, he, she, it, they

Verbs
facio, facere, feci, factus, to make, do
colo, colere, colui, cultus, to cherish, abide, cultivate, till, tend, care
for, inhabit, protect, worship
visito, visitare, visitavi, visitatus, to visit
odi, odisse, to hate (*this is a 3rd conjugation verb found only in the perfect, but translated as the present*)
diligo, diligere, dilexi, dilectus, to love
custodio, custodire, custodivi, custoditus, to keep, guard

Adverbs
desuper, above, from above
deorsum, below, from below

Conjunctions
nec, neque, nor

Exercitia

Translate the following.
1. Adorabis et coles.
2. Adoras et colis.
3. Adoravisti et coluisti.
4. Adorabit et colet.
5. Adorat et colit.
6. Adoravit et coluit.

7. Adorabo et colam.

8. Adoro et colo.

9. Adoravi et colui.

10. Adorabimus et colemus.

11. Adoramus et colimus.

12. Adoravimus et coluimus.

13. Adorabitis et coletis.

14. Adoratis et colitis.

15. Adoravistis et coluistis.

16. Adorabunt et colent.

17. Adorant et colunt.

18. Adoraverunt et coluerunt.

19. Non facio iniquitatem.

20. Faciam iniquitatem.

21. Feci iniquitatem.

22. Odi iniquitatem.

23. Odisti iniquitatem.

24. Odimus iniquitatem.

25. Facis sculptile magnum.

26. Facies sculptile magnum.

27. Fecisti hoc sculptile.

28. Facit praeceptum.

29. Faciet praeceptum.

30. Fecit hoc praeceptum.

31. Facimus praecepta misericordiae.

32. Faciemus haec paecepta misericordiae.

33. Fecimus praecepta misericordiae.

34. Facitis haec praecepta misericordiae.

35. Facietis praecepta misericordiae.

36. Fecistis haec praecepta misericordiae.

37. Faciunt praeceptum undecimum.

38. Facient hoc praeceptum decimum.

39. Fecerunt praeceptum nonum.

40. Diligo hanc filiam eorum.

41. Odi filiam eorum.

42. Diligo hunc patrem earum.

43. Odi matrem earum.
44. Diligo hanc matrem filiarum.
45. Odi fratrem filiarum.
46. Diligo haec praecepta ejus.
47. Diligo praecepta quae ejus sunt.
48. Diligo praecepta quae Domini sunt.
49. Odi terras quae ejus sunt.
50. Odi has aquas quae in terris ejus sunt.
51. Diligit terras quae in pace sunt.
52. Odit has terras quae non in pace sunt.
53. Diligunt terras in quibus aquae sunt.
54. Oderunt terras in quibus aquae sunt.
55. visitans et faciens
56. nomen viri visitantis
57. nomen matris vistantis
58. nomen hujus fratris visitantis
59. nomen patris facientis similitudinem
60. nomen hujus matris facientis panem
61. vir custodiens terram
62. viri custodientes hanc terram
63. Vir terram custodit.
64. Viri hanc terram custodiunt.
65. Visitat terram in quā aquae sunt.
66. Visitet hanc terram in quā aquae sint.
67. Visitabit terram in quā aquae sint.
68. Visitavit terram in quā aquae sunt.
69. Colit terras in quibus haec iniquitas non est.
70. Colet terras in quibus haec iniquitas non est.
71. Colat terras in quibus haec iniquitas non sit.
72. Coluit terras in quibus haec iniquitas non erat.
73. Dabit hoc sculptile huic matri quae praecepta Domini custodivit.
74. Dedit gloriam magnam huic viro, qui sedit in hac domo magnā.
75. Deus facit misericordiam his qui nomen sanctum ejus diligunt.

Schola Duodecima
The Twelfth Lesson

Lectio

This excerpt from Exodus 20:7–11 continues with the Second and Third Commandments.

Non assumes nomen Domini Dei tui in vanum: nec enim habebit insontem Dominus eum qui assumpserit nomen Domini Dei sui frustra. (v. 7)
Memento ut diem sabbati sanctifices. (v. 8)
Sex diebus operaberis et facies omnia opera tua. (v. 9)
Septimo autem die sabbatum Domini Dei tui est: non facies omne opus in eo, tu, et filius tuus et filia tua, servus tuus et ancilla tua, jumentum tuum, et advena qui est intra portas tuas. (v. 10)
Sex enim diebus fecit Dominus caelum et terram, et mare, et omnia quae in eis sunt, et requievit in die septimo: idcirco benedixit Dominus diei sabbati, et sanctificavit eum. (v. 11)

Translatio

You shall not take the name of the Lord your God for an empty thing: for the Lord shall not hold him guiltless who shall have taken the name of the Lord his God unto a deception. (v. 7)
Remember that you should hallow the day of the Sabbath. (v.8)
In six days you shall work and you shall do all your labors. (v.9)
However, on the seventh day is the Sabbath of the Lord your God: you shall not do any work on it, you, and your son and your daughter, your slave and your handmaiden, your beast of burden, and the stranger who is within your gates. (v. 10)
For in six days the Lord made the heaven and earth, and the sea, and all things that are in them, and he rested on the seventh day: therefore the Lord blessed the day of the Sabbath, and hallowed it. (v. 11)

Grammatica

The Future Perfect Tense

If you had been around in the streets of an Italian city during the classical period when everyone spoke Latin you would have faced a situation when you had to discuss an event whose action will be completed (perfect) in the future. This entailed a knowledge of the future perfect tense. We have seen the simple future tense, and its formation in the first and second, and third and fourth conjugations. We have also seen the perfect tense, formed on the third principal part of the verb, with the same endings in all conjugations. The future perfect tense is also formed on the perfect stem, with the same endings for all four conjugations. The future perfect is formed in English by using the auxiliary verbs *shall/will* and *have/had*, as in *before he will go to class, he shall have completed his homework*. The future perfect tense describes an action that took place before a simple future. In verse 7, for example, the future *habebit* is followed by *assumpserit* in the relative clause: *The Lord will not hold* (simple future) *him guiltless who shall have taken* (future perfect) *the name of the Lord his God for the purpose of deception*.

The future perfect is formed by taking the third principal part (the perfect), dropping the first person singular ending *-i*, and adding the endings in table 12.1.

Table 12.1

	Singular	Plural
1st	-ero	-erimus
2nd	-eris	-eritis
3rd	-erit	-erint

Note that these endings are, except for the third plural, the same as the future tense of the verb *sum, esse, fui, futurus* (*to be*). In the third plural, the future is *erunt*; in the future perfect, the ending becomes *-erint*. Table 12.2 shows the future perfect of the verb *sumo, sumere, sumpsi, sumptus* (*to take*).

Table 12.2

	Singular		Plural	
1st	sumps-ero	(I shall have taken)	sumps-erimus	(we shall have taken)
2nd	sumps-eris	(you etc.)	sumps-eritis	
3rd	sumps-erit		sumps-erint	

Note that the personal endings are the same as those for the present system of tenses. The perfect endings are used only in the perfect tense, not in the past perfect or future perfect. Note also that the verb *assumo* (sometimes written as *adsumo*), *assumere, assumpsi, assumptus* is composed of the verb *sumo* plus the preposition *ad* (*to*), with the *d* changing to match the initial *s* of sumo.

The verb *memento* is an impersonal third person imperative of the verb *memini* (*to remember*). This is a curious verb; like *odi* (*to hate*), it is found only in the perfect, but has a present tense meaning. Translate *memento* as *remember*. That which is to be remembered is given sometimes by an infinitive. Here the conjunction *ut* (*that, in order that*), which is followed by the subjunctive *sanctifices*, is used after *memento*. Table 12.3 is a review of the indicative and subjunctive present of the first conjugation.

Table 12.3

	Indicative	Subjunctive
Singular		
1st	sanctifico	sanctificem
2nd	sanctificas	sanctifices
3rd	sanctificat	sanctificet
Plural		
1st	sanctificamus	sanctificemus
2nd	sanctificatis	sanctificetis
3rd	sanctificant	sanctificent

Declensions

The word *dies, diei* (*day*) is a noun belonging to the fifth declension. Words belonging to this declension tend to be feminine. However, *dies* can be either feminine or masculine. In this passage, it is treated as masculine, as is evident from the adjective *septimo* in verse 10 and the pronoun *eum* at the end of verse 11. Table 12.4 presents the fifth declension.

Table 12.4

	Singular	Plural
Nominative	dies	dies
Genitive	diei	dierum
Dative	diei	diebus
Accusative	diem	dies
Ablative	die	diebus

In verse 8, the accusative, *diem* appears. In verses 9 and 11, the ablative plural *diebus* appears. This use of the ablative is that of *time within which something happens*. The adjective modifying *diebus* (*in days*), is the indeclinable cardinal number *sex* (*six*). The numbers one (*unus, -a, -um*), two (*duo, duae, duo*), and three (*tres, tres, tria*) are the only cardinal numbers that are declined. From four on, there are no declensional endings. The declension of *duo* preserves the endings of the dual number. At one time, Latin had different endings for singular, dual, and plural nouns and adjectives. The dual endings appear only in the declension of *duo* (see table 12.5).

Table 12.5

	Masculine	Feminine	Neuter
Nominative	duo	duae	duo
Genitive	duorum	duarum	duorum
Dative	duobus	duabus	duobus
Accusative	duos	duas	duo
Ablative	duobus	duabus	duobus

The cardinal number *tres* is declined like a plural adjective of the third declension (see table 12.6).

Table 12.6

	Masculine	Feminine	Neuter
Nominative	tres	tres	tria
Genitive	trium	trium	trium
Dative	tribus	tribus	tribus
Accusative	tres	tres	tria
Ablative	tribus	tribus	tribus

Similarly, table 12.7 shows the plural declension of the adjective *omnis, omne* (*all, every, any*).

Table 12.7

	Masculine & Feminine	Neuter
Nominative	omnes	omnia
Genitive	omnium	omnium
Dative	omnibus	omnibus
Accusative	omnes	omnia
Ablative	omnibus	omnibus

Third declension adjectives (including participles) and some nouns have *-ium* as the ending of the genitive plural. The nouns which have this ending in the genitive plural are nouns whose nominative and genitive singular have the same number of syllables, or nouns whose stems end in a double consonant, as long as the second letter of the stem is not *l* or *r*. This is a rather arcane rule, but it explains why the genitive plural of *pater, patris* is *patrum*, not *patrium*.

The neuter noun *mare, maris* (*sea*) appears in verse 11. The declension of neuter nouns of the third declension can be found in table 12.8. (Note that *mare, maris* has an equal number of syllables in the nominative and genitive singular, while *nomen, nominis* does not. This affects the genitive plural ending.)

Table 12.8

	Singular		Plural	
Nominative	mare	nomen	maria	nomina
Genitive	maris	nominis	marium	nominum
Dative	mari	nomini	maribus	nominibus
Accusative	mare	nomen	maria	nomina
Ablative	mare	nomine	maribus	nominibus

Deponent Verbs

We have already seen a deponent verb. These are verbs which appear only in the passive form, but are active in meaning. In verse 9, the verb *operaberis* appears. The principal parts are *operor, operari, operatus sum*, and it belongs to the first conjugation. Table 12.9 presents the forms of the present and future indicative *active* tenses of this verb (note the passive forms of the personal endings *-r, -ris/-re, -tur, -mur, -mini, -ntur*).

Table 12.9

	Present		Future	

		Singular		
1st	operor	(I work)	operabor	(I will work)
2nd	operaris / operare	(you etc.)	operaberis / operabere	
3rd	operatur		operabitur	

		Plural	
1st	operamur		operabimur
2nd	operamini		operabimini
3rd	operantur		operabuntur

In + Accusative

The prepositions *in* or *ad* with the accusative indicate motion toward or into something. These prepositions with the accusative (rather than the ablative) can also be used to indicate purpose, as *in vanum* (*for cheating, for deception*).

Vocabula

Nouns

vanum, -i, *n.,* emptiness, vanity, cheating, deception (*from the adjective* **vanus, -a, -um,** empty, vain)

dies, diei, *5th, m. & f.,* day

sabbatum, -i, *n.,* Sabbath, rest (*borrowed from Hebrew*)

opus, operis, *pl.* **opera, operum,** *n.,* work

ancilla, -ae, *f.,* handmaid

jumentum, -i, *n.,* beast of burden, draught animal

advena, -ae, *m.,* alien, stranger, sojourner

porta, -ae, *f.,* gate, door

mare, maris, *pl.* **maria, marium,** *n.,* sea

Adjectives

insons, *3rd in one ending, stem* **insont-,** innocent, guiltless

duodecimus, -a, -um, twelfth

sex, *indeclinable ordinal numeral,* six

Verbs

assumo (*or* adsumo), assumere, assumpsi, assumptus, to take

habeo, habēre, habui, habitus, to have, hold

memini, meminisse, *found only in the perfect tense,* to remember (*imperative form:* **memento**)

operor, operari, operatus sum, deponent, to work, labor

facio, facere, feci, factus, to do, make

requiesco, requiescere, requievi, requietus, to rest, repose

benedico, benedicere, benedixi, benedictus, to bless (*object in the dative case*)

Adverbs

frustra, in vain, for an empty use, in deception, in error

Prepositions

intra, + *accusative,* within

Conjunctions

idcirco, therefore

ut, that, in order that, so that

enim, for (*resumptive, or causative, but not temporal; postpositive, a word that can never be first in a sentence*)

autem, however

Exercitia

Translate the following.

1. Sex enim diebus fecit Dominus caelum et terram et mare.
2. Sex enim diebus facit Dominus caelum et terram et mare.
3. Sex enim diebus faciet Dominus caelum et terram et mare.
4. Tribus enim diebus fecit Dominus caelum et terram et mare.
5. Duobus enim diebus fecit Dominus caelum et terram et mare.
6. Uno enim die fecit Dominus caelum et terram et mare.
7. Septimo autem die non facies omne opus.
8. Decimo autem die non facies hoc tuum opus.
9. Undecimo autem die non facies haec tua opera.
10. Duodecimo autem die non facies omne opus.
11. Septimo autem die non operaberis.
12. Septimo autem die non operamini.

13. Septimo autem die non operaris.
14. Septimo autem die non operare.
15. Memento ut diem sabbati sanctifices.
16. Memento ut septimo die non opus facias.
17. Memento ut nomen Domini Dei vestri sanctificetis.
18. qui assumpserit nomen Domini frustra
19. qui assumit nomen Domini frustra
20. qui assumpsit nomen Domini frustra
21. qui assumet nomen Domini frustra
22. Requievit in die septimo.
23. Requiescit in hoc die septimo.
24. Requiescet in die septimo.
25. Requiescat in hoc die septimo.
26. Requiescat in pace.
27. Requieverit in pace.
28. omnia quae in eis sunt
29. omnia quae in his aquis
30. omnis fortis vir qui in hac domo erat
31. omnis femina quae in hac domo erit
32. omne peccatum quod in viro sit
33. omnia peccata quae in hoc viro sint
34. omnes fortes viri qui in domo erant
35. omnes feminae quae in domo erunt
36. omne peccatum omnium virorum
37. omnia peccata omnium feminarum
38. Benedixit Dominus diei septimo.
39. Benedicit Dominus omni diei.
40. Benedixerit Dominus omnibus diebus.
41. Benedicet Dominus diei septimo.
42. Benedicat Dominus huic diei septimo.
43. Sanctificavit septimum diem.
44. Sanctificat omnem diem.
45. Sanctificabit omnes dies.
46. Sanctificet omnes hos dies.
47. Sanctificetur septimus dies.
48. Sanctificentur omnes dies.

49. Non habebit eum insontem qui assumpserit nomen Domini in vanum.

50. Non habuit eum insontem qui assumpsit nomen Domini in vanum.

51. Nec habet eam insontem quae assumit nomen Domini in vanum.

52. Nec habebit eos insontes qui assumpserint nomen Domini in vanum.

53. Nec habebunt eas insontes quae assumpserint nomen Domini in vanum.

54. Non habent eos insontes qui assumunt nomen insontium frustra.

55. Habebunt eos insontes qui erunt intra portas eorum.

56. Habuerunt eos insontes qui erant intra portas eorum.

57. Habebo eos insontes qui dilexerint nomen Domini.

58. Habebis eum insontem qui dilexerit nomen Domini.

59. Habebimus eas insontes quae dilexerint nomen Domini.

60. Non habebitis eos insontes qui non dilexerint nomen Domini.

61. Hoc est nomen matris duorum filiorum qui tres domos habent.

62. Dominus regnum caelorum his qui diligunt duos aut tres discipulorum ejus dabit.

63. Dominus regnum caelorum duobus aut tribus bonis dabit.

64. Omnes qui diligunt Dominum habebunt regnum caelorum in duobus aut tribus diebus.

65. Dominus fortis et sanctus huic generationi mille misericordiarum dedit.

SCHOLA TERTIA DECIMA
THE THIRTEENTH LESSON

Lectio

Here is another selection from the Ten Commandments, Exodus 20:12–17. The translation is a bit awkward. The awkwardness reflects the Vulgate's Latin, which often translates Hebrew idioms woodenly into Latin in a literalistic manner. Jerome's other writings often exhibit a beautiful Latin style, but he opted for a stiffer one in the Vulgate.

Honora patrem tuum et matrem tuam, ut sis longaevus super terram, quam Dominus Deus tuus dabit tibi. (v. 12)
Non occides. (v. 13)
Non moechaberis. (v. 14)
Non furtum facies. (v. 15)
Non loqueris contra proximum tuum falsum testimonium. (v. 16)
Non concupisces domum proximi tui, nec desiderabis uxorem ejus, non servum, non ancillam, non bovem, non asinum, nec omnia quae illíus sunt. (v. 17)

Translatio

Honor your father and your mother, that you may be long-lived upon the land, which the Lord your God will give to you. (v. 12)
You shall not kill. (v. 13)
You shall not commit adultery. (v. 14)
You shall not make a theft. (v. 15)
You shall not speak false testimony against your neighbor. (v. 16)
You shall not covet your neighbor's house, nor shall you desire his wife, nor servant, nor handmaid, nor ox, nor ass, nor all things which are his. (v. 17)

Pronuntiatio

The letter *h* here found in the first conjugation imperative verb *honora* is generally not pronounced in Church Latin when it occurs at the beginning of a word. In classical pronunciation, the *h* is pronounced. The dropping of the *h* sound at the beginning of a word has led to some occasional spelling changes, as in the Aramaic word *hosanna*, which will appear in some Latin texts as *osanna*.

The deponent verb *moechor, moechari, moechatus sum* is a word borrowed from Greek. The diphthong *oe* is pronounced as the *a* in *bake* in Church Latin; in classical pronunciation it is pronounced as the *oy* in *boy*. *Ch* is pronounced as a hard *k*, it represents the Greek letter *chi*, χ. The verb *moechor* means *commit adultery*.

Grammatica

Deponent Verbs

This type of verb has appeared several times already, but a review never hurts. There are two deponent verbs in this selection, *moechaberis* and *loqueris*. Both occur in the second person singular future indicative. Remember that they are passive in form, but active in meaning. *Moechor, moechari, moechatus sum* belongs to the first conjugation, and *loquor, loqui, locutus sum* (*to speak, say*) is of the third conjugation. Note the infinitives of each: *moechari* and *loqui*. We have seen that the active infinitive (the second principal part) of all four conjugations ends in *-re*, as in *amare, habēre, ducere*, and *venire*. The passive infinitives of the first, second, and fourth conjugations end in *-ri*, as in *amari* (*to be loved*), *haberi* (*to be held*), and *audiri* (*to be heard*). Passive infinitives of the third conjugation end simply in an *-i*, as in *duci* (*to be led*), replacing the active *-ere* (*ducere*); hence the infinitive of *loquor* is *loqui* (*to speak*).

Table 13.1 shows the present passive indicative of all four conjugations.

Table 13.1

	First	Second	Third	Fourth
	amo (I love)	*habeo (I hold)*	*duco (I lead)*	*audio (I hear)*
Singular				
1st	amor	habeor	ducor	audior
2nd	amaris/-re	haberis/-re	duceris/-re	audiris/-re
3rd	amatur	habetur	ducitur	auditur
Plural				
1st	amamur	habemur	ducimur	audimur
2nd	amamini	habemini	ducimini	audimini
3rd	amantur	habentur	ducuntur	audiuntur

Now take a look at the present *active* indicative of the first and third conjugation deponent verbs *moechor* (*I commit adultery*) and *loquor* (*I speak*) found in table 13.2.

Table 13.2

	First	Third
Singular		
1st	moechor	loquor
2nd	moecharis/-re	loqueris/-re
3rd	moechatur	loquitur
Plural		
1st	moechamur	loquimur
2nd	moechamini	loquimini
3rd	moechantur	loquuntur

The forms are the same as the passive voice verbs, but the meaning is active.

Table 13.3 presents the future passive indicative of the first conjugation verb *amo* and the future active indicative of the first conjugation deponent verb *moechor*, along with the future passive indicative of the third conjugation verb *duco* and the future active of the third conjugation verb *loquor*.

Table 13.3

	First		Third	
Singular				
1st	amabor	moechabor	ducar	loquar
2nd	amaberis/-re	moechaberis/-re	duceris/-re	loqueris/-re
3rd	amabitur	moechabitur	ducetur	loquetur
Plural				
1st	amabimur	moechabimur	ducemur	loquemur
2nd	amabimini	moechabimini	ducemini	loquemini
3rd	amabuntur	moechabuntur	ducentur	loquentur

Ut + Subjunctive

We have already seen *ut* (*that, so that, in order that*) as a conjunction. *Ut* can introduce a number of different types of clauses. A clause has a subject and a verb. A clause which stands by itself is often termed a sentence. Sentences, however, may be made up of several clauses. When this is the case, a clause which could stand alone is termed the main clause, or an independent clause, as in the sentence *I went to the store*. A clause such as *to get some milk* could be added to the independent clause. This clause indicates the purpose for which the going to the store was done. Since *to get some milk* could not stand on its own as a sentence, it is termed a dependent clause. In Latin, such purpose clauses are introduced by *ut* and have a subjunctive verb.

In verse 12 of our *lectio*, the independent clause beginning *Honora patrem tuum* contains a verb which is imperative. *Honor your father and your mother* is the independent clause. The word *ut* with the subjunctive verb *sis* indicates the purpose clause, *so that you may be long-lived on the land*. Table 13.4 shows once again the subjunctive present active of all four conjugations. A clause that expresses a negative such as "I eat that I may not die" is introduced not by *ut*, but by *ne*.

Table 13.4

	First	Second	Third	Fourth
Singular				
1st	amem	habeam	ducam	veniam
2nd	ames	habeas	ducas	venias
3rd	amet	habeat	ducat	veniat
Plural				
1st	amemus	habeamus	ducamus	veniamus
2nd	ametis	habeatis	ducatis	veniatis
3rd	ament	habeant	ducant	veniant

More Pronouns

We have seen the third person pronoun *is, ea, id*. There are a number of other pronouns that can be translated as *he, she, it, they*, etc. In the last verse of the selection, the pronoun *illíus* appears. *Illíus* is the genitive singular masculine of the demonstrative pronoun *ille, illa, illum*. This pronoun often means *that*, as in *that car*. Hence it is called a demonstrative, since it points to a noun. *Ille, illa, illum* can also be used to mean *he, she, it.* Table 13.5 shows us the declension of *ille.* Note again the genitive and dative singulars.

Table 13.5

	Masculine	Feminine	Neuter
		Singular	
Nominative	ille	illa	illum
Genitive	illíus	illíus	illíus
Dative	illi	illi	illi
Accusative	illum	illam	illum
Ablative	illo	illā	illo
		Plural	
Nominative	illi	illae	illa
Genitive	illorum	illarum	illorum
Dative	illis	illis	illis
Accusative	illos	illas	illa
Ablative	illis	illis	illis

Vocabula

Nouns

furtum, -i, *n.,* theft, robbery, deceit, trick
proximus, -i, *m.,* neighbor (*from the adjective* **proximus, -a, -um,** nearest)
testimonium, -i, *n.,* testimony, witness (*as an act, not a person*)
uxor, -oris, *f.,* wife
asinus, -i, *m.,* ass
bos, bovis, *m.,* ox

Adjectives

longaevus, -a, -um, long-lived
proximus, -a, -um, nearest (*as a substantive,* neighbor)

Verbs

honoro, honorare, honoravi, honoratus, to honor, respect, adorn
do, dare, dedi, datus, to give
occido, occidere, occisi, occisus, to kill

moechor, moechari, moechatus sum, *1st deponent,* to commit adultery
loquor, loqui, locutus sum, *3rd deponent,* to talk, speak, say
concupisco, concupiscere, concupiscivi (*or* **concuposcii**)**, concupitus,**
to desire, covet, strive (*from* **cum** + **cupisco,** to wish, desire)
desidero, desiderare, desideravi, desideratus, to wish, desire
audio, audire, audivi, auditus, to hear

Prepositions
super, + *accusative,* over, above, on, upon
contra, + *accusative,* against

Conjunctions
ut, + *subjunctive,* in order that, so that

Exercitia

Translate the following.
1. Honora patrem tuum.
2. Honora matrem tuam.
3. Honora illum.
4. Honora illam.
5. Honora patres tuos.
6. Honora illos.
7. Honora matres tuas.
8. Honora illas.
9. Honorate illas.
10. Honora patrem tuum ut sis longaevus super terram tuam.
11. Honorate patres tuos ut sitis longaevi super terram vestram.
12. Honora matrem tuam ut sis longaeva super terram tuam.
13. Honorate matres tuas ut sitis longaevae super terram vestram.
14. Non occides ut sis longaevus in terrā tuā.
15. Non occidetis ut sitis longaevi in terrā vestrā.
16. Non occidam ut sim longaevus in domo meā.
17. Non occidemus ut simus longaevi in domo nostrā.
18. Non occidet ut sit longaeva in domo suā.
19. Non occident ut sint longaevi in domo suā.
20. Non occidit, honorat patrem et matrem ut sit proximus bonus.
21. Non occidunt, honorant patres et matres ut sint proximi boni.

22. Non furtum facies ut habeas nomen bonum.
23. Non furtum faciam ut habeam nomen bonum.
24. Non furtum facias ut habeas nomen bonum.
25. Non furtum faciunt nec occidunt ut habeant nomen bonum.
26. Non furtum fecit nec occisit in terrā quam Deus ei dedit.
27. Non furtum feci nec occisi in terrā quam Deus mihi dedit.
28. Non furtum fecerunt nec occiserunt in terris quas Deus eis dedit.
29. Non furtum facit nec occidit in terrā quam Deus illi dedit.
30. Non furtum facimus nec occidimus in terris quas Deus nobis dedit.
31. Non furtum faciamus nec occidamus in terris quas Deus nobis dedit.
32. Non furtum faciant nec occidant in terris quas Deus illis dedit.
33. Non furtum faciatis nec occidatis in terrā quam Deus vobis dedit.
34. Loquor et audis.
35. Loquimur et auditis.
36. Loquitur et audiunt.
37. Loquuntur et audiuntur.
38. Loquimini et audimini.
39. Loqueris et audiris.
40. Loquere et audire.
41. Loquor ut audias.
42. Loqueris ut audiat.
43. Loquitur ut audiam.
44. Loquimur ut audiant.
45. Loquimini ut audiat.
46. Loquuntur ut audiatis.
47. Loquor ut audiar.
48. Loquere ut audiaris.
49. Loquitur ut audiatur.
50. Loquimur ut audiamur.
51. Loquimini ut audiamini.
52. Loquuntur ut audiantur.
53. Non concupisco domum proximi mei.
54. Non concupiscis nec desideras domum proximi tui.
55. Non concupisces nec desiderabis domum proximi tui.
56. Non concupiscit nec desiderat domum proximi sui.

57. Non concupiscimus nec desideramus domum proximi nostri.
58. Non concupiscemus nec desiderabimus domum proximi nostri.
59. Non concupiscunt nec desiderant uxores proximorum illorum.
60. Non concupiscent nec desiderabunt uxores proximorum eorum.

Additional Reading

For additional practice translate these passages from Scripture. Unfamiliar words are defined below.

Matthew 5:21
Audistis quia dictum est antiquis: Non occides. . . .

Matthew 5:27
Audistis quia dictum est antiquis: Non
moechaberis.

Matthew 5:38
Audistis quia dictum est: Oculum pro oculo, et dentem pro dente.

Matthew 5:43
Audistis quia dictum est: Diliges proximum tuum, et odio habebis inimicum tuum. Ego autem dico vobis: Diligite inimicos vestros, benefacite his qui oderunt vos.

quia, *conjunction,* that
dictum est, *3rd person singular perfect passive of* **dico, dicere, dixi, dictus,** it was said
antiquus, -a, -um, ancient, old
oculus, -i, *m.,* eye
dens, dentis, *f.,* tooth
odium, -i, *n.,* hatred (*translate the ablative here as* "with hatred")
inimicus, -i, *m.,* enemy
autem, however
benefacio, benefacere, benefeci, benefactus, to do good

Schola Quarta Decima
The Fourteenth Lesson

Lectio

In this lesson, we transition from the Ten Commandments to Jesus' Sermon on the Mount, which begins in Matthew 5:1–3. Matthew places a collection of the teachings of Jesus in chapters 5 through 7. The Sermon begins with the Beatitudes. As the Ten Commandments are the heart of the Law, the Beatitudes are at the heart of Jesus' teachings on the life of discipleship.

Videns autem Jesus turbas, ascendit in montem, et cum sedisset, accesserunt ad eum discipuli ejus, (v. 1)
et aperiens os suum docebat eos dicens: (v. 2)
Beati pauperes spiritu: quoniam ipsorum est regnum caelorum. (v. 3)

Translatio

However, seeing the crowds, Jesus went up onto the mountain, and when he had sat, his disciples approached toward him, (v. 1)
and opening his mouth he taught them saying: (v. 2)
Blessed (are) the poor in spirit: for theirs is the kingdom of the heavens. (v. 3)

Grammatica

Present Active Participle

There are three present active participles in this *lectio*, *videns* in verse 1 and *aperiens* and *dicens* in verse 2. A participle is a verbal adjective. We have met participles before, now we will examine them a bit more closely. Since the participle retains the force of a verb, it can take an object, as in verse 1, *videns turbas* (*seeing the crowds*), or in verse 2, *aperiens os suum* (*opening his mouth*). Notice that the English participle does the same thing. The English present active participle is formed by adding *-ing* to a verbal stem. To form the Latin present active participle, take the present stem (the first principal part), drop the personal ending, add a connecting vowel (*-a-* for the first conjugation, *-e-* for the second and third, and *-ie-* for the fourth conjugation along with *-io* verbs of the third), and to the connecting vowels, *-ns* is added to give the nominative singular of the participle. Table 14.1 illustrates examples from all four conjugations.

Table 14.1

Conjugation	Principle Parts	Present Active Participle
First	amo, amare, amavi, amatus (to love)	amans (loving)
Second	habeo, habēre, habui, habitus (to have)	habens (having)
Third	dico, dicere, dixi, dictus (to say)	dicens (saying)
Third -io	facio, facere, feci, factus (to do)	faciens (doing)
Fourth	audio, audire, audivi, auditus (to hear)	audiens (hearing)

Deponent verbs, which have passive forms but active meanings, form their present active participles in exactly the same way. For example, the participle of *loquor, loqui, locutus sum* is *loquens* (*speaking*).

Participles are declined as third declension adjectives in one ending. Table 14.2 shows the declension of the participles *videns* (*seeing*, from *video, vidēre, visi, visus*), *aperiens* (*opening*, from *aperio, aperire, aperui, apertus*), and *dicens* (*saying*, from *dico, dicere, dixi, dictus*). The neuter is given only when it differs from the masculine and feminine.

Table 14.2

	M. & F.	N.	M. & F.	N.	M. & F.	N.
			Singular			
Nominative	videns		aperiens		dicens	
Genitive	videntis		aperientis		dicentis	
Dative	videnti		aperienti		dicenti	
Accusative	videntem	videns	aperientem	aperiens	dicentem	dicens
Ablative	vidente		aperiente		dicente	
			Plural			
Nominative	videntes	videntia	aperientes	aperientia	dicentes	dicentia
Genitive	videntium		aperientium		dicentium	
Dative	videntibus		aperientibus		dicentibus	
Accusative	videntem	videntia	aperientem	aperientia	dicentem	dicentia
Ablative	videntibus		aperientibus		dicentibus	

Note that the stem of the participle is actually -*nt*. In the nominative (and neuter accusative singular), the -*s* case ending has absorbed the sound of the **t**, and it has disappeared. (The ablative singular can also appear as *videnti, aperienti, dicenti,* but the ablative in *-e* is more common.)

The participle can be used as an ordinary adjective to describe a noun, as in *vir loquens* (*a man speaking*). The participle, unlike an adjective, can take an object, as in *viri loquentes verba* (*men speaking words*).

The Latin participle can also be translated into English as a relative clause, as in *vir loquens verba peccata dimisit* (*the man who was speaking the words forgave sins*). How the participle will be translated is dependent on the context and on the choice of the translator.

There are times when the participle can be translated in an adverbial manner, as in *puer dicens ad domum venit* (*speaking, the boy went to the house*).

The Imperfect Tense

We have seen that the simple future of the first and second conjugations is formed by adding *-a/e-bo, -a/e-bis, -a/e-bit,* etc. to the present stem. The imperfect is formed by taking the present stem, adding the proper connecting vowel for each conjugation, and then adding the tense sign *-ba-* plus the personal endings *-m, -s, -t, -mus, -tis, -nt.*

The imperfect or simple past tense can be translated by the English past, as in *videbam* (*I saw*), *amabam* (*I loved*), *faciebam* (*I made*). It indicates an action going on in the past, as in *I was seeing, I was loving, I was making.* It can also be translated by renderings such as *I used to see, I used to love, I used to make.* The imperfect can also have an incipient sense, as in *I began to see, I began to love, I began to make.* As with the use of participles, the way the imperfect is translated into English can vary with the perceptions and literary sense of the translator. The context of the sentence can offer a clue as to what choice the translator will make. For example, in verse 2, the clause *docebat eos dicens* which is translated above as *he taught them, saying* can be rendered as *he began to teach them, saying.*

Table 14.3 shows the conjugation of *amabam* (*I loved*), *docebam* (*I taught*), *ducebam* (*I led*), and *veniebam* (*I came*).

Table 14.3

	Singular			
1st	amabam	docebam	ducebam	veniebam
2nd	amabas	docebas	ducebas	veniebas
3rd	amabat	docebat	ducebat	veniebat
	Plural			
1st	amabamus	docebamus	ducebamus	veniebamus
2nd	amabatis	docebatis	ducebatis	veniebatis
3rd	amabant	docebant	ducebant	veniebant

The passive voice (active for deponent verbs!) is formed in exactly the same way, but with the passive personal endings *-r, -ris/-re, -tur, -mur, -mini, -ntur,* as in *amabar* (*I was being loved*), *docebar* (*I was being taught*), *loquebar* (*I was speaking*), *audiebar* (*I was being heard*).

The Pluperfect Subjunctive and Cum Clauses

The word *cum* can be a preposition meaning *with.* It is followed by the ablative case. It can also be a conjunction meaning *when.* In verse 1, such a clause occurs. In this passage, *cum* is introducing a clause which indicates the circumstance in which the later narration will occur, *when he had seated himself.* When *cum* introduces such a clause, a verb in the past tense will have to be in the subjunctive. If the verb were present or future, it would be in the indicative.

In verse 1, the tense used is the pluperfect, which describes an action in the past that happened before another past action. The pluperfect is formed in English by using the auxiliary verb *had,* as in *he had seen* or *he had seated himself.* In Latin, the indicative pluperfect active is formed by taking the perfect stem (by dropping the first person ending from the third principal part) and adding the past tense of the verb *to be* (*eram, eras, erat, eramus, eratis, erant*). The subjunctive pluperfect active is formed by taking the third principal part (including the first person ending), adding *-sse-,* then the active personal endings *-m, -s, -t, -mus, -tis, -nt.* Table 14.4 demonstrates the conjugation of *sedeo, sedēre, sedi, sessus* in the pluperfect active indicative and subjunctive.

Table 14.4

	Indicative	Subjunctive
	Singular	
1st	sederam	sedissem
2nd	sederas	sedisses
3rd	sederat	sedisset
	Plural	
1st	sederamus	sedissemus
2nd	sederatis	sedissetis
3rd	sederant	sedissent

Note that in English, the subjunctive after *cum* is translated as an indicative: *when he sat, when he had seated himself, when he had sat down* are all ways to translate *cum sedisset*. The pluperfect is used here because the action of the *cum* clause takes place before that of the main verb, *accesserunt* (*they approached*), which is in the perfect. In terms of time, the pluperfect describes an action that occurs before the perfect or imperfect.

Ablative of Respect

In the phrase *pauperes spiritu*, *spiritu* is in the ablative case. These people are *poor in respect to their spirit*, or *poor in spirit*. This is a common usage of the ablative case without a preposition.

Vocabula

Nouns
turba, -ae, *f.*, crowd
mons, montis, *f.*, mountain
discipulus, -i, *m.*, disciple
os, oris, *n.*, mouth

Adjectives
beatus, -a, -um, blessed
pauper, *gen.* **pauperis,** *3rd in one ending*, poor

Pronouns
ipse, ipsa, ipsum, *gen.* **ipsíus,** *dat.* **ipsi,** *intensive pronoun,* oneself, himself, herself, itself, themselves, etc. (*declined like* **ille***; can also be used as* he, she, it, they)

Verbs
ascendo, ascendere, ascendi, ascensus, to ascend, go up, rise
accedo, accedere, accessi, accesus, to go to, approach
aperio, aperire, aperui, apertus, to open

Conjunctions
cum, when
quoniam, because, for

Exercitia

Translate the following.
1. Ipse dixit.
2. Ipse dicit.
3. Ipse dixerat.
4. Cum ipse dixisset.
5. Cum ipse dicit.
6. Cum ipse dicet.
7. Ipsi dixerunt.
8. Ipsi dicunt.
9. Ipsi dixerant.
10. Cum ipsi dixissent.
11. Cum ipsi dicunt.
12. Cum ipsi dicent.
13. Videns turbas ascendit in montem.
14. Videntes turbas ascenderunt in montes.
15. Cum ascendisset in montem, aperuit os suum.
16. Cum ascendissent in montem, aperuerunt ora sua.
17. Cum vidisset turbas, ascendit in montem.
18. Cum vidisses turbas, ascendisti in montem.
19. Cum vidissem turbas, ascendi in montem.
20. Cum vidissemus turbas, ascendimus in montem.
21. Cum vidissetis turbas, ascendistis in montem.

22. Cum vidissent turbas, ascenderunt in montem.
23. Cum vidisset turbam magnam, ascendebat in montem.
24. Cum ascendisset in montem, aperuit os suum.
25. Cum ascendisset in montem, aperiebat os suum.
26. Cum aperuisset os suum, docebat ipsos.
27. Cum aperuisset os suum, docuit illos.
28. Cum docuisset eos, sedit in monte.
29. Cum docuisset eos, sedebat in monte.
30. Beatus pauper spiritu, ejus est regnum caeli.
31. Beati pauperes spiritu, eorum est regnum caelorum.
32. Beata alta spiritu, ejus est regnum caeli.
33. Beati sint pauperes spiritu, ipsorum est regnum caeli.
34. Beati erant pauperes spiritu, illorum est regnum caeli.
35. Beatae sunt pauperes spiritu, earum est regnum caeli.
36. Beatae sint pauperes spiritu, illarum est regnum caeli.
37. Beatae erant pauperes spiritu, ipsarum est regnum caelorum.
38. Aperiens os suum, docebat eos.
39. Aperientes ora sua, docebant illos.
40. Sedens in monte, docuit turbas magnas.
41. Sedentes in montibus, docuerunt turbas magnas.
42. ascendens in montem et aperiens os ejus
43. ascendentes in montes et aperientes ora eorum
44. Beati ascendentes in montem, quoniam vident turbam.
45. Beatus ascendens in montem, quoniam videt turbam.
46. Beatus sedens in monte, quoniam videt discipulos.
47. Beati discipuli sedentes in monte, quoniam vident caelum.
48. Beatus pauper spiritu sit, quoniam videt Deum.
49. Gloriam pauperi spiritu dedit cum vidisset eum.
50. Gloriam pauperibus spiritu dederunt cum vidissent eos.

Schola Quinta Decima
The Fifteenth Lesson

Lectio

In this passage from Matthew 5:4–9, the Sermon on the Mount continues with the Beatitudes.

Beati mites: quoniam ipsi possidebunt terram. (v. 4)
Beati qui lugent: quoniam ipsi consolabuntur. (v. 5)
Beati qui esuriunt et sitiunt justitiam: quoniam ipsi saturabuntur. (v. 6)
Beati misericordes: quoniam ipsi misericordiam consequentur. (v. 7)
Beati mundo corde: quoniam ipsi Deum videbunt. (v. 8)
Beati pacifici: quoniam filii Dei vocabuntur. (v. 9)

Translatio

Blessed (are) the mild: because they shall possess the land. (v. 4)
Blessed (are) those who mourn: because they shall be consoled. (v. 5)
Blessed (are) those who hunger and thirst (for) justice: for they shall be filled. (v. 6)
Blessed (are) the merciful: for they shall attain mercy. (v. 7)
Blessed (are those) with a clean heart: for they shall see God. (v. 8)
Blessed (are) the peacemakers: for they shall be called sons of God. (v. 9)

Grammatica

Review of the Future Tense

There are a number of future verbs in the active and passive forms in this *lectio*. They afford a good opportunity to review how the simple future tense is formed for the first and second conjugations, and for the third and fourth:

- *Possidebunt*, from *possideo, possidēre, possedi, possessus*, second conjugation (*to own, possess*). For the future, the second conjugation takes the present stem and adds *-ebo, -ebis, -ebit, -ebimus, -ebitis, -ebunt*.
- *Consolabuntur*, from *consolo, consolare, consolavi, consolatus*, first conjugation (*to cheer, comfort, console*). This verb can also appear as a deponent verb, *consolor, consolari, consolatus sum*, with the same meaning. However, deponent verbs cannot be used in a passive sense, even

though they have the passive form. Here, the verb is passive. Verbs of the first conjugation form their passive future by adding *-abor*, *-aberis*, *-abitur*, *-abimur*, *-abimini*, *-abuntur* to the present stem.

- *Saturabuntur*, from *saturo, saturare, saturavi, saturatus*, first conjugation (*to satiate, fill, glut*). This is, of course, formed exactly as consolabuntur.
- *Consequentur*, from the deponent verb *consequor, consequi, consecutus sum*, third conjugation (*to follow, pursue, imitate, obtain, attain*). The third and fourth conjugation verbs do not add the tense sign *-bi-*. They change their connecting vowels from the present tense *i* to an *e*, or an *ie* in the case of *-io* verbs of the third and all fourth conjugation verbs, then the personal endings, active or passive, are added. In the first person singular, however, third and fourth conjugation future verbs have the vowel *a* (or *ia*) rather than *e* (or *ie*).
- *Videbunt*, from *video, vidēre, vidi, visus*, second conjugation (*to see*). This is formed regularly as a second conjugation future active.
- *Vocabuntur*, from *voco, vocare, vocavi, vocatus*, first conjugation (*to call*). This is also formed regularly as a first conjugation future passive.

The Imperfect Indicative Active and Passive

We looked at the imperfect tense in *schola tertia decima*. It is formed by taking the present stem, adding the proper connecting vowel (first conjugation, *-a*; second conjugation, *-e*; third conjugation, *-e*; third conjugation *-io* verbs and fourth conjugation, *-ie*), then the tense sign *-ba-* plus the personal ending. This is true of both the active and passive voices.

The active voice endings are *-m, -s, -t, -mus, -tis, -nt* and the passive endings are *-r, -ris* or *-re, -tur, -mur, -mini, -ntur*. For example, the active and passive imperfect indicatives of *voco, vocare, vocavi, vocatus* (*to call*) are listed in table 15.1.

Table 15.1

	Active			Passive	
			Singular		
1st	vocabam	(I called)	vocabar	(I was called)
2nd	vocabas	(you called)	vocabaris	(you were called)
3rd	vocabat	(he, she, it called)	vocabatur	(he, she, it was called)
			Plural		
1st	vocabamus	(we called)	vocabamur	(we were called)
2nd	vocabatis	(you called)	vocabamini	(you were called)
3rd	vocabant	(they called)	vocabantur	(they were called)

The imperfect can be translated as a simple past tense, as in the paradigm above, or in a progressive sense as *I was calling* and *I was being called*. A sense of a continuous past action can be the sense of the imperfect, as in *I used to call* and *I used to be called*. The imperfect can have an incipient or beginning sense, as in *I began to call* and *I began to be called*. The sense will have to be taken from the context of the sentence or phrase in which the verb is found.

The Translation of Qui, Quae, Quod

The relative pronoun *qui* is usually translated as *who*, *which*, or *that* in the nominative case. There are cases, as in the passage from Matthew, in which *qui* needs to be translated as *they who* or *those who*. English usage needs the use of two pronouns at times, when Latin uses only one. A form of the verb *sum, esse, fui, futurus* (*to be*) may also need to be supplied in English.

Numerals

We have seen that the first three cardinal numerals are declined to agree with the noun that they describe. The number *sex* (*six*) has also previously appeared. It is never declined, so it retains the same form in all cases, numbers, and genders. Here are the remaining numerals from four through ten, all of them, like *sex*, indeclinable:

- quattuor (four)
- quinque (five)
- septem (seven)

- octo (eight)
- novem (nine)
- decem (ten)

Ablative of Description

Verse eight begins *beati mundo corde* (*blessed are the clean of heart*). As a noun, *mundus, -i* means *world*, as an adjective, *mundus, a, um* means *clean*. The ablative *mundo corde* can be translated *with a clean heart*. As in the ablative of respect, the ablative case without a preposition can be used to describe someone or something. The difference between this and the ablative of respect is that in the latter the adjective would be nominative plural, *mundi*, and the ablative of respect would be *corde*, yielding *blessed are those who are clean (in respect to) their heart*. In the present case of the ablative of description, the translation would read *blessed are those who are with a clean heart*, or simply, *blessed are the clean of heart*. Notice that the English *clean of heart* is a kind of genitive of respect or of description!

Vocabula

Nouns
justitia, -ae, *f.*, justice, righteousness
cor, cordis, *n.*, heart
misericordia, -ae, *f.*, mercy
mundus, -i, *m.*, world

Adjectives
mitis, -e, *3rd in two endings,* mild, mellow, ripe, soft, gentle
misericors, misericordis, -e, *3rd in two endings,* merciful
mundus, -a, -um, clean
pacificus, -a, -um, peace-making, peaceable

Verbs
possideo, possidēre, possedi, possessus, to own, possess
lugeo, lugēre, luxi, luctus, to mourn, lament, bewail
consolo, consolare, consolavi, consolatus, to comfort, cheer, console
consolor, consolari, consolatus sum, to deponent, comfort, cheer, console
esurio, esurire, esuritus, hunger, to be hungry, hunger for (*no perfect*)

sitio, sitire, sitivi or sitii, to thirst, be thirsty, be parched, thirst for
saturo, saturare, saturavi, saturatus, to satiate, glut, fill
consequor, consequi, consecutus sum, *deponent,* to follow, pursue,
attain, chase after
video, vidēre, vidi, visus, to see
voco, vocare, vocavi, vocatus, to call

Conjunctions
quoniam, for, because
quia, for, because

Exercitia

Translate the following.

1. Esuriunt et sitiunt.
2. Esuriebant et sitiebant.
3. Esurient et sitient.
4. Esurit et sitit.
5. Esuriebat et sitiebat.
6. Esuriet et sitiet.
7. Esurio et sitio.
8. Esuriebam et sitiebam.
9. Esuriam et sitiam.
10. Consequor et consolor.
11. Consequebamur et consolabamur.
12. Consequebantur et consolabantur.
13. Consequeris et consolare.
14. Consequentur et consolabuntur.
15. Consequetur et consolabitur.
16. Consequemini et consolabimini.
17. Consequebamini et consolabamini.
18. Beati sunt homines mundo corde, quia Deum videbunt.
19. Beati sunt homines mundo ore, quoniam Deum videbunt.
20. Beati homines misericordi ore, quoniam Deum viderunt.
21. Beati qui lugent, quoniam consolabuntur.
22. Beatae quae lugebunt, quoniam consolabuntur.
23. Beati qui lugetis, quoniam consolabimini.
24. Beati qui lugebitis, quoniam consolabimini.

25. Beatus qui luges, quia consolabaris.
26. Beata quae luges, quia consolabaris.
27. Beatus qui luget, quia consolatur.
28. Beata quae luget, quia consolatur.
29. Beatus qui esurit et sitit justitiam, quoniam ipse saturabitur.
30. Beata quae esurit et sitit justititam, quoniam ipsa saturabitur.
31. Beati qui esuriunt et sitiunt justitiam, quoniam ipsi saturabuntur.
32. Beatae quae esuriunt et sitiunt justitiam, quoniam ipsae saturabuntur.
33. Beati sunt qui esuriunt et sitiunt justitiam, quia illi saturabuntur.
34. Beatae sint quae esuriunt et sitiunt justitiam, quia illae saturabuntur.
35. Video illum panem.
36. Video illos duos panes.
37. Video illos tres panes.
38. Videbam illos quattuor panes.
39. Videbo illos quinque panes.
40. Vidi illos sex panes.
41. Videro illos septem panes.
42. Videam illos octo panes.
43. Vidissem illos novem panes.
44. Video illos decem panes.
45. Benedictus est unus vir mundo corde qui venit in nomine Domini.
46. Benedicti sunt duo viri mundo corde qui veniunt in nomine Domini.
47. Benedicti sunt tres viri mundo corde qui veniunt in nomine Domini.
48. Benedictae sunt quattuor matres mundo ore qui veniunt in nomine Domini.
49. Bendictae sunt quinque filiae mundo ore qui veniunt in nomine Domini.
50. Beati sunt sex filii mundo ore qui veniunt in nomine Domini.
51. Beata sint septem maria quae in mundo sunt.
52. Beati sunt octo agni qui in illā terrā sanctā sunt.
53. Beatae sunt novem filiae quarum pater in domo magnā est.
54. Beati sunt decem filii quorum mater in domo magnā est.

Additional Reading

Luke 6:20b–21a

Beati pauperes quia, vestrum est regnum Dei.
Beati qui nunc esuritis, quia saturabimini.

nunc, now

SCHOLA SEXTA DECIMA
THE SIXTEENTH LESSON

Lectio

We continue reading the Sermon on the Mount in this passage from Matthew 5:10–12.

Beati qui persecutionem patiuntur propter justitiam: quoniam ipsorum est regnum caelorum. (v. 10)
Beati estis cum maledixerint vobis, et persecuti vos fuerint, et dixerint omne malum adversum vos mentientes, propter me. (v. 11)
gaudete, et exultate, quoniam merces vestra copiosa est in caelis.
Sic enim persecuti sunt prophetas, qui fuerunt ante vos. (v. 12)

Translatio

Blessed are those who suffer persecution on account of justice: for theirs is the kingdom of the heavens. (v. 10)
Blessed are you when, lying, they shall have cursed you, and persecuted you, and said every evil against you, on account of me: (v. 11)
rejoice, and exult, because your reward is bountiful in the heavens.
For thus they persecuted the prophets who were before you. (v. 12)

Grammatica

The Future Perfect and the Perfect Subjunctive

The verbs *maledixerint, persecuti fuerint,* and *dixerint* are all third person plural future perfect indicatives. The future perfect is used to add vividness to a future happening or condition. The conjunction *cum* here indicates a conditional meaning of *when*, such as *whenever*. The future perfects in verse 11 can be translated into English as future perfect, as simple future, or even as present tense verbs.

Remember that the future perfect indicative is formed by taking the third principal part, dropping the first person perfect ending *-i*, and adding *-ero, -eris, -erit, -erimus, -eritis, -erint*. The endings, except for the first singular and third plural, are identical to the future of the verb *sum* (*to be*): *ero, eris, erit, erimus, eritis, erunt.*

The perfect active subjunctive looks almost entirely like the future perfect indicative. The only difference is in the first person singular, in which the perfect subjunctive has the ending *-erim* rather than *-ero*. Other than this, the perfect subjunctive and future perfect indicative are formed exactly alike.

The Perfect Tenses of Deponent Verbs and Passives of Normal Verbs

Deponent verbs use the third principal part to form the perfect tenses. The verb *persequor, persequi, persecutus sum* is a third conjugation verb meaning *to persecute*. It is made up of two elements, the preposition *per* (*through*) and the root verb *sequor, sequi, secutus sum* (*to follow, chase*). The perfect tense of deponent verbs is formed by taking the third principal part and a form of the verb *to be*. Very often the present tense of the verb *sum, esse, fui, futurus* is used to form the perfect, as shown in table 16.1.

Table 16.1

Singular		Plural	
persecutus sum	(I persecuted)	persecuti sumus	(we persecuted)
persecutus es	(you persecuted)	persecuti estis	(you persecuted)
persecutus est	(he, she, it persecuted)	persecuti sunt	(they persecuted)

This is also the way that normal verbs form the perfect passive, (but the passive participle for normal verbs is its *fourth* principal part). For example the verb *duco, ducere, duxi, ductus* forms its perfect passive as shown in table 16.2.

Table 16.2

Singular		Plural	
ductus sum	(I was led)	ducti sumus	(we were led)
ductus es	(you were led)	ducti estis	(you were led)
ductus est	(he, she, it was led)	ducti sunt	(they were led)

Of course, the gender and number of the perfect passive participle (the fourth principal part of normal verbs, the third part of deponent verbs) will vary according to the subject of the verb. The perfect passive participle can also function as an adjective, as in *benedicta tu* (*blessed are you*).

The perfect passive of normal verbs and the perfect active of deponent verbs can also be formed by taking the participle and adding the appropriate form of the perfect tense of the verb *sum, esse, fui, futurus* to it in place of the present tense form. The perfect of the verb to be is conjugated exactly as any other present active form, as shown in table 16.3.

Table 16.3

Singular		Plural	
fui	(I was, have been)	fuimus	(we were, have been)
fuisti	(you were, have been)	fuistis	(you were, have been)
fuit	(he, she, it has been)	fuerunt	(they were, have been)

The two verbs conjugated above, *persecutus sum* (*I persecuted*) and *ductus sum* (*I was led*), can also appear as *persecutus fui* and *ductus fui*. Both forms have exactly the same meaning.

The future perfect passive of normal verbs and the future perfect active of deponent verbs are formed by taking the perfect passive participle and adding the appropriate future form of the verb *sum*, namely, *ero, eris, erit, erimus, eritis, erunt*. But the future forms of *sum* can be replaced by the future perfect forms: *fuero, fueris, fuerit, fuerimus, fueritis, fuerint*. This is what has happened in verse 11, *persecuti fuerint* (*they shall have persecuted*). Verbs forms such as the future perfect active of deponent verbs or future perfect passives of normal verbs will be pointed out when they recur in the readings. Table 16.4 presents the two variant forms of the future perfect of the third conjugation deponent verb *patior, pati, passus sum* (*to suffer, allow*).

Table 16.4

	Singular		
1st	passus ero	passus fuero	(I will have suffered)
2nd	passus eris	passus fueris	(you will have suffered)
3rd	passus erit	passus fuerit	(he, she, it will have suffered)
	Plural		
1st	passi erimus	passi fuerimus	(we will have suffered)
2nd	passi eritis	passi fueritis	(you will have suffered)
3rd	passi erunt	passi fuerint	(they will have suffered)

Present Active Participles of Deponent Verbs

Remember that the present active participle is formed by taking the present stem of the verb, adding the proper connecting vowel for each conjugation, and then adding the nominative singular ending *-ns* for all three genders. For all other cases (except the neuter singular accusative, which is the same as the nominative) the ending is *-nt-*, as in *laudans* (praising), genitive *laudantis*.

Although deponent verbs have passive forms with active meanings, their present active participles are formed exactly as the participles of normal verbs. The verb *mentior, mentiri, mentitus sum* is a fourth conjugation deponent verb meaning *to cheat, lie*. *Mentientes* is the nominative masculine plural form of the participle, it is modifying the subject *they* of *maledixerint* and the other verbs in the sentence. It can be translated as the participle *lying*, or it could be treated as an adjective being used as a noun, *liars*, which would then render the sentence *when the liars curse you . . .*

Participles are treated as third declension adjectives in one ending; for review, in table 16.5 is the declension of *mentiens* (*lying*).

Table 16.5

	Singular	
	Masculine & Feminine	**Neuter**
Nominative	mentiens	mentiens
Genitive	mentientis	mentientis
Dative	mentienti	mentienti
Accusative	mentientem	mentiens
Ablative	mentiente/-i	mentiente/-i
	Plural	
Nominative	mentientes	mentientia
Genitive	mentientium	mentientium
Dative	mentientibus	mentientibus
Accusative	mentientes	mentientia
Ablative	mentientibus	mentientibus

Vocabula

Nouns
persecutio, -onis, *f.*, persecution
merces, mercedis, *f.*, pay, reward, wages, salary, fee
propheta, -ae, *m.*, prophet

Adjectives
copiosus, -a, -um, abundant, rich, plentiful, abounding

Verbs
patior, pati, passus sum, *deponent,* to suffer, allow
maledico, maledicere, maledixi, maledictus, + *dative or accusative,*
to curse
persequor, persequi, persecutus sum, *deponent,* to persecute
mentior, mentiri, mentitus sum, *deponent,* to cheat, lie, deceive
gaudeo, gaudēre, gavisus sum, *semideponent (deponent only in the*
perfect), to rejoice
exsulto, exsultare, exsultavi, exsultatus, to exult

Prepositions
propter, + *accusative,* on account of, because of
adversum, + *accusative,* against
ante, + *accusative,* before

Adverbs
sic, thus, so

Exercitia

Translate the following.
1. Beati estis cum maledixerint vobis.
2. Beati sunt cum maledixerint eis.
3. Beati sumus cum maledixeritis nobis.
4. Beati sumus cum maledixerit nobis.
5. Non beati sunt mentientes.
6. Non beatae sunt mentientes.
7. Non beatum est regnum mentientium.
8. Beatum est regnum laudantium.
9. Non benedicit mentientibus.

10. Benedicit docentibus.
11. Non benedicet mentientibus.
12. Benedicet docentibus.
13. Non benedixit mentientibus.
14. Benedixit docentibus pueros.
15. Non benedixerit mentientibus.
16. Benedixerit docentibus pueros.
17. Ne benedicat mentientibus.
18. Benedicat docentibus pueros.
19. Beatus qui persecutionem patitur.
20. Beatus qui persecutionem patior.
21. Beata quae persecutionem patitur.
22. Beata quae persecutionem patior.
23. Beatus qui persecutionem pateris.
24. Beata quae persecutionem patere.
25. Beati qui persecutionem patimur.
26. Beatae quae persecutionem patimur.
27. Beati qui persecutionem patimini.
28. Beatae quae perseutionem patimini.
29. Beati qui persecutionem patiuntur.
30. Beatae quae persecutionem patiuntur.
31. Mentior et persequor.
32. Mentiar et persequar.
33. mentiens et persequens
34. mentientes et persequentes
35. Mentiris et persequeris.
36. Mentieris et persequeris.
37. Mentitur et persequitur.
38. Mentietur et persequetur.
39. Mentimur et persequimur.
40. Mentiemur et persequemur.
41. Mentimini et persequimini.
42. Mentiemini et persequemini.
43. Mentiuntur et persequuntur.
44. Mentientur et persequentur.
45. Gaudens patior et exsulto.

46. Gaudentes patimur et exsultamus.
47. Gaudens patire et exsultas.
48. Gaudentes patimini et exsutatis.
49. Gaudens patitur et exsultat.
50. Gaudentes patiuntur et exsultant.
51. Gaudemus propter justitiam.
52. Gaudeamus propter justitiam.
53. Gaudetis propter justitiam.
54. Gaudeatis propter justitiam.
55. Gaudent propter justitiam.
56. Gaudeant propter justitiam.
57. Gaudete et exsultate quoniam merces vestra copiosa est in caelis.
58. Gaude et exsulta quoniam merces tua copiosa est in caelis.
59. Gaudete et exsultate quoniam merces vestra copiosa erit in caelis.
60. Gaude et exsulta quoniam merces tua copiosa erit in caelis.
61. Passus sum propter justitiam.
62. Gavisus sum propter justitiam.
63. Passus es propter justitiam.
64. Gavisus es propter justitiam.
65. Passus est propter justitiam.
66. Gavisus est propter justitiam.
67. Passi sumus propter justitiam.
68. Gavisi sumus propter justitiam.
69. Passi estis propter justitiam.
70. Gavisi estis propter justitiam.
71. Passi sunt propter justitiam.
72. Gavisi sunt propter justitiam.
73. Laudatus est propheta ante illos.
74. Laudatus fuit propheta ante eos.
75. Laudati sunt prophetae ante illos.
76. Laudati fuerunt prophetae ante eos.
77. Sanctificatus sum et sanctifico vos.
78. Sanctificatus fui et sanctifico vos.
79. Sanctificatus es et sanctificas nos.
80. Sanctificatus fuisti et sanctificas nos.
81. Sanctificatus est et sanctificat nos.

82. Sanctificatus fuit et sanctificat nos.
83. Sanctificati sumus et sanctificamus vos.
84. Sanctificati fuimus et sanctificamus vos.
85. Sanctificati estis et sanctificatis nos.
86. Sanctificati fuistis et sanctificatis nos.
87. Sanctificati sunt et sanctificant nos.
88. Sanctificati fuerunt et sanctificant nos.

Additional Reading

Luke 6:23

Gaudete in illā die, et exultate: ecce enim merces vestra multa est in caelo: secundum haec enim faciebant prophetis patres eorum.

ecce, behold
enim, for
secundum, +*accusative,* according to

Schola Septima Decima
The Seventeenth Lesson

Lectio

In this lesson we will examine Ecclesiastes 1:1–4, which begins with the realistic, but grim advice: the well-known "vanity of vanities, all is vanity." In Hebrew, this book is known as Qoheleth (the Preacher). It is one of the wisdom books of the Old Testament, along with Proverbs and Job. The Septuagint, or Greek version of the Old Testament adds Sirach and Wisdom of Solomon. Although written originally in Hebrew, Ecclesiastes reflects a time when Greek philosophy was becoming known to the Jewish people, perhaps in the third century before Christ.

Verba Ecclesiastae, filii David, regis Jerusalem. (v. 1)
Vanitas vanitatum, dixit Ecclesiastes, vanitas vanitatum, et omnia vanitas. (v. 2)
Quid habet amplius homo de universo labore suo quo laborat sub sole? (v. 3)
Generatio praeterit, et generatio advenit; terra vero in aeternum stat. (v. 4)

Translatio

The words of the Preacher, the son of David, king of Jerusalem. (v. 1)
Emptiness of emptinesses, said the Preacher, emptiness of emptinesses, and all things are emptiness. (v. 2)
What more does a man have from all his labor by which he works under the sun? (v. 3)
A generation passes, and a generation comes; truly the earth stands for ever. (v. 4)

Grammatica

Noun and Adjective Information

The word *ecclesiastes, -ae* is a word borrowed from Greek. An *ecclesiastes* is a person who addresses the *ecclesia*, or assembly. In both Greek and Latin *ecclesia* means the assembly of God's people, or the Church.

Both the words *David* and *Jerusalem* are Hebrew names that are not declined, here take them to be in the genitive case. (The name Jerusalem is found also as Hieruslem, a Greek rendering of the

Hebrew name. The Greek begins with "hiero," meaning "sacred" in Greek.) Note that both *filii* and *regis* are genitives which are in apposition to *ecclesiastae*, that is, they are nouns which further describe this particular noun, and must therefore be in the same case as the noun they are describing, or are in apposition to.

In verse 2, note that the verb *sunt* must be supplied for the adjective *omnia*, which is being used here as a noun, *all things*. Table 17.1 lists a review of the third declension adjective in two endings, *omnis, omne*, meaning *all, every*.

Table 17.1

| | Singular | |
	Masc. & Fem.	Neuter
Nominative	omnis	omne
Genitive	omnis	omnis
Dative	omni	omni
Accusative	omnem	omne
Ablative	omni	omni
	Plural	
Nominative	omnes	omnia
Genitive	omnium	omnium
Dative	omnibus	omnibus
Accusative	omnes	omnia
Ablative	omnibus	omnibus

Degrees of Comparison

In verse 3, *amplius* is an adverb meaning *more*. It is derived from the adjective *amplus, -a, -um* (*filled, enough, ample*). Adjectives in Latin can appear in degrees, or states of comparison, as in the English *nice, nicer, nicest* or *good, better, best*. The first degree or state of an adjective is called the positive degree, as in *deep* (*altus, -a, -um*). The second degree is called the comparative degree, as in *deeper* (*altior, altius*, third declension in two endings). The third degree is called the superlative, as in *deepest* (*altissimus, -a, -um*). Note that *altus, altior, altissimus* can also mean *high, higher, highest*.

The comparative degree is formed by taking the root of the adjective, such as *alt-*, and adding *-ior* for the masculine and feminine nominative and -*ius* for the neuter. Comparative degree adjectives are of the third declension, and the root used for adding the various endings is -*ior*-. The neuter nominative also serves as a comparative adverb. *Altius* can either be the neuter nominative or accusative singular adjective *deeper*, or the adverb *more deeply*.

Some adjectives, as in English, are irregular in their degrees. *Good, better, best*, for example, show no relation between the positive and comparative degrees. In Latin, these adjectives are also irregular: *bonus, -a, -um (good); melior, melius (better); optimus, -a, -um (best)*. Table 17.2 shows the declension of *melior, melius (better)*. While the root is irregular, the declension is perfectly regular for all comparative degree adjectives.

Table 17.2

	Singular	
	Masc. & Fem.	**Neuter**
Nominative	melior	melius
Genitive	melioris	melioris
Dative	meliori	meliori
Accusative	meliorem	melius
Ablative	meliore	meliore
	Plural	
Nominative	meliores	meliora
Genitive	meliorum	meliorum
Dative	melioribus	melioribus
Accusative	meliores	meliora
Ablative	melioribus	melioribus

The superlative degree is formed by adding -*issimus, -a, -um* to the stem of the positive degree, or, for adjectives ending in -*er*, such as *miser, misera, miserum (wretched)*, -*rimus*: *miserrimus, -a, -um, (most wretched)* An adjective whose root ends in *l*, such as *facilis*, easy, takes the form *facillimus*. The superlative degree is declined exactly as are adjectives of the first and second declensions.

Adverbs of the positive degree are often formed by adding -*e* to the stem of the adjective, as in *alte (deeply)*. This is also true of the superlative degree, as in *altissime (most deeply)*. Remember that the comparative degree of adverbs is simply the neuter nominative form, as in *altius* (*more deeply*).

The Verb Eo (to Go)

The verb of verse 4, *praeterit*, is formed from the preposition *praeter* (*past, beyond*) and the verb *eo, ire, ivi* (*ii*), *itus* (*to go*). In English, the principal parts of the verb *to go* are *go, went, gone*. The past tense has no obvious relationship to the present tense. In Latin, the verb *to go* also has irregular principal parts, but the conjugating of the verb is done regularly. The present, imperfect, and future indicative conjugations of the verb *eo* can be found in table 17.3. Notice that the imperfect and future tenses are formed on the root *i-*.

Table 17.3

	Singular		Plural	
		Present		
1st	eo	(I go)	imus	(we go)
2nd	is	(you go)	itis	(you go)
3rd	it	(he, she, it goes)	eunt	(they go)
		Imperfect		
1st	ibam	(I went)	ibamus	(we went)
2nd	ibas	(you went)	ibatis	(you went)
3rd	ibat	(he, she, it went)	ibant	(they went)
		Future		
1st	ibo	(I will go)	ibimus	(we will go)
2nd	ibis	(you will go)	ibitis	(you will go)
3rd	ibit	(he, she, it will go)	ibunt	(they will go)

The perfect tenses are formed regularly on the stem of *ivi* or *ii*. This verb is often prefixed with a preposition, giving various shades of meaning, such as *praetereo* (*I go past, I pass*), *exeo* (*I go out*), *ineo* (*I go in*), and so on.

The Interrogative Pronoun

Quid in verse 3 is the neuter singular interrogative pronoun. The relative pronoun connects two clauses, as in *this is the man whom you seek.* The interrogative pronoun asks a question, as in *whom do you seek?* The forms of the interrogative and relative pronouns are the same except for the nominative singular of all three genders and the neuter accusative singular. The masculine and feminine interrogative pronoun in the nominative singular is *quis* (*who?*). The neuter singular nominative and accusative is *quid* (*what?*). Compare this to the nominative relative pronoun forms *qui, quae, quod.* As has been mentioned, in all the other cases, both kinds of pronouns have the same forms: genitive *cujus*, dative *cui*, etc.

Vocabula

Nouns
verbum, -i, *n.,* word
ecclesiastes, -ae, *m.,* preacher
ecclesia, -ae, *f.,* assembly, church
Jerusalem, *indeclinable, can also be spelled Hierusalem or appear as the declined noun* **Hierosolyma, -ae** *or* **Hierosolymae, -arum**
vanitas, -atis, *f.,* emptiness, vanity, nullity
homo, hominis, *m.,* man, human being
labor, -is, *m.,* work, labor
sol, -is, *m.,* sun
generatio, -onis, *f.,* generation

Pronouns
quis, quid, *interrogative pronoun,* who? what?

Adjectives
amplus, -a, -um, ample, sufficient
universus, -a, -um, all
verus, -a, -um, true (*the ablative neuter* **vero,** *in truth, can be used as an adverb,* truly; *the true adverbial form is* **vere**)
aeternus, -a, -um, eternal, everlasting (**in aeternum,** forever)
melior, melius, better
optimus,-a, -um, best

Verbs
laboro, laborare, laboravi, laboratus, to work, labor
praetereo, praeterire, praeterivi, praeteritus, to pass, pass by, go past

Prepositions
de, + *ablative,* from
sub, + *ablative,* under, below
praeter, + *accusative,* past, beyond

Adverbs
amplius, more
vere, vero, truly

Exercitia

Translate the following.

1. vanitas vanitatum
2. vanitas vanitatis
3. illa vanitas
4. generatio generationum
5. generatio generationis
6. illa generatio
7. homo hominum
8. homo hominis
9. ille homo
10. labor laborum
11. Laborem laborat.
12. labor sub sole
13. homo de homine
14. Deus de Deo
15. verbum Dei
16. verbum aeternum Dei aeterni
17. Terra in aeternum sub sole est.
18. Terra sub sole aeterno erit.
19. In terram sub sole eunt.
20. In terram sub sole imus.
21. In terram sub sole itis.
22. In terram sub sole it.
23. Generatio praeterit.
24. Generatio advenit.
25. Generationes praetereunt.
26. Generationes adveniunt.
27. Generatio praeteribat.
28. Generatio adveniebat.
29. Generatio praeteribit.
30. Generatio adveniet.
31. Generationes praeteriverunt.
32. Generationes advenerunt.
33. Generatio praeterivit.
34. Generatio advenit.
35. In caelis altis cum sole.
36. In caelis altioribus cum sole.
37. In caelis altissimis cum sole.
38. In caelo alto cum sole bono.
39. In caelo altiore cum sole meliore.
40. In caelo altissimo cum sole optimo.

41. Quid habet amplius homo de universo labore suo?
42. Quid habet amplius homo de omni labore suo?
43. Quid habent amplius homines de universis laboribus suis?
44. Quid habent amplius homines de omnibus laboribus suis?
45. Vanitas vanitatis, omnia vanitas sunt.
46. Vanitas vanitatis, universa vanitas.
47. Vanitas vanitatum, omnia vanitas sunt.
48. Verbum verborum, omnia verbum sunt.
49. Verba ecclesiastae vere verba prophetae sunt.
50. Sol praeterit, sol advenit, verbum Dei aeternum est.

Additional Reading

Ecclesiastes 1:12–13

Ego Ecclesiastes fui rex Israël in Jerusalem; (v. 12)
et proposui in animo meo quaerere et investigare sapienter de omnibus
quae fiunt sub sole. (v. 13)

propono, proponere, proposui, propositus, to propose
animus, -i, *m.,* mind
quaero, quaerere, quaesivi, quaesitus, to enquire, look into, ask, seek
sapienter, wisely
fio, fieri, factus sum, to happen, occur, be made

Schola Duodevicesima
The Eighteenth Lesson

Lectio

In this reading from Ecclesiastes 3:1–8, we learn that there is a time for everything that life holds. It exemplifies the attitude of the wisdom literature that the experience of life is both pleasant and unpleasant, and it is wise not to be overly affected by either. This is also an attitude of Greek Stoic philosophy. For a similar idea, look at Job 1:21-22, and 2:9-10.

Omnia tempus habent, et suis spatiis transeunt universa sub caelo. (v. 1)
Tempus nascendi, et tempus moriendi;
tempus plantandi, et tempus evellendi quod plantatum est. (v. 2)
Tempus occidendi, et tempus sanandi;
tempus destruendi, et tempus aedificandi. (v. 3)
Tempus flendi, et tempus ridendi;
tempus plangendi, et tempus saltandi. (v. 4)
Tempus spargendi lapides, et tempus colligendi;
tempus amplexandi, et tempus longe fieri ab amplexibus. (v. 5)
Tempus acquirendi, et tempus perdendi;
tempus custodiendi, et tempus abjiciendi. (v. 6)
Tempus scindendi, et tempus consuendi;
tempus tacendi, et tempus loquendi. (v. 7)
Tempus dilectionis, et tempus odii;
tempus belli, et tempus pacis. (v. 8)

Translatio

All things have a time, and in their places all things pass under heaven. (v. 1)
A time of being born, and a time of dying;
a time of planting, and a time of ripping up what has been planted. (v. 2)
A time of killing, and a time of healing,
a time of tearing down, and a time of building. (v. 3)
A time of weeping, and a time of smiling;
a time of mourning, and a time of dancing. (v. 4)
A time of strewing stones, and a time of gathering;
a time of embracing, and a time to become far from embraces. (v. 5)
A time of acquiring, and a time of losing;
a time of keeping, and a time of casting away. (v. 6)

A time of ripping, and a time of sewing together;
a time of being silent, and a time of speaking. (v. 7)
A time of love, and a time of hate;
a time of war, and a time of peace. (v. 8)

Grammatica

The Gerund

A participle is a verbal adjective, as in *they used a <u>running</u> clock*. Similarly, the gerund is a verbal noun, as in *they gave me the gift <u>of running</u>*. Since it is derived from a verb, like the participle, the gerund can take a direct or indirect object. The gerund is formed by taking the first principal part, dropping the first person ending, adding the proper connecting vowel for each conjugation, then adding *-nd-* plus the case endings for neuter nouns of the second declension. In the passage for this lesson, all of the gerunds are in the genitive case. Gerunds are all formed alike, whether the root verb is normal or deponent. In verse 7, for example, the gerund *tacendi* (*of being silent*) is formed from the second conjugation verb *taceo, tacēre, tacui, tacitus* (*to be quiet*), and the gerund *loquendi* (*of speaking*) is from the third conjugation deponent verb *loquor, loqui, locutus sum* (*to speak*).

In verse 5, both *spargendi* (*of scattering*) and *colligendi* (*of collecting*) have *lapides* (*stones*) as their object. The object of *evellendi* (*of uprooting*) in verse 2 is the noun clause *quod plantatum est* (*that which was planted*).

Gerunds never appear in the nominative case. When a verbal noun is used as a subject, the infinitive serves the purpose. Gerunds generally appear only in the genitive, dative, ablative, and occasionally, accusative cases. The accusative of the gerund is generally used only after a preposition, otherwise the infinitive is more common as an object. Both the infinitive and the gerund are considered to be neuter nouns.

The Verb Fio

Fio, fieri, factus sum is the usual form of the passive of *facio, facere, feci, factus* (*to do* or *to make*). *Fio* can mean *I am made*. It can also mean *to become* or even, as in verse 5, *to be*, as in *tempus longe fieri a complexibus* (*a time to be far away from embraces*). The simple tenses of *fio* are formed on the stem *fi-*, as has already been seen. For a review, table 18.1 shows the indicative present tense.

Table 18.1

		Singular		Plural
1st	fio	I become	fimus	we become
2nd	fis	you become	fitis	you become
3rd	fit	he, she, it become	fiunt	they become

The imperfect is fiebam, I became, and the future fiebo, I will become. The subjunctive present forms are found in table 18.2.

Table 18.2

		Singular		Plural
1st	fiam	may I be, become	fiamus	may we be, become
2nd	fias	may you be, become	fiatis	may you be, become
3rd	fiat	may he become, let it be	fiant	may they become, let them be

The Fourth Declension

The noun *amplexus, -ūs* (*embrace*) is a masculine noun of the fourth declension. In v. 5 it is in the ablative plural following the preposition *a* (*ab* before a vowel, meaning *from*). This use of the ablative is the ablative of separation. Table 18.3 shows a review of the endings of the fourth declension.

Table 18.3

	Singular	Plural
Nominative	amplexus	amplexūs
Genitive	amplexūs	amplexuum
Dative	amplexui	amplexibus
Accusative	amplexum	amplexūs
Ablative	amplexu	amplexibus

Vocabula

Nouns

tempus, temporis, *n.,* time
spatium, -i, *n.,* place, space
lapis, lapidis, *m.,* stone
amplexus, -ūs, *m.,* embrace
dilectio, dilectionis, *f.,* love
odium, -i, *n.,* hate
bellum, -i, *n.,* war
pax, pacis, *f.,* peace

Verbs

transeo, transire, transivi, transitus, to pass, pass by, go across
(**trans + eo, ire**)
nascor, nasci, natus sum, to be born (*the past participle* **natus** *can mean*
a child)
morior, mori, mortuus sum, to die
planto, plantare, plantavi, plantatus, to plant, set
evello, evellere, evelli (*or* **evulsi**)**, evulsus,** to pull out, rip up
occido, occidere, occisi, occisus, to kill
sano, sanare, sanavi, sanatus, to heal
destruo, destruere, destruxi, destructus, to tear down, destroy
aedifico, aedificare, aedificavi, aedificatus, to build, build up
fleo, flēre, flevi, fletus, to weep
rideo, ridēre, risi, risus, to laugh
plango, plangere, planxi, planctus, to mourn, lament
salto, saltare, saltavi, saltatus, to dance, leap
spargo, spargere, sparsi, spartus, to strew, sprinkle, scatter
colligo, colligere, collegi, collectum, to collect, assemble, draw together
amplexor, amplexari, amplexatus sum, to embrace
fio, fieri, factus sum, to become, be made (*often used as the passive of*
facio)
acquiro (*for* **adquiro**)**, acquirere, acquisivi, acquisitus,** to acquire,
amass
perdo, perdere, perdidi, perditus, to destroy, ruin, waste, lose
custodio, custodire, custodivi, custoditus, to watch, defend, guard

abjicio (*or* **abicio**), **abjicere, abjeci, abjectus,** to cast away, throw, cast off
scindo, scindere, scidi, scissus, to cut, tear, rend asunder, split
consuo, consuere, consui, consutus, to sew, stitch, join together
taceo, tacēre, tacui, tacitus, to be silent, be quiet
loquor, loqui, locutus, to talk, say, speak

Adverbs
longe, afar, far away

Exercitia

Translate the following.
1. Laudare bonum est.
2. Laudare Deum bonum est.
3. Dilectio laudandi bona est.
4. Dilectio laudandi Deum bona est.
5. Loqui bonum est.
6. Loqui de Deo bonum est.
7. Dilectio loquendi bona est.
8. Dilectio loquendi de Deo bona est.
9. Sanare bonum est.
10. Sanare homines bonum est.
11. Dilectio sanandi bona est.
12. Dilectio sanandi homines bona est.
13. Omnia tempus habent.
14. Omnia tempora habent.
15. Universa tempus habent.
16. Universa tempora habent.
17. tempus amandi matrem
18. tempus amandi patrem
19. tempus filio amandi matrem
20. tempus filiae amandi patrem
21. odium spargendi lapides
22. Odium spargendi lapides mihi est.
23. Odium spargendi lapides filio est.
24. Odium spargendi lapides ei est.
25. Odium belli illis est.
26. Odium belli illis fiat.

27. Tempus pacis illis fiat.
28. Tempora pacis terrae fiant.
29. tempus fieri longe a bello
30. Tempus fieri longe a bello fiat.
31. tempus fieri longe a loquendo
32. Tempus fieri longe a loquendo fiat.
33. tempora fieri longe ab odio
34. Tempora fieri longe ab odio fiant.
35. tempus evellendi quod plantatum est
36. Tempus fiat evellendi quod plantatum est.
37. Tempora fiant evellendi quae plantata sunt.
38. Tempora bona fiant evellendi quae plantata sunt.
39. Tempus fiat consuendi quod scissum est.
40. Tempora fiant consuendi quae scissa sunt.
41. Tempus fiat consuendi quod scissum fuit.
42. Tempora fiant consuendi quae scissa fuerunt.
43. Tempus est fieri longe a scindendo.
44. Tempus sit fieri longe a spargendo lapides.
45. Tempus sit fieri longe a faciendo debita.
46. Tempus est fieri longe a spargendo lapides.
47. Tempora sunt fieri longe a faciendo debita.
48. Loqui bonum est, melius est tacēre.
49. Nasci bonum est, melius est mori in Christo.
50. Flēre non bonum est, melius est ridēre.

Additional Reading

Ecclesiastes 7:10–11

Ne sis velox ad irascendum, quia ira in sinu stulti requiescit. (v. 10)
Ne dicas: Quid putas causae est quod priora tempora meliora fuere quam
nunc sunt? Stulta enim est hujuscemodi interrogatio. (v. 11)

ne, *a conjunction indicating a negative wish or command,*
followed by the subjunctive
velox, *3rd in one ending,* swift
irascor, irasci, iritus sum, to be angry, be in a rage
ira, -ae, *f.,* wrath, anger

quia, because
sinus, -ūs, *m.,* fold, bosom, bay, place of concealment
stultus, -a, -um, stupid
requiesco, requiescere, requievi, requietus, to rest, repose
puto, putare, putavi, putatus, to think
causa, -ae, *f.,* cause, reason (**quid causae,** what of a reason, *or* why?)
quod, that
prior, prius, *comparative adjective,* earlier
fuere, *an alternative of* fuerunt
quam, than
hujuscemodi, of this sort
interrogatio, -onis, *f.,* question

Ecclesiastes 11:1

Mitte panem tuum super transeuntes aquas, quia post tempora multa invenies illum.

mitto, mittere, misi, missus, to send, cast
transeuns, transeuntis, the present active participle of **transeo**

Schola Undevicesima
The Nineteenth Lesson

Lectio

This selection is a medieval text, De bono fidei, *sometimes attributed to St. Thomas Aquinas. Although probably not written by St. Thomas, it is found in his opuscula (minor works). It is an example of medieval scholastic Latin. It shows how a medieval author would approach biblical exegesis, often by quoting verses out of their context. The saint himself would probably have been more subtle in his writing, but this seems to be a good place to begin reading a medieval text, since it will be both unfamiliar and yet not overly difficult for the student*

Primum quod est necessarium Christiano est fides, sine quā nullus dicitur fidelis Christianus. Fides autem facit quattuor bona. Primum est quod per fidem anima conjungitur Deo, nam per fidem anima Christiana facit quasi quoddam matrimonium cum Deo. "Sponsabo te mihi in fide." Et inde est quod quando homo baptizatur, primo confitetur fidem cum dicitur ei: "Credis in Deum?" quia baptismus est primum sacramentum fidei. Et ideo dicit Dominus: "Qui crediderit et baptizatus fuerit salvus erit."

Translatio

St. Thomas Aquinas, On the Good of Faith

The first thing that is necessary for a Christian is faith, without which no one is called a faithful Christian. Faith, however, makes four goods. The first is that through faith the soul is joined to God, for through faith the Christian soul makes, as it were, a kind of marriage with God. "I will espouse you to me in faith." And from this it is that when a man is baptized he first confesses the faith, when it is said to him: "Do you believe in God?", because baptism is the first sacrament of faith. And therefore the Lord says: "He who shall have believed and shall have been baptized will be saved."

Grammatica

The Indefinite Pronoun

We have seen the relative and interrogative pronouns in earlier chapters. The indefinite pronoun is basically the same as the relative pronoun, with the addition of -*dam*. The indefinite pronoun *quidam*, *quaedam*, *quoddam* can be translated as *a certain, a sort of, a kind of*. *Quoddam matrimonium* is *a kind of marriage*. Table 19.1 shows the declension of the indefinite pronoun.

Table 19.1

	Masculine	Feminine	Neuter
		Singular	
Nominative	quidam	quaedam	quoddam
Genitive	cujusdam	cujusdam	cujusdam
Dative	cuidam	cuidam	cuidam
Accusative	quemdam	quamdam	quoddam
Ablative	quodam	quadam	quodam
		Plural	
Nominative	quidam	quaedam	quaedam
Genitive	quorumdam	quarumdam	quorumdam
Dative	quibusdam	quibusdam	quibusdam
Accusative	quosdam	quasdam	quaedam
Ablative	quibusdam	quibusdam	quibusdam

The Conjunctions Quod and Quia

In the first line of the text, *quod* appears as a neuter relative pronoun: *primum quod est necessarium* (*the first thing which is necessary*). In the second and fourth lines, *quod* appears as a conjunction, meaning *that*, which introduces a clause, as in *primum est quod per fidem* (*the first is that through faith*) and *inde est quod quando homo baptizatur* (*from this it is that when a man is baptized*). You have to be careful to differentiate between *quod* as a neuter relative pronoun and *quod* as a conjunction. The conjunction, of course, never changes its form.

The conjunction *quia* can also function as a conjunction meaning *that*. It can also mean *because*, as it appears in line five. *Quod* can also mean *because*. The context of the sentence will tell you which meaning of *quod* or *quia* to use.

There is a third conjunction, *quoniam*, which can also introduce a subordinate clause. Its meaning is *that* or *because*. These three conjunctions meaning *that* are somewhat peculiar to medieval or ecclesiastical Latin. Classical Latin prefers other constructions to introduce subordinate clauses.

A Review of the Fifth Declension

The word *fides* appears a number of times in the *lectio* selection. It is a fifth declension noun meaning *faith*. Most fifth declension nouns are feminine in gender. Table 19.2 is a review of the fifth declension.

Table 19.2

	Singular	Plural
Nominative	fides	fides
Genitive	fidei	fiderum
Dative	fidei	fidebus
Accusative	fidem	fides
Ablative	fide	fidebus

Vocabula

Nouns
fides, -ei, *f.,* faith
anima, -ae, *f.,* soul (*dat. and abl. pl.* **animabus** *rather than* **animis**)
matrimonium, -i, *n.,* marriage, matrimony
homo, hominis, *m.,* man, human being
baptismus, -i, *m.,* baptism
sacramentum, -i, *n.,* sacred oath, sacrament

Adjectives
necessarius, -a, -um, needful, necessary
nullus, -a, -um, no one, nothing (*gen. sing.* **nullíus**, *dat. sing.* **nulli** *in all genders*)
fidelis, fidele, *3rd in two endings,* faithful, believing
salvus, -a, -um, safe, saved

Prepositions
sine, + *ablative,* without
per, + *accusative,* through

Verbs
conjungo, conjungere, conjunxi, conjunctus, to join, unite
sponso, sponsare, sponsavi, sponsatus, to betroth, marry
baptizo, baptizare, baptizavi, baptizatus, to baptize
confiteor, confiteri, confessus sum, *deponent,* to profess, confess, avow
credo credere credidi creditus, to believe

Adverbs
primo, first
quasi, as if, as it were

Conjunctions
quod, that, because
quia, that, because
quoniam, that, because
autem, however
nam, for
inde, from this
quando, when
ideo, therefore

Exercitia

Translate the following.
1. Nullus dicitur fidelis Christianus.
2. Nulli dicuntur fideles Christiani.
3. Nulla dicitur fidelis Christiana.
4. Nullae dicuntur fideles Christianae.
5. Dicit nullum fidelem Christianum.
6. Dicit nullam fidelem Christianam.
7. Dicunt nullos fideles Christianos.
8. Dicunt nullas fideles Christianas.
9. Nomen nullíus est fidele.
10. Nomina nullorum sunt fidelia.
11. Dat nomen nulli.
12. Dat nomina nullis.
13. Dicit quod baptizatus est a nullo.
14. Dicit quia baptizatus est a nullo.

15. Dicunt quoniam baptizati sunt a nullis.
16. Baptizat quia fidelis est.
17. Confitetur fidem quia fidelis est.
18. Confitentur fidem quia fideles sunt.
19. Credo in unum Deum.
20. Credimus in unum Deum.
21. Credidimus in unum Deum quia baptizati sumus.
22. Baptizati sumus, inde credidimus in unum Deum.
23. In baptismo, anima Deo conjungitur.
24. Quoniam baptizatur, anima Christiana Deo conjungitur.
25. Quando confitemur fidem, dicimus quod credimus in Deum.
26. Quia confessi sumus fidem Christianam, diximus quia credidimus in Deum.
27. Sine fide, Christiani dicunt quia nullus salvus erit.
28. Sine baptismo, nullus Christianus erit.
29. Per fidem et baptismum salvi erimus.
30. Anima Christiana facit quoddam matrimonium cum Deo.
31. Animae Christianae faciunt quoddam matrimonium cum Deo.
32. Illi habent quamdam fidem, inde credunt in quemdam Deum.
33. Quando homo baptizatur, primo confitetur fidem.
34. Quando quidam homo baptizatur, primo confitetur quamdam fidem.
35. Dicunt quod quando homines baptizantur, primo confitentur fidem veram.
36. Quia dicunt quod illi confitentur fidem, inde baptizentur.

Additional Reading

St. Cyprian of Carthage, De oratione dominicā

St. Cyprian lived during the first half of the third century. He died in 258, during a period of persecution. He studied oratory and pleaded in the law courts (we would call that becoming a lawyer today.) He was converted by a priest named Caecilius, and within a few years of his conversion he was elected the bishop of Carthage in North Africa. Like the later St. Augustine, his Latin displays a beautiful classical style.

Voluntas autem Dei est quam Christus et fecit et docuit. Humilitas in conversatione, stabilitas in fide, verecundia in verbis, in factis justitia, in operibus misericordia, in moribus disciplina.

quam, *translate as* that which
et . . . et, both . . . and
verecundia, -ae, *f.,* modesty
factum, -i, *n.,* deed
mos, moris, *f.,* custom (*pl.* morals, ethics)

Schola Vicesima
The Twentieth Lesson

Lectio

In this lectio, we continue with our reading of De bono fidei.

Baptismus enim sine fide non prodest. Et ideo sciendum est quod nullus est acceptus a Deo sine fide. "Sine fide impossibile est placēre Deo." Et ideo dicit Augustinus super illud, "Omne quod non est ex fide, peccatum est; Ubi non est aeternae et incommutabilis veritatis agnitio, falsa est virtus etiam in optimis moribus."

Translatio

For baptism without faith is of no avail. And therefore it must be known that no one has been accepted by God without faith. "Without faith, it is impossible to please God." And therefore Augustine says concerning it, "Everything which is not from faith, is sin; Where there is not a recognition of eternal and unchangeable truth, virtue is false even in the best morals."

Grammatica

The Gerundive

The gerundive is a verbal adjective. It looks and is formed like a gerund, but has the force of a future passive participle, and especially in the nominative and accusative, the gerund expresses necessity. *Sciendum* is the gerundive of *scio, scire, scivi, scitum* (*to know*). *Sciendum est* expresses the idea *it must be known, it has to be known.* This use of the gerund is called as the passive periphrastic. Unlike the gerund, the gerundive can modify nouns, as in *scientia scienda* (*a knowledge which must be known*) or *mater amanda est* (*a mother must be loved*). If a noun and gerundive is preceded by *ad*, the construction indicates purpose, as in *ad scientiam sciendam* (*for the purpose of knowledge being known*) or in *ad Deum laudandum* (*so that God should be praised*).

    If the gerundive, being passive, is accompanied by a noun indicating agency, that noun will be in the dative case, as in *Deus populo laudandus est* (*God must be praised by the people*). This use of the gerund is known as the dative of agency. In other passive situations, the agent is in the ablative case. (A noun that is the performer of an action in the passive voice is described as an "agent," and in English is often indicated by the preposition "by." If the verb were in the active voice, an agent would usually be the subject, as in "The people must praise God," compared with "God must be praised by the people.")

The Infinitive

The construction *impossibile est* (*it is impossible*) is followed by an infinitive, as in *impossibile est placēre Deo* (*it is impossible to please God*). The verb *placeo, placēre, placui, placitus* (*to please, to be pleasing*) is followed by the dative case.

The adjective *impossibilis, impossibile* is a third declension adjective in two endings. It is ultimately derived from the verb *possum, posse, potui*, which means *can, to be able*. It is also followed by an infinitive. The verb *possum* is made up of the prefix *pot-*, indicating ability, and the verb *sum*. Its conjugation is formed by placing *pot-* before the forms of the verb *to be*. When the verb begins with an *s*, as in *sum* or *sunt*, the *t* of *pot-* becomes an *s*. Table 20.1 illustrates the present tense conjugation of *possum* (*I can, I am able*).

Table 20.1

	Singular	Plural
1st	possum	possumus
2nd	potes	potestis
3rd	potest	possunt

Similarly, the imperfect forms are *poteram* (*I was able*), *poteras, poterat, poteramus, poteratis, poterant*, and the future forms are *potero* (*I will be able*), *poteris, poterit, poterimus, poteritis, poterunt*.

Similar in formation to this is the verb *prosum, prodesse, profui* (*to be of avail, to be of profit, to be of advantage*). This verb is followed by the dative. It appears in the first sentence of the *lectio*: *baptismus sine fide non prodest* (*baptism without faith is of no use*).

Vocabula

Nouns
peccatum, -i, *n.,* sin, error, mistake

veritas, veritatis, *f.,* truth
agnitio, agnitionis, *f.,* recognition
virtus, virtutis, *f.,* virtue
mos, moris, *m.,* custom, usage, conduct, law, rule, *pl.* morals, ethics
scientia, -ae, *f.,* knowledge

Adjectives
impossibilis, impossibile, *3rd in two endings,* impossible
incommutabilis, -e, *3rd in two endings,* unchangeable, immutable
falsus, -a, -um, false

Verbs
prosum, prodesse, profui, to avail, to be of help
scio, scire, scivi, scitus, to know
accipio, accipere, accepi, acceptus, to take, receive
placeo, placēre, placui, placitus, to please, be pleasing to

Prepositions
super, + *accusative,* above, upon, over, + *ablative,* concerning, about
e, ex *before vowels,* out of, from

Adverbs
ubi, where

Exercitia

Translate the following.
1. Non prodest.
2. Non prosunt.
3. Non prodest mihi.
4. Non prosunt nobis.
5. Non prodest filio.
6. Non prosunt matri.
7. Sciendum est quod nullum impossibile Deo est.
8. Loquendum est quod nullum impossibile Deo est.
9. Loquendum est quia nullum impossibile Deo facere est.
10. Sciendum est quia Deus amandus est.
11. Dilectio Dei loquenda est fidelibus Christianis.
12. Placet Deo amare mundum.

13. Placet hominibus amare Deum.
14. Sine dilectione Dei, nullus placet Domino.
15. Per dilectionem Dei, homines placent Domino.
16. Patri prodest amare filios suos.
17. Filiis prodest amare patrem suum.
18. Pater potest amare filios suos.
19. Filii possunt amare patrem suum.
20. Quando homini odium est, impossibile est ei amare Deum.
21. Dicit quod Deus omnibus amandus est quia fecit omnia.
22. Dixit quod Deus omnibus amandus est quoniam fecit universa.
23. Dicet quod Christus adorandus est quoniam sanavit nos.
24. Dicat quod Christus adorandus est quoniam sanat nos.
25. Christus ad mundum sanandum venit.
26. Spiritus Sanctus ad mundum sanctificandum venit.
27. Loquitur ad Deum sciendum in mundo.
28. Loquitur ad scientiam sciendam in mundo.
29. Loquitur ad veritatem sciendam in mundo.
30. Loquitur ad veritatis agnitionem sciendam in mundo.
31. Dicit ad dilectionem laudandi Deum sciendam in mundo.
32. Dicit ad dilectionem orandi sciendam in mundo.
33. Ubi dilectio Dei scita est, prodest hominibus orare.
34. Ubi dilectio Dei dicitur, prodest hominibus laudare.
35. Ubi Deus amatus est, homines amandi sunt.

Additional Reading

St. Cyprian, De oratione dominica, *continued*

Injuriam facere non nosse et factam posse tolerare, cum fratribus pacem tenēre, Deum toto corde diligere, amare in illo quod Pater est, timēre quod Deus est, Christo nihil omnino praeponere, quia nec nobis quidquam ille praeposuit, caritati ejus inseparabiliter adhaerēre, cruci ejus fortiter et fidenter assistere quando de ejus nomine et honore certamen est, exhibēre in sermone constantiam quē confitemur, in quaestione fiduciam quē congredimur, in morte patientiam quē coronamur. Hoc est coheredem Christi esse velle, hoc est praeceptum Dei facere, hoc est voluntatem Patris adimplēre.

nosse, *infinitive,* to have known
factam, *accusative singular feminine passive participle of* **facio,** having been done, *refers to* **injuriam**
tolero, tolerare, toleravi, toleratus, to bear, tolerate
teneo, tenēre, tenui, tentus, to hold, keep
diligo, diligere, dilexi, dilectus, to love
timeo, timēre, timui, to fear
nihil, *indeclinable,* nothing
omnino, *adverb,* at all
praepono, praeponere, praeposui, praepositus, to place before
nec = non
quidquam, anything at all
caritas, -atis, *f.,* love, charity
inseperabiliter, inseparably
adhaereo, adhaerēre, adhaesi, adhaesus, to cling, cleave, stick
crux, -cis, *f.,* cross
fidenter, faithfully
assisto, assistere, astiti, to stand by, place oneself
certamen, -inis, *n.,* struggle, fight, contention
exhibeo, exhibēre, exhibui, exhibitus, to produce, bring forth, show
sermo, -onis, *m.,* speech
constantia, -ae, *f.,* firmness, perseverance
quā, when
confiteor, confiteri, confessus sum, *deponent,* to confess, acknowledge
fiducia, -ae, *f.,* confidence, trust, reliance
congredior, congredi, congressus sum, to engage, contend, meet in combat, dispute
mors, -tis, *f.,* death
patientia, -ae, *f.,* endurance, long-suffering
corono, coronare, coronavi, coronatus, to crown
coheres, coheredis, coheir
volo, velle, volui, to wish, desire
adimpleo, adimplēre, adimplevi, adimpletus, to fill, fulfill, fill up

Schola Vicesima Prima
The Twenty-First Lesson

Lectio

In this lesson, we continue with De bono fidei *attributed to St. Thomas Aquinas.*

Secundo quia per fidem inchoatur in nobis vita aeterna, nam vita aeterna nihil aliud est quam cognoscere Deum. Unde dicit Dominus, "Haec est vita aeterna, ut cognoscant te solum verum Deum." Haec autem cognitio Dei incipit hīc per fidem, sed perficitur in vītā futurā, in quā cognoscimus eum sicuti est. Et ideo dicitur, "Fides est substantia sperandarum rerum." Nullus ergo potest pervenire ad beatudinem, quae est vera cognitio Dei, nisi primo cognoscat per fidem. "Beati qui non viderunt, et crediderunt."

Translatio

Secondly, that eternal life is begun in us through faith, for eternal life is nothing other than to know God. Whence the Lord says, "This is eternal life, that they should know you, the only true God." However, this knowledge of God begins here through faith, but is perfected in the life to come, in which we know him as he is. And therefore it is said, "Faith is the substance of things to be hoped for." No one, therefore, is able to attain to beatitude, which is the true knowledge of God, unless he first knows through faith. "Blessed are those who have not seen, and have believed."

Grammatica

The Adjective Alius, Alia, Aliud

This adjective means *other* or *another*. Like *unus*, *alius* is treated as an adjective of the first and second declensions except for the genitive and dative singular. Here are six adjectives that have this peculiarity. We have seen some of them; here are all six of them:

- alius, alia, aliud (other, another)
- alter, altera, alterum (other [of two], second)
- nullus, -a, -um (no one, nothing, not any)
- solus, -a, -um (only, alone)
- totus, -a, -um (whole, entire, all)

• unus, -a, -um (one)

Table 20.1 shows the declension of *alius, alia, aliud*. All six of these adjectives have the same genitive and dative singular endings, and other than the neuter *aliud*, the other cases are exactly those of the first and second declensions.

Table 20.1

	Singular		
	Masculine	**Feminine**	**Neuter**
Nominative	alius	alia	aliud
Genitive	alíus	alíus	alíus
Dative	alii	alii	alii
Accusative	alium	aliam	aliud
Ablative	alio	aliā	alio
	Plural		
Nominative	alii	aliae	alia
Genitive	aliorum	aliarum	aliorum
Dative	aliis	aliis	aliis
Accusative	alios	alias	alia
Ablative	aliis	aliis	aliis

Ut with the Subjunctive

In the quote from St. John's Gospel, *Haec est vita aeterna, ut cognoscant te solum verum Deum* (*This is eternal life, that they should know you, the only true God*), the conjunction *ut* (*that*) is introducing a noun clause which is in apposition to the independent clause *haec est vita aeterna* (*this is eternal life*). The dependent clause explains the independent clause, *that they should know you* . . . Generally in clauses of this sort, the verb of the *ut* clause is in the subjunctive mood.

Ut with the subjunctive can also be found in result clauses, in which case *ut* is often translated as *in order that* or *so that*, as in *I am studying so that I may learn Latin*.

Clauses with *ut* following verbs of command or request also usually have the subjunctive, as in *I ask that you would bring me water*. Various types of nominal or noun clauses with *ut* will occur in later readings, you should simply be aware for now that they exist.

Nisi with the Subjunctive

The conjunction *nisi* means *unless*. It is also followed by the subjunctive, as in the sentence *Nullus ergo potest pervenire ad beatudinem . . . nisi primo cognoscat per fidem* (*No one is able to arrive at beatitude . . . unless he first should know through faith*). In both the *ut* and *nisi* clauses in this selection, the verb is a form of *cognosco, cognoscere, cognovi, cognitus*, a third conjugation verb meaning to know, investigate, *learn thoroughly*. The third person indicative forms are *cognoscit* (*he knows*) and *cognoscunt* (*they know*). The subjunctive forms are *cognoscat* and *cognoscant*. Note yet once again the change of the connecting vowel that produces the present subjunctive.

Comparisons with Quam

The adverb *quam* (*than*) is used in comparisons, as in *I like vanilla more than chocolate*, or *two heads are better than one*. In the clause *nam vita aeterna nihil aliud est quam cognoscere Deum* (*For eternal life is nothing other than to know God*), *nihil aliud* (*nothing other*) implies a comparison. Here, *quam* is followed by the infinitive *cognoscere*. Note that the infinitive is also used after *potest* (*is able*); the same constructions exist in English.

Vocabula

Nouns
nihil, *n., indeclinable,* nothing
cognitio, cognitionis, *f.,* knowledge, learning
substantia, -ae, *f.,* substance
res, rei, *f.,* thing
beatitudo, beatitudinis, *f.,* beatitude, blessedness

Adjectives
alius, alia, aliud, other, another (with peculiar gen. and dat. sing.)
solus, -a, -um, sole, only (with peculiar gen. and dat. sing.)
futurus, -a, -um, future, about to be, participle of sum, esse, fui, futurus
melior, melius, *3rd in two endings,* better
major, majus, *3rd in two endings,* greater, larger
minor, minus, *3rd in two endings,* less, smaller

Verbs
inchoo, inchoare, inchoavi, inchoatus, *also found as* **incoho, incohare, etc.,** to begin, commence
cognosco, cognoscere, cognovi, cognitus, to know, learn
incipio, incipere, incepi, inceptus, to begin
perficio, perficere, perfeci, perfectus, to perfect, make perfect, complete
spero, sperare, speravi, speratus, to hope, hope for
pervenio, pervenire, perveni, perventus, to reach, attain, arrive at
possum, posse, potui (pot- + sum), to be able, can

Adverbs
quam, than (*in comparisons*)
unde, from this, whence
hīc, here (*don't confuse this with the demonstrative pronoun* **hic,** this)
sicuti *or* **sicut,** as

Conjunctions
nam, for
ideo, therefore
ergo, therefore

Prepositions
per, + *accusative,* through

Exercitia

Translate the following.

1. Nam vita aerterna nihil aliud est quam cognoscere Deum.
2. Nam vita aeterna nihil aliud est quam amare Deum.
3. Nam vita aeterna nihil aliud est quam diligere Deum.
4. Nam regnum caelorum nihil aliud est quam laudare Deum.
5. Nam regnum caeli nihil aliud est quam glorificare Deum.
6. Haec est vita aeterna, ut cognoscant te solum verum Deum.
7. Haec est vita aeterna, ut cognoscat te solum verum Deum.
8. Hoc est regnum caelorum, ut cognoscam te solum verum Deum.
9. Hoc est regnum caelorum, ut cognoscamus te solum verum Deum.
10. Haec est beatitudo, ut cognoscas me solum verum Deum.
11. Haec est beatitudo, ut cognoscatis me solum verum Deum.
12. In vitā futurā cognoscimus eum sicuti est.

13. In vitā futurā cognosco eum sicuti est.
14. In vitā futurā cognoscit eum sicut est.
15. In vitā futurā cognscunt eum sicut est.
16. In vitā futurā cognoscet eum sicuti est.
17. In vitā futurā cognoscent eum sicut est.
18. In vitā futurā cognoscat eum sicut est.
19. In vitā futurā cognoscant eum sicuti est.
20. Possum cognoscere Deum.
21. Possumus cognoscere Deum.
22. Potes cognoscere Deum.
23. Potestis cognoscere Deum.
24. Potest cognoscere Deum.
25. Possunt cognoscere Deum.
26. Poteram cognoscere Deum.
27. Poteramus facere bonum.
28. Poteras facere bonum.
29. Poteratis facere melius.
30. Poterat facere melius.
31. Poterant facere melius.
32. Potero cognoscere hanc substantiam.
33. Poterimus cognoscere illam.
34. Poteris cognoscere hanc substantiam rerum sperandarum.
35. Poteritis cognoscere hanc substantiam rerum sperandarum.
36. Poterit cognosecere illam substantiam rerum sperandarum meliorum.
37. Poterunt cognoscere substantiam meliorem bonorum sperandorum.
38. Cognoscimus substantiam majorem rerum amandarum.
39. Cognoscamus hanc substantiam minorem rerum laudandarum.
40. Nullus ergo potest pervenire ad beatitudinem, nisi primo cognoscat per fidem.
41. Nullus ergo potest pervenire ad cognitionem, nisi primo amet Deum.
42. Nulli ergo possunt pervenire ad cognitionem, nisi primo ament Deum.
43. Vos ergo non potestis advenire ad beatitudinem, nisi primo amestis Deum.

44. Tu ergo non potes pervenire ad cognitionem Dei, nisi primo credas in nomine uníus veri Dei.

45. Nos ergo non possumus pervenire ad beatitudinem, nisi primo credamus in nomine solíus veri Filii Dei.

46. Nullus ergo potest pervenire ad beatitudinem, nisi primo credat in nomine uníus veri Filii Dei.

47. Nulli ergo possunt pervenire ad cognitionem Dei, nisi primo credant per fidem in nomine uníus Dei.

48. Hīc incipit vita fidei majoris.

49. Hīc inchoat vita fidei melioris.

50. Baptismus sacramentum est, unde vita melior fidei incipit in nobis.

Additional Reading

Egeria lived during the second half of the fourth century. Not a lot is known about her (her name was sometimes given by patristic or medieval commentators as Etheria or even Sylvia!). Around 380 she made a tour of the eastern Mediterranean, and left a long letter, sometimes termed a "diary," concerning her trip or pilgrimage. The letter may have been sent back to her Christian friends at home, which may have been in southern France or Spain. The "diary" is important in that it records the celebrations of the Holy Week liturgies in Jerusalem toward the end of the fourth century. Her Latin at times departs from a classical model, but offers insights into how a less formal Latin writing style would have appeared.

Cum ergo perventum fuerit in Gethsemani, fit primum oratio apta; sic dicitur hymnus, item legitur ille locus de evangelio ubi comprehensus est Dominus. Qui locus ad quod lectus fuerit, tantus rugitus et mugitus totíus populi est cum fletu ut forsitan porro ad civitatem gemitus populi omnis auditus sit. Et jam illā horā itur ad civitatem pedibus cum hymnis; pervenitur ad portam eā horā quā incipit quasi homo hominem cognoscere; inde totum per mediam civitatem omnes usque ad unum, majores atque minores, divites, pauperes, toti ibi parati; specialiter illā die nullus recedit a vigiliis usque in mane. Sic deducitur episcopus a Gethsemani usque ad portam et inde per totam civitatem usque ad Crucem.

perventum fuerit, *literally* it had been arrived—*a similar impersonal passive idiom with verbs of motion can be found in* **illā horā itur** (at that hour it was gone) *and in* **pervenitur** (it was arrived); *English would demand the third person plural,* when they had arrived, at that hour they went, they arrived, etc.

aptus, -a, -um, proper, fitting

item, likewise, besides, also, similarly

comprehendo, comprehendere, comprehendi, comprehensus, to seize, lay hold of

ad quod = cum, when—*in the sentence* **Qui locus ad quod . . .** *translate* **qui** *as* that, *and put* **ad quod** *at the beginning,* When that place . . .

lego, legere, lexi, lectus, to read

tantus, -a, -um, so much

rugitus, -ūs, *m.,* roaring, rumbling

mugitus, -ūs, *m.,* lowing, bellowing

fletus, -ūs, *m.,* weeping

forsitan, perhaps, seemingly

porro, farther, far away

gemitus, -ūs, *m.,* sigh, sighing, groan, groaning

pes, pedis, *m.,* foot—*here, she is using the ablative plural* "with feet," *translate* on foot

quasi, as if

totum, *used as an adverb,* completely

medius, -a, -um, middle—*the Latin idiom* **per mediam civitatem** *is* through the middle of the city

usque ad, all the way up to—*think of* **unum** *as standing for* **unum locum**

major, majus, greater, older, *comparative degree of* **magnus, -a, -um**

minor, minus, lesser, younger, *comparative of* **parvus, -a, -um,** small

dives, divitis, rich, rich man

vigilia, -ae, *f.,* sleeplessness, wakefulness, vigil (*sometimes plural,* night watch, vigils)

mane, *indeclinable,* morning, early in the morning

Schola Vicesima Secunda
The Twenty-Second Lesson

Lectio

In this lesson, we conclude our reading of De bono fidei.

Tertio quod fides dirigit vitam praesentem. Nam ad hoc quod homo bene vivat, oportet quod sciat necessaria ad bene vivendum. Et si deberet omnia necessaria ad bene vivendum per studium addiscere, vel non potest pervenire, vel post longum tempus, fides autem docet omnia necessaria ad bene vivendum. Ipsa enim docet quod est unus Deus, qui est remunerator bonorum et punitor malorum, et quod est alia vita, et hujusmodi, quibus satis allicimur ad bonum et vitamus malum, "Justus meus ex fide vivit."

   Et hoc etiam patet quia nullus philosophorum ante adventum Christi cum toto conatu suo potuit tantum scire de Deo, et de necessariis ad vitam aeternam, quantum post adventum Christi scit una vetula per fidem, et ideo dicitur: "Repleta est terra scientiā Domini."

Translatio

Thirdly, that faith directs the present life. For (it is) toward this (purpose) that a man should live well, (that) it is proper that he know the necessary things for living well. And if he should need to learn through exertion all the necessary things for living well, either he is unable to attain (it), or (only) after a long time; faith, however, teaches all things necessary for living well. For she herself teaches that there is one God, who is the repayer of the good and the punisher of the evil; and that there is another life, and of what sort; by which things we are allured enough to the good and we avoid the bad, "My just one lives by faith."

   And this also is clear, that none of the philosophers before the coming of Christ was able, with all his effort, to know as much about God and about the things necessary for eternal life, as after the coming of Christ one old woman knows through faith, and therefore it is said: "The earth is filled with the knowledge of the Lord."

Grammatica

Impersonal Verbs with the Accusative and Infinitive

There are, in both English and Latin, verbs that do not have a discernible subject. *It is raining, it is necessary that, it is helpful to* are examples in English. The verb *oportet* is an impersonal verb meaning *it behooves, it is necessary, it is proper.* The verb *oportet* can be followed by the accusative and the infinitive construction. The subject of an infinitive is in the accusative, not the nominative case. This text does not follow this rule, as is obvious in the clause *oportet quod sciat necessaria ad bene vivendum* (*it is needful that one know the things necessary for living well*). In classical Latin, this would appear as *oportet eum scire necessaria ad bene vivendum.* However, here we have *quod* (*that*) followed by the present subjunctive, *sciat.* The verb *scio, scire, scivi, scitum* is a fourth conjugation verb meaning *to know.* Verbs of knowing or thinking can also take the accusative and infinitive construction.

Contrary to Fact Conditions

The sentence beginning *Et si deberet . . . addiscere* (*and if he should need to learn . . .*) is the beginning of a condition. The verb *debeo, debēre, debui, debitum* is a second conjugation verb meaning *to owe.* It also indicates necessity, as in *debet* (*one should, one ought, one has to*). In this sentence, *deberet* is the imperfect subjunctive form. This tense and mood of the verb is used in conditions that want to indicate something that is contrary to what the facts are. *If I were a rich man* in English has the definite idea that the speaker of the sentence is not rich. Similarly here, the notion is that if one needed to learn all the things for living well, it would not be possible without the knowledge that comes through Christ's revelation.

Generally, in a contrary to fact present condition, the verb of the *si* (*if*) clause (the dependent clause, or the *protasis*) is in the imperfect subjunctive. The verb of the independent clause (the *apodosis*, the *then* clause) should also be in the subjunctive. In Medieval Latin, the *then* clause can appear in the indicative in these contrary to fact conditions.

The Formation of the Imperfect Subjunctive

The imperfect tense of the subjunctive is formed by taking the active infinitive (second principal part) and adding to it the personal endings

-m, -s, -t, -mus, -tis, -nt for the active and -r, -ris/-re, -tur, -mur, -mini, -ntur for the passive. Table 22.1 shows the active imperfect subjunctive forms of each conjugation.

Table 22.1

1st	2nd	3rd	3rd -io	4th
		Active		
laudarem	monerem	ducerem	caperem	audirem
laudares	moneres	duceres	caperes	audires
laudaret	moneret	duceret	caperet	audiret
laudaremus	moneremus	duceremus	caperemus	audiremus
laudaretis	moneretis	duceretis	caperetis	audiretis
laudarent	monerent	ducerent	caperent	audirent
		Passive		
laudarer	monerer	ducerer	caperer	audirer
laudareris/-re	monereris/-re	ducereris/-re	capereris/-re	audireris/-re
laudaretur	moneretur	duceretur	caperetur	audiretur
laudaremur	moneremur	duceremur	caperemur	audiremur
laudaremini	moneremini	ducemini	caperemini	audiremini
laudarentur	monerentur	ducerentur	caperentur	audirentur

For deponent verbs, a hypothetical active infinitive form must be created. Notice that in the third conjugation, deponent verbs have an infinitive which does not have the usual *-ri* ending, as in *patior, pati.* The imperfect subjunctive of *patior* is *paterer* in the first person singular.

Table 22.2 shows the imperfect subjunctive forms of the third conjugation deponent verb *loquor, loqui, locutus sum (to speak).*

Table 22.2

loquerer	loqueremur
loquereris/-re	loqueremini
loqueretur	loquerentur

Similarly, a first conjugation deponent verb such as *miror, mirari* forms its first person imperfect subjunctive as *mirarer*, and a fourth conjugation deponent verb such as *experior, experiri (to try)* forms it as *experirer.*

Vocabula

Nouns
studium, -i, *n.,* zeal, effort
tempus, -oris, *n.,* time
remunerator, -is, *m.,* repayer, rewarder
punitor, -is, *m.,* punisher
philosophus, -i, *m.,* philosopher
adventus, -ūs, *m.,* arrival
conatus, -ūs, *m.,* attempt, effort, exertion
vetula, -ae, *f.,* old woman
scientia, -ae, *f.,* knowledge
hujusmodi, *gen. of* **hic** *and* **modus,** of this sort, of what sort

Adjectives
praesens, *3rd in one ending,* present, in sight, at hand (*a participle of*
praesum)
necessarius, -a, -um, unavoidable, inevitable, necessary (*used as a noun
in the neuter plural*)
alius, -a, -um, other, another
tantus . . . quantus, correlative adjectives, so much . . . as much, or
so great . . . as great.

Verbs
dirigo, dirigere, direxi, directus, to direct, guide
praesum, praeesse, praefui, praefuturus, to be set over, preside, rule
over, superintend (*participle* **praesens,** present)
vivo, vivere, vixi, victus, to live, be alive
oportet, *impersonal, perfect:* **oportuit,** it behooves, it is proper, it is
needful (*followed by the accusative and infinitive construction or by a
clause in the subjunctive*)
scio, scire, scivi, scitus, to know
debeo, debēre, debui, debitum, to owe, ought, to be bound to
addisco, addiscere, addidici, addictus, to learn in addition, learn further,
hear, to be informed

disco, discere, didici, to learn
pervenio, pervenire, perveni, perventum, to arrive, reach
allicio, allicere, allexi, allectus, to draw, attract, draw to one's self

vito, vitare, vitavi, vitatus, to avoid, shun

pateo, patēre, patui, to be open, (to open), lie open, be accessible
(it is clear)

Exercitia

Translate the following.
1. Nam ad hoc quod homo bene vivat.
2. Nam ad hoc quod homines bene vivant.
3. Nam ad hoc quod homo bene oret.
4. Nam ad hoc quod homines bene orent.
5. Nam ad hoc quod homo bene laudet.
6. Nam ad hoc quod homines bene laudent.
7. Nam ad hoc quod homo bene discat.
8. Nam ad hoc quod homines bene discant.
9. Nam ad hoc quod homo bene sciat.
10. Nam ad hoc quod homines bene sciant.
11. Oportet quod sciat necessaria ad bene vivendum.
12. Oportet eum scire omnia necessaria ad bene vivendum.
13. Oportet quod sciant omnia necessaria ad bene vivendum.
14. Oportet eos scire omnia necessaria ad bene vivendum.
15. Oportet quod discant omnia necessaria ad bene dirigendum.
16. Oportet eos discere omnia necessaria ad bene dirigendum.
17. Oportet quod dicat omnia necessaria ad bene sciendum Deum.
18. Oportet eum dicere omnia necessaria ad bene sciendum Deum.
19. Oportet quod pateant portae caeli.
20. Oportet portas caeli patēre.
21. Si deberet addiscere omnia necessaria ad bene vivendum, non potest pervenire.
22. Si deberet addiscere omnia necessaria ad bene sciendum, non possit pervenire.
23. Si addisceret omnia necessaria ad bene vivendum, sit in gloriā.
24. Si perveniret ad gloriam, sciverimus nomen ejus.
25. Si pervenirent ad gloriam, sciverint nomina illorum.
26. Si portae caeli paterent, Christus non veniret ad salvationem hominum.
27. Si discerem bene linguam Latinam, veniam ad Romam.

28. Si disceremus bene linguam Latinam, venerimus ad Romam.
29. Scio quod alia vita est, et hujusmodi.
30. Scio aliam vitam esse, et hujusmodi.
31. Sciat quod alia vita est, et hujusmodi.
32. Sciat aliam vitam esse, et hujusmodi.
33. Scio quod vitem peccatum et faciam bonum.
34. Scimus quod vitemus peccatum et faciamus bonum.
35. Scio vitare peccatum et facere bonum.
36. Scimus vitare peccatum et facere bonum.
37. Patet quia nullus philosophorum potuit scire tantum de Deo, quantum vetula per fidem scit.
38. Patet quod ego non possum scire tantum de fide, quantum Aquinas scivit.

Additional Reading

From the Diary of Egeria

Ante crucem autem ubi ventum fuerit, jam lux quasi clara incipit esse. Ibi denuo ille locus de evangelio ubi adducitur Dominus ad Pilatum, et omnia quaecumque scripta sunt Pilatum ad Dominum dixisse aut ad Judaeos, totum legitur. Postmodum autem alloquitur episcopus populum confortans eos, quoniam et totā nocte laboraverint et adhuc laboraturi sint ipsā die, ut non lassentur, sed habeant spem in Deo, qui eis pro eo labore majorem mercedem redditurus sit. Et sic confortans eos, ut potest ipse, alloquens dicit eis: "Ite interim nunc unusquisque ad domumcellas vestras, sedete vobis et modico, et ad horam prope secundam diei omnes parati estote hīc, ut de eā horā usque ad sexta[m] sanctum lignum Crucis possitis vidēre, ad salutem sibi unusquisque nostrum credens profuturum. De horā enim sextā denuo necesse habemus hīc omnes convenire in isto loco, id est ante Crucem, ut lectionibus et orationibus usque ad noctem operam demus."

clarus, -a, -um, bright
incipio, incipere, incepi, inceptus, to begin, *followed by the infinitive*
denuo, again
adduco, adducere, adduxi, adductus, to lead to

quaecumque, *neuter pl. of* **quicumque, quaecumque, quodcumque** (*declined like the relative pronoun with cumque added to it*), whoever, whatever

scribo, scribere, scripsi, scriptus, to write

dixisse, *perfect infinitive of* **dico, dicere, dixi, dictus,** to have written—*translate this passage as* . . . and all the various things that were written that Pilate had said to the Lord or to the Jews . . . (*the subject of an infinitive is always in the accusative case; the perfect infinitive is formed by adding* **-isse** *to the perfect stem of a verb*)

totum, *used as an adverb,* completely

legitur—*this is the present tense, treat it as a historical present and translate it with a past tense*

postmodum, after, afterward

alloquor, alloqui, allocutus sum (ad + loquor), to address, speak to

conforto, confortare, confortavi, confortatus, to strengthen, encourage (*not used in classical Latin*)

quoniam, because, *used here with the subjunctive*

laboraturi sint—This is a late form of a future subjunctive! *Laboraturus* is the future participle, meaning *about to work.* The future active participle is formed by taking the passive participle (the fourth principal part), dropping the case ending, and adding *-urus, -a, -um* to it. The usage here is definitely not classical. Translate *laboraturi sint* as *they would be about to work.* A rough translation of the subordinate clause is *since they had been at it the whole night, and would be busy on that day* . . . In later Latin, the future tense is sometimes replaced by the future participle and a form of the verb *sum,* so *veniet* (*he will come*) is replaced by *venturus est.* Notice *redditurus sit* in the next line. The verb is *reddo, reddere, redidi, reditus* (*to give back, repay*). The same construction is found here, a future participle (*redditurus*) and a form of the verb *to be* (*sit*), *he would pay back.*

lasso, lassare, lassavi, lassus, tire, make weary, become weary

interim meanwhile

unusquisque, everyone

domumcella, -ae, *f.,* room (*usually found simply as* **cella**)

modico, for a short while, *from* **modicus, -a, -um,** moderate, proper (*here the ablative is used as an adverb*)

prope, near, nearly, close

estote, *pl. imperative of* **sum** (*the singular is* **esto**)

hīc, here

lignum, -i, *n.,* wood

salus, -utis, *f.,* salvation

profuturum, *the future active participle of* **prosum,** to help, avail, be of use, *here referring to* **lignum crucis,** the wood of the cross—*the sentence reads something like* each one believing that it (*i.e.,* the wood) will be of use to each (*sibi*) for our salvation

necesse, *usually found in the form* **necesse est,** it is necessary, there is need, *followed by an infinitive (here she has combined this adjective with* **habemus** *and has turned the adjective into a noun,* we have need, we must)

convenio, convenire, conveni, conventus, to meet, assemble

iste, ista, istud, *like* **ille,** that, this

operam dare, + *dat.,* to work at, give attention to

lectio, -onis, *f.,* reading

Schola Vicesima Tertia
The Twenty-Third Lesson

Lectio

In this lesson, we begin reading from the account of the Scillitan martyrs. A dozen Christians were executed for their faith at Carthage in North Africa on July 17, 180. The account (acta—deeds) of the martyrdom exists in several different forms, both in Greek and Latin. The martyrs are known as Scillitans from the town of Scillium in Numidia. The persecution that they were caught in had begun under Marcus Aurelius, although he died before the trial recorded here. His son, Commodus, had become emperor, but had not yet ended the persecution.

Praesente bis et Claudiano consulibus, XVI Kalendas Augustas, Kartagine in secretario inpositis Sperato, Nartzalo et Cittino, Donatā, Secundā, Vestiā, Saturninus proconsul dixit, "Potestis indulgentiam domini nostri imperatoris promereri, si ad bonam mentem redeatis."

    Speratus dixit, "Numquam malefacimus, iniquitati nullam operam praebuimus. Numquam maledeximus, sed male accepti gratias egimus, propter quod imperatorem nostrum observamus."

    Saturninus proconsul dixit, "Et nos religiosi sumus, et simplex est religio nostra. Et juramus per genium domini nostri imperatoris, et pro salute ejus supplicamus, quod et vos facere debetis."

    Speratus dixit, "Si tranquillas praebueris aures tuas, dico mysterium simplicitatis."

    Saturninus dixit, "Initianti tibi mala de sacris nostris aures non praebeo, sed potius jura per genium domini nostri imperatoris."
Speratus dixit, "Ego imperium hujus saeculi non cognosco, sed magis illi Deo servio quem nemo hominum vidit nec vidēre his oculis potest. Furtum non feci, sed siquid emero, teloneum reddo, quia cognosco domini meum regem regum et imperatorem omnium gentium."

Translatio

When Praesens, for the second time, and Claudianus were consuls, sixteen days before the Kalends of August [July 17, 180], at Carthage, when Speratus, Nartzalus and Cittinus, Donata, Secunda, and Vestia were set in the council chamber, Saturninus the proconsul said, "You are able to gain the forgiveness of our lord the emperor, if you return to good sense."

Speratus said, "We have never done anything wrong, we have offered no opportunity for evil. We have never cursed, but treated badly we
have given thanks, on account of this we have respected our emperor."

Saturninus the proconsul said, "We are also god-fearing, and our
religious obligation is simple. We both swear by the guardian spirit of
our lord the emperor, and we pray for his health, which you also ought
to do."

Speratus said, "If you would offer quiet ears, I would tell you
the mystery of innocence."

Saturninus said, "I will not offer ears to you who originate evils
concerning our holy things, but rather, swear by the guardian spirit of
our lord the emperor."

Speratus said, "I do not recognize the rule of this world, but I
rather serve that God whom no one sees nor is able to see with these
eyes. I have not stolen, but if I shall have bought anything, I pay the
tax, because I recognize my Lord is the king of kings and emperor of
all peoples."

Grammatica

The Ablative Absolute

In the first paragraph of the English translation there are two temporal clauses beginning with the conjunction when: *When Praesens
and Claudianus were consuls, when Speratus et al. were set.* In the Latin
text, there is no word meaning *when* present. The Latin text is using a
construction called the ablative absolute. This construction is formed
by nouns, or nouns modified by adjectives or participles, placed in the
ablative case but grammatically unrelated to the rest of the sentence.
For example, *Claudiano consule* is an ablative absolute. It can be translated as *Claudianus being consul* or *when Claudianus was consul.* Note
that in our text the ablative absolute is in the plural, since two men
are mentioned, *Praesente et Claudiano consulibus.* The ablative absolute
is often used in place of a temporal clause or some other descriptive
clause. Here are some examples:

- cenā finitā, *the dinner being finished, when dinner was finished*
- Caesare duce, *Caesar being leader, when Caesar was leader*
- puero legente, *the boy reading, while the boy was reading*
- Mariā orante, *Mary praying, when Mary was praying*
- Jesu baptizato, *Jesus having been baptized, when Jesus was baptized*

- apostolis electis, *the apostles being chosen, when the apostles were chosen*
- oratione dictā, *the prayer being said, when the prayer was said*
- orationibus dictis, *the prayers being said, when the prayers were said*

Roman Dates

The Roman year was divided into twelve months, originally corresponding to the waxing and waning of the moon (the Latin word for *month* is *mensis*). The first month was originally March (*Martius*), and many of the month names were simply numbers, such as September, the seventh month, October, the eighth month. July was originally *Quintilis*, the fifth month, and August *Sextilis*, the sixth month. These names were changed to honor Julius and Augustus Caesar (July and August).

In the Roman year, there were no weeks of seven days; this is a Hebrew custom. Instead, the Romans divided the month according to days known as the kalends (*Kalendae*) which referred to the beginning of a month, originally associated with the sight of the new moon. The ides were at the full moon, or the middle of the month, and the nones were placed nine days before the ides. The days were counted backwards from the major parts of the month. For example, *XVI (ante) Kalendas Augustas* was sixteen days before the kalends of August. The day before the kalends was the *pridie*, the day before that *III ante Kalendas*, and so on. There is probably no reason at this point to learn this rather arcane system, other than to know why the sixteenth day before the kalends of August is actually July 17.

The Romans reckoned their years in numerical succession from the reputed founding of the city, *ab urbe condita (from the city being founded)*, which was in 753 BC according to our calendar. Ordinary references to a year, however, were usually based on the names of the two consuls chosen for that year. The two consuls were originally executive officers elected to that position, and together held a great deal of authority. During the period of the principate (after Julius Caesar) the consulate became a weakened office, with executive power in the hands of the emperor (*imperator*, originally a military title, *commander.*) Hence the year AD 180 is, in Roman reckoning, *Praesente bis et Claudiano consulibus (when Praesens, for the second time, and Claudianus were consuls)*. *Bis* is an adverb meaning *twice*.

Conditions Revisited

There are three conditional sentences in this selection, two of them reversing the protasis and apodosis (the *si* or *if* clause, the protasis, comes last instead of first). In the first one, which is at the end of the first paragraph, the dependent clause is *si ad bonam mentem redeatis* (*if you would return to a proper disposition*). The verb is from *redeo, redire*, a compound of *re + eo, ire, ivi, itus* (*to go back, return*). In the reading it is in the present subjunctive. The verb of the apodosis is in the indicative, *potestis* (*you are able*)—with the infinitive *promereri*, from *promereor* (*to earn, merit, gain*). In ecclesiastical Latin, if the verb of the independent clause (apodosis) is in the indicative, it indicates nothing as to whether or not the condition will be fulfilled, it is an open possibility. If the verb of the apodosis is in the subjunctive, it indicates that the condition is not or will not be fulfilled.

The first conditional sentence can be translated as *you can gain the favor of the emperor if you would return to a good disposition*, or the future could be used, *you will be able to gain*, or a subjunctive *you would be able to gain*.

The second condition is found in the fourth paragraph, and the verb is in the future perfect, *si praebueris* (*if you would offer, if you were to offer your ears*), and once again, the apodosis has the verb in the indicative, *dico*. In English, *dico* needs to be rendered either by the future, *I will tell*, or the subjunctive, *I would tell*.

The third condition is found in the last paragraph, *siquid emero, teleonum reddo* (*if I should buy anything, I pay the tax*). Here the verb of the protasis is again in the future perfect indicative. The use of the future or future perfect indicates a more vivid sense to the condition (*siquid = si + quid*).

The Locative Case

The locative case indicates a place where. In Latin it is usual only with proper names of cities or places. In the first and second declension, the locative singular looks like the genitive, *Romae* (*at Rome*), *Ephesi* (*at Ephesus*). In the plural of these declensions, it looks like the ablative, *Athenis* (*at Athens*; nominative, *Athenae*). In the third declension, singular or plural, the locative has the same ending as the corresponding ablative, so *Carthagine* (*at Carthage*; nominative, *Carthago*). The locative indicates a place where, it never indicates motion toward a city.

Vocabula

Nouns

consul, -is, *m.,* consul

Carthago, -inis, *f.,* Carthage, *alternate spelling* **Kartago,** *perhaps with the K here influenced by the word* **Kalendas** (*ordinarily, the use of K was replaced in Latin by C, except for the word* **Kalendae** *and some Greek loan words*)

secretarium, -i, *n.,* inner room, council chamber

proconsul, -is, *m.,* proconsul, *a former consul who was given administrative work in the provinces*

indulgentia, -ae, *f.,* mercy, clemency, favor

mens, -ntis, *f.,* mind, disposition, heart

iniquitas, -atis, *f.,* evil, iniquity

opera, -ae, *f.,* pains, effort, trouble, time, opportunity

imperator, -is, *m.,* commander, emperor

religio, -onis, *f.,* religious awe, scrupulosity, conscientiousness, sacred obligation, religious worship

genius, -i, *m.,* guardian spirit, tutelary deity

salus, -utis, *f.,* health, salvation

auris, -is, *f.,* ear

simplicitas, -tis, *f.,* guilelessness, moral simplicity, frankness, innocence

sacra, -orum, *n.,* holy things, rites

imperium, -i, *n.,* rule, empire

nemo, -inis, *m.,* no one

oculus, -i, *m.,* eye

furtum, -i, *n.,* theft

teleonum, -i, *n.,* tax

gens, -tis, *f.,* people, nation

Adjectives

nullus, -a, -um, none (*declined like* **unus** *or* **alius,** *the genitive is* **nullíus,** *the dative* **nulli**)

religiosus, -a, -um, god-fearing, scrupulous, conscientious as to ritual

simplex, *3rd in one ending,* simple

tranquillus,- a, -um, tranquil, quiet, peaceful

Verbs
inpono, inponere, inposui, inpositus, to place, set, put in
promereor, promereri, promissus sum, to earn, gain, merit
redeo, redire, redivi, reditus, *(an intransitive verb, indicating motion only)* to go back, return
praebeo, praebēre, praebui, praebitus, to grant, offer, proffer, hold out, exhibit
malefacio, malefacere, malefeci, malefactus, to do evil, do wrong
observo, observare, obervavi, observatus, to watch, respect
juro, jurare, juravi, juratus, to swear
supplico, supplicare, supplicavi, supplicatus, to beg, pray
initio, initiare, initiavi, initiatus, to begin, originate
cognosco, cognoscere, cognovi, cognotus, to recognize
servio, servire, servivi, servitus, to serve
emo, emere, emi, emptum, to buy, purchase

Adverbs
bis, twice
numquam, never
potius, rather
magis, rather

Exercitia

Translate the following.
1. Praesente consule
2. Claudiano consule
3. Praesente et Claudiano consulibus
4. Praesente bis et Claudiano consulibus
5. Petro capto
6. Paulo dicente
7. Petro et Paulo scribentibus
8. Johanne baptizante
9. Johanne baptizato
10. Johanne et Petro baptizantibus
11. Johanne et Petro baptizatis
12. Johanne et Petro bis baptizatis
13. Johanne bis et Petro baptizantibus multos

14. Johanne et Petro multos Romae baptizantibus
15. Petro et Paulo majores Carthagine baptizantibus
16. Paulo multa dicente populo Athenis, redivit ad Hierusalem.
17. Sperato in secretario Carthagine inposito, Saturninus proconsul introivit.
18. Donatā in secretario Carthagine inpositā, Saturninus proconsul redivit.
19. Sperato et Donatā in secretario inpositis, Saturninus eis locutus est.
20. Sperata et Donatā locutis, Valerianus in secretarium venit.
21. Iniquitati nullam operam praebuimus.
22. Iniquitati nullam operam praebemus.
23. Iniquitati nullam operam praebebimus.
24. Iniquitati nullam operam praebeamus.
25. Iniquitati nullam operam praebueramus.
26. Iniquitati nullam operam praebuerimus.
27. Si mentem tuam redeatis, potestis indulgentiam domini imperatoris promerēri.
28. Si ad domum illíus domini redeam, possum indulgentiam imperatoris promerēri.
29. Nisi ad domum illíus domini redeam, non possum indulgentiam promerēri.
30. Juramus per genium imperatoris, quod et vos facere debetis.
31. Jurant per genium imperatoris, quod et tu facere debes.
32. Jurabatis per genium imperatoris, quod et illi facere debent.
33. Juremus per genium imperatoris, quod et vos facere debetis.
34. Si tranquillas aures praebueris, dico tibi mysterium simplicitatis.
35. Si tranquillas aures praebueritis, dicimus vobis mysterium regni caeli.
36. Si tranquillas aures praeberunt, dico eis mysterium magnum.
37. Si quid emero, teleonum imperatori do.
38. Si quid emerit in Romā, teleonum imoeratori dat.
39. Si vivero in Italiā, beatissimus sum.

Additional Reading

From the Martyrdom of Cyprian *(September 14, 258). The Martyrdom records some of the trial and execution of St. Cyprian, bishop of Carthage, during the persecution of Valerian.*

Et ita alterā die, octavā decimā Kalendarum Octobrium, mane multa turba convenit ad Sexti secundum praeceptum Galeri Maximi proconsulis. Et ita idem Galerius Maximus proconsul eādem die Cyprianum sibi offerri praecepit in atrio Sauciolo sedenti. Cumque oblatus fuisset, Galerius proconsul episcopo dixit, "Tu es Thascius Cyprianus?"

Cyprianus episcopus respondit, "Ego sum."

Galerius Maximus proconsul dixit, "Tu papam te sacrilegae mentis hominibus praebuisti?"

Cyprianus episcopus respondit, "Ego."

Galerius Maximus proconsul dixit, "Jusserunt te sacratissimi imperatores caerimoniari."

Cyprianus episcopus dixit, "Non facio."

Galerius Maximus ait, "Consule tibi."

Cyprianus episcopus respondit, "Fac quod tibi praeceptum est. In re tam justā nulla est consultatio."

Galerius Maximus collocutus cum concilio sententiam vix et aegre dixit verbis hujusmodi: "Diu sacrilegā mente vixisti et plurimos nefariae conspirationis homines adgregasti et inimicum te diis Romanis et religionibus sacris constituisti, nec te pii et sacratissimi principes Valerianus et Gallienus Augusti et Valerianus nobilissimus Caesar ad sectam caerimoniarum suarum revocare potuerunt. Et ideo cum sis nequissimorum criminum auctor et signifer deprehensus, eris ipse documento his quos scelere tuo tecum adgregasti; sanguine tuo sancietur disciplina." Et, his dictis, decretum ex tabellā recitavit: "Thascium Cyprianum gladio animadverti placet."

Cyprianus episcopus dixit, "Deo gratias."

mane, early in the morning
turba, -ae, *f.,* crowd
ad sexti, *i.e.,* **ad domum Sexti**
isdem, eadem, idem (is, ea, id + dem), the same
sibi, *dative,* to himself, *i.e., the proconsul* (*note the participle* **sedenti** *modifies* **sibi**)
offero, offerre, obtuli, oblatus, to present, offer, bring; **offerri:** *passive infitive*; **oblatus fuisset:** *passive pluperfect subjunctive*
praecipio, praecipere, praecepi, praeceptus, to command, order

atrium, -i, hall, court, vestibule (*what exactly is meant by the* **atrium Sauciolum** *is unknown, presumably the name of the hall where trials were held*)

papa, -ae, *m., from the Greek,* father, bishop, presbyter, pastor, *in apposition to* **te,** yourself

sacrilegus, -a, -um, sacrilegious, robbing a temple

jubeo, jubēre, jussi, jussus, to command, order, bid

caerimonior, -ari, -atus sum, to perform the customary rites

ait, *found only in this form in the present =* **dicit,** he says, he said

consulo, consulere, consului, consultus, to consider, reflect, deliberate

consultatio, -onis, *f.,* deliberation, consideration

colloquor, colloqui, collocutus sum, to speak, speak with

consilium, -i, *n.,* council, counsel

sententia, -ae, *f.,* opinion, judgment

vix, *adv.,* with great difficulty, barely

aeger, aegra, aegrum, ill, sick, unwilling, reluctant, **aegre** *is the adverbial form*

hujusmodi, of this sort, of this kind

diu, *adv.,* for a long time

vivo, vivere, vixi, victus, to live

plurimus, -a, -um, *superlative of* **multus,** very many

nefarius, -a, -um, impious, heinous

conspiratio, -onis, *f.,* plot, conspiracy

adgrego (aggrego), adgregare, -avi, -atus, to gather together, assemble (*note the perfect here is* **adgregasti** *for* **adgregavisti**)

inimicus, -i, enemy

constituo, constituere, constitui, constitutus, to put, place, station, establish

pius, -a, -um, dutiful, devout, conscientious

princeps, principis, *m.,* leading citizen, the n leader, prince

augustus, -a, -um, venerable, majestic, *a name given to Julius Caesar's adopted son Octavian* (*in the third century, the empire was being governed by 4 emperors: 2 senior* **Augusti,** *and 2 younger* **Caesares;** *both* **Augustus** *and* **Caesar** *were names that became titles—here, two* **Augusti** *and one* **Caesar** *are mentioned*)

secta, -ae, *f.,* path, way

caerimonia, -ae, *f., also found as* **caerimonium, -i,** *n.,* rite, religious usage

revoco, revocare, revocavi, revocatus, to call back

nequissimus, -a, -um, most worthless
crimen, -inis, *n.,* charge, accusation, crime
auctor, -is, *m.,* source, maker, creator
signifer, -is, *m.,* standard-bearer (*military usage*)
deprehendo, -ere, -endi, -ensus, to take, seize, snatch
documentum, -i, *n.,* pattern, warning, proof (*here translate as* an example)
scelus, -eris, *n.,* crime
sanguis, -inis, *m.,* blood
sancio, sancire, sanxi, sanctus, to render inviolate, enact, confirm
disciplina, -ae, *f.,* instruction, *here* sentence
decretum, -i, *n.,* decree
tabella, -ae, *f.,* writing tablet (of wax)
gladius, -i, *m.,* sword
animadverto, animadvertere, animadversi, animadversus, to regard, observe, punish with death (*here, the passive infinitive following* **placet**)

Schola Vicesima Quarta
The Twenty-Fourth Lesson

Lectio

We conclude our reading from the account of the early Christian martyrs from Scillita.

Saturninus proconsul dixit ceteris, "Desinite hujus esse persuasionis."

Speratus dixit, "Mala est persuasio homicidium facere, falsum testimonium dicere."

Saturninus proconsul dixit, "Nolite hujus dementiae esse participes."

Cittinus dixit, "Nos non habemus alium quem timeamus, nisi Dominum Deum nostrum qui est in caelis."

Donata dixit, "Honorem Caesari quasi Caesari; timorem autem Deo."

Vestia dixit, "Christiana sum."

Secunda dixit, "Quod sum, ipsud volo esse."

Saturninus proconsul Sperato dixit, "Perseveras Christianus?"

Speratus dixit, "Christianus sum."

Et cum eo omnes consenserunt.

Saturninus procunsul dixit, "Numquid ad deliberandum spatium vultis?"

Speratus dixit, "In re tam justā, nulla est deliberatio."

Saturninus proconsul dixit, "Quae sunt res in capsā vestrā?"

Speratus dixit, "Libri et epistulae Pauli viri justi."

Saturninus proconsul dixit, "Moram XXX dierum habete et recordemini."

Speratus iterum dixit, "Christianus sum."

Et cum eo omnes consenserunt.

Saturninus proconsul decretum ex tabellā recitavit, "Speratum, Nartzalum, Cittinum, Donatam, Vestiam, Secundam, et ceteros ritu Christiano se vivere confessos, quoniam oblatā sibi facultate ad Romanorum mores redeundi obstinanter perseveraverunt, gladio animadverti placet."

Speratus dixit, "Deo gratias agimus."

Nartzalus dixit, "Hodie martyres in caelis sumus, Deo gratias."

Saturninus proconsul per praeconem dici jussit, "Speratum, Nartzalum, Cittinum, Veturium, Felicem, Aquilinum, Laetantium, Januariam, Generosam, Vestiam, Donatam, Secundam duci jussi."

Universi dixerunt, "Deo gratias."

Et ita omnes simul martyrio coronati sunt, et regnant cum Patre et Filio et Spiritu Sancto per omnia saecula saeculorum. Amen.

Translatio

Saturninus the proconsul said to the others, "Cease to be of this belief."

Speratus said, "The belief to do murder, to speak false witness is evil."

Saturninus the proconsul said, "Do not will to be sharers of this madness."

Cittinus said, "We have no other whom we should fear, except our Lord God who is in the heavens."

Donata said, "(We give) honor to Caesar as to Caesar, but reverence to God."

Vestia said, "I am a Christian."

Secunda said, "What I am, that I wish to be."

Saturninus the proconsul said to Speratus, "Do you remain a Christian?"

Speratus said, "I am a Christian."

And all agreed with him.

Saturninus the proconsul said, "Do you want time for considering?"

Speratus said, "In a matter so right, there is no considering."

Saturninus the proconsul said, "What are the things in your case?"

Speratus said, "Books and the letters of Paul, a just man."

Saturninus the proconsul said, "Take a delay of thirty days and think."

Speratus again said, "I am a Christian."

And they all agreed with him.

Saturninus the proconsul read the decree from the writing tablet: "It is pleasing for Speratus, Nartzalus, Cittinus, Donata, Vestia, Secunda, and the others to be killed by the sword, having admitted that they live in the Christian observance, because, with the possibility offered them of returning to the ways of the Romans, they stubbornly persisted."

Speratus said, "We give thanks to God."

Nartzalus said, "Today we are martyrs in heaven, thanks be to God."

Saturninus the proconsul ordered to be said through the herald: "I have ordered Speratus, Nartzalus, Cittinus, Veturius, Felix, Aquilinus, Januaria, Generosa, Vestia, Donata, and Secunda to be led away."

They all said, "Thanks be to God."

And so they were all crowned with martyrdom at the same time, and they reign with the Father and the Son and the Holy Spirit through all ages of ages. Amen.

Grammatica

The Verbs Volo and Nolo

Volo means *I wish, I will, I want,* and *nolo, I do not wish, I do not will, I do not want.* The principal parts of *volo* are *volo, velle, volui,* and of *nolo* they are *nolo, nolle, nolui.* Note the formation of the infinitives of each verb. In all but the present tense, the verb *volo* is conjugated as if it belonged to the third conjugation. Table 24.1 illustrates the present tense, indicative and subjunctive, of *volo* and *nolo.*

Table 24.1

Indicative		Subjunctive	
volo	nolo	velim	nolim
vis	non vis	velis	nolis
vult	non vult	velit	nolit
volumus	nolumus	velimus	nolimus
vultis	non vultis	velitis	nolitis
volunt	nolunt	velint	nolint

In all other tenses, the verb is regular. *Nolo* is a verb of the third conjugation.

Both of these verbs are generally followed by an infinitive. The imperative of *nolo* plus an infinitive is used to form a negative command. The negative command can also be formed by using *ne* plus the subjunctive. For example, the command, *do not teach* can be formed as *ne doceas* or as *noli docēre.* In the plural, these would appear as *ne doceatis* and *nolite docēre.* This construction appears in the third line of the text, *nolite hujus dementiae esse participes,* which is literally *be unwilling to be partakers of this madness,* and which could be translated simply as *do not be partakers of this madness.*

The Accusative with the Infinitive

Since an infinitive is a verb, it can have a subject. When this is the case, the subject of an infinitive is always in the accusative case, not the nominative. This construction often occurs after verbs of saying, knowing, or sensing. For example, in the reading of the sentence on the martyrs, where it is noted that they, having confessed themselves to be Christians, *confessos se vivere ritu Christiano, se (themselves)* is in the accusative case as both the object of the participle *confessos* (*having admitted*) and the subject of the infinitive *vivere* (*to live*).

Similarly, look at the following examples. *Peter thought that John was an apostle* would be *Petrus putabat Joannem apostolum esse.* Literally, this would read *Peter thought John to be an apostle*, and in English this makes sense. Similarly *Lawrence says that Peter is in Asia* would be *Laurentius dicit Petrum in Asiā esse.* Again, literally it reads *Lawrence says Peter to be in Asia.*

Medieval Latin seems to prefer a clause with *quia* or *quod* (*Petrus putabat quod Joannes apostolus erat*), but the classical construction of accusative and the infinitive is still sometimes used.

Questions

The word *numquid* or *num* is used in introducing a question to which a negative reply is expected. In the reading, Saturninus is expecting that the martyrs will refuse some time for consideration when he asks *numquid ad deliberandum spatium vultis?* If he were to expect a positive answer, the question would have begun with *nonne. Nonne ad deliberandum spatium vultis* could be translated as *is it not the case that you would wish a time for deliberating?*

Questions can also be formed simply be placing the suffix *-ne* after the first word of the sentence, and often by making the verb the first word, as in *vultisne ad deliberandum spatium?* (*do you want some time to deliberate?*) In the case of using *-ne*, no information is given as to what kind of reply is expected.

Vocabula

Nouns

persuasio, -nis, *f.,* belief, persuasion
homocidium, -i, *n.,* murder, homicide
testimonium, -i, *n.,* witness
dementia, -ae, *f.,* madness
particeps, -ipis, sharer, partaker
honor, -is, *m.,* honor
timor, -is, *m.,* fear, awe
spatium, -i, *n.,* space
deliberatio, -nis, *f.,* consideration, deliberation

capsa, -ae, *f.,* case
liber, libri, *m.,* book
epistula, -ae, *f.,* letter
mora, -ae, *f.,* delay
decretum, -i, *n.,* decree, sentence
tabella, -ae, *f.,* wax tablet for writing and reading
ritus, -ūs, *m.,* rite, religious custom
facultas, -atis, *f.,* possibility, capability, opportunity
gladius, -i, *m.,* sword
praeco, -onis, *m.,* herald
martyr, -is, witness, martyr (*from Greek*)
martyrium, -i, *n.,* martyrdom

Adjectives
ceterus, -a, -um, other
triginta, *indeclinable,* thirty (*written* **XXX,** *pronounced as* **triginta**)

Verbs
desino, desinere, desinii, desitus, to leave off, stop, cease (+ *infinitive*)
timeo, timēre, timui, timitus, to fear, dread
nolo, nolle, nolui, to be unwilling, to not want
volo, velle, volui, to wish, will, want
persevero, perseverare, -avi, -atus, to persist, remain, continue, finish
consentio, consentire, consensi, consensus, to agree, harmonize with
recordor, recordari, recordatus sum, to think over
recito, recitare, recitavi, recitatus, to read aloud, recite
confiteor, confiteri, confessus sum, to profess, confess, admit
vivo, vivere, vixi, victus, to live
offero, offerre, obtuli, oblatus (ob + fero, ferre, tuli, latus), to bear, present, offer
redeo, redire, redii, reditus, to go back, return
animadverto, -ere, -si, -tus, to pay attention, see, understand, punish
jubeo, jubēre, jussi, jussus, to command, order
corono, -are, avi, atus, to crown

Exercitia

Translate the following.

1. Desinite hujus persuasionis esse.
2. Desinite hujus esse persuasionis.
3. Nolite hujus persuasionis esse.
4. Nolite hujus esse persuasionis.
5. Nolite hujus dementiae participes esse.
6. Noli hujus dementiae esse.
7. Perseveras Christianus?
8. Perseverasne Christianus?
9. Vultisne ad deliberandum spatium?
10. Numquid ad deliberandum spatium vultis?
11. Nonne ad deliberandum spatium vultis?
12. Saturninus putabat Christianos ad deliberandum spatium velle.
13. Saturninus dixit eos ad deliberandum spatium nolle.
14. Quae est haec res in capsā tuā?
15. Quae sunt res in capsā vestrā?
16. Ille dicit has res in capsā esse.
17. Dicitne has res in capsā meā esse?
18. In re tam justā nulla est deliberatio.
19. Estne in re tam justā delberatio?
20. Numquid in re tam justā deliberatio est?
21. Nonne in re tam justā deliberatio est?
22. Si deliberatio in re tam justā esset, necesse esset spatium ad deliberandum.
23. Nisi deliberatio in re tam justā esset, non poteramus facere justitiam.
24. Nisi bonum hominibus faceres, non poteras Deum vidēre.
25. Sententiā ex tabellā recitatā, martyres gladio animadversi sunt.
26. Cum sententia ex tabellā recitaretur, martyres gladio animadversi sunt.
27. Epistulis lectis, Saturninus dixit Speratum Christianum esse.
28. Cum epistulae lectae essent, Saturninus dixit se putare Speratum Christianum esse.
29. Saturninus Speratum, Narztalum, et Cittinum duci jussit.
30. Saturninus Speratum, Narztalum, et Cittinum gladio animadverti jussit.

Additional Reading

A letter of St. Gregory the Great to Mellitus, (601) Gregory the Great lived in the second half of the 6th century. He was trained in grammar and rhetoric and became a monk. In 590 he was elected Pope. He is noted for his encouragement of liturgical renewal and missionary zeal. He sent the monk Augustine to England with a company of Benedictines to convert the inhabitants. Among the over 800 of his letters that survive is this one to Mellitus, another Benedictine who was being sent to join the mission in England. Gregory's advice makes good pastoral sense: don't destroy the culture, baptize it.

Cum ergo Deus omnipotens vos ad reverentissimum virum, fratrem nostrum Augustinum episcopum perduxerit, dicite ei quid diu mecum de causā Anglorum cogitans tractavi, videlicet, quia fana idolorum destrui in eadem gente minime debeant, sed ipsa quae in eis sunt idola destruantur.

Aqua benedicta fiat, in eisdem fanis aspergatur. Altaria construantur, reliquiae ponantur. Quia si fana eadem bene constructa sunt, necesse est ut a cultu daemonum in obsequium veri Dei debeant commutari. Ut dum gens ipsa eadem fana sua non videt destrui, de corde errorem deponat et Deum verum cognoscens ac adorans ad loca quae consuevit familiarius concurrat.

Et quia boves solent in sacrificio daemonum multos occidere, debet eis etiam hāc de re aliquā sollemnitas immutari, ut die dedicationis vel natalitii sanctorum martyrum, quorum illic reliquiae ponuntur.

Tabernacula sibi circa easdem ecclesias, quae ex fanis commutatae sunt, de ramis arborum faciant, et religiosis conviviis sollemntitatem celebrent, nec diabolo jam animalia immolent, sed ad laudem Dei in esu suo animalia occident, et donatori omnium de satietate suā gratias referent, ut dum eis aliqua exterius gaudia reservantur, ad interiora gaudia consentire facilius valeant.

Nam duris mentibus simul omnia impossibile esse dubium non est, quia et is qui summum locum ascendere nititur gradibus vel passibus, non autem saltibus, elevatur.

cum . . . perduxerit, *temporal clause with the future perfect,* when
    God . . . shall have brought
videlicet, namely
fana, *neuter plural of* **fanum**
destrui, *passive infinitive of* **destruo**
ipsa *and* **idola** *go together,* those idols which are in them

ut dum . . . , so that while the people do not see their shrines de-
stroyed . . . [they] would remove error (*notice that, while* **gens** *is singular
in Latin, the English uses a plural, similarly* **consuevit . . . concurrat,**
they may more familiarly come together at the places where they were
accustomed—**consuevit** *is from* **consuesco, consuescere, consuevi**)
bos, bovis, bullock, cow
natalitius, -a, -um (*usually* **natalicius, -a, -um**), pertaining to a birthday
hāc de re . . . the festival ought to be changed for them from whatever it was, as a day of consecration . . .
esus, -ūs, *m.,* act of eating, food
gratias refero = gratias ago
dubium non est . . . For there is no doubt furthermore that all things
are impossible for hardened minds, and he who strives to rise to the
highest place is raised by stairs or footsteps, but not by jumps . . .
simul . . . et = etiam
nitor, niti, nisus *or* **nixus sum,** *deponent,* to press forward with effort

Schola Vicesima Quinta
The Twenty-Fifth Lesson

Lectio

In this last lesson, we'll read the text of the Pange lingua, *a hymn written by St. Thomas Aquinas. Thomas lived in the thirteenth century, and wrote this hymn for the new feast of Corpus Christi. It is often sung during the procession with the Eucharist to the place of repose on Holy Thursday. The most familiar verses are the last two, which are often sung during Benediction of the Blessed Sacrament. The hymn expresses the theme of transubstantiation, namely that the bread and wine become the Body and Blood of Christ during the consecration of the Mass.*

1. Pange, lingua, gloriosi
   corporis mysterium,
   sanguinisque pretiosi,
   quem in mundi pretium
   fructus ventris generosi
   Rex effudit gentium.

2. Nobis datus, nobis natus,
   ex intactā Virgine,
   et in mundo conversatus,
   sparso verbi semine,
   sui moras incolatūs
   miro clausit ordine.

3. In supremae nocte cenae
   recumbens cum fratribus,
   observatā lege plene
   cibis in legalibus,
   cibum turbae duodenae
   se dat suis manibus.

4. Verbum caro panem verum
   verbo carnem efficit,
   fitque sanguis Christi merum,
   et si sensus deficit,
   ad firmandum cor sincerum
   sola fides sufficit.

5. Tantum ergo sacramentum
   veneremur cernui,
   et antiquum documentum
   novo cedat ritui;
   praestet fides supplementum
   sensuum defectui.

6. Genitori Genitoque
   laus et jubilatio,
   salus, honor, virtus quoque
   sit et benedictio;
   procedenti ab utroque
   compar sit laudatio.

Translatio

1. Sing, O tongue, the mystery of the glorious body, and of the precious blood, that the King of the nations, the fruit of a noble womb, poured out for the price of the world.

2. Given to us, born for us, from an untouched Virgin, and having lived in the world, when the seed of the word was spread, he closed in a wondrous order the times of his own sojourn.

3. On the night of the last supper, reclining with the brothers, with the full law being kept in lawful foods, he gives himself with his own hands (as) food for the crowd of twelve.

4. The Word, flesh, makes real bread flesh by (his) word, and wine becomes the blood of Christ, and if sense fails, faith alone avails for a genuine heart to be strengthened.

5. Bowing, therefore, let us revere such a sacrament, and let the ancient example yield to the new rite; let faith furnish a supply for the failing of the senses.

6. To the Begetter and to the Begotten may there be praise and rejoicing, salvation, honor and strength, also blessing; to the One proceeding from both may there be equal praise.

Grammatica et Poetica

Word Order in Poetry

In the Latin prose readings encountered so far, adjectives have generally been close to the nouns they modify, as are nouns in the genitive case to the ones they accompany. The verbs tend to appear at the end of a sentence. In poetry, word order is sacrificed for the sake of meter and sound play. This, along with the use of elevated language and, at times, rare words, makes poetry in any language more difficult to read than prose.

Poetry sometimes leaves out words that one would expect, as in verse 4, in which the subject is *Verbum caro* (literally, *the Word, flesh*). This is often translated as "the Word made flesh," which is probably the intention of the author, but the meter would not allow it.

The translation given above is a literal one. Notice that there is no rhyme or meter in the English, as there is in the Latin. In classical Latin poetry, rhyme is generally not an element of a work. In later Latin it often appears as a poetic fixture.

The Rhythm of the Poem

There have been claims that the rhythms of this work are based on an old marching song that goes back to the time of Caesar. The beginning of that song is

Ēccĕ Cāēsār nūnc trĭūmphăt, quī sŭbēgĭt Gāllĭās,
Ēccĕ tūrbām nūnc rĕdūcĭt quāē rĕfērt vīctōrĭ ăm.

Behold, Caesar now triumphs, who subdues the Gauls,
Behold, he now leads back the host that carries the victory.

As a processional song, the *Pange lingua* has the rhythm of marching feet:

Pāngĕ līnguā glōrĭōsī cōrpŏrīs mȳstērĭūm,
Sānguĭnīsquē prētĭōsī quēm īn mūndī prētĭūm.

A syllable in Latin is long if its vowel is long, and short if its vowel is short. Vowels are either long by nature (as the *a* in the infinitve *portāre*) or by position. A vowel before two consonants is long by position (as the *u* in *tūrbam*). A vowel before another vowel is short by position (as the first *i* in *gloriosi*). The rhythm of the *Pange lingua* is a long followed by a short, then a long followed by either a long or a short (-‿-x). The last foot has three beats to it, -‿-.

The Particle *-que*

In *sanguinisque pretiosi* (*and of the precious blood*), the word *and* is not *et*, but the suffix *-que* that is added to *sanguinis*. This is a fairly common usage, especially if there is a string of words which would be connected by *and*. The ancient Roman acronym SPQR, for example, stands for *senatus populusque Romanus* (*the Roman senate and people*). The *-que* always appears on the last word of the connected series, and never earlier. Another example occurs in verse 6, Genitori Genitoque (*to the Father and the Son*).

Notae

Verse 1

The object of *pange* (*sing*) is *mysterium*. *Mysterium* has two genitives attached to it, one before (*gloriosi corporis*) and one after (*sanguinis pretiosi*). Note the *-que* attached to *sanguinis*.

In pretium indicates purpose (*for the cost of the world*).

Notice the "sandwiching" of *effudit* (*he poured out*) between *Rex* and *gentium* (*King of the nations*).

Verse 2

The participles *datus* and *natus* give an internal rhyme, along with the double use of *nobis*. *Conversatus* is the perfect participle of the deponent verb *conversor* (*to dwell, live*), and so must be translated actively (*having dwelt*). *Sparso verbi semine* is an ablative absolute (*when the seed of the Word is spread*). *Moras*, the accusative plural of *mora* (*delay*), can be translated as *time*. *Incolatūs* is the genitive singular modifying *moras*.

Verse 3

Observata lege plene is another ablative absolute. *Cibis in legalibus* (*with legal foods*) indicates that the ritual laws of the Passover were observed. The word *duodenae* is from *duodeni*, a plural adjective meaning "twelve each." It is being used here as a substitute for the usual *duodecim* (*twelve*). *Se* (*himself*), an accusative, is in apposition to *cibum* (*food—he gives himself as food*).

Verse 4

Caro (*flesh*) is in apposition to *Verbum* (*the Word, flesh, makes true bread flesh by a word*). Often in English translations, something is added here, such as "the Word *made* flesh," but the Latin simply juxtaposes the two words. Notice another *-que* in *fitque* (*and it becomes*). *Ad firmandum* is a case of *ad* + the accusative to indicate purpose, in this case the gerundive is modifying *cor*.

Notice in this verse the verbs made from prepositions and *facio*: *efficio, deficio, sufficio*. The third person singulars of each form part of the rhyme of this verse.

Verse 5

Cernui looks like a fourth declension dative singular, but it is the nominative masculine plural of the adjective *cernuus* (*kneeling*). It does rhyme with *ritui* and *defectui*, both of which are fourth declension singular datives. A *documentum* is a type or example, a bit different than its descendant in English, document.

Verse 6

Genitor and the passive participle *genitus* (from *geno*) are used, for the sake of meter (and the *-oque* rhyme), for *Pater* and *Filius*. *Genitor* and *genitus* are derived from theological Trinitarian language, not from biblical usage. *The begetter* and *the begotten*, are generally not found in liturgical language, but they are in theological treatises. Notice again the use of *-que*.

The Holy Spirit is referred to as *procedenti ab utroque* (*to the one proceeding from both*), also a theological usage rather than a liturgical one. *Procedenti* is the dative active participle from *procedo*.

Vocabula

Verse 1

pango, pangere, panxi (*or* pegi, pepegi), panctus (*or* pactus), to make, compose, sing

lingua, -ae, *f.,* tongue, language

corpus, corporis, *n.,* body

mysterium, -i, *n.,* mystery

pretiosus, -a, -um, costly, precious

pretium, -i, *n.,* price, cost

venter, -ntris, *m.,* womb

generosus, -a, -um, noble

rex, regis, *m.,* king

effundo, effundere, effudi, effusus, to pour out, shed, spill

gens, gentis, *f.,* nation, people, clan

Verse 2

intactus, -a, -um, untouched

conversor, conversari, conversatus sum, *deponent,* to dwell, live

spargo, spargere, sparsi, sparsus, to sow, scatter, strew

semen, seminis, *n.,* seed, offspring

mora, -ae, *f.,* delay; *in this reading pl.,* times

incolatus, -ūs, *m.,* sojourn, stay, residing

mirus, -a, -um, wonderful

claudo, claudere, clausi, clausus, to close, shut

ordo, ordinis, *m.,* order, rank, rite

Verse 3
supremus, -a, -um, last, final, supreme
nox, noctis, *f.,* night
cena, -ae, *f.,* supper, meal
recumbo, recumbere, recubui, to recline
observo, observare, observavi, observatus, to keep, observe
plene, *adverb,* fully
cibus, -i, *m.,* food, meat
legalis, -e, lawful, legal
turba, -ae, *f.,* crowd
duodeni, -ae, -a, *(only plural),* twelve each; *in this reading,* the twelve
manus, -ūs, *f.,* hand

Verse 4
verbum, -i, *n.,* word
caro, carnis, *f.,* flesh, meat
efficio, efficere, effeci, effectus, to make, effect
merum, -i, *n.,* wine
sensus, -ūs, *m.,* sense, feeling, perception, mind
deficio, deficere, defeci, defectus, to fail, faint, be lacking
firmo, firmare, firmavi, firmatus, to strengthen, establish
cor, cordis, *n.,* heart
sincerus, -a, -um, guileless, innocent, sincere
sufficio, sufficere, suffeci, suffectus, to be enough, suffice

Verse 5
tantus, -a, -um, such
veneror, venerari, veneratus sum, *deponent,* to adore, venerate
cernuus, -a, -um, kneeling
documentum, -i, *n.,* example, type, specimen
cedo, cedere, cessi, cessus, to yield, withdraw, grant
ritus, -ūs, *m.,* rite, ceremony
praesto, praestare, praestiti, praestitus, to furnish, grant, guarantee,
serve, stand out
supplementum, -i, *n.,* supply, supplement
defectus, -ūs, *m.,* need, lack

Verse 6

generator, -is, *f.,* generator, father, begetter
geno, genere, genui, genitus, to generate, beget, bear
laus, laudis, *f.,* praise
salus, -utis, *f.,* health, salvation
virtus, -utis, *f.,* strength, virtue
quoque, also
procedo, procedere, processi, processus, to proceed, go forth
uterque, utraque, utrumque, both, each of two
compar, *3rd declension adjective in one ending,* equal

Exercitia

Translate the following.

1. Pange lingua corporis sanguinisque mysterium.
2. Pango corporis sanguinisque mysterium.
3. Pango corporis mysterium sanguinisque.
4. Pangis gloriosi corporis mysterium sanguinisque pretiosi.
5. Pangit gloriosi corporis mysterium sanguinisque pretiosi.
6. In mundo conversatus, moras incolatūs clausit.
7. In mundo conversatus, sparso verbi semine, moras incolatūs clausit.
8. In mundo conversabatur, spargebat semen verbi, claudebatque moras incolatūs.
9. In mundo conversabitur, sparget semen verbi, claudetque moras incolatūs.
10. In mundo conversatus est, verbo evangelii sparso, moras incolatūs clausit.
11. Verbo evangelii sparso, miro ordine moras incolatūs clausit.
12. Verbo evengelii sparso, miro ordine tempus vitae claudebatur.
13. Verbo gratiae sparso, generoso ordine tempus vitae suae clausum est.
14. Verbo Dei in mundo sparso, genersoso ordine tempus vitae suae clausum est.
15. Verbum Dei in mundo sparsit, clausitque dies vitae suae miro ordine.
16. Observatā lege in cibis legalibus, cibum dat turbae.
17. Observatis legibus in cibo legali, se cibum dat turbae duodecim.

18. Observato praecepto in cibis legalibus, se suis manibus cibum turbae dedit.

19. Observatā lege plene in cibis legalibus, se cibum manibus suis turbae dabat.

20. Legem in cibis legalibus observavit deditque se cibum manibus suis turbae.

21. Panem verum carnem Christi efficit fitque sanguis Christi merum.

22. Verbo panem verum carnem effecit et sanguis Christi merum factum est.

23. Si sensus deficit, sola fides ad firmandum cor sufficit.

24. Si sensūs deficiunt, sola fides ad firmandum cor sufficit.

25. Si sensūs deficiunt, sola fides ad firmandam animam sufficit.

26. Cernui veneremur tantum sacramentum.

27. Cernui veneramur tantum sacramentum donumque.

28. Cernui venerati sumus tantum sacramentum donumque.

29. Cernuus veneratus sum tantum sacramentum donumque.

30. Cernuus venerer tantum sacramentum et Deo gratias agam.

31. Cernui veneremur tantum sacramentum et Deo gratias agamus.

32. Patri Filioque sint laus jubilatioque.

33. Genitori Genitoque sit benedictio, et procedenti ab utroque.

34. Compar laudatio sit procedenti ab utroque.

35. Compar laudatio sit sedenti ad dexteram Genitoris.

36. Compar laudatio sit Genitoque Patris supremi.

37. Compar laudatio sit nomini Geniti Filii.

38. Honor virtusque nomini Genitoris Genitique, et procedentis ab utroque.

39. Genitorem, Genitum, et procedentem ab utroque ecclesia laudat.

40. Gloria a Genito nomini Genitoris datur, in potestate procedentis ab utroque.

Additional Reading

Rabanus Maurus, Veni Creator Spiritus
Rabanus Maurus lived during the late eighth and mid–ninth centuries. He was a Benedictine monk and abbot, eventually becoming archbishop of Mainz in 847. He wrote many commentaries on biblical books, a work on the philosophy of nature, and a series of intricate poems on the Cross. He is

best known for this hymn, Veni Creator Spiritus. It is used at Pentecost, at ordinations, and at the time of the election of a pope.

1. Veni, Creator Spiritus,
   mentes tuorum visita,
   imple supernā gratiā
   quae tu creasti pectora.
2. Qui diceris Paraclitus,
   altissimi donum Dei,
   fons vivus, ignis, caritas,
   et spiritalis unctio.
3. Tu septiformis munere,
   digitus paternae dexterae,
   tu rite promissum Patris,
   sermone ditans guttura.
4. Accende lumen sensibus,
   infunde amorem cordibus,
   infirma nostri corporis,
   virtute firmans perpeti.

5. Hostem repellas longius,
   pacemque dones protinus,
   ductore sic te praevio,
   vitemus omne noxium.
6. Per te sciamus, da, Patrem,
   noscamus atque Filum,
   teque utriusque Spiritum,
   credamus omni tempore.
7. Deo Patri sit gloria,
   et Filio, qui a mortuis
   surrexit, ac Paraclito,
   in saeculorum saecula.

Verse 1
tuorum, *needs a noun to be supplied, such as* of your people
imple, fill, *has the object* **pectora,** from **pectus, -oris**
creasti, *a shortening of* **creavisti**

Verse 2
diceris, you are called

Verse 3
septiformis, *adjective,* sevenfold, + *ablative,* sevenfold in . . .
munere, *ablative of* **munus, muneris**
digitus, *for the sake of meter, can be elided to* **ditus** *in pronunciation*
ditans, *active participle of* **dito, -are,** to enrich
sermone, *ablative following* **ditans,** enriching with speech

Verse 4
infunde amorem, *usually pronounced* **infundamorem,** *the* **e** *is elided for the sake of meter*
infirma, *neuter plural adjective, used substantively as* weaknesses
perpeti, *ablative of the adjective* **perpes** (*stem* **perpet-**), *modifying* **virtute**

Verse 5

ductore . . . praevio, *an ablative absolute*
utriusque, *genitive of* **uterque**

Verse 6

da, grant, *followed by* **sciamus** *and* **noscamus,** *both in the subjunctive,*
add *that* to we may know

Stephen Langton, Veni Sancte Spiritus

*This hymn serves as a liturgical Sequence (a hymn between the readings)
for Pentecost. It is generally attributed to Stephen Langton, who lived
from 1150 to 1228. He was elected as archbishop of Canterbury in 1208,
but King John refused to recognize him. Pope Innocent III placed England
under an interdict until the king relented in 1213. The archbishop returned
to England, and his first act was to forgive the king, who, two years later,
would sign the Magna Carta. Stephen Langton is noted for introducing the
practice of dividing the biblical books into chapters. His divisions are still
used, as is his hymn.*

1. Veni, sancte Spiritus,
   et emitte caelitus
   lucis tuae radium.
2. Veni pater pauperum,
   veni dator munerum,
   veni lumen cordium.
3. Consolator optime,
   dulcis hospes animae,
   dulce refrigerium.
4. In labore requies,
   in aestu temperies
   in fletu solatium.
5. O lux beatissima,
   reple cordis intima
   tuorum fidelium.

6. Sine tuo numine,
   nihil est in homine,
   nihil est innoxium.
7. Lava quod est sordidum,
   riga quod est aridum,
   sana quod est saucium.
8. Flecte quod est rigidum,
   fove quod est frigidum,
   rege quod est devium.
9. Da tuis fidelibus
   in te confidentibus
   sacrum septenarium.
10. Da virtutis meritum,
    da salutis exitum,
    da perenne gaudium.

Verse 6

numine, *distinguish carefully from* **nomine**

Verse 9

septenarius, -a, -um, containing seven, *a word such as "gifts" should be
   understood with it*

Morphology

Nouns

Latin nouns have number, gender, and case. The number of a noun is either singular or plural. The gender can be masculine, feminine, or neuter. The case indicates the use of a noun in a sentence: nominative (subject), genitive (possession), dative (indirect object), accusative (direct object, and after prepositions of motion), ablative (used with prepositions, also indicates separation, description, and various other uses), vocative (direct address, usually the same as the nominative, except in the second declension), and locative (rarely used, and only with names of cities to indicate place where).

There are five declensions of nouns. All nouns fall into one of the five types modeled by each declension. Note that the long marks used in the models are not used throughout the text, except to distinguish some similar cases.

The First Declension

Nouns in this declension are feminine, unless they refer to a specifically male person such as *papa* (*pope*) or *nauta* (*sailor*).
Example: **glōria, -ae,** glory

	Singular	Plural
Nominative	glōria	glōriae
Genitive	glōriae	glōriārum
Dative	glōriae	glōriīs
Accusative	glōriam	glōriās
Ablative	glōriā	glōriīs

The vocative is the same as the nominative, the locative for singular names of cities is the same is the genitive, so *Rōmae* (*at Rome*); for plural names of cities the locative is the same as the ablative, so *Athēnīs* (*at Athens*; nominative *Athēnae*).

The Second Declension

Nouns in this declension are either masculine or neuter. Most masculine nouns have their nominative singular in *-us*, neuters are in *-um*. Examples: **servus, -i,** servant; **bellum, -i,** war

	Singular	Plural	Singular	Plural
Nominative	servus	servi	bellum	bella
Genitive	servī	servōrum	bellī	bellōrum
Dative	servō	servīs	bellō	bellīs
Accusative	servum	servōs	bellum	bellōs
Ablative	servō	servīs	bellō	bellīs

The vocative of second declension masculine singular nouns ends in *-e*, as in *serve* (*O servant!*). The plural vocative is the same as the nominative, as are neuter vocatives. The locative of singular names of cities is the same as the genitive, as in *Ephesī* (*at Ephesus*).

There are also masculine nouns of the second declension whose nominative singular ends in *-r*, such as *puer* (*boy*), or *–ir* as in *vir* (*man*) . The other case endings are the same as normal second declension nouns, so *puerī, puerō,* etc.

The Third Declension

Nouns of this declension are either masculine, feminine, or neuter. The stem for these nouns is taken from the genitive form.
Examples: **dux, ducis,** leader (m.); **pāx, pācis,** peace (f.); **lūmen, lūminis,** light (n.)

	Singular	Plural	Singular	Plural	Singular	Plural
Nominative	dux	ducēs	pāx	pācēs	lūmen	lūmina
Genitive	ducis	ducum	pācis	pācum	lūminis	lūminum
Dative	ducī	ducibus	pācī	pācibus	lūminī	lūminibus
Accusative	ducem	ducēs	pācem	pācēs	lūmen	lūmina
Ablative	duce	ducibus	pāce	pācibus	lūmine	lūminibus

Certain nouns of this declension have the genitive plural in *-ium*. These are nouns which either have an equal number of syllables in the nominative and genitive singular, such as *panis, panis* (*bread*), genitive plural *panium*, or have a stem that ends in two consonants, as long as the second consonant is not an *l* or an *r*, such as *pars, partis*, genitive plural *partium*.

There are a handful of neuter nouns which also have the genitive in *-ium*. These also have the ablative singular in *-i* rather than *-e*, and the nominative and accusative plural in *-ia* rather than *-a*. One example is *mare, maris* (*sea*), plural *maria* in the nominative and accusative, and *marium* in the genitive.

The Fourth Declension

Nouns of this declension are generally masculine, but a few are feminine. Neuter nouns have slight variants in their declension.
Examples: **frūctus, -ūs,** fruit (m.); **genū, -ūs,** knee (n.)

	Singular	Plural	Singular	Plural
Nominative	frūctus	frūctūs	genū	genua
Genitive	frūctūs	frūctuum	genūs	genuum
Dative	frūctuī	frūctibus	genū	genibus
Accusative	frūctum	frūctūs	genū	genua
Ablative	frūctū	frūctibus	genū	genibus

The Fifth Declension

Most nouns of this declension are feminine, a few are masculine.
Example: **fidēs, fidei,** faith

	Singular	Plural
Nominative	fidēs	fidēs
Genitive	fideī	fidērum
Dative	fideī	fidēbus
Accusative	fidem	fidēs
Ablative	fidē	fidēbus

Adjectives

Adjectives of the First and Second Declension

Example: **beātus, -a, -um,** blessed, happy

	Singular M.	F.	N.	Plural M.	F.	N.
Nominative	beātus	beāta	beātum	beātī	beātae	beāta
Genitive	beātī	beātae	beātī	beātōrum	beātārum	beātōrum
Dative	beātō	beātae	beātō	beātīs	beātīs	beātīs
Accusative	beātum	beātam	beātum	beātōs	beātās	beāta
Ablative	beātō	beātā	beātō	beātīs	beātīs	beātīs

Adjectives of the Third Declension

These adjectives are in one, two, or three endings. This refers to the nominative singular. One ending adjectives have one nominative singular form for all genders, two endings have the same ending in the nominative singular for the masculine and feminine, and another for the neuter. Three endings adjectives have different endings for each gender in the nominative singular.

Participles are treated as adjectives of one ending.

Example: **omnis, -e,** all, every

	Singular M.	F.	N.	Plural M.	F.	N.
Nominative	omnis	omnis	omne	omnēs	omnēs	omnia
Genitive	omnis	omnis	omnis	omnium	omnium	omnium
Dative	omnī	omnī	omnī	omnibus	omnibus	omnibus
Accusative	omnem	omnem	omne	omnēs	omnēs	omnia
Ablative	omnī	omnī	omnī	omnibus	omnibus	omnibus

Example: **amāns**, loving, *participle of* **amō, amāre, amāvi, amātus**

	Singular			Plural		
	M.	**F.**	**N.**	**M.**	**F.**	**N.**
Nominative	amāns	amāns	amāns	amāntēs	amāntēs	amāntia
Genitive	amāntis	amāntis	amāntis	amāntium	amāntium	amāntium
Dative	amāntī	amāntī	amāntī	amāntibus	amāntibus	amāntibus
Accusative	amāntem	amāntem	amāns	amāntēs	amāntēs	amāntia
Ablative	amānte	amānte	amānte	amāntibus	amāntibus	amāntibus

The ablative singular of the participle can also be found in -*ī*.

Demonstrative Adjectives and Pronouns

The third person pronoun (he, she, it, they), also used as a demonstrative (this, that, these, those):

	Singular			Plural		
	M.	**F.**	**N.**	**M.**	**F.**	**N.**
Nominative	is	ea	id	eī, iī	eae	ea
Genitive	ejus	ejus	ejus	eōrum	eārum	eōrum
Dative	eī	eī	eī	eīs, iīs	eīs, iīs	eīs, iīs
Accusative	eum	eam	id	eōs	eās	ea
Ablative	eō	eā	eō	eīs, iīs	eīs, iīs	eīs, iīs

The demonstrative adjective (this, these), is also used as a third person pronoun (he, she, it, they):

	Singular			Plural		
	M.	**F.**	**N.**	**M.**	**F.**	**N.**
Nominative	hic	haec	hoc	hī	hae	haec
Genitive	hujus	hujus	hujus	hōrum	hārum	hōrum
Dative	huic	huic	huic	hīs	hīs	hīs
Accusative	hunc	hanc	hoc	hōs	hās	haec
Ablative	hōc	hāc	hōc	hīs	hīs	hīs

The demonstrative adjective (that, those), also used as a third person pronoun (he, she, it, they):

	Singular			Plural		
	M.	**F.**	**N.**	**M.**	**F.**	**N.**
Nominative	ille	illa	illum	illī	illae	illa
Genitive	illīus	illīus	illīus	illōrum	illārum	illōrum
Dative	illī	illī	illī	illīs	illīs	illīs
Accusative	illum	illam	illum	illōs	illās	illa
Ablative	illō	illā	illō	illīs	illīs	illīs

The demonstrative *iste, ista, istud* and the reflexive *ipse, ipsa, ipsum* are declined like *ille, illa, illud.*

The relative pronoun (who, which, that) and the interrogative adjective (which?):

	Singular			Plural		
	M.	**F.**	**N.**	**M.**	**F.**	**N.**
Nominative	quī	quae	quod	quī	quae	quae
Genitive	cujus	cujus	cujus	quōrum	quārum	quōrum
Dative	cui	cui	cui	quibus	quibus	quibus
Accusative	quem	quam	quod	quōs	quās	quae
Ablative	quō	quā	quō	quibus	quibus	quibus

The interrogative pronoun (who? which?) is declined similarly, with the exception of the masculine and feminine nominative singular, which is *quis* rather than *quī* and *quae.*

Variations of these pronouns such as *quisquam, quaedam, quidquam* (*anyone, anything*); *quisque, quaeque, quodque* (*whoever, whatever, each*); and so on, are all similarly declined, with the particle added to the various case forms.

First and Second Person Pronouns

	First Person		Second Person	
	Singular	**Plural**	**Singular**	**Plural**
Nominative	ego	nōs	tū	vōs
Genitive	meī	nostrī, nostrum	tuī	vestrī, vestrum
Dative	mihi	nōbis	tibi	vōbis
Accusative	mē	nōs	tē	vōs
Ablative	mē	nōbis	tē	vōbis

The personal pronouns in the genitive case are rarely used for possession. Instead, the possessive pronouns are used.

Verbs

Verbs have person, number, tense, voice, and mood. In the simple tenses (present, imperfect, and future) the first principal part is used. In the perfect active tenses (perfect, pluperfect, and future perfect) the third principal part is used. In the perfect passive tenses, the fourth principal part, which is the passive participle, and an appropriate form of the verb *to be* is used.

The irregular verb sum, **esse, fuī, futūrus**, simple tenses:

	Indicative Mood		Subjunctive Mood	
	Singular	**Plural**	**Singular**	**Plural**
	Present Tense			
1st	sum	sumus	sim	sīmus
2nd	es	estis	sīs	sītis
3rd	est	sunt	sit	sint
	Imperfect Tense			
1st	eram	erāmus	essem	essēmus
2nd	erās	erātis	essēs	essētis
3rd	erat	erant	esset	essent
	Future Tense			
1st	erō	erimus		
2nd	eris	eritis		
3rd	erit	erunt		

The irregular verb **eō, īre, īvī (iī), itus** (*to go*), simple tenses:

	Indicative Mood		Subjunctive Mood	
	Singular	**Plural**	**Singular**	**Plural**
	Present Tense			
1st	eō	īmus	eam	eāmus
2nd	īs	ītis	eās	eātis
3rd	it	eunt	eat	eant
	Imperfect Tense			
1st	ībam	ībāmus	īrem	īrēmus
2nd	ībās	ībātis	īrēs	īrētis
3rd	ībat	ībant	īret	īrent
	Future Tense			
1st	ībō	ībimus		
2nd	ībis	ībitis		
3rd	ībit	ībunt		

The Regular Verb, All Conjugations, Simple Tenses, Indicative Mood, Active Voice

The regular verb is found in four varieties, depending on a dominant vowel in the infinitive. The third conjugation has a subvariety, called -*io* verbs, which is a mixture of the third and fourth conjugation.

Examples:

1. **amō, amāre, amāvī, amātus,** to love

2. **habeō, habēre, habuī, habitus,** to have, hold

3. **agō, agere, ēgī, actus,** to do, drive, treat, wage

3. -*io*, **facio, facere, fēcī, factus,** to do, make

4. **veniō, venīre, vēnī, ventus,** to come

	1.	2.	3.	3. -io	4.
			Present Tense		
1st S.	amō	habeō	agō	faciō	veniō
2nd S.	amās	habēs	agis	facis	venīs
3rd S.	amat	habet	agit	facit	venit
1st P.	amāmus	habēmus	agimus	facimus	venīmus
2nd P.	amātis	habētis	agitis	facitis	venītis
3rd P.	amant	habent	agunt	faciunt	veniunt
			Imperfect Tense		
1st S.	amābam	habēbam	agēbam	faciēbam	veniēbam
2nd S.	amābās	habēbās	agēbās	faciēbās	veniēbās
3rd S.	amābat	habēbat	agēbat	faciēbat	veniēbat
1st P.	amābāmus	habēbāmus	agēbāmus	faciēbāmus	veniēbāmus
2nd P.	amābātis	habēbātis	agēbātis	faciēbātis	veniēbātis
3rd P.	amābant	habēbant	agēbant	faciēbant	veniēbant
			Future Tense		
1st S.	amābō	habēbō	agam	faciam	veniam
2nd S.	amābis	habēbis	agēs	faciēs	veniēs
3rd S.	amābit	habēbit	aget	faciet	veniet
1st P.	amābimus	habēbimus	agēmus	faciēmus	veniēmus
2nd P.	amābitis	habēbitis	agētis	faciētis	veniētis
3rd P.	amābunt	habēbunt	agent	facient	venient

Simple Tenses, Subjunctive Mood, Active Voice

	1.	2.	3.	3. -io	4.
			Present Tense		
1st S.	amem	habeam	agam	faciam	veniam
2nd S.	amēs	habeās	agās	faciās	veniās
3rd S.	amet	habeat	agat	faciat	veniat
1st P.	amēmus	habeāmus	agāmus	faciāmus	veniāmus
2nd P.	amētis	habeātis	agātis	faciātis	veniātis
3rd P.	ament	habeant	agant	faciant	veniant
			Imperfect Tense		
1st S.	amārem	habērem	agerem	facerem	venīrem
2nd S.	amārēs	habērēs	agerēs	facerēs	venīrēs
3rd S.	amāret	habēret	ageret	faceret	venīret
1st P.	amārēmus	habērēmus	agerēmus	facerēmus	venīrēmus
2nd P.	amārētis	habērētis	agerētis	facerētis	venīrētis
3rd P.	amārent	habērent	agerent	facerent	venīrent

Simple Tenses, Indicative Mood, Passive Voice (and Deponents)

Examples: 1, 2, 3, as above

3. *-io*, **capio, capere, cēpī, captus,** to take

4. **audiō, audīre, audīvī, audītus,** to hear

	1.	2.	3.	3. -io	4.
			Present Tense		
1st S.	amor	habeor	agor	capior	audior
2nd S.	amāris/-re	habēris/-re	ageris/-re	caperis/-re	audīris/-re
3rd S.	amātur	habētur	agitur	capitur	audītur
1st P.	amāmur	habēmur	agimur	capimur	audīmur
2nd P.	amāminī	habēminī	agiminī	capiminī	audīminī
3rd P.	amantur	habentur	aguntur	capiuntur	audiuntur
			Imperfect Tense		
1st S.	amābar	habēbar	agēbar	capiēbar	audiēbar
2nd S.	amābāris/-re	habēbāris/-re	agēbāris/-re	capiēbāris/-re	audiēbāris/-re
3rd S.	amābātur	habēbātur	agēbātur	capiēbātur	audiēbātur
1st P.	amābāmur	habēbāmur	agēbāmur	capiēbāmur	audiēbāmur
2nd P.	amābāminī	habēbāminī	agēbāminī	capiēbāminī	audiēbāminī
3rd P.	amābantur	habēbantur	agēbantur	capiēbantur	audiēbantur
			Future Tense		
1st S.	amābor	habēbor	agar	capiar	audiar
2nd S.	amāberis/-re	habēberis/-re	agēris/-re	capiēris/-re	audiēris/-re
3rd S.	amābitur	habēbitur	agētur	capiētur	audiētur
1st P.	amābimur	habēbimur	agēmur	capiēmur	audiēmur
2nd P.	amābiminī	habēbiminī	agēminī	capiēminī	audiēminī
3rd P.	amābuntur	habēbuntur	agentur	capientur	audientur

Simple Tenses, Subjunctive Mood, Passive Voice (and Deponents)

	1.	2.	3.	3. -io	4.
			Present Tense		
1st S.	amer	habear	agar	capiar	audiar
2nd S.	amēris/-re	habeāris/-re	agāris/-re	capiāris/-re	audiāris/-re
3rd S.	amētur	habeātur	agātur	capiātur	audiātur
1st P.	amēmur	habeāmur	agāmur	capiāmur	audiāmur
2nd P.	amēminī	habeāminī	agāminī	capiāminī	audiāminī
3rd P.	amentur	habeantur	agantur	capiantur	audiantur
			Imperfect Tense		
1st S.	amārer	habērer	agerer	caperer	audīrer
2nd S.	amārēris/-re	habērēris/-re	agerēris/-re	caperēris/-re	audīrēris/-re
3rd S.	amārētur	habērētur	agerētur	caperētur	audīrētur
1st P.	amārēmur	habērēmur	agerēmur	caperēmur	audīrēmur
2nd P.	amārēminī	habērēminī	agerēminī	caperēminī	audīrēminī
3rd P.	amārentur	habērentur	agerentur	caperentur	audīrentur

Perfect Tenses, Indicative and Subjunctive Moods, Active Voice

All conjugations form these tenses with the same endings on the third principal part of the verb.

Example: **dūco, dūcere, duxi, ductus,** to lead

	Indicative Mood		Subjunctive Mood	
	Singular	**Plural**	**Singular**	**Plural**
		Perfect Tense		
1st	duxī	duximus	duxerim	duxerimus
2nd	duxistī	duxistis	duxeris	duxeritis
3rd	duxit	duxērunt	duxerit	duxerint
		Pluperfect Tense		
1st	duxeram	duxerāmus	duxissem	duxissēmus
2nd	duxerās	duxerātis	duxissēs	duxissētis
3rd	duxerat	duxerant	duxisset	duxissent
		Future Perfect Tense		
1st	duxerō	duxerimus		
2nd	duxeris	duxeritis		
3rd	duxerit	duxerint		

Perfect Tenses, Indicative Mood, Passive Voice

All conjugations form these tenses with the same endings on the fourth principal part, the passive participle, and a form of the verb *sum, esse, fuī, futūrus.*

	Singular	Plural
	Perfect Tense	
1st	ductus, -a, -um sum / fuī	ducti, -ae, -a sumus / fuimus
2nd	ductus, -a, -um es / fuistī	ducti, -ae, -a estis / fuistis
3rd	ductus, -a, -um est / fuit	ducti, -ae, -a sunt / fuērunt
	Pluperfect Tense	
1st	ductus, -a, -um eram / fueram	ducti, -ae, -a erāmus / fuerāmus
2nd	ductus, -a, -um erās / fuerās	ducti, -ae, -a erātis / fuerātis
3rd	ductus, -a, -um erat / fuerat	ducti, -ae, -a erant / fuerant
	Future Perfect Tense	
1st	ductus, -a, -um erō / fuerō	ducti, -ae, -a erimus / fuerimus
2nd	ductus, -a, -um eris / fueris	ducti, -ae, -a eritis / fueritis
3rd	ductus, -a, -um erit / fuerit	ducti, -ae, -a erunt / fuerunt

Perfect Tenses, Subjunctive Mood, Passive Voice

	Singular	Plural
		Perfect Tense
1st	ductus, -a, -um sim	ducti, -ae, -a sīmus
2nd	ductus, -a, -um sīs	ducti, -ae, -a sītis
3rd	ductus, -a, -um sit	ducti, -ae, -a sint
		Pluperfect Tense
1st	ductus, -a, -um essem / fuissem	ducti, -ae, -a essēmus / fuissēmus
2nd	ductus, -a, -um essēs / fuissēs	ducti, -ae, -a essētis / fuissētis
3rd	ductus, -a, -um esset / fuisset	ducti, -ae, -a essent / fuissent

Imperatives

	Active		Passive	
	Singular	**Plural**	**Singular**	**Plural**
1.	amā	amāte	amāre	amāminī
2.	habē	habēte	habēre	habēminī
3.	age	agite	agere	agiminī
4.	audī	audīte	audīre	audīminī

Answer Key

This key to the exercises is not intended to give a definitive translation for the drills. It serves as a guide to measuring the general accuracy of a student's translation. Context often determines a translation, and these drills do not have a larger context to them. For example, the use or lack of a definite article, or the subject of a third person singular verb (he, she, it) could be determined by a larger context. In these translations, third person singular verbs without an expressed subject are given the subject "he." The student may choose to use "she" or "it." The genitive case may appear as the English possessive case or as a phrase with "of." Verbs may be translated in a number of forms in English; for example, laudas may appear as "you praise," "you are praising," or "you do praise." The purpose of the exercises is to provide drills for practicing vocabulary, grammar, and usage, not to be great literature.

Schola Prima

1. in the holy name
2. in the holy name of the Father
3. in the holy name of the holy Father
4. in the name of the Spirit
5. in the holy name of the Spirit
6. in the holy name of the Holy Spirit
7. in the first lesson
8. in the sister's first lesson
9. in the first sister's first lesson
10. the father's holy name
11. the holy name of the first father
12. the first brother's holy name
13. with the name of the first mother
14. with the first brother's first lesson
15. without the holy name of the son
16. without the holy son's holy name

17. without the father's sister's first lesson
18. without the first holy father
19. without the holy mother
20. with the first sister
21. with the first brother
22. with the son's first brother
23. with the first son of the first brother
24. with the mother's first sister
25. with the first sister of the first mother
26. without the holy brother of the first father
27. both glory and the name of the mother
28. both glory and the first brother's name
29. both the glory of the name and a father's glory
30. the holy name of the first glory
31. with a father's glory and a son's name
32. without the name of the mother and sister

Schola Secunda

1. both war and peace
2. either war or peace
3. both now and always
4. either now or always
5. War has a beginning (There is a beginning to war).
6. The war had a beginning.
7. There is a beginning for peace.
8. May peace have a beginning.
9. The good mother has a daughter.
10. May the good mother have a daughter.
11. The good mother had a daughter.
12. The good father has a son.
13. The good father had a son.
14. May the good father have a son.
15. The glory of peace is in the land.
16. The glory of peace was in the land.
17. May the glory of peace be on the earth.
18. May God have glory on the earth.

19. May the Lord God have glory on the earth.
20. May glory be to the Holy Spirit.
21. May the Holy Spirit have glory in peace.
22. The good God has glory in peace.
23. May God have glory forever.
24. God has glory forever (*or*, may God have glory forever).
25. either glory or a name
26. both glory and a name
27. May the good Lord God have glory both in peace and in war, forever.
28. May the good Lord God have glory both in peace and in war, unto ages of ages.
29. May the good Lord God have a good name forever and ever.
30. The mother has a first and second son.
31. The father has a first and second daughter.
32. The brother has a good beginning in the first lesson.
33. The sister had a good beginning in the second lesson.
34. May the daughter have a good beginning in the second lesson.
35. In the first lesson may there be a good beginning for the second son.

Schola Tertia

1. Hail, daughter!
2. Hail, son!
3. Hail, mother!
4. Hail, father!
5. Hail, teacher!
6. Hail, master!
7. Hail, daughter and son!
8. Hail, mother and father!
9. Hail, heaven's Queen!
10. Hail, Queen of heaven!
11. Your queen is in heaven.
12. Your (*pl.*) queen is in heaven.
13. Your queen was in heaven.
14. May your war be on land.

15. Hail queen, full of grace.
16. The Lord God is worthy of glory.
17. May the land be worthy of peace.
18. May the land be worthy of a queen.
19. May your land be worthy of peace.
20. May your land be worthy of a queen.
21. May your land be worthy of a good queen.
22. May there be peace in your land.
23. May there be peace in your land, as there is in heaven.
24. May your land be full of peace.
25. May the Lord be with you.
26. The Lord is with you.
27. May peace be with you.
28. May peace be with you now and always.
29. Your boy was worthy of you.
30. Your daughter is worthy of you.
31. May your mother be full of glory.
32. May your father be full of glory.
33. May your beginning be full of glory.
34. Your start is worthy of glory.
35. May your name be worthy of glory.
36. May your name be always worthy of you.
37. God's heaven is now full of peace.
38. May God's heaven be full of peace.
39. May God's heaven be full of peace and glory now and always and forever.
40. The Lord's field is full of your war.
41. Hail, teacher of peace!
42. There is a war in the field.
43. In the field full of glory, there is war.
44. The master of the field is a good lord.
45. May you have glory, O master!
46. May peace be to you, O mother!
47. May peace be with you, master.
48. May peace be with you, daughter and son!
49. May the Lord be with you, O queen!
50. The teacher is with you in the third lesson.

51. The third lesson is full of glory.
52. The Lord be (*or,* is) with you.
53. The Lord is with you.
54. May the Lord be with you.
55. The Lord was with you.
56. The Lord be (is) with you.
57. The Lord is with you.
58. The Lord be with you.
59. The Lord was with you.

Schola Quarta

1. I am blessed (*or,* I am Benedict).
2. May I be blessed.
3. I was blessed.
4. You are blessed.
5. May you be blessed.
6. You were blessed.
7. He is blessed.
8. May he be blessed.
9. He was blessed.
10. I (*f.*) am holy (*or,* I am a saint).
11. May I be holy.
12. I was holy.
13. You are a holy woman.
14. May you be holy.
15. You were a holy woman.
16. She is holy.
17. May she be holy.
18. She was holy.
19. Hail, daughter.
20. Hail, holy name!
21. Hail, holy son!
22. Hail, holy queen.
23. Hail, name of God.
24. Hail, holy God.
25. Hail, O Lord.

26. Hail, daughter and son.
27. Hail, mother and father.
28. Glory be to the father.
29. Glory be to the son.
30. Glory be to the spirit.
31. The mother had a name.
32. The sister had a name.
33. The brother had a name.
34. May the mother have a name.
35. May the daughter have a name.
36. May a name be to the son.
37. In the beginning God had glory.
38. In the beginning, you were blessed.
39. In the name of Jesus may you be blessed.
40. In the name of Jesus may I be blessed.
41. Mary was full of sorrow.
42. The son is full of sorrow.
43. The father was full of sorrow.
44. You (*f.*) are full of sorrow.
45. Blessed be the womb of Mary.
46. Mary's name was blessed.
47. You are blessed, holy Lord.
48. May you be blessed, holy Son.
49. Blessed be the holy name of the Lord, now and unto ages of ages.
50. Blessed be the fruit of Mary's womb.
51. The Lord's fruit is full of grace.

Schola Quinta

1. Pray for us.
2. Pray (*pl.*) for us.
3. Praise God!
4. Praise (*pl.*) the Lord.
5. Praise the queen.
6. Praise the God of heaven.
7. I do not praise you.
8. I do not praise you (*pl.*).
9. You are praising God.

10. You praise Mary.
11. You praise God's mother.
12. You pray to the Son of God.
13. I praise not death.
14. You do not praise death.
15. He (*or,* she, it) does not praise death.
16. He prays for you.
17. You are praying for us.
18. Pray for women!
19. Our queen prays for us.
20. In the hour of our death, our queen prays for us.
21. Holy God, I praise you.
22. Holy God, your son praises you.
23. The fourth son of the fifth mother praises God.
24. The fifth daughter of our sister is blessed.
25. May the third daughter of your mother be blessed.
26. Your brother praises our Lord.
27. Your mother's sister prays for sinners at the hour of death.
28. The sinner's mother sins not, she prays for sinners.
29. Son of God, Mary's father praises you in the hour of death.
30. Your daughter praises us.
31. Your son is full of grace, hail, holy mother.
32. Your sons are full of sorrow, may they now be full of glory.

Schola Sexta

1. May your will be done.
2. May the will of God be done.
3. May the Spirit's will happen.
4. May your kingdom come.
5. May God's kingdom come.
6. May the Son's kingdom come.
7. You kingdom is coming.
8. The kingdom of God comes.
9. The kingdom of the Son comes.
10. Your kingdom comes.
11. God's kingdom is coming.

12. The kingdom of the Son comes.
13. May the kingdom of heaven come.
14. May the will of heaven come.
15. May the name of God come.
16. May Jesus' name come.
17. Mary's name comes.
18. The Son's name is coming.
19. The Spirit's name sanctifies.
20. The name of God hallows.
21. The name of Jesus makes holy.
22. May the name of the Spirit of God sanctify.
23. May the name of Jesus sanctify in heaven.
24. May the Kingdom of God sanctify in the skies.
25. Your will is being hallowed.
26. May your will be hallowed.
27. Your kingdom is sanctified.
28. May your kingdom be sanctified.
29. Your kingdom is sanctified in the heavens.
30. May your kingdom be sanctified in the heavens.
31. Your kingdom is being sanctified on earth.
32. May your kingdom be sanctified in the lands.
33. The will of God is made holy on the earth.
34. May God's will be made holy in the lands.
35. The kingdom of your will is sanctified on earth and in heaven.
36. May the kingdom of your will be hallowed on earth and in heaven.
37. The kingdom of your will is hallowed in the lands and in the heavens.
38. May the kingdom of your will be sanctified in the lands and in the heavens.
39. May the kingdom of your will come to be on earth and in heaven.
40. May the kingdom of your will come to be in the lands and in the skies.
41. The kingdom of the will of the Son is made in the lands and in the heavens.
42. May the kingdom of the name of God's Son come and be done on earth and in heaven.

43. The kingdom of your name comes and is made in the lands and in the skies.
44. The name of the sixth son is praised in the fifth lesson.
45. May the name of the sixth son be praised in the fifth lesson.
46. You are in the skies.
47. You who are in the heavens.
48. You who are on the earth.
49. You who are Mary's son.
50. You who are Mary's daughter.
51. You who are blessed.
52. You who are a blessed woman.
53. You that are a blessed thing.
54. You that are the fourth thing.
55. You who are blessed on earth as in the heavens.

Schola Septima

1. I lead.
2. I do not lead.
3. May I lead.
4. May I not lead.
5. You lead.
6. You lead not.
7. May you lead.
8. You should not lead.
9. He leads.
10. He does not lead.
11. May he lead.
12. May he not lead.
13. We lead.
14. We do not lead.
15. We should lead.
16. We should not lead.
17. I forgive.
18. I do not forgive.
19. May I forgive.
20. May I not forgive.

21. You are forgiving.
22. You do not forgive.
23. You should forgive.
24. You may not forgive.
25. He forgives.
26. He does not forgive.
27. May he forgive.
28. May he not forgive.
29. Forgive!
30. Forgive (*pl.*)! (*Note the vowel change: dimit**te** to dimit**tite**.*)
31. Free!
32. Set free (*pl.*)!
33. Give!
34. Give (*pl.*)!
35. Lead!
36. Lead (*pl.*)!
37. May you not forgive.
38. You should not lead.
39. May you not free.
40. May you not give.
41. our bread
42. our Father
43. our temptation
44. our debt
45. Free us from evil.
46. Free (*pl.*) us from evils.
47. Do not free us from grace.
48. Lead us into grace.
49. Lead us not into evil.
50. Give us good bread.
51. Do not give us bad bread.
52. The debtor owes a debt.
53. The debtor does not owe the debt.
54. I owe a debt to the father.
55. You owe a debt to the mother.
56. He owes a debt to the brother.

57.   We owe a debt to the sister.

Schola Octava

1.   I thank you.
2.   You give thanks to the Father.
3.   He thanks the mother.
4.   We thank you (*pl.*).
5.   May we thank you.
6.   Let me thank you.
7.   You thank the all-powerful Father.
8.   May you thank the all-powerful Father.
9.   He gives thanks to the heavenly Father.
10.   May he thank the heavenly father.
11.   We thank the all-powerful God.
12.   Let us thank our God.
13.   We thank the great God on account of his own great glory.
14.   Let us thank the great God on account of his own great glory.
15.   They give great thanks to the heavenly God because of the glory of his own name.
16.   May they give great thanks to the heavenly God on account of the glory of his great name.
17.   You give great thanks to the heavenly God because of the great glory of his great name.
18.   May you give great thanks to the heavenly God on account of the great glory of his great name.
19.   You (*pl.*) give great thanks to the heavenly God because of the great glory of his holy name.
20.   May you (*pl.*) give thanks to the all-powerful God because of the great glory of his reign.
21.   We thank the holy Father because of the great glory of his kingdom.
22.   Let us thank the all-powerful Son because of the great glory of his kingdom.
23.   Let us thank the Holy Spirit because of his great grace.
24.   We glorify the all-powerful God on account of his holy Son.

25. Let us glorify the all-powerful God on account of his heavenly name.
26. We praise you, all-powerful God, on account of your heavenly name.
27. May we praise you, all-powerful God, on account of the heavenly name of your Son.
28. We praise you, good God, on account of the heavenly name of your Son.
29. Let us praise you, good Jesus, on account of the glory of your Father's name.
30. Let us bless the Lord on account of his great glory.
31. May all glory be yours.
32. All glory is to you.
33. all glory in every land
34. all glory in all lands
35. God's glory is his own.
36. God's name is his own.
37. God's Son is his.
38. Mary's son is hers.
39. Mary's daughter is hers.
40. Mary's name is her own.
41. I thank God.
42. Let me thank the Holy Spirit.
43. Jesus sits in heaven.
44. May Mary sit in heaven.
45. You sit on the earth.
46. May you sit in your land.
47. I sit in every land.
48. May I sit in every land.
49. We sit in the heavens.
50. May we sit in the heavens.
51. You sit in the holy land.
52. May you sit in a holy land.
53. They sit in their own land.
54. Let them sit in their own land.
55. You adore God in the highest,
56. May you adore God in the highest.

57. We adore God in the highest.
58. May we adore God in the highest.
59. They adore God in the highest.
60. Let them adore God in the highest.

Schola Nona

1. you who take away the sins
2. he who takes away the sins
3. I who take away the sins
4. you (*f.*) who take away the bread
5. she who takes away the bread
6. I (*f.*) who take away the bread
7. you (*n.*) who take away
8. it that takes away
9. I (*n.*) that take away
10. whose sins you take away
11. whose sins he takes away
12. whose sins I take away
13. whom you take away
14. whom (*f.*) he takes away
15. what I take away
16. I sit at the right hand.
17. I sit at the left hand.
18. You sit at the right hand.
19. You sit at the left hand.
20. He sits at the right hand.
21. He sits at the left hand.
22. We sit at the right hand.
23. We sit at the left hand.
24. You (*pl.*) sit at the right hand.
25. You (*pl.*) sit at the left hand.
26. They sit at the right hand.
27. They sit at the left hand.
28. You are most high.
29. I am the highest.
30. He is the most high.
31. You are a most holy woman.

32. I (*f.*) am most holy.
33. She is the holiest.
34. Receive our prayer.
35. Receive my prayer.
36. I receive our prayer.
37. You receive our prayer.
38. He receives my prayer.
39. We receive your prayer.
40. You (*pl.*) receive my prayer.
41. They receive your prayer.
42. Have mercy on us.
43. Have mercy on the daughter.
44. Have mercy on the mother.
45. I pity the daughter.
46. I pity the son.
47. I have mercy on the mother.
48. Have mercy on the world.
49. Have mercy on the sin.
50. Have mercy on the daughter.
51. The only son of the only Father.
52. The only daughter of the only mother.
53. The only begotten son of the one Father.
54. The one daughter of the one mother.
55. Glory be to the only begotten Son.
56. Glory be to the one Son.
57. Glory be to the one Father.
58. Glory be to the one Holy Spirit.
59. In the name of the one Father.
60. In the name of the one Holy Spirit.

Schola Decima

1. in front of me
2. before you
3. before God
4. out of Egypt
5. out of deepest Egypt

6. from the house
7. from the high house
8. out of my house
9. out of your house
10. I am the one who led you out.
11. You are the one who led me out.
12. It is Moses who led us out.
13. It is we who led you out.
14. It is you who led us out.
15. They led us out from the land of Egypt.
16. Moses teaches instruction and law.
17. Moses has taught instruction and law.
18. Moses will teach instruction and law.
19. Moses sits in our house.
20. Moses will sit in our house.
21. Moses sat in our house.
22. The slave has a foreign law.
23. The slave has had a foreign law.
24. The slave will have a foreign law.
25. I have good instruction.
26. I will have good instruction.
27. I have had good instruction.
28. I come from the house of slavery.
29. You come from the house of slavery.
30. He comes from the house of slavery.
31. We come from the house of slavery.
32. You (*pl.*) come from the house of slavery.
33. They come from the house of slavery.
34. I have come from a most holy land.
35. You have come from a most holy land.
36. He has come from a most holy land.
37. We have come from a most holy land.
38. You (*pl.*) have come from a most holy land.
39. They have come from a most holy land.
40. I praise the fruit of Egypt.
41. You praise the fruit of Egypt.

42. He praises the fruit of Egypt.
43. We praise the fruit of Egypt.
44. You (*pl.*) praise the fruit of Egypt.
45. They praise the fruit of Egypt.
46. I will praise the tenth law.
47. You will praise the ninth law.
48. He will praise the eighth law.
49. We will praise the sixth law.
50. You (*pl.*) will praise the fifth law.
51. They will praise the fourth law.
52. Moses will teach the third instruction.
53. You will teach the second instruction.
54. I will teach the first law.
55. They will teach the instruction to the servant.
56. You will teach the instruction to the servant.
57. We shall teach the instruction to the slave.
58. I taught law in the land.
59. You taught the law on the earth.
60. He has taught the law in the house.
61. We have taught the law in the house.
62. You (*pl.*) have taught instruction in Egypt.
63. They taught instruction in Egypt.
64. I thank the Lord God.
65. Let me thank the Lord God.
66. I thanked the Lord God.
67. We give thanks to the Lord God.
68. Let us thank the Lord God.
69. We have given thanks to the Lord God.
70. They thank the Lord God.
71. May they thank the Lord God.

Schola Undecima

1. You will adore and will worship.
2. You adore and worship.
3. You have adored and have worshipped.
4. He will adore and worship.

5. He adores and worships.
6. He has adored and has worshipped.
7. I shall adore and shall worship.
8. I adore and worship.
9. I have adored and have worshipped.
10. We shall adore and shall worship.
11. We adore and worship.
12. We have adored and have worshipped.
13. You (*pl.*) will adore and will worship.
14. You adore and worship.
15. You have adored and have worshipped.
16. They will adore and will worship.
17. They adore and worship.
18. They have adored and have worshipped.
19. I do not commit evil.
20. I will do iniquity.
21. I have done evil.
22. I hate evil.
23. You hate evil.
24. We hate iniquity.
25. You are making a large statue.
26. You will make a large statue.
27. You have made this statue.
28. He makes a commandment.
29. He will make a commandment.
30. He has made this precept.
31. We make commandments of mercy.
32. We will make these commandments of mercy.
33. We have made precepts of mercy.
34. You do these precepts of mercy.
35. You will do precepts of mercy.
36. You have done these commandments of mercy.
37. They do the eleventh commandment.
38. They will do this tenth commandment.
39. They have done the ninth commandment.
40. I love this daughter of theirs.

41. I hate their daughter.
42. I love this father of theirs (*f.*).
43. I hate their mother.
44. I love this mother of the daughters.
45. I hate the daughters' brother.
46. I love these precepts of his.
47. I love the commandments that are his.
48. I love the commandments that are the Lord's.
49. I hate the lands that are his.
50. I hate these waters that are in his lands.
51. He loves the lands that are in peace.
52. He hates these lands that are not in peace.
53. They love the lands in which there are waters.
54. They hate the lands in which there are waters.
55. visiting and doing
56. the name of the man visiting
57. the name of the mother visiting
58. the name of this visiting brother
59. the name of the father making a likeness
60. the name of this mother making bread
61. a man guarding the land
62. men guarding this land
63. The man guards the land.
64. Men guard this land.
65. He visits the land in which there are waters.
66. He may visit this land in which there may be waters.
67. He will visit the land in which there may be waters.
68. He has visited a land in which there are waters.
69. He cares for the lands in which this evil is not.
70. He will cultivate the lands in which this iniquity is not.
71. May he till the lands in which this evil may not be.
72. He has cultivated the lands in which this evil was not.
73. He will give this statue to this mother who has kept the Lord's precepts.
74. He has given great glory to this man, who sat in this big house.
75. God performs mercy to those who love his holy name.

Schola Duodecima

1. For in six days the Lord made the sky and the land and the sea.
2. For in six days the Lord makes the sky and the land and the sea.
3. For in six days the Lord will make the sky and the land and the sea.
4. For in three days the Lord has made the sky and the land and the sea.
5. For in two days the Lord made the sky and the land and the sea.
6. For in one day the Lord made the sky and the land and the sea.
7. However on the seventh day you shall not do any work.
8. However on the tenth day you shall not do this your work.
9. However on the eleventh day you shall not do these your works.
10. However on the twelfth day you shall not do any work.
11. However on the seventh day you shall not work.
12. However on the seventh day you (*pl.*) do not labor.
13. However on the seventh day you do not labor.
14. However on the seventh day you work not.
15. Remember that you should hallow the day of the Sabbath.
16. Remember that on the seventh day you should not do work.
17. Remember that you should hallow the name of the Lord your God.
18. who shall have taken the name of the Lord in vain
19. who takes the name of the Lord in vain
20. who has taken the name of the Lord in vain
21. who will take the name of the Lord in vain
22. He rested on the seventh day.
23. He rests on this seventh day.
24. He will rest on the seventh day.
25. May he rest on this seventh day.
26. Let him rest in peace.
27. He shall have rested in peace.
28. all things that are in them
29. all things that are in these waters
30. every strong man who was in this house
31. every woman who will be in this house
32. every sin that may be in a man.
33. all the sins that are in this man
34. all strong men who were in the house

35. all the women who will be in the house
36. every sin of all the men
37. all the sins of all the women
38. The Lord blessed the seventh day.
39. The Lord blesses every day.
40. The Lord shall have blessed all days.
41. The Lord will bless the seventh day.
42. May the Lord bless this seventh day.
43. He has sanctified the seventh day.
44. He hallows every day.
45. He will make all days holy.
46. May he hallow all these days.
47. Let the seventh day be sanctified.
48. Let all days be hallowed.
49. He will not hold him blameless who shall have taken the Lord's name in vain.
50. He has not held him blameless who has taken the Lord's name in vain.
51. Nor does he hold her innocent who has taken the Lord's name in vain.
52. Nor will he hold them blameless who will have taken the Lord's name in vain.
53. Nor will they hold them (*f.*) innocent who will have taken the Lord's name in vain.
54. They hold them not blameless who take the name of the innocent in vain.
55. They will hold them innocent who will be within their gates.
56. They have held them blameless who were within their gates.
57. I will hold them innocent who shall have loved the Lord's name.
58. You will hold him innocent who shall have loved the Lord's name.
59. We shall hold them (*f.*) innocent who shall have loved the Lord's name.
60. You shall not hold them innocent who shall not have loved the Lord's name.
61. This is the name of the mother of the two sons who have three houses.

62. The Lord will give the kingdom of the heavens to those who love two or three of his disciples.
63. The Lord will give the kingdom of the heavens to two or three good people.
64. All those who love the Lord will have the kingdom of the heavens in two or three days.
65. The holy and strong Lord gave a thousand mercies to this generation.

Schola Tertia Decima

1. Honor your father.
2. Honor your mother.
3. Honor him.
4. Honor her.
5. Honor your fathers.
6. Honor them.
7. Honor your mothers.
8. Honor those women.
9. Honor (*pl.*) them.
10. Honor your father that you may be long-lived upon your land.
11. Honor (*pl.*) your fathers that you may be long-lived upon your land.
12. Honor your mother that you may be long-lived upon your land.
13. Honor (*pl.*) your mothers that you may be long-lived upon your land.
14. You shall not kill that you may be long-lived in your land.
15. You (*pl.*) shall not kill that you may be long-lived in your land.
16. I shall not kill that I may be long-lived in my house.
17. We shall not kill that we may be long-lived in our house.
18. She shall not kill that she may be long-lived in her house.
19. They shall not kill that they may be long-lived in their house.
20. He kills not, he honors his father and mother that he may be a good neighbor.
21. They do not kill, they honor (their) fathers and mothers that they may be good neighbors.
22. You shall not commit a theft that you may have a good name.
23. I shall not commit a theft that I may have a good name.

24. You shall not steal that you may have a good name.
25. They do not steal nor kill that they may have a good name.
26. He did not steal nor kill in the land that God gave him.
27. I stole not nor did I kill in that land that God gave to me.
28. They have not stolen nor killed in the lands that God gave them.
29. He neither steals nor kills in the land that God gave him.
30. We do not steal nor kill in the lands that God gave us.
31. Let us not steal nor kill in the lands that God gave us.
32. Let them not steal nor kill in the lands that God gave them.
33. You (*pl.*) should not steal nor kill in the land that God gave you.
34. I speak and you hear.
35. We speak and you (*pl.*) hear.
36. He speaks and they hear.
37. They speak and they hear.
38. You (*pl.*) speak and are heard.
39. You speak and are heard.
40. You speak and are heard.
41. I speak that you may hear.
42. You speak that he may hear.
43. He speaks that I may hear.
44. We speak that they may hear.
45. You (*pl.*) speak that he may hear.
46. They speak that you (*pl.*) may hear.
47. I speak to be heard.
48. You speak that you may be heard.
49. He speaks that he may be heard.
50. We speak that we may be heard.
51. You (*pl.*) speak that you may be heard.
52. They speak that they may be heard.
53. I do not desire my neighbor's house.
54. You do not covet nor desire your neighbor's house.
55. You shall not covet nor desire his neighbor's house.
56. He covets not nor desires his neighbor's house.
57. We do not covet nor desire our neighbor's house.
58. We shall not covet nor desire our neighbor's house.
59. They do not covet nor desire the wives of those neighbors.
60. They shall not covet nor desire the wives of their neighbors.

Schola Quarta Decima

1. He himself has spoken.
2. He speaks.
3. He had spoken.
4. When he himself spoke.
5. When he speaks.
6. When he will speak.
7. They themselves have spoken.
8. They speak.
9. They had spoken.
10. When they had spoken.
11. When they themselves speak.
12. When they will speak.
13. Seeing the crowds, he went up on the mountain.
14. Seeing the crowds, they went up on the mountains.
15. When he had gone up onto the mountain, he opened his mouth.
16. When they had gone up onto the mountain, they opened their mouths.
17. When he had seen the crowds, he went up on the mountain.
18. When you had seen the crowds, you went up on the mountain.
19. When I had seen the crowds, I went up on the mountain.
20. When we had seen the crowds, we went up onto the mountain.
21. When you (*pl.*) had seen the crowds, you went up onto the mountain.
22. When they had seen the crowds, they went up on the mountain.
23. When he had seen the large crowd, he went up on the mountain.
24. When he had gone up on the mountain, he opened his mouth.
25. When he had gone up on the mountain, he was opening his mouth.
26. When he had opened his mouth, he was teaching them.
27. When he had opened his mouth, he taught them.
28. When he had taught them, he sat on the mountain.
29. When he had taught them, he was sitting on the mountain.
30. Blessed is the poor in spirit, his is the kingdom of heaven.
31. Blessed are the poor in spirit, theirs is the kingdom of heaven.
32. Blessed is the deep in spirit, hers is the kingdom of heaven.

33. Blessed be the poor in spirit, theirs is the kingdom of heaven.
34. Blessed were the poor in spirit, theirs is the kingdom of heaven.
35. Blessed are the women poor in spirit, theirs is the kingdom
     of heaven.
36. Blessed be the women poor in spirit, theirs is the kingdom
     of heaven.
37. Blessed were the women poor in spirit, theirs is the kingdom of
     the heavens.
38. Opening his mouth, he taught them.
39. Opening their mouths, they taught them.
40. Sitting on the mountain, he taught the large crowds.
41. Sitting on the mountains, they taught the large crowds.
42. ascending the mountain and opening his mouth
43. going up on the mountains and opening their mouths
44. Blessed are those going up onto the mountain, because they see
     the crowd.
45. Blessed is he going up on the mountain, for he sees the crowd.
46. Blessed be the one who is sitting on the mountain, because he sees
     the disciples.
47. Blessed are the disciples who are sitting on the mountain, for they
     see the sky.
48. Blessed be the poor in spirit, for he sees God.
49. He gave glory to the one poor in spirit when he had seen him.
50. They gave glory to those poor in spirit when they had seen them.

Schola Quinta Decima

1.   They hunger and thirst.
2.   They were hungry and thirsty.
3.   They will hunger and thirst.
4.   He hungers and thirsts.
5.   He hungered and thirsted.
6.   He will hunger and thirst.
7.   I hunger and thirst.
8.   I was hungry and thirsty.
9.   I will hunger and thirst.
10. I follow and console (*or*, am consoled).

11. We followed and consoled.
12. They followed and consoled.
13. You follow and console.
14. They will follow and console.
15. He will follow and will console.
16. You (*pl.*) will follow and will console.
17. You (*pl.*) followed and consoled.
18. Blessed are the men with a clean heart, for they shall see God.
19. Blessed are the men with a clean mouth, for they shall see God.
20. Blessed are men with a merciful mouth, because they have seen God.
21. Blessed are those who mourn, because they will be consoled.
22. Blessed are the women who will mourn, for they will be consoled.
23. Blessed are you who mourn, for you shall be consoled.
24. Blessed are you who will mourn, for you shall be consoled.
25. Blessed are you who mourn, for you shall be consoled.
26. Blessed are you (*f.*) who mourn, for you shall be consoled.
27. Blessed is he who mourns, for he is consoled.
28. Blessed is she who mourns, for she is consoled.
29. Blessed is he who hungers and thirsts for justice, because he will be filled.
30. Blessed is she who hungers and thirsts for justice, for she will be filled.
31. Blessed are they who hunger and thirst for justice, for they shall be filled.
32. Blessed are the women who hunger and thirst for justice, because they shall be filled.
33. Blessed are those who hunger and thirst for justice, because they will be filled.
34. Blessed be the women who hunger and thirst for justice, for they will be filled.
35. I see that bread.
36. I see those two loaves.
37. I see those three loaves.
38. I saw those four loaves.
39. I will see those five loaves.

40. I have seen those six loaves.
41. I will have seen those seven loaves.
42. May I see those eight loaves.
43. I would have seen those nine loaves.
44. I see those ten loaves.
45. Blessed is the one man with a clean heart who comes in the name of the Lord.
46. Blessed are the two men with a clean heart who come in the name of the Lord.
47. Blessed are the three men with a clean heart who come in the name of the Lord.
48. Blessed are the four mothers with a clean mouth who come in the Lord's name.
49. Blessed are the five daughters with a clean mouth who come in the Lord's name.
50. Blessed are the six sons with a clean mouth who come in the Lord's name.
51. Blessed be the seven seas that are in the world.
52. Blessed are the eight lambs that are in that holy land.
53. Blessed are the nine daughters whose father is in the large house.
54. Blessed are the ten sons whose mother is in the large house.

Schola Sexta Decima

1. Blessed are you when they shall have cursed you.
2. Blessed are they when they shall have cursed them.
3. Blessed are we when you shall have cursed us.
4. Blessed are we when he shall have cursed us.
5. Those who lie are not blessed.
6. Lying women are not blessed.
7. The kingdom of liars is not blessed.
8. The kingdom of those who praise is blessed.
9. He does not bless lying people.
10. He blesses those who teach.
11. He will not bless liars.
12. He will bless those who teach.
13. He has not blessed those who lie.

14. He has blessed those who teach children.
15. He shall not have blessed lying people.
16. He shall have blessed those teaching children.
17. May he not bless liars.
18. May he bless those who teach boys.
19. Blessed is he who suffers persecution.
20. Blessed am I who suffer persecution.
21. Blessed is she who suffers persecution.
22. Blessed am I (*f.*) who suffer persecution.
23. Blessed are you who suffer persecution.
24. Blessed are you (*f.*) who suffer persecution.
25. Blessed are we who suffer persecution.
26. Blessed are we women who suffer persecution.
27. Blessed are you who suffer persecution.
28. Blessed are you women who suffer persecution.
29. Blessed are they who suffer persecution.
30. Blessed are the women who suffer persecution.
31. I lie and persecute.
32. I will lie and persecute.
33. lying and persecuting
34. those lying and persecuting
35. You lie and persecute.
36. You will lie and persecute.
37. He lies and persecutes.
38. He will lie and persecute.
39. We lie and persecute.
40. We will lie and persecute.
41. You lie and persecute.
42. You will lie and persecute.
43. They lie and persecute.
44. They will lie and persecute.
45. Rejoicing, I suffer and exult.
46. Rejoicing, we suffer and exult.
47. Rejoicing, you suffer and exult.
48. Rejoicing, you suffer and exult.
49. Rejoicing, he suffers and exults.

50. Rejoicing, they suffer and exult.
51. We rejoice because of justice.
52. Let us rejoice on account of justice.
53. You rejoice because of righteousness.
54. May you rejoice because of righteousness.
55. They rejoice because of justice.
56. May they rejoice because of justice.
57. Rejoice and exult because your reward is abundant in heaven.
58. Rejoice and exult because your reward is abundant in heaven.
59. Rejoice and exult because your reward will be abundant in heaven.
60. Rejoice and exult for your reward will be abundant in heaven.
61. I have suffered on account of justice.
62. I have rejoiced on account of justice.
63. You have suffered on account of justice.
64. You have rejoiced on account of justice.
65. He has suffered on account of justice.
66. He has rejoiced on account of justice.
67. We have suffered on account of justice.
68. We have rejoiced on account of justice.
69. You have suffered on account of justice.
70. You have rejoiced on account of justice.
71. They have suffered on account of justice.
72. They have rejoiced on account of justice.
73. The prophet has been praised before them.
74. The prophet has been praised before them.
75. The prophets have been praised before them.
76. The prophets have been praised before them.
77. I have been sanctified and I sanctify you.
78. I have been sanctified and I sanctify you.
79. You have been sanctified and you sanctify us.
80. You have been sanctified and you sanctify us.
81. He has been sanctified and he sanctifies us.
82. He has been sanctified and he sanctifies us.
83. We have been sanctified and we sanctify you.
84. We have been sanctified and we sanctify you.
85. You have been sanctified and you sanctify us.

86. You have been sanctified and you sanctify us.
87. They have been sanctified and they sanctify us.
88. They have been sanctified and they sanctify us.

Schola Septima Decima

1. vanity of vanities
2. emptiness of emptiness
3. that emptiness
4. generation of generations
5. a generation of a generation
6. that generation
7. man of men
8. a man of a man
9. that man
10. work of works
11. He works a work.
12. work under the sun
13. a man from a man
14. God from God
15. God's word
16. the eternal word of the eternal God
17. The land is under the sun forever.
18. The land will be under the eternal sun.
19. They go into the land under the sun.
20. We go into the land under the sun.
21. You go into the land under the sun.
22. He goes into the land under the sun.
23. A generation goes by.
24. A generation comes.
25. Generations go by.
26. Generations come.
27. A generation was passing by.
28. A generation was coming.
29. A generation will pass by.
30. A generation will come.
31. Generations have passed by.

32. Generations have come.
33. A generation has passed.
34. A generation has come.
35. In the high heavens with the sun.
36. In the higher heavens with the sun.
37. In the highest heavens with the sun.
38. In the high heaven with the good sun.
39. In the higher heaven with a better sun.
40. In the highest heaven with the best sun.
41. What more has a man from all his labor?
42. What more has a man from all his labor?
43. What more do men have from all their work?
44. What more do men have from all their work?
45. Emptiness of emptiness (vanitatis is singular) all things are an emptiness.
46. Vanity of vanity (vanitatis is singular) all things are a vanity.
47. Vanity of vanities, all things are a vanity.
48. Word of words, all things are a word.
49. The words of the preacher are truly the words of a prophet.
50. The sun passes by, the sun comes, the word of God is eternal.

Schola Duodevicesima

1. To praise is good.
2. To praise God is good.
3. The love of praising is good.
4. The love of praising God is good.
5. To speak is good.
6. To speak about God is good.
7. The love of speaking is good.
8. The love of speaking about God is good.
9. To heal is good.
10. To heal men is good.
11. The love of healing is good.
12. The love of healing human beings is good.
13. All things have a time.
14. All things have times.

15. All things have a time.
16. All things have times.
17. the time of loving a mother
18. a time of loving a father
19. a time for a son of loving (his) mother
20. a time for a daughter of loving a father
21. the hatred of throwing stones
22. I have a hatred of throwing stones.
23. The son has a hatred of throwing stones.
24. He has a hatred of throwing stones.
25. They have a hatred of war.
26. May they have a hatred of war.
27. May there be a time of peace for them.
28. May there be for the land a time of peace.
29. a time to be far away from war
30. May there be a time to be far from war.
31. a time to be far from speaking
32. May there be a time to be far from speaking,
33. times to be far from hatred
34. May there be times to be far from hatred.
35. a time of pulling up what has been planted
36. May there be a time of pulling up what has been planted.
37. May there be times of pulling up the things that have been planted.
38. May there be good times of pulling up the things that have been planted.
39. May there be a time of sewing together what has been torn.
40. May there be times of sewing together the things that have been torn.
41. May there be a time of sewing together what has been torn.
42. May there be times of sewing together the things that have been torn.
43. There is a time to be far from ripping.
44. May there be a time to be far from throwing stones.
45. May there be a time to be far from making debts.
46. There is a time to be far from throwing stones.

47. There are times to be far from making debts.
48. To speak is good, it is better to be silent.
49. To be born is good, it is better to die in Christ.
50. It is not good to weep, it is better to laugh.

Schola Undevicesima

1. No one is called a faithful Christian.
2. None are called faithful Christians.
3. No woman is called a faithful Christian.
4. No women are called faithful Christians.
5. He calls no one a faithful Christian.
6. He calls no woman a faithful Christian.
7. They call none faithful Christians.
8. They call no women faithful Christians.
9. The name of no one is faithful.
10. The names of none are faithful.
11. He gives a name to no one.
12. He gives names to none.
13. He says that he has been baptized by no one.
14. He says that he has been baptized by no one.
15. They say that they have been baptized by no one.
16. He baptizes because he is faithful.
17. He professes the faith because he is faithful.
18. They profess the faith because they are faithful.
19. I believe in one God.
20. We believe in one God.
21. We have believed in one God because we have been baptized.
22. We have been baptized, therefore we believe in one God.
23. In baptism, the soul is joined to God.
24. Because it is baptized, the Christian soul is joined to God.
25. When we profess the faith, we say that we believe in God.
26. Because we have professed the Christian faith, we have said that we have believed in God.
27. Without faith, Christians say that no one will be saved.
28. Without baptism, no one will be a Christian.
29. We will be saved through faith and baptism.

30. A Christian soul makes a kind of marriage with God.
31. Christian souls make a kind of marriage with God.
32. They have a sort of faith, therefore they believe in some sort of God.
33. When a man is baptized, he first professes the faith.
34. When a certain man is baptized, he first professes a kind of faith.
35. They say that when people are baptized, they first profess the true faith.
36. Because they say that they profess the faith, from this let them be baptized.

Schola Vicesima

1. It is not of help.
2. They avail not.
3. It doesn't help me.
4. They do not help us.
5. It is not a help for the son.
6. They do not avail the mother.
7. It must be known that nothing is impossible for God.
8. It must be said that nothing is impossible for God.
9. It must be said that nothing is impossible for God to do.
10. It must be known that God must be loved.
11. The love of God must be spoken of by faithful Christians.
12. It pleases God to love the world.
13. It is pleasing to people to love God.
14. Without the love of God, no one pleases the Lord.
15. Through the love of God, people please the Lord.
16. It is of help to the father to love his sons.
17. It is of help for the sons to love their father.
18. The father can love his sons.
19. The sons are able to love their father.
20. When a man has hatred, it is impossible for him to love God.
21. He says that God is to be loved by all because he made all things.
22. He has said that God is to be loved by all because he made all things.
23. He will say that Christ is to be adored because he has healed us.

24. Let him say that Christ is to be adored because he heals us.
25. Christ came for the hallowing of the world.
26. The Holy Spirit came for the hallowing of the world.
27. He speaks so that God may be known in the world.
28. He speaks that knowledge may be known in the world.
29. He speaks that truth should be known in the world.
30. He speaks so that the recognition of truth be known in the world.
31. He speaks so that the love of praising God is known in the world.
32. He speaks so that the love of praying be known in the world.
33. Where the love of God has been known, it avails people to pray.
34. Where the love of God is being spoken, it avails people to praise.
35. Where God has been loved, people are to be loved.

Schola Vicesima Prima

1. For eternal life is nothing other than to know God.
2. For eternal life is nothing other than to love God.
3. For eternal life is nothing other than to love God.
4. For the kingdom of the heavens is nothing other than to praise God.
5. For the kingdom of heaven is nothing other than to glorify God.
6. This is eternal life, that they should know you, the only true God.
7. This is eternal life, that he should know you, the only true God.
8. This is the kingdom of the heavens, that I should know you, the only true God.
9. This is the kingdom of the heavens, that we should know you, the only true God.
10. This is blessedness, that you should know me, the only true God.
11. This is blessedness, that you should know me, the only true God.
12. In the future life, we know him as he is.
13. In the future life, I know him as he is.
14. In the future life, he knows him as he is.
15. In the future life they know him as he is.
16. In the future life, he will know him as he is.
17. In a future life they shall know him as he is.
18. In a future life he may know him as he is.
19. In a future life they may know him as he is.

20. I can know God.
21. We are able to know God.
22. You can know God.
23. You are able to know God.
24. He can know God.
25. They can know God.
26. I was able to know God.
27. We were able to know God.
28. You were able to do good.
29. You were able to better.
30. He was able to do better.
31. They were able to do better.
32. I will be able to know this substance.
33. We will be able to know her.
34. You will be able to know this substance of things to be hoped for.
35. You will be able to know this substance of things to be hoped for.
36. He will be able to know that substance of better things to be hoped for.
37. They will be able to know the better substance of good things to be hoped for.
38. We know the greater substance of things that must be loved.
39. We may know this lesser substance of things that must be praised.
40. Therefore no one can arrive at blessedness, unless he first knows through faith.
41. Therefore no one can arrive at knowledge, unless he first loves God.
42. None, therefore, are able to arrive at knowledge, unless they first love God.
43. Therefore you cannot arrive at beatitude, unless you first love God.
44. You, therefore, cannot arrive at the knowledge of God, unless you first believe in the name of the one true God.
45. Therefore we are unable to arrive at blessedness, unless we first believe in the name of the only true Son of God.
46. Therefore no one can attain beatitude, unless he first believes in the name of the one true Son of God.

47. None, therefore, can arrive at the knowledge of God, unless they first believe through faith in the name of the one God.
48. Here begins the life of greater faith.
49. Here begins the life of better faith.
50. Baptism is a sacrament from which the better life of faith begins in us.

Schola Vicesima Secunda

1. For toward this that a man should live well.
2. For toward this that people should live well.
3. For toward this that a man should pray well.
4. For toward this that people should pray well.
5. For toward this that a man should praise well.
6. For toward this that people should praise well.
7. For toward this that a man should learn well.
8. For toward this that people should learn well.
9. For toward this that a man should know well.
10. For toward this that people should know well.
11. It is proper that he should know the things necessary for living well.
12. It behooves him to know all things necessary for living well.
13. It is proper that they know all things necessary for living well.
14. It behooves them to know all things necessary for living well.
15. It is fitting that they learn all things necessary for directing well.
16. It behooves them to learn all things necessary for directing well.
17. It is fitting that he say all things necessary for knowing God well.
18. It behooves him to say all things necessary for knowing God well.
19. It is proper that the gates of heaven.
20. It behooves the gates of heaven should lie open to be open.
21. If he ought to learn in addition all things necessary for living well, he cannot attain it.
22. If he ought to learn in addition all things necessary for knowing well, he could not attain it.
23. If he would have learned in addition all things necessary for living well, he should be in glory.

24. If he had arrived at glory, we would have known his name.
25. If they had arrived at glory, they would have known their names.
26. If the gates of heaven were open, Christ would not have come for the salvation of men.
27. If I learned the Latin language well, I would go to Rome.
28. If we learned the Latin language well, we would have gone to Rome.
29. I know that there is another life, and of what sort.
30. I know there is another life, and of what sort.
31. Let him know that there is another life, and of what sort.
32. Let him know there is another life, and of what sort.
33. I know that I should avoid sin and do good.
34. We know that we should avoid sin and do good.
35. I know to avoid sin and to do good.
36. We know to avoid sin and to do good.
37. It is clear that none of the philosophers was able to know as much about God as an old woman knows through faith.
38. It is clear that I cannot know as much about faith as Aquinas knew.

Schola Vicesima Tertia

1. Praesens being the consul
2. when Claudianus was consul
3. when Praesens and Claudianus were consuls
4. when Praesens for the second time and Claudianus were consuls
5. Peter having been captured
6. when Paul was saying
7. when Peter and Paul were writing
8. while John was baptizing
9. John having been baptized
10. when John and Peter were baptizing
11. John and Peter having been baptized
12. John and Peter having been baptized for the second time
13. when John for the second time and Peter were baptizing many
14. while John and Peter were baptizing many at Rome
15. when Peter and Paul were baptizing more people at Carthage

16. When Paul had spoken many things to the people at Athens, he returned to Jerusalem.
17. With Speratus having been set in the council chamber, Saturninus the proconsul entered.
18. When Donata was placed in the council chamber at Carthage, Saturninus the proconsul returned.
19. When Speratus and Donata were placed in the council chamber, Saturninus spoke to them.
20. When Speratus and Donata had spoken, Valerianus went into the council chamber.
21. We have offered no opportunity for wickedness.
22. We offer no opportunity for wickedness.
23. We will offer no opportunity for wickedness.
24. Let us offer no opportunity for wickedness.
25. We had offered no opportunity for wickedness.
26. We shall have offered no opportunity for wickedness.
27. If you return to your senses (mind), you can earn the forgiveness of the lord emperor.
28. If I return to the house of that lord, I can gain the emperor's forgiveness.
29. Unless I return to that lord's house, I cannot gain forgiveness.
30. We swear through the guardian spirit of the emperor, which you also ought to do.
31. They swear through the guardian spirit of the emperor, which you also ought to do.
32. You swear through the genius of the emperor, which they also ought to do.
33. Let us swear through the genius of the emperor, which you also ought to do.
34. If you offer undisturbed ears, I am telling to you the mystery of innocence.
35. If you offer undisturbed ears, we are telling to you the mystery of the kingdom of heaven.
36. If they offer undisturbed ears, I am telling them a great mystery.
37. If I should have bought anything, I give the tax to the emperor.

38. If he should have bought anything in Rome, he pays the tax to the emperor.
39. If I were living in Italy, I would be most happy.

Schola Vicesima Quarta

1. Cease to be of this belief.
2. Cease to be of this belief.
3. Be unwilling to be of this belief.
4. Be unwilling to be of this belief.
5. Be unwilling to be sharers of this madness.
6. Be unwilling to be of this madness.
7. Do you remain a Christian?
8. Do you remain a Christian?
9. Do you wish a space for deliberation?
10. Do you want time for considering?
11. Don't you want time for consideration?
12. Saturninus thought that the Christians wanted time for consideration.
13. Saturninus said that they did not want time for consideration.
14. What is this thing in your case?
15. What are the things in your container?
16. He said that these things are in the case.
17. Does he say that these things are in my case?
18. In a matter so just, there is no deliberating.
19. Is there deliberating in a matter so just?
20. Is there deliberation in a matter so just?
21. Isn't there consideration in a matter so just?
22. If there were deliberation in a matter so just, there would be time necessary for considering.
23. Unless there were deliberation in a matter so just, we could not do justice.
24. Unless you do good to people, you would not be able to see God.
25. With the verdict read from the tablet, the martyrs were punished with the sword.
26. When the verdict was read from the tablet, the martyrs were punished by the sword.

27. When the letters were read, Saturninus said that Speratus was a Christian.

28. When the letters were read, Saturninus said that he thought that Speratus was a Christian.

29. Saturninus ordered Speratus, Nartzalus, and Cittinus to be led away.

30. Saturninus ordered Speratus, Nartzalus, and Cittinus to be punished by the sword.

Schola Vicesima Quinta

1. Sing, tongue, the mystery of the body and of the blood.

2. I sing the mystery of the body and of the blood.

3. I sing the mystery of the body and of the blood.

4. You sing the mystery of the glorious body and the precious blood.

5. He sings the mystery of the glorious body and the precious blood.

6. Having dwelt in the world, he closed the times of sojourn.

7. Having dwelt in the world, with the seed of the word sown, he closed the times of (his) stay.

8. He dwelt in the world, he spread the seed of the word, and closed the times of (his) sojourn.

9. He will dwell in the world, he will spread the seed of the word, and he will close the times of (his) sojourn.

10. He has dwelt in the world, with the word of the gospel sown, he has closed the times of staying.

11. With the word of the gospel sown, in wonderful order he closed the times of sojourn.

12. With the word of the gospel sown, in wonderful order he closed the time of life.

13. With the word of grace sown, with a noble order the time of his life was closed.

14. With the word of God sown in the world, with a noble order the time of his life has been closed.

15. He spread the word of God in the world, and closed his days of his life with a wonderful order.

16. With the law having been kept with lawful foods, he gives food to the crowd.

17. With the laws having been kept with lawful food, he gave himself as food to the crowd of twelve.
18. When the precept was kept with lawful foods, he gave himself as food to the crowd with his own hands.
19. With the law fully kept with lawful foods, he gave himself as food to the crowd with his own hands.
20. He kept the law with licit foods and gave himself as food to the crowd with his own hands.
21. He makes bread the true flesh of Christ and wine becomes the blood of Christ.
22. With a word he has made bread the true body, and wine has become the blood of Christ.
23. If sense fails, faith alone is enough for a heart to be strengthened.
24. If the senses fail, faith alone suffices to strengthen a heart.
25. If the senses fail, faith alone is enough for a soul to be strengthened.
26. Kneeling, let us adore such a sacrament.
27. Kneeling, we venerate such a sacrament and gift.
28. Kneeling we have adored such a sacrament and gift.
29. Kneeling, I have venerated such a sacrament and gift.
30. Kneeling, let me adore such a sacrament and give thanks to God.
31. Kneeling, let us adore such a sacrament and give thanks to God.
32. May there be praise and rejoicing to the Father and the Son.
33. May there be blessing to the Begetter and the Begotten, and to the one who proceeds from them both.
34. May there be equal praise to the one proceeding from them both.
35. May there be equal praise to the one sitting at the right hand of the Begetter.
36. May there be equal praise to the One Begotten of the supreme Father.
37. May there be equal praise to the name of the begotten Son.
38. Honor and strength to the name of the Begetter and the Begotten, and to the one who proceeds from them both.
39. The church praises the Begetter, the Begotten, and the one proceeding from them both.
40. Glory is given by the Begotten to the name of the Begetter, in the power of the one proceeding from both.

Glossary

A

a (*before a consonant*), ab, abs
(*before a vowel*), + *ablative*, by, from,
away from

abjicio (*or* abicio), abjicere, abjeci,
abjectus, 3, to cast away, throw,
cast off

accedo, accedere, accessi, accessus, 3,
to go to, approach

accendo, accendere, accensis, accensus,
3, to inflame, enkindle, set fire to

accipio, accipere, accepi, acceptus, 3,
to take, receive

acquiro, acquirere, acquisivi,
acquisitus, 3, to acquire, amass

addisco, addiscere, addidici, addictus,
3, to learn in addition, learn further,
hear, be informed

adduco, adducere, adduxi, adductus, 3,
to lead to

adgrego (*or* aggrego), adgregare,
adgregavi, adgregatus, 1, to gather
together, assemble

adhaereo, adhaerēre, adhaesi,
adhaesus, 2, to cling, cleave, stick

adimpleo, adimplēre, adimplevi,
adimpletus, 2, to fill, fulfill, fill up

adoro, adorare, adoravi, adoratus, 1,
to adore

adsumo (*or* assumo), adsumere,
adsumpsi, adsumptus, 3, to take

advenio, advenire, adveni, adventus, 4,
to come, arrive

adventus, -ūs, *m.*, 4, arrival

adversum, + *accusative*, against

aedifico, aedificare, aedificavi,
aedificatus, 1, to build, build up

aeger, aegra, aegrum, *adjective*, ill, sick,
unwilling, reluctant

aegre, *adverb*, unwillingly, reluctantly,
sickly

Aegyptus, -i, *f.*, 2, Egypt

aestus, -ūs, *m.*, 4, heat

aeternus, -a, -um, *adjective*, eternal,
everlasting; in aeternum, forever

ager, agri, *n.*, field, *pl.*, countryside

agnitio, -ionis, *f.*, 3, recognition

agnus, -i, *m.*, 2, lamb (*vocative same as the
nominative*)

ago, agere, egi, actus, 3, to do, drive,
treat, act; *with* gratias, give thanks

ait, he says, he said (*found only in this
form in the present*)

alienus, -a, -um, *adjective*, foreign,
strange, alien

aliquis, aliquis, aliquid, someone,
something, anyone, anything

alius, -a, -um, *adjective*, other, another

allicio, allicere, allexi, allectus, 3, to
draw, attract, draw to one's self

alloquor, alloqui, allocutus sum, 3,
deponent, to address, speak to

altare, -is, *n.*, 3, altar, *pl.*, altaria

alter, altera, alterum, *adjective*, other (of
two), second (*gen. sing.* alteríus, *dat.
sing.* alteri)

altus, -a, -um, *adjective*, high, deep

amicus, -i, *m.*, 2, friend

amo, amare, amavi, amatus, 1, to love

amor, -is, *m.*, 3, love

amplexor, amplexari, amplexatus sum,
1, *deponent*, to embrace

amplius, *adverb*, more (*also*, amplior,
amplius, *comparative of* amplus)

amplus, -a, -um, *adjective*, ample,
sufficient

ancilla, -ae, *f.*, 1, handmaid

anima, -ae, *f.*, 1, soul (*dat. and abl. pl.*
animabus)

animadverto, animadvertere,
animadversi, animadvertus, 3, to
punish with death, regard, observe

animal, -is, *n.*, 3, animal, beast

animus, -i, *m.*, 2, mind

ante, + *accusative*, before

antiquus, -a, -um, *adjective*, old, ancient

aperio, aperire, aperui, apertus, *4,* to open
aptus, -a, -um, *adjective,* fitting, proper
aqua, -ae, *f., 1,* water
arbor, -is, *f., 3,* tree
aridus, -a, -um, *adjective,* dry
ascendo, ascendere, ascendi, ascensus, *3,* to ascend, go up, rise
asinus, -i, *m., 2,* ass
aspergo, aspergere, aspersi, aspersus, *3,* to sprinkle
assisto, assistere, astiti, _____ (ad + sto), to stand by, place oneself
assumo, *cf.* **adsumo,** to take
atrium, -i, *n., 2,* hall, court, vestibule
auctor, -is, *m., 3,* source, maker, creator
audio, audire, audivi, auditus, *4,* to hear
auris, -is, *f., 3,* ear
aut, *conjunction,* or; **aut . . . aut,** either . . . or
autem, *conjunction,* however
ave, *pl.,* **avete,** hail, greetings, be well

B

baptismus, -i, *m., 2,* baptism
baptizo, baptizare, baptizavi, baptizatus, *1,* to baptize
beatudo, -inis, *f., 3,* beatitude, blessedness
beatus, -a, -um, *adjective,* blessed, happy
bellum, -i, *n., 2,* war
benedico, benedicere, benedixi, benedictus, *3,* to bless (*object is usually dative*)
benedictio, -ionis, *f., 3,* blessing
benedictus, -a, -um, *adjective,* blessed
benefacio, benefacere, benefeci, benefactus, *3,* to do good
bis, *adverb,* twice
bonus, -a, -um, *adjective,* good
bos, bovis, *m. & f., 3,* bovine, cow, ox

C

caelestis, -e, *adjective, 3 in two endings,* heavenly, of heaven
caelitus, *adverb,* from heaven
caelum (*or* coelum), -i, *n.* (*pl. usually masc.,* **caeli**), sky, heavens

caeremonia, -ae, *f., 1,* rite, religious usage (*also found as* **caerimonium, -i,** *n.*)
caerimonior, caerimoniari, caerimoniatus sum, *1, deponent,* to perform the customary rites
capsa, -ae, *f., 1,* case, container
caritas, -atis, *f., 3,* love, charity
caro, carnis, *f., 3,* flesh, meat
causa, -ae, *f., 1,* cause, reason; **quid causae,** why?; **causā,** + *genitive,* for the sake of
cedo, cedere, cessi, cessus, *3,* to yield, withdraw, grant
cella, -ae, *f., 1,* room
cena (*or* coena), -ae, *f., 1,* supper, meal, banquet
cernuus, -a, -um, *adjective,* kneeling
certamen, -inis, *n., 3,* struggle, fight, contention
ceterus, -a, -um, *adjective,* other
cibus, -i, *m., 2,* food, meat
circa, + *accusative,* around, about, in respect to
clarus, -a, -um, *adjective,* bright, shining, famous
claudo, claudere, clausi, clausus, *3,* to close, shut
cognitio, -ionis, *f., 3,* knowledge, learning
cognosco, cognoscere, cognovi, cognitus, *3,* to know, learn, recognize
coheres, coheredis, *m., 3,* coheir
colligo, colligere, collexi, collectus, *3,* to collect, assemble, draw together
colloquor, colloqui, collocutus sum, *3, deponent,* to speak, speak with
colo, colere, colui, cultus, *3,* to cultivate, till, tend, care for, cherish, abide, inhabit, care for, protect, worship
commuto, commutare, commutavi, commutatus, *1,* to change, transform
compar, *3 adjective in one ending* (*gen.* **comparis**), like, equal
complexus, -ūs, *m., 4,* embrace
comprehendo, comprehendere, comprehendi, comprehensus, *3,* to seize, lay hold of
conatus, -ūs, *m., 4,* attempt, effort, exertion

concupisco, concupiscere, concupiscivi (-ii), concupitus, *3*, to desire, covet, strive

concurro, concurrere, concurri, concursus, *3*, to assemble, concur, meet, join

confido, confidere, confisus sum, *3 semideponent*, to trust, hope

confiteor, confiteri, confessus sum, *2*, to profess, confess, avow, admit

conforto, confortare, confortavi, confortatus, *1*, to strengthen, encourage

congredior, congredi, congressus sum, *3, deponent*, to engage, contend, meet in combat, dispute

conjungo, conjungere, conjunxi, conjunctus, *3*, to join, unite

conor, conari, conatus sum, *1, deponent*, to try, attempt

consentio, consentire, consensi, consensus, *4*, to agree, harmonize with

consequor, consequi, consecutus sum, *3, deponent*, to follow, pursue, attain, chase after

consilium, -i, *n.*, *2*, council, counsel

consolo, consolare, concolavi, consolatus, *1*, to comfort, cheer, console (*also can appear in a deponent form*, consolor, consolari, consolatus sum)

consolator, -is, *m.*, *3*, consoler

conspiratio, -nis, *f.*, *3*, plot, conspiracy

constantia, -ae, *f.*, *1*, firmness, perseverance

constituo, constituere, constitui, constitutus, *3*, to put, place, establish, station

construo, construere, construxi, constructus, *3*, to build, frame together, construct

consuesco, consuescere, consuevi, consuetus, *3*, to be accustomed

consul, -is, *m.*, *3*, consul

consulo, consulere, consului, consultus, *3*, to consider, reflect, deliberate

consultatio, -nis, *f.*, *3*, deliberation, consultation

consuo, consuere, consui, consutus, *3*, to sew, stitch, join together

contra, + *accusative*, against

convenio, convenire, conveni, conventus, *4*, to meet, assemble

conversor, conversari, conversatus sum, *1, deponent*, to dwell, live

convivium, -i, *n.*, *2*, banquet

cor, cordis, *n.*, *3*, heart

coram, + *ablative*, before, in front of

corono, coronare, coronavi, coronatus, *1*, to crown

corpus, corporis, *n.*, *3*, body

cotidianus, -a, -um, *adjective*, daily, of the day

credo, credere, credidi, creditus, *3, usually takes dative*, to believe

creo, creare, creavi, creatus, *1*, to create

crimen, -inis, *n.*, *3*, charge, accusation, crime

crux, crucis, *f.*, *3*, cross

cultus, -ūs, *m.*, *4*, worship, cult

cum, (1) + *ablative*, with (2) *conjunction*, when

cupisco, cupiscere, cupiscivi (cupiscii), cupitus, *3*, to wish, desire

custodio, custodire, custodivi (custodii), custoditus, *4*, to keep, guard

D

daemon, -onis, *m.*, *3*, evil spirit, demon

dator, -is, *m.*, *3*, giver

de, + *ablative*, from, down from, about, concerning

debeo, debēre, debui, debitus, *2*, to owe, ought, be bound to

debitor, -is, *m.*, *3*, debtor, ower

debitum, -i, *n.*, *2*, debt, obligation

decem, *indeclinable adjective*, ten

decimus, -a, -um, *adjective*, tenth

decretum, -i, *n.*, *2*, decree

dedicatio, -ionis, *f.*, *3*, dedication

defectus, -ūs, *m.*, *4*, need, lack

deficio, deficere, defeci, defectus, *3,* to fail, faint, be lacking

dementia, -ae, *f., 1,* madness

dens, dentis, *f., 3,* tooth

denuo, *adverb,* again

deorsum, *adverb,* below, from below

deprecatio, -ionis, *f., 3,* prayer, supplication

deprehendo, deprehendere, deprehendi, deprehensus, *3,* to take, seize, snatch

desidero, desiderare, desideravi, desideratus, *1,* to wish, desire

desino, desinere, desii, desitus, *3,* to leave off, stop, cease (*followed by infinitive*)

destruo, destruere, destuxi, destructus, *3,* to tear down, destroy

desuper, *adverb,* from above, above

Deus, -i, *m., 2,* God (*vocative same as the nominative*)

devius, -a, -um, *adjective,* astray, off the path

dexter, -tra, -trum, *adjective,* right (*opposite of* **sinister,** left); **ad dexteram,** at the right hand

diabolus, -i, *m., 2,* devil

dico, dicere, dixi, dictus, *3,* to say, speak

dies, -ei, *m. or f., 5,* day

digitus, -i, *m., 2,* finger, toe

dignus, -a, -um, *adjective,* worthy, worthy of (+ *ablative*)

dilectio, -ionis, *f., 3,* love

diligo, diligere, dilexi, dilectus, *3,* to love

dimitto, dimittere, dimisi, dimissus, *3,* to send away, forgive

dirigo, dirigere, direxi, directus, *3,* to direct, guide

disciplina, -ae, *f., 1,* instruction

disco, discere, didici, _____, *3,* to learn

discipulus, -i, *m., 2,* disciple

dito, ditare, ditavi, ditatus, *1,* to enrich, endow

diu, *adverb,* for a long time

dives, divitis, *m., 3,* rich, rich man

do, dare, dedi, datus, *1,* to give, put, place

doceo, docēre, docui, doctus, *2,* to teach

doctrina, -ae, *f., 1,* teaching, instruction, doctrine

documentum, -i, *n., 2,* example, warning, proof, pattern

dolor, -is, *m., 3,* sorrow, pain, sadness

dominus, -i, *m., 2,* lord, master, the Lord

domumcella, -ae, *f., 1,* room

domus, -i, *f., 2,* house

donator, -is, *m., 3,* giver, donator

duco, ducere, duxi, ductus, *3,* to lead

ductor, -is, *m., 3,* leader, commander

dulcis, -e, *3 adjective in two endings,* sweet

durus, -a, -um, *adjective,* hard, difficult

duo, duae, duo, *adjective,* two (*cf. p. XX for declension*)

duodecimus, -a, -um, *adjective,* twelfth

dux, ducis, *m., 3,* leader, commander

E

e (*before a consonant*), **ex** (*before a vowel*), + *ablative,* out of, from

ecce, *imperative,* behold!

ecclesia, -ae, *f., 1,* church, assembly

ecclesiastes, -ae, *m., 1,* preacher

educo, educere, eduxi, eductus, *3,* to lead out

efficio, efficere, effeci, effectus, *3,* to make, effect

effundo, effundere, effudi, effusus, *3,* to pour out, spill, shed

ego, *first person singular pronoun,* I (*gen.* **mei,** *dat.* **mihi,** *acc.* **me,** *abl.* **me**)

elevo, elevare, elevavi, elevatus, *1,* to raise, raise up, elevate

emitto, emittere, emisi, emissus, *3,* to send out

emo, emere, emi, emptus, *3,* to buy

enim, *conjunction,* for

epistula, -ae, *f., 1,* letter

ergo, *conjunction,* therefore

error, -is, *m., 3,* error, deception, mistake

esurio, esurire, _____, esuritus, *4,* to hunger, be hungry, hunger for

esus, -ūs, *m., 4,* act of eating

et, *conjunction,* and; **et . . . et,** both . . . and

evello, evellere, evelli (evulsi), evulsus, *3,* to pull up, rip out

excelsus, -a, -um, *adjective*, high, lofty, exalted

exhibeo, exhibēre, exhibui, exhibitus, 2, to produce, bring forth, show

exitus, -ūs, *m.*, 4, outcome, departure, end, death

exsulto, exsultare, exsultavi, exsultatus, 1, to exult

exterior, exterius, outer, exterior (*comparative adjective of* exterus, -a, -um, outside)

F

facilis, -e, 3 *adjective in two endings,* easy; *comp. adv.* facilius, more easily

facio, facere, feci, factus, 3, to make, do

factum, -i, *n.*, 2, deed

facultas, -atis, *f.*, 3, possibility, capability, opportunity

falsus, -a, -um, *adjective,* false

familiaris, -e, 3 *adjective in two endings,* familiar, friendly; *comp. adv.* familiarius, more familiarly

fanum, -i, *n.*, 2, temple, shrine

fidelis, -e, 3 *adjective in two endings,* faithful, believing

fidenter, *adverb,* faithfully

fides, -ei, *f.*, 5, faith, trust

fiducia, -ae, *f.*, 1, confidence, trust, reliance

filia, -ae, *f.*, 1, daughter

filius, -i, *m.*, 2, son

fio, fieri, factus sum, 3, to become, be made, happen (*used as the passive of* facio)

firmo, firmare, firmavi, firmatus, 1, to strengthen, establish

flecto, flectere, flexi, flectus, 3, to bend

fleo, flere, flevi, fletus, 2, to weep

fletus, -ūs, *m.*, 4, weeping

fons, fontis, *f.*, 3, fountain, source

forsitan, *adverb,* perhaps, seemingly

fortis, -e, 3 *adjective in two endings,* strong, mighty

foveo, fovēre, fovi, fotus, 2, to warm, heat up

frater, -tris, *m.*, 3, brother

frigidus, -a, -um, *adjective,* cold

fructus, -ūs, *m.*, 4, fruit

frustra, *adverb,* in vain

furtum, -i, *n.*, 2, theft, robbery, deceit, trick

futurus, -a, -um, *adjective (participle of* sum*)*, future, about to be

G

gaudeo, gaudēre, gavisus sum, 2, *semideponent,* to rejoice

gemitus, -ūs, *m.*, 4, sigh, sighing, groan, groaning

generatio, -nis, *f.*, 3, generation

generator, -is, *m.*, 3, generator, father

generosus, -a, -um, *adjective,* noble

genius, -i, *m.*, 2, guardian spirit, tutelary deity

geno, genere, genui, genitus, 3, to beget, bear, generate

gens, -ntis, *f.*, 3, people, nation, clan

gladius, -i, *m.*, 2, sword

gloria, -ae, *f.*, 1, glory

glorifico, glorificare, glorificavi, glorificatus, 1, to glorify

gloriosus, -a, -um, *adjective,* glorious

gradus, -ūs, *m.*, 4, step, stair

gratia, -ae, *f.*, 1, grace, favor; ago gratias, I give thanks

guttur, -is, *n.*, 3, throat

H

habeo, habēre, habui, habitus, 2, to have, hold

hic, haec, hoc, *demonstrative adjective/ pronoun,* this, these; *personal pronoun,* he, she, it, they

hīc, *adverb,* here

Hierosolyma, -ae, *or* Hierosolymae, -arum, *f.*, 1, Jerusalem

Hierusalem, *indeclineable,* Jerusalem

hodie, *adverb,* today

homo, -inis, *m.*, 3, man, human being

homocidium, -i, *n.*, 2, murder, homicide

honor, -is, *m.*, 3, honor, distinction

honoro, honorare, honoravi, honoratus,
    1, to honor, respect, adorn
hora, -ae, *f., 1,* hour, time, season
hospes, hospitis, *m. & f.,* guest, host
hostis, -is, *m., 3,* enemy
hujuscemodi, of this sort (*cf.* **modus, hic;**
    also **hujusmodi**)

I

ibi, *adverb,* there
idcirco, *conjunction,* therefore
ideo, *conjunction,* therefore
idolum, -i, *n., 2,* idol, false god
ignis, -is, *m., 3,* fire
ille, illa, illum, *demonstrative adjective/*
    pronoun, that, those; *personal pronoun,*
    he, she, it, they
illic, *adverb,* there
immolo, immolare, immolavi,
    immolatus, *1,* to sacrifice, immolate
immuto, immutare, immutavi,
    immutatus, *1,* to change into
imperator, -is, *m., 3,* commander,
    emperor
imperium, -i, *n., 2,* rule, empire
impleo, implēre, implevi, impletus, *2,*
    to fill, accomplish
impossibilis, -e, *3 adjective in two*
    endings, impossible
in, + *ablative,* in, on; + *accusative,* into,
    onto
inchoo, inchoare, inchoaci, inchoatus,
    1, to begin, commence
incipio, incipere, incepi, inceptus, *3,* to
    begin, commence
incolatus, -ūs, *m., 4,* sojourn, stay, act of
    residence
incommutabilis, -e, *3 adjective in two*
    endings, unchangeable, immutable
inde, *conjunction,* from this
induco, inducere, induxi, inductus, *3,* to
    lead into
infirmo, inirmare, infirmavi,
    infirmatus, *1,* to weaken
infirmus, -a, -um, *adjective,* weak
infundo, infundere, infudi, infusus, *3,*
    to pour into

indulgentia, -ae, *f., 1,* mercy, clemency,
    favor
inimicus, -i, *m., 2,* enemy
iniquitas, -atis, *f., 3,* iniquity, evil
initio, initiare, initiavi, initiatus, *1,* to
    begin, originate
innoxius, -a, -um, *adjective,* harmless
inpono, inponere, inposui, inpositus, *3,*
    to place, set, put in
inseperabiliter, *adverb,* inseparably
insons, *3 adjective in one ending,*
    innocent, guileless
intactus, -a, -um, *adjective,* untouched
inter, + *accusative,* between, among
interim, *adverb,* meanwhile
interior, interius, *comparative adjective,*
    interior, inward
interrogatio, -ionis, *f., 3,* question
intimus, -a, -um, *adjective,* innermost,
    most secret; **intima,** *neuter pl.,* bowels,
    inmost parts
intra, + *accusative,* within
ipse, ipsa, ipsum, *intensive pronoun,*
    oneself, himself, etc.; *personal pronoun,*
    he, she, it, they
ira, -ae, *f., 1,* anger, wrath
irascor, irasci, iratus sum, *3, deponent,* to
    be angry, be in a rage
is, ea, id, *demonstrative adjective/pronoun,*
    this, that; *personal pronoun,* he, she, it,
    they (*gen. sing.* **ejus,** *dat. sing.* **ei**)
isdem, eadem, idem, *pronoun,* the same
iste, ista, istud, *demonstrative adjective/*
    pronoun, that
item, likewise besides, also, similarly

J

Jesus (*gen., dat., abl., voc.* **Jesu,** *acc.*
    Jesum), Jesus
jubeo, jubēre, jussi, jussus, *2,* to
    command, order, bid
jubilatio, -ionis, *f., 3,* rejoicing
jumentum, -i, *n., 2,* beast of burden,
    draught animal
juro, jurare, juravi, juratus, *1,* to swear
justitia, -ae, *f., 1,* justice, righteousness

K

Kalendae, -arum, *f., 1,* the kalends of
the month, beginning of a month

L

labor, -is, *m., 3,* work, labor
laboro, laborare, laboravi, laboratus, *1,*
to work, labor
lapis, lapidis, *m., 3,* stone
lasso, lassare, lassavi, lassatus, *1,* to tire,
make weary, become weary
laudatio, -ionis, *f., 3,* praise
laudo, laudare, laudavi, laudatus, *1,* to
praise
laus, laudis, *f., 3,* praise
lavo, lavare, lavavi, lavatus, *1,* to wash
lectio, -ionis, *f., 3,* reading
legalis, -e, *3 adjective in two endings,*
legal, lawful
lego, legere, lexi, lectus, *3,* to read
lex, legis, *f., 3,* law
liber, libera, liberum, *adjective,* free; *as a
noun,* child
liber, libri, *m., 2,* book
libero, liberare, liberavi, liberatus, *1,* to
free, deliver, liberate
lignum, -i, *n., 2,* wood
lingua, -ae, *f., 1,* tongue, language
locus, -i, *m., 2,* place; *pl. neuter,* **loca,
-orum**
longe, *adverb,* from afar, afar, far away;
comparative adverb **longius,** farther
away
longevus, -a, -um, *adjective,* long-lived
longus, -a, -um, *adjective,* long
loquor, loqui, locutus sum, *3, deponent,*
to talk, speak, say
lugeo, lugēre, luxi, luctus, *2,* to mourn,
lament, bewail
lumen, -inis, *n., 3,* light

M

magis, *adverb,* rather
magister, -tri, *m., 2,* master, teacher
major, majus, *comparative adjective of*
magnus, greater, larger

**maledico, maledicere, maledixi,
maledictus,** *3,* to curse
**malefacio, malefacere, malefeci,
malefatus,** *3,* to do evil, do wrong
malus, -a, -um, *adjective,* bad, evil
mane, *adverb,* early, early in the morning
manus, -ūs, *f., 4,* hand
mare, -is, *n., 3,* sea (*pl.* **maria, marium**)
martyrium, -i, *n., 2,* martyrdom
martyrus, -i, *m., 2,* martyr, witness
mater, -tris, *f., 3,* mother
matrimonium, -i, *n., 2,* marriage
medius, -a, -um, *adjective,* middle
melior, melius, *comparative of* **bonus,**
better
memini, meminisse, to remember (*found
only in the perfect forms; imperative*
memento)
mens, mentis, *f., 3,* mind, disposition,
heart
mensis, -is, *m., 3,* month
mentior, mentiri, mentitus sum, *4,
deponent,* to cheat, lie, deceive
merces, mercedis, *f., 3,* pay, reward,
wages, salary, fee
meritum, -i, *n., 2,* merit
merus, -i, *n., 2,* wine
mille, *n., 3,* thousand, *pl.* **millia** *or* **milia**
minimus, -a, -um, *superlative adjective of*
parvus, least (*adverb* **minime**)
minor, minus, *comparative adjective of*
parvus, lesser, smaller
mirus, -a, -um, *adjective,* wonderful
misereor, misereri, misertus sum, *2,
deponent,* to have mercy (+ *gen. or dat.*)
misericordia, -ae, *f., 1,* mercy
misericors, -cordis, -e, *3 adjective in two
endings,* merciful
mitis, -e, *3 adjective in two endings,* mild,
mellow, soft, ripe, gentle
mitto, mittere, misi, missus, *3,* to send,
cast
modicus, -a, -um, *adjective,* moderate,
proper
modus, -i, *m., 2,* way, manner
(**hujuscemodi,** of this sort)
moechor, moechari, moechatus sum, *1,
deponent,* to commit adultery

mons, -ntis, *f., 3,* mountain
mora, -ae, *f., 1,* delay
morior, mori, mortuus sum, *3, deponent,* to die
mors, -rtis, *f., 3,* death
mortuus, -a, -um (*from* **morior**), dead
mos, moris, *f., 3,* custom, *pl.* **mores, -ium,** ethics, morals
mugitus, -ūs, *m., 4,* lowing, bellowing
mulier, -is, *f., 3,* woman
mundus, -a, -um, *adjective,* clean
mundus, -i, *m., 2,* world
munus, muneris, *n., 3,* gift, offering, task, duty

N

nam, *conjunction,* for
nascor, nasci, natus sum, *3, deponent,* to be born
natalicius (natalitius), -a, -um, pertaining to a birthday
natus or **nata** (*from* **nascor**), child
ne, *adverb (+ subjunctive),* not; *conjunction,* lest
nec, *adverb,* not; **nec . . . nec,** neither . . . nor
necessarius, -a, -um, *adjective,* needful, necessary, unavoidable, inevitable
necesse est, *impersonal verb,* it is necessary, there is need (+ *infinitive*)
nefarious, -a, -um, *adjective,* impious, heinous
nemo, neminis, *m., 3,* no one
nequissimus, -a, -um, *superlative adjective,* most worthless
nihil, *indeclinable,* nothing
nitor, niti, nisus sum, *3, deponent,* to endeavor, strive, lean upon, rest
nolo, nolle, nolui, *3,* to be unwilling, to not want (*imperative* **noli, nolite** + *infinitive used as negative command*)
nomen, -inis, *n., 3,* name
non, *adverb,* not
nonus, -a, -um, *adjective,* ninth
nos, *first person plural pronoun,* we (*gen.* **nostri, nostrum,** *dat. and abl.* **nobis,** *acc.* **nos**)

nosco, noscere, novi, notus, *3,* to know, recognize
novem, *indeclinable adjective,* nine
nox, noctis, *f., 3,* night
noxius, -a, -um, *adjective,* noxious, harmful, evil
nullus, -a, -um, *adjective,* no one, none, nothing (*gen. sing.* **nullíus,** *dat. sing.* **nulli**)
numen, -inis, *n., 3,* divinity, Godhead
numquam, *adverb,* never
nunc, *adverb,* now

O

obsequium, -i, *n., 2,* homage, service, worship, respect
observo, observare, observavi, observatus, *1,* to watch, respect, keep
occido, occidere, occisi, occisus, *3,* to kill
octavus, -a, -um, *adjective,* eighth
octo, *indeclinable adjective,* eight
oculus, -i, *m., 2,* eye
odi, odisse, *3,* to hate (*found only in the perfect form, but with present meaning*)
odium, -i, *n., 2,* hatred
offero, oferre, obtuli, oblatus (ob + fero), *3,* to present, offer, bring
omnino, *adverb,* at all
omnipotens, *3 adjective in one ending,* all-powerful, omnipotent
omnis, -e, *3 adjective in two endings,* all, every
opera, -ae, *f., 1,* pains, effort, trouble, time; **dare operam,** pay attention to
operor, operari, operatus sum, *1, deponent,* to work, labor
oportet, *imprsonal verb,* it behooves, it is proper, it is needful (+ *accusative and infinitive; perfect* **oportuit**)
optimus, -a, -um, *superlative of* **bonus,** best
opus, operis, *n., 3,* work (*pl.* **opera, -um**)
ordo, -inis, *m., 3,* order, rank, rite
oro, orare, oravi, oratus, *1,* to pray
os, oris, *n., 3,* mouth

P

pacificus, -a, -um, adjective, peaceful,
peace-making, peaceable

pango, pangere, panxi (or **pegi,** or
pepigi), panctus (or **pactus),** *3,* to
make, compose, sing

panis, -is, *m., 3,* bread (gen. pl. panium)

papa, -ae, *m., 1,* father, bishop, presbyter,
pastor

paraclitus, -i, *m., 2,* advocate, helper

particeps, *3 adjective in one ending,*
sharing, participating; *as a noun,*
sharer, partaker

parvus, -a, -um, *adjective,* small, little

passus, -ūs, *m., 4,* pace, foot step

pateo, patēre, patui, _____, 2, to be
open, lie open, be accessible

paternus, -a, -um, *adjective,* of the father,
fatherly

patientia, -ae, *f., 1,* endurance, long-
suffering

patior, pati, passus sum, *3, deponent,* to
suffer, allow

pauper, *3 adjective in one ending,* poor

pax, pacis, *f., 3,* peace

peccator, -is, *m., 3,* sinner

peccatum, -i, *n., 2,* sin, error

pecco, peccare, peccavi, peccatus, *1,* to
sin, err, make a mistake

pectus, pectoris, *n., 3,* breast, heart

per, + *accusative,* through

perdo, perdere, perdidi, perditus, *3,* to
destroy, ruin, waste, lose

perduco, perducere, perduxi, perductus,
3, to lead through, bring to

perennis, -e, *3 adjective in two endings,*
everlasting

perficio, perficere, perfeci, perfectus, *3,*
to complete, make perfect, perfect

perpes, *3 adjective in one ending,*
unending, perpetual (*gen.* **perpetis**)

persecutio, -nis, *f., 3,* persecution

persequor, persequi, persecutus sum, *3,*
deponent, to persecute

persevero, perseverare, perseveravi,
perseveratus, *1,* to persist, continue,
finish

persuasio, -nis, *f., 3,* belief, persuasion

pervenio, pervenire, perveni,
perventus, *4,* to reach, attain, arrive
at

pes, pedis, *f., 3,* foot

philosopus, -i, *m., 2,* philosopher

pius, -a, -um, *adjective,* dutiful, devout,
conscientious

placeo, placēre, placui, placitus, *2,* (+
dat.) to please, be pleasing to;
(*impersonal use*) **placet** + *infinitive,* it is
pleasing

plango, plangere, planxi, planctus, *3,* to
mourn, lament

planto, plantare, plantavi, plantatus, *1,*
to plant, set

plenus, -a, -um, *adjective* (+ *abl.*), full,
full of; *adverb* **plene,** fully

plurimus, -a, -um, *superlative adjective of*
multus, very many

porro, *adverb,* farther, far away

porta, -ae, *f., 1,* gate, door

possideo, possidēre, possedi, possessus,
2, to own, possess

possum, potesse, potui (pot + sum), to
be able, can (+ *infinitive*)

postmodum, *adverb,* after, afterward

potius, *adverb,* rather

praebeo, praebēre, praebui, praebitus,
2, to grant, offer, proffer, hold out,
exhibit

praeceptum, -i, *n., 2,* commandment,
precept

praecipio, praecipere, praecepi,
praeceptus, *3,* to command, order

praeco, praeconis, *m., 3,* herald

praepono, praeponere, praeposui,
praepositus, *3,* to place before

praesens, *3 adjective* (*participle*) *in one*
ending (*from* **praesum**), present

praesto, praestare, praestiti, praestitus,
1, to furnish, grant, guarantee, serve,
stand out

praesum, praeesse, praefui,
praefuturus, (prae + sum), to be set
over, preside, rule over

praeter, + *accusative,* past, beyond

praetereo, praeterire, praeterivi,
praeteritus, (praeter + eo), to pass,
pass by, go past

praevius, -a, -um, *adjective,* preceding, leading
pretiosus, -a, -um, *adjective,* precious, costly
pretium, -i, *n.,* 2, cost, price
primo, *adverb,* first, at first
primus, -a, -um, *adjective,* first
princeps, -ipis, *m.,* 3, leading citizen, prince
principium, -i, *n.,* 2, beginning, start, origin
prior, prius, *comparative adjective,* earlier, prior
pro, + *ablative,* for, on behalf of, before, in place of
procedo, procedere, processi, processus, 3, to proceed, go forth
proconsul, -is, *m.,* 3, former consul, governor of a province
promeror, promereri, promissus sum, 2, *deponent,* to earn, gain, merit
promissum, -i, *n.,* 2, promise
prope, *adverb,* near, nearby, close
propheta, -ae, *m.,* 1, prophet
propono, proponere, proposui, propositus, 3, to propose
propter, + *accusative,* on account of, because
prosum, prodesse, profui, profuturus (pro + sum), to avail, be of help (+ *dat.*)
protinus (protenus), *adverb,* constantly, immediately, forward, further
proximus, -a, -um, *adjective,* nearest; *as a noun,* neighbor
puer, -i, *m.,* 2, boy, servant
punitor, -is, *m.,* 3, punisher
puto, putare, putavi, putatus, 1, to think

Q

qua, *adverb,* when
quaero, quaerere, quaesivi, quaesitus, 3, to inquire, look into, ask, seek
quam, *adverb,* than
quando, *conjunction,* when
quartus, -a, -um, *adjective,* fourth
quasi, *adverb,* as if, as it were

quattuor, *indeclinable adjective,* four
qui, quae, quod, *relative pronoun,* who, which, that
quia, *conjunction,* that, because
quicumque, quaecumque, quodcumque, *relative pronoun,* whatever, whoever
quidam, quaedam, quoddam, *indefinite pronoun,* certain, sort of, kind of
quinque, *indeclinable adjective,* five
quintus, -a, -um, *adjective,* fifth
quis, quis, quid, *interrogative pronoun,* who? what?
quisquam, quaequam, quidquam, *indefinite pronoun,* any at all
quod, *conjunction,* that, because
quoniam, *conjunction,* because, for, that
quotidianus, -a, -um, *adjective,* daily, of the day

R

radius, -i, *m.,* 2, ray
ramus, -i, *m.,* 2, branch, twig
recito, recitare, recitavi, recitatus, 1, to read aloud, recite
recordor, recordari, recordatus sum, 1, *deponent,* to think over
recumbo, recumbere, recubui, _____, 3, to recline
reddo, reddere, redidi, reditus, 3, to give back, repay
redeo, redire, redivi, reditus (re + eo), to go back, return
refrigerium, -i, *n.,* 2, consolation, cooling, refreshment
regina, -ae, *f.,* 1, queen
regnum, -i, *n.,* 2, kingdom, rule, reign
rego, regere, rexi, rectus, 3, to rule, guide, govern
religio, -ionis, *f.,* 3, religious awe, scrupulosity, conscientiousness, sacred obligations, worship
religiosus, -a, -um, *adjective,* god-fearing, scrupulous, conscientious as to ritual
reliquia, -ae, *f.,* 1, remains, relic, remnant

remunerator, -is, *m.*, *3*, rewarder, repayer

repello, repellere, repuli, repulsus, *3*, to repel, overcome, reject, drive away

repleo, replēre, replevi, repletus, *2*, to fill, complete

requies, -ei, *f.*, *5*, rest, quiet

requiesco, requiescere, requievi, requietus, *3*, to rest, repose

res, rei, *f.*, *5*, thing, affair

reservo, reservare, reservavi, reservatus, *1*, to save, preserve, hold back, keep

revoco, revocare, revocavi, revocatus, *1*, to call back

rex, regis, *m.*, *3*, king

rideo, ridēre, risi, risus, *2*, to laugh

rigidus, -a, -um, *adjective*, stiff

rigo, rigare, rigavi, rigatus, *1*, to wet, water

rite, *adverb*, duly, properly, rightly

ritus, -ūs, *m.*, *4*, religious custom, rite

rugitus, -ūs, *m.*, *4*, roaring, rumbling

S

sabbatum, -i, *2*, Sabbath, Sabbath Day

sacra, -orum, *n.*, *pl.*, *2*, holy things, rites

sacramentum, -i, *n.*, *2*, sacrament, holy oath

sacrilegus, -a, -um, *adjective*, sacrilegious, robbing a temple

saeculum, -i, *n.*, *2*, world, age

salto, saltare, saltavi, saltatus, *1*, to dance, leap

saltus, -ūs, *m.*, *4*, jump, leap

salus, -utis, *f.*, *3*, salvation, health

salveo, salvēre, _____, *2*, to be well, be in good health; *imperative* salve, *pl.* salvete, used as a greeting upon arrival or departure

salvus, -a, -um, *adjective*, safe, saved

sancio, sancire, sanxi, sanctus, *4*, to render inviolate, enact, confirm

sanctifico, sanctificare, sanctificavi, sanctificatus, *1*, to hallow, make holy, sanctify

sanctus, -a, -um, *adjective*, holy; as a noun, saint

sanguis, sanguinis, *m.*, *3*, blood

sano, sanare, sanavi, sanatus, *1*, to heal

sapiens, *3 adjective in one ending*, wise

sapienter, *adverb*, wisely

satietas, -atis, *f.*, *3*, abundance, sufficiency

saturo, saturare, saturavi, saturatus, *1*, to satiate, glut, fill

saucius, -a, -um, *adjective*, wounded

scelus, sceleris, *n.*, *3*, crime

schola, -ae, *f.*, *1*, lesson, school, class

scientia, -ae, *f.*, *1*, knowledge

scindo, scindere, scidi, scissus, *3*, to cut, tear, rend asunder, split

scio, scire, scivi, scitus, *4*, to know

scribo, scribere, scripsi, scriptus, *3*, to write

sculptile, -is, *n.*, *3*, carving, graven image, statue

secretarium, -i, *n.*, *2*, inner room, council chamber

secta, -ae, *f.*, *1*, path, way

secundum, + *accusative*, following, according to

secundus, -a, -um, *adjective*, second, following

sedeo, sedēre, sedi, sessus, *2*, to sit

semen, -inis, *m.*, *3*, seed, offspring, descendants

semper, *adverb*, always

sensus, -ūs, *m.*, *4*, sense, feeling, perception, mind

sententia, -ae, *f.*, *1*, opinion, judgment

septem, *indeclinable adjective*, seven

septenarius, -a, -um, *adjective*, containing seven

septiformis, -e, *3 adjective in two endings*, sevenfold

septimus, -a, -um, *adjective*, seventh

sermo, -onis, *f.*, *3*, speech

servio, servire, servivi, servitus, *4*, to serve

servitus, -utis, *f.*, *3*, slavery, servitude

servo, servare, servavi, servatus, *1*, to save, preserve

servus, -i, *m.*, *2*, servant, slave

sex, *indeclinable adjective*, six

sextus, -a, -um, *adjective*, sixth

sic, *adverb*, thus, so

sicut, *adverb*, as, just as (*also appears as* **sicuti**)

signifer, -is, *m., 3*, standard-bearer

similitudo, -inis, *f., 3*, likeness

simplex, *3 adjective in one ending*, simple

simplicitas, -atis, *f., 3*, guilelessness, frankness, innocence

sincerus, -a, -um, *adjective*, guileless, innocent, sincere

sine, + *ablative*, without

sinister, -tra, -trum, *adjective*, left (*opposite of* **dexter,** right)

sinus, -ūs, *m., 4*, fold, bosom, bay, place of concealment

sitio sitire, sitivi (sitii), _____, *4*, to thirst, be thirsty, be parched, thirst for

sol, solis, *m., 3*, sun

solatium, -i, *n., 2*, comfort, solace

sollemnitas, -atis, *f., 3*, festival, solemnity

solus, -a, -um, *adjective*, sole, only, alone (*gen.* **solíus,** *dat.* **soli**)

sordidus, -a, -um, *adjective*, filthy

soror, -is, *f., 3*, sister

spargo, spargere, sparsi, sparsus, *3*, to strew, sprinkle, scatter

spatium, -i, *n., 2*, space, place

spero, sperare, speravi, speratus, *1*, to hope, hope for

spes, -ei, *f., 5*, hope

spiritualis, -e, *3 adjective in two endings*, spiritual

spiritus, -ūs, *m., 4*, wind, breath, spirit

sponso, sponsare, sponsavi, sponsatus, *1*, to betroth

sto, stare, steti, status, *1*, to stand

studium, -i, *n., 2*, zeal, effort

stultus, -a, -um, *adjective*, stupid

sub, + *ablative*, under, below

substantia, -ae, *f., 1*, substance

sufficio, sufficere, suffeci, suffectus, *3*, to be enough, suffice

sum, esse, fui, futurus, to be (*impf.* **eram, eras,** *etc.; fut.* **ero, eris,** *etc.; pres. subj.* **sim, sis,** *etc.*)

super, + *accusative*, over, above, on, upon; + *ablative*, about, concerning

supernus, -a, -um, *adjective*, heavenly, celestial

supplementum, -i, *n., 2*, supply, supplement

supplico, supplicare, supplicavi, supplicatus, *1*, to beg, pray

supremus, -a, -um, *superlative adjective*, last, latest, highest, extreme, greatest, supreme

surgo, surgere, surrexi, surrectus, *3*, to rise

suspicio, suscipere, suscepi, susceptus (sub + capio), *3*, to receive, take

sustuli, sublatus (perfect form of tollo, tollere), to take away

suus, -a, -um, *reflexive adjective*, one's own (*may refer to any person or number; so,* his own, her own, your own, *etc.*)

T

tabella, -ae, *f., 1*, wax writing tablet

tabernaculum, -i, *n., 2*, tent, pavilion, hut

taceo, tacēre, tacui, tacitus, *2*, to be silent, be quiet

tantus, -a, -um, *adjective*, so much, such

tantus . . . quantus, *correlative adjectives*, so much . . . as much, or so great . . . as great

tecum (cum te), with you

teleonum, -i, *n., 2*, tax

temperies, -ei, *f., 5*, tempering

tempus, temporis, *n., 3*, time

teneo, tenēre, tenui, tentus, *2*, to hold, keep

tentatio, -ionis, *f., 3*, temptation

terra, -ae, *f., 1*, land, earth

tertius, -a, -um, *adjective*, third

testimonium, -i, *n., 2*, witness, testimony

timeo, timēre, timui, timitus, *2*, to fear

timor, -is, *m., 3*, fear, awe

tolero, tolerare, toleravi, toleratus, *1*, to bear, tolerate

tollo, tollere, sustuli, sublatus, *3*, to take away

totus, -a, -um, *adjective*, all (*gen. sing.* **totíus,** *dat. sing.* **toti**)

tracto, tractare, tractavi, tractatus, *1,* to treat, deal with, handle, draw, drag

tranquillus, -a, -um, *adjective,* tranquil, quiet, peaceful

trans, + *accusative,* across

transeo, transire, transivi (ii), transitus (trans + eo), to pass, pass by, go across

tres, tres, tria, *3 adjective in two endings,* three

triginta, *indeclinable adjective,* thirty

tu, *second person singular pronoun,* you (*gen.* **tui,** *dat.* **tibi,** *acc. and abl.* **te)**

turba, -ae, *f., 1,* crowd, throng

tuus, -a, -um, *adjective,* your, yours (*referring to a singular person*)

U

ubi, *(interrogative) adverb,* where (?); *conjunction,* when, as soon as

unctio, -ionis, *f., 3,* anointing

unde, *adverb,* from this, whence

undecimus, -a, -um, *adjective,* eleventh

unigenitus, -a, -um, *adjective,* only-begotten

universus, -a, -um, *adjective,* all

unus, -a, -um, *adjective,* one, single (*gen.* **uníus,** *dat.* **uni)**

unusquisque, unaquaeque, unumquidque (unumquodque), every, everyone

usque, *adverb,* as far as, all the way

ut, *conjunction,* that, in order that, so that, as

uterque, utraque, utrumque, *adjective,* both, each of two

uxor, -is, *f., 3,* wife

V

valeo, valére, valui, valitus, *2,* to be well, healthy, be able (*imperative* **vale,** *pl.* **valete,** farewell)

vanitas, -atis, *f., 3,* emptiness, vanity, nullity

vanus, -a, -um, *adjective,* empty, vain

vanum, -i, *n., 2,* emptiness, vanity, cheating, deception

velox, *3 adjective in one ending,* swift

veneror, venerari, veneratus sum, *1, deponent,* to adore, venerate

venia, -ae, *m., 1,* alien, stranger, sojourner

venio, venire, veni, ventus, *4,* to come, arrive

venter, -tris, *m., 3,* womb

verbum, -i, *n., 2,* word

vere (*or* **vero),** *adverb,* truly

verecundia, -ae, *f., 1,* modesty

veritas, -atis, *f., 3,* truth

verus, -a, -um, *adjective,* true

vester, vestra, vestrum, *adjective,* your, yours (*referring to plural persons*)

vetula, -ae, *f., 1,* old woman

videlicet, *used adverbially,* namely

video, vidēre, vidi, visus, *2,* to see

vigilia, -ae, *f., 1,* sleeplessness, wakefulness, vigil; *pl.,* night watch, vigils

vir, -i, *m., 2,* man, male

virgo, virginis, *f., 3,* maiden, young woman, virgin

virtus, -tutis, *f., 3,* virtue, strength

visito, visitare, visitavi, visitatus, *1,* to visit

vito, vitare, vitavi, vitatus, *1,* to shun, avoid

vivo, vivere, vixi, victus, *3,* to live, be alive

vivus, -a, -um, *adjective,* living

vix, *adverb,* with great difficulty, barely

vobiscum (cum vobis), with you

voco, vocare, vocavi, vocatus, *1,* to call

volo, velle, volui, _____, to wish, desire (*present* **volo, vis, vult, volumus, vultis, volunt)**

voluntas, -atis, *f., 3,* will, desire

vos, *second person plural pronoun,* you (*gen.* **vestri, vestrum,** *dat. and abl.* **vobis,** *acc.* **vos)**

Z

zelotes, -ae, *m., 1,* jealous person, one who loves zealously

About the Liturgical Institute

The Liturgical Institute, founded in 2000 by His Eminence Francis Cardinal George of Chicago, offers a variety of options for education in liturgical studies. A unified, rites-based core curriculum constitutes the foundation of the program, providing integrated and balanced studies toward the advancement of the renewal promoted by the Second Vatican Council. The musical, artistic, and architectural dimensions of worship are given particular emphasis in the curriculum. Institute students are encouraged to participate in its "liturgical heart" of daily Mass and Morning and Evening Prayer. The academic program of the Institute serves a diverse, international student population—laity, religious, and clergy—who are preparing for service in parishes, dioceses, and religious communities. Personalized mentoring is provided in view of each student's ministerial and professional goals. The Institute is housed on the campus of the University of St. Mary of the Lake/Mundelein Seminary, which offers the largest priestly formation program in the United States and is the center of the permanent diaconate and lay ministry training programs of the Archdiocese of Chicago. In addition, the University has the distinction of being the first chartered institution of higher learning in Chicago (1844), and one of only seven pontifical faculties in North America.

For more information about the Liturgical Institute and its programs, contact: usml.edu/liturgicalinstitute. Phone: 847-837-4542. Email: litinst@usml.edu.

Msgr. Reynold Hillenbrand
1904-1979

Monsignor Reynold Hillenbrand, ordained a priest by Cardinal George Mundelein in 1929, was Rector of St. Mary of the Lake Seminary from 1936 to 1944.

He was a leading figure in the liturgical and social action movement in the United States during the 1930s and worked to promote active, intelligent, and informed participation in the Church's liturgy.

He believed that a reconstruction of society would occur as a result of the renewal of the Christian spirit, whose source and center is the liturgy.

Hillenbrand taught that, since the ultimate purpose of Catholic action is to Christianize society, the renewal of the liturgy must undoubtedly play the key role in achieving this goal.

Hillenbrand Books strives to reflect the spirit of Monsignor Reynold Hillenbrand's pioneering work by asking available innovative and scholarly resource that advance the liturgical and sacramental life of the Church.

STATISTICS OF
DIRECTIONAL DATA

Probability and Mathematical Statistics

A Series of Monographs and Textbooks

Editors

Z. W. Birnbaum
University of Washington
Seattle, Washington

E. Lukacs
Catholic University
Washington, D.C.

1. Thomas Ferguson. Mathematical Statistics: A Decision Theoretic Approach. 1967
2. Howard Tucker. A Graduate Course in Probability. 1967
3. K. R. Parthasarathy. Probability Measures on Metric Spaces. 1967
4. P. Révész. The Laws of Large Numbers. 1968
5. H. P. McKean, Jr. Stochastic Integrals. 1969
6. B. V. Gnedenko, Yu. K. Belyayev, and A. D. Solovyev. Mathematical Methods of Reliability Theory. 1969
7. Demetrios A. Kappos. Probability Algebras and Stochastic Spaces. 1969, 1970
8. Ivan N. Pesin. Classical and Modern Integration Theories. 1970
9. S. Vajda. Probabilistic Programming. 1972
10. Sheldon Ross. Introduction to Probability Models. 1972
11. Robert B. Ash. Real Analysis and Probability. 1972
12. V. V. Fedorov. Theory of Optimal Experiments. 1972
13. K. V. Mardia. Statistics of Directional Data. 1972

In Preparation

Tatsuo Kawata. Fourier Analysis and Probability Theory

Fritz Oberhettinger. Tables of Fourier Transforms and Their Inverses

H. Dym and H. P. McKean, Jr. Fourier Series and Integrals

STATISTICS OF
DIRECTIONAL DATA

K. V. MARDIA

Department of Mathematical Statistics
The University, Hull, England

1972

ACADEMIC PRESS London and New York

ACADEMIC PRESS INC. (LONDON) LTD.
24/28 Oval Road,
London NW1

United States Edition published by
ACADEMIC PRESS INC.
111 Fifth Avenue
New York, New York 10003

Library of Congress Catalog Card Number: 72–77853
ISBN: 0–12–471150–2

Printed in Great Britain by
ROYSTAN PRINTERS LIMITED
Spencer Court, 7 Chalcot Road
London NW1

To PAVAN

PREFACE

The aim of this book is to give a systematic account of statistical theory and methodology for observations which are directions. The directions are usually regarded as points on a circle in 2 dimensions or on a sphere in 3 dimensions. While unifying the work of many researchers, the presentation keeps the requirements of students of mathematical statistics and of scientific workers from various disciplines very much in the foreground. To this end, the book gives the underlying theory of each technique, and applications are illustrated by working through a number of real life examples. Some chapters are devoted exclusively to applications. This presentation is adopted because of the belief that students will appreciate the techniques fully only after grasping the motivation behind them, whereas scientific workers will need some knowledge of the underlying assumptions in order to apply the methods safely.

Chapters 1–7 deal with the statistics of circular data while Chapters 8 and 9 deal with the statistics of spherical data. Chapters 1 and 2 are primarily concerned with the diagrammatical representations of circular data and diagnostic tools, respectively. Chapter 1 contains examples of angular data from various scientific fields. Mathematical justifications of the results used in Chapter 2 are differed until Chapter 3. Chapters 3 and 4 are on probability theory on the circle; several probability models are discussed in Chapter 3 including the von Mises distribution which has the same statistical role on the circle as the normal distribution on the line (see Section 3.4.10). Chapter 4 includes certain sampling distributions for von Mises populations. Chapters 5–7 are on inference on the circle and they deal with estimation, hypothesis testing for samples from von Mises distributions and non-parametric methods respectively. Chapter 8 deals with diagrammatical representations, diagnostic tools, probability models and certain sampling distributions on the sphere. The Fisher distribution is of central importance on the sphere and Chapter 9 deals with inference problems associated with samples from this distribution. Appendix 1 provides a list of formulae for Bessel functions which are collected together to facilitate the manipulation of the von Mises distribution. Appendices 2 and 3 give tables for fitting, estimation and testing problems on the circle and on the sphere respectively. The bibliography is fairly exhaustive as far as theoretical papers are concerned and also serves as an author index. In addition to a subject index, an index of the principal notation is also given with an indication of their meaning.

The book assumes a basic knowledge of mathematical statistics at under-graduate level. Calculus and matrix algebra are used at a level similar to that required for undergraduate statistics courses. To understand only the statistical applications, elementary training in mathematics and statistics is sufficient.

The material of this book can be used as (i) a graduate text (ii) a research monograph (iii) a user's manual or (iv) an elementary methods text. We now suggest how to use this book for each of these four purposes and note some points which may prove helpful.

(i) *As a graduate text*

A course of two hours per week for two terms should cover Chapters 3–9 (excluding Sections 4.6, 8.2, 8.3, 8.6.3b), but if a shorter course is preferred so as to supplement an existing course, there are several possibilities available. For examples, a course on distribution theory may include Chapter 3 (Sections 3.1–3.3, Sections 3.4.2–3.4.5, 3.4.8d–e, 3.4.9, 3.5, 3.6), Chapter 4 and Chapter 8 (Sections 8.5–8.8), while a course on statistical inference may include Chapter 3 (Sections 3.3, 3.4.4, 3.4.9), Chapters 5–7, Chapter 8 (Sections 8.4, 8.5) and Chapter 9. The results from the excluded sections may be quoted where relevant. I have found in giving the latter course to M.Sc. students that a minimum of two hours per week for one term is required.

While treating the circular case, we have alluded to the corresponding methods on the line and it may be useful to elaborate these points. In a similar way, when dealing with the spherical case, the corresponding results for the circular case are referred to for details and illumination. No mathe-matical examples are spelled out formally but at various places we have left out detailed derivations and the filling in of these details using the hints provided, constitutes good example material. The von Mises and the Fisher distributions are particular cases of a distribution on a *p*-dimensional hypersphere (see Section 8.8). As a consequence, various results for the two distributions can be unified but this is not done here partly because it has no known application for higher dimensions. Nevertheless, this unification also provides material for good examples.

(ii) *As a research monograph*

Specialists will find a good coverage of existing results as well as various new results. A serious attempt is made to unify the results and many proofs have been simplified. Several new results are included, primarily to fill gaps in the subject. [In particular, the following results are new. Sections 2.5.1, 2.6.1–3, 2.7.2, 3.3.3–4, 3.4.9f (entropy), 3.4.9h, 3.5.2, 3.7; Eqns (4.2.6), (4.2.28); Section 4.3.3 (formulation), Eqns (4.5.7), (4.5.12); Sections 4.5.5, 4.6.2, 4.7.1; Eqns (4.7.11), (4.8.8); Sections 4.9.4, 5.1, 5.6, 6.2.2a, 6.2.2b(1), 6.3.1c, 6.3.2b–2c (cases I, II); optimum properties in Sections 6.2.2b(2), 6.2.3a, b; tests defined by (6.3.37), (6.3.38), (6.4.6), (6.4.11), (6.4.12); Eqns (7.4.15), (7.4.17), (8.5.21), (8.6.8), (8.6.17), (8.6.39), (9.3.7), (9.3.16); Section 9.4.2a (cases I, II), tests defined by (9.4.20), (9.4.21), (9.5.3), (9.5.8)–(9.5.10).]. Almost all theoretical contributions are reviewed.

(iii) *As a user's manual*

It is assumed that the reader has a familiarity with statistical terms on the line such as probability distributions (normal, χ^2 and F distributions in particular), confidence intervals and statistical tests to the extent that he will be able to formulate his problem in a statistical framework. For example, whether he needs a one-sample or a two-sample test, whether he is interested in comparing two means or two variances etc. etc. In addition to the usual mathematical knowledge required for elementary statistics, his familiarity with the trigonometric functions is assumed.

Analogues of almost every univariate method are available for the circular and the spherical cases. There are also techniques which arise only for the circular and the spherical cases such as testing for uniformity. The introductory remarks to Chapters 6–9 contain comments on such situations. All techniques given in the book are illustrated fully with the help of real data, drawn from many fields of application. Appropriate tables are provided in Appendices 2 and 3. Although these examples deal with data obtained from biology, geology, meteorology, medicine, crystallography, astronomy ect., workers in other fields should have no difficulty in translating them into terms which are more familiar to their own disciplines. Section 1.5 may be useful for this purpose since it summarizes applications from various fields.

The von Mises distribution is as important on the circle as the normal distribution is on the line (Section 3.4.9) while the Fisher distribution is important on the sphere (Section 8.5). Examples of fitting these distributions are provided (Sections 5.4, 9.2). There are various one-sample non-parametric tests and the comparisons given in Section 7.2.6 will be useful for deciding which one to use for any given problem. There exist various co-ordinate systems on the sphere and Section 8.2 relates some of them to the standard polar co-ordinates.

As yet there are no standard statistical packages available on computers for directional data techniques but programming them is not too difficult. For large data, as well as for techniques involving eigen values and vectors, such programming is desirable but for small samples, the use of a desk calculator is adequate. The amount of labour involved will be minimized by using the tabular methods illustrated in the examples.

(iv) *As an elementary methods text*

A course which assumes a basic knowledge of statistical methods on the line can be developed. Chapters 1 and 2, Section 3.4.9 (explaining the von Mises distribution with the help of the figures), the solved examples in Chapters 5–7, Sections 8.1, 8.4, the figures of Section 8.5 and the solved examples in Chapter 9 should provide good material. The course must give emphasis to geometrical pictures. Some prior knowledge of the trigonometric functions is needed. Various points mentioned under (iii) are also relevant.

The author will be most grateful to readers who draw his attention to any errors, or obscurities in the book or suggest any other improvements.

February, 1972   K. V. Mardia

ACKNOWLEDGEMENTS

I am deeply indebted to all those statisticians who developed techniques for analysing directional data and to all those scientific workers who drew attention to the need for such techniques; in particular, I should mention E. Batschelet, R. A. Fisher, E. J. Gumbel, E. Irving, M. A. Stephens, G. S. Watson and E. J. Williams.

I am also grateful to those authors and editors who generously granted me permission to reproduce certain charts, figures and tables which add greatly to the value of the book and, likewise, it is a pleasure to thank those authors who sent me copies of their unpublished work. Where such material appears in the book, credit is given to the original source.

My greatest debt is to Professor T. Lewis for his valuable help and encouragement throughout this project. Thanks are also due to my other colleagues Dr. M. S. Bingham, Dr. E. A. Evans and Dr. J. W. Thompson for their support, and to Professor E. Batschelet, Dr. C. Bingham and Dr. J. S. Rao for their help. I am also grateful to Professor E. S. Pearson for his helpful advice. Parts of the draft were read by Dr. M. S. Bingham and Mr. B. D. Spurr and their comments led to substantial improvements. Finally, my thanks go to Miss T. Blackmore and Miss L. Robinson for typing the difficult manuscript with great skill.

K. V. M.

CONTENTS

INTRODUCTION

1. The Background

The interest in developing techniques to analyse directional data is as old as the subject of mathematical statistics itself. Indeed, the theory of errors was developed by Gauss primarily to analyse certain directional measurements in astronomy. It is a historical accident that the observational errors involved were sufficiently small to allow Gauss to make a linear approximation and, as a result, he developed a linear rather than a directional theory of errors. In many applications, however, we meet directional data which cannot be treated in this manner, e.g. orientation data in biology, dip and declination data in geology, seasonal fluctuation data in medicine and wind direction data in meteorology. The temptation to employ conventional linear techniques can lead to paradoxes; for example, the arithmetic mean of the angles 1° and 359° is 180° whereas by geometrical intuition the mean ought to be 0°.

2. Directions

Directions may be visualized in a space of any number of dimensions but practical situations almost invariably give rise to directions in two or three dimensional space where they may be represented by points on the circumference of a circle or on the surface of a sphere respectively. In general, directions can be regarded as points on the surface of a hypersphere. Sometimes, the orientation of an undirected line is of interest, e.g. in determining a crystal axis, or in dealing with hinge lines. Such observations can be described as *axes* rather than directions. In representing axial data on the surface of a hypersphere, the undirected lines are extended to cut the hypersphere and no distinction is made between the two diametrically opposite points which correspond to any given undirected line. Alternatively, axial data can be represented as a set of points on the surface of a semi-hypersphere.

3. LINEAR VERSUS DIRECTIONAL STATISTICS

Since the circle is a closed curve but the line is not, we anticipate differences between the theories of statistics on the line and on the circle. For example, it is necessary to define distribution functions, characteristic functions and moments in a way that takes account of the natural periodicity of the circle. The compactness of the circle leads to a simpler treatment of the convergence in law of random variables. The different algebraic structures of the circle and the line, the circle having only one operation (viz., addition modulo 2π) and the line having two operations (viz., addition and multiplication), produce different forms of central limit theorems and stability. On the circle, there are difficulties in ordering observations and this necessitates the use of special tools in non-parametric methods. Similar remarks apply to the hyperspherical case when it is compared with the usual multivariate analysis for Euclidean spaces.

4. HISTORICAL NOTES

Early developments in the subject were mainly for uniformly distributed random vectors. As early as 1734, Daniel Bernoulli discussed a solution to the problem of whether the close coincidence of the orbital planes of the six planets then known could have arisen by chance. Each orbital plane can be identified by its normal which in turn corresponds to a point on the surface of a sphere. Bernoulli's assertion then amounts to the hypothesis that these points are uniformly distributed on the surface of the unit sphere. A natural test-statistic is the resultant length of the normal vectors to the orbital planes. Rayleigh (1880) was the first to study the distribution of the resultant length of such vectors (in two dimensions) for a problem in sound although statisticians were not generally aware of his solution until 1905 when he responded to a letter of K. Pearson in *Nature* which posed the problem of the isotropic random walk on a circle. Rayleigh's solution was approximate but an exact solution was produced promptly by Kluvyer (1905). K. Pearson (1906) provided another approximate solution. Rayleigh (1919) gave an exact solution to the problem of the uniform random walk on the sphere together with an approximation for large samples.

The underlying population distributions in the above work were of course uniform. Non-uniform distributions started appearing only after 1900. Interest in Brownian motion on the circle and the sphere led to wrapped normal distributions (cf. Perrin, 1928). Von Mises (1918) in investigating whether the atomic weights were integers subject to errors introduced a distribution on the circle by using a characterization analogous to the Gauss characterization of the normal distribution on the line. Langevin (1905) in the study of magnetism introduced a distribution on the sphere which was shown by Arnold (1941) to possess a Gauss-type characterization on the sphere. Meanwhile, the need for techniques of analysing directional data was strongly felt especially by the earth scientists (see Steinmetz, 1962 for references). However, real progress was made neither in statistical inference for this distribution on the sphere, nor in the subject of orientation analysis as a whole, until an epoch making paper of R. A. Fisher appeared in 1953. He was attracted to this field by a problem of Hosper (1955) in paleomagnetism. At the same time, E. J. Gumbel, D. Durand and J. A. Greenwood were producing results for the von Mises distribution and Fisher's method helped Greenwood and Durand (1955) to make progress towards a distribution theory for the circular case.

A remarkable paper by Watson and Williams (1956) not only unified the inference problems for the von Mises and the Fisher distributions but also brought a wealth of new results and ideas. Since then, thanks mostly to G. S. Watson and his co-workers, the growth and dissemenation of the subject have been rapid; Watson introducing analysis of variance type techniques, various parametric and non-parametric tests, M. A. Stephens making various other major contributions to the small sample theory and applications, and J. Beran unifying the treatment of non-parametric tests. E. Irving, who had attracted the attention of G. S. Watson in 1956 to the subject, illuminated various techniques on the sphere in his book of 1964 which was written especially for geologists. E. Batschelet unified and simplified methodology for the circular case in his 1965 monograph primarily for biologists. There are other notable contributions to this field in the last two decades including those of B. Ajne, T. W. Anderson, C. Bingham, E. Breitenberger, E. J. Burr, E. Dimroth, T. D. Downs, A. L. Gould, J. L. Hodges, Jr., N. L. Johnson, N. H. Kuiper, U. R. Maag, E. S. Pearson, C. R. Rao, J. S. Rao, S. Schach, B. Selby and G. J. G. Upton.

The theory of errors was developed by Gauss primarily in relation to the needs of astronomers and surveyors, making rather accurate angular measurements. Because of this accuracy it was appropriate to develop the theory in relation to an infinite linear continuum, or, as multivariate errors came into view, to a Euclidean space of the required dimensionality. The actual topological framework of such measurements, the surface of a sphere, is ignored in the theory as developed, with a certain gain in simplicity.

It is, therefore, of some little mathematical interest to consider how the theory would have had to be developed if the observations under discussion had in fact involved errors so large that the actual topology had had to be taken into account. The question is not, however, entirely academic, for there are in nature vectors with such large natural dispersions.

R. A. Fisher

1

ANGULAR DATA
AND FREQUENCY DISTRIBUTIONS

1.1 INTRODUCTION

Angular observations arise from random experiments in various different ways. They may be direct measurements such as wind directions or vanishing angles of migrating birds. They may arise indirectly from the measurement of times reduced modulo some period and converted into angles, e.g. the incidence rate of a particular disease in each calendar month over a number of years. Rounding errors in numerical calculations converted into angles also form such observations.

We may regard the angular observations as observations on a circle of unit radius. A single observation $\theta°$ $(0° < \theta° \leqslant 360°)$ measured in degrees is then a unit vector and the data can be described as circular data. Further, $\theta°$ represents the angle made by the vector with the positive x-axis in the anti-clockwise direction. The cartesian co-ordinates of the vector are $(\cos \theta°, \sin \theta°)$ while the polar co-ordinates are $(1, \theta°)$. If the vector is not directed, i.e. if the angles $\theta°$ $(0 < \theta° \leqslant 180°)$ and $180° + \theta°$ are not distinguished, the data can be described as axial data.

1.2. DIAGRAMMATICAL REPRESENTATION

1.2.1. Ungrouped Data

The angular observations can be represented in two ways. They can be represented by points on the circumference of a unit circle, the same mass

1

being assigned to each observation. Figure 1.1 illustrates this method for the following example.

Example 1.1. A roulette wheel was allowed to revolve and its stopping positions were measured in angles with a fixed direction. The measurements in 9 trials were 43°, 45°, 52°, 61°, 75°, 88°, 88°, 279°, 357°. Its representation in Fig. 1.1 shows that the wheel seems to have a *preferred* direction.

FIG. 1.1. Circular plot of the roulette data of Example 1.1.

Alternatively, we can represent the data by drawing the radii of a unit circle, obtained by joining the origin to the observed points on the circumference. Figure 1.2 shows this representation of Example 1.1. Its relation with the rose diagram (see Section 1.2.2) can be noted; the vectors are of unit length in our case. The first method is analogous to that which is commonly used for data on a line and is preferred.

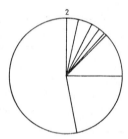

FIG. 1.2. Rose diagram of the roulette data of Example 1.1.

1.2.2. Grouped Data

Circular Histograms. Angular data can be grouped by adopting the same procedure as on the real line. The range (0°, 360°) can be divided into a certain number of class-intervals and the frequency corresponding to each class can be counted. Choice of class-limits and length of class-intervals require the same consideration as for linear data. However, in the circular case there can be an interval such as 330°–30° which contains simultaneously the angles 359° and 0°.

TABLE 1.1   Vanishing angles of 714 British mallards
(adapted from Matthews, 1961)

Direction	Number of birds	Direction	Number of birds
0°—	40	180°—	3
20°—	22	200°—	11
40°—	20	220°—	22
60°—	9	240°—	24
80°—	6	260°—	58
100°—	3	280°—	136
120°—	3	300°—	138
140°—	1	320°—	143
160°—	6	340°—	69
		Total	714

Table 1.1 shows the frequencies of the vanishing angles of 714 non-migratory British mallards with 0° as the north. The birds were displaced under sunny conditions from Slimbridge, Gloucestershire, by distances of between 30 km. and 250 km. in different directions over one year. We can represent this data on a histogram similar to that used on a line. We take a unit circle and, corresponding to each interval, construct a block on its circumference whose area is proportional to the frequency in that interval. Figure 1.3 gives a *circular histogram* of the data given in Table 1.1. The corresponding frequency polygon can be constructed by joining the mid-points of the summits of the blocks. The latter presentation on a circle is complicated and does not elicit additional information.

Linear Histograms. Another useful representation is to unroll the circular histogram so that it sits on a segment of width 360°. The point of cut used in unrolling the circle should be selected carefully. If the data has a mode (a preferred direction) then it is wiser to use a cut such that the centre of the *linear* histogram approximately corresponds to this mode. A cut near the mode would give an erroneous impression of the data. Further,

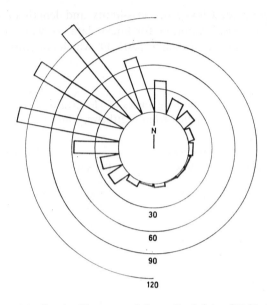

Fig. 1.3. Circular histogram of the mallard data of Table 1.1.

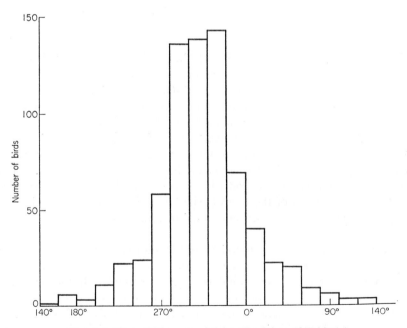

Fig. 1.4. Linear histogram of the mallard data of Table 1.1.

the ends of the axis exist only as a convenience and a linear histogram for circular data should be judged after imagining it to be wrapped around the circumference of a circle. To emphasize this fact, the first block can be repeated at the other end. Further, the linear histogram is preferred to the circular histogram partly because of our competence to interpret such histograms. Figure 1.4 shows a linear histogram of the data in Table 1.1.

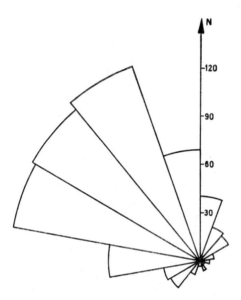

FIG. 1.5. Rose diagram of the mallard data of Table 1.1.

Rose Diagrams. Another natural representation is a rose diagram. Corresponding to each interval, we construct a sector with apex at the origin, radius proportional to the class frequency and arc substending the class interval. Figure 1.5 gives a rose diagram of the data in Table 1.1. The angles are measured in the clockwise direction with the north as 0°. If the observations take values in the interval (0°, 180°) then linear histograms can be drawn as usual. To draw a rose diagram for such data, we can construct that half of the diagram corresponding to the range 0° to 180° and obtain the other half by reflection through the origin. Figure 1.6 gives a rose diagram for the data in Table 1.6.

The area of each sector in the type of rose diagram described above varies as the square of the frequency. In order to make the areas proportional to the square roots of the frequencies instead of the frequencies themselves, the square roots of the frequencies should be taken as the radii. The resulting diagram can be described as an equi-areal rose diagram. The graphic comparisons between observed and expected frequencies in such presentations is hardly satisfactory, since a given arithmetic difference between the frequencies is represented by decreasing intervals on the polar radii as the frequency increases. Of course, linear histograms conserve areas and are comparatively simple to construct.

Rose diagrams and circular histograms are sometimes described as polar-wedge diagrams.

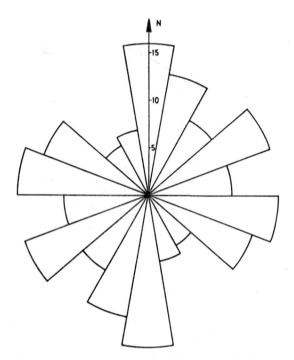

FIG. 1.6. Rose diagram of the pebbles data of Table 1.6.

1.3 INTERRELATIONS BETWEEN DIFFERENT UNITS OF ANGULAR MEASUREMENT

1.3.1. Radians

For theoretical purposes, it is preferred that the angle $\theta°$ in degrees is converted into the angle θ in radians. We, of course, have

$$\theta° = 180\,\theta/\pi, \qquad \theta = \pi\theta°/180. \qquad (1.3.1)$$

The range of θ is $0 < \theta \leqslant 2\pi$ corresponding to the range $0° < \theta° \leqslant 360°$ of

$\theta°$. If an arc of a circle with unit radius substends an angle of θ radians at the centre of the circle, then the length of the arc is θ.

TABLE 1.2   Orientations of sand-grains of Recent Gulf Coast beach
(Curray, 1956)

Class interval	Number of grains	Class interval	Number of grains
0°—	244	90°—	401
10°—	262	100°—	382
20°—	246	110°—	332
30°—	290	120°—	322
40°—	284	130°—	295
50°—	314	140°—	230
60°—	326	150°—	256
70°—	340	160°—	263
80°—	371	170°—	281
		Total	5439

The observations may be concentrated on $(0°, 90°)$ or $(0°, 180°)$. For example, axial data are concentrated on $(0°, 180°)$. Table 1.2 shows orientation of the least projection elongations of sand grains in thin sections, cut parallel to the laminations, of Recent Gulf Coast beach sand. This data with angles in $(0°, 180°)$ can be converted to the range of $(0°, 360°)$ by doubling each angle. Further, the range $0°$ to $360°/l$ of $\theta°$ can be converted to the range $(0, 2\pi)$ by

$$\theta = l\pi\theta°/180. \tag{1.3.2}$$

1.3.2. Time Period

Now, we consider conversion of the measurements of times reduced modulo some period into angles. The length of the time period can be identified with $360°$. The usual time period is either a day or a year. We first consider data where the period is a day. Table 1.3 shows the number of occasions on which thunder was heard during each two hourly interval of the day at Kew (England) during summer from 1910–1935. In this case, $15°$ corresponds to 1 hour and $1°$ corresponds to 4 minutes, so that the conversion is straightforward. The conversion of the data in Table 1.3 is shown in the second column of the table.

TABLE 1.3   The number of occasions on which thunder was heard at Kew in the summers of 1910–1935 (adapted from Bishop, 1947)

G.M.T.	Angle	Frequency	G.M.T.	Angle	Frequency
00–	0°–	26	12–	180°–	133
02–	30°–	24	14–	210°–	149
04–	60°–	14	16–	240°–	122
06–	90°–	15	18–	270°–	80
08–	120°–	14	20–	300°–	61
10–	150°–	65	22–	330°–	22
				Total	725

Next, we consider the case when the period is a year. Table 1.4 shows the number of occurrences of rainfall of 1″ or more per hour in the U.S.A. during 1908–1937, classified according to the twelve months. For a non-leap year, the tth day can be related to the angles by

$$\theta° = 360 \times t/365. \tag{1.3.3}$$

A similar conversion can be done for a leap year. However, when the data is classified into months, the class-intervals and the mid-points obtained by using (1.3.3) are not easy to handle. For example, the class-interval for the

TABLE 1.4   The number of occurrences of rainfall of 1″ or more per hour in the U.S.A., 1908–37 (Dyck and Mattice, 1941)

Month	Angle	Frequency (Unadjusted)	Frequency (Adjusted)
JAN.	0°–	101	101
FEB.	30°–	94	104
MARCH	60°–	232	231
APRIL	90°–	406	406
MAY	120°–	685	683
JUNE	150°–	1225	1225
JULY	180°–	1478	1475
AUG.	210°–	1384	1381
SEPT.	240°–	907	907
OCT.	270°–	383	382
NOV.	300°–	195	195
DEC.	330°–	145	145
Total		7235	7235

month of February is $30° 35'–58° 12'$. In addition, the lengths of the months vary. To overcome these difficulties, we can adjust the frequencies such that they correspond to 360 days with each month of the same length. Then $1°$ will correspond to 1 day. The adjustment is as follows. Let the observed frequencies for January, March, May, July, August, October and December be multiplied by

$$c = 30/31 = 0·96774$$

and let the frequency for February be multiplied by

$$d = 30/28 = 1·07143.$$

Let n_i be the original frequencies and let n_i' be the frequencies so adjusted. We then have reduced the year to 360 days but $N \neq N'$ where $N = \Sigma n_i$ and $N' = \Sigma n_i'$. To preserve the sum N, the final adjusted frequencies are obtained on multiplying n_i' by N/N'.

For the data in Table 1.4, we have

$$N = 7235, \qquad N' = 7101·5, \qquad N/N' = 1·03103.$$

These corrections are essential when the differences between the frequencies are of the order 10 per cent or less, since the differences between the lengths of the months can themselves produce such irregularities. In particular, the month of February has 10 per cent fewer days than January.

For the data in Table 1.4, the adjusted frequencies are shown in the fourth column and the corresponding class-intervals in terms of the angles are given in the second column. In the month of February, the adjusted frequency is 104 compared with the unadjusted frequency of 94. For January, the observed frequency remains 101 and so the month with minimum frequency becomes January instead of February.

The above cycles are the most frequent in practice but the same principle can be used to reduce any other periodic data into angles.

1.4 FORMS OF FREQUENCY DISTRIBUTIONS

The forms of the circular distributions appearing in practice can roughly be identified from the linear histograms just as in the case of linear data. As pointed out before, the linear histogram should be obtained from the circular histogram by cutting the circle at a suitable point such that the maximum concentration on the linear histogram appears around its centre. The data considered in this section will be visualized in this way.

1.4.1. Unimodal Distributions

Each of the frequency distributions given in Table 1.1 to Table 1.4 is unimodal. The frequencies tail off uniformly giving rise to a minimum in the corresponding circular histogram. This point of minimum is called the antimode in contrast to the mode which is, of course, the point of maximum. The frequency distribution in Table 1.1 and Table 1.2 are somewhat symmetrical. The distribution of the directions of birds in Table 1.1 has a high peak and the frequencies tail off uniformly to zero. The birds have a preferred direction between 280°–340°, i.e. there is a tendency to select a N–W course. The distributions in Table 1.3 and Table 1.4 are slightly asymmetrical and are positively skew since the rise to the maximum is more rapid than the fall. In Table 1.3 the main period of thunderstorm activity is 2 p.m. to 4 p.m.

TABLE 1.5   Azimuths of cross-beds in the upper Kamthi river
(Sengupta and Rao, 1966)

Azimuth	Frequency	Azimuth	Frequency
0°–	75	180°–	0
20°–	75	200°–	21
40°–	15	220°–	8
60°–	25	240°–	24
80°–	7	260°–	16
100°–	3	280°–	36
120°–	3	300°–	75
140°–	0	320°–	90
160°–	0	340°–	107
		Total	580

Table 1.5 gives an example of an asymmetrical distribution which is negatively skew. The data gives azimuths of cross-beds in the upper Kamthi river, India. As on the line, symmetrical distributions on the circle are comparatively rare.

TABLE 1.6   Horizontal directions of 100 outwash Wisconsin pebbles
(adapted from Krumbein, 1939)

Mid-points	0°	20°	40°	60°	80°	100°	120°	140°	160°	Total
Frequency	16	13	9	14	9	14	12	6	7	100

Table 1.6 gives horizontal directions of outwash pebbles from a late Wisconsin outwash terrace along Fox River, near Cary, Illinois. The directions are distributed almost uniformly over the range of (0°, 180°). (In fact, the observed value of χ^2 under this hypothesis is 8·72. The 5% value of χ^2

with 8 degrees of freedom is 15·5.) Table 1.7 shows the month of onset of lymphatic leukemia in the U.K. during 1946–1960. The distribution is unimodal but does not tail off to zero.

TABLE 1.7   Month of onset of lymphatic leukemia in the U.K., 1946–60
(Lee, 1963)

Month	Number of cases	Month	Number of cases
Jan.	40	July	51
Feb.	34	Aug.	55
March	30	Sept.	36
April	44	Oct.	48
May	39	Nov.	33
June	58	Dec.	38
		Total	506

In the strict sense, there are no J or U shaped distributions on a circle if the observations are distributed on the complete range of $(0, 2\pi)$. However, a J-shaped or U-shaped linear histogram will arise from a unimodal circular distribution if the cut point is selected near to the mode.

1.4.2. Multi-modal Distributions

So far we have discussed unimodal distributions. Multi-modal distributions also occur in practice. Table 1.8 and Table 1.9 give typical examples. Table 1.8 shows orientations of 76 turtles after treatment. It can be observed that

TABLE 1.8   Orientations of 76 turtles after treatment
(Gould's data cited by Stephens, 1969f)

Direction	Number of turtles	Direction	Number of turtles
0°—	8	180°—	1
30°—	18	210°—	5
60°—	18	240°—	6
90°—	12	270°—	1
120°—	1	300°—	1
150°—	3	330°—	2
		Total	76

the distribution is bimodal and the two modes are roughly 180° apart. The dominant mode is in the interval 60°–90° and the subsidiary mode is in the interval 240°–270°. The data indicates that the turtles have a preferred direction (the homeward direction) but a substantial minority seem to prefer

TABLE 1.9   Geostrophic wind directions at Crawley for the 25 months, November–March, 1957–61 (Findlater *et al.* 1966)

Direction	Frequency	Direction	Frequency
0°–	27	180°–	27
20°–	23	200°–	43
40°–	44	220°–	69
60°–	42	240°–	69
80°–	25	260°–	53
100°–	20	280°–	38
120°–	20	300°–	37
140°–	11	320°–	39
160°–	19	340°–	40
		Total	646

the direction exactly opposite this homeward direction. Table 1.9 shows wind directions at Crawley, England. The data is bimodal and the two modes are again 180° apart, implying two opposite regimes of wind direction.

1.5 FURTHER EXAMPLES OF ANGULAR DATA

Some actual examples giving rise to angular data are described in Sections 1.2–1.4. We now give further examples involving angular data. Although these experiments belong to different scientific disciplines and therefore seem to be quite different, they all give rise to angular data and are abstractly equivalent from the statistical point of view.

1.5.1. Geology

Angular data appear in investigations of various geological processes since these involve transporting matter from one place to another in time. (The term fabrics, or vectorial fabrics, is sometimes used by geologists to describe geological orientation data.) Studies of the directions of remnant magnetism are used to interpret paleomagnetic current and possible magnetic pole wandering during geological times. Studies of the orientations of fractures and fabric elements in deformed rocks are used to interpret tectonic forces. Orientations of cross-bedding and other structures, and particle long axes in undeformed sediments, are used to interpret the directions of depositing currents of wind or water. For further details, see Curray (1956) and Pincus (1953, p. 584). Tables 1.2, 1.5 and 1.6 give some examples in the above category.

Data for the above situations are likely to consist of measurements of planar and linear features at given geographical points. Planar features may include foliation planes, bedding planes, planes of cross-stratification, cleavage planes, fold axial planes, joints and faults while linear features may include fold and other tectonic axes, cleavage-bedding intersections, mineral, fossile or pebble elongations, and other sedimentary and tectonic lineations (Loudon, 1964). Watson (1970) has given an excellent account of geological terms and concepts.

The above measurements can be expressed in terms of azimuth and angle of dip so that circular distributions appear only as marginal distributions. The joint distribution will be discussed in Chapters 8 and 9 which also contain various examples.

1.5.2. Meteorology

A natural source of angular data is, of course, wind directions and we have already considered such data in Table 1.9. A distribution of wind directions may arise either as a marginal distribution of the wind speed and direction as in Table 1.9, or as a conditional distribution for a given speed as in Table 1.10. Wind directions are usually represented clockwise on the map from north (0°) to east (90°), south (180°), west (270°) and back to north (360°). The bearings N32°E and S29°E are therefore 32° and 151° respectively. This representation is used in Table 1.9 and Table 1.10.

TABLE 1.10 Wind directions at Larkhill with speeds between 27 and 41 knots, March–May, 1940–45 (Tucker, 1960)

Direction	N	NE	E	SE	S	SW	W	NW	Total
Mid-points	0°	45°	90°	135°	180°	225°	270°	315°	—
Frequency	20	5	7	4	16	32	43	26	153

The thunderstorms data of Table 1.3 and the rainfall data of Table 1.4 are examples where the circular distribution also appear naturally. Similar data appears for the monthly run-off for a watershed, for the monthly evaporation from a reservoir and in other hydrologic cycles.

1.5.3. Biology

The study of bird orientation in homing or migration leads to angular data. The birds are released from a point and the bearings of their flights, called vanishing angles, are recorded just as they vanish in the distance. Table 1.1 gives an example. There are various important experiments on birds to answer questions such as whether the sun-azimuth-compass hypothesis is obeyed, whether celestial cues are utilized for orientation, whether the flight directions are random under certain conditions etc. For an excellent discussion of various developments and investigations in this field, the reader is referred to Schmidt-Koenig (1965). Chapters 6 and 7 contain various examples from this area.

There are similar investigations on orientation of surface animals. The turtle data in Table 1.8 is such an example.

TABLE 1.11   Angles between the swimming directions of *Daphnia* and the plane of polarization of light (Waterman and Jander's data, cited in Waterman, 1963)

Direction	Frequency	Direction	Frequency
0°—	65	90°—	208
10°—	17	100°—	81
20°—	12	110°—	73
30°—	16	120°—	43
40°—	22	130°—	50
50°—	51	140°—	35
60°—	58	150°—	24
70°—	67	160°—	29
80°—	105	170°—	44
		Total	1000

The study of the effects of polarized light on the orientation of marine animals also gives rise to angular data. Table 1.11 gives data consisting of angles between the swimming directions of *Daphnia* and the plane of polarization, the degree of polarization being 27°. The distribution is bimodal and the modes are roughly 90° apart. This typical characteristic of bimodal data has already been noted in Section 1.4. For another type of investigation under polarized light, giving rise to angular data, see Jaffe (1956).

1.5.4. Geography

Orientation data appear naturally when readings consist of longitudes and latitudes. For example, in the study of the occurrence of earthquakes in a region, the longitude and latitude of each shock (its epicentre) are recorded.

On the other hand, the data may be cyclic as in studying the variation of the number of earthquakes from year to year or from day to day after a large main shock. Angular observations also arise in daily determinations of micro-seismic directions at a particular location (Jensen, 1959).

1.5.5. Economic Time-series

If an economic time-series is a random perturbation of a periodic phenomenon with known period, the random times associated with it could be described by circular distributions. Table 1.12 gives a series of the production of buses in the U.S.A. which forms a genuine circular distribution consisting of discrete, countable units. Although only few series of prices, production or trade may sensibly be viewed in this way, further examples have been given by Gumbel (1954).

TABLE 1.12   The production of buses in the U.S.A. in 1948–50 (from *Automobile Facts and Figures*, 1951, AMA, New York)

Month	Frequency	Month	Frequency
Jan.	1120	July	1435
Feb.	985	Aug.	1589
March	1223	Sept.	1453
April	1200	Oct.	1523
May	1197	Nov.	1251
June	1527	Dec.	1192
		Total	15695

1.5.6. Physics

Von Mises (1918) proposed to test the hypothesis that atomic weights are integers subject to error. All weights can be reduced to angular deviations such as 8·25 to 90°, 8·75 to 270°, 9·00 to 0°, 9·25 to 90° and so on. The physical problem is not clear but statistically it reduces to testing whether the circular distribution has a mode at 0° (see Example 6.1).

Angular data also appears in determining a preferred direction for optical axes of crystals in rock specimens. The distribution of the resultant of a random sample of unit vectors arises in representing sound waves or molecular links (Rayleigh, 1919). It also arises in various problems related to the interference among oscillations with random phases (Beckmann, 1959). Studies of rotary Brownian motion also involve problems in this area.

Angular data also arises in experiments with a bubble chamber, where points representing events are observed through a circular window. If each point is moved radially to the circumference of the circle, we have angular observations.

1.5.7. Psychology

The perception of direction under varying experimental conditions leads to angular data (Ross *et al.*, 1969). For example, to simulate zero-gravity in space travel, experiments on divers and swimmers are performed under water to assess their ability in perceiving the true horizontal and vertical in the absence of a visual cue. The data consists of their deviations from the true direction. Studies to compare relative performances in perceiving the true vertical under water and on land also give rise to angular data.

1.5.8. Medicine

The number of deaths due to a disease or the number of onsets of a disease in each month over years forms a circular distribution. The data in Table 1.7 is such an example.

Monthly death rates can be regarded as constituting a circular distribution under the assumption that the underlying population is stationary so that the rates are proportional to the numbers of deaths. Under a similar assumption, mean percentages of deaths due to a particular disease constitutes a circular distribution. Gumbel (1954) has given various examples.

Cardiology is a field in which angular variates are prominent especially in the vector cardiogram which is the three-dimensional analogue of the usual one-dimensional cardiogram (see Downs and Liebman, 1969; Gould, 1969). Gould (1969) has given an excellent discussion of the problems involved and Downs and Liebman (1969) contains various references dealing with vector cardiographic data.

1.5.9. Astronomy

The theory of errors as developed by Gauss was primarily for the analysis of astronomical measurements which consisted of points on the celestial sphere. The surface of the celestial sphere can be approximated locally by a tangent plane with the probability concentrated in the neighbourhood of the point of contact. Hence, the actual manifold, the surface of the sphere, was ignored in the theory and this lead to the development of the theory of Statistics on Euclidean spaces.

Bernoulli (1734) enquired whether the close coincidence of the orbital planes of the six planets known at that time could have arisen by chance.

Each orbital plane can be regarded as a point on the sphere (see Example 9.4) and his hypothesis is equivalent to the statement that the points are distributed uniformly on the sphere. Watson (1970) has discussed this problem for the nine planets. Pólya (1919) enquired whether the stars are distributed at random over the celestial sphere.

1.5.10. Sampling

A roulette wheel usually has 37 equally spaced positions on the circumference of a circle. In an unbiased wheel, each position is equally likely. In general, we can consider a wheel with scale graduated from 0 to 2π. The stopping position of the wheel gives rise to a random point on the circle.

Consider a circular disc on which beads are dropped, while the tray is agitated in its plane. The chance of a bead coming off depends on the angle made by the disc with the horizontal plane.

The generation of random numbers with a given base leads to a circular distribution in view of the periodicity of the remainders. We will see in Section 4.3.4 that the behaviour of the distribution of the first digit selected at random from a large compendium such as a census register can be explained by regarding it as a distribution on a circle.

2

DESCRIPTIVE MEASURES

2.1. INTRODUCTION

We have seen in Section 1.4 that the most common circular frequency distributions are (i) uniform (ii) unimodal (symmetrical, skew or peaked) and (iii) bimodal (especially with the modes at 180° apart). We may include the multi-modal distributions to complete this list.

As in the linear case, our main emphasis will be on unimodal distributions. To describe unimodal circular distributions we shall need some measures like the mean, variance etc. These will also be useful in making comparisons between unimodal distributions.

2.1.1. Linear Measures

It is tempting to use the conventional measures on the line for a circular distribution. A drawback of such measures can be seen by considering an extreme example. Let us assume that the observed angles in a sample of size 2 are 1° and 359°. The arithmetic mean and the sample variance give absurd results. Although intuitively we will infer that the mean direction is in some sense 0° and the deviation about the mean is roughly 1°. We will get a sensible answer by selecting the zero direction as the y-axis in place of the x-axis, since the data then reduces to 269° and 271°. Hence, the usual linear measures depend heavily on the choice of the zero direction and are therefore inappropriate for circular distributions.

2.1.2. Notations

We shall assume that $\theta_1, ..., \theta_n$ is a random sample of size n from a circular population with distribution function $F(\theta)$. (For the definition of $F(\theta)$, see Section 3.1.) The angles $\theta_1, ..., \theta_n$ are measured from the x-axis OX in the anti-clockwise direction. We may also imagine the angle θ_i as representing the unit vector $\overline{OP_i}$ making angle θ_i with the x-axis in the positive direction where P_i is the point θ_i on the unit circle, $i = 1, ..., n$ (see Fig. 2.1). If the data is grouped, we shall assume that there are k class-intervals of lengths h. Then θ_i will denote the mid-point of the ith class-interval, f_i the observed frequency in the ith interval and n the sum of the frequencies. In our terminology, we regard descriptive measures as statistics. This approach helps not only to study their population counter-parts but also to remind us that we are dealing with sampling variations.

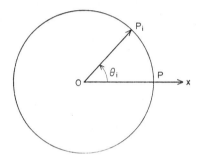

FIG. 2.1. Representations of the ith sample point θ_i . $OP = 1$.

2.2. A MEASURE OF LOCATION

2.2.1. A Property of Measures of Location

Let $x_1, ..., x_n$ be n observations on the line and let $x_1', ..., x_n'$ represent the same observations when the distances are measured from O' instead of O along the x-axis, put $OO' = a$. If L is a sensible measure of location on the line then we should have

$$L(x_1', ..., x_n') = L(x_1, ..., x_n) - a. \qquad (2.2.1)$$

This property implies that the position of the point whose x co-ordinate is $L(x_1, ..., x_n)$ remains invariant under the choice of origin. Similarly, it is desirable that the position of the direction corresponding to the direction represented by a measure of circular location should not depend upon the choice of the zero direction. Let $\theta_1', ..., \theta_n'$ be the angles obtained from

$\theta_1, \ldots, \theta_n$ with respect to a new zero direction OA. Suppose that $\angle XOA = \alpha$. Then we should have

$$L(\theta_1{}', \ldots, \theta_n{}') = \{L(\theta_1, \ldots, \theta_n) - \alpha\} \bmod 2\pi. \tag{2.2.2}$$

The contrast between (2.2.1) and (2.2.2) clearly indicates the different natures of the problems on the line and on the circle.

2.2.2. The Mean Direction

Let P_i be the point on the circumference of the unit circle corresponding to the angle θ_i, $i = 1, \ldots, n$. Then the mean direction $\bar{x}_0$ of $\theta_1, \ldots, \theta_n$ is defined to be the direction of the resultant of the unit vectors $\overline{OP}_1, \ldots, \overline{OP}_n$. The cartesian co-ordinates of P_i are $(\cos \theta_i, \sin \theta_i)$, $i = 1, \ldots, n$ so that the centre of gravity of these points is $(\bar{C}, \bar{S})$ where

$$\bar{C} = \frac{1}{n} \sum_{i=1}^{n} \cos \theta_i, \qquad \bar{S} = \frac{1}{n} \sum_{i=1}^{n} \sin \theta_i. \tag{2.2.3}$$

Therefore, if

$$\bar{R} = (\bar{C}^2 + \bar{S}^2)^{\frac{1}{2}} \tag{2.2.4}$$

then $R = n\bar{R}$ is the length of the resultant and $\bar{x}_0$ is the solution of the equations

$$\bar{C} = \bar{R} \cos \bar{x}_0, \qquad \bar{S} = \bar{R} \sin \bar{x}_0. \tag{2.2.5}$$

We now show that $\bar{x}_0$ has some desirable properties as a measure of location. Let $\theta_1{}', \ldots, \theta_n{}'$ be the angles obtained from $\theta_1, \ldots, \theta_n$ when the new zero direction is α. Let

$$\bar{C}' = \frac{1}{n} \sum_{i=1}^{n} \cos \theta_i{}', \qquad \bar{S}' = \frac{1}{n} \sum_{i=1}^{n} \sin \theta_i{}'.$$

We have

$$\theta_i{}' = (\theta_i - \alpha) \bmod 2\pi \tag{2.2.6}$$

so that

$$\bar{C}' = \bar{R} \cos (\bar{x}_0 - \alpha), \qquad \bar{S}' = \bar{R} \sin (\bar{x}_0 - \alpha). \tag{2.2.7}$$

Let us write

$$\bar{C}' = \bar{R}' \cos \bar{x}_0{}', \qquad \bar{S}' = \bar{R}' \sin \bar{x}_0{}' \tag{2.2.8}$$

then from (2.2.7) we have

$$\bar{x}_0{}' = (\bar{x}_0 - \alpha) \bmod 2\pi, \qquad \bar{R}' = \bar{R}. \tag{2.2.9}$$

Hence Eqn (2.2.2) is satisfied.

Further, from (2.2.4) and (2.2.5), we have

$$\sum_{i=1}^{n} \sin (\theta_i - \bar{x}_0) = 0. \qquad (2.2.10)$$

This corresponds to the equation in the linear case

$$\sum_{i=1}^{n} (x_i - \bar{x}) = 0,$$

i.e. the sum of deviations about the mean equals zero. We will show in the next section that the mean direction minimizes a suitable measure of dispersion.

2.3. THE CIRCULAR VARIANCE

2.3.1. Definition

Let P_i be the point corresponding to θ_i on the unit circle and let α be a fixed direction. Let us assume initially that $\alpha = 0$ and suppose that P is the corresponding point on the circle. A measure of the circular dispersion between P and P_i is the smaller of the two angles that OP_i makes with OP, say ξ_i. (See Fig. 2.1.)

We have

$$\xi_i = \min (\theta_i, 2\pi - \theta_i) = \pi - |\pi - \theta_i|. \qquad (2.3.1)$$

Since $1 - \cos \xi_i$ is a monotonically increasing function of ξ_i, we may take

$$D = \frac{1}{n} \sum_{i=1}^{n} (1 - \cos \xi_i) \qquad (2.3.2)$$

as a measure of dispersion of the points P_i. Using (2.3.1) in (2.3.2), we have, after shifting the zero direction to α with the help of (2.2.6),

$$D = \frac{1}{n} \sum_{i=1}^{n} \{1 - \cos (\theta_i - \alpha)\}. \qquad (2.3.3)$$

2.3.2. A Minimization Property

We now show that the dispersion D is minimized at $\alpha = \bar{x}_0$. On equating the derivative of (2.3.3) with respect to α to zero, we have

$$\Sigma \sin (\theta_i - \alpha) = 0.$$

This expression is equivalent to (2.2.6) so that the dispersion is smallest about $\bar{x}_0$. This minimization property is similar to that of the ordinary sample variance. Let us write the value of D about $\bar{x}_0$ by S_0 so that

$$S_0 = 1 - \frac{1}{n} \sum_{i=1}^{n} \cos(\theta_i - \bar{x}_0). \qquad (2.3.4)$$

Using (2.2.5), we have

$$S_0 = 1 - \bar{R}. \qquad (2.3.5)$$

We will call S_0 the *circular variance* and $\bar{R}$ the mean resultant length. For inference problems, $\bar{R}$ is of interest rather than S_0.

From (2.2.9), it can be seen that S_0 is invariant under a change of the zero direction.

Let R be the length of the resultant of the vectors $\overline{OP_i}$, i.e.

$$R = n\bar{R} \qquad (2.3.6)$$

then

$$S_0 = 1 - R/n. \qquad (2.3.7)$$

We see immediately that

$$0 \leqslant S_0 \leqslant 1. \qquad (2.3.8)$$

If the n observed directions are tightly clustered about the mean direction $\bar{x}_0$ then the length R will be almost as large as n so that S_0 will be nearly zero. On the other hand, if the directions are widely dispersed then R will be small, so that S_0 will be nearly 1.

Example 2.1. To calculate $\bar{x}_0$ and S_0 for the data in Example 1.1. (The observations are also given in the first column of Table 2.1.)

TABLE 2.1   Calculations of $\bar{x}_0$ and S_0 for the data in Example 1.1.

θ_i	$\cos\theta_i$	$\sin\theta_i$
43°	0·7314	0·6820
45°	0·7071	0·7071
52°	0·6157	0·7880
61°	0·4848	0·8746
75°	0·2588	0·9659
88°	0·0349	0·9994
88°	0·0349	0·9994
279°	0·1564	−0·9877
357°	0·9986	−0·0523
Totals	4·0226	4·9764

Using Table 2.1, we have

$$n = 9, \qquad \bar{C} = 4 \cdot 0226/9 = 0 \cdot 4470, \qquad \bar{S} = 4 \cdot 9764/9 = 0 \cdot 5529.$$

Hence

$$\bar{R} = (\bar{C}^2 + \bar{S}^2)^{\frac{1}{2}} = 0 \cdot 7110,$$

$$\cos \bar{x}_0 = \bar{C}/\bar{R} = 0 \cdot 6287, \qquad \sin \bar{x}_0 = \bar{S}/\bar{R} = 0 \cdot 7776.$$

Consequently,

$$\bar{x}_0 = 51 \cdot 0°, \qquad S_0 = 0 \cdot 2889.$$

Figure 2.2 shows $\bar{x}_0$ and $\bar{R}$ for this data.

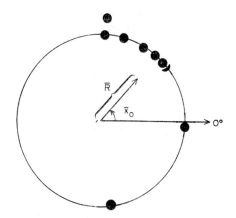

FIG. 2.2. The mean direction $\bar{x}_0$ and the mean resultant length $\bar{R}$ for the data in Example 2.1.

2.3.3. The Analysis of Variance Property

We now give an important property of S_0. Let μ_0 be the true mean direction. Then, from (2.3.3), the dispersion about μ_0 is

$$D_0 = 1 - \frac{1}{n} \sum_{i=1}^{n} \cos(\theta_i - \mu_0), \qquad (2.3.9)$$

or, equivalently,

$$D_0 = 1 - C'/n, \qquad (2.3.10)$$

where C' is the length of the resultant with μ_0 as the zero direction. We have $0 \leqslant D_0 \leqslant 2$ although $0 \leqslant S_0 \leqslant 1$.

In the usual notation, we have for the linear case

$$\frac{1}{n} \sum_{i=1}^{n} (x_i - \mu)^2 = \frac{1}{n} \sum_{i=1}^{n} (x_i - \bar{x})^2 + (\bar{x} - \mu)^2 \qquad (2.3.11)$$

so that the total variation about the true mean is decomposed into two important components. Now,

$$n - C' = (n - R) + (R - C') \tag{2.3.11}'$$

so that from (2.3.4) and (2.3.9), we have

$$D_0 = S_0 + 2(R/n) \sin^2 \tfrac{1}{2} (\bar{x}_0 - \mu_0). \tag{2.3.12}'$$

There is an anology between (2.3.11) and (2.3.12)' as follows. Equation (2.3.12)' indicates that the total variation about the mean direction is decomposed into two parts. The first part represents the deviation of the sample about the sample mean direction and the second part measures the deviation of the sample mean from the true mean direction. We shall see that the equivalent relation (2.3.11)' plays an important role in the analysis of circular variance.

2.3.4. Transformation to the Standard Deviation

From (2.3.8), S_0 takes values in $(0, 1)$ unlike S^2 on the line whose range is $(0, \infty)$. We shall show later (Section 3.7.1) that an appropriate transformation of S_0 to the range $(0, \infty)$ is given by

$$s_0 = \{-2 \log_e (1 - S_0)\}^{\frac{1}{2}}. \tag{2.3.12}$$

The measure s_0 is somewhat analogous to the ordinary sample standard deviation on the line. Nevertheless, S_0 and R are more useful than s_0 for theoretical investigations.

For small S_0, (2.3.12) reduces to

$$s_0 = (2S_0)^{\frac{1}{2}}. \tag{2.3.13}$$

In (2.3.12), we have assumed that the range of θ is $(0, 2\pi)$. If the range of θ is $(0, 2\pi/l)$ then (see Section 3.7.1) we define

$$s_0 = \{-2 \log_e (1 - S_0)\}^{\frac{1}{2}}/l. \tag{2.3.14}$$

2.3.5. Change of the Zero Direction

We have already obtained some basic results on changing the zero direction in Section 2.2.2. We now indicate some applications. Let $\bar{x}_0'$ and S_0' be the values of the mean direction and circular variance after a shift of α. From (2.2.9), we have

$$\bar{x}_0 = (\bar{x}_0' + \alpha) \bmod 2\pi, \qquad S_0 = S_0' \tag{2.3.15}$$

so that, given the values of $\bar{x}_0'$ and S_0', $\bar{x}_0$ and S_0 can be obtained.
    Further, the result

$$\bar{C}' = \bar{R} \cos (\bar{x}_0 - \alpha), \qquad \bar{S}' = \bar{R} \sin (\bar{x}_0 - \alpha) \tag{2.3.16}$$

can be used when the components are required relative to a fixed direction α. For example, if α is the homeward direction then $\bar{C}'$ will be the component in the homeward direction and, from (2.3.3), $1 - \bar{C}'$ will measure the deviation in this direction.

2.4. CALCULATION OF THE MEAN DIRECTION AND THE CIRCULAR VARIANCE

With the help of four typical examples on grouped data, we illustrate how $\bar{x}_0$ and S_0 can be obtained for different situations. The first three examples are on unimodal data covering the cases (i) when the range of the angles is $(0, 360°)$, (ii) when the range is $(0, 180°)$ and (iii) when the period is time. The fourth example is on bimodal data with the modes $180°$ apart.

We have

$$\bar{C} = \frac{1}{n} \Sigma f_i \cos \theta_i, \qquad \bar{S} = \frac{1}{n} \Sigma f_i \sin \theta_i, \qquad \bar{R} = (\bar{C}^2 + \bar{S}^2)^{\frac{1}{2}}. \qquad (2.4.1)$$

TABLE 2.2   Calculation of $\bar{x}_0$ and S_0 for the mallard data in Table 1.1.

θ_i (Mid-point)	f_i	$\cos \theta_i$	$f_i \cos \theta_i$	$\sin \theta_i$	$f_i \sin \theta_i$
10°	40	0·9848	39·3920	0·1736	6·9440
30	22	0·8660	19·0520	0·5000	11·0000
50	20	0·6428	12·8560	0·7660	15·3200
70	9	0·3420	3·0780	0·9397	8·4573
90	6	0·0000	0·0000	1·0000	6·0000
110	3	−0·3420	−1·0260	0·9397	2·8191
130	3	−0·6428	−1·9284	0·7660	2·2980
150	1	−0·8660	−0·8660	0·5000	0·5000
170	6	−0·9848	−5·9088	0·1736	1·0416
190	3	−0·9848	−2·9544	−0·1736	−0·5208
210	11	−0·8660	−9·5260	−0·5000	−5·5000
230	22	−0·6428	−14·1416	−0·7660	−16·8520
250	24	−0·3420	−8·2080	−0·9397	−22·5528
270	58	0·0000	0·0000	−1·0000	−58·0000
290	136	0·3420	46·5120	−0·9397	−127·7992
310	138	0·6428	88·7064	−0·7660	−105·7080
330	143	0·8660	123·8380	−0·5000	−71·5000
350	69	0·9848	67·9512	−0·1736	−11·9784
Totals	714		356·8264		−366·0312

Then

$$\cos \bar{x}_0 = \bar{C}/\bar{R}, \qquad \sin \bar{x}_0 = \bar{S}/\bar{R}, \qquad S_0 = 1 - \bar{R}. \qquad (2.4.2)$$

To obtain $\bar{x}_0$, it is convenient to use

$$\bar{x}_0 = \begin{cases} \bar{x}_0' & \text{if} \quad \bar{S} > 0, \quad \bar{C} > 0, \\ \bar{x}_0' + \pi & \text{if} \quad \bar{C} < 0, \\ \bar{x}_0' + 2\pi & \text{if} \quad \bar{S} < 0, \quad \bar{C} > 0 \end{cases}$$

where

$$\bar{x}_0' = \arctan (\bar{S}/\bar{C}), \qquad -\frac{\pi}{2} < \bar{x}_0' < \frac{\pi}{2}. \qquad (2.4.3)$$

Example 2.2. To calculate $\bar{x}_0$ and S_0 for the mallard data in Table 1.1. Using Table 2.2, we have

$$\bar{C} = 356 \cdot 8264/714 = 0 \cdot 4998, \qquad \bar{S} = -366 \cdot 0312/714 = -0 \cdot 5126$$

Consequently,

$$\bar{R} = 0 \cdot 7159, \qquad \cos \bar{x}_0 = 0 \cdot 6981, \qquad \sin \bar{x}_0 = -0 \cdot 7160$$

so that

$$\bar{x}_0 = 314 \cdot 3°, \qquad S_0 = 0 \cdot 2841.$$

Further, from (2.3.12),

$$s_0 = 0 \cdot 8176 \text{ radians, i.e. } s_0 = 46 \cdot 8°.$$

Example 2.3. To calculate the circular mean and variance for the distribution in Table 1.2.

Since the range of the angles is $(0°, 180°)$, we first *double* the angles. Let $\theta_i' = 2\theta_i$ be the new mid-point of the ith interval. We then carry out similar calculations to those in Example 1.1 using the frequencies f_i corresponding to the mid-points θ_i'. Let $\bar{C}', \bar{S}', \bar{x}_0'$, etc. be the quantities for θ_i' corresponding to $\bar{C}, \bar{S}, \bar{x}_0$, etc. An appropriate measure of the circular mean $\tilde{x}_0$ for the θ_i can intuitively be taken as

$$\tilde{x}_0 = \bar{x}_0'/2.$$

A theoretical justification of this result will be given in Section 3.5.2. Further, it will be shown that an appropriate measure of the circular variance $\tilde{S}_0$ for θ_i is

$$\tilde{S}_0 = 1 - (1 - S_0')^{\frac{1}{4}}.$$

We have

$$\bar{C}' = -0 \cdot 10055, \quad \bar{S}' = 0 \cdot 01772, \quad \bar{R}' = 0 \cdot 1021, \quad \bar{x}_0' = 170°, \quad \bar{S}_0' = 0 \cdot 8969.$$

Hence

$$\tilde{x}_0 = 85°, \qquad \tilde{S}_0 = 0\cdot4333.$$

Further, using (2.3.14) with $l = 2$, we have

$$s_0 = 1\cdot0681 \text{ radians, i.e. } s_0 = 61°.$$

Example 2.4. To calculate $\bar{x}_0$ and S_0 for the rainfall data in Table 1.4.

We take our class-intervals as the angles given in the second column of Table 1.4 and take the f_i as the adjusted frequencies given in the fourth column. On proceeding as in Example 2.3, we find that

$$\bar{C} = -0\cdot5247, \qquad \bar{S} = -0\cdot1746, \qquad \bar{R} = 0\cdot553.$$

Hence

$$\bar{x}_0 = 198\cdot4°, \qquad S_0 = 0\cdot447, \qquad s_0 = 1\cdot166.$$

It is important to express these in terms of days, i.e. using (1.3.4)

$$\bar{x}_0 = 198\cdot4 \times 365/360 = 201\text{st day.}$$

Hence $\bar{x}_0$ is 20 July. Similarly, s_0 is 67·7 days.

If the time period is a day as in the distribution of thunderstorms in Table 1.3, the procedure for conversion is much simpler. The quantities $\bar{x}_0$ and s_0 can be converted into hours and minutes by using the fact that 1° corresponds to 4 minutes.

Example 2.5. To calculate the circular mean and variance for the turtle data in Table 1.8.

TABLE 2.3   Calculations of $\bar{x}_0$ and S_0 for the turtle data in Table 1.8

Direction	Frequency	Frequency at 180° to (1)	New frequency (2) + (3)	New mid-points θ_i	Double angles θ_i'
(1)	(2)	(3)	(4)		
0°—	8	1	9	15°	30°
30°—	18	5	23	45°	90°
60°—	18	6	24	75°	150°
90°—	12	1	13	105°	210°
120°—	1	1	2	135°	270°
150°—	3	2	5	165°	330°
			Total 76		

The information that the two modes are 180° apart can be utilized by combining the observations on θ and on $\theta + 180°$. The range of the angles then reduces to $(0°, 180°)$ and we can therefore calculate $\tilde{x}_0$ and $\tilde{S}_0$ as in Example 2.3. We regard the data as arising from two unimodal components with the same variance but with the modes 180° apart. These now represent the appropriate mean and variance of one of the components. A theoretical justification may be found in Section 3.6.

Table 2.3 illustrates the conversion to the range $(0°, 180°)$ for this example. Column 4 shows the new frequencies f_i obtained by adding the pairs of frequencies corresponding to class-intervals 180° apart. The new mid-points θ_i are shown in Column 5. Working on f_i and θ_i' as in Example 2.3, we find that

$$\bar{x}_0' = 122\cdot9°, \qquad S_0' = 0\cdot4750.$$

Consequently,

$$\tilde{x}_0 = 61\cdot4° \quad \text{and} \quad \tilde{S}_0 = 0\cdot1698.$$

This procedure can easily be modified to cover similar cases such as bimodal data in the range $(0°, 180°)$. The data on swimming directions of *Daphnia* in Table 1.11 is such an example. The new frequencies f_i in this case will be obtained by adding the pairs of frequencies which are 90° apart and then we would work on f_i and $\theta_i' = 4\theta_i$. Finally, the mean direction and the circular variance are obtained from $\tilde{x}_0 = \bar{x}_0'/4$ and $\tilde{S}_0 = 1 - (1 - S_0')^{1/16}$.

2.5. SOME OTHER MEASURES OF LOCATION

2.5.1. A Median Direction

Suppose we are given a set of sample points on the unit circle. Any one point P of these given points which has the properties that (i) half of the sample points are on each side of the diameter PQ through P and (ii) the majority of the sample points are nearer to P than to Q, is called a median of the sample. The vector $\overline{OP}$ is called a median direction of the sample.

A population median direction ξ_0 is any solution of

$$\int_{\xi_0}^{\xi_0 + \pi} f(\theta)\, d\theta = \int_{\xi_0 + \pi}^{\xi_0 + 2\pi} f(\theta)\, d\theta = \tfrac{1}{2}, \qquad (2.5.1)$$

with the parent density $f(\theta)$ satisfying

$$f(\xi_0) > f(\xi_0 + \pi).$$

For a symmetrical distribution, the median direction will be in the axis of symmetry. We shall show in Section 2.6.2 that the circular mean deviation is a minimum about ξ_0. This property is analogous to the well-known property of the linear median. A median may not be unique in general. However, we prove in Section 3.3.4 that each unimodal distribution has a unique median.

We denote the sample median direction by M_0. The indeterminacy of the circular median for grouped data can be removed by adopting the convention used for the linear median. The method is illustrated in the following examples.

Example 2.7. To obtain the median direction for the data in Example 1.1.
   The observations (in degrees) are 43, 45, 52, 61, 75, 88, 88, 279, 357. From Fig. 1.1, we see that the median direction is 52°. The median of these points when considered on the line is 75°.

Example 2.8. To find the median direction for the mallard data given in Table 1.1.
   The calculations required for M_0 are shown in Table 2.4. Column 3 shows the cumulative frequencies. The first half of this column is repeated in Column

TABLE 2.4   Calculation of the median direction for the mallard data in Table 1.1.

(1) Upper class-limit θ_i (in degrees)	(2) Frequency	(3) Cumulative Frequency	(4) Frequency below $\theta_i - 180°$	(5) Frequency in $(\theta_i - 180°, \theta_i)$	(6) Interval $(\theta_i - 180°, \theta_i)$
20	40	40			
40	22	62			
60	20	82			
80	9	91			
100	6	97			
120	3	100			
140	3	103			
160	1	104			
180	6	110	0	110	(0, 180)
200	3	113	40	73	(20, 200)
220	11	124	62	62	(40, 220)
240	22	146	82	64	(60, 240)
260	24	170	91	79	(80, 260)
280	58	228	97	131	(100, 280)
300	136	364	100	264	(120, 300)
320	138	502	103	399	(140, 320)
340	143	645	104	541	(160, 340)
360	69	714	110	604	(180, 360)

4 which lists the cumulative frequencies of angles below $\theta_i - 180°$ where θ_i is the upper-limit of the ith class-interval. The frequency in $(\theta_i - 180°, \theta_i)$ is obtained by subtracting the entries of Column 4 from those of Column 3. Now, half of the total frequency of 714 is 357 which, from Column 5, lies between the frequencies corresponding to the intervals $(120°, 300°)$ and $(140°, 320°)$. As the frequencies are greater in the lower half of the circle, the median direction lies in the interval $(300°, 320°)$ rather than $(120°, 140°)$. Since there are 264 observations in $(120°, 300°)$ and 399 observations in $(140°, 320°)$, the median direction is

$$M_0 = 300 + \frac{357 - 264}{399 - 264} \times 20 = 313 \cdot 8°.$$

The mean direction (Example 2.2) of this data is $314 \cdot 3°$ which is practically the same.

2.5.2. The Mode

The mode of a given frequency distribution can be obtained by the same procedure as on the line, after selecting the cut point so that the maximum concentration appears in the centre of the distribution. Consequently, for grouped data,

$$\text{Mode} = l + \frac{f_0 - f_{-1}}{2f_0 - f_{-1} - f_{+1}} \times h, \tag{2.5.2}$$

where l is the lower limit of the modal class, f_0 is the frequency in the modal class, f_{-1} and f_{+1} are respectively the frequencies in the classes preceding and following the modal class, and h is the length of the class-interval.

Example 2.9. To calculate the mode of the mallard data in Table 1.1. From Table 2.4, we have

$$l = 320, \quad f_0 = 143, \quad f_{-1} = 138, \quad f_{+1} = 69, \quad h = 20$$

so that the mode is $321 \cdot 3°$.

2.6. SOME OTHER MEASURES OF DISPERSION

2.6.1. The Circular Mean Deviation

Let α be a fixed direction. Taking α as the zero direction, the angle θ_i becomes θ_i' where

$$\theta_i' = (\theta_i - \alpha) \bmod 2\pi. \tag{2.6.1}$$

Let ξ_i be the deviation of θ_i' as defined by (2.3.1) so that

$$\xi_i = \min (\theta_i', 2\pi - \theta_i'). \tag{2.6.2}$$

This deviation itself can be regarded as a measure of circular distance and consequently, we may define a measure of dispersion

$$d_0 = \frac{1}{n} \sum_{i=1}^{n} \xi_i, \tag{2.6.3}$$

or, equivalently,

$$d_0 = \pi - \frac{1}{n} \sum_{i=1}^{n} |\pi - \theta_i'|. \tag{2.6.4}$$

Using (2.6.1), we find from (2.6.4) that

$$d_0 = \pi - \frac{1}{n} \sum_{i=1}^{n} |\{\pi - |\theta_i - \alpha|\}|, \tag{2.6.5}$$

which has a form very similar to the ordinary mean deviation and can be described as the circular mean deviation about α.

A Minimization Property. The population circular mean deviation is given by

$$\delta_0 = \pi - E|(\pi - |\theta - \alpha|)|, \tag{2.6.6}$$

which reduces to

$$\delta_0 = \int_0^\pi \theta\, dF(\theta + \alpha) + \int_\pi^{2\pi} (2\pi - \theta)\, dF(\theta + \alpha). \tag{2.6.7}$$

The first and the second derivatives of (2.6.7) with respect to α are

$$-\int_0^\pi dF(\theta + \alpha) + \int_\pi^{2\pi} dF(\theta + \alpha), \qquad 2\{f(\alpha) - f(\pi + \alpha)\}$$

so that δ_0 is minimized at

$$\int_0^\pi dF(\theta + \alpha) = \int_\pi^{2\pi} dF(\theta + \alpha) = \tfrac{1}{2}, \tag{2.6.8}$$

where

$$f(\alpha) > f(\pi + \alpha).$$

It can be seen that (2.6.8) is equivalent to (2.5.1). Hence the mean deviation is a minimum when measured from the median direction.

We denote d_0 by d_0' when $\alpha = \bar{x}_0$ in (2.6.5). By analogy with the linear case, we shall use d_0' rather than the mean deviation d_0 about the median direction. The population circular mean deviation about the true mean direction will be denoted by δ_0'.

Example 2.10. To calculate the circular mean deviation about the mean direction for the mallard data in Table 1.1.

TABLE 2.5 Calculation of the circular mean deviation for the mallard data in Table 1.1.

θ_i (in degrees)	θ_i' (in degrees)	ξ_i (in degrees)	η_i	f_i	$f_i \eta_i$
10	55·7	55·7	−3	40	−120
30	75·7	75·7	−4	22	−44
50	95·7	95·7	0	20	0
70	115·7	115·7	1	9	9
90	135·7	135·7	2	6	12
110	155·7	155·7	3	3	9
130	175·7	175·7	4	3	12
150	195·7	164·3	4	1	4
170	215·7	144·3	3	6	18
190	235·7	124·3	2	3	6
210	255·7	104·3	1	11	11
230	275·7	84·3	0	22	0
250	295·7	64·3	−1	24	−24
270	315·7	44·3	−2	58	−116
290	335·7	24·3	−3	136	−408
310	355·7	4·3	−4	138	−552
330	15·7	15·7	−1	143	−143
350	35·7	35·7	−2	69	−138

We already know from Example 2.2 that $\bar{x}_0 = 314\cdot3°$. The values of θ_i' and ξ_i with $\alpha = 314\cdot3°$ are shown in Table 2.5. To calculate d_0', we divide the data into two parts one consisting of the mid-points θ_i from 330° to 130° and the other part from 150° to 310° so that

$$d_0' = \frac{1}{n}\Sigma f_i \xi_i = \frac{n_1 \bar{d}_1 + n_2 \bar{d}_2}{n},$$

where $\bar{d}_1$ and $\bar{d}_2$ are the means of the two parts, $n_1 = 315$, and $n_2 = 399$. On changing the scale and the origin for each part separately (see Column 4 of Table 2.5), we obtain after using Column 6

$$\bar{d}_1 = 95\cdot7 - \frac{20 \times 403}{315} = 70\cdot1; \qquad \bar{d}_2 = 84\cdot3 - \frac{20 \times 1061}{399} = 31\cdot1.$$

Consequently, $d_0' = 48\cdot3°$.

2.6.2. The Quartile Deviation

Let M_0 be the median direction of n observations. We can define the first and the third quartile directions $Q_1{}^0$ and $Q_3{}^0$ as the values of the $n/4$th observations from the median direction M_0 in the clockwise and the anti-clockwise senses respectively. Then the quartile deviation is the arc length from $Q_1{}^0$ to $Q_3{}^0$ which contains M_0.

For a population with distribution function $F(\theta)$, we define $\xi_1{}^0$ and $\xi_3{}^0$ by

$$\int_{\xi_0 - \xi_1{}^0}^{\xi_0} dF(\theta) = \tfrac{1}{4}, \qquad \int_{\xi_0}^{\xi_0 + \xi_3{}^0} dF(\theta) = \tfrac{1}{4}. \qquad (2.6.9)$$

This approach can be extended to define other quantiles.

Example 2.11. To calculate $Q_1{}^0$ and $Q_3{}^0$ for the mallard data in Table 1.1. $Q_1{}^0$ the 178·5th observation below M_0 in the sense defined above. From Table 2·4, the number of observations from 300° to M_0 is 357–264 = 93 so that $Q_1{}^0$ is the 178·5–93 = 85·5th observation below M_0. Consequently,

$$Q_1{}^0 = 300 - \frac{85\cdot5}{136} \times 20 = 287\cdot4°.$$

Similarly, $Q_3{}^0$ is the 178·5 – (138 – 93) = 133·5th observation above M_0 so

$$Q_3{}^0 = 320 + \frac{133\cdot5}{143} \times 20 = 338\cdot7°.$$

Thus the quartile deviation is 51·3°.

2.6.3. The Circular Mean Difference

Let ξ_{ij} be the deviation between θ_i and θ_j as described in Section 2.6.1. That is,

$$\xi_{ij} = \pi - |\{\pi - |\theta_i - \theta_j|\}|.$$

We can, therefore, define

$$\bar{D}_0 = \frac{1}{n^2} \sum_{i=1}^{n} \sum_{j=1}^{n} \{\pi - |(\pi - |\theta_i - \theta_j|)|\} \qquad (2.6.10)$$

as the circular mean difference. This does not depend on any measure of location.

It is interesting to note that when the distance between θ_i and θ_j is taken as $1 - \cos(\theta_i - \theta_j)$, the alternative measure

$$\frac{1}{n^2} \Sigma\Sigma \{1 - \cos(\theta_i - \theta_j)\}$$

of dispersion reduces to $1 - \bar{R}^2$.

For a population with distribution function $F(\theta)$, the circular mean difference is given by

$$\Delta_0 = \pi - E\{|(\pi - |\theta_1 - \theta_2|)|\}, \qquad (2.6.11)$$

where θ_1 and θ_2 are independently distributed as $F(\theta)$. We find that (2.6.11) reduces to

$$\Delta_0 = \pi - \int_0^{2\pi} \int_0^{2\pi} |\pi - \theta| \, dF(\xi) \, dF(\theta + \xi). \qquad (2.6.12)$$

2.6.4. The Circular Range

We can define the circular range as the length of the smallest arc which encompasses all the sample observations. Let $\theta_{(1)}, ..., \theta_{(n)}$ be the linear order statistics for $\theta_1, ..., \theta_n$ $(0 < \theta_i \leqslant 2\pi)$. Define

$$T_i = \theta_{(i+1)} - \theta_{(i)}, \qquad i = 1, ..., n-1; \qquad T_n = 2\pi - \theta_{(n)} + \theta_{(1)}.$$

These measure the arc lengths between adjacent points. The circular range w is then given by

$$w = 2\pi - \max(T_1, ..., T_n). \qquad (2.6.13)$$

For continuous circular distributions, the support is usually $(0, 2\pi)$ so that the range is 2π.

Example 2.12. To obtain the circular range for the data in Example 1.1.
We have

$$\theta_{(i)} : 43, 45, 52, 61, 75, 88, 88, 279, 357.$$

$$T_i : 2, 7, 9, 14, 13, 13, 191, 78, 46.$$

Hence, we have $w = 360° - 191° = 169°$. This result is obvious from Fig. 1.1 since the maximum arc without any mass point is from 88° to 279°.

2.7. TRIGONOMETRIC MOMENTS

2.7.1. Definitions

We have seen in Sections 2.2–2.4 that the moments

$$\bar{C} = \frac{1}{n}\Sigma\cos\theta_i, \qquad \bar{S} = \frac{1}{n}\Sigma\sin\theta_i$$

play key roles in defining the mean direction and the circular variance. Let us write

$$\mathbf{m_1}' = \bar{C} + i\bar{S}.$$

Then we have

$$\mathbf{m_1}' = \bar{R}e^{i\bar{x}_0}. \tag{2.7.1}$$

We can call m_1' the first trigonometric moment. Extending this notion, we can define the pth trigonometric moment about the zero direction as

$$\mathbf{m_p}' = a_p + ib_p, \tag{2.7.2}$$

where

$$a_p = \frac{1}{n}\sum_{i=1}^{n}\cos p\theta_i, \qquad b_p = \frac{1}{n}\sum_{i=1}^{n}\sin p\theta_i. \tag{2.7.3}$$

This can also be expressed as

$$\mathbf{m_p}' = \bar{R}_p\, e^{im_p^0}, \tag{2.7.4}$$

where R_p is the length of the pth mean resultant and m_p^0 is its direction. From (2.7.3) and (2.7.4), we have

$$a_p = \bar{R}_p\cos m_p^0, \qquad b_p = \bar{R}_p\sin m_p^0. \tag{2.7.5}$$

Of course,

$$a_1 = \bar{C}, \qquad b_1 = \bar{S}, \qquad R_1 = \bar{R}, \qquad m_1^0 = \bar{x}_0.$$

We can also define the pth trigonometric moment about the mean direction $\bar{x}_0$ as

$$\mathbf{m_p} = \bar{a}_p + i\bar{b}_p, \tag{2.7.6}$$

where

$$\bar{a}_p = \frac{1}{n}\sum_{i=1}^{n}\cos p(\theta_i - \bar{x}_0), \qquad \bar{b}_p = \frac{1}{n}\sum_{i=1}^{n}\sin p(\theta_i - \bar{x}_0). \tag{2.7.7}$$

From (2.7.5) and (2.7.7), we find that

$$\mathbf{m}_p = \bar{R}_p\, e^{i(m_p{}^0 - p\bar{x}_0)} \tag{2.7.8}$$

so that we have the following useful results.

$$\bar{a}_p = \bar{R}_p \cos (m_p{}^0 - p\bar{x}_0), \qquad \bar{b}_p = \bar{R}_p \sin (m_p{}^0 - p\bar{x}_0). \tag{2.7.9}$$

It can be seen that

$$|\mathbf{m}_p'| \leqslant 1, \qquad |\mathbf{m}_p| \leqslant 1. \tag{2.7.10}$$

2.7.2. Measures of Skewness and Kurtosis

We have used the first trigonometric moment to define the mean direction and circular variance. The approach suggests that the second trigonometric moment may be used to define some suitable measures of skewness and kurtosis for circular distributions. We shall show in Section 3.7 that appropriate measures are

$$g_1{}^0 = \bar{R}_2 \sin (m_2{}^0 - 2\bar{x}_0)/S_0{}^{3/2} \tag{2.7.11}$$

and

$$g_2{}^0 = [\bar{R}_2 \cos (m_2{}^0 - 2\bar{x}_0) - (1 - S_0)^4]/S_0{}^2. \tag{2.7.12}$$

For unimodal symmetric frequency distributions, $g_1{}^0$ will be nearly zero. We would expect $g_2{}^0$ to be nearly zero for unimodal distributions having a normal peak. If $g_2{}^0 > 0$ the distribution may be described as leptokurtic whereas if $g_2{}^0 < 0$ the distribution may be described as platykurtic.

Example 2.13. To calculate the first two trigonometric moments and the measures of skewness and kurtosis for the mallard data in Table 1.1
We have already calculated the first trigonometric moment (Example 2.2):

$$\mathbf{m}_1' = (0 \cdot 4998) - (0 \cdot 5126)\, i.$$

Also,

$$\bar{x}_0 = 314 \cdot 3°, \qquad S_0 = 0 \cdot 2841.$$

From Table 2.6,

$$a_2 = -28 \cdot 1362/714 = -0 \cdot 0394, \qquad b_2 = -272 \cdot 7020/714 = -0 \cdot 3819.$$

TABLE 2.6   Calculation of the second trigonometric moment for the mallard data in Table 1.1.

θ_i (mid-point)	f_i	$2\theta_i$	$\cos 2\theta_i$	$f_i \cos 2\theta_i$	$\sin 2\theta_i$	$f_i \sin 2\theta_i$
10°	40	20	0·9397	37·5880	0·3420	13·6800
30	22	60	0·5000	11·0000	0·8660	19·0520
50	20	100	−0·1736	−3·4720	0·9848	19·6960
70	9	140	−0·7660	−6·8940	0·6428	5·7852
90	6	180	−1·0000	−6·0000	0·0000	0·0000
110	3	220	−0·7660	−2·2980	−0·6428	−1·9284
130	3	260	−0·1736	−0·5208	−0·9848	−2·9544
150	1	300	0·5000	0·5000	−0·8660	−0·8660
170	6	340	0·9397	5·6382	−0·3420	−2·0520
190	3	20	0·9397	2·8191	0·3420	1·0260
210	11	60	0·5000	5·5000	0·8660	9·5260
230	22	100	−0·1736	−3·8192	0·9848	21·6656
250	24	140	−0·7660	−18·3840	0·6428	15·4272
270	58	180	−1·0000	−58·0000	0·0000	0·0000
290	136	220	−0·7660	−104·1760	−0·6428	−87·4208
310	138	260	−0·1736	−23·9568	−0·9848	−135·9024
330	143	300	0·5000	71·5000	−0·8660	−123·8380
350	69	340	0·9397	64·8393	−0·3420	−23·5980
Totals	714			−28·1362		−272·7020

Hence, using (2.7.5), we obtain

$$m_2^{\ 0} = 272 \cdot 1°, \qquad \bar{R}_2 = 0 \cdot 3840,$$

and therefore

$$\bar{a}_2 = 0 \cdot 3828, \qquad \bar{b}_2 = 0 \cdot 0487$$

by (2.7.9). Finally, from (2.7.11) and (2.7.12) we have

$$g_1^{\ 0} = 0 \cdot 3217, \qquad g_2^{\ 0} = 1 \cdot 4882,$$

indicating that the distribution is fairly symmetric and rather leptokurtic. These findings are consistent with Figure 1.4.

2.8. CORRECTIONS FOR GROUPING

Let each class-interval be of the same length h where h is measured in radians. It will be shown in Section 3.8.2 that $m_p^{\ 0}$ does not require a

Sheppard-type correction for grouping whereas $\bar{R}_p$ does need such a correction. The corrected values of R_1 and R_2 are

$$\tilde{R}_1 = a(h)\,\bar{R}_1 \tag{2.8.1}$$

and

$$\tilde{R}_2 = a(2h)\,\bar{R}_2, \tag{2.8.2}$$

where

$$a(h) = h/(2\sin\tfrac{1}{2}h).$$

Hence S_0 and $g_2{}^0$ both need Sheppard-type corrections but $\bar{x}_0$ does not. Table 2.7 gives some selected values of the correction factor $a(h)$.

TABLE 2.7 The multiplier in the Sheppard-type correction

Class-length h	Multiplier $a(h)$	Class-length h	Multiplier $a(h)$
3°	1·0001	20°	1·0051
4°	1·0002	24°	1·0073
5°	1·0003	30°	1·0115
6°	1·0005	36°	1·0166
8°	1·0008	40°	1·0206
9°	1·0010	45°	1·0262
10°	1·0013	60°	1·0472
12°	1·0018	72°	1·0690
15°	1·0029	90°	1·1107
18°	1·0041	120°	1·2092

Example 2.14. To obtain the first two corrected trigonometric moments for the mallard data in Table 1.1.
From Table 2.7, we have for $h = 20°$

$$\tilde{R}_1 = 1\cdot0051\,\bar{R}_1, \qquad \tilde{R}_2 = 1\cdot0013\,\bar{R}_2.$$

Consequently, using Example 2.13, it is found that

$$m_1{}^0 = 314\cdot3°, \qquad \tilde{R}_1 = 0\cdot7196,$$
$$m_2{}^0 = 272\cdot1°, \qquad \tilde{R}_2 = 0\cdot3890.$$

The corrected values of S_0, s_0, $g_1{}^0$ and $g_2{}^0$ are

$$S_0 = 0\cdot2804, \qquad s_0 = 0\cdot8112, \qquad g_1{}^0 = 0\cdot3298, \qquad g_2{}^0 = 1\cdot4644.$$

Hence, the findings of Example 2.13 remain the same.

3

BASIC CONCEPTS AND THEORETICAL MODELS

3.1. THE DISTRIBUTION FUNCTION

Let Z be a random variable which takes values on the circumference of the unit circle $x^2 + y^2 = 1$ in the plane. We may identify the possible values of Z with angles measured anti-clockwise from the positive x-axis so that the angle θ represents the point $(\cos \theta, \sin \theta)$, $0 < \theta \leqslant 2\pi$. With this representation we may define the distribution function F of Z by the equation

$$F(\theta) = \Pr (0 < Z \leqslant \theta), \qquad 0 < \theta \leqslant 2\pi.$$

However, it is unnatural to restrict the domain of definition of F to the interval $(0, 2\pi)$ because of the special relationship between the two end points which, of course, correspond to the same point on the circle. We therefore extend the domain of definition to the whole real line by the equation

$$F(\theta + 2\pi) - F(\theta) = 1, \qquad -\infty < \theta < \infty. \qquad (3.1.1)$$

The function F defined in this way is called the distribution function (d.f.) of Z on the circle. Equation (3.1.1) reflects the fact that any arc of the unit circle subtending an angle of 2π radians at the origin is the whole of the circumference of the circle and the total probability around the circumference is unity.

Before considering the probability that θ takes a value in an arc, we develop a suitable notation. Let α, β be two angles such that $-\infty < \alpha, \beta < \infty$ and $|\alpha - \beta| < 2\pi$. Suppose that A, B are the two points on the unit circle represented by α, β respectively. We denote the arc

39

consisting of the points from A to B in the anti-clockwise direction by arc (α, β) with the convention that the point A is excluded. Denote by X the point on the unit circle corresponding to the zero direction, i.e. X is the point where the positive x-axis meets the circle. If $0 < \alpha < \beta < 2\pi$, then arc (α, β) is that arc AB of the unit circle which does not contain X whereas arc (β, α) is the arc BXA containing X. In the first case the point A is deleted while in the second case the point B is deleted. In these two cases, we may simply denote the arcs by $\alpha < \theta \leqslant \beta$ and $\beta < \theta \leqslant \alpha$ respectively.

For $-\infty < \alpha < \beta < \infty$ and $\beta - \alpha < 2\pi$, it can be shown that the d.f. F has the property

$$\Pr\{\theta \in \text{arc}\,(\alpha, \beta)\} = F(\beta) - F(\alpha) = \int_{\alpha+}^{\beta} dF(\theta), \qquad (3.1.2)$$

where the integral is a Lebesgue–Stieltjes integral. The d.f. F is a right continuous function of θ but in contrast with d.f.'s on the real line,

$$\lim_{\theta \to \infty} F(\theta) = \infty, \qquad \lim_{\theta \to -\infty} F(\theta) = -\infty.$$

However,

$$F(0) = 0, \qquad F(2\pi) = 1.$$

It should be noted that although the function F depends on the choice of the zero direction, (3.1.2) shows that $F(\beta) - F(\alpha)$ is independent of this choice. Thus changing the zero direction simply adds a constant to F. It will sometimes be convenient to define the d.f. F by initially considering θ in the range $-\pi < \theta \leqslant \pi$ so that $F(-\pi) = 0$ and $F(\pi) = 1$. This amounts to adding the constant $\Pr\{\theta \in \text{arc}\,(-\pi, 0)\}$ to the d.f. defined previously.

If the d.f. F is absolutely continuous, it has a probability density function (p.d.f.) f such that

$$\int_{\alpha}^{\beta} f(\theta)\, d\theta = F(\beta) - F(\alpha), \qquad -\infty < \alpha < \beta < \infty.$$

A given function f is the p.d.f. of an absolutely continuous distribution if and only if

$$\text{(i)} \qquad f(\theta) \geqslant 0, \qquad -\infty < \theta < \infty,$$

$$\text{(ii)} \qquad f(\theta + 2\pi) = f(\theta), \qquad -\infty < \theta < \infty,$$

and

$$\text{(iii)} \qquad \int_0^{2\pi} f(\theta)\, d\theta = 1.$$

In this case, we shall describe θ as a continuous random variable.

An alternative way of looking at a distribution on the unit circle is to consider it as a bivariate singular distribution on the plane with mass concentrated on the circumference of the unit circle. This representation will, however, be used only occasionally.

3.2 THE CHARACTERISTIC FUNCTION

3.2.1. Definition

If Z is a random variable with values on the unit circle, we shall identify Z with a random variable θ, $0 < \theta \leqslant 2\pi$ such that

$$Z = e^{i\theta}.$$

Notationally, we shall not distinguish between a random variable and its values.

In analogy with real line, let us consider the function

$$\phi(t) = E(e^{it\theta}) = \int_0^{2\pi} e^{it\theta}\, dF(\theta),$$

where $F(\theta)$ is the circular d.f. of θ. Using (3.1.1), it is easy to see that

$$\int_0^{2\pi} e^{it(\theta+2\pi)}\, dF(\theta) = \int_0^{2\pi} e^{it\theta}\, dF(\theta)$$

so that

$$e^{2\pi it} = 1$$

whenever there is a ϕ with $|\phi(t)| \neq 0$. This suggests that the function $\phi(t)$ should only be defined for integer values of t. In fact, the theory of Fourier series for periodic functions shows that it is sufficient to take t as an integer. Accordingly, the characteristic function (c.f.) ϕ_p of θ is defined by

$$\phi_p = \int_0^{2\pi} e^{ip\theta}\, dF(\theta), \qquad p = 0, \pm 1, \pm 2, \dots . \tag{3.2.1}$$

We obviously have

$$\phi_0 = 1, \qquad \bar{\phi}_p = \phi_{-p}, \qquad |\phi_p| \leqslant 1. \tag{3.2.2}$$

We shall write

$$\phi_p = \alpha_p + i\beta_p, \tag{3.2.3}$$

where

$$\alpha_p = E(\cos p\theta) = \int_0^{2\pi} \cos p\theta \, dF(\theta) \tag{3.2.4}$$

and

$$\beta_p = E(\sin p\theta) = \int_0^{2\pi} \sin p\theta \, dF(\theta). \tag{3.2.5}$$

We have

$$\alpha_{-p} = \alpha_p, \quad \beta_{-p} = -\beta_p, \quad |\alpha_p| \leqslant 1, \quad |\beta_p| \leqslant 1. \tag{3.2.6}$$

3.2.2. Fourier–Stieltjes Series

The similarity of the function ϕ_p to the coefficients of the Fourier–Stieltjes series of F is evident (Zygmund, 1959, p. 11). In fact, the numbers $2\pi\phi_p$ are the Fourier–Stieltjes coefficients of F and

$$dF(\theta) \sim \frac{1}{2\pi} \sum_{p=-\infty}^{\infty} \phi_p e^{-ip\theta}, \tag{3.2.7}$$

where the notation $\sim$ means that the ϕ_p are related to F by the formula (3.2.1). It does not carry any implication that the series is convergent, still less that it converges to F. However, if $\sum_{p=1}^{\infty} (\alpha_p^2 + \beta_p^2)$ is convergent, the random variable θ has a density which is defined almost everywhere by

$$f(\theta) = \frac{1}{2\pi} \sum_{p=-\infty}^{\infty} \phi_p e^{-ip\theta}. \tag{3.2.8}$$

A proof is given in Section 4.2.2. Its similarity with the inversion theorem for continuous random variables on the line is clearly evident. We can rewrite (3.2.8) as

$$f(\theta) = \frac{1}{2\pi} \left[1 + 2 \sum_{p=1}^{\infty} (\alpha_p \cos p\theta + \beta_p \sin p\theta) \right]. \tag{3.2.9}$$

Further, the d.f. of θ is simply given by

$$F(\theta) = \frac{1}{2\pi} \left[\theta + 2 \sum_{p=1}^{\infty} \{\alpha_p \sin p\theta + \beta_p(1 - \cos p\theta)\}/p \right]. \tag{3.2.10}$$

Conversely, if $f(\theta)$ is of bounded variation then the Fourier-series (3.2.8) is valid by Jordan's test (Titchmarsh, 1958, p. 406) provided

$$f(\theta) = \tfrac{1}{2}\{f(\theta + 0) + f(\theta - 0)\}.$$

Further, by Dirichlet's test (Titchmarsh, 1958, p. 407), the representation is also valid if $f(\theta)$ has only a finite number of maxima and minima and a finite number of discontinuities in the interval $(0, 2\pi)$.

3.2.3. Independence and Convolution

Let θ_1 and θ_2 be two angular random variables. Their joint c.f. is defined by

$$\phi_{p,q} = E(e^{ip\theta_1 + iq\theta_2}),$$

where p and q are integers. The variable (θ_1, θ_2) takes values on a torus. Let ϕ_p and ϕ_q' be the marginal c.f.'s of (θ_1, θ_2). Then the variables θ_1 and θ_2 are independent if and only if

$$\phi_{p,q} = \phi_p \phi_q'. \tag{3.2.11}$$

In the famous Buffon's needle problem, the direction of the needle and the centre of the needle are two such angular variables. Their independence is always assumed.

Let $\theta_1, \ldots, \theta_n$ be random variables on the circle. The sum

$$S_n = (\theta_1 + \ldots + \theta_n) \bmod 2\pi$$

is an analog of the sum of random variables on the line. If $\theta_1, \ldots, \theta_n$ are distributed independently, the c.f. of S_n is the product of the c.f.'s of $\theta_1, \ldots, \theta_n$. Further, if the θ_i are identically distributed with the common c.f. ϕ_p, the c.f. of S_n is simply $\phi_p{}^n$. When the series $\Sigma|\phi_p|^2$ is convergent, the p.d.f. of S_n is

$$(2\pi)^{-1} \Sigma \phi_p{}^n e^{-ip\theta}.$$

Let θ and ξ be two independent random variables with corresponding d.f.'s F_1 and F_2. By following the same method as on the line, the distribution of $\zeta = (\theta + \xi) \bmod 2\pi$ is given by

$$\int_0^{2\pi} dF_2(\zeta - \theta) \, dF_1(\theta). \tag{3.2.12}$$

If one of the random variables has a density, the convolution also has a density. When θ and ζ both have densities, (3.2.12) reduces to

$$\int_0^{2\pi} f_1(\theta) f_2(\zeta - \theta) \, d\theta. \tag{3.2.13}$$

It is interesting that if one of the two random variables is uniformly distributed, their convolution has the uniform density. A proof is given in Section 3.4.4.

In Chapter 4, Sections 4.2 and 4.3, we shall deal with various other properties of the c.f. including the uniqueness theorem and a limit theorem for sequences of random variables.

3.3. MOMENTS AND MEASURES OF LOCATION AND DISPERSION

3.3.1. Trigonometric Moments

In this section, we define the population characteristics corresponding to various sample characteristics given in Chapter 2 and we study their properties. We have already defined

$$\alpha_p = E(\cos p\theta), \quad \beta_p = E(\sin p\theta), \quad \mu_p' = \phi_p = E(e^{ip\theta}). \quad (3.3.1)$$

Hence, the sequence of trigonometric moments of θ is the c.f. of θ. Consequently, all the results for the c.f. apply to the moments. In particular, in contrast to distributions on the line, a circular distribution is always uniquely defined by its moments.

Let us write

$$\phi_p = \rho_p e^{i\mu_p^0}, \quad p \geqslant 0. \quad (3.3.2)$$

For $p = 1$, we shall write

$$\alpha_1 = \alpha, \quad \beta_1 = \beta, \quad \rho_1 = \rho, \quad \mu_1^0 = \mu_0.$$

The pth central trigonometric moment can be defined as

$$\mu_p = E\{e^{ip(\theta-\mu_0)}\} = \bar\alpha_p + i\bar\beta_p. \quad (3.3.3)$$

From (3.3.2) and (3.3.3), we have the relations

$$\mu_p = \phi_p e^{ip\mu_0},$$
$$\bar\alpha_p = \rho_p \cos(\mu_p^0 - p\mu_0), \quad \bar\beta_p = \rho_p \sin(\mu_p^0 - p\mu_0).$$

In particular

$$\bar\alpha_1 = \rho, \quad \bar\beta_1 = 0.$$

Considering

$$E\{a_0 + a_1 \sin(\theta - \mu_0) + a_2 \cos(\theta - \mu_0)\}^2 \geqslant 0$$

for all real a_0, a_1 and a_2, we have the following inequality satisfied by the moments up to the second order.

$$1 - \bar\alpha_2^2 - \bar\beta_2^2 - 2\bar\alpha_1^2(1 - \bar\alpha_2) \geqslant 0. \quad (3.3.4)$$

Let v be the new zero direction when the transformed random variable is

$$\theta^* = (\theta - v) \bmod 2\pi. \tag{3.3.5}$$

If ϕ_p^* is the pth moment of θ^* then

$$\phi_p^* = e^{-ivp} \phi_p. \tag{3.3.6}$$

The central moments are invariant under this transformation.

3.3.2. The Mean Direction and Circular Variance

We summarize the main properties of the mean direction and the circular variance. Let us write

$$\phi_1 = \rho e^{i\mu_0}. \tag{3.3.7}$$

Then μ_0 is the mean direction of θ, ρ is the resultant length and

$$E\{\sin (\theta - \mu_0)\} = 0. \tag{3.3.8}$$

Further, the circular variance of θ is

$$V_0 = 1 - \rho = 1 - E\{\cos (\theta - \mu_0)\}. \tag{3.3.9}$$

We have

$$0 \leqslant V_0 \leqslant 1.$$

The circular variance about $\theta = v$ is given by

$$V_0' = 1 - E\{\cos (\theta - v)\}.$$

The quantities V_0' and V_0 are related by

$$V_0' = V_0 + 2\rho \sin^2 \tfrac{1}{2}(\mu_0 - v). \tag{3.3.10}$$

Further, V_0' has a minimum at $v = \mu_0$.
    Under the transformation (3.3.5), we have

$$\mu_0^* = (\mu_0 - v)(\bmod 2\pi), \qquad \rho^* = \rho, \qquad V_0^* = V_0. \tag{3.3.11}$$

Hence, V_0 is invariant under any change of zero direction.
    We shall show in Section 3.4.2 that $V_0 = 0$ if and only if the distribution is concentrated at one single point $\theta = \mu_0$. This property is again similar to that of σ^2 on the line. If $V_0 = 1$, we may say that the distribution has maximum variation and is so scattered that there is no concentration around any particular direction.

3.3.3. A Tschebycheff-type Inequality

We show that

$$\Pr\{|\sin\tfrac{1}{2}(\theta - \mu_0)| \geqslant \varepsilon\} \leqslant V_0/2\varepsilon^2, \qquad 0 < \varepsilon < 1. \qquad (3.3.12)$$

Without any loss of generality, let us take μ_0 as the zero direction and let us measure θ in the range $(-\pi, \pi)$. Then

$$V_0 = 2\int_{-\pi}^{+\pi} \sin^2 \tfrac{1}{2}\theta \; dF(\theta) \geqslant 2\int_{|\sin\frac{1}{2}\theta| \geqslant \varepsilon} \sin^2 \tfrac{1}{2}\theta \; dF(\theta)$$

$$\geqslant 2\varepsilon^2 \Pr\{|\sin\tfrac{1}{2}\theta| \geqslant \varepsilon\}. \qquad (3.3.13)$$

Hence the inequality (3.3.12) is established.

The inequality (3.3.12) cannot be improved upon as is shown by the following discrete distribution.

$$\Pr(\theta = 0) = 1 - (V_0/2\varepsilon^2), \qquad \Pr(\theta = \pm 2\arcsin\varepsilon) = V_0/2\varepsilon^2.$$

The similarity between the inequality (3.3.12) and the standard Tschbeycheff inequality on the line is evident. We can put (3.3.12) in a more manageable form as follows. Assume again that $\mu_0 = 0$ and $-\pi < \theta \leqslant \pi$ and let $a = (V_0/2)^{\frac{1}{2}}$. From (3.3.13), we have

$$\Pr\{|\theta| \geqslant 2\arcsin(\varepsilon a)\} \leqslant 1/\varepsilon^2. \qquad (3.3.14)$$

For other inequalities on the circle, the reader is referred to Marshall and Olkin (1961) who also deal with a general method of constructing sharp inequalities on the circle.

3.3.4. Other Measures

We have already defined and studied the circular median, the mean deviation, the quartile deviation and the mean difference for θ in Sections 2.5–2.6. In this section, we prove only one additional result, viz., the median of a unimodal distribution is unique.

Let $f(\theta)$ be the density of a unimodal distribution with mode at $\theta = \theta_0$. Suppose that $\theta = \theta^*$ is the anti-mode. By definition, $f(\theta)$ monotonically increases from θ^* to θ_0 and decreases monotonically from θ_0 to θ^*. We then show that $f(\theta)$ must have a unique median.

If possible, let there be two medians θ_1, θ_2 defined by

$$\int_{\theta_1}^{\theta_3} f(\theta)\,d\theta = \tfrac{1}{2} = \int_{\theta_2}^{\theta_4} f(\theta)\,d\theta, \qquad (3.3.15)$$

where $\theta_3 = \theta_1 + \pi$, $\theta_4 = \theta_2 + \pi$. For our proof, it is not necessary to specify the two medians further by the order of the a_i where

$$f(\theta_i) = a_i, \qquad i = 1, 2, 3, 4. \qquad (3.3.16)$$

Consequently, we select the directions θ_1, θ_2 such that $0 < \theta_1 < \pi < \theta_2 < 2\pi$. By rotation, we can always take $\theta_0 = 0$. Let A_i be the event that θ lies in arc (θ_i, θ_{i+1}), $i = 1, 2, 3, 4$, where $\theta_5 = \theta_1$.

In view of (3.3.15), we have

$$\mathrm{Pr}\,(A_1) = \mathrm{Pr}\,(A_3), \qquad \mathrm{Pr}\,(A_2) = \mathrm{Pr}\,(A_4). \qquad (3.3.17)$$

Let M be the point on the unit circle corresponding to θ. There are four possible cases to consider according as M lies in (i) arc (θ_2, θ_3), (ii) arc (θ_1, θ_2), (iii) arc (θ_1, θ_4), or (iv) arc (θ_3, θ_4). We give a proof only for Case (i). The proofs for the other cases follow by similar arguments.

We have

$$a_1 > a_2, \quad a_4 > a_3. \qquad (3.3.18)$$

Let us first assume that $a_2 < a_3$, i.e. it is the smallest of (a_1, a_2, a_3, a_4). Now, if $a_1 > a_3$ then the values of $f(\theta)$ in A_2 cannot exceed a_3 while the values of $f(\theta)$ in A_4 are greater than min (a_1, a_4). But min $(a_1, a_4) > a_3$ so that

$$\mathrm{Pr}\,(A_2) < \mathrm{Pr}\,(A_4). \qquad (3.3.19)$$

This inequality contradicts equation (3.3.17) so we must have $a_1 < a_3$. But, if $a_1 < a_3$, a similar argument leads to the inequality

$$\mathrm{Pr}\,(A_3) < \mathrm{Pr}\,(A_1), \qquad (3.3.20)$$

which again contradicts (3.3.17). Therefore, it is impossible that $a_2 < a_3$. Similarly, if $a_3 < a_2$ it may be shown that (3.3.19) must hold when $a_4 > a_2$ and (3.3.20) holds when $a_4 < a_2$ so that (3.3.17) is again contradicted. Hence, there can only be one median.*

3.3.5. Symmetric Distributions

Let us assume that the range of θ is $-\pi < \theta \leqslant \pi$. The distribution of θ is symmetric about $\theta = 0$ if the distribution is invariant under the transformation

$$\theta' = -\theta \,(\mathrm{mod}\, 2\pi). \qquad (3.3.21)$$

We can define symmetry about $\theta = v$ by selecting the zero direction as $\theta = v$. For a symmetric random variable θ with density $f(\theta)$, we have

$$f(\theta - v) = f(v - \theta). \qquad (3.3.22)$$

*This proof was communicated to me by Dr. J. W. Thompson.

If a distribution is symmetric about $\theta = v$ then it is also symmetric about $\theta = v + \pi$. Further, if the distribution is unimodal, the mean direction, the circular median and the mode are all equal. We have the central sine moments

$$\bar{\beta}_p = 0 \qquad (3.3.23)$$

so that the Fourier expansion (3.2.9) simplifies for $\mu_0 = 0$ to

$$f(\theta) = \frac{1}{2\pi}\left(1 + 2 \sum_{p=1}^{\infty} \alpha_p \cos p\theta\right). \qquad (3.3.24)$$

Further, the inequality (3.3.4) on moments reduces to

$$1 + \bar{\alpha}_2 \geqslant 2\bar{\alpha}_1^{\,2}. \qquad (3.3.25)$$

3.4. CIRCULAR MODELS

3.4.1. Introduction

Most of the basic models on the circle have been derived either from transformations of the standard univariate (or bivariate) models or as circular analogues of important univariate characterizations. Investigations of fundamental theorems on the circle such as the central limit theorem, Brownian motion etc., have strengthened the usefulness of some models. However, in contrast with the linear case, statistical sampling distributions on the circle have not led to tractable distributions analogous to χ^2, t and F on the line.

Sections 3.4.2., 3.4.3., 3.4.8c give discrete models. Other sections deal with continuous models. The von Mises distribution studied in Section 3.4.9 plays a key role in statistical inference on the circle and its importance on the circle is somewhat similar to that of the normal distribution on the line. Some reasons for this predominance are given in Section 3.4.10. For a reader interested in statistical applications, a working knowledge of the uniform distribution, the von Mises distribution and the wrapped normal distribution will be sufficient (viz., Section 3.4.4, 3.4.8d, 3.4.9a, b). The wrapped Cauchy distribution (Section 3.4.8e) and the lattice distributions (Section 3.4.3) are useful in theoretical investigations (see Sections 4.2.1, 4.3.2).

For any unimodal symmetric distribution about $\theta = v$, we have seen in Section 3.3.5 that v is the mode of the distribution and v is also the mean direction μ_0. With the help of the transformation

$$\theta' = (\theta - \mu_0)\,(\mathrm{mod}\,2\pi)$$

we can shift the mean direction to zero. Therefore, we shall assume for unimodal symmetric distributions that $\mu_0 = 0$.

3.4.2. Point Distributions

Consider the distribution concentrated at one single point $\theta = \mu_0$ so that

$$\Pr\,(\theta = \mu_0) = 1. \tag{3.4.1}$$

Its c.f. is given by

$$\phi_p = e^{ip\mu_0}.$$

It can be seen easily that $V_0 = 0$. We now show that if $V_0 = 0$ for a distribution then the distribution must be a point distribution. We have

$$\int_0^{2\pi} \{1 - \cos(\theta - \mu_0)\}\,dF(\theta) = 0. \tag{3.4.2}$$

Since the function $1 - \cos(\theta - \mu_0)$ is continuous and non-negative, the distribution with d.f. F must be concentrated at the point θ for which $\cos(\theta - \mu_0) = 1$. Hence we get (3.4.1).

For $\mu_0 = 0$,

$$\phi_p = 1, \qquad \alpha_p = 1, \qquad \beta_p = 0$$

so that the Fourier expansion of this distribution is simply

$$p(\theta) = \frac{1}{2\pi}\left(1 + 2\sum_{p=1}^{\infty} \cos p\theta\right). \tag{3.4.3}$$

3.4.3. Lattice Distributions

Let us consider a discrete distribution with

$$\Pr\,(\theta = v + 2\pi r/m) = p_r, \qquad r = 0, 1, \ldots, m - 1, \tag{3.4.4}$$

and

$$p_r \geqslant 0, \qquad \Sigma p_r = 1.$$

The points $v + 2\pi r/m$ are equidistant on the unit circle and the distribution may be imagined as concentrated on the vertices of an m-sided regular polygon. In particular, if all the weights are equal then

$$p_r = 1/m. \tag{3.4.5}$$

This distribution will be called the discrete uniform distribution. For $m = 37$, we have the distribution of an unbiased roulette wheel.

Let us take $v = 0$. Then the c.f. of (3.4.5) is given by

$$\phi_p = \sum_{r=0}^{m-1} p_r\, e^{2\pi r p i/m}. \tag{3.4.6}$$

We have

$$\phi_p = 1 \quad \text{for} \quad p = 0 \,(\text{mod}\, m). \tag{3.4.7}$$

For the discrete uniform distribution, (3.4.6) reduces to

$$\phi_p = 1 \quad \text{if} \quad p = 0 \bmod m; = 0, \quad \text{otherwise.} \tag{3.4.8}$$

For a roulette wheel having $2n + 1$ points with bias at $\theta = 0$, two suitable models are

$$\Pr\,(\theta = \pm r) = c_1 p^{r+1}, \qquad r = 0, \pm 1, ..., \pm n,$$

and

$$\Pr\,(\theta = 0) = c_2 p, \qquad \Pr\,(\theta = \pm r) = c_2 p/|r|, \qquad r = \pm 1, ..., \pm n.$$

Of course, c_1 and c_2 are selected in such a way that the total probability is one.

A Poisson distribution on the circle will be given in Section 3.4.8c. For a distribution of the first digits in random sampling, see Section 4.3.4.

3.4.4. The Uniform Distribution

Let θ be distributed uniformly over $(0, 2\pi)$ so that the p.d.f. of θ is

$$f(\theta) = \frac{1}{2\pi}, \qquad 0 < \theta \leqslant 2\pi. \tag{3.4.9}$$

We have

$$\phi_p = (e^{2\pi pi} - 1)/2\pi pi, \qquad p \neq 0.$$

Consequently,

$$\phi_p = 1 \quad \text{if} \quad p = 0;$$
$$= 0 \quad \text{if} \quad p \neq 0. \tag{3.4.10}$$

We have $V_0 = 1$ so that there is no concentration about any particular direction.

Let $\theta_1, \ldots, \theta_n$ be n independent uniform random variables with the common c.f. ϕ_p. The c.f. of the sum $S = (\theta_1 + \ldots + \theta_n)(\text{mod } 2\pi)$ is $\phi_p{}^n$. From (3.4.10),

$$\phi_p{}^n = 1 \quad \text{if} \quad p = 0;$$
$$= 0 \quad \text{if} \quad p \neq 0,$$

which is similar to (3.4.10). Hence from the uniqueness theorem (Section 4.2.1), S_n is again uniformly distributed over $(0, 2\pi)$. In fact, under a mild condition, we shall see in Section 4.3.2a that this result is true for any independent and identically distributed random variables $\theta_1, \ldots, \theta_n$ as $n \to \infty$.

Furthermore, let θ_1 be distributed uniformly and let θ_2 have any distribution whatsoever. If θ_1 and θ_2 are independently distributed, the c.f. of $\xi = \theta_1 + \theta_2 \,(\text{mod } 2\pi)$ is unity if $p = 0$ and is zero otherwise. Hence, by the uniqueness theorem (Section 4.2.1), ξ is distributed uniformly over $(0, 2\pi)$.

3.4.5. The Cardioid Distribution

Let

$$f(\theta) = (2\pi)^{-1} [1 + 2\rho \cos(\theta - \theta_0)], \qquad 0 < \theta \leqslant 2\pi, \quad |\rho| < \tfrac{1}{2}. \quad (3.4.11)$$

The polar representation of this density is a cardioid curve. The distribution was introduced by Jeffreys (1948, p. 302).

The distribution is symmetrical and unimodal. For $\rho = 0$, it reduces to the uniform distribution and, therefore, for small ρ it represents a slight departure from uniformity. We have $\theta_0 = \mu_0$ and $V_0 = 1 - \rho$. From (2.6.5), its mean deviation about the direction $\theta_0 = 0$ is given by

$$\delta_0 = E\{\pi - |\pi - \theta|\} = \frac{\pi}{2} - \frac{4}{\pi} + \frac{4V_0}{\pi}. \quad (3.4.12)$$

3.4.6. Triangular Distributions

Consider

$$f(\theta) = \frac{1}{8\pi} \{4 - \pi^2\rho + 2\pi\rho \,|\pi - \theta|\}, \qquad 0 < \theta \leqslant 2\pi, \quad \rho \leqslant 4/\pi^2. \quad (3.4.13)$$

The distribution is symmetric about $\theta = 0$. We have

$$\alpha_{2p-1} = \rho/(2p - 1)^2, \qquad \alpha_{2p} = 0, \qquad \beta_p = 0. \quad (3.4.14)$$

For the asymmetric distribution with p.d.f.

$$f(\theta) = \frac{1}{2\pi}\{1 + \rho(\theta - \pi)\}, \qquad 0 < \theta \leqslant 2\pi, \quad 0 < \rho \leqslant 1/\pi, \qquad (3.4.15)$$

we have

$$\alpha_p = 0, \qquad \beta_p = (-1)^{p-1}\rho/p, \qquad (3.4.16)$$

and

$$\mu_0 = \pi/2, \qquad V_0 = 1 - \rho.$$

Their Fourier expansions are immediate from (3.4.14) and (3.4.16).

3.4.7. The Offset Normal Distribution

Let $\phi(x, y; \mathbf{\mu}, \mathbf{\Sigma})$ be the p.d.f. of the bivariate normal distribution with mean vector $\mathbf{\mu} = (\mu, v)$ and covariance matrix $\mathbf{\Sigma}$. Let ρ denote the correlation between the variables and let σ_1^2 and σ_2^2 be their variances. Suppose that $\Phi(x)$ is the d.f. of $N(0, 1)$. On using the result

$$d^2 \int_0^\infty r \exp\{-\tfrac{1}{2}d^2(r^2 - 2br)\}\, dr = 1 + (2\pi)^{\frac{1}{2}} bd\, e^{\frac{1}{2}b^2 d^2}\, \Phi(bd),$$

and $x = r\cos\theta$, $y = r\sin\theta$, we find that the p.d.f. of θ is given by

$$p(\theta; \mu, v, \sigma_1, \sigma_2, \rho) = \{C(\theta)\}^{-1}\{\phi(\mu, v; 0, \mathbf{\Sigma}) + aD(\theta)\, \Phi\{D(\theta)\}$$
$$\times\, \phi[a\{C(\theta)\}^{-\frac{1}{2}}(\mu\sin\theta - v\cos\theta)]\}, \qquad (3.4.17)$$

where

$$a = \{\sigma_1\sigma_2(1 - \rho^2)^{\frac{1}{2}}\}^{-1},$$

$$C(\theta) = a^2(\sigma_2^2\cos^2\theta - \rho\sigma_1\sigma_2\sin 2\theta + \sigma_1^2\sin^2\theta),$$

$$D(\theta) = a^2\{C(\theta)\}^{-\frac{1}{2}}\{\mu\sigma_2(\sigma_2\cos\theta - \rho\sigma_1\sin\theta) + v\sigma_1(\sigma_1\sin\theta - \rho\sigma_2\cos\theta)\},$$

and $\phi(x)$ is the p.d.f. of $N(0, 1)$. Particular cases of interest are

$$p(\theta; 0, 0, 1, 1, \rho) = (1 - \rho^2)^{\frac{1}{2}}/\{2\pi(1 - \rho\sin 2\theta)\}, \qquad (3.4.18)$$

$$p(\theta; \mu, 0, 1, 1, 0) = (2\pi)^{-\frac{1}{2}}\phi(\mu) + \mu\cos\theta\, \phi(\mu\sin\theta)\, \Phi(\mu\cos\theta), \quad (3.4.19)$$

and

$$p(\theta; 0, 0, \sigma_1, \sigma_2, 0) = (1 - b^2)^{\frac{1}{2}}/\{2\pi(1 - b\cos 2\theta)\}, \qquad (3.4.20)$$

where

$$b = (\sigma_1^2 - \sigma_2^2)/(\sigma_1^2 + \sigma_2^2), \qquad |b| \leqslant 1.$$

Further, (3.4.17) reduces to the uniform distribution if and only if $\mu = v = 0$, $\sigma_1 = \sigma_2$ and $\rho = 0$.

The distribution (3.4.20) is the asymptotic distribution of the mean direction under certain conditions (Section 4.8). The distribution (3.4.19) appears in studying the power of a test (Klotz, 1964). In the study of wind directions, (3.4.20) is generally used by meteorologists since it is the p.d.f of the wind direction under the assumption that the x and y components of the wind velocity are independently distributed as $N(0, \sigma_1)$ and $N(0, \sigma_2)$, respectively. However, the distribution theory necessary for statistical inference under this assumption is formidable.

3.4.8. Wrapped Distributions

3.4.8a. *Definition*

Given a distribution on the line, we can wrap it around the circumference of the circle of unit radius. That is, if x is a random variable on the line with d.f. $F(x)$, the random variable x_w of the wrapped distribution is given by

$$x_w = x \,(\mathrm{mod}\,2\pi),\qquad\qquad (3.4.21)$$

and the d.f. of x_w is given by

$$F_w(\theta) = \sum_{k=-\infty}^{\infty} \{F(\theta + 2\pi k) - F(2\pi k)\}, \qquad 0 < \theta \leqslant 2\pi. \qquad (3.4.22)$$

In particular, if x has a distribution concentrated on the points $x = k/(2\pi m)$, $k = 0, \pm 1, \pm 2, \dots$ and m is an integer, we have

$$p_w(\theta = 2\pi r/m) = \sum_{k=-\infty}^{\infty} p(\theta + 2\pi k), \qquad r = 0, 1, \dots, m-1, \qquad (3.4.23)$$

where p and p_w are the probability functions of x and x_w respectively. Similarly, if x has a p.d.f. $f(x)$, the corresponding p.d.f. of x_w is

$$f_w(\theta) = \sum_{k=-\infty}^{\infty} f(\theta + 2\pi k). \qquad (3.4.24)$$

3.4.8b. *Properties*

(a)   If $\phi(t)$ is the c.f. of x then the c.f. of x_w is simply $\phi(p)$. Since,

$$\phi_p = \int_0^{2\pi} e^{ip\theta}\,\mathrm{d}F_w(\theta) = \sum_{k=-\infty}^{\infty} \int_{2\pi k}^{2\pi(k+1)} e^{ip\theta}\,\mathrm{d}F(\theta)$$

$$= \int_{-\infty}^{\infty} e^{ipx}\,\mathrm{d}F(x) = \phi(p). \qquad (3.4.25)$$

(b) If $\phi(t)$ is integrable then x has a density and

$$f_w(\theta) = \sum_{k=-\infty}^{\infty} f(\theta + 2\pi k) = \frac{1}{2\pi}\left[1 + 2\sum_{p=1}^{\infty} (\alpha_p \cos p\theta + \beta_p \sin p\theta)\right], \quad (3.4.26)$$

where $\phi(p) = \alpha_p + i\beta_p$.

Since $\phi(t)$ is integrable, we have

$$\Sigma|\phi_p|^2 < \Sigma|\phi_p| < \int_{-\infty}^{\infty}|\phi(t)|\,dt.$$

Therefore the series $\Sigma(\alpha_p^2 + \beta_p^2)$ is convergent and the result follows from (3.2.9) and (3.4.24). It can also be derived from the Poisson summation formula.

(c) If x is infinitely divisible then x_w is also infinitely divisible.

(d) The wrapping of the fractional part of a random variable x can be achieved simply by the transformation

$$\theta = 2\pi(x - [x]),$$

where $[x]$ denotes the integral part of x.

(e) The process of unwrapping a distribution on the circle does not lead to a unique distribution on the line so that the process of wrapping is not reversible.

Let $g(\theta)$ be the p.d.f. of a distribution on the circle. We can construct the following p.d.f.* on the line which when wrapped leads to $g(\theta)$.

$$f(x) = p_r g(x), \qquad 2\pi r < x \leqslant 2\pi(r + 1), \qquad r = 0, \pm1, \pm2, \ldots$$

where p_r are any non-negative numbers such that $\Sigma p_r = 1$.

We now consider some important particular cases.

3.4.8c. The Wrapped Poisson Distribution

Consider the probability function of the Poisson distribution

$$p(x; \lambda) = e^{-\lambda}\lambda^x/x!, \qquad x = 0, 1, \ldots; \quad \lambda > 0. \qquad (3.4.27)$$

From (3.4.23), the wrapped Poisson distribution is defined by

$$\text{Pr}\,(\theta = 2\pi r/m) = \sum_{k=0}^{\infty} p(r + km; \lambda), \qquad r = 0, 1, \ldots, m - 1,$$

where m is an integer. It can be seen that the probabilities are decreasing

*This example was communicated to me by Dr. M. S. Bingham.

functions of r. From (3.4.25), the c.f. of θ is

$$\phi_p = \exp\left(-\lambda + \lambda e^{2\pi p i/m}\right).$$

Hence, it possesses the additive property.

This distribution appears in the study of distributions of triangular arrays on the circle (Lévy, 1939).

3.4.8d. *The Wrapped Normal Distribution*

Let x be $N(0, \sigma)$. From (3.4.24), the p.d.f. of the wrapped normal distribution is given by

$$f_w(\theta) = \frac{1}{\sigma\sqrt{2\pi}} \sum_{k=-\infty}^{\infty} \exp\left(-\frac{1}{2}\frac{(\theta + 2\pi k)^2}{\sigma^2}\right), \qquad 0 < \theta \leq 2\pi. \qquad (3.4.28)$$

Since the c.f. of $N(0, \sigma)$ is $\exp\left(-\frac{1}{2}t^2\sigma^2\right)$, (3.4.25) gives

$$\phi_p = \alpha_p = e^{-\frac{1}{2}p^2\sigma^2}, \qquad \beta_p = 0. \qquad (3.4.29)$$

On using this result in (3.4.26), we obtain a useful representation of the density

$$f_w(\theta) = \left(1 + 2\sum_{p=1}^{\infty} \rho^{p^2} \cos p\theta\right)\Big/(2\pi), \qquad 0 < \theta \leq 2\pi, \quad 0 \leq \rho \leq 1, \qquad (3.4.30)$$

where

$$\rho = e^{-\frac{1}{2}\sigma^2}, \qquad \sigma^2 = -2\log\rho. \qquad (3.4.31)$$

This relation between (3.4.28) and (3.4.31) is a famous transformation formula from the theory of theta functions (Bellman, 1961, p.11). We further have

$$\mu_0 = 0, \quad \alpha = \rho, \quad \alpha_2 = \rho^4, \quad V_0 = 1 - \rho, \quad \sigma = \{-2\log(1 - V_0)\}^{\frac{1}{2}},$$
$$(3.4.32)$$

where ρ is given by (3.4.31).

The distribution is unimodal and is symmetric about $\theta = 0$. As $\rho \to 0$ it tends to the uniform distribution while as $\rho \to 1$ it is concentrated at one single point. The distribution in general has two points of inflection. The d.f. can be obtained on integrating the series (3.4.30) term by term.

Numerical values of the p.d.f. (3.4.28) can be obtained on using the relation

$$f_w(\theta) = (2\pi)^{-1}\, \vartheta_3(\theta, \rho),$$

where ϑ_3 is a zeta function. Schuler and Gebelein (1955, Tables 3 and 4) have tabulated

$$\vartheta_3(\tfrac{1}{2}\cos^{-1} x, \rho), \qquad -1 \leqslant x \leqslant 1, \qquad 0 \leqslant \rho \leqslant 0.5.$$

For practical purposes, the first three terms of (3.4.30) suffice for $\sigma^2 \geqslant 2\pi$ while for $\sigma^2 \leqslant 2\pi$ the central term of (3.4.28) can be used.

The distribution possesses the additive property. Let $\theta_1, ..., \theta_n$ be independent variables and let θ_i have the p.d.f. (3.4.30) with $\rho = \rho_i$. The c.f. of the sum of $\theta_1, ..., \theta_n$ is

$$\left(\prod_{i=1}^{n} \rho_i\right)^{p^2}.$$

Hence by the uniqueness theorem and (3.4.29), the distribution is again of the form (3.4.30).

The wrapped normal distribution appears in the central limit theorem on the circle (Section 4.3.2b). It also appears in Brownian motion on the circle. In fact, if in a continuous time random walk (i) a particle starts at $\theta = 0$ at time $t = 0$, (ii) the particle moves infinitesimal distances in infinitesimal time periods, and (iii) the mean zero and the variance is $\sigma^2 = ct$ at time t, then the p.d.f. of the position of the particle at time t is given by (3.4.28) with $\sigma^2 = ct$. This result was first obtained by de Hass–Lorentz (1913, pp. 24–25). Stephens (1963a) has given a proof in which it is assumed that the steps are symmetrically distributed. The result may also be derived as a special case of Theorem 6.2 of M. S. Bingham (1971).

Amongst others, Zernkie (1928), Wintner (1933) and Lévy (1939) have studied this distribution.

3.4.8e. *The Wrapped Cauchy Distribution*

Consider, the Cauchy distribution on the real line with density

$$f(\theta; a) = \frac{1}{\pi} \frac{a}{a^2 + x^2}, \qquad -\infty < x < \infty, \quad a > 0.$$

Its c.f. is $e^{-a|t|}$. Consequently, from (3.4.26), we find that the wrapped Cauchy distribution has the density

$$c(\theta; \rho) = \sum_{k=-\infty}^{\infty} f(\theta + 2\pi k; a) = (2\pi)^{-1}\left(1 + 2\sum_{p=1}^{\infty} \rho^p \cos p\theta\right), \qquad (3.4.33)$$

where $\rho = e^{-a}$. By considering the real part of the geometric series

$$\sum_{p=1}^{\infty} \rho^p e^{-ip\theta}$$

(3.4.33) reduces to

$$c(\theta; \rho) = \frac{1}{2\pi} \frac{1 - \rho^2}{1 + \rho^2 - 2\rho \cos \theta}, \qquad 0 < \theta \leqslant 2\pi, \quad 0 \leqslant \rho \leqslant 1. \qquad (3.4.34)$$

Further,

$$\phi_p = \rho^{|p|}, \quad \alpha_p = \rho^p, \quad \beta_p = 0, \quad V_0 = 1 - \rho. \qquad (3.4.35)$$

This distribution is again unimodal and symmetric. As $\rho \to 0$, it tends to the uniform distribution and as $\rho \to 1$ it is concentrated at the point $\theta = 0$. Its d.f. is given by

$$C(\theta; \rho) = (2\pi)^{-1} \arccos \left\{ \frac{(1 + \rho^2) \cos \theta - 2\rho}{1 + \rho^2 - 2\rho \cos \theta} \right\}, \qquad 0 \leqslant \theta \leqslant 2\pi \qquad (3.4.36)$$

It possesses the additive property. The p.d.f. $c(\theta; \rho)$ as a function of θ and ρ is the Poisson kernel (see Section 4.2.1).

This distribution was first introduced by Lévy (1939) and has also been studied by Wintner (1947). Using the c.f. of the most general stable univariate distribution (Lukacs, 1970, p. 136), we find that the p.d.f. of the corresponding wrapped distribution is

$$(2\pi)^{-1} [1 + 2\Sigma \rho^{p^a} \cos \{p(\theta - \theta_0) + bp^a\}], \qquad 0 < \theta \leqslant 2\pi, \quad 0 \leqslant a \leqslant 2.$$

For $b = 0$, Wintner (1947) proves that the distribution has a unique mode at $\theta = \theta_0$. This density, of course, includes the wrapped normal and the wrapped Cauchy distributions. The wrapped Karl Pearson family is more complicated (Mardia, 1971).

3.4.9. The von Mises Distribution

3.4.9a. *Definition*

A circular random variable θ is said to have a von Mises distribution if its p.d.f. is given by

$$g(\theta; \mu_0, \kappa) = \frac{1}{2\pi I_0(\kappa)} e^{\kappa \cos(\theta - \mu_0)}, \qquad 0 < \theta \leqslant 2\pi, \quad \kappa > 0, \quad 0 \leqslant \mu_0 < 2\pi, \qquad (3.4.37)$$

where $I_0(\kappa)$ is the modified Bessel function of the first kind and order zero, i.e.

$$I_0(\kappa) = \sum_{r=0}^{\infty} \frac{1}{r!^2} (\tfrac{1}{2}\kappa)^{2r}. \qquad (3.4.38)$$

The parameter μ_0 is the mean direction while the parameter κ is described as the concentration parameter for the reason given in Sections 3.4.9b and

3.4.9c. If a random variable θ has its p.d.f. of the form (3.4.37), we will say that it is distributed as $M(\mu_0, \kappa)$.*

This distribution was introduced by von Mises (1918) to study the deviations of measured atomic weights from integral values. It plays a prominent role in statistical inference on the circle and its importance there is almost the same as that of the normal distribution on the line. Various characterizations of this distribution, analogous to those of the linear normal distribution, are given in Section 3.4.9f. Section 3.4.10 discusses the question of its appropriateness as the 'normal distribution on the circle'. Examples 5.2–5.3 discuss the fitting of this distribution to typical data.

We now verify that for the distribution (3.4.37) the total probability is unity, i.e.

$$\int_0^{2\pi} e^{\kappa \cos \theta} \, d\theta = 2\pi I_0(\kappa). \tag{3.4.39}$$

Expanding the exponential term in the left-hand side, it becomes

$$\sum_{r=0}^{\infty} \frac{\kappa^r}{r!} T_r, \tag{3.4.40}$$

where

$$T_r = \int_0^{2\pi} \cos^r \theta \, d\theta.$$

On integrating by parts (one of the parts being $\cos \theta$), we have

$$T_r = \{(r-1)/r\} \, T_{r-2}$$

so that

$$T_{2r} = 2\pi \binom{2r}{r} \bigg/ 2^{2r}, \qquad T_{2r+1} = 0.$$

Substituting this result in (3.4.40) and using (3.4.38), we obtain (3.4.39).

We now give various properties of this distribution.

3.4.9b. *The Shape of the Distribution*

The distribution is unimodal and is symmetrical about $\theta = \mu_0$. The mode is at $\theta = \mu_0$ and the antimode is at $\theta = \mu_0 + \pi$. The ratio of the density at the mode to the density at the antimode is given by $e^{2\kappa}$ so that the larger the value of κ, the greater is the clustering around the mode. Let $\mu_0 = 0$. It has two inflexion points which are given by

$$\pm \arccos \left\{ -\frac{1}{2\kappa} + \left(1 + \frac{1}{4\kappa^2} \right)^{\frac{1}{2}} \right\} .$$

*Note that $M(\mu_0 + \pi, \kappa)$ and $M(\mu_0, -\kappa)$ are the same distribution. To eliminate this indeterminancy of the parameters μ_0, κ, we shall always take $\kappa > 0$ and $0 \leqslant \mu_0 < 2\pi$.

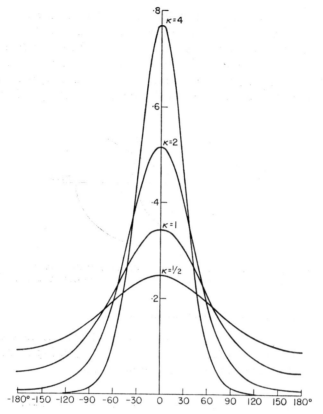

FIG. 3.1. Density of the von Mises distribution for $\mu_0 = 0°$ and $\kappa = \frac{1}{2}, 1, 2, 4$.

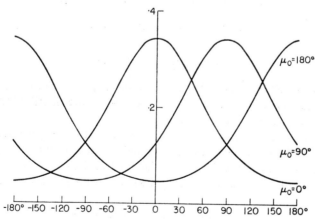

FIG. 3.2. Density of the von Mises distribution for $\kappa = 1$ and $\mu_0 = 0°, 90°, 180°$.

For large values of κ, the points reduce to $\pm\kappa^{-\frac{1}{2}}$ which are comparable to the inflexion points $\pm\sigma$ for $N(0, \sigma)$. Hence, for large κ the distribution is clustered around the mean direction. Figure 3.1 shows the density for $\mu_0 = 0$ and $\kappa = \frac{1}{2}, 1, 2, 4$. For $\kappa = 4$, the distribution lies almost within the arc $(270°, 90°)$. Figure 3.2 shows the density for $\kappa = 1$ and $\mu_0 = 0°, 90°, 180°$. Figure 3.3 gives a polar representation of the density for $\mu_0 = 0$ and $\kappa = 1$.

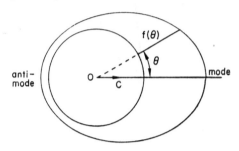

FIG. 3.3. Polar diagram of the density of the von Mises distribution for $\mu_0 = 0°$ and $\kappa = 1$. The mean vector is represented by $\overline{OC}$, $\rho = OC = 0.45$. (Batschelet, 1965).

3.4.9c. *Its Relation with Other Distributions*

For $\kappa = 0$, we see from (3.4.37) that $M(\mu_0, \kappa)$ reduces to the uniform distribution. For small values of κ, we find on neglecting terms of order κ^2, κ^4, ... that it reduces to the cardioid distribution

$$f(\theta) = \frac{1}{2\pi}\{1 + \tfrac{1}{2}\kappa \cos(\theta - \mu_0)\}, \qquad 0 < \theta \leqslant 2\pi.$$

Let $\theta - \mu_0 = \xi/\kappa^{\frac{1}{2}}$ where κ is large. Then from (3.4.37)

$$g(\xi) = \text{const. exp}\{\kappa \cos(\xi/\kappa^{\frac{1}{2}})\}. \qquad (3.4.41)$$

Now,

$$\cos(\xi/\kappa^{\frac{1}{2}}) \doteq 1 - (\xi^2/2\kappa)$$

so that from (3.4.41), ξ is $N(0, 1)$. Hence for large κ, the random variable θ is distributed as $N(\mu_0, 1/\kappa^{\frac{1}{2}})$. Further, as $\kappa \to \infty$, the distribution becomes concentrated at the point $\theta = \mu_0$.

The von Mises distribution is also related to the bivariate normal distribution as follows. Let x and y be independent normal variables with means $(\cos \mu_0, \sin \mu_0)$ and equal variances $1/\kappa$. This construction ensures that the mean lies on the unit circle. The p.d.f. of the polar variables (r, θ) is

$$\text{const. } r \exp\left[-\frac{\kappa}{2}\{r^2 - 2r \cos(\theta - \mu_0)\}\right]. \qquad (3.4.42)$$

Since the range of r does not depend on θ, the conditional distribution of θ for $r = 1$ is $M(\mu_0, \kappa)$. This construction follows from an argument of Fisher (1959, p. 137).

The above relations of the von Mises distribution with other distributions and the properties in Section 3.4.9b clearly indicate that μ_0 behaves like the mean while $1/\kappa$ influences the von Mises distribution in the same way as σ^2 influences the normal distribution. For $\kappa = 0$ the distribution is uniform while for large κ the distribution is clustered around the direction μ_0. Consequently, κ is generally described as the concentration parameter. Its relation with V_0, which is not simple, is given below in (3.4.47).

We shall give the relation of the von Mises distribution with the wrapped normal distribution in Section 3.4.9g.

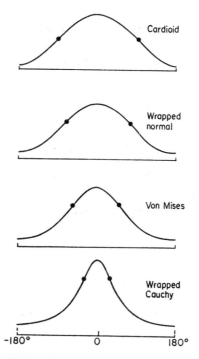

FIG. 3.4. A comparison of four unimodal symmetric distributions with $\mu_0 = 0°$, $\rho = 0.45$ ($\kappa = 1$). The dots are the points of inflexion (Batschelet, 1965).

Figure 3.4 gives a comparison of four important symmetric unimodal distributions with the same values of the ρ. Their shapes differ somewhat as is evident from their points of inflexion.

3.4.9d. *Characteristic Function and Moments*

Let us take $\mu_0 = 0$. Since the distribution is symmetrical about $\theta = 0$, we have

$$\beta_p = E\,(\sin p\theta) = 0. \qquad (3.4.43)$$

Consequently,

$$\phi_p = \alpha_p = \frac{1}{2\pi I_0(\kappa)} \int_0^{2\pi} \cos p\theta \; e^{\kappa \cos \theta} \, d\theta.$$

On expanding the exponential term, we have

$$\phi_p = \sum_{r=0}^{\infty} \frac{\kappa^r}{r!} \, T_{r,p}, \qquad (3.4.44)$$

where

$$T_{r,p} = \int_0^{2\pi} \cos^r \theta \cos p\theta \, d\theta.$$

On integrating $T_{r,p}$ by parts twice ($\cos p\theta$ and $\sin p\theta$ being the successive part integrated), we have

$$T_{r,p} = \{r(r-1)/(r^2 - p^2)\} \, T_{r-2,p}, \quad r \neq p,$$

and

$$T_{p,p} = \tfrac{1}{2} T_{p-1,p-1}.$$

Consequently,

$$T_{r,p} = 0 \quad \text{if} \quad r < p,$$

and

$$T_{2r+p,p} = 2\pi \binom{2r+p}{r} \Big/ 2^{2r+p}, \quad T_{2r+1+p,p} = 0.$$

Hence, we find from (3.4.44) that

$$\phi_p = \alpha_p = I_p(\kappa)/I_0(\kappa), \qquad (3.4.45)$$

where

$$I_p(\kappa) = \sum_{r=0}^{\infty} \{(\Gamma(p + r + 1)\,\Gamma(r + 1)\}^{-1} \left(\frac{\kappa}{2}\right)^{2r+p}. \qquad (3.4.46)$$

The function $I_p(\kappa)$ is the modified Bessel function of the first kind and of the pth order.

In particular, we have for $\mu_0 \neq 0$,

$$\alpha = A(\kappa) \cos \mu_0, \quad \beta = A(\kappa) \sin \mu_0, \quad \rho = A(\kappa), \quad V_0 = 1 - A(\kappa), \quad (3.4.47)$$

where we shall always denote the ratio (for the resultant length ρ)

$$I_1(\kappa)/I_0(\kappa) = A(\kappa).$$

The relation between V_0 and A is hardly simple. However, its behaviour for small κ can be studied from

$$A(\kappa) = \tfrac{1}{2}\kappa\,[1 - \tfrac{1}{8}\kappa^2 + \tfrac{1}{48}\kappa^4 - \ldots]. \qquad (3.4.48)$$

This relation follows upon using the series definitions $I_0(\kappa)$ and $I_1(\kappa)$ given by (3.4.46). For large κ, we have the following asymptotic series (see, Abramowitz and Stegun, 1965, p. 377)

$$I_p(\kappa) \sim (2\pi\kappa)^{-\frac{1}{2}} e^\kappa \left\{ 1 - \frac{(m-1)}{8\kappa} + \frac{(m-1)(m-9)}{2!(8\kappa)^2} \right.$$
$$\left. - \frac{(m-1)(m-9)(m-25)}{3!(8\kappa)^3} + \ldots \right\}, \qquad (3.4.49)$$

where $m = 4p^2$. On using this expansion, we have

$$A(\kappa) \sim 1 - \frac{1}{2\kappa} - \frac{1}{8\kappa^2} - \frac{1}{8\kappa^3} + o(\kappa^{-3}). \qquad (3.4.50)$$

Further, we show that

$$\alpha_2 = I_2(\kappa)/I_0(\kappa) = 1 - 2\{A(\kappa)/\kappa\}. \qquad (3.4.51)$$

By directly differentiating the series for $I_1(\kappa)$ given in (3.4.46) we find that

$$\frac{d}{d\kappa}\{\kappa I_1(\kappa)\} = \kappa I_0(\kappa), \qquad \frac{d}{d\kappa}\{I_1(\kappa)/\kappa\} = I_2(\kappa)/\kappa. \qquad (3.4.52)$$

On eliminating the derivative of $I_1(\kappa)$, we obtain

$$I_2(\kappa) = I_0(\kappa) - \{2I_1(\kappa)/\kappa\} \qquad (3.4.53)$$

which establishes (3.4.51).

In passing we note that the von Mises distribution may be regarded as the wrapped distribution of the random variable on the line having the c.f. $I_{|t|}(\kappa)/I_0(\kappa)$, although, as we have seen in Section 3.4.8b, the process of unwrapping is not unique.

3.4.9e. *The Distribution Function*

From (3.2.9) and (3.4.45), we have the Fourier expansion for the p.d.f. of $M(0, \kappa)$ as

$$g(\theta; 0, \kappa) = \frac{1}{2\pi I_0(\kappa)} \left\{ I_0(\kappa) + 2 \sum_{p=1}^{\infty} I_p(\kappa) \cos p\theta \right\}. \qquad (3.4.54)$$

Consequently, the corresponding d.f. is

$$G(\theta;0,\kappa) = \frac{1}{2\pi I_0(\kappa)} \left[\theta I_0(\kappa) + 2 \sum_{p=0}^{\infty} \{I_p(\kappa)\sin p\theta\}/p \right]. \qquad (3.4.55)$$

This expression has been used by Gumbel, et al. (1953) for calculating the distribution function. The d.f. can also be expressed in terms of the incomplete beta function, viz.

$$G(\theta;0,\kappa) = \frac{1}{4\pi I_0(\kappa)} \left[\sum_{p=0}^{\infty} \frac{\kappa^p}{p!} \int_0^{\sin^2\theta} x^{-\frac{1}{2}}(1-x)^{\frac{1}{2}p-\frac{1}{2}} dx \right].$$

The result follows on using the definition of the d.f., expanding the exponential term and integrating it term by term.

Gumbel *et al.* (1953) have tabulated $2G(\theta;0,\kappa)$ for $\theta = 0°(5°)180°$, $\kappa = 0(\cdot 2)4$. Batschelet (1965) has given $G(\theta;\pi,\kappa)$ for $\theta = 0°(5°)360°$, $\kappa = 0(\cdot 2)10$. An excerpt of this table is in Appendix 2.1 which gives

$$G(\alpha;0,\kappa) = \Pr(-\pi < \theta < -\pi + \alpha), \qquad 0 \leqslant \alpha \leqslant \pi, \quad \kappa \leqslant 10,$$

where the range of θ is $(-\pi, \pi)$. The values of G for $\alpha \geqslant \pi$ may be obtained from

$$\Pr(-\pi < \theta < -\pi + \alpha) = 1 - G(2\pi - \alpha;0,\kappa).$$

From $\kappa > 10$, the distribution can be approximated satisfactorily by $N(\mu_0, \{\kappa - \frac{1}{2}\}^{-\frac{1}{2}})$. This approximation for large κ was derived in Section 3.4.9c.

3.4.9f. *Some Characterizations*

We now give two characterizations of the von Mises distribution which on the line produce the normal distribution. The first characterization is due to von Mises (1918) while the second characterization is new. We also discuss some other characterizations.

The Maximum Likelihood Characterization. Let $f(x - \mu)$ be a p.d.f. on the line. Gauss proved that the sample mean $\bar{x}$ is the maximum likelihood estimate of μ if and only if the random variable x is normal. Analogously, let $g(\theta - \mu_0)$ be a p.d.f. on the circle and let us assume that the maximum likelihood estimate of μ_0 is the sample mean direction $\bar{x}_0$ so that

$$\sum_{i=1}^{n} g'(\theta_i - \bar{x}_0)/g(\theta_i - \bar{x}_0) = 0 \qquad (3.4.56)$$

where, by the definition of $\bar{x}_0$ (Section 2.2.2.),

$$\sum_{i=1}^{n} \sin (\theta_i - \bar{x}_0) = 0. \tag{3.4.57}$$

Since the equations (3.4.56) and (3.4.57) are identical for each n, we have

$$g'(\theta - \bar{x}_0)/g(\theta - \bar{x}_0) = \text{const. } \sin (\theta - \bar{x}_0).$$

Replacing $\bar{x}_0$ by μ_0, we observe that $g(\theta)$ is the p.d.f. of a von Mises distribution. Hence, we get the characterization due to von Mises (1918).

The Maximum Entropy Characterization. The entropy of a distribution with p.d.f. $f(\theta)$ is defined to be

$$-\int_0^{2\pi} f(\theta) \log f(\theta)\, d\theta. \tag{3.4.58}$$

We show that the von Mises distribution has the maximum entropy under the condition that the mean direction and the circular variance are fixed, i.e.

$$\int_0^{2\pi} \cos \theta f(\theta)\, d\theta = \rho \cos \mu_0, \quad \int_0^{2\pi} \sin \theta f(\theta)\, d\theta = \rho \sin \mu_0, \tag{3.4.59}$$

where ρ and μ_0 have preassigned values. From Information Theory, we have (see Rao, 1965, p. 47)

$$-\int_0^{2\pi} f \log (f/g)\, d\theta \leqslant 0, \tag{3.4.60}$$

where f and g are two densities. The equality holds only when f and g are almost everywhere equal.

Let us choose $g(\theta)$ as

$$\log g(\theta) = b \cos (\theta - v) + c, \tag{3.4.61}$$

where b, v and c are determined such that $g(\theta)$ satisfies (3.4.59) and the total probability is one. That is,

$$v = \mu_0, c = - \log \{2\pi I_0(b)\} \tag{3.4.62}$$

and b is the solution of the equation

$$\{I_1(b)/I_0(b)\} = \rho. \tag{3.4.63}$$

On using (3.4.61) in (3.4.60), we obtain

$$-\int_0^{2\pi} f\log f\,d\theta \leqslant -\int_0^{2\pi}(b\cos\theta\cos v + b\sin\theta\sin v + c)f\,d\theta$$

which with the help of (3.4.59) and (3.4.62) reduces to

$$-\int_0^{2\pi} f\log f\,d\theta \leqslant -(b\rho + 2\pi c) = D, \quad \text{say.}$$

Consequently, D is a fixed upper bound to the entropy under the condition (3.4.59). Using (3.4.62) and (3.4.63), it can easily be seen that this bound is actually attained when f is chosen as g. Hence, we get the required result.

If f is not restricted by the condition (3.4.59), the entropy is maximum for the uniform distribution on $(0, 2\pi)$ by a similar argument. The normal distribution maximises the entropy on the line when μ and σ^2 are fixed (see Rao, 1965, pp. 131–132).

In Section 3.4.9c, we have obtained the von Mises distribution as a conditional distribution. The construction is, of course, not unique. For example, a bivariate normal distribution with mean vector $\{(\cos\mu_0)/\kappa,$ $(\sin\mu_0)/\kappa\}$, variances $1/\kappa^2$ and correlation coefficient zero again leads to the von Mises distribution. Downs (1966) has given a converse result.

Pólya (1930) has shown that the distribution on the line for which the mean and the mode of the likelihood function are equal leads to the normal distribution as a limiting case. Its circular analogue produces the von Mises distribution.

3.4.9g. Relation with the Wrapped Normal Distribution

The wrapped normal and the von Mises distributions can be made to approximate each other closely (Stephens, 1963a). By equating their first trigonometric moments, we can relate their parameters. In fact, from (3.4.31) and (3.4.47)

$$e^{-\frac{1}{2}\sigma^2} = A(\kappa). \tag{3.4.64}$$

As $\kappa \to 0$ then $\sigma \to \infty$ and both distributions tend to the uniform distribution while as $\kappa \to \infty$ then $\sigma \to 0$ and both distributions tend to the same point distribution. Hence there is exact agreement for the extreme cases. Stephens (1963a) has also verified numerically that the agreement is satisfactory for intermediate values.

This relationship can be used to draw a random sample from $M(\mu_0, \kappa)$. For given κ, we obtain the corresponding σ from (3.4.64). By following any standard method, a random sample from $N(\mu_0, \sigma)$ can then be drawn which, with the help of the transformation

$$x_\omega = x \,(\text{mod } 2\pi),$$

leads to a random sample from the wrapped normal distribution. In view of the approximation above, this random sample from the wrapped normal distribution may be regarded as a random sample from $M(\mu_0, \kappa)$.

3.4.9h. *Convolutions of von Mises Distributions*

Let θ_1 and θ_2 be independently distributed as $M(\mu_0, \kappa_1)$ and $M(v_0, \kappa_2)$ respectively. On using the convolution formula (3.2.13) the p.d.f. of $\theta = \theta_1 + \theta_2 \,(\text{mod } 2\pi)$ is given by

$$\{4\pi^2 I_0(\kappa_1) I_0(\kappa_2)\}^{-1} \int_0^{2\pi} e^{r \cos(\xi - \beta)} \, d\xi,$$

where

$$r \cos \beta = \kappa_1 + \kappa_2 \cos(\theta - \alpha), \quad r \sin \beta = \kappa_2 \sin(\theta - \alpha), \quad \alpha = \mu_0 + v_0.$$

With the help of the result (3.4.39), the p.d.f. of θ simplifies to

$$h(\theta) = \{2\pi I_0(\kappa_1) I_0(\kappa_2)\}^{-1} I_0[\{\kappa_1^2 + \kappa_2^2 + 2\kappa_1\kappa_2 \cos(\theta - \alpha)\}^{\frac{1}{2}}], \qquad (3.4.65)$$

where $\alpha = \mu_0 + v_0$. For $\kappa_1 = \kappa_2 = \kappa$, the expression within the square brackets reduces to $2\kappa \cos \frac{1}{2}(\theta - \alpha)$ but the distribution still remains complicated. Further, the convolution of von Mises distributions is not von Mises distribution. However, we can approximate (3.4.65) by a von Mises distribution. Without any loss of generality, let us assume that μ_0 and v_0 are zero. From Section 3.4.9g, the distributions $M(0, \kappa_1)$ and $M(0, \kappa_2)$ can be approximated by the wrapped normal distributions with σ_1^2 and σ_2^2 defined by (3.4.64). In view of the additive property of the wrapped normal distribution (Section 3.4.8d), the convolution of these two distributions is again a wrapped normal distribution with parameter $\sigma_3^2 = \sigma_1^2 + \sigma_2^2$ which in turn can be approximated by $M(0, \kappa_3)$ where κ_3 is the solution of

$$A(\kappa_3) = A(\kappa_1) A(\kappa_2). \qquad (3.4.66)$$

Thus

$$\theta_1 + \theta_2 \,(\text{mod } 2\pi) \simeq M(\mu_0 + v_0, \kappa_3). \qquad (3.4.67)$$

Numerical studies have shown that this approximation is quite satisfactory (see Stephens, 1963a).

The p.d.f. of an n-fold convolution of von Mises distributions can easily be obtained on substituting the c.f. of the sum into the Fourier series (3.2.9). On equating this expression for $n = 2$ to (3.4.65), we get a simple proof of the famous von Neumann addition formula

$$I_0\{(\kappa_1{}^2 + \kappa_2{}^2 + 2\kappa_1\kappa_2 \cos \theta)^{\frac{1}{2}}\} = I_0(\kappa_1)I_0(\kappa_2) + 2 \sum_{p=1}^{\infty} I_p(\kappa_1)I_p(\kappa_2) \cos p\theta \tag{3.4.68}$$

which is also valid for any complex numbers κ_1 and κ_2. The Fourier series for the p.d.f. of the n-fold convolution does not simplify for $n > 2$ but it can again be approximated by a von Mises distribution.

It can be seen from the c.f. method that the distribution of the difference $\theta_1 - \theta_2 \pmod{2\pi}$ has the p.d.f. given by (3.4.65) with $\alpha = \mu_0 - \nu_0$. Hence, from (3.4.67) we deduce that

$$\theta_1 - \theta_2 \pmod{2\pi} \simeq M(\mu_0 - \nu_0, \kappa_3), \tag{3.4.69}$$

where κ_3 is given by (3.4.66). The result can also be obtained by using the fact that the distribution of the difference of two independent wrapped normal variables is again wrapped normal.

3.4.10. Appropriate Circular Normal Distribution

There will be no difficulty in accepting a distribution as the "normal distribution on the circle" if it has properties analogous to all the important characterizations of the linear normal distribution. However, such an ideal situation does not exist. The von Mises distribution has some but not all of these desirable properties and the wrapped normal distribution has some of the others.

The von Mises distribution, as we have seen, not only depends on two parameters, but its behaviour is also governed by these parameters in a way similar to that of $N(\mu, \sigma)$ with regard to μ and σ. Further, we have seen in Section 3.4.9c that the von Mises distribution can be constructed as a conditional distribution of a bivariate normal distribution and it tends to a normal distribution of large κ. Analogously to the linear normal distribution, it possesses the maximum likelihood characterization in estimating the shift-parameter on the circle and it also maximizes the entropy for a fixed circular mean and variance (Section 3.4.9f). On the other hand, the wrapped normal distribution is a natural adaptation of the linear normal distribution to the circle. Brownian motion on the circle (Section 3.4.8d) and a variant form of the central limit theorem on the circle (Section 4.3.2b) both lead to this distribution. The wrapped normal distribution possesses the additive property. Further, the independence of $f(\theta_1) + f(\theta_2)$ and $f(\theta_1) - f(\theta_2)$, where

f is an arbitrary function and θ_1 and θ_2 are independent, also leads to the wrapped normal (Kac and van Kampen, 1939).

We have seen in Section 3.4.9g that these two distributions can be made to approximate each other closely. We may, therefore, assume that the properties of the wrapped normal are approximately enjoyed by the von Mises distribution and vice versa. Consequently we may select either one of these two distributions as an appropriate normal distribution depending on which is more convenient for the problem in hand. The von Mises leads to tractable sampling distributions in problems of hypothesis testing whereas the wrapped normal does not. It also provides simpler maximum likelihood estimates. However, the trigonometric moments are simpler for the wrapped normal so that the wrapped normal distribution is preferable as a diagnostic aid. In fact, we shall define a circular standard deviation and a measure of circular kurtosis with the help of this distribution (Section 3.7).

Another circular distribution which has some important properties analogous to those of the linear normal distribution is the uniform distribution. The uniform distribution is stable (Section 4.2.4) but neither the wrapped normal nor the von Mises distribution shares this property. It also appears as the limiting distribution in a central limit theorem on the circle (Section 4.3.2a). In spite of these properties, the uniform distribution can hardly be regarded as a serious contender.

3.5. ANGULAR DISTRIBUTIONS ON THE RANGE $(0, 2\pi/l)$

3.5.1. Construction

We have already come across some examples of angular frequency distributions on $(0, \pi)$ and $(0, \pi/2)$ in Chapter 1. More generally, let us consider a continuous random variable θ^* which is observed modulo $2\pi/l$ where l is a positive integer. The variable θ^* can be regarded as a random variable with values in the interval $0 < \theta^* \leqslant 2\pi/l$ on the line. If we define

$$\theta' = l\theta^* \qquad (3.5.1)$$

then the random variable θ' has values in the range $0 < \theta' \leqslant 2\pi$ and, by wrapping this interval around the unit circle, θ' may be interpreted as a circular random variable whose p.d.f. is given by

$$f(\theta') = g(\theta'/l)/l, \qquad (3.5.2)$$

where g is the p.d.f. of θ^* on the line. This suggests that the c.f. of θ^* may be defined as

$$E(e^{ilp\theta^*}). \qquad (3.5.3)$$

Conversely, given a circular random variable θ we can construct a distribution on $(0, 2\pi/l)$ with the help of the transformation $\theta^* = \theta/l$, $0 < \theta \leqslant 2\pi$. For example, the p.d.f. of θ^* obtained from $M(0, \kappa)$ by this method gives the p.d.f. of the *von Mises type angular distribution* as

$$g(\theta^*) = \{l/2\pi I_0(\kappa)\}\, e^{\kappa \cos l\theta^*}, \qquad 0 < \theta^* \leqslant 2\pi/l. \qquad (3.5.4)$$

For $l = 2$, this density was first suggested by Arnold (1941). Alternatively, we can construct a distribution on $(0, 2\pi/l)$ by the transformation $\theta^* = \theta(\mathrm{mod}\,(2\pi/l))$. The resulting distributions for $l = 2$ will be discussed further in Section 3.6. In this case we may view angular distributions as the circular distributions having antipodal symmetry and are called axial.

3.5.2. Mean and Variance of θ^*

Suppose that μ_0' and V_0' are the mean and variance of θ'. How can we obtain suitable measures of the mean and variance of θ^* in terms of μ_0' and V_0'? This problem has some relevance in Data Analysis.

In view of (3.5.5), it is natural to define the mean direction $\tilde{\mu}_0$ of θ^* by

$$E\{\sin l(\theta^* - \tilde{\mu}_0)\} = 0. \qquad (3.5.5)$$

On comparing this equation with the result

$$E\{\sin (\theta' - \mu_0')\} = 0 \qquad (3.5.6)$$

we may take

$$\tilde{\mu}_0 = \mu_0'/l, \qquad 0 < \tilde{\mu}_0 \leqslant 2\pi/l. \qquad (3.5.7)$$

This measure for $l = 2$ has been widely used. Its use was introduced by Krumbein (1939) on intuitive grounds.

It is not easy to construct an appropriate function of V_0' which can be regarded as a circular variance of θ^*. For a distribution concentrated on a sufficiently small arc about μ_0', $2V_0'$ behaves like σ^2 (see Section 3.7.1) so that for this limiting case, we may define the circular variance $\tilde{V}_0$ of θ^* by

$$\tilde{V}_0 = V_0'/l^2. \qquad (3.5.8)$$

We can obtain a general relation by considering the wrapped normal distribution as follows. On wrapping $N(0, \sigma)$ on the range $(0, 2\pi/l)$, we have the p.d.f. of θ^* as

$$g_w(\theta^*) = (2\pi\sigma^2)^{-\frac{1}{2}} \sum_{k=-\infty}^{\infty} \exp\left[-\{\theta^* + (2k\pi/l)\}^2/2\sigma^2\right], \qquad 0 < \theta^* \leqslant 2\pi/l,$$

which implies that $\theta' = l\theta^*$ has the circular wrapped normal distribution with σ^2 replaced by $l^2\sigma^2$. Consequently, from (3.4.31) and (3.4.32),

$$V_0' = 1 - E(\cos l\theta) = 1 - e^{-\frac{1}{2}l^2\sigma^2}. \tag{3.5.9}$$

The standard deviation σ of θ^* is thus known in terms of V_0'. On using the relationship between the circular variance and standard deviation of the wrapped normal distribution which is precisely (3.5.9) with $l = 1$, we may define the circular variance $\tilde{V}_0$ by

$$\tilde{V}_0 = 1 - e^{-\frac{1}{2}\sigma^2}. \tag{3.5.10}$$

Finally, on eliminating σ from (3.5.9) and (3.5.10), we have

$$\tilde{V}_0 = 1 - (1 - V_0')^{1/l^2}. \tag{3.5.11}$$

For large l, it reduces to (3.5.8). For small l, $\tilde{V}_0$ tends to unity which is precisely the variance of the uniform distribution.

For $l = 2$, it is customary to use (3.5.8) but the circular variance of θ^* is not adjusted and is taken as V_0'. The relation (3.5.11) provides a method of obtaining the circular variance of θ^* in terms of V_0' which is acceptable at least for the wrapped normal and the von Mises distributions.

3.6. MIXTURES AND MULTI-MODAL DISTRIBUTIONS

We may regard multi-modal distributions as mixtures of unimodal distributions. In particular, a bimodal distribution may be regarded as a mixture of two unimodal distributions. We shall consider here only bimodal distributions with modes π radians apart. Let $f(\xi)$ be the p.d.f. of a unimodal distribution. The mixture with p.d.f.

$$g(\theta) = \lambda f(\theta) + (1 - \lambda)f(\theta + \pi), \quad 0 < \theta \leqslant 2\pi, \quad 0 < \lambda < 1, \tag{3.6.1}$$

has in general two modes π radians apart. If ϕ_p is the c.f. of ξ then the c.f. of θ is simply

$$\{\lambda + (1 - \lambda)(-1)^p\} \phi_p. \tag{3.6.2}$$

Under the transformation

$$\theta^* = \theta \text{ if } 0 < \theta \leqslant \pi, \quad \theta^* = \theta - \pi \text{ if } \pi < \theta \leqslant 2\pi,$$

i.e. $\theta^* = \theta \pmod{\pi}$,

the p.d.f. of θ^* is given by

$$h(\theta^*) = f(\theta^*) + f(\theta^* + \pi), \qquad 0 < \theta^* \leqslant \pi, \qquad (3.6.3)$$

which does not depend on λ. Under the assumption that g has two modes π radians apart, we find, on considering (3.6.1) with $\lambda = \frac{1}{2}$, that h is unimodal. Further,

$$E(e^{ip\theta^*}) = \phi_p \quad \text{if } p \text{ is even;} \quad = 0 \text{ otherwise.} \qquad (3.6.4)$$

Since θ^* is on the range $(0, \pi)$, we may obtain its mean direction and circular variance with the help of (3.5.7) and (3.5.11) respectively. Consequently, if μ_0' is the mean direction of $\theta' = 2\theta^*$, the two mean directions of the mixture may be defined as

$$\tilde{\mu}_0 = \tfrac{1}{2}\mu_0', \quad \pi + \tfrac{1}{2}\mu_0'. \qquad (3.6.5)$$

For $\lambda = \frac{1}{2}$, the p.d.f. given by (3.6.1) reduces to

$$g(\theta) = \tfrac{1}{2}\{f(\theta) + f(\theta + \pi)\}, \qquad 0 < \theta \leqslant 2\pi. \qquad (3.6.6)$$

Since $g(\theta) = g(\theta + \pi)$, the p.d.f. corresponds to a bimodal antipodally symmetric distribution. Further, the conditional p.d.f. of θ given $0 < \theta \leqslant \pi$ is $h(\theta)$ where the function h is defined by (3.6.3). In view of this relationship between (3.6.3) and (3.6.6), we may define the circular variance of the bimodal symmetric variable θ by

$$\tilde{V}_0 = 1 - (1 - V_0')^{1/4}, \qquad (3.6.7)$$

where V_0' is the circular variance of $\theta' = 2\theta^*$. If the p.d.f. f corresponds to $M(0, \kappa)$, (3.6.6) reduces to

$$g(\theta) = \cosh(\kappa \cos \theta)/\{2\pi I_0(\kappa)\}, \qquad 0 < \theta \leqslant 2\pi. \qquad (3.6.8)$$

We shall show that this bimodal symmetric distribution can be approximated by another density which is easier to handle for inference problems.

A Multi-modal Distribution of von Mises Type. Multimodal distributions can also be obtained by extending the range of unimodal distributions on

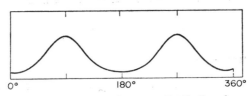

FIG. 3.5. Density of the bimodal von Mises type distribution for $\kappa = 1$ and $\mu_0 = 90°$ (Batschelet, 1965).

$(0, 2\pi/l)$ to $(0, 2\pi)$. For example, from the von Mises distribution on $(0, 2\pi/l)$ given at (3.5.4), we have a multi-modal density (see Fig. 3.5 for $l = 2$)

$$u(\theta) = \{1/2\pi I_0(\kappa)\} e^{\kappa \cos l(\theta - \mu_0)}, \qquad 0 < \theta \leqslant 2\pi, \quad 0 < \mu_0 < 2\pi/l. \quad (3.6.9)$$

It has l modes situated $2\pi/l$ radians apart with the first mode at $\theta = \mu_0$. We now show that it possesses certain properties similar to that of the von Mises distribution. The distribution has a maximum likelihood characterization similar to that for the von Mises distribution given in Section 3.4.9f. If the maximum likelihood estimate of μ_0 for a given density $g(\theta - \mu_0)$ is $m_l{}^0$ defined by

$$\sum_{i=1}^{n} \sin l(\theta_i - m_l{}^0) = 0,$$

it can be shown on following the reasoning of Section 3.4.9f that $g(\theta)$ must be of the form (3.6.9). Further, as in Section 3.4.9c, we find for large κ, θ is distributed approximately as $N(\mu_0, 1/l\kappa^{\frac{1}{2}})$. In view of these properties, (3.6.9) will be described as a multi-modal distribution of von Mises type. Similar properties also hold for the p.d.f. on $(0, 2\pi/l)$ given by (3.5.4).

For $l = 2$, we are also interested in the distribution of θ given by (3.6.8) but inference problems for this distribution cannot be solved easily. The problems are much easier to handle for (3.6.9). For $l = 2$ we write (3.6.9) as

$$u(\xi) = \{1/2\pi I_0(\kappa_1)\} e^{\kappa_1 \cos 2\xi}, \qquad 0 < \xi \leqslant 2\pi. \quad (3.6.10)$$

We now show that the distribution of θ and ξ given by (3.6.8) and (3.6.10) respectively, can be made to approximate each other closely. From the approximation of the wrapped normal distribution to the von Mises distribution (Section 3.4.9g), we note that if

$$A_1(\kappa) = e^{-\frac{1}{2}\sigma^2}, \quad (3.6.11)$$

then

$$A_p(\kappa) = I_p(\kappa)/I_0(\kappa) \doteq e^{-\frac{1}{2}p\sigma^2}. \quad (3.6.12)$$

For the random variable θ, we define σ for given κ by (3.6.11). Similarly, for ξ, let us define σ_1 by (3.6.11) when $\kappa = \kappa_1$ so that

$$A_p(\kappa_1) \doteq e^{-\frac{1}{2}p\sigma_1^2}. \quad (3.6.13)$$

The c.f.'s of θ and ξ are respectively $A_p(\kappa)$ and $A_{\frac{1}{2}p}(\kappa_1)$ for even p and are zero otherwise. Using (3.6.12) and (3.6.13), we easily see that these c.f.'s are identical for all p if $\sigma_1 = 2\sigma$. Hence, on relating σ to σ_1 by $\sigma_1 = 2\sigma$, the two distributions can be made to approximate each other closely. This procedure amounts to relating κ and κ_1 approximately by $A_1(\kappa) = A_2(\kappa_1)$.

Using this result, it can easily be shown that the distributions of $\theta^* = \theta \,(\text{mod}\,\pi)$ and $\tilde{\theta} = \xi\,(\text{mod}\,\pi)$ can be made to approximate each other closely where θ and ξ have the p.d.f.'s given by (3.6.8) and (3.6.10), respectively.

3.7. CIRCULAR STANDARD DEVIATION, SKEWNESS AND KURTOSIS

3.7.1. Transformation of V_0

We know that V_0 lies in the range $(0, 1)$. To relate V_0 to the standard deviation on the line, it is natural to use the following result for the wrapped normal distribution

$$1 - V_0 = e^{-\frac{1}{2}\sigma^2}.$$

We can therefore define the circular standard deviation σ_0 as

$$\sigma_0 = \{- 2 \log (1 - V_0)\}^{\frac{1}{2}}. \tag{3.7.1}$$

The range of σ_0 is, of course, $(0, \infty)$. For small V_0, (3.7.1) reduces to

$$\sigma_0 \doteq (2V_0)^{\frac{1}{2}}. \tag{3.7.2}$$

This is consistent with the following inequality deduced for small ε from the Tchebycheff-type inequality given by (3.3.14).

$$\Pr\{|\theta| \geqslant \varepsilon(2V_0)^{\frac{1}{2}}\} \leqslant \frac{1}{\varepsilon^2}.$$

Hence (3.7.1) is certainly adequate for small V_0. A further justification will be given below. The transformation (3.7.2) was first suggested by von Mises (1918).

For a variable θ^* concentrated on the range $(0, 2\pi/l)$, (3.5.10) and (3.5.11) imply that

$$\sigma_0^* = \{- 2 \log (1 - V_0')\}^{\frac{1}{2}}/l, \tag{3.7.3}$$

where V_0' is the circular variance for $\theta' = l\theta^*$. This transformation is consistent with the property $\sigma' = l\sigma^*$.

These results have already been applied in Section 2.4.

3.7.2. Skewness

On the line, the measure of skewness commonly used is

$$\gamma_1 = E(x - \mu)^3/\sigma^3 \tag{3.7.4}$$

which is motivated by the fact that the third central moment is the lowest order vanishing odd moment for the symmetric distributions and is divided by σ^3 to render γ_1 invariant under a change of scale. For circular symmetric distributions, we have from (3.3.23)

$$\bar{\beta}_p = 0.$$

Therefore, by analogy, a function of $\bar{\beta}_2$ can be taken as a measure of circular skewness. An appropriate function can be selected as follows.

Consider the transformation

$$x = \delta\theta, \qquad -\pi < \theta \leqslant \pi, \qquad (3.7.5)$$

where δ is small. It transforms the circular variable θ into a variable x concentrated on an arc of the circle so that as $\delta \to 0$ the distribution of x must behave like an ordinary distribution on the line. In particular, if μ_c, σ_c^2 and γ_1^c are some suitable measures of circular location, dispersion and skewness, then for x we must ensure that

$$\mu_c \doteq \mu, \qquad \sigma_c^2 \doteq \sigma^2, \qquad \gamma_1^c \doteq \mu_3/\sigma^3. \qquad (3.7.6)$$

We first verify that μ_0 and V_0 do possess this property. Let μ_0 and V_0 be the mean direction and circular variance of x. Using

$$\sin\theta = \theta - \frac{\theta^3}{3!} + ..., \qquad \cos\theta = 1 - \frac{\theta^2}{2!} + \frac{\theta^4}{4!} - ... , \qquad (3.7.7)$$

we have

$$\mu_0 = \mu + o(\delta), \qquad 2V_0 = \sigma^2 + o(\delta^2). \qquad (3.7.8)$$

Hence μ_0 and $2V_0$ do satisfy (3.7.6).

Let $\bar{\beta}_2$ be the second sine moment of x and let $\mu_0 = 0$. On using (3.7.7), we find that

$$\bar{\beta}_2 = E(\sin 2x) = E(\sin 2\delta\theta - 2\sin\delta\theta) = -\mu_3 + o(\delta^3).$$

Hence a circular measure of skewness satisfying (3.7.6) is proportional to

$$\gamma_1^{\,0} = \bar{\beta}_2/V_0^{\,3/2}. \qquad (3.7.9)$$

If $V_0 = 1$ then we have maximum dispersion and $\gamma_1^{\,0}$ will have no meaning. The uniform distribution is such a distribution.

3.7.3. Kurtosis

Similarly, we have

$$2E(\cos 2x - 4\cos x + 3) = \mu_4 + o(\delta^4)$$

and again ignoring the constant multiplier, a suitable measure of kurtosis can be taken as

$$(\bar{\alpha}_2 - 4\bar{\alpha}_1 + 3)/V_0^2. \qquad (3.7.10)$$

It is desirable to adjust the measure such that its value reduces to zero for the von Mises distribution. The value of $\bar{\alpha}_2$ is complicated for the von Mises distribution but since the wrapped normal distribution approximates this distribution closely (Section 3.4.9g), we may take $\bar{\alpha}_2 = (1 - V_0)^4$. Consequently, we take our measure of kurtosis as

$$\gamma_2^0 = \{\bar{\alpha}_2 - (1 - V_0)^4\}/V_0^2. \qquad (3.7.11)$$

We denote $\bar{\alpha}_2/V_0^2$ by $\bar{\gamma}_2^0$.

The sample counterparts of γ_1^0 and γ_2^0 have already been used in Section 2.7.2. An inequality involving γ_1^0, γ_2^0 and V_0 can be obtained easily from (3.3.4).

Let us consider some examples. For the uniform distribution and for nearly uniform distributions such as

$$f(\theta) = (1 + a \sin 3\theta)/2\pi$$

we will have $\gamma_1^0 = \gamma_2^0 = 0$. Consequently, these measures are not meaningful for large values of V_0. For the distribution with p.d.f.

$$f(\theta) = (2\pi)^{-1}[1 + 2(1 - V_0)\cos\theta + 2V_0^{3/2} a \sin 2\theta + 2V_0^2 b \cos 2\theta],$$

where the constants V_0, a and b are selected suitably so that the total probability is one. For this distribution, $\gamma_1^0 = a$ and $\bar{\gamma}_2^0 = b$. All the trigonometric moments of order higher than two are zero. For the triangular distribution given by (3.4.15), we have

$$\gamma_1^0 = \tfrac{1}{2}\rho/(1 - \rho)^{3/2} \quad \text{and} \quad \bar{\gamma}_2^0 = 0.$$

It is interesting to note that μ_0, V_0, γ_1^0 and γ_2^0 use only the first two trigonometric moments. However, we have disregarded constant multipliers in defining γ_1^0 and γ_2^0. Also, we could have used σ_0^2 in the place of V_0, or we may not have standardized $\bar{\alpha}_2$ and $\bar{\beta}_2$ at all. The final choice, of course, would rest on the relative simplicity of the sampling distributions of their sample counterparts.

Batschelet (1965) first initiated the study of measures of skewness and proposed $\bar{\beta}_2$ as a measure of skewness.

3.8. CORRECTIONS FOR GROUPING

3.8.1. A General Result

Let us assume that the p.d.f. $f(x)$ is continuous and is concentrated on (a, b). Let $g(x)$ be a continuous function of x then we have

$$E\{g(x)\} = \int_a^b g(x) f(x)\, dx. \qquad (3.8.1)$$

However, if the range (a, b) is divided into n intervals of length h then the expected value of $g(x)$ after the grouping is

$$E^*\{g(x)\} = \sum_{i=1}^n u(x_i), \qquad (3.8.2)$$

where $x_i = a + (i - \tfrac{1}{2})h$ and

$$u(x) = g(x) \int_{-\frac{1}{2}h}^{\frac{1}{2}h} f(x + y)\, dy. \qquad (3.8.3)$$

We now obtain a relation between (3.8.1) and (3.8.2) by following a method of Kendall and Stuart (1969, pp. 75–76). In their case, $g(x) = x^r$. From the Euler–Maclaurin sum formula (Milne–Thomson, 1933, Section 7.5), using the continuity of $f(x)$ and $g(x)$ and assuming that $u(x)$ has derivatives up to order $2m$, we obtain

$$\frac{1}{h} \int_a^b u(x)\, dx = \sum_{i=1}^n u(x_i) - R_n, \qquad (3.8.4)$$

where R_n is a remainder term. We have

$$R_n = S_{2m} + \sum_{i=1}^m \frac{h^{2i-1}}{(2i)!} \{u^{(2i-1)}(b) - u^{(2i-1)}(a)\} B_{2i}(\tfrac{1}{2}), \qquad (3.8.5)$$

where $u^{(i)}$ is the ith derivative of $u(x)$, $B_i(\tfrac{1}{2})$ is the value of the ith Bernoulli polynomial at $\tfrac{1}{2}$ and

$$S_{2m} = \frac{nh^{2m}}{(2m)!} B_{2m}(\tfrac{1}{2}) u^{(2m)}(a + nh\delta), \qquad 0 < \delta < 1. \qquad (3.8.6)$$

If R_n can be neglected, then on substituting (3.8.4) into (3.8.2) we have, after changing the order of the integration,

$$E^*\{g(x)\} = \frac{1}{h} \int_a^b \left\{ \int_{-\frac{1}{2}h}^{\frac{1}{2}h} g(x - y)\, dy \right\} f(x)\, dx. \qquad (3.8.7)$$

Assuming

$$\int g(x)\,dx = g_1(x),$$ (3.8.8)

we can write (3.8.7) as

$$E^*\{g(x)\} = E\{g_1(x + \tfrac{1}{2}h) - g_1(x - \tfrac{1}{2}h)\}/h.$$ (3.8.9)

For particular functions $g(.)$, (3.8.9) can be expressed in terms of $E\{g(x)\}$ defined by (3.8.1).

3.8.2. The Circular Case

Let us take

$$g(x) = \cos px, \qquad p = 0, \pm 1, \dots$$

which is, of course, a continuous function of x. We have from (3.8.8)

$$g_1(x) = (\sin px)/p.$$

Considering $f(x)$ as a distribution concentrated on the interval $(0, 2\pi)$, (3.8.9) gives

$$\alpha_p^* = \{2 \sin (\tfrac{1}{2}ph)/ph\}\alpha_p,$$

where α_p^* is the cosine-moment after grouping and α_p is the corrected cosine-moment. Now, $h = 2\pi/n$ so that if p is not a multiple of n, we have

$$\alpha_p = a(h)\alpha_p^*,$$ (3.8.10)

where

$$a(h) = \tfrac{1}{2}ph(\sin \tfrac{1}{2}ph)^{-1}.$$ (3.8.11)

Similarly, we have

$$\beta_p = a(h)\beta_p^*.$$ (3.8.12)

Further,

$$\mu_p = a(h)\mu_p^*, \quad \rho_p = a(h)\rho_p^*.$$ (3.8.13)

The quantity μ_p^0 does not need a correction. These results have already been used in Section 2.8.

Let us examine the validity of neglecting the remainder term R_n given by (3.8.5). In our cases, $u(x)$ is a function of period 2π so that R_n simply becomes S_{2m}. From Kendall and Stuart (1969, p. 77), we have

$$|R| = |S_{2m}| < \{4n\,h^{2m}/(2\pi)^{2m}\}\,|u^{(2m)}(\theta)|, \qquad 0 < \theta < 2\pi$$

which in turn depends on h and on the behaviour of $f^{(2m-1)}(\theta)$. Hence, for small h and moderately large m, S_{2m} will certainly be negligible.

In practice, it is found that the correction (3.8.13) leads to improvements in accuracy if the distribution is either symmetrical or moderately skew but not if the distribution is extremely skew.

The result (3.8.13) is due to Greenwood (1959a) who uses a different approach. Gilroy (1965) has obtained the same result as an average correction and has also studied the effect of this correction on certain important models.

4

FUNDAMENTAL THEOREMS AND DISTRIBUTION THEORY

4.1. INTRODUCTION

We have already studied some basic properties of the characteristic function (c.f.) for circular distributions in Section 3.2. It turns out that the c.f. and the trigonometric moments are identical. In Sections 4.2 and 4.3, we deal with the uniqueness theorem, inversion formulae, a limit theorem on sequences of random variables, central limit theorems on the circle and Poincaré's theorem. In the subsequent sections, we give the distribution theory for the sample resultant and for related statistics. The isotropic random walk is treated first. Sampling distributions of various statistics from the uniform and von Mises distributions receive special attention.

4.2. THEOREMS ON THE CHARACTERISTIC FUNCTION

4.2.1. The Uniqueness Theorem

We show that a distribution function F on the circle is uniquely determined by its c.f.

$$\phi_p = \int_0^{2\pi} e^{ip\theta}\, dF(\theta). \tag{4.2.1}$$

In fact, our proof also gives an inversion formula for F.

Consider the family of functions

$$u_\rho(\xi) = \frac{1}{2\pi} \sum_{p=-\infty}^{\infty} \phi_p \, \rho^{|p|} \, e^{-ip\xi}, \qquad 0 \leqslant \rho < 1. \qquad (4.2.2)$$

Since the sequence ϕ_p is bounded, the series (4.2.2) always converges to a continuous function of ξ. (The limiting function is also differentiable.) The series may or may not converge for $\rho = 1$. However, even if there is not ordinary convergence at $\rho = 1$, the series may still be Abel summable there, i.e. $\lim_{\rho \to 1^-} u_\rho(\xi)$ may still exist.

On taking $\phi_p = 1$ we find that (4.2.2) reduces to the Fourier expansion

$$\frac{1}{2\pi} \sum_{p=-\infty}^{\infty} \rho^{|p|} \, e^{-ip\xi} = c(\xi; \rho), \qquad 0 \leqslant \rho < 1, \qquad (4.2.3)$$

of the wrapped Cauchy distribution with p.d.f. $c(\xi; \rho)$; see (3.4.33) and (3.4.34). On substituting (4.2.1) into (4.2.2) and then using (4.2.3), we obtain

$$u_\rho(\xi) = \int_0^{2\pi} c(\xi - \theta; \rho) \, \mathrm{d}F(\theta). \qquad (4.2.4)$$

Let us define the random variable $\zeta = \xi + \theta \pmod{2\pi}$ where ξ and θ are independent and ξ has the p.d.f. $c(\xi; \rho)$ while θ has the d.f. F. The sum $\zeta = \xi + \theta \pmod{2\pi}$ will have a density whether F has a density or not. Further, (4.2.4) is precisely the p.d.f. of ζ (see the convolution formula (3.2.12)). We have from (4.2.4),

$$\lim_{\rho \to 1} \int_0^\theta u_\rho(\xi) \, \mathrm{d}\xi = \int_0^{2\pi} \left(\lim_{\rho \to 1} \int_{-\phi}^{\theta - \phi} c(\xi; \rho) \, \mathrm{d}\xi \right) \mathrm{d}F(\phi),$$

where the change in the order of integration is justified by Fubini's theorem and the interchange of the limit with integration is permissible by the dominated convergence theorem. Since ξ becomes concentrated at the point $\xi = 0$ as $\rho \to 1$ as seen in Section 3.4.8e, we have

$$\lim_{\rho \to 1} \int_{-\phi}^{\theta - \phi} c(\xi; \rho) \, \mathrm{d}\xi = 1 \quad \text{if} \quad -\phi < 0 \leqslant \theta - \phi; \quad = 0, \text{ otherwise.}$$

Hence we obtain

$$\lim_{\rho \to 1} \int_0^\theta u_\rho(\xi) \, \mathrm{d}\xi = F(\theta). \qquad (4.2.5)$$

Consequently, $F(\theta)$ can be obtained by a limiting process from the functions $u_\rho(\xi)$ which by (4.2.2) themselves depend only on ϕ_p. Therefore, the result follows.

Since ϕ_p is also the pth trigonometric moment, this theorem implies that the trigonometric moments uniquely determine the distribution. Such an unconditional result does not exist for the moments on the line.

4.2.2. Inversion Formulae

For a given c.f. ϕ_p, we have from (4.2.5) and (4.2.2)

$$F(\theta + h) - F(\theta) = \lim_{\rho \to 1} \frac{1}{2\pi} \left[h + \sum_{\substack{p=-\infty \\ p \neq 0}}^{\infty} \frac{1 - e^{-iph}}{ip} \phi_p \rho^{|p|} e^{-ip\theta} \right] \quad (4.2.6)$$

provided that θ and $\theta + h$ are continuity points of F and $h > 0$. In particular, if the series $\Sigma |\phi_p|^2$ is convergent, F has a density f defined almost everywhere by

$$f(\theta) = (2\pi)^{-1} \sum_{p=-\infty}^{\infty} e^{-ip\theta} \phi_p$$

$$= (2\pi)^{-1} \left[1 + 2 \sum_{p=1}^{\infty} (\alpha_p \cos p\theta + \beta_p \sin p\theta) \right], \quad (4.2.7)$$

where $\phi_p = \alpha_p + i\beta_p$. This result also follows from Riesz–Fischer theorem (Titchmarsh, 1958, p. 423).

We now derive the following alternative inversion formula.

$$F^*(\theta) = \tfrac{1}{2}\{F(\theta + 0) + F(\theta - 0)\}$$

$$= \frac{\theta}{2\pi} + \frac{1}{\pi} \sum_{p=1}^{\infty} \{\alpha_p \sin p\theta + \beta_p(1 - \cos p\theta)\}/p. \quad (4.2.8)$$

Since $F^*(\theta)$ is a function of bounded variation on $(0, 2\pi)$, we have the Fourier expansion (Jordan's test, Titchmarsh, 1958, p. 407):

$$F^*(\theta) - c_0 \theta = \alpha_0' + \sum_{p=1}^{\infty} \alpha_p' \cos p\theta + \sum_{p=1}^{\infty} \beta_p' \sin p\theta \quad (4.2.9)$$

which on using the conditions $F^*(0) = 0$, $F^*(2\pi) = 1$ gives

$$c_0 = 1/(2\pi), \qquad \alpha_0' = - \Sigma \alpha_p'. \quad (4.2.10)$$

Further,

$$\alpha_p' = \frac{1}{\pi} \int_0^{2\pi} \{F^*(\theta) - c_0\theta\} \cos p\theta \, d\theta.$$

On integrating it by parts, we find that

$$\alpha_p' = -\frac{1}{\pi p}\int_0^{2\pi} \sin p\theta \, dF^*(\theta) = -\beta_p/\pi p.$$

(4.2.11)

Similarly,

$$\beta_p' = \alpha_p/\pi p.$$

(4.2.12)

On using (4.2.10)–(4.2.12) in (4.2.9), we obtain (4.2.8).

4.2.3. Polar Distributions and the Characteristic Function

Let $\psi(t_1, t_2)$ be the c.f. of a continuous two-dimensional random variable (x, y) and suppose that $\psi(t_1, t_2)$ is integrable. We obtain the distribution of (r, θ) where

$$x = r \cos \theta, \qquad y = r \sin \theta.$$

(4.2.13)

By the inversion theorem, the p.d.f. of (x, y) is given by

$$(2\pi)^{-2}\int_{-\infty}^{\infty}\int_{-\infty}^{\infty} e^{-it_1 x - it_2 y}\, \psi(t_1, t_2)\, dt_1\, dt_2.$$

(4.2.14)

Using (4.2.13) and putting

$$t_1 = \rho \cos \Phi, \qquad t_2 = \rho \sin \Phi$$

$$\psi(t_1, t_2) = E[\exp\{i\rho r \cos (\theta - \Phi)\}] \equiv \bar{\psi}(\rho, \Phi),$$

(4.2.15)

we find that the joint density of r and θ is given by

$$p(r, \theta) = (2\pi)^{-2} r \int_0^{\infty}\int_0^{2\pi} e^{-i\rho r \cos(\theta - \Phi)}\, \rho\bar{\psi}(\rho, \Phi)\, d\rho\, d\Phi.$$

(4.2.16)

On integrating over θ and interchanging the order of integration, the density of r is found to be

$$p_1(r) = (2\pi)^{-2} r \int_0^{\infty}\int_0^{2\pi} \left\{\int_0^{2\pi} e^{-i\rho r \cos(\theta - \Phi)}\, d\theta\right\} \rho\bar{\psi}(\rho, \Phi)\, d\rho\, d\Phi.$$

Since θ has a distribution on the circle, the inner integral does not depend on Φ. Its value is given by

$$2\pi I_0(i\rho r) = 2\pi J_0(\rho r), \quad \text{say}.$$

(4.2.17)

Hence, we have

$$p_1(r) = (2\pi)^{-1} r \int_0^\infty \int_0^{2\pi} J_0(\rho r)\, \bar{\psi}(\rho, \theta)\, \rho \, d\rho \, d\theta, \qquad (4.2.18)$$

where $J_0(x)$ is the standard Bessel function of zero order and from (4.2.17) it is given by

$$J_0(x) = \sum_{k=0}^\infty \frac{(-1)^k}{k!\,k!} (\tfrac{1}{2}x)^{2k}. \qquad (4.2.19)$$

The formula (4.2.18) may be described as an inversion formula for the distribution of r. We can rewrite it as

$$p_1(r) = r \int_0^\infty J_0(\rho r)\, \bar{\psi}_1(\rho) \rho \, d\rho, \qquad (4.2.20)$$

where

$$\bar{\psi}_1(\rho) = (2\pi)^{-1} \int_0^{2\pi} \bar{\psi}(\rho, \Phi)\, d\Phi. \qquad (4.2.21)$$

We now express $\bar{\psi}_1(\rho)$ in terms of $p_1(r)$. From (4.2.15), we have

$$\bar{\psi}(\rho, \Phi) = \int_0^\infty \int_0^{2\pi} e^{i\rho r \cos(\theta - \Phi)}\, p(r, \theta)\, dr \, d\theta.$$

On substituting for $\bar{\psi}$ in (4.2.21) and integrating over Φ using the same method as in (4.2.16) to integrate over θ, we obtain

$$\bar{\psi}_1(\rho) = \int_0^\infty J_0(r\rho)\, p_1(r)\, dr. \qquad (4.2.22)$$

This is related to the Hankel transform of $p_1(r)$ with (4.2.20) as its inverse. Applications of the Hankel transform in such a context are given in Lord (1954). We can also establish (4.2.22) by using the following relation from G. N. Watson (1948, p. 453) for any function $v(R)$ satisfying a certain convergence condition.

$$\int_0^\infty \int_0^\infty v(R)\, J_0(uR)\, J_0(ur)\, uR \, du \, dR = v(r). \qquad (4.2.23)$$

Let μ_k' be the kth moment of r. On using the expansion (4.2.19) for J_0 in (4.2.22), we obtain

$$\bar{\psi}_1(\rho) = \sum_{k=0}^\infty (-1)^k \frac{\mu_{2k}'\, \rho^{2k}}{2^{2k}\, k!^2}. \qquad (4.2.24)$$

Thus the moments of r^2 can be derived from $\bar\psi_1(\rho)$. In view of this property, $\bar\psi_1(\rho)$ is described as the polar moment generating function.

Similarly, we can obtain the marginal density of θ from (4.2.16). It can be simplified easily when the range of r is finite. Further, we find that the joint c.f. of r and θ can be expressed as

$$E(e^{itr+ip\theta}) = \int_0^{2\pi} \int_{0^-}^{\infty} e^{itr+ip\theta}\,\psi_2(r,\theta)\,dr\,d\theta,$$

where

$$\psi_2(r,\theta) = r\int_0^{\infty} I_p(i\rho r)\,\bar\psi(\rho,\theta)\rho\,d\rho,$$

and the Bessel function $I_p(.)$ is defined by (3.4.46). It is interesting to note that the moment generating function of $\cos\theta$ is simply

$$(2\pi)^{-1}\left\{I_0(t) + 2\sum_{p=1}^{\infty}\alpha_p I_p(t)\right\}, \tag{4.2.25}$$

where α_p is the real part of the c.f. of θ. This result follows on using the Fourier expansion for the p.d.f. of θ together with the c.f. of the von Mises distribution. It can be used to obtain the moments of $\Sigma\cos\theta_i$ where $\theta_1,\theta_2\ldots$ are independent observations on θ.

The Distribution of R. Suppose that $\theta_j, j=1,\ldots,n$ are distributed independently with p.d.f. $f_j(\theta), j=1,\ldots,n$. We give a general method to obtain the distribution of R where

$$R^2 = C^2 + S^2, \quad C = \sum_{j=1}^{n} l_j\cos\theta_j, \quad S = \sum_{j=1}^{n} l_j\sin\theta_j,$$

where l_j are given constants. The joint c.f. of (C, S) is

$$\prod_{j=1}^{n}\bar\psi_j(\rho,\Phi), \tag{4.2.26}$$

where $\bar\psi_j(\rho,\Phi)$ is the joint c.f. of $(l_j\cos\theta_j, l_j\sin\theta_j)$, i.e.

$$\bar\psi_j(\rho,\Phi) = E[\exp\{i\rho l_j\cos(\theta_j - \Phi)\}]. \tag{4.2.27}$$

Hence, from the inversion formula (4.2.18) the p.d.f. of R is given by

$$p(R) = (2\pi)^{-1}R\int_0^{\infty}\int_0^{2\pi} J_0(\rho R)\left\{\prod_{j=1}^{n}\bar\psi_j(\rho,\Phi)\right\}\rho\,d\rho\,d\Phi. \tag{4.2.28}$$

This method will be used subsequently to obtain the distribution of R for various particular cases.

4.2.4. Further Properties of the c.f.

(a) We have obtained an inequality on moments [see (3.3.4)] which may be extended as follows. Since,

$$E\left[\left|\sum_{p=1}^{m} e^{ip\theta} z_p\right|^2\right] \geq 0$$

for all complex $z_1, z_2, ..., z_m$, we obtain

$$\sum_{p,q=1}^{m} \phi_{p-q} z_p \bar{z}_q \geq 0.$$

Consequently, the sequence $\{\phi_p\}$ can be described as positive definite. If $a_{pq} = \phi_{p-q}$, $p, q = 1, ..., m$, then the mth order determinant

$$D_m = |a_{pq}| \geq 0 \qquad (4.2.29)$$

for all circular distributions. For symmetric distributions, (4.2.29) holds with a_{pq} replaced by α_{p-q}.

The following converses are true. If $\{\phi_p\}$ is a positive definite sequence of complex numbers with $\phi_0 = 1$, it represents the Fourier coefficients of a circular distribution. Further, if $D_m > 0$ for $m = 1, ..., p$ and $D_m = 0$ for $m = p + 1, p + 2, ...$, the circular distribution is a discrete distribution on exactly p points. These results are due to Hurwitz (1903) and Herglotz (1911). For a proof, the reader is referred to Shohat and Tamarkin (1943, p. 7).

(b) We can define a stable distribution function F on the circle by the convolution property

$$F(x - c_1) * F(x - c_2) = F(x - c).$$

Since there is no scaling reduction possible on a circle, this definition seems to be the most general. Let ϕ_p be the c.f. of F and $v = (c - c_1 - c_2)$ (mod 2π). Then

$$\phi_p^2 = \phi_p e^{ipv}$$

and its solutions are

$$\phi_p = 0, \quad p \neq 0 \quad \text{or} \quad \phi_p = e^{ipv}.$$

Hence from Sections 3.4.3 and 3.4.4 we deduce that the stable circular distributions are precisely the discrete uniform distributions concentrated on $\theta_r = v + 2\pi r/m$ and the uniform distribution on $(0, 2\pi)$.

(c) Let $f(\theta)$ and $g(\theta)$ be two densities with c.f.'s ϕ_p and $\phi_p{}'$. The Parseval formula is (Titchmarch, 1958, p. 425):

$$2\pi \int_0^{2\pi} f(\theta)\, g(\theta)\, d\theta = \sum_{p=-\infty}^{\infty} \phi_p \bar{\phi}_p{}'. \tag{4.2.30}$$

In particular,

$$\pi \int_0^{2\pi} \{f(\theta)\}^2\, d\theta = \tfrac{1}{2} + \sum_{p=1}^{\infty} (\alpha_p{}^2 + \beta_p{}^2).$$

(d) From the Riemann–Lebesgue theorem (Titchmarch, 1958, p. 403) for absolutely continuous F, we know that

$$\lim_{p \to \infty} \phi(p) = 0. \tag{4.2.31}$$

For discrete F, we have

$$\lim_{p \to \infty} \sup |\phi(p)| = 1. \tag{4.2.32}$$

These results can be deduced from the corresponding results on the line (Lukacs, 1970, pp. 19–20) by unwrapping the circle on to the interval $(0, 2\pi)$. Similarly, for singular distributions

$$\lim_{p \to \infty} \sup |\phi(p)| = L, \qquad 0 \leqslant L \leqslant 1. \tag{4.2.33}$$

These relations can be used to investigate the type of a distribution whose c.f. is given.

Further, from Lukacs (1970, pp. 17–18), we deduce that ϕ_p is the c.f. of a lattice distribution if and only if

$$|\phi(p)| = 1 \quad \text{for some} \quad p \neq 0. \tag{4.2.34}$$

4.3. LIMIT THEOREMS

4.3.1. The Continuity Theorem (Theorem of Carathéodory)

Let $\{\phi_p(m),\ m = 1, 2, \ldots\}$ be the sequence of c.f.'s corresponding to a sequence of d.f.'s $\{F_m(\theta),\ m = 1, 2, \ldots\}$. We prove that the convergence of $F_m(\theta)$ to a d.f. $F(\theta)$ with c.f. ϕ_p implies that

$$\lim_{m \to \infty} \phi_p(m) = \phi_p. \tag{4.3.1}$$

Conversely, if (4.3.1) holds for each p for a sequence $\{\phi_p(m)\}$ then it will be shown that there exists a d.f. $F(\theta)$ such that $F_m(\theta)$ converges to $F(\theta)$ at all the points of continuity of $F(\theta)$.

The first part follows immediately from Helly's second theorem (Lukacs, 1970, p. 45).

To prove the converse, we assume if possible that there exists a continuity point ξ $(0 < \xi \leqslant 2\pi)$ of F such that $F_m(\xi)$ does not converge to $F(\xi)$, i.e. by hypothesis

$$F_m(\xi) \nrightarrow F(\xi). \tag{4.3.2}$$

By the Helly selection theorem, we can find then a subsequence $\{F_{m_k}\}$ such that the limit of $F_{m_k}(\xi)$ exists but it differs from $F(\xi)$. For definiteness, assume that

$$\lim F_{m_k}(\xi) > F(\xi). \tag{4.3.3}$$

Again, it is possible to select a subsequence $\{F_{s_k}(\theta)\}$ of $\{F_{m_k}(\theta)\}$ such that

$$\lim F_{s_k}(\theta) = G(\theta), \tag{4.3.4}$$

at every continuity point θ of G, G being a d.f. The c.f.'s of both F and G are ϕ_p from the first part and therefore from the uniqueness theorem

$$F(\theta) \equiv G(\theta). \tag{4.3.5}$$

However, from (4.3.3) and (4.3.4), we have

$$G(\xi) = \lim F_{s_k}(\xi) = \lim F_{m_k}(\xi) > F(\xi). \tag{4.3.6}$$

Therefore, (4.3.5) cannot hold and this in turn implies that (4.3.2) is false. Hence the limiting distribution is uniquely determined by the limits of the trigonometric moments.

The reader will have observed that the proof of the continuity theroem is much simpler for circular distributions than for distributions on the line. This is because any pointwise limit of circular c.f.'s is itself a circular c.f. whereas on the line it is necessary to add the condition that the limit be continuous at $t = 0$. Roughly speaking, it is not possible for the probability mass to "escape to infinity" on the circle.

4.3.2. Central Limit Theorems

4.3.2a. *Uniform Distribution*

Let $\theta_1, ..., \theta_n$ be independent and identically distributed random variables with the common d.f. $F(\theta)$. We show that the distribution of the sum

$$S_n = (\theta_1 + ... + \theta_n) \,(\text{mod } 2\pi) \tag{4.3.7}$$

converges to the uniform distribution provided that F does not correspond to a lattice distribution on the circle.

Let ϕ_p be the c.f. corresponding to $F(\theta)$. Since F is not a lattice distribution, we have from (4.2.34)

$$|\phi_p| < 1, \quad \text{for all} \quad p \neq 0.$$

Hence, the c.f. $\phi_p{}^n$ of S_n tends to zero for all $p \neq 0$. From (3.4.10), this limiting c.f. is the c.f. of the uniform distribution. Therefore, the result follows on using the continuity theorem.

We now show that if F has a lattice distribution on the circle with zero as a lattice point, the distribution of the sum S_n converges to a discrete uniform distribution.

Let $p_0, ..., p_{m-1}$ be the probability at the points $2\pi r/m$, $r = 0, 1, ..., m-1$ with $p_0 \neq 0$. From (3.4.6) the c.f. of F is given by

$$\phi_p = \sum_{r=0}^{m-1} p_r \, \xi_r{}^p,$$

where $\xi_r = \exp\{2\pi r i/m\}$. We have

$$\phi_p = 1 \quad \text{for} \quad p = 0 \, (\text{mod } m).$$

We show that for this case

$$|\phi_p| < 1 \quad \text{if and only if} \quad p \neq \text{mod } m. \tag{4.3.8}$$

Consider $|\phi_p| = 1$ which is equivalent to

$$\{p_0 + \Sigma p_r \cos (2\pi r/m)\}^2 + \{\Sigma p_r \sin (2\pi r/m)\}^2 = (p_0 + \Sigma p_r)^2,$$

where the subscript r runs from 1 to $m-1$. On simplification, we find that

$$2p_0 \, \Sigma p_r \sin^2 (\pi pr/m) + \Sigma p_r p_{r'} \sin^2 \{\pi p(r - r')/m\} = 0.$$

Since p_0 and p_r are positive numbers, we must have

$$\sin (\pi pr/m) = \sin \{\pi p(r - r')/m\} = 0, \quad r, r' = 1, ..., m-1,$$

which are satisfied if and only if $p = 0 \, (\text{mod } m)$. Hence (4.3.8) follows. On using (4.3.8), we obtain

$$\lim_{n \to \infty} \phi_p{}^n = 0. \quad p \neq \text{mod } m; = 1, \quad p = 0 \, (\text{mod } m).$$

From (3.4.8), this is the c.f. of the discrete uniform distribution on m points. Hence, the result follows from the continuity theorem.

Convergence need not occur if the point $\theta = 0$ is not a lattice point. Consider a distribution with

$$\Pr(\theta = c) = p_1, \qquad \Pr(\theta = c + \pi) = p_2, \qquad c \neq 0, \pi,$$

where c is an irrational number, $p_1 > 0$ and $p_1 + p_2 = 1$. We have $\phi_{2p} = e^{2pci}$ so that $\lim_{n \to \infty} \phi_{2p}^{n}$ oscillates.

4.3.2b. *Wrapped Normal Distribution*

So far we have considered the limiting distribution of the sum S_n without any scaling factor. On the circle, there is no scaling operation which can reduce the variance of the sum as can be done on the line. In view of this shortcoming, the following result is interesting.

Let $\theta_j, j = 1, ..., n$ be independent and identically distributed random variables with $-\pi < \theta_j \leqslant \pi$ for each j and let $F(\theta)$ be their common d.f. Suppose also that $E(\theta) = 0$. Then the distribution of

$$S_n^* = (\Sigma \theta_j / n^{\frac{1}{2}}) \;(\text{mod } 2\pi)$$

tends to the wrapped normal distribution with the parameter $\sigma^2 = E(\theta^2)$.

The c.f. of S_n^* is given by

$$\phi_p^* = [E\{\cos (p\theta/n^{\frac{1}{2}}) + i \sin (p\theta/n^{\frac{1}{2}})\}]^n, \qquad -\pi < \theta \leqslant \pi. \qquad (4.3.9)$$

We have

$$\cos (p\theta/n^{\frac{1}{2}}) = 1 - \frac{p^2\theta^2}{2n} + o\left(\frac{1}{n}\right), \quad \sin (p\theta/n^{\frac{1}{2}}) = \frac{p\theta}{n^{\frac{1}{2}}} + o\left(\frac{1}{n}\right)$$

so that (4.3.9) becomes

$$\phi_p^* = \exp \left\{ n \log \left[1 - \frac{p^2\sigma^2}{2n} + o\left(\frac{1}{n}\right) \right] \right\}.$$

Hence, we obtain

$$\lim_{n \to \infty} \phi_p^* = \exp \{- \tfrac{1}{2}p^2\sigma^2\}. \qquad (4.3.10)$$

On comparing (4.3.10) with the c.f. of the wrapped normal distribution given at (3.4.29), we obtain the desired result.

Since the range of θ is finite, $E(\theta^2)$ always exists. For a given density, $E(\theta^2)$ can be obtained easily. Let

$$f(\theta) = \frac{1}{2\pi} [1 + 2 \sum_{p=1}^{\infty} (\alpha_p \cos p\theta + \beta_p \sin p\theta)], \qquad -\pi < \theta \leqslant \pi.$$

After some straightforward integration, we have

$$E(\theta^2) = \frac{\pi^2}{3} + 4 \sum_{p=1}^{\infty} (-1)^p \alpha_p/p^2. \tag{4.3.11}$$

In particular, for the cardioid distribution

$$E(\theta^2) = \frac{\pi^2}{3} - 4\rho.$$

For the wrapped normal distribution and the von Mises distribution, (4.3.11) does not simplify.

We have considered the central limit theorems for equal components. For the central limit theorem for non-identical random variables, the reader is referred to Lévy (1939) and Dvoretzky and Wolfowitz (1951). The latter reference deals with discrete random variables. We can deduce a Lindberg-type central limit theorem on the circle from Parthasarathy (1967, pp. 115–116) who gives such a theorem for an arbitrary locally compact abelian group. The limiting distribution in this case is wrapped normal. The asymptotic distribution of the sample mean direction, which differs from the asymptotic distribution of S_n^*, is given in Section 4.9.

4.3.3. Poincaré's Theorem

Poincaré (1912) considered the following problem as an illustration of his general result. Let a needle be free to rotate about the centre of a disc which is divided into a hundred sectors alternatively red and black. Poincaré has shown that the distribution of the stopping position of the needle is uniform in general. This problem can be formulated as follows. Let the continuous random variable x denote the total distance covered by a point on the rim of a roulette wheel of unit radius after a push. The final stopping position x_w is measured by

$$x_w = x \,(\mathrm{mod}\, 2\pi).$$

That is, the random variable x_w corresponds to the wrapped distribution of x. Poincaré's result then states that the variable x_w is distributed nearly as a uniform variable if the spread of the variable x is large.

We reformulate this problem as follows. Let us define

$$x' = cx. \tag{4.3.12}$$

We show that the distribution of the wrapped variable

$$x_w' = x' \,(\mathrm{mod}\, 2\pi) \tag{4.3.13}$$

tends to the uniform distribution as $c \to \infty$. This construction implies that the density of x is spread out in the limit. Suppose that $\phi(t)$ is the c.f. of x. Then the c.f. of x_w is simply $\phi(cp)$. Since x is a continuous random variable, the Lebesgue–Riemann theorem [see (4.2.31)] gives

$$\lim_{|t| \to \infty} \phi(t) = 0,$$

which implies that for the c.f. of x_w', we have

$$\lim_{c \to \infty} \phi(cp) = 0, \quad \text{for all } p \neq 0.$$

Consequently, the distribution of x_w' tends to the uniform distribution.

This result has already been demonstrated for the wrapped normal distribution (Section 3.4.8d) and for the wrapped Cauchy distribution (Section 3.4.8e) when $\sigma \to \infty$ and $a \to \infty$ respectively. Feller (1966, pp. 62–63) has given another version of this problem and assumes that the maximum of the density of x is small.

4.3.4. The Distribution of First Significant Digits

Let us consider the distribution of the first significant digits from a large body of data such as from a Census report. Let x be the random variable which generates the data. The random variable

$$x_w = \log_{10} x \,(\text{mod } 1)$$

has a uniform distribution on the circle of unit length by Poincaré's theorem since the spread of x will be very large. Now, the first digit of x is i, $i = 1$, $2, \ldots, 9$ if and only if

$$i \times 10^r \leqslant x < (i + 1) \times 10^{r+1},$$

where r is a suitably chosen integer. Consequently,

$$\Pr(\text{the first digit of } x = i) \equiv \Pr\{\log_{10} i \leqslant x_w < \log_{10}(i + 1)\}$$
$$= \log_{10}(i + 1) - \log_{10} i, \quad i = 1, 2, \ldots, 9. \quad (4.3.14)$$

The above result is due to Pinkham (1961) who also discusses its applications in inventory problems and in the generation of pseudorandom numbers. Benford (1938) arrived at this model through empirical studies of various such data. Table 4.1 reproduces one of his examples which gives a complete count (except for dates and page numbers) of an issue of the Reader's Digest. The expected frequencies obtained from (4.3.14) are shown in Column

3. The observed value of χ^2 is 3·30 and $\Pr(\chi_8^2 > 15·51) = 0·05$ so that the fit is satisfactory.

TABLE 4.1. The frequencies of first digits from large numbers in an issue of the Reader's Digest (Benford, 1938)

First digit	Observed frequency	Expected frequency
1	103	92·7
2	57	54·2
3	38	38·5
4	23	29·9
5	22	24·3
6	20	20·6
7	17	17·9
8	15	15·7
9	13	14·2
Total	308	308

4.4. THE ISOTROPIC RANDOM WALK ON THE CIRCLE

4.4.1. The Problem

We assume that a random walk starts from the origin $(0, 0)$ in the plane. Let $l_1, l_2, \ldots$ be the lengths of successive steps whose directions $\theta_1, \theta_2, \ldots$ relative to a fixed x-axis are distributed independently and uniformly. We obtain the distribution of the distance from the origin after n steps, assuming that the l_i are fixed, $i = 1, \ldots, n$.

We have

$$f(\theta_i) = 1/(2\pi), \qquad 0 < \theta_i \leqslant 2\pi. \tag{4.4.1}$$

Let C and S be the x and y coordinates of the point reached after the nth step so that

$$C = \sum_{i=1}^{n} l_i \cos \theta_i, \quad S = \sum_{i=1}^{n} l_i \sin \theta_i$$

and the distance travelled after n steps is the length of their resultant, viz.

$$R = (C^2 + S^2)^{\frac{1}{2}}.$$

Let $\bar{x}_0$ be the angle made by the resultant with the x-axis so that

$$\cos \bar{x}_0 = C/R, \qquad \sin \bar{x}_0 = S/R.$$

The statistic $\bar{x}_0$ is, of course, the sample mean direction if the l's are equal.

4.4.2. The Distribution of $\bar{x}_0$ and R

We first obtain the distribution of R by following the characteristic function method of Section 4.2.3. Using (4.4.1) in (4.2.27), the c.f. of $(l_j \cos \theta_j, l_j \sin \theta_j)$ is

$$\bar{\psi}_j(\rho, \Phi) = (2\pi)^{-1} \int_0^{2\pi} e^{i\rho l_j \cos (\theta - \Phi)} \, d\theta, \tag{4.4.2}$$

where we have used the notation of (4.2.15). Since θ has a distribution on the circle, the integral in (4.4.2) does not depend on Φ. On substituting its value from (4.2.17), we have

$$\bar{\psi}_j(\rho, \Phi) = J_0(l_j \rho). \tag{4.4.3}$$

Hence, the c.f. of (C, S) is given by

$$\prod_{j=1}^{n} J_0(l_j \rho) \tag{4.4.4}$$

which does not depend on Φ. On substituting (4.4.4) into the inversion formula (4.2.28) for R, we find that the p.d.f. of R is given by

$$p(R) = R \int_0^\infty u \, J_0(Ru) \prod_{i=1}^{n} J_0(l_i u) \, du. \tag{4.4.5}$$

From (4.2.16), it follows that the distribution of $\bar{x}_0$ is uniform and the random variables $\bar{x}_0$ and R are distributed independently.

We have $R \leqslant n$ so in (4.4.5)

$$p(R) = 0 \quad \text{for} \quad R > n$$

which implies that the integral on the right vanishes for $R > n$.

Equal Lengths. For $l_1 = \ldots = l_n = 1$, the p.d.f. of R given by (4.4.5) reduces to

$$h_n(R) = R \int_0^\infty u J_0(Ru) J_0^{\,n}(u) \, du = R\phi_n(R^2), \quad \text{say.} \tag{4.4.6}$$

Particular cases of this p.d.f. are discussed below.

From (4.4.4), the polar moment generating function of R is

$$J_0{}^n(\rho),\tag{4.4.7}$$

which is also the c.f. of (C, S).

We now obtain the d.f. of R. Let

$$J_1(x) = \sum_{k=0}^{\infty} \frac{(-1)^k}{k!(k+1)!} (\tfrac{1}{2}x)^{2k+1}$$

be the standard Bessel function of order one. We have similar to (3.4.52)

$$d\{xJ_1(x)\}/dx = xJ_0(x)\tag{4.4.8}$$

so that the d.f. corresponding to $h_n(R)$ can be written as

$$H_n(R) = \int_0^\infty \left[\int_0^R \frac{dJ_1(u\rho)u\rho}{d(u\rho)} \, d\rho \right] J_0{}^n(u) \, du.$$

Therefore,

$$H_n(R) = R \int_0^\infty J_1(uR) J_0{}^n(u) \, du.\tag{4.4.9}$$

By using the fact that $R^2 = 2(1 - \cos\theta)$, where θ, the angle between the first two steps is uniformly distributed, we have

$$h_2(R) = 2\{\pi(4 - R^2)^{\frac{1}{2}}\}^{-1}, \qquad 0 < R < 2.\tag{4.4.10}$$

For $n = 3$, the p.d.f. can be expressed in terms of elliptic functions, viz.

$$\begin{aligned} h_3(R) &= \pi^{-2} mR^{\frac{1}{2}}K(m) && \text{if } R < 1, \\ &= \pi^{-2} R^{\frac{1}{2}} K(1/m) && \text{if } R > 1, \end{aligned}\tag{4.4.11}$$

where

$$m = 4\{R/(3-R)(1+R)^3\}^{\frac{1}{2}}, K(m) = \int_0^1 \{(1-t^2)(1-m^2t^2)\}^{-\frac{1}{2}} \, dt.$$

As $R \to 1$, $h_3(R) \to \infty$. For details of the derivation, see Stephens (1962a). For $n = 4(1)7$, the p.d.f. has been calculated by K. Pearson (1906) who also gave a series expansion which was used later by Greenwood and Durand (1955) to tabulate the distribution for $n = 6(1)24$. Durand and Greenwood (1957) have examined the adequacy of some approximations by truncating Pearson's series expansion and compared various methods of approximation.

For large n, a chi-square approximation can be used (see Section 4.9). Johnson (1966) has given a beta approximation and Stephens (1969d) has fitted Pearson curves (see Section 4.7).

The above problem of the random walk on the circle was proposed by K. Pearson (1905) in a letter to *Nature*. Its asymptotic solution had been obtained already by Rayleigh (1880) and was reported in response to Pearson's letter in Rayleigh (1905). The exact solution was obtained by Kluyver (1906) and Pearson (1906) gave another proof of Kluyver's result. Later Markov (1912) and Rayleigh (1919) studied this problem. Our solution seems to require a minimum of Bessel function theory.

4.4.3. The Distribution of C and S

We now obtain the joint p.d.f. of

$$C = \Sigma \cos \theta_i \quad \text{and} \quad S = \Sigma \sin \theta_i.$$

From Section 4.4.2, the joint p.d.f. of $(\bar{x}_0, R)$, where $C = R \cos \bar{x}_0$ and $S = R \sin \bar{x}_0$, is given by

$$R\phi_n(R^2)/2\pi, \quad 0 < \bar{x}_0 \leqslant 2\pi, \quad R > 0, \tag{4.4.12}$$

with ϕ_n as in Eqn (4.4.6). Consequently, the joint p.d.f. of (C, S) is simply

$$g_0(C, S) = (2\pi)^{-1} \phi_n(C^2 + S^2). \tag{4.4.13}$$

We shall obtain the marginal distributions of C and S in Section 4.5.4.

4.5. DISTRIBUTION OF C, S AND R FOR A VON MISES POPULATION

4.5.1. Introduction

In all subsequent sections, we shall write

$$C = \sum_{i=1}^{n} \cos \theta_i, \quad S = \sum_{i=1}^{n} \sin \theta_i, \quad R = (C^2 + S^2)^{\frac{1}{2}}.$$

We now assume that $\theta_1, \dots, \theta_n$ is a random sample from a von Mises distribution with p.d.f.

$$g(\theta; \mu_0, \kappa) = \{2\pi I_0(\kappa)\}^{-1} \exp \{\kappa \cos (\theta - \mu_0)\}, \quad 0 < \theta \leqslant 2\pi. \tag{4.5.1}$$

That is, θ is distributed as $M(\mu_0, \kappa)$.

In Section 4.5.5, we deal with some sampling distributions for a multimodal von Mises-type distribution.

4.5.2. The Joint Distribution of C and S

The joint p.d.f. $g_\kappa(C, S)$ of (C, S) can be obtained by integrating the likelihood function of $\theta_1, \ldots, \theta_n$ keeping C and S fixed. Thus

$$g_\kappa(C, S) = \{I_0(\kappa)\}^{-n} e^{\kappa\mu C + \kappa\nu S} \int \ldots \int \prod_{i=1}^{n} \frac{d\theta_i}{2\pi}, \qquad (4.5.2)$$

where

$$\mu = \cos \mu_0, \qquad \nu = \sin \mu_0, \qquad (4.5.3)$$

and the integral is taken over $\theta_1, \ldots, \theta_n$ with C and S held constant. The integral represents the density of (C, S) when $\theta_1, \ldots, \theta_n$ is a random sample from the uniform population, i.e. it is equal to $g_0(C, S)$ given by (4.4.13). On substituting (4.4.13) into (4.5.2), we have

$$g_\kappa(C, S) = [2\pi I_0{}^n(\kappa)]^{-1} e^{\kappa\mu C + \kappa\nu S} \phi_n(C^2 + S^2). \qquad (4.5.4)$$

The marginal distributions of C and S cannot be obtained in a useful form from (4.5.4). We shall obtain them in Section 4.5.4 by a different approach.

4.5.3. Distributions of $\bar{x}_0$ and R

On transforming C and S to $\bar{x}_0$ and R by $C = R \cos \bar{x}_0$ and $S = R \sin \bar{x}_0$ in (4.5.4), the joint p.d.f. of $\bar{x}_0$ and R is seen to be

$$g(\bar{x}_0, R) = [2\pi I_0{}^n(\kappa)]^{-1} e^{\kappa R \cos (\bar{x}_0 - \mu_0)} h_n(R), \qquad 0 < \bar{x}_0 \leqslant 2\pi, \quad 0 < R < n.$$

$$(4.5.5)$$

On integrating with respect to $\bar{x}_0$, we see easily that the p.d.f. of R is given by

$$p(R) = \{I_0(\kappa)\}^{-n} I_0(\kappa R) h_n(R), \qquad 0 < R < n, \qquad (4.5.6)$$

where $h_n(R)$ is the p.d.f. of R for the uniform case and is given by (4.4.6). It can be verified that the total probability is unity by using (4.2.23). For $n = 2$ and $n = 3$, we can simplify (4.5.6) with the help of (4.4.10) and (4.4.11). Another proof of (4.5.6) will appear in Section 4.6.1.

The result (4.5.6) is due to Greenwood and Durand (1955). Section 4.9 discusses the limiting distribution of $(\bar{x}_0, R)$ and some approximations.

It seems that the marginal p.d.f. of $\bar{x}_0$ cannot be simplified. However, using (4.5.5) and (4.5.6), we obtain the important result that the conditional distribution of $\bar{x}_0$ given R is $M(\mu_0, \kappa R)$, i.e.

$$f(\bar{x}_0|R) = \{2\pi I_0(\kappa R)\}^{-1} \exp \{\kappa R \cos (\bar{x}_0 - \mu_0)\}, \qquad 0 < \bar{x}_0 \leqslant 2\pi. \quad (4.5.7)$$

4.5.4. Marginal Distributions of C and S

The c.f. of $\cos \theta$ is given by

$$\phi(t) = \{2\pi I_0(\kappa)\}^{-1} \int_0^{2\pi} \exp \{it \cos \theta + \kappa \cos (\theta - \mu_0)\} \, d\theta. \quad (4.5.8)$$

To evaluate this integral, we note that

$$\int_0^{2\pi} \exp (a \cos \theta + ib \sin \theta) \, d\theta = 2\pi J_0\{(b^2 - a^2)^{\frac{1}{2}}\} \quad (4.5.9)$$

which can be verified by expanding the exponential term and using

$$\int_0^{2\pi} (a \cos \theta + ib \sin \theta)^r \, d\theta = \begin{cases} 2 \beta(\tfrac{1}{2}, m + \tfrac{1}{2})(a^2 - b^2)^m, & \text{if } r = 2m \\ 0, & \text{if } r = 2m + 1. \end{cases}$$

Thus (4.5.8) reduces to

$$\phi(t) = J_0\big(\{(t - i\kappa\mu)^2 - \kappa^2 v^2\}^{\frac{1}{2}}\big)/I_0(\kappa). \quad (4.5.10)$$

The c.f. of C is $\phi^n(t)$ so that, by the inversion theorem, the p.d.f. of C is

$$g(C) = \{2\pi I_0{}^n(\kappa)\}^{-1} \int_{-\infty}^{\infty} e^{-iCt} J_0{}^n\big(\{(t - i\kappa\mu)^2 - \kappa^2 v^2\}^{\frac{1}{2}}\big) \, dt.$$

By contour integration of the integrand around the rectangle with vertices $(\pm c, 0)$, $(\pm c, \kappa\mu)$ and letting $c \to \infty$, we find that

$$g(C) = \{2\pi I_0{}^n(\kappa)\}^{-1} e^{\kappa\mu C} \int_{-\infty}^{\infty} e^{-iCt} J_0{}^n\{(t^2 - \kappa^2 v^2)^{\frac{1}{2}}\} \, dt. \quad (4.5.11)$$

Since the integrand is an even function of t, we have finally

$$g(C) = \{\pi I_0{}^n(\kappa)\}^{-1} e^{\kappa\mu C} \int_0^{\infty} \cos Ct \, J_0{}^n\{(t^2 - \kappa^2 v^2)^{\frac{1}{2}}\} \, dt. \quad (4.5.12)$$

For $\mu_0 = 0$, we have $v = 0$ so that (4.5.12) reduces to the p.d.f. given by Greenwood and Durand (1955):

$$g(C) = \{\pi I_0{}^n(\kappa)\}^{-1} e^{\kappa C} \int_0^{\infty} \cos Ct \, J_0{}^n(t) \, dt. \quad (4.5.13)$$

Further, for $\kappa = 0$, we get the p.d.f. of Lord (1948) for the isotropic case:

$$g(C) = \pi^{-1} \int_0^\infty \cos Ct \, J_0{}''(t) \, dt. \qquad (4.5.14)$$

Some approximations to (4.5.13) and (4.5.14) are discussed in Section 4.9.

We may obtain the p.d.f. of S by replacing μ_0 by $\tfrac{1}{2}\pi - \mu_0$ in (4.5.12). Thus the p.d.f. of S is

$$g(S) = \{\pi I_0{}''(\kappa)\}^{-1} e^{\kappa v S} \int_0^\infty \cos St \, J_0{}''\{(t^2 - \kappa^2 \mu^2)^{\frac{1}{2}}\} \, dt. \qquad (4.5.15)$$

Putting $\kappa = 0$, we get the p.d.f. of S for the uniform case.

4.5.5. Distributions for a Multi-modal von Mises-type population

Let $\theta_1, \ldots, \theta_n$ be a random sample from a population with p.d.f.

$$u(\theta) = \{1/2\pi I_0(\kappa)\} e^{\kappa \cos l(\theta - \mu_0)}, \qquad 0 < \theta \leqslant 2\pi, \quad \kappa > 0, \qquad (4.5.16)$$

where l is a positive integer (Section 3.6). Let

$$\Sigma \cos l\theta_i = R_l \cos m_l{}^0, \quad \Sigma \sin l\theta_i = R_l \sin m_l{}^0. \qquad (4.5.17)$$

Using the method of Section 4.4, the c.f. of $(\cos l\theta, \sin l\theta)$ for the uniform variable θ is found to be

$$(2\pi)^{-1} \int_0^{2\pi} e^{i\rho \cos(l\theta - \Phi)} \, d\theta.$$

After transforming the variable θ to $\theta' = l\theta$, the new integral can be split into the sum of l integrals over $(2\pi i, 2\pi i + 2\pi)$, $i = 0, 1, \ldots, l - 1$. Each of the integrals has the same value and we find that the c.f. reduces to $J_0(\rho)$. Consequently, the c.f. of (4.5.17) is given by (4.4.7). Thus the p.d.f. of R_l is given precisely by (4.4.6). Further, the method of Section 4.5.2. is again applicable to (4.5.16) and we deduce that the joint p.d.f. of R_l and $m_l{}^0$ is also given by (4.5.5). The marginal p.d.f. of R_l is the same as (4.5.6) while the conditional distribution of $m_l{}^0$ given R_l is $M(l\mu_0, \kappa R_l)$.

4.6. DISTRIBUTIONS RELATED TO THE MULTI-SAMPLE PROBLEM FOR VON MISES POPULATIONS

Let θ_{jk}, $k = 1, \ldots, n_j$, $j = 1, \ldots, q$, be independent random samples of sizes $n_1, \ldots, n_q$ from $M(\mu_{0,j}, \kappa_j)$, $j = 1, \ldots, q$, respectively. Let $\bar{x}_{0,j}$ and R_j be the mean direction and resultant of the jth sample. We shall write

$$\mathbf{R}^* = (R_1, ..., R_q), \quad \boldsymbol{\mu}_0 = (\mu_{0,1}, ..., \mu_{0,q}), \quad \boldsymbol{\kappa} = (\kappa_1, ..., \kappa_q),$$

$$C_j = \sum_{k=1}^{n_j} \cos \theta_{jk}, \quad S_j = \sum_{k=1}^{n_j} \sin \theta_{jk}, \quad C = \Sigma C_j,$$

$$S = \Sigma S_j, \quad n = \Sigma n_j. \tag{4.6.1}$$

Let $\bar{x}_0$ and R be the mean direction and resultant of the combined sample. We have

$$R^2 = C^2 + S^2, \quad C = \Sigma R_j \cos \bar{x}_{0,j}, \quad S = \Sigma R_j \sin \bar{x}_{0,j}. \tag{4.6.2}$$

4.6.1. The Distribution of R

We again utilize the c.f. method used in Section 4.4 for the distribution of R for the uniform case. In the notation of (4.2.15), the c.f. of $(\cos \theta, \sin \theta)$ is defined by

$$\bar{\psi}(\rho, \Phi) = E[\exp \{i\rho \cos (\theta - \Phi)\}]$$

which, after using the transformation $\theta' = \theta - \Phi$, reduces to

$$\bar{\psi}(\rho, \Phi) = \{2\pi I_0(\kappa)\}^{-1} \int_0^{2\pi} \exp \{i\rho \cos \theta + \kappa \cos (\theta - \mu_0 + \Phi)\} \, d\theta.$$

On substituting the value of this integral from (4.5.9), we obtain

$$\bar{\psi}(\rho, \Phi) = J_0[\{\rho^2 - \kappa^2 - 2i\rho\kappa \cos (\Phi - \mu_0)\}^{\frac{1}{2}}]/I_0(\kappa). \tag{4.6.3}$$

Hence, the joint c.f. of C and S is given by

$$\prod_{j=1}^{q} J_0^{n_j}(w_j) \Big/ \prod_{j=1}^{q} I_0^{n_j}(\kappa_j), \tag{4.6.4}$$

where

$$w_j = \{\rho^2 - \kappa_j^2 - 2i\rho\kappa_j \cos (\Phi - \mu_{0,j})\}^{\frac{1}{2}}. \tag{4.6.5}$$

On using (4.6.4) in the inversion formula (4.2.28), we obtain the p.d.f. of R as

$$f(R) = \left\{ 2\pi \prod_{j=1}^{q} I_0^{n_j}(\kappa_j) \right\}^{-1} R\Psi_1(R; \boldsymbol{\mu}_0, \boldsymbol{\kappa}), \tag{4.6.6}$$

where

$$\Psi_1(R; \boldsymbol{\mu}_0, \boldsymbol{\kappa}) = \int_0^{\infty} \int_0^{2\pi} J_0(R\rho) \prod_{j=1}^{q} J_0^{n_j}(w_j) \rho \, d\rho \, d\Phi. \tag{4.6.7}$$

In fact, by using the method of Section 4.6.3 it can be shown that for $q = 1$ (4.6.7) reduces to the p.d.f. of R for the von Mises distribution given by (4.5.6).

4.6.2. The Distribution of $(R, \mathbf{R}^*)$

Let us first obtain the conditional distribution of R given $\mathbf{R}^*$. Since by (4.5.7), the conditional distribution of $\bar{x}_{0,j}$ given R_j is $M(\mu_{0,j}, \kappa_j R_j)$, the c.f. of $(R_j \cos \bar{x}_{0,j}, R_j \sin \bar{x}_{0,j})$ can be obtained from (4.6.3) on replacing μ_0, κ and ρ by $\mu_{0,j}, \kappa_j R_j$ and ρR_j respectively. Consequently, using the representation (4.6.2) of C and S, the c.f. of (C, S) for given $\mathbf{R}^*$ is simply

$$\prod_{j=1}^{q} \{J_0(w_j R_j)/I_0(\kappa_j R_j)\}. \tag{4.6.8}$$

Substituting this c.f. in the inversion formula (4.2.28), we have the conditional distribution of R given $\mathbf{R}^*$ as

$$f(R|\mathbf{R}^*) = \left\{2\pi \prod_{j=1}^{q} I_0(\kappa_j R_j)\right\}^{-1} R\Psi_2(R, \mathbf{R}^*; \mu_0, \kappa), \tag{4.6.9}$$

where

$$\Psi_2(R, \mathbf{R}^*; \mu_0, \kappa) = \int_0^\infty \int_0^{2\pi} J_0(R\rho) \left\{\prod_{j=1}^{q} J_0(w_j R_j)\right\} \rho \, d\rho \, d\Phi. \tag{4.6.10}$$

Using the independence of $R_1, \ldots, R_q$, we obtain the p.d.f. of $\mathbf{R}^*$ from (4.5.6) which when multiplied by (4.6.9) gives the joint p.d.f. of R and $\mathbf{R}^*$ as

$$f(R, \mathbf{R}^*; \mu_0, \kappa) = \left\{2\pi \prod_{j=1}^{q} I_0^{n_j}(\kappa_j)\right\}^{-1} \left\{\prod_{j=1}^{q} h_{n_j}(R_j)\right\} R\Psi_2(R, \mathbf{R}^*; \mu_0, \kappa). \tag{4.6.11}$$

Finally, on dividing (4.6.11) by (4.6.6), it follows that the conditional p.d.f. of $\mathbf{R}^*$ given R is

$$f(\mathbf{R}^*|R, \mu_0, \kappa) = \left\{\prod_{j=1}^{q} h_{n_j}(R_j)\right\} \{\Psi_2(R, \mathbf{R}^*; \mu_0, \kappa)\}/\Psi_1(R; \mu_0, \kappa), \tag{4.6.12}$$

where Ψ_1 and Ψ_2 are given by (4.6.7) and (4.6.10) respectively. The p.d.f.'s (4.6.9), (4.6.11), (4.6.12) involve the quantities w_j defined by (4.6.5). The dependence on the functions Ψ_1 and Ψ_2 makes these distributions difficult to handle in general. We now consider some particular cases.

4.6.3. Distributions for the Homogeneous Case

We now assume that $\mu_{0,1} = \ldots = \mu_{0,q} = \mu_0$ and $\kappa_1 = \ldots = \kappa_q = \kappa$. For this case, the distribution of R is given by (4.5.6). On using this result in

(4.6.6), we obtain

$$\Psi_1(R; \mu_0 \mathbf{1}, \kappa \mathbf{1}) = 2\pi I_0(\kappa R) h_n(R)/R, \qquad (4.6.13)$$

where $\mathbf{1}$ is a vector of q 1's. Let us next consider Ψ_2. We can take $\mu_0 = 0$ by making a shift of the origin of Φ. Further, on transforming (ρ, Φ) to cartesian co-ordinates (x, y) and performing the same contour integration with respect to x as carried out for (4.5.11), we have

$$\Psi_2(R, \mathbf{R}^*; \mu_0 \mathbf{1}, \kappa \mathbf{1})$$

$$= \int_{-\infty}^{\infty} \int_{-\infty}^{\infty} J_0[\{(x + i\kappa)^2 + y^2\}^{\frac{1}{2}}] \prod_{j=1}^{q} J_0\{R_j(x^2 + y^2)^{\frac{1}{2}}\} \, dx \, dy.$$

Transforming (x, y) to polar co-ordinates and using the result

$$\int_0^{2\pi} J_0\{R(\rho^2 - \kappa^2 + 2i\kappa\rho \cos \Phi)^{\frac{1}{2}}\} \, d\Phi = 2\pi J_0(R\rho) I_0(\kappa R), \qquad (4.6.14)$$

obtained from the von Neumann addition formula (3.4.68), we find that

$$\Psi_2(R, \mathbf{R}^*; \mu_0 \mathbf{1}, \kappa \mathbf{1}) = 2\pi I_0(\kappa R) \int_0^{\infty} J_0(R\rho) \left\{ \prod_{j=1}^{q} J_0(R_j \rho) \right\} \rho \, d\rho. \quad (4.6.15)$$

With the help of the simplified versions of Ψ_1 and Ψ_2 given by (4.6.13) and (4.6.15), various distributions related to $(R, \mathbf{R}^*)$ can be obtained. In particular, from (4.6.12), the conditional p.d.f. of $\mathbf{R}^*$ given R is

$$f(\mathbf{R}^*|R) = R\left[\left\{ \prod_{j=1}^{q} h_{n_j}(R_j) \right\} \Big/ h_n(R) \right] \int_0^{\infty} J_0(R\rho) \left\{ \prod_{j=1}^{q} J_0(R_j \rho) \right\} \rho \, d\rho. \quad (4.6.16)$$

We now simplify this distribution for $q = 2$. Consider the conditional distribution of R given R_1 and R_2 for $\kappa = 0$ so that the angles are uniformly distributed. We have

$$R^2 = R_1^2 + R_2^2 - 2R_1 R_2 \cos \lambda, \qquad 0 < \lambda \leqslant \pi, \qquad (4.6.17)$$

where $(\pi - \lambda)$ is the angle between R_1 and R_2. It can be seen that the angle λ is distributed uniformly from 0 to π. Hence, on using the transformation (4.6.17) from λ to R, we find that the conditional p.d.f. of R given R_1 and R_2 is

$$R/(\pi R_1 R_2 \sin \lambda), \quad |R_1 - R_2| < R < R_1 + R_2, \quad 0 < R_1 < n_1, \quad 0 < R_2 < n_2,$$
$$(4.6.18)$$

where, from (4.6.17),

$$\sin \lambda = \{[(R_1 + R_2)^2 - R^2][R^2 - (R_1 - R_2)^2]\}^{\frac{1}{2}}/(2R_1 R_2). \qquad (4.16.19)$$

The fact that the p.d.f. of R given by (4.6.18) is identical to (4.6.9) with $q = 2$ and $\kappa = 0$ implies that

$$\int_0^\infty J_0(R\rho) J_0(R_1 \rho) J_0(R_2 \rho)\rho \, d\rho = 1/(\pi R_1 R_2 \sin \lambda). \qquad (4.6.20)$$

On substituting (4.6.20) in (4.6.16) with $q = 2$, the p.d.f. of R_1 and R_2 given R reduces to

$$f(R_1, R_2|R) = Rh_{n_1}(R_1)h_{n_2}(R_2)/\{\pi R_1 R_2 h_n(R) \sin \lambda\}, \qquad (4.6.21)$$

where $0 < |R_1 - R_2| < R$, $0 < R_1 + R_2 < n$ and $\sin \lambda$ is given by (4.6.19). Other distributions connected with R, R_1 and R_2 can be simplified similarly.

The results (4.6.16) and (4.6.21) are of practical interest because they do not involve the parameters μ_0 and κ. The result (4.6.21) was obtained by Watson and Williams (1956) who obtained it by first considering the uniform case and then the von Mises case. The approach is basically similar to that adopted in Section 4.5 for the distribution of R. (Their result should be multiplied by a factor of 2). The generalization of this result to (4.6.16) is due to J. S. Rao (1969) who also uses Watson and Williams' approach.

4.6.4. The Two-sample Case

We now consider the distributions associated with R, R_1 and R_2 when the μ_0's and κ's are not restricted. We first establish that

$$a_p = \int_0^\infty J_0(R\rho) \prod_{j=1}^2 J_p(R_j \rho)\rho \, d\rho = (\cos p\lambda)/(\pi R_1 R_2 \sin \lambda), \qquad (4.6.22)$$

where p is an integer and λ is defined by (4.6.17) and (4.6.19). On equating the value of Ψ_2 from (4.6.15) and (4.6.10) for $q = 2$ and using (4.6.20), we obtain the identity

$$\int_0^\infty \int_0^{2\pi} J_0(R\rho) \left\{ \prod_{j=1}^2 J_0(R_j w) \right\} \rho \, d\rho \, d\Phi = 2I_0(R\kappa)/(R_1 R_2 \sin \lambda), \qquad (4.6.23)$$

where

$$w = (\rho^2 - \kappa^2 - 2i\rho\kappa \cos \Phi)^{\frac{1}{2}}.$$

Applying the von Neumann addition formula (3.4.68) to $J_0(R_1 w)$ and $J_0(R_2 w)$, interchanging the summation and integration signs and integrating with respect to Φ, the left-hand side of (4.6.23) becomes

$$2\pi \left[I_0(\kappa R_1) I_0(\kappa R_2) a_0 + 2 \sum_{p=1}^\infty I_p(\kappa R_1) I_p(\kappa R_2) a_p \right], \qquad (4.6.24)$$

while, on substituting for R from (4.6.17) and again using the von Neumann addition formula, the right-hand side of (4.6.23) becomes

$$2\left[I_0(\kappa R_1) I_0(\kappa R_2) + 2 \sum_{p=1}^{\infty} I_p(\kappa R_1) I_p(\kappa R_2) \cos p\lambda\right]\bigg/(R_1 R_2 \sin \lambda). \quad (4.6.25)$$

Since (4.6.24) is identically equal to (4.6.25) for all values of κ, we obtain (4.6.22).

Let us now simplify (4.6.10) for $q = 2$ with unrestricted μ's and κ's. On applying the von Neumann addition formula to $J_0(R_1 w_1)$ and $J_0(R_2 w_2)$ and integrating with respect to Φ under the summation sign, we find, after using (4.6.22) together with the addition formula, that

$$\Psi_2(R, \mathbf{R}^*; \boldsymbol{\mu}_0, \boldsymbol{\kappa}) = \{I_0(w_1') + I_0(w_2')\}/(R_1 R_2 \sin \lambda), \quad (4.6.26)$$

where

$$w_1' = \{\kappa_1{}^2 R_1{}^2 + \kappa_2{}^2 R_2{}^2 - 2\kappa_1\kappa_2 R_1 R_2 \cos (\lambda - d)\}^{\frac{1}{2}},$$

$$w_2' = \{\kappa_1{}^2 R_1{}^2 + \kappa_2{}^2 R_2{}^2 - 2\kappa_1\kappa_2 R_1 R_2 \cos (\lambda + d)\}^{\frac{1}{2}}$$

and

$$d = \mu_{0,1} - \mu_{0,2}.$$

The expression for Ψ_1 given by (4.6.7) for $q = 2$ can be shown to depend only on κ_1 and κ_2 although no further simplification is possible. For the particular case of $\kappa_1 = \kappa_2 = \kappa$, the conditional p.d.f. of R_1 and R_2 given R is, from (4.6.12) and (4.6.26),

$$f(R_1, R_2|R)$$
$$= h_{n_1}(R_1) h_{n_2}(R_2)\{I_0[\kappa\{R_1{}^2 + R_2{}^2 - 2R_1 R_2 \cos (\lambda - d)\}^{\frac{1}{2}}]$$
$$+ I_0[\kappa\{R_1{}^2 + R_2{}^2 - 2R_1 R_2 \cos (\lambda + d)\}^{\frac{1}{2}}]\}/\{R_1 R_2 \Psi_1(R; \kappa, \boldsymbol{\mu}) \sin \lambda\},$$

$$(4.6.27)$$

where w_1 and w_2 in the expression (4.6.7) for $\Psi_1(R; \kappa, \boldsymbol{\mu})$ are now given by

$$w_1 = \{\rho^2 - \kappa^2 - 2i\rho\kappa \cos (\Phi - d)\}^{\frac{1}{2}}, \qquad w_2 = \{\rho^2 - \kappa^2 - 2i\rho\kappa \cos \Phi\}^{\frac{1}{2}}.$$

Unless $d = 0$, the p.d.f. (4.6.27) depends on κ.

It should be noted that the distribution theory treated here extends immediately to the multi-modal case on adopting the approach of Section 4.5.5. An approximation to the distribution of $(R, \mathbf{R}^*)$ will be given in Section 4.9.4.

4.7. MOMENTS OF R

4.7.1. A General Case

Let $\theta_1, ..., \theta_n$ be independent and identically distributed random variables. Let

$$x_j = e^{i\theta_j}, \qquad y_k = e^{-i\theta_k}.$$

Then we have $x_k y_k = 1$. If $j \neq k$ then x_j and y_k are distributed independently. Now,

$$R^2 = n + \Sigma x_j y_k, \qquad (4.7.1)$$

where Σ will always denote the summation over unequal subscripts. The sum may be described as an augmented symmetric function. On taking the expectation of (4.7.1), we obtain

$$E(R^2) = n + n(n-1)\rho^2, \qquad (4.7.2)$$

where $\rho^2 = \alpha^2 + \beta^2$. Squaring both sides of (4.7.1) and taking expectations, we find that

$$E(R^4) = n^2 + 2n^2(n-1)\rho^2 + E(D), \qquad (4.7.3)$$

where

$$D = \sum_{j \neq k} \sum_{j' \neq k'} x_j y_k x_{j'} y_{k'}. \qquad (4.7.4)$$

The quantity D is, in terms of the augmented symmetric functions,

$$D = \Sigma x_j y_k x_{j'} y_{k'} + \Sigma x_j y_{j'} x_{j'} y_{k'} + \Sigma x_j y_{k'}^2 x_{j'}$$
$$+ \Sigma x_j^2 y_k y_{k'} + \Sigma x_j y_k x_{j'} y_j + \Sigma x_j^2 y_k^2 + \Sigma x_j y_j x_k y_k. \qquad (4.7.5)$$

We have

$$E(\Sigma x_j y_k x_{j'} y_{k'}) = n^{(4)} \{E(x)\}^2 \{E(y)\}^2,$$

where

$$n^{(4)} = n(n-1)(n-2)(n-3), \qquad x = e^{i\theta}, \qquad y = e^{-i\theta}.$$

We can calculate the expectations of the other terms in (4.7.5) similarly. We then find that

$$E(D) = n^{(4)} \rho^4 + 2n^{(3)} \rho^2 + 2n^{(2)}\{\alpha_2(\alpha^2 - \beta^2) + 2\alpha\beta\beta_2\}$$
$$+ n^{(2)}(\alpha_2^2 + \beta_2^2) + n(n-1). \qquad (4.7.6)$$

Hence, we can obtain $E(R^4)$ from (4.7.4) and, using (4.7.2), deduce that

$$\text{var}\,(R^2) = 2n^{(3)}\{\alpha_2(\alpha^2 - \beta^2) + 2\alpha\beta\beta_2 + \rho^2\}$$
$$+ n^{(2)}(1 + \alpha_2{}^2 + \beta_2{}^2) + (6 - 4n)\rho^4. \qquad (4.7.7)$$

For symmetrical distributions, $\beta = \beta_2 = 0$ so that (4.7.2) and (4.7.7) simplify to

$$E(R^2) = n + n(n - 1)\alpha^2 \qquad (4.7.8)$$

and

$$\text{var}\,(R^2) = 2n^{(3)}(\alpha_2 + 1)\,\alpha^2 + n^{(2)}(1 + \alpha_2{}^2) + (6 - 4n)\alpha^4. \qquad (4.7.9)$$

4.7.2. The von Mises Distribution

In particular, for the von Mises distribution $M(0, \kappa)$ we can obtain $E(R^2)$ and var (R^2) from (4.7.8) and (4.7.9) by using

$$\alpha_p = I_p(\kappa)/I_0(\kappa), \qquad p = 1, \dots, n.$$

The higher moments of R^2 can be obtained as follows. Let

$$\mu_s = E(R^s), \qquad v_s = E\{R^s A(\kappa R)\},$$

where $A(\kappa) = I_1(\kappa)/I_0(\kappa)$. We write the expressions for μ_s and v_s with the help of the p.d.f. of R given by (4.5.6) and differentiate these with respect to κ. Using the results

$$I_0{}'(\kappa) = I_1(\kappa), \quad I_1{}'(\kappa) = I_0(\kappa) - \{I_1(\kappa)/\kappa\}, \qquad (4.7.10)$$

obtained by differentiating the series for $I_0(\kappa)$ and $I_1(\kappa)$ given in (3.4.46), we find that

$$v_s = \mu'_{s-1} + nA(\kappa)\mu_{s-1}, \qquad \mu_{s+1} = [\{1 + n\kappa A(\kappa)\}/\kappa]v_s + v_s'.$$

Using the first of these equations to eliminate v_s and v_s' from the second one, we obtain the recurrence relation

$$\mu_{2s} = \mu''_{2s-2} + \{(1 + 2nA\kappa)/\kappa\}\,\mu'_{2s-2} + n(1 - A^2 + nA^2)\mu_{2s-2}, \qquad (4.7.11)$$

where $A = A(\kappa)$, μ'_{2s-2} and μ''_{2s-2} denote the first and the second derivatives of μ_{2s-2} with respect to κ. For $s = 1$, we have

$$\mu_2 = n + n(n - 1)\,A^2.$$

Higher moments can be obtained recursively by this process.

4.7.3. The Uniform Distribution

For the uniform distribution with p.d.f.

$$f(\theta) = (2\pi)^{-1}, \qquad 0 < \theta \leqslant 2\pi,$$

we have

$$\alpha_i = \beta_i = 0, \qquad i \geqslant 1. \tag{4.7.11}'$$

Hence, from (4.7.8) and (4.7.9),

$$E(R^2) = n, \qquad \mathrm{var}\,(R^2) = n(n-1). \tag{4.7.12}$$

The distribution of R has been obtained in Section 4.4.2 but it is not easy to calculate the moments directly from its p.d.f. We can obtain the higher moments using the polar moment generating function (4.4.7) together with (4.2.24). However, a direct method is as follows. From (4.7.1) and (4.7.11)$'$, the even moments of R^2 about its mean are given by

$$\mu_s(R^2) = E\{R^2 - E(R^2)\}^{2s} = E(\Sigma x_j y_k)^s. \tag{4.7.13}$$

Of course, the odd moments of R^2 are zero. In view of (4.7.11)$'$ and the definitions of x_j and y_k, the non-zero contribution to $\mu_3(R^2)$ will come only from the term

$$2\Sigma x_j y_j x_k y_k x_l y_l$$

in the expansion of $(\Sigma x_j y_k)^3$. The factor 2 appears because $x_j y_{j'} x_k y_{k'} x_l y_{l'}$ with $j' \neq j$, $k' \neq k$, $l' \neq l$ reduces to $x_j y_j x_k y_k x_l y_l$ if either $j' = k$, $k' = l$, $l' = j$ or $j' = l$, $k' = j$, $l' = k$. Hence,

$$\mu_3(R^2) = 2n(n-1)(n-2). \tag{4.7.14}$$

This process is tedious for larger values of s. It is then convenient to work with

$$\mu_s'(R^2) = E\{S_{10}S_{01}\}^s,$$

where $S_{10} = \Sigma x_i$, $S_{01} = \Sigma y_i$. We can obtain the coefficients of the non-zero terms by expanding $\{S_{10}S_{01}\}^s$ into augmented symmetric functions. For example, from David et al. (1966, pp. 165–179)

$$\mu_4'(R^2) = E\{[44] + 16[33,11] + 18[(22)^2] + 72[22,(11)^2] + 24[(11)^4]\},$$

where $[(44)] = \Sigma x_j^4 y_j^4$, $[(11)^4] = \Sigma x_j y_j x_k y_k x_l y_l x_m y_m$, etc. Hence

$$\mu_4'(R^2) = 24n^{(4)} + 72n^{(3)} + 34n^{(2)} + n. \tag{4.7.15}$$

Using (4.7.12), (4.7.14) and (4.7.15) we obtain

$$\mu_4(R^2) = 3n(n-1)(3n^2 - 11n + 11). \tag{4.7.16}$$

Apparently, these moments for the uniform case were first obtained by Haldane (1960). They have been derived elegantly by Johnson (1966) who investigated a much more general problem. Stephens (1969d) has given another derivation. These proofs are different from ours.

We have given details of certain approximations to the distribution of R for the uniform case in Section 4.4. Some of these approximations use the moments derived above. Johnson (1966) has used the first two moments to approximate the distribution of R by the beta distribution and Stephens (1969d) has fitted Pearson curves. Stephens (1969a) has also fitted Pearson curves to the distribution of R for samples from von Mises populations.

4.8. THE MOMENTS OF C AND S

It is much easier to obtain the moments of C and S. Since each of C and S is a sum of independent and identically distributed random variables, the usual technique can be used. Thus

$$E(C) = n\alpha, \qquad \text{var}(C) = \frac{n}{2}(1 + \alpha_2 - 2\alpha^2), \tag{4.8.1}$$

$$E(S) = n\beta, \qquad \text{var}(S) = \frac{n}{2}(1 - \alpha_2 - 2\beta^2). \tag{4.8.2}$$

$$\text{cov}(C, S) = \frac{n}{2}(\beta_2 - 2\alpha\beta). \tag{4.8.3}$$

The third and the fourth moments can also be obtained by using the univariate results

$$\mu_3(\Sigma x_i) = n\mu_3, \qquad \mu_4(\Sigma x_i) = n\{\mu_4 + 3(n-1)\mu_2^2\}. \tag{4.8.4}$$

For the uniform case, all the odd moments of C and S are zero by symmetry. Further, the moments of C and S are equal. In particular,

$$\text{var}(C) = \text{var}(S) = n/2. \tag{4.8.5}$$

Further,

$$E(\cos^2 \theta) = 1/2, \qquad E(\cos^4 \theta) = 3/8$$

so that from (4.8.3) we have

$$\mu_4(C) = \mu_4(S) = 3n(2n - 1)/8. \tag{4.8.6}$$

We now investigate the moments of C for the von Mises distribution with $\mu_0 = 0$. From (4.5.10), the moment generating function of $\cos \theta$ is $I_0(t + \kappa)/I_0(\kappa)$ so that its cumulant generating function is given by

$$C(\kappa) = n\{\log I_0(t + \kappa) - \log I_0(\kappa)\}.$$

Let κ_r be the rth cumulant of C. Then

$$\kappa_{r+1} = n\left[\frac{\partial^r}{\partial t^r}\left(\frac{\partial}{\partial t}\log I_0(t + \kappa)\right)\right]_{t=0} = n\frac{d^{r+1}\{\log I_0(\kappa)\}}{d\kappa^{r+1}}. \tag{4.8.7}$$

Consequently,

$$\kappa_{r+1} = \frac{d\kappa_r}{d\kappa}, \qquad (r \neq 0). \tag{4.8.8}$$

From (4.8.7) and (3.4.52), we have

$$\kappa_1 = nA \tag{4.8.9}$$

and

$$dI_1(\kappa)/d\kappa = I_0(\kappa) - \{I_1(\kappa)/\kappa\}, \tag{4.8.10}$$

respectively. Using these results in (4.8.8), we obtain

$$\kappa_2 = n\{1 - A^2 - (A/\kappa)\}. \tag{4.8.11}$$

Similarly, it can be shown that

$$\kappa_3 = -\frac{2\kappa_1\kappa_2}{n} - \frac{\kappa_2}{\kappa} + \frac{\kappa_1}{\kappa^2}, \tag{4.8.12}$$

and

$$\kappa_4 = -\frac{2\kappa_1\kappa_3}{n} - \frac{2\kappa_2^2}{n} - \frac{\kappa_3}{\kappa} + \frac{2\kappa_2}{\kappa^2} - \frac{2\kappa_1}{\kappa^3}. \tag{4.8.13}$$

For the uniform case, Durand and Greenwood (1957) examine approximations to the distribution of C with the help of an Edgeworth expansion and a Fisher–Cornish expansion while Stephens (1969d) has fitted Pearson curves. Stephens (1969a) has also fitted Pearson curves to the distribution of C for samples from the von Mises distribution.

4.9. LIMITING DISTRIBUTIONS OF ANGULAR STATISTICS

4.9.1. The Joint Distribution of C and S

By the central limit theorem, the joint distribution of $\bar{C} = C/n$ and $\bar{S} = S/n$ is asymptotically normal. From (4.8.1)–(4.8.3), their asymptotic means, variances and covariance are

$$E(\bar{C}) = \alpha, \qquad E(\bar{S}) = \beta \qquad\qquad (4.9.1)$$

$$\operatorname{var}(\bar{C}) = \frac{1}{2n}(1 + \alpha_2 - 2\alpha^2), \qquad \operatorname{var}(\bar{S}) = \frac{1}{2n}(1 - \alpha_2 - 2\beta^2),$$

$$\operatorname{cov}(\bar{C}, \bar{S}) = \frac{1}{2n}(\beta_2 - 2\alpha\beta), \qquad\qquad (4.9.2)$$

In particular, the asymptotic marginal distributions of $\bar{C}$ and $\bar{S}$ are normal. For the uniform case when n is large, $\bar{C}$ and $\bar{S}$ are distributed independently and are both asymptotically $N(0, 1/(2n)^{\frac{1}{2}})$. However, the distribution of $(\bar{x}_0, R)$ is not as simple and depends on whether ρ is zero or not.

4.9.2. The Distributions of $\bar{x}_0$ and R

Case I: $\rho \neq 0$. If $\rho^2 = \alpha^2 + \beta^2 \neq 0$ then we show that the joint distribution of $\bar{x}_0$ and $\bar{R} = R/n$ is asymptotically bivariate normal with

$$E(\bar{x}_0) = \mu_0, \qquad E(\bar{R}) = \rho, \qquad\qquad (4.9.3)$$

$$\operatorname{var}(\bar{x}_0) = \frac{1}{2n\rho^4}\{\rho^2 + \alpha_2(\beta^2 - \alpha^2) - 2\alpha\beta\beta_2\}, \qquad\qquad (4.9.4)$$

$$\operatorname{var}(\bar{R}) = \frac{1}{2n\rho^2}\{\rho^2(1 - 2\rho^2) + \alpha_2(\alpha^2 - \beta^2) + 2\alpha\beta\beta_2\}, \qquad (4.9.5)$$

and

$$\operatorname{cov}(\bar{x}_0, \bar{R}) = \frac{1}{2n\rho^3}\{\beta_2(\alpha^2 - \beta^2) - 2\alpha\beta\alpha_2\}. \qquad\qquad (4.9.6)$$

If arctan (θ) is measured in the interval $(0, \pi)$, we have

$$\bar{x}_0 = \begin{cases} \arctan(\bar{S}/\bar{C}) & \text{if } \bar{C} > 0, \\ \pi + \arctan(\bar{S}/\bar{C}) & \text{if } \bar{C} < 0. \end{cases}$$

Since $\rho \neq 0$, we can assume $\alpha > 0$ by selecting the zero direction suitably so that with probability 1

$$\bar{x}_0 = \arctan(\bar{S}/\bar{C}). \tag{4.9.7}$$

Further,

$$\bar{R} = (\bar{S}^2 + \bar{C}^2)^{\frac{1}{2}}. \tag{4.9.8}$$

Consequently, $\bar{x}_0$ and $\bar{R}$ are functions of $\bar{C}$ and $\bar{S}$. The results (4.9.3)–(4.9.6) follow on using the following well-known lemma together with (4.9.1) and (4.9.2).

Lemma. Let $g(T_1, ..., T_k)$ be a differentiable function of k random variables $T_1, ..., T_k$ with (i) $E(T_i) = \theta_i$, and (ii) var (T_i) of order n^{-1}. Then

$$E(g) = g(\theta_1, ..., \theta_k) + \tfrac{1}{2}\Sigma g^{(ij)} \sigma_{ij} + O(n^{-3/2}), \tag{4.9.9}$$

and

$$\text{var}(g) = \Sigma g^{(i)} g^{(j)} \sigma_{ij} + O(n^{-3/2}), \tag{4.9.10}$$

where $\sigma_{ii} = \text{var}(T_i)$, $\sigma_{ij} = \text{cov}(T_i, T_j)$, $g^{(i)} = \partial g/\partial \theta_i$, $g^{(ij)} = \partial^2 g/\partial \theta_i \partial \theta_j$, $g \equiv g(\theta_1, ..., \theta_k)$, and the summation is extended over all values of $i, j = 1, ..., k$. Further, if h is another differentiable function of $T_1, ..., T_k$, then

$$\text{cov}(g, h) = \Sigma g^{(i)} h^{(j)} \sigma_{ij} + O(n^{-3/2}). \tag{4.9.11}$$

The joint distribution of (g, h) is asymptotically bivariate normal if (a) the leading terms in $E(g)$ and $E(h)$ are finite and (b) the variances of g and h are of the form c_1/n and c_2/n with $c_1, c_2 > 0$.

Symmetrical Distributions. For symmetrical distributions about zero, $\beta = \beta_2 = 0$, and so (4.9.3)–(4.9.6) simplify to

$$E(\bar{x}_0) = 0, \qquad E(\bar{R}) = \alpha, \tag{4.9.12}$$

$$\text{var}(\bar{x}_0) = \frac{1}{2n\alpha^2}(1 - \alpha_2), \quad \text{var}(\bar{R}) = \frac{1}{2n}(1 - 2\alpha^2 + \alpha_2), \quad \text{cov}(\bar{x}_0, \bar{R}) = 0. \tag{4.9.13}$$

From (4.9.9),

$$E(\bar{x}_0) = 0 + O(n^{-2}), \qquad E(\bar{R}) = \alpha + \frac{1}{4n\alpha}(1 - \alpha_2) + O(n^{-3/2}). \tag{4.9.14}$$

Case II: $\rho = 0$. When $\rho = 0$, $\bar{x}_0$ and R do not satisfy the condition (b) of the lemma given above and therefore we use a different approach.

First, let us consider samples from the uniform population. The distribution of $\bar{x}_0$ is itself uniform (Section 4.4.2). Since $(C/n^{\frac{1}{2}}, S/n^{\frac{1}{2}})$ is asymptotically distributed as bivariate normal with zero means, variances 2 and correlation zero,

$$U^2 = 2R^2/n \tag{4.9.15}$$

is asymptotically distributed as a chi-square variable with 2 degrees of freedom.

Next, let $\rho = 0$ but $\alpha_2 \neq 0$. Initially, let us assume that $\beta_2 = 0$. The variables $C' = (2/n)^{\frac{1}{2}}C$ and $S' = (2/n)^{\frac{1}{2}}S$ are asymptotically independent normal with zero means and with variances

$$\sigma_1^2 = 1 + \alpha_2, \qquad \sigma_2^2 = 1 - \alpha_2. \tag{4.9.16}$$

On transforming C', S' to the polar co-ordinates $\bar{x}_0, U$ given by

$$C' = U \cos \bar{x}_0, \qquad S' = U \sin \bar{x}_0 \tag{4.9.17}$$

we can obtain the p.d.f. of $(\bar{x}_0, U)$. Integrating this density with respect to $\bar{x}_0$ and using the integral for $I_0(x)$, we see that the p.d.f. of U is given by

$$|a^2 - b^2|^{\frac{1}{2}} U e^{-\frac{1}{2}aU^2} I_0(\tfrac{1}{2}bU^2), \qquad a > 0, \quad U > 0, \tag{4.9.18}$$

where

$$a = (\sigma_1^2 + \sigma_2^2)/2\sigma_1^2\sigma_2^2, \qquad b = (\sigma_1^2 - \sigma_2^2)/2\sigma_1^2\sigma_2^2, \tag{4.9.19}$$

and σ_1 and σ_2 are given by (4.9.16). The p.d.f. of U^2 can be expressed as that of an infinite series of chi-square variables with even d. of fr. Further, the p.d.f. of $\bar{x}_0$ is a particular case of the off-set normal and is of the form (3.4.20). The distribution (4.9.18) has been studied by Hoyt (1947) in connection with another problem. We can express U as a weighted sum of chi-square variables and by a suitable transformation it can therefore be shown that for $\beta_2 \neq 0$, the distribution of U is again of the form (4.9.18) but with different a and b (see Mardia, 1972). Also, the distribution of

$$U/(1 - \alpha_2^2)^{\frac{1}{2}}$$

is of the form (4.9.18) with $a = 1$ and $b = \alpha_2$. For $b = 0$ we, of course, have the uniform case.

Hence, in contrast with the situation when $\rho \neq 0$, the asymptotic distribution of R for $\rho = 0$ is not normal. This difference in behaviour of the distribution of R has a profound effect on testing procedures and usually leads to separate treatments of the two cases.

4.9.3. The von Mises Population

Let us assume that the parent population is $M(0, \kappa)$. We now obtain various asymptotic results and then discuss some approximations. We shall take $\kappa > 0$ throughout.

(a) Since $\rho > 0$, the joint distribution of $\bar{x}_0$ and R can be obtained from case I of Section 4.9.2. The asymptotic means and variances are given by (4.9.12)–(4.9.14). From (3.4.51),

$$\alpha_2 = 1 - 2A/\kappa,$$

where

$$\alpha = A = A(\kappa) = I_1(\kappa)/I_0(\kappa).$$

Consequently,

$$\text{var}\,(\bar{x}_0) \doteq \frac{1}{nA\kappa}, \tag{4.9.20}$$

Further, from (4.9.14),

$$E(\bar{R}) \doteq A + \frac{1}{2n\kappa}. \tag{4.9.21}$$

Using the exact value of $E(\bar{R}^2)$ given by (4.7.8), and using (4.9.21), we have, to the order n^{-2},

$$\text{var}\,(\bar{R}) = \frac{1}{n\kappa}\{\kappa(1 - A^2) - A\} - \frac{1}{4n^2\kappa^2}. \tag{4.9.22}$$

By using further terms in (4.9.10), we also have, to the order n^{-2},

$$\text{var}\,(\bar{x}_0) = \frac{1}{nA\kappa} + \frac{1}{n^2A^3\kappa^2}\{3\kappa(1 - A^2) - 5A\}. \tag{4.9.23}$$

For large κ, (4.9.21)–(4.9.23) can be simplified by using the expansion for A given by (3.4.50), i.e.

$$A = 1 - \frac{1}{2\kappa} - \frac{1}{8\kappa^2} + \dots. \tag{4.9.24}$$

For example,

$$\text{var}\,(\bar{x}_0) \doteq \frac{1}{n\kappa}\left\{1 + \frac{1}{2\kappa}\right\}. \tag{4.9.25}$$

(b) *Distribution of n − C.* We show that for large κ, $2\kappa(n - C)$ is distributed as χ_n^2. Our proof depends on the result that if θ is distributed as $M(0, \kappa)$ then for large κ,

$$\xi = 2\kappa(1 - \cos \theta)$$

is distributed as χ_1^2. The m.g.f. of ξ is

$$\phi(t) = e^{2t\kappa} I_0\{(1 - 2t)\kappa\}/I_0(\kappa). \qquad (4.9.26)$$

From (3.4.49), we have

$$I_0(\kappa) \doteq \{2\pi\kappa\}^{-\frac{1}{2}} e^{\kappa}$$

for large κ so that (4.9.26) reduces to

$$\phi(t) \doteq (1 - 2t)^{-\frac{1}{2}}.$$

Hence*, for large κ

$$\xi = 2\kappa(1 - \cos \theta) \simeq \chi_1^2. \qquad (4.9.27)$$

Now, we can write

$$2\kappa(n - C) = \sum_{i=1}^{n} \xi_i,$$

where $\xi_i = 2\kappa(1 - \cos \theta_i)$ are distributed independently and identically. Hence, using the above result together with the additive property of χ^2, we have

$$2\kappa(n - C) \simeq \chi_n^2. \qquad (4.9.28)$$

(c) *Distribution of R − C.* For large κ, we now show that

$$2\kappa(R - C) \simeq \chi_1^2. \qquad (4.9.29)'$$

It can be seen that

$$2\kappa(R - C) = 2\kappa R(1 - \cos \bar{x}_0).$$

Now, from (4.5.7), the conditional distribution of $\bar{x}_0$ given R is $M(0, \kappa R)$. On using (4.9.27), we see that the conditional distribution of $2\kappa(R - C)$ for given R is χ_1^2 which does not depend on R. Hence (4.9.28) follows.

(d) *Distribution of n − R.* We have the identity

$$2\kappa(n - C) = 2\kappa(R - C) + 2\kappa(n - R). \qquad (4.9.30)'$$

Hence using (4.9.28) and (4.9.29)' in a variant form of the Cochran theorem, we have

$$2\kappa(n - R) \simeq \chi_{n-1}^2 \qquad (4.9.31)'$$

*Alternatively, we can use $\xi \doteq \kappa\theta^2$ where θ is $N(0, \kappa^{-\frac{1}{2}})$.

and the random variables $2\kappa(R - C)$ and $2\kappa(n - R)$ are distributed independently.

This important result is a particular case of a result by Watson and Williams (1956) for higher dimensions but the proof given above differs from theirs.

The result (4.9.31)' is what may be expected from (4.9.28) since

$$n - R = \sum_{i=1}^{n} \{1 - \cos (\theta_i - \bar{x}_0)\}$$

which is equivalent to $n - C$ except that μ_0 is estimated by $\bar{x}_0$. Further, the decomposition (4.9.30)' not only behaves like the similar identity in the analysis of variance on the line (Section 2.3.3) but for large κ, the distribution theory of the components is identical.

(e) *Approximations to $n - C$.* In practice, the asymptotic result (4.9.28) is not adequate for moderately large values of κ. It is desirable to obtain an approximation such that the identity (4.9.30)' remains valid. This can be achieved by selecting γ such that

$$E\{2\gamma(n - C)\} = n.$$

The right-hand side of this expression is the expected value of a chi-square variable with n d. of fr. Using $E(C) = nA$ and the expansion (4.9.24) for large values of κ, we have

$$\gamma^{-1} = \kappa^{-1} + \tfrac{1}{4}\kappa^{-2}. \tag{4.9.29}$$

Also, on identifying the expression for $n\,\mathrm{var}\,(\bar{x}_0)$ given by (4.9.25) with $1/\gamma$, we have

$$\gamma^{-1} = \kappa^{-1} + \tfrac{1}{2}\kappa^{-2}. \tag{4.9.30}$$

Stephens (1969a) found that the average value of γ from (4.9.29) and (4.9.30) gives a good approximation. Hence,

$$2\gamma(n - C) \simeq \chi_n^2, \qquad 2\gamma(n - R) \simeq \chi_{n-1}^2, \qquad 2\gamma(R - C) \simeq \chi_1^2, \tag{4.9.31}$$

where

$$\gamma^{-1} = \kappa^{-1} + \tfrac{3}{8}\kappa^{-2}. \tag{4.9.32}$$

This approximation can be used for $\kappa \geqslant 2$.

We can also approximate the distribution of $n - C$ by the distribution of $\gamma_1^{-1} \chi_f^2$ using the relations

$$E(n - C) = f/\gamma_1, \qquad \mathrm{var}\,(n - C) = 2f/\gamma_1^2.$$

On substituting the moments (4.8.9) and (4.8.11), we have

$$\gamma_1(n - C) \simeq \chi_f{}^2, \tag{4.9.33}$$

where

$$\gamma_1{}^{-1} = (\kappa - A - A^2\kappa)/2\kappa(1 - A), \qquad f = n(1 - A)\gamma_1. \tag{4.9.34}$$

Further, $\gamma_1(n - R)$ can be taken as $\chi_{f_1}{}^2$ so from (4.9.21),

$$f_1 = \gamma_1\{2\kappa n(1 - A) - 1\}/(2\kappa). \tag{4.9.35}$$

Consequently, $\gamma_1(R - C)$ has a χ^2 distribution with $f - f_1$ d. of fr. However, the d. of fr. $f - f_1$ may be fractional.

(f) *Approximations in the multi-sample case.* We use the notation of Section 4.5. From the above discussion, it follows that for large κ

$$2\kappa(n - R) \simeq \chi_{n-1}^2, \qquad 2\kappa(n_j - R_j) \simeq \chi_{n_j-1}^2, \qquad j = 1, ..., q. \tag{4.9.36}$$

Therefore, we have

$$2\kappa\left(n - \sum_{j=1}^{q} R_j\right) \simeq \chi_{n-q}^2, \qquad 2\kappa\left(\sum_{j=1}^{q} R_j - R\right) \simeq \chi_{q-1}^2 \tag{4.9.37}$$

and we may regard these two statistics as being independently distributed. Further approximations will be discussed in Chapter 6.

4.9.4. Higher Moments

The method given in Section 4.9.2 is obviously applicable to higher moments. In particular, when the parent population is symmetric, we have for the measures of skewness and kurtosis (Sections 2.7.2 and 3.7) for large n:

$$E(g_1{}^0) = 0, \qquad E(g_2{}^0) = (\alpha_2 - \alpha^4)/(1 - \alpha)^4, \tag{4.9.38}$$

$$\text{var}(g_1{}^0) = \frac{1}{2n\alpha^2(1 - \alpha)^3}\{\alpha^2(1 - \alpha_4) + 4\alpha_2{}^2(1 - \alpha_2) - 4\alpha\alpha_2(\alpha - \alpha_3)\} \tag{4.9.39}$$

and

$$\text{var}(g_2{}^0) = \frac{1}{2n(1 - \alpha)^6}[4(1 + \alpha_2 - 2\alpha^2)\{\alpha_2 - \alpha^3(2 - \alpha)\}^2 + (1 - \alpha)^2$$
$$\times (1 + \alpha_4 - 2\alpha_2{}^2) + 4(1 - \alpha)\{\alpha_2 - \alpha^3(2 - \alpha)\}(\alpha + \alpha_3 - 2\alpha\alpha_2)]. \tag{4.9.40}$$

For the wrapped normal distribution, we have for large n, on using (3.4.29),

$$E(g_1{}^0) = 0, \qquad E(g_2{}^0) = 0, \tag{4.9.41}$$

$$\text{var}\,(g_1{}^0) = \frac{(1 + \alpha)(1 + \alpha^2)}{2n(1 - \alpha)^2}\{(1 + \alpha^4)(1 + \alpha^8 - 4\alpha^4) + 4\alpha^6\}, \tag{4.9.42}$$

and

$$\text{var}\,(g_2{}^0) = \frac{(1 + \alpha)^2}{2n(1 - \alpha)^2}\{16\alpha^6 + (1 + \alpha^2)^2\,(1 + \alpha^4)^2\,(1 - 8\alpha^4)\}. \tag{4.9.43}$$

The last expression is positive for $\alpha < 0.6$ but may not be positive beyond this range.

5

POINT ESTIMATION

5.1. A CRAMÉR–RAO TYPE BOUND

Let $\theta_1, \ldots, \theta_n$ be a random sample from a circular population with p.d.f. $f(\theta; \theta_0)$. We assume that the p.d.f. f is periodic in θ_0 of period 2π. For example, the parameter θ_0 may represent the mean direction. Let us describe θ_0 as an angular parameter. The classical definition of unbiasedness does not have any meaning in estimating θ_0 but it can be modified as follows. Let (r, t) be the polar co-ordinates of a vector based on the observations $\theta_1, \ldots, \theta_n$. We may call the statistic t an angular unbiased estimate of θ_0 if

$$E(e^{it}|r) = |E(e^{it}|r)|\, e^{i\theta_0}. \qquad (5.1.1)$$

That is, if t_1 and t_2 are two statistics such that

$$t_1 = r \cos t, \qquad t_2 = r \sin t,$$

we keep the length $r = (t_1{}^2 + t_2{}^2)^{\frac{1}{2}}$ fixed in estimating the direction θ_0 by a direction t. From (5.1.1), we have

$$E\{\sin(t - \theta_0)|r\} = 0. \qquad (5.1.2)$$

To derive a Cramér–Rao type bound, we follow the method which is generally used to obtain the Cramér–Rao bound on the line. Since the range of the circular variable θ does not depend on θ_0, we find after differentiating (5.1.2) with respect to θ_0 under the integral sign

$$E\{\cos(t - \theta_0)|r\} = \mathrm{cov}\left\{\sin(t - \theta_0), \frac{\partial \log L}{\partial \theta_0}\,\middle|\, r\right\}, \qquad (5.1.3)$$

118

where

$$L = \prod_{i=1}^{n} f(\theta_i; \theta_0)$$

is the likelihood function. Let us assume that the circular variance of $t|r$ is not unity, i.e.

$$V_0(t|r) = 1 - E\{\cos(t - \theta_0)|r\} \neq 1. \tag{5.1.4}$$

Using the well-known inequality

$$\{\text{cov}(X, Y)\}^2 \leqslant \text{var}(X)\,\text{var}(Y)$$

in (5.1.3), we obtain

$$\text{div}(t, \theta_0|r) \geqslant 1/E\left[\left(\frac{\partial \log L}{\partial \theta_0}\right)^2 \middle| r\right], \tag{5.1.5}$$

where

$$\text{div}(t, \theta_0|r) = E\{\sin^2(t - \theta_0)|r\}/\{1 - V_0(t|r)\}^2. \tag{5.1.6}$$

The inequality (5.1.5) is analogous to the Cramér–Rao inequality and we may describe the quantity $\text{div}(t, \theta_0|r)$ as the divergence of an angular unbiased estimate t of θ_0 when r is given. In analogy with the line, we may say that the estimate t is best for θ_0 if the equality in (5.1.5) holds. We also have

$$\text{div}(t, \theta_0|r) < 1/\{1 - V_0(t|r)\}^2 \tag{5.1.7}$$

so that a bound for $V_0(t|r)$ can be obtained with the help of (5.1.5).

The equality in (5.1.5) holds if and only if

$$\frac{\partial \log L}{\partial \theta_0} = b(r) \sin(t - \theta_0), \tag{5.1.8}$$

where $b(r)$ is a function of r only.

We now consider two examples.

The von Mises Distribution. Let $f(\theta; \mu_0)$ be the p.d.f. corresponding to $M(\mu_0, \kappa)$ with κ known. Suppose that

$$C = R \cos \bar{x}_0, \quad S = R \sin \bar{x}_0.$$

Since the distribution of $\bar{x}_0$ given R from (4.5.7) is $M(\mu_0, \kappa R)$, we have on using (3.4.47) and (3.4.51),

$$E\{\cos(\bar{x}_0 - \mu_0)|R\} = A(\kappa R), \quad E(\sin^2(\bar{x}_0 - \mu_0)|R\} = A(\kappa R)/\kappa R, \tag{5.1.9}$$

where $A(\kappa) = I_1(\kappa)/I_0(\kappa)$. Further,

$$\frac{\partial \log L}{\partial \mu_0} = \kappa R \sin (\bar{x}_0 - \mu_0)$$

and using (5.1.9), we obtain

$$E\left\{\left(\frac{\partial \log L}{\partial \mu_0}\right)^2 \middle| R\right\} = \kappa R A(\kappa R).$$

Consequently, the bound (5.1.5) is attained if $\kappa > 0$.

For $\kappa = 0$, the underlying population reduces to the uniform population. In this case, we find from (5.1.9) that the condition (5.1.4) is no longer satisfied.

A Multi-modal von Mises Distribution. Suppose that the population has

$$f(\theta; \mu_0) = \{1/2\pi I_0(\kappa)\} e^{\kappa \cos l(\theta - \mu_0)}, \qquad 0 < \theta \leqslant 2\pi, \quad \kappa > 0, \qquad (5.1.10)$$

where l is a positive integer. Let κ and l be known. Define R_l and $m_l{}^0$ by

$$R_l \cos m_l{}^0 = \Sigma \cos l\theta_i, \qquad R_l \sin m_l{}^0 = \Sigma \sin l\theta_i. \qquad (5.1.11)$$

From Section 4.5.5, the distribution of $m_l{}^0$ given R_l is $M(l\mu_0, \kappa R_l)$. On applying the method used for the von Mises case, we find that the bound (5.1.5) is attained in estimating $\theta_0 = l\mu_0$ by $m_l{}^0$.

The above discussion succeeds in showing that $\bar{x}_0$ is optimum as an estimate of μ_0 for the von Mises population. However, the definition of unbiasedness given by (5.1.2) is restrictive since $\bar{x}_0$ may not be an angualr unbiased estimate of μ_0 in general. We may define a *weak* angular unbiased estimate t of θ_0 by

$$E(r e^{it}) = |E(r e^{it})| e^{i\theta_0}. \qquad (5.1.12)$$

In this sense $\bar{x}_0$ is an angular unbiased estimate of μ_0. It is easy to see that (5.1.2) implies (5.1.12) but not vice versa. A bound similar to (5.1.5) follows immediately from (5.1.12) but it is not attained for the examples considered above.

5.2. THE METHOD OF MOMENTS

Suppose that $f(\theta; \theta_0, \rho_0)$ is the p.d.f. of a population which depends only on two parameters θ_0 and ρ_0. Let

$$E(\cos \theta) = a(\theta_0, \rho_0), \quad E(\sin \theta) = b(\theta_0, \rho_0), \qquad (5.2.1)$$

where a and b are not identically equal to zero. The estimates of θ_0 and ρ_0 by the method of moments are the solution of

$$\bar{C} = a(\theta_0, \rho_0), \quad \bar{S} = b(\theta_0, \rho_0). \tag{5.2.2}$$

This method applies immediately to the wrapped normal, the wrapped Cauchy, the cardioid and the von Mises distributions.

It can be seen that these estimates minimize the distance (J. S. Rao, 1969)

$$\sum_{i=1}^{n} [\{\cos\theta_i - a(\theta_0, \rho_0)\}^2 + \{\sin\theta_i - b(\theta_0, \rho_0)\}^2]$$

provided that the Jacobian $|\partial(a, b)/\partial(\theta_0, \rho_0)|$ is non-zero. Further, from Section 4.9.2, the estimates are consistent and are asymptotically normal. The method can easily be extended to the case when even numbers of parameters are to be estimated (cf. Section 5.6). On the line, the method of moments is dubious because of the moments may not exist. The trigonometric moments do not have this disadvantage. This method also gives a natural way to combine estimates on the circle. For example, let

$$E(t_i) = \rho_0 \cos\theta_0, \qquad E(t_i') = \rho_0 \sin\theta_0, \qquad i = 1, 2.$$

If no further information is given, better estimates of θ_0 and ρ_0 can be obtained on solving

$$t_1 + t_2 = 2\rho_0 \cos\theta_0, \qquad t_1' + t_2' = 2\rho_0 \sin\theta_0.$$

5.3. SUFFICIENCY

Let us again consider a population with p.d.f. $f(\theta; \theta_0, \rho_0)$. From the standard estimation theory, it follows that C and S are jointly complete sufficient statistics for θ_0 and ρ_0 if

$$f(\theta; \theta_0, \rho_0) = p(\theta) \exp\{a_1(\theta_0, \rho_0)\cos\theta + a_2(\theta_0, \rho_0)\sin\theta + q(\theta_0, \rho_0)\}. \tag{5.3.1}$$

The von Mises distribution and the multi-modal von Mises distribution (5.1.8) are of this form. Further, $\bar{x}_0$ is the maximum likelihood estimate of θ_0 if and only if (Greenwood, 1959b):

$$a_1(\theta_0, \rho_0) = \int_0^{\theta_0} a_0(t, \rho_0) \sin t \, dt, \quad a_2(\theta_0, \rho_0) = \int_0^{\theta_0} a_0(t, \rho_0) \cos t \, dt$$

and

$$q(\theta_0, \rho_0) = q_0(\rho_0).$$

We have already dealt with the particular case of the von Mises distribution in Section 3.4.9f.

5.4. THE VON MISES DISTRIBUTION

5.4.1. The Maximum Likelihood Estimates

Two Parameter Estimation. Let $\theta_1, ..., \theta_n$ be a random sample from $M(\mu_0, \kappa)$. We find

$$\log L = -n\log(2\pi) - n\log I_0(\kappa) + \kappa \sum_{i=1}^{n} \cos(\theta_i - \mu_0). \qquad (5.4.1)$$

On differentiating (5.4.1) with respect to μ_0 and κ, and using,

$$I_0'(x) = I_1(x), \qquad (5.4.2)$$

we obtain

$$\frac{\partial \log L}{\partial \mu_0} = \kappa \sum_{i=1}^{n} \sin(\theta_i - \mu_0) \qquad (5.4.3)$$

and

$$\frac{\partial \log L}{\partial \kappa} = -nA(\kappa) + \sum_{i=1}^{n} \cos(\theta_i - \mu_0), \qquad (5.4.4)$$

where

$$A(\kappa) = I_1(\kappa)/I_0(\kappa). \qquad (5.4.5)$$

The relation (5.4.2) follows easily on differentiating the series expansion for $I_0(x)$ given by (3.4.46). Hence the maximum likelihood estimate $\hat{\mu}_0$ of μ_0 is

$$\cos \hat{\mu}_0 = C/R, \qquad \sin \hat{\mu}_0 = S/R,$$

which implies that

$$\hat{\mu}_0 = \bar{x}_0. \qquad (5.4.6)$$

Further, the maximum likelihood estimate $\hat{\kappa}$ of κ is the solution of

$$A(\hat{\kappa}) = \bar{R}.$$

That is,

$$\hat{\kappa} = A^{-1}(\bar{R}). \qquad (5.4.7)$$

The solution of (5.4.7) can only be obtained numerically. Some selected values of the functions A and A^{-1} are given in Appendix 2.2 and Appendix 2.3 respectively. We know that $0 \leqslant \bar{R} \leqslant 1$. For the extreme cases, approximate solutions to (5.4.7) can be obtained as follows. For small values of R, we have from the expansion (3.4.48)

$$\bar{R} \doteq \tfrac{1}{2}\hat{\kappa}\, \{1 - \tfrac{1}{8}\hat{\kappa}^2 + \tfrac{1}{48}\hat{\kappa}^4\}$$

and on inverting the series (see, for example Abramowitz and Stegun, 1965, p.16) we obtain

$$\hat{\kappa} \doteq \tfrac{1}{6}\bar{R}(12 + 6\bar{R}^2 + 5\bar{R}^4). \tag{5.4.8}$$

This approximation yields at least two figure accuracy if $\bar{R} < 0.45$. For very small $\bar{R}$, we have simply

$$\hat{\kappa} \doteq 2\bar{R}. \tag{5.4.9}$$

For large values of $\bar{R}$, from the expansion (3.4.50),

$$\bar{R} \doteq 1 - \frac{1}{2\hat{\kappa}} - \frac{1}{8\hat{\kappa}^2} - \frac{1}{8\hat{\kappa}^3}.$$

Again on inverting the series, we have

$$\frac{1}{\hat{\kappa}} \doteq 2(1 - \bar{R}) - (1 - \bar{R})^2 - (1 - \bar{R})^3 \tag{5.4.10}$$

which yields at least three figure accuracy for $\bar{R} > 0.8$. Further, for $\bar{R}$ very nearly 1, we have

$$\hat{\kappa} = 1/2(1 - \bar{R}). \tag{5.4.11}$$

Example 5.1. Obtain the maximum likelihood estimates of μ_0 and κ for the data in Example 2.1.

We have shown in Example 2.1 that $\bar{R} = 0.7110$. From Appendix 2.3, we have $\hat{\kappa} = 2.07685$ for $\bar{R} = 0.71$ while $\hat{\kappa} = 2.14359$. for $\bar{R} = 0.72$. By linear interpolation, we find that $\hat{\kappa} = 2.08362$. The maximum likelihood estimate $\bar{x}_0$ of μ_0 by Example 2.1 is $51.0°$.

Example 5.2. Table 5.1 gives vanishing angles of homing pigeons in a clock resetting experiment (adapted from Fig. 24B of Schmidt–Koenig, 1965). Obtain the maximum likelihood estimates of μ_0 and κ and examine the goodness of fit using these estimates.

On the following the method of Example 2.2, we find that

$$C = -7.2098, \qquad S = 67.3374, \qquad \bar{R} = 0.3240.$$

Hence, $\bar{x}_0 = 96.1°$. From Appendix 2.3, $\hat{\kappa} = 0.6854$. On using these estimates, we computed the expected frequencies by numerical integration and these frequencies are shown in Table 5.1. These expected frequencies can be obtained from the distribution function given in Appendix 2.1 if we follow the method used in fitting the normal distribution. The value of χ^2 for the goodness of fit test is found to be 10.21. The 5% value of χ_9^2 is 16.92 and

TABLE 5.1.   Observed vanishing angles of homing pigeons (adapted from Schmidt–Koenig, 1965) and the corresponding expected frequencies from a von Mises distribution

Direction (degrees)	Observed frequency	Expected frequency	Direction (degrees)	Observed frequency	Expected frequency
0−	26	17·3	180−	14	14·1
30−	22	23·9	210−	11	10·2
60−	26	29·3	240−	12	8·3
90−	30	30·4	270−	5	8·0
120−	29	26·4	300−	5	9·2
150−	18	19·9	330−	11	12·2
			Total	209	209·2

therefore the fit is satisfactory. Under the hypothesis of uniformity, the value of χ^2 is found to be 51·27. Hence, we reject the hypothesis strongly.

Example 5.3. Obtain the maximum likelihood estimates of μ_0 and κ for the sand-grains data in Table 1.2 and test the goodness of fit.

We double the angles and fit a von Mises distribution to the resulting data. That is, we are fitting the distribution given by (5.1.10) when $l = 2$. We find that $\bar{x}_0 = 180\cdot8°$, $\bar{R} = 0\cdot1018$. Therefore from Appendix 5.3, $\hat{\kappa} = 0\cdot2047$. By following the method of Examples 5.2, we obtain the corresponding expected frequencies and these frequencies are shown in Table 5.2. The observed value of χ^2 is 24·65 whereas $\chi_{15}^2 = 25\cdot00$. Hence, the null hypothesis is just accepted at the 5% level of significance. The hypothesis of uniformity is again found to be strongly rejected. The value of χ^2 being 140·00.

TABLE 5.2. Observed orientations of sand-grains and, after doubling the angles for the data given in Table 1.2, the corresponding expected frequencies from a von Mises distribution

Orientation (degrees)	Observed frequency	Expected frequency	Orientation (degrees)	Observed frequency	Expected frequency
0−	244	244·6	90−	401	365·6
10−	262	250·3	100−	382	357·2
20−	246	261·8	110−	332	341·6
30−	290	278·2	120−	322	321·5
40−	284	298·3	130−	295	299·9
50−	314	319·8	140−	230	279·7
60−	326	340·2	150−	256	262·9
70−	340	356·2	160−	263	251·0
80−	371	365·3	170−	281	244·8
			Total	5439	5438·9

Gumbel (1954) has shown by graphical comparisons that the von Mises distribution provides a good fit to various data from meteorology, medicine and economic time series.

Asymptotic Properties. We now consider some asymptotic properties of $\hat{\mu}_0$ and $\hat{\kappa}$. From (5.4.3), we have

$$E\left\{-\frac{\partial^2 \log L}{\partial \mu_0{}^2}\right\} = n\kappa E\{\cos(\theta - \mu_0)\} = n\kappa A,$$

so that for large n,

$$\text{var}(\hat{\mu}_0) \doteq 1/n\kappa A. \tag{5.4.12}$$

Similarly, using (4.7.10) we have

$$\text{var}(\hat{\kappa}) \doteq \kappa/n(\kappa - \kappa A^2 - A), \qquad \text{cov}(\hat{\mu}_0, \hat{\kappa}_0) = 0. \tag{5.4.13}$$

Hence for large n, $\hat{\mu}_0$ and $\hat{\kappa}_0$ are independently distributed as normal with means μ_0 and κ and variances (5.4.12) and (5.4.13) respectively. In fact, we can improve these results with the help of Section 4.9. From (4.9.14) and (4.9.23), we have

$$E(\hat{\mu}_0) = \mu_0 + O(n^{-2}), \tag{5.4.14}$$

and

$$\text{var}(\hat{\mu}_0) = \frac{1}{nA\kappa} + \frac{1}{n^2 A^3 \kappa^2}\{3\kappa(1 - A^2) - 5A\} + O(n^{-3}). \tag{5.4.15}$$

Using the approximation for A given by (3.4.48) and (3.4.50), we have var $(\hat{\mu}_0) = 2/n\kappa^2$, when κ is small, $= 1/n\kappa$ for large κ. Thus μ_0 can be estimated with much lesser precision for small κ than for large κ. This behaviour is not surprising since as $\kappa \to 0$, the von Mises distribution tends to the uniform distribution. The preceding conclusion can also be reached from the circular variance for $\hat{\mu}_0$ given by

$$V_0 = 1 - E\{\cos(\bar{x}_0 - \mu_0)\} = 1 - E\{A(\kappa R)\}. \tag{5.4.16}$$

From (4.9.9), we have to order n^{-1}

$$E(\hat{\kappa}) = \kappa - \tfrac{1}{2}\{A''/(A')^3\} \text{var}(\bar{R}),$$

where A' and A'' are derivatives of A with respect to κ. On substituting var $(\bar{R})$ from (4.9.22), we find that

$$E(\hat{\kappa}) \doteq \kappa + \frac{1}{2nB^2}\{2\kappa^2 A(1 - A^2) - 3A^2\kappa + \kappa - 2A\}, \tag{5.4.17}$$

where

$$B = \kappa(1 - A^2) - A. \tag{5.4.18}$$

Hence, the bias in $\hat{\kappa}$ is not negligible unless n is very large.

Single Parameter Estimation. We now consider the case when one of the parameters μ_0 and κ is known. If κ is given then the maximum likelihood estimate of μ_0 remains unaltered. However, if μ_0 is given, we may take it to be zero. In this case, the maximum likelihood estimate $\hat{\kappa}_0$ of κ_0 is given by

$$A(\hat{\kappa}_0) = \bar{C}, \qquad \hat{\kappa}_0 = A^{-1}(\bar{C}) \tag{5.4.19}$$

which reduces to (5.4.7) when $\bar{C}$ is replaced by $\bar{R}$. Thus the estimate $\hat{\kappa}$ can be obtained by following the same procedure as for $\hat{\kappa}$. In particular, the approximations (5.4.8) and (5.4.9) can be used. We have

$$E\{A(\hat{\kappa}_0)\} = E(\bar{C}) = A(\kappa) \tag{5.4.20}$$

so that $A(\hat{\kappa}_0)$ is an unbiased estimate of $A(\kappa)$. For large n, the bias in estimating κ turns out to be precisely the expression (5.4.17), since var $(\bar{R})$ and var $(\bar{C})$ are identical up to order n^{-1} by (4.8.11) and (4.9.22). (We shall show in Section 5.4.2 that (5.4.19) is the best estimate of $A(\kappa)$). Further, var $(\hat{\kappa}_0)$ to order n^{-1} is given by (5.4.13). Hence, $\hat{\kappa}_0$ is asymptotically distributed as $N\big(\kappa, \kappa^{\frac{1}{2}}/\{n(\kappa - \kappa A^2 - A)\}^{\frac{1}{2}}\big)$.

5.4.2. Other Methods of Estimation

First, let us consider the method of moments (Section 5.2). The estimates of μ_0 and κ by this method are the solutions of

$$\bar{C} = A \cos \mu_0, \qquad \bar{S} = A \sin \mu_0$$

which coincide with the maximum likelihood estimates.

We can show easily that $\bar{x}_0$ and R are jointly complete sufficient statistics for μ_0 and κ (see, for example, Hogg and Craig, 1965, pp. 229–230). The joint distribution of $\bar{x}_0$ and R given by (4.5.5) is of exponential form as would be expected. Their completeness can be proved using this density. However, if κ is given then $R \cos \bar{x}_0$ and $R \sin \bar{x}_0$ are minimal sufficient statistics for μ_0 which implies that $\bar{x}_0$ itself does not contain all the information about μ_0. This fact underlines the difficulty in constructing an optimality criterion for estimating the circular mean direction. But if μ_0 is given, on taking $\mu_0 = 0$ we see that C is a complete sufficient statistic for κ. This result also follows from the p.d.f. of C given by (4.5.13). Since by (5.4.20) $\bar{C}$ is an unbiased estimate of $A(\kappa)$, we deduce from the Rao–Blackwell theorem that $A(\hat{\kappa}_0)$ is the best unbiased estimate of $A(\kappa)$.

5.4.3. The Multi-modal von Mises-type Distribution

Let $\theta_1, ..., \theta_n$ be a random sample from the multi-modal von Mises-type distribution given by (5.1.10). Assuming that l is known, the problem of estimation for this distribution can be solved simply by following the method used for the von Mises distribution. In particular, the maximum likelihood estimates of μ_0 and κ are

$$\hat{\mu}_0 = m_l{}^0/l, \qquad \hat{\kappa} = A^{-1}(\bar{R}_l), \tag{5.4.21}$$

where $\bar{R}_l = R_l/n$, $m_l{}^0$ and R_l are defined by (5.1.11), and A^{-1} is defined by (5.4.7). Hence, $\hat{\kappa}$ can be obtained from Appendix 2.3. The approximations (5.4.8)–(5.4.11) are also applicable for this case on replacing $\bar{R}$ by $\bar{R}_l$. Further,

$$\text{var}\,(\hat{\mu}_0) \doteq 1/n\kappa A l^2. \tag{5.4.22}$$

Also, the asymptotic correlation between $\hat{\kappa}$ and $\hat{\mu}_0$ is again zero and the asymptotic variance of $\hat{\kappa}$ is precisely given by (5.4.13).

5.5. A REGRESSION MODEL

A natural analogue of the normal theory linear regression for circular variables is as follows (Gould, 1969). Let θ_i, $i = 1, ..., n$ be independently distributed as $M(\mu_0 + \beta t_i, \kappa)$ $i = 1, ..., n$ where $t_1, ..., t_n$ are known numbers while μ_0, β and κ are unknown parameters. We shall be concerned with the maximum likelihood estimates of μ_0 and β. The logarithm of the likelihood function for estimating μ_0 and β is

$$\text{const} + \kappa \sum_{i=1}^{n} \cos\,(\theta_i - \mu_0 - \beta t_i). \tag{5.5.1}$$

Hence, the maximum likelihood estimates $\hat{\mu}_0$ and $\hat{\beta}$ of μ_0 and β are the solutions of

$$\sum_{i=1}^{n} \sin\,(\theta_i - \hat{\mu}_0 - \hat{\beta} t_i) = 0, \tag{5.5.2}$$

and

$$\sum_{i=1}^{n} t_i \sin\,(\theta_i - \hat{\mu}_0 - \hat{\beta} t_i) = 0. \tag{5.5.3}$$

From (5.5.2), we have

$$\tan \hat{\mu}_0 = \Sigma \sin\,(\theta_i - \hat{\beta} t_i)/\Sigma \cos\,(\theta_i - \hat{\beta} t_i). \tag{5.5.4}$$

We can obtain $\hat{\beta}$ by an iterative procedure as follows. Let $\bar{\beta}$ be an initial estimate of β and let $\bar{\mu}_0$ be the corresponding value of $\hat{\mu}_0$ from (5.5.4). Let $\Delta = \hat{\beta} - \bar{\beta}$. From (5.5.3), we have

$$\Sigma t_i \sin\,(\theta_i - \bar{\mu}_0 - \bar{\beta} t_i) \cos \Delta t_i = \Sigma t_i \cos\,(\theta_i - \bar{\mu}_0 - \bar{\beta} t_i) \sin \Delta t_i. \tag{5.5.5}$$

For small Δ, (5.5.5) gives

$$\hat{\beta} = \bar{\beta} + \{\Sigma\, t_i \sin(\theta_i - \bar{\mu}_0 - \bar{\beta}t_i)/\Sigma\, t_i^2 \cos(\theta_i - \bar{\mu}_0 - \bar{\beta}t_i)\}. \qquad (5.5.6)$$

Consequently, $\hat{\beta}$ can be obtained. The iteration is continued until the values of $\hat{\mu}_0$ and $\hat{\beta}$ stabilize. However, (5.5.4) will have two roots. Using the definition of the circular variance, we see that the quantity

$$1 - \frac{1}{n}\sum_{i=1}^{n}\cos(\theta_i - \bar{\mu}_0 - \bar{\beta}t_i) \qquad (5.5.7)$$

measures the angular deviations of the observations from their predicted values, i.e. it corresponds to the residual. We select that root $\bar{\mu}_0$ which makes (5.5.7) positive.

The above estimation procedure depends heavily on the choice of initial estimates. For finite samples, the procedure may lead to two different curves but it is not difficult to rule out one of the curves on practical grounds (Gould, 1969).

We now show that this method of estimation coincides with the least square method. Let $\mathbf{x}_i' = (\cos\theta_i, \sin\theta_i)$ and $\mathbf{v}_i' = \{\cos(\mu_0 + \beta t_i), \sin(\mu_0 + \beta t_i)\}$. We have

$$\frac{1}{2}\sum_{i=1}^{n}(\mathbf{x}_i - \mathbf{v}_i)'(\mathbf{x}_i - \mathbf{v}_i) = n - \sum_{i=1}^{n}\mathbf{x}_i'\mathbf{v}_i. \qquad (5.5.8)$$

Consequently, we deduce that minimizing (5.5.8) is the same as maximizing (5.5.1).

5.6. MIXTURES OF VON MISES DISTRIBUTIONS

Let us consider the problem of estimating parameters for the mixture of von Mises distributions having p.d.f.

$$\lambda f_1(\theta) + (1 - \lambda)f_2(\theta), \qquad 0 < \lambda < 1, \quad 0 < \theta \leqslant 2\pi, \qquad (5.6.1)$$

where

$$f_i(\theta) = \{1/2\pi I_0(\kappa_i)\}\exp\{\kappa_i \cos(\theta - \mu_{0,i})\}, \qquad i = 1, 2. \qquad (5.6.2)$$

The maximum likelihood equations for estimating the five parameters can be obtained but these cannot be solved analytically even when $\mu_{0,2} = \mu_{0,1} + \pi$ and $\kappa_1 = \kappa_2$. Jones and James (1969) use a combination of the gradient method and the Newton–Raphson method to obtain the maximum likelihood estimates numerically.

The method of moments is not easily applicable in the general case. There is also the problem of selecting an appropriate set of moments to estimate the five parameters. We can use the first two sine and cosine moments but the fifth equation cannot be constructed in any symmetrical manner. For the important particular case of $\kappa_1 = \kappa_2$ and $\mu_{0,2} = \mu_{0,1} + \pi$, we can obtain the estimates by the method of moments as follows. For this case, we can take the density (5.6.1) as

$$g(\theta) = \{1/2\pi I_0(\kappa)\}[\lambda \exp\{\kappa \cos(\theta - \mu_0)\} + (1 - \lambda) \exp\{-\kappa \cos(\theta - \mu_0)\}].$$
(5.6.3)

On using the transformation $\theta^* = \theta \pmod{\pi}$, (5.6.3) reduces to

$$h(\theta^*) = [1/2\pi I_0(\kappa)] \cosh\{\kappa \cos(\theta^* - \mu_0)\}, \qquad 0 < \theta^* \leqslant \pi. \qquad (5.6.4)$$

These distributions (5.6.3) and (5.6.4) have been studied in Section 3.6. The distribution of θ^* does not depend on λ and we can estimate the parameters μ_0 and κ by using the first trigonometric moment of $\theta' = 2\theta^*$, i.e. by (3.6.4) the moment estimates $\bar{\mu}_0$, $\bar{\kappa}$ of μ_0 and κ are the solutions of

$$\sum_{i=1}^{n} \sin 2(\theta_i^* - \mu_0) = 0, \qquad \frac{1}{n}\sum_{i=1}^{n} \cos 2(\theta_i^* - \mu_0) = A_2(\kappa) = I_2(\kappa)/I_0(\kappa),$$

where from (3.4.53)

$$A_2(\kappa) = 1 - 2\{A(\kappa)/\kappa\}.$$

Let

$$\Sigma \sin 2\theta_i^* = \bar{R}' \sin \bar{x}_0', \qquad \Sigma \cos 2\theta_i^* = \bar{R}' \cos \bar{x}_0'. \qquad (5.6.5)$$

We then have $\bar{\mu}_0 = \frac{1}{2}\bar{x}_0$ while $\bar{\kappa}$ is a solution of

$$\bar{R}' = 1 - 2\{A(\kappa)/\kappa\}. \qquad (5.6.6)$$

An estimate $\bar{\lambda}$ of λ can now be obtained on using the first trigonometric central moment of θ from (3.6.2), i.e. $\bar{\lambda}$ is a solution of

$$\frac{1}{n}\Sigma \cos(\theta_i - \bar{\mu}_0) = (2\bar{\lambda} - 1)A(\bar{\kappa}) = \bar{C}\cos\bar{\mu}_0 + \bar{S}\sin\bar{\mu}_0. \qquad (5.6.7)$$

Another method of estimation is given by Stephens (1969f).

Equation (5.6.7) should be ignored if λ is known to be $\frac{1}{2}$. The asymptotic variances and covariances of the above estimates can be obtained on using the lemma in Section 4.9.2.

Example 5.4. Obtain the moment estimates of μ_0, κ and λ for the turtle data in Table 1.8.

From Example 2.5, we have

$$\bar{\mu}_0 = \tfrac{1}{2}\bar{x}_0' = 61\cdot4°, \qquad \bar{R}' = 1 - S_0' = 0\cdot5250.$$

On substituting this value in (5.6.6), we find that $\bar{\kappa}$ is a solution of $A(\kappa)/\kappa = 0\cdot2375$. From Appendix 2.2,

$$A(\kappa)/\kappa = 0\cdot2403 \text{ for } \kappa = 3\cdot5, \qquad A(\kappa)/\kappa = 0\cdot2350 \text{ for } \kappa = 3\cdot6.$$

Hence, by linear interpolation $\bar{\kappa} = 3\cdot553$. Applying the method of Example 2.2 to the data given in Table 1.8, it is found that $\bar{C} = 0\cdot2006$ and $\bar{S} = 0\cdot4405$. On substituting the values of $\bar{\mu}_0$, $\bar{\kappa}$, $\bar{C}$ and $\bar{S}$ into (5.6.7), we have $\bar{\lambda} = 0\cdot78$. Hence, the proportion of turtles going forward is $0\cdot78$. Boneva *et al.* have studied the data by fitting a histospline.

6

TESTS FOR SAMPLES
FROM VON MISES POPULATIONS

6.1. INTRODUCTION

We shall assume that the underlying population is von Mises $M(\mu_0, \kappa)$ with p.d.f.

$$\{2\pi I_0(\kappa)\}^{-1} \exp\{\kappa \cos(\theta - \mu_0)\}, \qquad 0 < \theta \leqslant 2\pi, \quad \kappa > 0,$$

where μ_0 is the mean direction and κ is the concentration parameter. We give tests which are analogues of the standard normal theory tests viz., test of preassigned mean direction and of preassigned concentration parameter, tests of equality of two mean directions and of equality of two concentration parameters, tests of homogeneity etc. These tests are modified when the data is either multi-modal or axial. We also consider another situation which is peculiar to circular distributions, viz. to test whether the data is uniformly distributed.

Watson and Williams (1956) laid foundation to most of the parametric problems.

We shall discuss the optimum properties of the tests and illustrate them with the help of appropriate examples. As one would expect, all the tests depend on the sample mean direction or on the resultant length or on both. Example 2.1 shows the necessary calculations to obtain these quantities for ungrouped data. The maximum likelihood estimate of κ is sometimes used and its method of calculation for the same data is given in Example 5.1. For grouped data, these quantities can be obtained as in Examples 2.2 and 5.2.

6.2. SINGLE SAMPLE TESTS

6.2.1. Tests of Uniformity

Let $\theta_1, ..., \theta_n$ be a random sample from a population with p.d.f. $f(\theta)$. We are interested in testing the null hypothesis

$$H_0 : f(\theta) = 1/2\pi, \qquad 0 \leqslant \theta \leqslant 2\pi, \qquad (6.2.1)$$

against the alternative

$$H_1 : f(\theta) = g(\theta), \qquad (6.2.2)$$

where $g(\theta)$ has the given form but may contain unknown parameters. For most of our discussion in this section, we shall assume that $g(\theta)$ is the p.d.f. corresponding to $M(\mu_0, \kappa)$.

6.2.1a. *The Uniformly Most Powerful Test when the Mean Direction is given*

Let us consider the problem of testing

$$H_0 : \mu_0 = 0, \quad \kappa = 0, \quad \text{against} \quad H_1 : \mu_0 = 0, \quad \kappa = \kappa_1 \neq 0, \qquad (6.2.3)$$

which implies that the mean direction is taken to be zero when it exists. Under H_0, the likelihood function is

$$L_0 = 1/(2\pi)^n$$

while under H_1,

$$L_1 = e^{n\kappa_1 \bar{C}}/\{2\pi I_0(\kappa_1)\}^n,$$

where

$$\bar{C} = C/n, \quad C = \sum_{i=1}^{n} \cos \theta_i. \qquad (6.2.4)$$

Since the hypotheses are simple, the best critical region (BCR) by the Neyman–Pearson lemma is

$$\log L_0 - \log L_1 = -n\kappa_1 \bar{C} + n \log I_0(\kappa_1) < K.$$

Hence the BCR is

$$\bar{C} > K, \qquad (6.2.5)$$

where K is given by

$$\Pr(\bar{C} > K \mid H_0) = \alpha.$$

We shall use K as a generic constant in similar contexts. In fact, the test can easily be seen to be uniformly most powerful (UMP) test.

The p.d.f.'s of C under H_0 and under H_1 are given by (4.5.14) and (4.5.13) respectively. From (4.5.13), the power of the test can be obtained. Appendix 2.4 gives its critical values. From Section 4.9.1, for large n, $\bar{C}$ is distributed as $N(0, (2n)^{-\frac{1}{2}})$. A better approximation is given by (Durand and Greenwood, 1957):

$$\Pr[(2n)^{\frac{1}{2}} \bar{C} \geqslant K] = 1 - \Phi(K) + \phi(K)\{(3K - K^3)/16n$$
$$+ (15K + 305K^3 - 125K^5 + 9K^7)/4608 \, n^2\},$$

where $\Phi(\cdot)$ and $\phi(\cdot)$ are the d.f. and the p.d.f. of $N(0, 1)$.

For simplicity, we have taken the given mean direction μ_0' as zero. To test $\mu_0 = \mu_0'$, the criterion of (6.2.5) becomes

$$\bar{C}' = \frac{1}{n} \sum_{i=1}^{n} \cos(\theta_i - \mu_0') = R \cos(\bar{x}_0 - \mu_0'). \qquad (6.2.6)$$

Example 6.1. It was speculated in the 1920's that the atomic weights were integers subject to errors. Table 6.1 shows 360° times the fractional parts of the atomic weights (as then known) of the 24 lightest elements (von Mises, 1918). Test the hypothesis of uniformity.

TABLE 6.1. Angular deviations of the atomic weights (as known in the 1920's) of the 24 lightest elements.

Angular deviations	0°	3°36′	36°	72°	108°	169°12′	324°	Total
Frequency	12	1	6	1	2	1	1	24

We have here $\mu_0 = 0$. The hypotheses H_0 and H_1 defined by (6.2.3) are appropriate in this case. We find that $\bar{C} = 0.724$. From Appendix 2.4, the 1% value of $\bar{C}$ for $n = 24$ is 0.334. Hence, we reject the null hypothesis strongly. In fact, $(2n)^{\frac{1}{2}}\bar{C} = 5.02$ and by using the normal approximation, the probability of exceeding this value is found to be 10^{-7}.

6.2.1b. *The Rayleigh Test*

Let us now assume that μ_0 is unknown in hypotheses (6.2.3) so that under H_1, κ and μ_0 are both unknown. We now obtain the likelihood ratio test for this situation. The value of L_0 remains the same whereas using the maximum likelihood estimates of μ_0 and κ given at (5.4.6) and (5.4.7), we find under the alternative that

$$\max L_1 = \{2\pi I_0(\hat{\kappa})\}^{-n} \exp(n\hat{\kappa}\bar{R}),$$

where

$$A(\hat{\kappa}) = \bar{R} \qquad (6.2.7)$$

and

$$\bar{R}^2 = \bar{C}^2 + \bar{S}^2, \qquad \bar{S} = \frac{1}{n} \Sigma \sin \theta_i, \qquad \bar{C} = \frac{1}{n} \Sigma \cos \theta_i. \qquad (6.2.8)$$

Consequently, the likelihood ratio statistic is given by

$$\lambda = \{I_0(\hat{\kappa})\}^n \exp(-n\hat{\kappa}\bar{R}).\qquad (6.2.9)$$

We now show that λ is a monotonically decreasing function of $\bar{R}$ alone. Using (6.2.7) in (6.2.9), we have

$$\log \lambda = n\{\log I_0(\hat{\kappa}) - \hat{\kappa}A(\hat{\kappa})\}.$$

Using from (5.4.2),

$$I_0'(\kappa) = I_1(\kappa)\qquad (6.2.10)$$

we obtain,

$$d(\log \lambda)/d\hat{\kappa} = -n\hat{\kappa}A'(\hat{\kappa}).\qquad (6.2.11)$$

Since $\bar{R} \geqslant 0$, from (6.2.7) we have $\hat{\kappa} \geqslant 0$. Hence to show (6.2.11) to be negative, it remains to establish

$$A'(\kappa) \geqslant 0.\qquad (6.2.12)$$

If θ is distributed as $M(0, \kappa)$, we have from (3.4.47)

$$A(\kappa) = E(\cos \theta),\qquad (6.2.13)$$

that is

$$A(\kappa) = \{2\pi I_0(\kappa)\}^{-1} \int_0^{2\pi} \cos \theta \exp\{\kappa \cos \theta\}\, d\theta.$$

On differentiating both sides with respect to κ and using (6.2.10) and (6.2.13), we find that

$$A'(\kappa) = \text{var}(\cos \theta).\qquad (6.2.14)$$

Hence (6.2.12) follows. It may be noted that if we use the cosine moments given by (3.4.45) in (6.2.14), the following important relation is obtained

$$I_1'(\kappa) = \tfrac{1}{2}\{I_0(\kappa) + I_2(\kappa)\}.\qquad (6.2.15)$$

Using (6.2.12) in (6.2.11), we find that λ is a monotonically decreasing function of $\hat{\kappa}$. Finally, on differentiating (6.2.7) with respect to $\hat{\kappa}$ and using (6.2.12), it is found that $\hat{\kappa}$ is a monotonically increasing function of $\bar{R}$ and therefore the result follows. Further, the critical region (CR) $\lambda < K$ reduces to

$$\bar{R} > K,\qquad (6.2.16)$$

where $\bar{R}$ is given by (6.2.8). This test is what one expects intuitively since under the hypothesis of uniformity, the values of R will be small.

The p.d.f.'s of R under H_0 and under H_1 are given by (4.4.6) and (4.5.6) respectively. Hence, the power of the test can be obtained. Appendix 2.5 gives its critical values. For large n, we use the approximation (4.9.15), viz. $2n\bar{R}^2$ is distributed as chi-square with 2 d. of fr. A better approximation is (K. Pearson, 1906, Greenwood and Durand, 1955):

$$\Pr(n\bar{R}^2 \geqslant K) = e^{-K}[1 + (2K - K^2)/4n$$
$$- (24K - 132K^2 + 76K^3 - 9K^4)/288n^2].$$

An optimum property of this test is discussed in the next section.

Example 6.2. In an experiment in pigeon homing, the vanishing angles of 10 birds were found to be (Schmidt–Koenig, 1963)

$$55°, 60°, 65°, 95°, 100°, 110°, 260°, 275°, 285°, 295°.$$

Is there evidence that the directions were selected randomly?

We have $n = 10$, $C = 1.4884$, $S = 1.6590$ so that $\bar{R} = 0.2229$. From Appendix 2.5, the 5% value of $\bar{R}$ is 0.540. Hence the directions seem to have been selected randomly.

Example 6.3. For the leukemia data in Table 1.7, test for possible seasonal effects.

Suppose that there is no seasonal variation under the null hypothesis. Hence, we may regard the sample as being drawn from the uniform population on $(0, 2\pi)$ where the period of a year is identified with 2π. The data after adjustment for the lengths of months is shown in Columns 2 and 5 of Table 6.2. where the first interval $(0°, 30°)$ corresponds to the month of January and so on. We find on following the method of calculating used in Example 2.2, that

$$C = -48.2777, \quad S = -16.0046, \quad \bar{R} = 0.1005.$$

Hence $2n\bar{R}^2 = 10.22$. The 1% value of χ_2^2 is 9.21 so we reject the null hypothesis strongly. Thus there is evidence of a cyclic trend. It may be noted that if we use the Sheppard-type correction (Section 2.8), the value of $2n\bar{R}^2$ increases to 10.46.

Since the data is large, we may look into the question of whether the von Mises distribution provides a good fit. Following Example 5.2, we have $\bar{x}_0 = 198.3°$ and $\hat{\kappa} = 0.2021$. The corresponding expected frequencies are shown in Columns 3 and 6 of Table 6.2. The value of χ^2 for the goodness of fit test is found to be 9.6 whereas, under the hypothesis of uniformity, the value is 20.5. The 5% value of χ_9^2 is 16.92 so that the von Mises distribution provides a good fit but the hypothesis of uniformity is again rejected.

TABLE 6.2.   Observed frequencies for the leukemia data in Table 1.7 and the corresponding expected frequencies from a von Mises Distribution

Mid-points	Observed frequency	Expected frequency	Mid-points	Observed frequency	Expected frequency
15°	39	34·2	195°	50	51·0
45°	37	34·9	225°	54	49·9
75°	29	37·4	255°	37	46·6
105°	45	41·3	285°	47	42·2
135°	38	45·7	315°	34	38·2
165°	59	49·3	345°	37	35·3
			Total	506	506·0

Hence, we may say that the number of cases per month have a cyclic trend with maximum at 20th July ($= 365 \bar{x}_0/360$) and a ratio of the highest incidence to the lowest incidence $\exp\{2\hat{\kappa}\} = 1.50$.

Edwards (1961) has given an approximate test for testing uniformity against the cardioid distribution as the alternative. Both alternatives imply a cyclic movement with an annual peak period. Edwards (1961) also refers to other techniques. The above data has been analysed by David and Newell (1965) using another technique (see Example 7.5).

6.2.1c. Invariant Tests

Following Ajne (1968), we show that the invariance principle (Lehmann, 1959, Chapter 6) also leads to the Rayleigh test. Let H_0 be defined by (6.2.1). We consider the general alternative H_1' specifying a class of p.d.f.'s $g(\theta)$ which is invariant under a change of zero direction. Let

$$\xi_i = (\theta_i - \nu)(\mathrm{mod}\, 2\pi), \qquad i = 1, \dots, n.$$

Then the critical function ϕ of a test H_0 against H_1' must satisfy for every real constant ν

$$\phi(\theta_1, \dots, \theta_n) = \phi(\xi_1, \dots, \xi_n).$$

Consequently, ϕ must depend only on $n - 1$ variables $u_1, \dots, u_{n-1}$ defined by

$$u_j = (\theta_j - \theta_n)(\mathrm{mod}\, 2\pi), \qquad j = 1, \dots, n - 1, \tag{6.2.17}$$

where θ_n is selected as the new zero direction. In other words, $(u_1, \dots, u_{n-1})$ is a maximal invariant under the group of rotations. The joint density of $u_1, \dots, u_{n-1}$ is

$$L^*(u_1, \dots, u_{n-1}) = \int_0^{2\pi} g(\theta_n) \prod_{j=1}^{n-1} g(\theta_n + u_j) \, d\theta_n. \tag{6.2.18}$$

Under H_0, L^* reduces to a constant. Therefore, by the Neyman–Pearson lemma, the critical region of a most powerful invariant test is given by

$$L^*(u_1, ..., u_{n-1}) > K$$

which on using (6.2.17) and (6.2.18) reduces to

$$\int_0^{2\pi} \prod_{i=1}^n g(x + \theta_i)\, dx > K. \qquad (6.2.19)$$

For the von Mises population $M(\mu_0, \kappa)$,

$$\prod_{i=1}^n g(x + \theta_i) = \exp\{\kappa R \cos(x - \mu_0 - \bar{x}_0)\}/\{2\pi I_0(\kappa)\}^n$$

so that (6.2.19) becomes

$$I_0(\kappa R)/\{I_0(\kappa)\}^n > K.$$

Since $I_0'(\kappa) = I_1(\kappa) \geq 0$, $I_0(\kappa R)$ is a monotonically increasing function of κ for $\kappa > 0$. Hence, the critical region of the test is given by $R > K$ which is precisely that obtained from the likelihood ratio. Further, the critical region does not depend on κ and so the Rayleigh test is the uniformly most powerful (UMP) invariant test.

Bhattacharyya and Johnson (1969) have shown that the Rayleigh test is locally most powerful invariant for the offset normal distribution (Section 3.4.7) as the alternative.

6.2.2. Tests for the Mean Direction

We now assume that $\theta_1, ..., \theta_n$ is a random sample from $M(\mu_0, \kappa)$ with $\kappa \neq 0$ so that the possibility of uniformity is ruled out. Under the null hypothesis the value of μ_0 will be specified and, for simplicity, we take it as zero.

6.2.2a. *Concentration Parameter Known*

(1) *The Neyman–Pearson Approach.* Suppose that we wish to test

$$H_0 : \mu_0 = 0 \quad \text{against} \quad H_1 : \mu_0 = \mu_0', \quad 0 < \mu_0' < 2\pi. \qquad (6.2.20)$$

From the Neyman–Pearson lemma, we find that the best critical region (BCR) is given by

$$R\{\cos(\bar{x}_0 - \mu_0') - \cos \bar{x}_0\} > K.$$

This is equivalent to

$$R \sin(\bar{x}_0 - \tfrac{1}{2}\mu_0') > K. \qquad (6.2.21)$$

Hence, there are no UMP regions for testing H_0 against one-sided composite hypotheses $0 < \mu_0' < \pi$ and $\pi < \mu_0' < 2\pi$.

The likelihood ratio criterion for testing

$$H_0 : \mu_0 = 0 \quad \text{against} \quad H_1 : \mu_0 \neq 0, \quad 0 < \mu_0 < 2\pi, \qquad (6.2.22)$$

gives the CR as

$$R - C > K. \qquad (6.2.23)$$

For $\kappa > 2$, we can obtain K by using Stephen's approximation (4.9.31)

$$2\gamma(R - C) \simeq \chi_1^2, \qquad \gamma^{-1} = \kappa^{-1} + \tfrac{3}{8}\kappa^{-2}. \qquad (6.2.24)$$

For small κ, the percentage points of $R - C$ are not available. However, an alternative unbiased test developed below can always be used.

(2) *The Fisher Ancillary Principle.* Let g_2 be the p.d.f. of R given by (4.5.6) and let g_1 be the p.d.f. of $\bar{x}_0$ given R which from (4.5.7) corresponds to $M(\mu_0, \kappa R)$. We find that the likelihood function of $\theta_1, ..., \theta_n$ can be expressed as

$$L = g_1(\bar{x}_0 | R; \mu_0, \kappa) g_2(R; \kappa) h(\theta), \qquad (6.2.25)$$

where $h(\theta)$ is a function of $\theta_1, ..., \theta_n$ only. For this situation the Fisher ancillary principle (Fisher, 1959, Section IV 4; Kendall and Stuart, 1967, pp. 217–8) states that the conditional statistics $\bar{x}_0 | R$ should be used to test hypotheses about μ_0. Since no inferences about μ_0 are possible if only R is given, the observed R determines the precision with which inferences about μ_0 can be made. This principle is conceptually appealing because it takes into account the actual precision achieved. Therefore, when testing (6.2.20) we need only consider the distribution of $\bar{x}_0 | R$ which has the p.d.f.

$$g_1(\bar{x}_0 | R; \mu_0, \kappa') = \{2\pi I_0(\kappa')\}^{-1} \exp\{\kappa' \cos(\bar{x}_0 - \mu_0)\},$$
$$0 < \bar{x}_0 \leqslant 2\pi, \qquad \kappa' > 0, \qquad (6.2.26)$$

where $\kappa' = \kappa R$. From the Neyman–Pearson lemma, the best critical region (BCR) reduces to

$$\sin(\bar{x}_0 - \tfrac{1}{2}\mu_0') > K. \qquad (6.2.27)$$

Equivalently, the conditional BCR becomes

$$\bar{x}_0 \in \omega, \qquad (6.2.28)$$

where

$$\omega = \text{arc}\left[\{\tfrac{1}{2}(\pi + \mu_0') - \delta\}(\text{mod } 2\pi), \quad \{\tfrac{1}{2}(\pi + \mu_0') + \delta\}(\text{mod } 2\pi)\right],$$
$$0 < \delta < \tfrac{1}{2}\pi, \qquad (6.2.29)$$

which does not contain $\bar{x}_0 = \frac{1}{2}\mu_0'$. Let θ be distributed as $M(0, \kappa')$. The constant δ is then determined from

$$\Pr(\theta \in \omega) = \alpha, \tag{6.2.30}$$

where ω is given by (6.2.29).

Similarly, the power of the test at $\mu_0 = \mu_0'$ is given by

$$P(\mu_0') = \Pr(\theta \in \omega'), \tag{6.2.31}$$

where

$$\omega' = \text{arc} \left[\{\tfrac{1}{2}(\pi - \mu_0') - \delta\}(\text{mod } 2\pi), \quad \{\tfrac{1}{2}(\pi - \mu_0') + \delta\}(\text{mod } 2\pi)\right] \tag{6.2.32}$$

denotes the arc obtained on shifting the zero direction to μ_0' in (6.2.29). In practice, the CR and the power function defined by (6.2.30) and (6.2.31) can be obtained from Appendix 2.1.

Example 6.4. Given $\kappa' = 1$ and $\alpha = 0\cdot05$, obtain the critical regions ω when (i) $\mu_0 = 90°$ (ii) $\mu_0 = 270°$ and   (iii) $\mu_0 = 180°$.

(i) From (6.2.29), the CR ω is $(135° - \delta, 135° + \delta)$ where δ is obtained from

$$\Pr(\theta \in \omega) = 0\cdot05.$$

From Appendix 2.1, we have for $\kappa = 1$,

$$\Pr(\theta \in \omega) = 0\cdot04434 \text{ when } \delta = 20°, \qquad \Pr(\theta \in \omega) = 0\cdot05618 \text{ when } \delta = 25°.$$

By linear interpolation, we find that $\delta = 22\cdot4°$ so that ω is $(135° \pm 22\cdot4°)$ and the CR is

$$112\cdot6° \leqslant \bar{x}_0 \leqslant 157\cdot4°.$$

In Fig. 3.2, the curve for $\mu_0 = 0°$ corresponds to the p.d.f. of $\bar{x}_0|R$ under H_0 while the curve for $\mu_0 = 90°$ corresponds to the p.d.f. under H_1. It is interesting to note that the CR does not contain the mode $\mu_0 = 90°$ of the distribution under H_1.

(ii) Using the value of ω obtained in (i), the CR with $\mu_0' = 90° + 180°$ is simply $(90° + 135° \pm 22\cdot4)$.

(iii) For $\mu_0' = 180°$, the CR is $\omega = (180° \pm \delta)$. It always contains the mode $\mu_0 = 180°$ of the distribution under H_1. (The curves in Fig. 3.2 for $\mu_0 = 0$ and $\mu_0 = 180°$ are relevant here). Further, the distribution under H_0 is symmetric about $\bar{x}_0 = 180°$ so that the constant δ can be determined from

$$\Pr(180° - \delta < \bar{x}_0 < 180°) = 0\cdot025.$$

In this case, we can use Appendix 2.6. It is seen that for $\kappa = 1$, $\delta = 29 \cdot 6°$ so the CR is $(150 \cdot 4°, 209 \cdot 6°)$.

(3) *A Conditional Unbiased Test.* The conditional test defined by (6.2.28) depends on μ_0. We now derive a conditional unbiased test against the composite hypothesis $\mu_0 \neq 0$. Using the conditional distribution of $\bar{x}_0 | R$ given by (6.2.26), we find that for testing

$$H_0 : \mu_0 = 0 \quad \text{against} \quad H_1 : \mu_0 \neq 0, \tag{6.2.33}$$

the likelihood ratio test becomes

$$\cos \bar{x}_0 < K,$$

because under H_1 the maximum likelihood estimate of μ_0 is $\bar{x}_0$. Hence the CR of size α is given by (see Fig. 6.1)

$$\pi - \delta < \bar{x}_0 < \pi + \delta, \tag{6.2.34}$$

where the arc contains π, and δ is determined from

$$\{2\pi I_0(\kappa')\}^{-1} \int_{\pi}^{\pi + \delta} \exp(\kappa' \cos \theta) \, d\theta = \tfrac{1}{2}\alpha. \tag{6.2.35}$$

A critical region of this type has already appeared in Example 6.3(iii) as the conditional BCR against the simple alternative $\mu_0 = \pi$. The null distribution of $\bar{x}_0$ is symmetric about $\bar{x}_0 = \pi$ and we can therefore describe this test as an equal tails test.

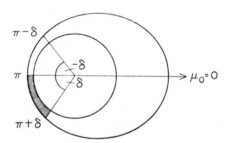

FIG. 6.1. Density of $\bar{x}_0 | R$ for $\mu_0 = 0$ and $\kappa' = 1$. Shaded area $= \tfrac{1}{2}\alpha$. Area between $(\pi - \delta, \pi + \delta)$ containing π is the critical region of size α.

We now show that among all the CR of size α containing the point $\bar{x}_0 = \pi$, only the equal tails test is unbiased against H_1. Of course, this result is intuitively expected. Let the CR of size α be defined by

$$\pi - d_1 \leqslant \bar{x}_0 \leqslant \pi + d_2, \tag{6.2.36}$$

where the arc contains π,

$$\Pr(\pi - d_1 \leqslant \bar{x}_0 < \pi) = \alpha_1, \qquad \Pr(\pi < \bar{x}_0 \leqslant \pi + d_2) = \alpha_2, \qquad \alpha_1 + \alpha_2 = \alpha.$$

Let

$$G(d) = \{2\pi I_0(\kappa')\}^{-1} \int_0^d \exp(-\kappa' \cos \theta) \, d\theta.$$

We take $0 \leqslant d_1 \leqslant d_2 < \pi$ without any loss of generality. The constants d_1 and d_2 are obtained from

$$G(d_1) = \alpha_1, \qquad G(d_2) = \alpha_2. \tag{6.2.37}$$

The power of this test is seen to be

$$P(\mu_0) = G(d_2 - \mu_0) + G(d_1 + \mu_0). \tag{6.3.38}$$

On differentiating (6.2.31) with respect to μ_0, we have

$$P'(\mu_0) = \{2\pi I_0(\kappa')\}^{-1} \left[\exp\{-\kappa' \cos(d_1 + \mu_0)\} - \exp\{-\kappa' \cos(d_2 - \mu_0)\}\right]. \tag{6.2.39}$$

On equating (6.2.39) to zero, the stationary values of $P(\mu_0)$ are given by

$$\mu_0 = \tfrac{1}{2}(d_2 - d_1), \qquad \mu_0 = \tfrac{1}{2}(d_2 - d_1) + \pi.$$

Let us denote these points by $\mu_{0,1}$ and $\mu_{0,2}$ respectively. On taking the first derivative of (6.2.39), we find that

$$P''(\mu_{0,1}) > 0, \qquad P''(\mu_{0,2}) < 0$$

if $0 < d_1 + d_2 < 2\pi$. Hence $\mu_{0,1}$ denotes a point of minimum of $P(\mu_0)$ while $\mu_{0,2}$ denotes a point of maximum. Consequently, from (6.2.39), the unique minimum occurs at $\mu_0 = 0$ if and only if $d_1 = d_2$. Finally, using (6.2.37), we conclude that the test (6.2.36) is unbiased against H_1 only when $\alpha_1 = \alpha_2$.

Selected critical values for the test defined by (6.2.34) and 6.2.35) are given in Appendix 2.6. For $\kappa > 10$, θ can be approximated by $N\{0, (\kappa - \tfrac{1}{2})^{-\frac{1}{2}}\}$. Of course, here κ is to be taken as κR.

Example 6.5. From a large scale-survey, it is known that the dip-directions of cross-beds of a section of a river have $\mu_0 = 342°$ and $\kappa = 0\cdot 8$. In a small-scale pilot survey ($n = 10$) of a neighbouring section of the river, it was found that $\bar{x}_0 = 278°$ and $\bar{R} = 0\cdot 35$. Can the mean direction for the neighbouring section be also taken as $342°$?

Let us take $\mu_0 = 342°$ under the null hypothesis. We have $\kappa' = \kappa R = 2·8$. From Appendix 2.6, for $\kappa = 2·8$ and $\mu_0 = 0$, the CR of size $0·05$ defined by (6.2.34) is $(180° \pm 101·3°)$. Hence the CR for $\mu_0 = 342°$ becomes $(342° - 180° \pm 101·3°)$ i.e. the CR is $60·7° \leqslant \bar{x}_0 \leqslant 263·3°$. Consequently, we accept the null hypothesis at the 5% level of significance.

6.2.2b. Concentration Parameter Unknown

(1) *One-sided* UMP *Similar Tests.* Let us consider the problem of testing

$$H_0 : \mu_0 = 0 \quad \text{against} \quad H_1 : \mu_0 \neq 0, \quad 0 < \mu_0 < \pi, \qquad (6.2.40)$$

when κ is unknown. Let $\mu = \cos \mu_0$ and $v = \sin \mu_0$. To develop a similar test, free (under H_0) from the nuisance parameter κ, we note from (4.5.4) and (4.5.12) that the conditional p.d.f. of S given C and the marginal p.d.f. of C are respectively

$$g_4(S|C; \mu_0, \kappa) = e^{\kappa vS} \phi_n(C^2 + S^2)/a(C; \mu_0, \kappa), \quad 0 < S^2 + C^2 < n^2, \quad (6.2.41)$$

and

$$g_3(C; \mu_0, \kappa) = \{2\pi I_0{}^n(\kappa)\}^{-1} e^{\kappa \mu C} a(C; \mu_0, \kappa), \qquad (6.2.42)$$

where

$$a(C; \mu_0, \kappa) = 2 \int_0^\infty \cos Ct \, J_0{}^n\{(t^2 - \kappa^2 v^2)^{\frac{1}{2}}\} \, dt \qquad (6.2.43)$$

and $\phi_n(\cdot)$, which does not depend on κ, is given by (4.4.6). Consequently, the null distribution of S given C does not depend on κ. (It depends of course on the value of μ_0 under H_0 through C). Further, it was shown in Section 5.4.2 that C is a complete sufficient statistic for κ when H_0 is true— a fact which can also be verified with the help of (6.2.42). Hence, the use of the conditional distribution of S given C is the only way of obtaining similar tests (see Lehmann, 1959, p.130). Further, to obtain the BCR, we need only consider the problem of testing the simple hypothesis

$$H_0 : \mu_0 = 0, \qquad H_1 : \mu_0 = \mu_0', \qquad \mu_0' \neq 0,$$

where κ and C are given. That is, it reduces to the problem of testing the simple hypothesis (6.2.20) when κ and C are given. Similar reduction appears in the one-sample problem for samples from normal population with unknown σ (see Kendall and Stuart, 1967, pp. 196–97, Example 23.7). Now, from (6.2.21), the BCR for (6.2.20) is precisely

$$S \cos \tfrac{1}{2}\mu_0' - C \sin \tfrac{1}{2}\mu_0' \geqslant K.$$

Since C is given, the BCR reduces to

$$S \cos \tfrac{1}{2}\mu_0' \geqslant K$$

which for $0 < \mu_0' < \pi$ reduces to

$$S \geqslant K. \tag{6.2.44}$$

Hence, the test (6.2.44) is a UMP similar test for testing the alternatives H_1. Similarly,

$$S \leqslant K \tag{6.2.45}$$

is a UMP similar test for testing

$$H_0 : \mu_0 = 0 \quad \text{against} \quad H_1' : \mu_0 \neq 0, \quad \pi < \mu_0 < 2\pi,$$

when κ is unspecified.

Let K be obtained from $\Pr(S \geqslant K|C) = \alpha$ when the null hypothesis is true. From (6.2.41), the power of the test (6.2.44) depends only on the parameter $\lambda = \kappa \sin \mu_0$ and is given by

$$P(C, \lambda) = \int_K^{\sqrt{(n^2 - C^2)}} g_4(S|C; \mu_0, \kappa) \, dS. \tag{6.2.46}$$

The power of the test (6.2.45) can be obtained similarly.

(2) *A UMP Invariant Two-sided Test.* We now consider the problem of testing

$$H_0 : \mu_0 = 0 \quad \text{against} \quad H_1 : \mu_0 \neq 0, \tag{6.2.47}$$

where κ is unspecified. For this purpose, it is convenient to take the ranges of θ and μ_0 as $-\pi$ to π instead of 0 to 2π.

We show that this testing problem is invariant under the transformation

$$\theta_i^* = -\theta_i, \quad i = 1, \ldots, n. \tag{6.2.48}$$

It can be seen that $\theta_1^*, \ldots, \theta_n^*$ are again independently distributed as $M(\mu_0^*, \kappa)$ where $\mu_0^* = -\mu_0$. The parameter μ_0 also ranges over $-\pi$ to π which implies that the parameter space of all possible values of (μ_0^*, κ) is the same as that for (μ_0, κ). Further, the null hypothesis $\mu_0 = 0$ is equivalent to $\mu_0^* = 0$ in the transformed space. Hence, the test situation is invariant under the transformation (6.2.48).

We know from Section 5.4.2 that C and S are sufficient for (μ_0, κ) and therefore the test function ϕ must satisfy

$$\phi(C, S) = \phi(C, -S).$$

That is, for given C, the test function must depend only on $|S|$. By the Neymann–Pearson lemma, the best invariant CR is given by

$$g_4(S|C; \mu_0, \kappa) + g_4(-S|C; \mu_0, \kappa) \geqslant K g_4(S|C; 0, \kappa),$$

where g_4 is the p.d.f. of $S|C$. On substituting for g_4 from (6.2.41), we obtain

$$\cosh(\kappa v S)/a(C; \mu_0, \kappa) > K. \tag{6.2.49}$$

Since $a(C; \mu_0, \kappa)$ is a factor in the p.d.f. of C given by (6.2.42), it must be positive. Consequently, for given C, (6.2.49) implies

$$|S| \geqslant K \tag{6.2.50}$$

provided that $\mu_0 \neq 0$ and $-\pi < \mu_0 < \pi$. Hence the best invariant CR turns out to be an equal tails test. The CR does not depend on (μ_0, κ) so the test is a UMP invariant test. Further, if K is obtained from $\Pr(|S| \geqslant K|C) = \alpha$ then the power of this test is $P(C, -\lambda) + P(C, \lambda)$ where P is defined by (6.2.46). The parameter λ may be described as a non-centrality parameter.

Similarities between these tests and the usual t-tests may be noted. The two-sided t-test is also a UMP invariant test with respect to certain transformations (Lehmann, 1959, p. 251, Example 10) and its power depends on a non-centrality parameter. However, in contrast, these tests are conditional and the likelihood function cannot be put into the usual two-parameter exponential family

$$h(\theta) q(\phi, \psi) \exp\{\phi U(\theta) + \psi T(\theta)\}$$

for which various general results are known (Lehmann, 1959, p. 134). In our case, the parameter ϕ as well as ψ is a function of both μ_0 and κ.

(3) *Confidence Intervals for* μ_0. Under the null hypothesis, we can obtain S_α such that

$$\Pr(|S| > S_\alpha|C) = \alpha \tag{6.2.51}$$

which is equivalent to obtaining R_α from

$$\Pr(R > R_\alpha|C) = \alpha, \tag{6.2.52}$$

where $R_\alpha = (S_\alpha^2 + C^2)^{\frac{1}{2}}$. For fixed n and α, let us imagine a graph of (C, R_α) with $C > 0$. For the observed value of $R = R_0$, we can obtain the corresponding value of C, C_α say, from the graph. Let δ be the solution of

$$C_\alpha = R_0 \cos \delta, \qquad 0 < \delta < \tfrac{1}{2}\pi. \tag{6.2.53}$$

In view of (6.2.52) and the relation

$$C = R \cos (\bar{x}_0 - \mu_0).$$ (6.2.54)

the arc containing $\bar{x}_0$

$$\text{arc } (\bar{x}_0 - \delta, \bar{x}_0 + \delta)$$ (6.2.55)

is a $(1 - \alpha)$-confidence interval for μ_0 (see Fig. 6.2).

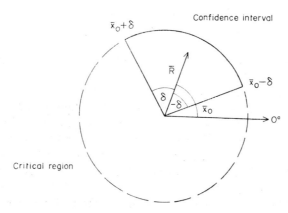

FIG. 6.2. Confidence interval $(\bar{x}_0 + \delta, \bar{x}_0 - \delta)$ for the mean direction μ_0 and the critical region.

Appendices 2.7a–2.7b give the values of δ for $\alpha = 0.05, 0.01$ when $\bar{R}$ is given. For $n > 30$, the following approximation can be used. Let $\hat{\kappa}$ be the maximum likelihood estimate of κ (see Section 5.4.1). Obtain $\kappa' = R\hat{\kappa}$. Let θ be distributed as $M(0, \kappa')$ and let δ' be the solution of

$$\text{Pr} (\pi - \delta' < \theta < \pi) = \tfrac{1}{2}\alpha.$$

A $(1 - \alpha)$-confidence interval for μ_0 is then arc $(\bar{x}_0 + \delta' - \pi, \bar{x}_0 - \delta' + \pi)$. This approximation is found to be adequate at least for $n > 30$. It can be used for moderately small n to obtain δ for those values of $\bar{R}$ which give δ greater than $\tfrac{1}{2}\pi$. The adequacy of this approximation is not surprising. After all, the above confidence interval will be asymptotically equivalent to the confidence interval obtained from the conditional test for the mean direction for given R (Section 6.2.2a(3)). Further for small samples, it involves replacing κ by its maximum likelihood estimate $\hat{\kappa}$ which depends only on R. In practice, $\hat{\kappa}$ can be obtained by the method given in Section 5.4.1 and δ' can then be obtained from Appendix 2.6 as in Section 6.2.2a(3).

Obviously, the above tests on the mean direction can be carried out once a relevant confidence interval has been obtained. For example, to test the two-sided alternatives at the 5% level of significance, the value of α is 0.05

whereas to test the one-sided alternatives at the same level, the value of α is 0·10 since

$$\Pr(S > S_\alpha | C) = \alpha \quad \text{implies} \quad \Pr(R > R_\alpha | C) = 2\alpha.$$

Example 6.6. In an experiment on homing pigeons (Schmidt–Koenig, 1963), the vanishing angles of 15 birds, released at 16·25 km south of their loft, were

$$85°, \ 135°, \ 135°, \ 140°, \ 145°, \ 150°, \ 150°, \ 150°,$$
$$160°, \ 185°, \ 200°, \ 210°, \ 220°, \ 225°, \ 270°.$$

The home direction was 149°. Was there any preference for the home direction?

We find that $n = 15$, $\bar{x}_0 = 168·5°$, $\bar{R} = 0·74$. First we test the hypothesis of uniformity. Since the 1% value of $\bar{R}$ is 0·540 from Appendix 2.5, we reject the hypothesis of uniformity, i.e. there is a preferred direction. To obtain 95% confidence interval for μ_0 under the plausible assumption of the von Mises population, we note from Appendix 2.7a for $\bar{R} = 0·74$, $\delta = 25·5°$ when $n = 14$ and $\delta = 23°$ when $n = 16$. Hence, for our case, $\delta = 24°$ approximately. Therefore, the 95% confidence interval from (6.2.55) is (144·5°, 192·5°). Since $\mu_0 = 149°$ is in this interval, we accept the null hypothesis at the 5% level of significance, i.e. there is a preference for the home direction.

To use the approximation just described, we find from Appendix 2.3 that for $\bar{R} = 0·74$, $\hat{\kappa} = 2·29$. Hence $\kappa' = n\bar{R}\hat{\kappa} = 25·42$. By using the normal approximation, the 95% confidence interval is $(\bar{x}_0 \pm 1·96/\sqrt{\kappa'})$ in radians, i.e. (146·2°, 190·8°). This again leads to the same conclusion.

(4) *An Alternative Testing Procedure.* It is clear from the preceding discussion that the tests for the mean direction can be based on the statistic $R|C$ instead of $S|C$ after taking the sign of S into account. In fact, Watson and Williams (1956) introduced the test based on $R|C$ for the two-sided alternatives. To test the hypothesis when $n < 15$, we can again use Appendices 2.7a–2.7b. For $n \geqslant 15$, we can also test the hypothesis after calculating R_α in (6.2.52) by using the following approximations of Stephens (1962a). The approximations depend on the value of C. Alternatively, we can use the nomograms of $R|C$ of Stephens (1962a) for $\alpha = 0·1, 0·05, 0·01$.

(i) For $0 < C \leqslant \frac{1}{3}n$, use

$$R_\alpha = \{C^2 + \tfrac{1}{2}n \chi_1^2(\alpha)\}^{\frac{1}{2}}, \tag{6.2.56}$$

where $\chi_1^2(\alpha)$ denote the upper $100\alpha\%$ point of the χ^2 distribution with 1 d. of fr.

(ii) For $\frac{1}{3}n < C < \frac{1}{2}n$, use

$$R_\alpha = \frac{1}{2}(R_{\alpha,1} + R_{\alpha,2}),$$

where $R_{\alpha,1}$ denotes the R_α defined by (6.2.56) and $R_{\alpha,2}$ is obtained from

$$F_{2,2n-2}(\alpha) = (n-1)(R_{\alpha,2} - C)/(n - R_{\alpha,2}), \tag{6.2.57}$$

where $F_{2,2n-2}(\alpha)$ is the upper $100\alpha\%$ point of the F-distribution with 2 and $2n - 2$ d. of fr.

(iii) For $\frac{1}{2}n \leqslant C \leqslant \frac{3}{4}n$, use $R_\alpha = R_{\alpha\,2}$ defined by (6.2.57).

(iv) For $\frac{3}{4}n < C < \frac{5}{6}n$, use

$$R_\alpha = \frac{1}{2}(R_{\alpha,2} + R_{\alpha,3}),$$

where $R_{\alpha,2}$ is defined by (6.2.53) and $R_{\alpha,3}$ is obtained from

$$F_{1,n-1}(\alpha) = (n-1)(R_{\alpha,3} - C)/(n - R_{\alpha,3}). \tag{6.2.58}$$

(v) For $C \geqslant \frac{5}{6}n$, use $R_\alpha = R_{\alpha,3}$ defined by (6.2.58).

The procedure is somewhat cumbersome in comparison to the approximation given above which uses only the von Mises distribution. The approximation (6.2.56) follows from the asymptotic distribution of S under uniformity (see Section 4.9.1) whereas the approximation (6.2.58), for large κ, follows from result (d) of Section 4.9.3. The approximation (6.2.58) also provides a motivation for (6.2.57).

The approximation (6.2.58) was first suggested by Watson and Williams (1956). Its use can also be understood as follows. We have

$$2\kappa(n - C) = 2\kappa(R - C) + 2\kappa(n - R) \tag{6.2.59}$$

and, for large κ, by Section 4.9.3, it obeys the χ^2-decomposition property parallel to

$$\frac{1}{\sigma^2}\Sigma(x_i - \mu)^2 = \frac{n}{\sigma^2}(\bar{x} - \mu)^2 + \frac{1}{\sigma^2}\Sigma(x_i - \bar{x})^2, \tag{6.2.60}$$

where $x_1 \ldots x_n$ is a random sample from $N(\mu, \sigma)$. Of course, we use t^2 (or the t-statistic) for the latter situation which is the ratio of the first term to the second term on the right-hand side of (6.2.60). When such a ratio is formed from (6.2.59), we are led to (6.2.58). It is therefore natural to use (6.2.58) for large κ. Upton (1970) gives approximations to the LR tests.

Example 6.7. Solve Example 6.6 by using the above approximations.
    We have

$$n = 15, \quad R = 10\cdot95, \quad \bar{x}_0 = 168\cdot5°, \quad \mu_0 = 149°,$$

so that from (6.2.54), $C = 10\cdot32$. Since, $\frac{1}{2}n < C < \frac{3}{4}n$, we should use the approximation (iii). From F-tables, the upper 5% value of $F_{2,28} = 3\cdot34$. On substituting for n, C, R and F into (6.2.57), we get $R_{\alpha,2} = 11\cdot22$ which is greater than $R = 10\cdot95$. Hence we accept the null hypothesis as in Example 6.6.

6.2.3. Tests for the Concentration Parameter

Let $\theta_1, ..., \theta_n$ be a random sample from $M(\mu_0, \kappa)$. The test statistics for hypothesis regarding κ should naturally depend on the appropriate circular variance, i.e. on C or R depending on whether μ_0 is known or not. This fact was first noted by Watson and Williams (1956). We show that the best tests in a certain sense depend only on C or R.

6.2.3a. *Mean Direction Known*

We shall assume throughout that $\mu_0 = 0$. Consider

$$H_0 : \kappa = \kappa_0 \quad \text{against} \quad H_1 : \kappa = \kappa_1.$$

By the Neyman–Pearson lemma, we find that the BCR is

$$(\kappa_0 - \kappa_1) C < K.$$

Hence,

$$C > K \tag{6.2.61}$$

is the UMP for testing H_0 against the alternatives $\kappa > \kappa_0$. Similarly, the UMP test for testing H_0 against the alternatives $\kappa < \kappa_0$ is $C < K$.
    We now show that for testing

$$H_0 : \kappa = \kappa_0 \quad \text{against} \quad H_1 : \kappa \neq \kappa_0$$

there exists a UMP unbiased test. The statistic C is sufficient for κ as noted in Section 6.2.2b(1). Further, from (6.2.42), the p.d.f. of C is given by

$$g(C; \kappa) = \{\pi I_0{}^n(\kappa)\}^{-1} e^{\kappa C} \int_0^\infty \cos Ct \, J_0{}^n(t) \, dt, \quad -n < C < n, \tag{6.2.62}$$

which belongs to the standard exponential family. Therefore, there exists a UMP unbiased test (see Lehmann, 1959, p. 126) and its acceptance region is

$$K_1 < C < K_2 \qquad (6.2.63)$$

where K_1 and K_2 are given by

$$\int_{K_1}^{K_2} g(C;\kappa_0)\,dC = 1 - \alpha \qquad (6.2.64)$$

and

$$\int_{K_1}^{K_2} Cg(C;\kappa_0)\,dC = (1 - \alpha)\,E(C|H_0) = n(1 - \alpha)\,A(\kappa_0). \qquad (6.2.65)$$

The second result in (6.2.65) follows from (4.8.9). On substituting for $g(C;\kappa_0)$ from (6.2.62) and interchanging the order of integration, we can integrate with respect to C. The resulting expression however is complicated.

For $\kappa_0 > 2$, we can use Stephen's approximation (4.9.31)

$$2\gamma_0(n - C) \simeq \chi_n^2, \qquad \gamma_0^{-1} = \kappa_0^{-1} + \tfrac{3}{8}\kappa_0^{-2}. \qquad (6.2.66)$$

Alternatively, we can use the approximation (4.9.33). For $\kappa_0 < 2$, the percentage points of C obtained from Pearson curve approximations by Stephens (1969a) can be used. For the two-sided alternatives, we can use the unbiased UMP region of the usual χ^2 test for unknown σ (see Lehmann, 1959, pp. 129–30) which may be considered as an approximation to (6.2.63). The latter test can be approximated by an equal tails chi-square test if n is not too small. Further, the power function obtained from (6.2.62) can also be approximated by the chi-square approximation (6.2.66) where κ_0 is replaced by κ. Problems with μ_0 known rarely occur in practice but we shall see below that this treatment helps us in understanding similar problems when μ_0 is unknown.

6.2.3b. Mean Direction Unknown

When μ_0 is unspecified, the likelihood ratio criterion for testing the null hypothesis $\kappa = \kappa_0$ against the alternative $\kappa > \kappa_0$ leads to the test

$$R > K. \qquad (6.2.67)$$

For $\kappa < \kappa_0$, the inequality in (6.2.67) is reversed. We now show that the test (6.2.67) is a UMP invariant test. The hypothesis $\kappa \geq \kappa_0$ remains invariant under the transformations $\theta_i' = (\theta_i + v) \pmod{2\pi}$, $i = 1, \ldots, n$. From Section 5.4.2, $\bar{x}_0$ and R are sufficient statistics for μ_0 and κ which under the transformation reduce to $\bar{x}_0' = (\bar{x}_0 + v) \pmod{2\pi}$ and $R' = R$. Now, R is a maximal invariant and consequently the invariant tests for this situation depend only on R. From (4.5.6), the p.d.f. of R is

$$f(R; \kappa) = \{I_0(\kappa)\}^{-n} I_0(\kappa R) h_n(R), \qquad (6.2.68)$$

where $h_n(R)$ does not depend on κ. We find that

$$\partial^2 \log f(R; \kappa)/\partial R\, \partial \kappa = A(\kappa R) + \kappa R A'(\kappa R).$$

This is non-negative for κ, $R \geqslant 0$ since $A(\kappa R)$ is non-negative by its definition while $A'(\kappa R)$ is non-negative by (6.2.12). Hence, the density f has a monotone likelihood ratio in κ (see Lehmann, 1959, p. 111, Ex. 6). On applying the Neyman–Pearson lemma to (6.2.68), we therefore obtain the desired result. We can deal similarly with the case for the alternative hypothesis $\kappa < \kappa_0$. An analogous theory problem in testing σ is well known (see Lehmann, 1959, p. 219, Example 5).

For the two-sided alternative $\kappa \neq \kappa_0$, we consider a locally UMP unbiased test. Let $K_1 < R < K_2$ be its acceptance region. We have

$$\int_{K_1}^{K_2} f(R; \kappa_0)\, dR = 1 - \alpha. \qquad (6.2.69)$$

Further, the derivative of the power will be zero at $\kappa = \kappa_0$. On writing the power function from (6.2.68) and differentiating it under the integral sign, we find that

$$\int_{K_1}^{K_2} RA(R\kappa_0) f(R; \kappa_0)\, dR = n(1 - \alpha) A(\kappa_0). \qquad (6.2.70)$$

Hence, K_1 and K_2 can be obtained numerically from (6.2.69) and (6.2.70). For n not too small, we expect as in Section 6.2.3a that this test can be approximated by the equal tails test. Further, the result established in the preceding section where μ_0 was specified suggests that the test is the UMP unbiased test.

Appendices 2.8a–2.8b give the 90% and 98% confidence intervals for κ based on the equal tails. For $\kappa > 2$, we can use Stephen's approximation of Section 4.9.3(e)

$$2\gamma(n - R) \simeq \chi^2_{n-1}, \qquad \gamma^{-1} = \kappa^{-1} + \tfrac{3}{8}\kappa^{-2}. \qquad (6.2.71)$$

On using this approximation, we now show that the $(1 - \alpha)$-confidence interval for κ based on the equal tails, is simply

$$[\{1 + (1 + 3a)^{\frac{1}{2}}\}/4a, \{1 + (1 + 3b)^{\frac{1}{2}}\}/4b], \qquad (6.2.72)$$

where $a = (n - R_0)/\chi_{n-1}^2(1 - \frac{1}{2}\alpha)$, $b = (n - R_0)/\chi_{n-1}^2(\frac{1}{2}\alpha)$, with $\chi_{n-1}^2(\alpha)$ being the upper $\alpha\%$ point of χ_{n-1}^2 and R_0 being the observed value of R. From (6.2.71), we have

$$\Pr(a^{-1} < 2\gamma < b^{-1}) = 1 - \alpha.$$

The inequality $2\gamma < b^{-1}$ implies that $16b\kappa^2 - 8\kappa - 3 < 0$. The roots of the quadratic equation $16b\kappa^2 - 8\kappa - 3 = 0$ are of opposite signs and if β is the positive root then $\kappa < \beta$. Similarly, the case $2\gamma > a^{-1}$ can be dealt with. Hence the result follows.

We can test $\kappa = \kappa_0$ against the one-sided alternatives at the 5% level of significance by obtaining the 90% confidence interval for κ on following the above method. For $\kappa_0 > 2$, we can use the approximation (6.2.71). (For large n, the normal approximation for $\bar{R}$ with mean and variance given by (4.9.21) and (4.9.22) is satisfactory. The latter approximation involves the quantity $A(\kappa)$ which is tabulated in Appendix 2.2). Stephens (1969a) has given the critical values of $\bar{R}$ for $\alpha = 0.01, 0.05, 0.95, 0.99$ which are based on Pearson-curve approximations. For $\kappa_0 \leqslant 2$, approximations of Section 6.3.2b can be used.

Example 6.8. In a pigeon homing experiment, the vanishing angles for 15 birds were found to be

$$115°, 120°, 120°, 130°, 135°, 140°, 150°, 150°,$$
$$150°, 165°, 185°, 210°, 235°, 270°, 345°.$$

Obtain a 90% confidence interval for the concentration parameter (Batschelet, 1971).

We have $n = 15$ and $\bar{R} = 0.6264$. Let κ_l and κ_u be the lower and the upper 90% confidence limits respectively. From the lower curves in Appendix 2.8a at $\bar{R} = 0.6264$, we find that $\kappa_l = 0.44$ for $n = 10$ and $\kappa_l = 0.88$ for $n = 20$. Hence, for $n = 15$ we have $\kappa_l = 0.66$. Similarly, from the upper curves at $\bar{R} = 0.6264$, $\kappa_u = 2.62$ for $n = 10$ and $\kappa_u = 2.40$ for $n = 20$. Consequently, for $n = 15$, we have $\kappa_u = 2.51$. Hence, a 90% confidence interval for κ is

$$0.66 < \kappa < 2.51.$$

From Appendix 2.3 for $\bar{R} = 0.6264$ we have after linear interpolation $\hat{\kappa} = 1.629$ which is included in the confidence interval but for obvious reasons, it is not the mid-point of the interval.

For illustrative purposes, we also give the 90% confidence interval for

κ from (6.2.72). It is not expected to give good results because $\hat{\kappa}$ is less than 2. We have

$$n - R_0 = 5 \cdot 6040, \qquad \chi_{14}^2(0 \cdot 05) = 23 \cdot 68 \quad \text{and} \quad \chi_{14}^2(0 \cdot 95) = 6 \cdot 57.$$

Consequently, $a = 0 \cdot 8530$ and $b = 0 \cdot 2367$. The 90% confidence interval, from (6.2.72), for κ is therefore approximately $(0 \cdot 85, 2 \cdot 44)$.

6.3. TWO-SAMPLE TESTS

Suppose that $\theta_{i1}, \ldots, \theta_{in_i}$, $i = 1, 2$ be independent random samples of sizes n_1, n_2 from $M(\mu_{0, i}, \kappa_i)$, $i = 1, 2$ respectively. Let the corresponding sample mean directions be $\bar{x}_{0,1}$, $\bar{x}_{0,2}$ and let the lengths of their resultants be R_1, R_2. Suppose that the mean direction and the length of the resultant of the combined sample are $\bar{x}_0$ and R respectively. Let the sums of the cosines and sines of the observations in the two samples be denoted by (C_1, S_1) and (C_2, S_2) respectively. This notation has been used already in Section 4.6 for the multi-sample case.

6.3.1. Tests for Mean Directions

We shall assume in this section that the concentration parameters κ_1 and κ_2 are equal, the common value being κ. We are interested in testing

$$H_0 : \mu_{0,1} = \mu_{0,2} = \mu_0, \tag{6.3.1}$$

against

$$H_1 : \mu_{0,1} \neq \mu_{0,2}, \tag{6.3.2}$$

where μ_0 and κ are unknown.

6.3.1a. *Non-existence of UMP Similar Tests*

We show that there does not exist a UMP similar test for this problem. We know from Section 5.4.2 that $\bar{x}_0$ and R are jointly complete sufficient statistics for μ_0 and κ. Hence, for all similar tests, we must keep $(\bar{x}_0, R)$ fixed. Further, the problem reduces to testing the simple null hypothesis

$$H_0^* : \mu_{0,1} = \mu_{0,2} = \mu_0, \qquad \kappa_1 = \kappa_2 = \kappa,$$

against the simple alternative

$$H_1^* : \mu_{0,1} = \mu_0, \quad \mu_{0,2} = \mu_0 + \delta, \qquad \delta \neq 0, \quad 0 < \delta < 2\pi,$$

where μ_0, δ and κ are fixed. From the Neyman–Pearson lemma, the BCR is found to be

$$R_2 \sin (\bar{x}_{0,2} - v) \geq K, \qquad (6.3.3)$$

where $v = \mu_0 + \frac{1}{2}\delta$. The BCR depends on v and therefore there is no UMP similar test. The situation is different for the normal theory two-sample problem where Student's t-test provides a UMP similar test (see Kendall and Stuart, 1967, pp. 197–8). We may therefore say that there is no strict analogue of Student's t-test for the two-sample problem on the circle.

6.3.1b. *A Two-sample Similar Test of Watson and Williams*

(1) *The Test.* We have shown in Section 4.6.3 that the conditional distribution of (R_1, R_2) given R (see Equation (4.6.21)) does not depend on κ when H_0 is true. Hence, for given R, we can construct a similar test for the two-sample problem by selecting a suitable function of R_1 and R_2. Watson and Williams (1956) have suggested rejecting H_0 for large values of $R_1 + R_2$ when R is fixed. That is, the critical region is

$$R_1 + R_2 > K, \qquad (6.3.4)$$

where, under H_0,

$$\Pr (R_1 + R_2 > K | R) = \alpha. \qquad (6.3.5)$$

Some justification for these tests are as follows. We have (see Fig. 6.3)

$$R^2 = R_1{}^2 + R_2{}^2 + 2R_1R_2 \cos (\bar{x}_{0,2} - \bar{x}_{0,1}).$$

So that if the difference $\bar{x}_{0,1}$ and $\bar{x}_{0,2}$ is zero in probability then $R_1 + R_2 = R$ in probability otherwise $R_1 + R_2 > R$. Hence, for given

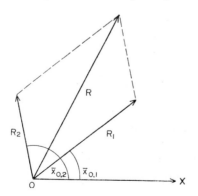

FIG. 6.3 The combined resultant length R.

$R, R_1 + R_2$ will be much larger for unequal mean directions. Further, when κ is known the likelihood ratio test for testing H_0 against H_1 at (6.3.1) and (6.3.2) is given by

$$- \log \lambda = \kappa(R_1 + R_2 - R) > K, \qquad (6.3.6)$$

which reduces to (6.3.4) for given R. Another justification appears in Section 6.3.1d.

(2) *The Null Distribution and the Power*. On transforming the variables R_1 and R_2 to

$$u = R_1 + R_2, \qquad v = R_1 - R_2$$

in the p.d.f. of (R_1, R_2) given R at (4.6.21), we obtain the p.d.f. of (u, v) given R. On integrating this p.d.f. with respect to v, we find that the p.d.f. of u given R under H_0 is

$$R/\{\pi h_n(R)(u^2 - R^2)^{\frac{1}{2}}\} \int_{-R}^{R} h_{n_1}\{\tfrac{1}{2}(u + v)\} h_{n_2}\{\tfrac{1}{2}(u - v)\}/(R^2 - v^2)^{\frac{1}{2}} \, dv,$$
$$R < u < n, \qquad (6.3.7)$$

where $h_n(\cdot)$ is given by (4.4.6). The latter is the p.d.f. of R for the uniform case. It is tedious to evaluate the integral in (6.3.7) numerically but calculations can be simplified by using the approximation of Greenwood and Durand (1955) for $h_n(\cdot)$ (See section 6.2.1b).

By the same method, the p.d.f. under the alternative can be obtained from (4.6.27). Hence, the power of the test is known formally.

We now consider some approximations to (6.3.7). For large κ, we have from Watson and Williams' approximation (4.9.37) that

$$2\kappa(R_1 + R_2 - R) \simeq \chi_1^2 \qquad (6.3.8)$$

and

$$2\kappa(n - R_1 - R_2) \simeq \chi_{n-2}^2. \qquad (6.3.9)$$

Further, these statistics are independently distributed for large κ. Hence, under the null hypothesis

$$F_{1,n-2} = (n - 2)(R_1 + R_2 - R)/(n - R_1 - R_2), \qquad (6.3.10)$$

where $F_{1,n-2}$ has an F-distribution with 1 and $n - 2$ d. of fr. From likelihood ratio theory and (6.3.6), we have asymptotically, under H_0,

$$2\kappa(R_1 + R_2 - R) \simeq \chi_1^2 \qquad (6.3.11)$$

for all values of κ. For $\kappa > 2$, we have from Stephens' approximation given by (4.9.31) that

$$2\gamma(n_i - R_i) \simeq \chi^2_{n_i-1}, \qquad \gamma^{-1} = \kappa^{-1} + \tfrac{3}{8}\kappa^{-2}. \qquad (6.3.12)$$

Hence, for $\kappa > 2$, we obtain from (6.3.11) and (6.3.12) that

$$F_{1,n-2} = \left(1 + \frac{3}{8\kappa}\right) \{(n-2)(R_1 + R_2 - R)/(n - R_1 - R_2)\}. \qquad (6.3.13)$$

The unknown κ can be replaced by its maximum likelihood estimate, viz.,

$$\hat{\kappa} = A^{-1}(\bar{R}), \qquad \bar{R} = R/n. \qquad (6.3.14)$$

Monte Carlo trials (Stephens, 1969e) support this approximation for $\hat{\kappa} > 2$, i.e. for $\bar{R} > 0.7$. This approximation does not differ from (6.3.10) for $\hat{\kappa} > 10$, i.e. $\bar{R} > 0.95$.

(3) *A Test Procedure.* Let $n_1 \leqslant n_2$ and let $r = n_1/n$, $0 < r < \tfrac{1}{2}$. Suppose that $\bar{R} = R/n$, $\bar{R}' = (R_1 + R_2)/n$. Appendices 2.9a–2.9b give the 5% critical values for the test for $r = \tfrac{1}{2}$ and $r = \tfrac{1}{3}$ respectively, i.e. for $n_1 = n_2$ and $2n_1 = n_2$. For $0 < \bar{R} < 0.4$ and $\tfrac{1}{3} < r < \tfrac{1}{2}$, we read the values of $\bar{R}'$ from Appendices 2.9a and 2.9b for $r = \tfrac{1}{2}$ and $\tfrac{1}{3}$ respectively and then obtain the value of $\bar{R}'$ for given r by interpolation. For $\bar{R} > 0.4$ and any moderate value of r, Appendix 2.9a can be used. For $\bar{R} > 0.7$ and any value of r, we use the F-approximation (6.3.13) where κ is estimated from (6.3.14). If $\bar{R} > 0.95$, the F-approximation given by (6.3.10) is sufficient. For $0 < \bar{R} < 0.4$ and $r < \tfrac{1}{3}$, we can use the result of Section 6.3.1c. Example 6.9 illustrates this procedure.

(4) *Relation with the Most General Similar Test.* In view of the completeness and sufficiency of $(\bar{x}_0, R)$ for (μ_0, κ), all similar tests must be conditional on $\bar{x}_0$ and R. However, the similar test of Watson and William is conditional only on R. This behaviour of Watson and William's test is explained by the fact that under H_0 the conditional distribution of (R_1, R_2) given $(\bar{x}_0, R)$ does not depend on $\bar{x}_0$. This result can be proved as follows. The joint p.d.f. of $\bar{x}_{0,1}$, $\bar{x}_{0,2}$, R_1 and R_2 from (4.5.5) is

$$\{(2\pi)^2 I_0{}''(\kappa)\}^{-1} \exp\left[\kappa\{R_1 \cos(\bar{x}_{0,1} - \mu_0)\right.$$
$$\left. + R_2 \cos(\bar{x}_{0,2} - \mu_0)\}\right] h_{n_1}(R_1) h_{n_2}(R_2).$$

On transforming the variables $\bar{x}_{0,1}$, $\bar{x}_{0,2}$, R_1 and R_2 to $\bar{x}_0$, R, R_1 and R_2 defined by

$$\begin{aligned}R_1 \cos \bar{x}_{0,1} + R_2 \cos \bar{x}_{0,2} &= R \cos \bar{x}_0, \\ R_1 \sin \bar{x}_{0,1} + R_2 \sin \bar{x}_{0,2} &= R \sin \bar{x}_0,\end{aligned} \qquad (6.3.15)$$

we find that the joint p.d.f. of $\bar{x}_0$, R, R_1 and R_2 can be written as

$$f(R_1, R_2|R)\, g(\bar{x}_0, R),\qquad\qquad(6.3.16)$$

where f and g are the p.d.f. of (R_1, R_2) given R and of $(\bar{x}_0, R)$ and are given by (4.6.21) and (4.5.5). Hence, the result follows.

6.3.1c. *An Approximate Confidence Interval*

We now give a method of obtaining an approximate $(1 - \alpha)$-confidence interval for the difference

$$\delta = (\mu_{0,1} - \mu_{0,2})\,(\mathrm{mod}\,2\pi).$$

From (4.5.7), $\bar{x}_{0,1}|R_1$ and $\bar{x}_{0,2}|R_2$ are distributed as $M(\mu_{0,1}, \kappa R_1)$ and $M(\mu_{0,2}, \kappa R_2)$ respectively. Hence, from (3.4.69) the difference

$$d = (\bar{x}_{0,1} - \bar{x}_{0,2})\,(\mathrm{mod}\,2\pi)$$

is approximately distributed as $M(\delta, \kappa^*)$ where κ^* is given by

$$A(\kappa^*) = A(\kappa R_1)\, A(\kappa R_2).\qquad\qquad(6.3.17)$$

In practice, we may replace κ by its m.l.e. $\hat{\kappa}$ given by

$$A(\hat{\kappa}) = (R_1 + R_2)/n.\qquad\qquad(6.3.18)$$

That is, the distribution of d can be approximated by $M(\delta, \hat{\kappa}^*)$ where $\hat{\kappa}^*$ is defined by

$$A(\hat{\kappa}^*) = A(\hat{\kappa}R_1)\, A(\hat{\kappa}R_2).\qquad\qquad(6.3.19)$$

Let θ be distributed as $M(0, \kappa^*)$ and suppose that, for given α, v is given by

$$\mathrm{Pr}\,(\pi - v < \theta < \pi + v) = \alpha,\qquad\qquad(6.3.20)$$

where the arc includes π. Therefore, an approximate $(1 - \alpha)$-confidence interval for δ is simply

$$\mathrm{arc}\,\{(d + \pi - v)(\mathrm{mod}\,2\pi),\quad (d + \pi + v)(\mathrm{mod}\,2\pi)\},\qquad(6.3.21)$$

where the arc includes d. This method is illustrated below, and can easily be modified if κ is known.

Example 6.9. In an experiment on pigeon-homing (Schmidt–Koenig, 1958), the 'internal clocks' of 10 birds were reset by 6 hours clockwise while the clocks of 9 birds were left unaltered. It is predicted from sun-azimuth compass theory that the mean direction of the vanishing angles in the experimental group should deviate by about $90°$ in the anti-clockwise direction with respect to the mean direction of the angles of the birds in the control group. The vanishing angles of the birds for this experiment are given below, measured in the clockwise-sense.

Control Group (θ_{i1}): $75°, 75°, 80°, 80°, 80°, 95°, 130°, 170°, 210°$

Experimental Group (θ_{i2}): $10°, 50°, 55°, 55°, 65°, 90°, 285°, 285°, 325°, 355°$.

Does the data support sun–azimuth compass theory?

We may assume that the two samples come from two von Mises distributions with equal concentration parameters (see Example 6.10). We first test the equality of the population mean directions with the help of the test procedure given in Section 6.3.1b(3). We have

$$n_1 = 9, \; n_2 = 10, \; C_1 = -1.5424, \; S_1 = 6.3320, \; C_2 = 5.5304, \; S_2 = 1.8917,$$
$$R_1 = 6.507, \quad R_2 = 5.845, \quad R = 9.131, \quad \bar{R} = 0.48, \quad \bar{R}' = 0.65.$$

Since $\bar{R} > 0.4$, we only use Appendix 2.9a. For $n = 16$ and $\bar{R} = 0.48$, the 5% value of $\bar{R}'$ is 0.59 while for $n = 20$ and $\bar{R} = 0.48$, the 5% value of $\bar{R}'$ is 0.57. Hence, for $n = 19$ and $\bar{R} = 0.48$, the 5% value of $\bar{R}'$ is 0.57. Consequently, the mean directions are significantly different. However, it is more appropriate to assume $\delta = 90°$ under the null hypothesis, i.e. to test equality of the mean directions after transforming θ_{i2} to $(\theta_{i2} + 90°)(\mod 2\pi)$. The values of R_1 and R_2 remain the same but

$$R = \{(C_1 - S_2)^2 + (S_1 + C_2)^2\}^{\frac{1}{2}} = 12.340.$$

Hence, the value of $\bar{R}$ under the hypothesis $\delta = 90°$ is $\bar{R} = 0.65$. Again, $\bar{R} > 0.4$ and we find for this value of R from Appendix 2.9a that the 5% value of $\bar{R}'$ for $n = 16$ and $n = 20$ are 0.72 and 0.71 respectively. Therefore, the 5% value of $\bar{R}'$ for $n = 19$ is 0.71. Hence, the data supports sun–azimuth compass theory.

For this example, we now obtain an approximate 95% confidence interval for δ on applying the method of Section 6.3.1c. We have

$$\bar{x}_{0,1} = 103.7° \quad \text{and} \quad \bar{x}_{0,2} = 18.9° \quad \text{so that} \quad d = 84.8°.$$

By using (6.3.18) and Appendix 2.3, we find that $\hat{\kappa} = 1.7394$. Appendix 2.2 gives $A(\hat{\kappa}R_1) = 0.9548$ and $A(\hat{\kappa}R_2) = 0.9499$. Hence, from (6.3.19), $A(\hat{\kappa}^*) = 0.9006$ which gives $\hat{\kappa}^* = 5.67$ from Appendix 2.3. Using Appendix 2.6, we find that v satisfying (6.3.20) is $49.7°$. Hence, from (6.3.21) an approximate

95% confidence interval for δ is simply $(35 \cdot 1°, 134 \cdot 5°)$. It can be seen that $\delta = 90°$ is included in this interval but $\delta = 0°$ is not.

6.3.1d. *The Likelihood Ratio Test*

For testing H_0 against H_1 defined by (6.3.1) and (6.3.2), we can obtain the LR test but its null distribution is intractable and its optimum properties are unknown. However, for large κ, it can be shown by using

$$A(\kappa) \doteq 1 - \tfrac{1}{2}\kappa^{-1}, \quad I_0(\kappa) \doteq (2\pi\kappa)^{-\frac{1}{2}} e^{\kappa}, \tag{6.3.22}$$

that the LR criterion is a monotonic function of the F-statistic given by (6.3.10). For small κ, on using

$$A(\kappa) \doteq \tfrac{1}{2}\kappa, \quad I_0(\kappa) \doteq 1 + \tfrac{1}{4}\kappa^2, \tag{6.3.23}$$

we find that

$$-2\log_e \lambda \doteq \frac{2}{n}\{(R_1 + R_2)^2 - R^2\}.$$

For these extreme cases, the LR criterion for given R is a function of $R_1 + R_2$ which supports the two-sample test criterion of Watson and Williams.

6.3.2. Tests for Concentration Parameters

Let us consider the problem of testing

$$H_0 : \kappa_1 = \kappa_2 = \kappa \quad \text{against} \quad H_1 : \kappa_1 \neq \kappa_2, \tag{6.3.24}$$

where $\mu_{0,1}$, $\mu_{0,2}$ and κ are unknown. Since R_1 and R_2 are invariant under rotations, by the invariance principle the test statistics for this problem should be a function of R_1 and R_2 only.

6.3.2a. *Non-existence of Exact Similar Tests*

By using the following p.d.f. of R_1 and R_2 for $n_1 = n_2 = 2$ obtained from (4.5.6) and (4.4.10), it can be seen that a similar test cannot be constructed.

$$f(R_1, R_2) = \{2/\pi I_0{}^2(\kappa)\}^2 I_0(\kappa R_1) I_0(\kappa R_2)/\{(4 - R_1{}^2)(4 - R_2{}^2)\}^{\frac{1}{2}},$$
$$0 < R_1, R_2 < 2.$$

In particular, the p.d.f. of the ratio R_1/R_2 also depends on κ. This behaviour is not surprising because under the null hypothesis $\bar{x}_{0,1}$, $\bar{x}_{0,2}$, R_1 and R_2 are minimal sufficient for $(\mu_{0,1}, \mu_{0,2}, \kappa)$ but are not boundedly complete. The latter result can be verified by noting that

$$(R_1{}^2 - n)/\{n_1(n_1 - 1)\} - (R_2{}^2 - n_2)/\{n_2(n_2 - 1)\}$$

will have a zero expectation under H_0 by (4.7.2). However, we shall be able to derive approximate similar tests from certain approximations to the distribution of R given in the next section.

6.3.2b. *Approximations to the Distribution of R*

From (4.9.31), an adequate approximation to the distribution of R is given by

$$2\gamma(n - R) \simeq \chi^2_{n-1}, \quad \gamma^{-1} = \kappa^{-1} + \tfrac{3}{8}\kappa^{-2}, \qquad (6.3.25)$$

when $\kappa > 2$. We now obtain approximation to the distribution of R when (i) $0 < \kappa < 1$ and (ii) $1 \leqslant \kappa \leqslant 2$. We know from Section 4.9.3 that $\bar{R}$ is asymptotically normal with

$$E(\bar{R}) = \rho, \qquad \text{var}\,(\bar{R}) = \frac{1}{n}\{1 - \rho^2 - (\rho/\kappa)\}, \qquad (6.3.26)$$

where $\rho = A(\kappa)$. By following the usual method for variance-stabilizing transformations (see Rao, 1965, p. 357), we obtain, for each range of κ, a function of $\bar{R}$ whose asymptotic variance is independent of ρ, i.e. of κ. These transformations to normality, after modifying the asymptotic variances, provide adequate approximations.

Case I. $0 < \kappa < 1$. On using the approximation

$$A(\kappa) = \frac{\kappa}{2}\left(1 - \frac{\kappa^2}{8}\right)$$

from (3.4.48) in (6.3.26), we find for small κ that

$$\tilde{R} = 2\bar{R} \simeq N(\kappa, \{2(1 - a^2\kappa^2)/n\}^{\frac{1}{2}}), \qquad a = (\tfrac{3}{8})^{\frac{1}{2}} = 0\cdot61237. \qquad (6.3.27)$$

The functional form of the transformation is

$$g_1(\kappa) = c(n/2)^{\frac{1}{2}} \int (1 - a^2\kappa^2)^{-\frac{1}{2}}\, d\kappa = \sin^{-1}(a\kappa), \qquad (6.3.28)$$

where c is given below. Therefore, the statistics

$$g_1(\tilde{R}) = \sin^{-1}(a\tilde{R}) \qquad (6.3.29)$$

has mean $g_1(\kappa)$ and

$$\text{var}\,\{g_1(\tilde{R})\} \doteq c^2 = 3/4n.$$

On comparing the exact tail area of $\bar{R}$ with various approximations obtained on modifying the variance of $g_1(\tilde{R})$, it is found that the approximation with

$$\text{var}\,\{g_1(\tilde{R})\} \doteq 3/\{4(n-4)\},\tag{6.3.30}$$

is quite satisfactory for n as low as 8. For κ very near 1, the approximation given below in case II is recommended. For $n > 40$, the normal approximation with mean and variance given by (6.3.26) is adequate.

The asymptotic mean given above can be improved. Substituting the asymptotic variance of $\bar{R}$ given by (6.3.27) into the asymptotic formula for the mean (4.9.9), we find that

$$E\{g_1(\tilde{R})\} = g_1(\kappa) + \frac{1}{n}a^3\kappa(1-a^2\kappa^2)^{-\frac{1}{4}}$$

which for small κ, reduces to

$$E\{g_1(\tilde{R})\} \doteq g_1(\kappa) + \frac{1}{n}a^3\kappa.\tag{6.3.31}$$

It may be noted that the same constant 'a' appears in (6.3.27) and Stephens' approximations (6.3.25).

Case II. $1 \leqslant \kappa \leqslant 2$. Using (6.3.26), the variance-stabilizing transformation is seen to be

$$g_2(\kappa) = cn^{\frac{1}{2}} \int \{1-\rho^2 - (\rho/\kappa)\}^{-\frac{1}{4}}\,d\rho.\tag{6.3.32}$$

Consider the term ρ/κ. Let $\kappa^* = \kappa - d$, $d = 1\cdot5$. In the neighbourhood of $\kappa = d$, we have

$$\frac{1}{\kappa} = \frac{1}{d}\left(1 - \frac{\kappa^*}{d}\right),$$

where κ^* is given by

$$\rho = A(d) + \kappa^*A'(d).$$

On substituting the resulting value of $1/\kappa$ in terms of ρ into (6.3.32), we find after some simplification

$$g_2(\kappa) = \sinh^{-1}\{(\rho - c_1)/c_2\}, \quad c_1 = 1\cdot08940, \quad c_2 = 0\cdot25789,\tag{6.3.33}$$

and

$$c = c_3/n^{\frac{1}{2}}, \quad c_3 = 0\cdot89325.$$

Hence, the transformation is

$$g_2(\bar{R}) = \sinh^{-1}\{(\bar{R} - c_1)/c_2\} \qquad (6.3.34)$$

with

$$\text{var}\,\{g_2(\bar{R})\} \doteq c_3{}^2/n.$$

Again, on comparing the exact tail area of $\bar{R}$ with the approximation obtained after modifying the variance to

$$\text{var}\,\{g_2(\bar{R})\} = c_3{}^2/(n - 3), \qquad (6.3.35)$$

it is found that the modified approximation is quite adequate for n as low as 8.

The above method of approximating (6.3.32) is, of course, general. Also, on proceeding as in (6.3.31), we have to order n^{-1}

$$E\{g_2(\bar{R})\} = g_2(\rho) - \frac{1}{n}[c_3{}^2(\rho - c_1)/2\{c_2{}^2 + (\rho - c_1)^2\}^{\frac{1}{2}}]. \qquad (6.3.36)$$

6.3.2c. A Two-sample Test

We now obtain a suitable two-sample test with the help of these approximations. Under H_0, $\kappa_1 = \kappa_2 = \kappa$ where κ is unknown. The boundary values of κ for the above approximations are $\kappa = 1$ and $\kappa = 2$ which in practice correspond to $\bar{R} = 0.45$ and $\bar{R} = 0.70$ respectively.

Case I. $\bar{R} < 0.45$. Under H_0, we can use the statistics

$$(2/\sqrt{3})\{g_1(\tilde{R}_1) - g_1(\tilde{R}_2)\}/\{(n_1 - 4)^{-1} + (n_2 - 4)^{-1}\}^{\frac{1}{2}} \qquad (6.3.37)$$

which is distributed as $N(0, 1)$ and where $g_1(\cdot)$ is defined by (6.3.29), $\tilde{R}_1 = 2\bar{R}_1$ and $\tilde{R}_2 = 2\bar{R}_2$. The critical region consists of the equal tails. If $n_1 = n_2$, the mean of this statistic is zero up to order n^{-1} but if $n_1 \neq n_2$, the bias in $g_1(\tilde{R}_1) - g_2(\tilde{R}_2)$ to order n^{-1} is from (6.3.31)

$$\left(\frac{1}{n_1} - \frac{1}{n_2}\right)a^3\kappa.$$

This bias is negligible either if κ is small or if n_1 and n_2 are nearly equal.

Case II. $0.45 \leqslant \bar{R} \leqslant 0.70$. For this case, we take our test-statistics as

$$\{g_2(\bar{R}_1) - g_2(\bar{R}_2)\}/[c_3\{(n_1 - 3)^{-1} + (n_2 - 3)^{-1}\}^{\frac{1}{2}}], \qquad (6.3.38)$$

where the function $g_2(\cdot)$ is defined by (6.3.34) and $c_3 = 0.89325$. Under H_0, this statistic is distributed as $N(0, 1)$. For $n_1 \neq n_2$, the bias to order n^{-1} can be obtained from (6.3.36). Example 6.10 illustrates this test.

Case III. $\bar{R} > 0.70$. From (6.3.25), we have under H_0,

$$F_{n_1-1, \, n_2-1} = \{(n_1 - R_1)(n_2 - 1)\}/\{(n_2 - R_2)(n_1 - 1)\}. \qquad (6.3.39)$$

The critical region consists of the equal tails of the F-distribution. Monte Carlo investigations have shown that this approximation is adequate. This test is illustrated in Example 6.15.

We can write down the likelihood ratio test for this problem but it is again complicated. However, on following the method of Section 6.3.1d, we find that λ is a monotonic function of the F-statistic for large κ and it is given by (6.3.39). For small κ

$$- 2 \log_e \lambda \doteq \frac{2n_1 n_2}{n} (\bar{R}_1 - \bar{R}_2)^2. \qquad (6.3.40)$$

In fact, for large n and very small κ, (6.3.37) reduces to the square root of (6.3.40).

Example 6.10. Test the equality of the concentration parameters for the data in Example 6.9.

We have $\bar{R} = 0.48$, $\bar{R}_1 = 0.7230$, $\bar{R}_2 = 0.5845$, $n_1 = 9$, $n_2 = 10$. Since $\bar{R} > 0.45$, we use the test (6.3.38). It is found that

$$g_2(\bar{R}_1) = - 1.1500, \qquad g_2(\bar{R}_2) = - 1.4246.$$

In calculating g_2, we can use the relation

$$g_2 = \log_e \{x + (1 + x^2)^{\frac{1}{2}}\}.$$

The value of the denominator in (6.3.38) is 0.4969. Consequently, the value of the criterion is 0.553 which is less than 1.96 and so the null hypothesis is accepted.

6.4. MULTI-SAMPLE TESTS

Let $\theta_{i1}, ..., \theta_{in_i}$, $i = 1, ..., q$ be q independent random samples of sizes n_i from $M(\mu_{0,i}, \kappa_i)$, $i = 1, ..., q$. Suppose that R_i is the length of the resultant of the ith sample, $i = 1, ..., q$ and R is the length of the resultant of the combined sample. We have in the notation of Section 4.6,

$$R_i^2 = C_i^2 + S_i^2, \qquad R^2 = C^2 + S^2, \qquad (6.4.1)$$

where C_i, S_i are the sums of the cosines and sines of the angles in the ith sample and C, S are the corresponding sums for the combined sample.

6.4.1. One-way Classification

Let us assume that $\kappa_1 = \ldots = \kappa_q = \kappa$ where κ is unknown. We wish to test

$$H_0 : \mu_{0,1} = \ldots = \mu_{0,q} \qquad (6.4.2)$$

against the alternative that at least one of the equalities does not hold. We can construct a similar test on extending the approach of the two-sample case. In fact, from (4.6.16), the p.d.f. of $R_1, \ldots, R_q$ given R is independent of κ, we can therefore take our critical region as

$$R_1 + \ldots + R_q > K \qquad (6.4.3)$$

for given R. The critical points for this case are not yet available but this difficulty can be overcome by using the alternative procedure described below.

Let $\kappa \geqslant 1$, $q > 2$. On following precisely the same argument as for the modified F-approximation (6.3.13), we find under H_0 that

$$\left(1 + \frac{3}{8\hat{\kappa}}\right) \{(n - q)(\Sigma R_i - R)/(n - \Sigma R_i)(q - 1)\} \simeq F_{q-1, n-q}, \qquad (6.4.4)$$

where $\hat{\kappa}$ is the m.l.e. of κ based on $\bar{R}$, and is given by (6.3.14). It is found from Monte Carlo trials that this approximation (Stephens, 1969e) is adequate for $\kappa \geqslant 1$, i.e. $\bar{R} \geqslant 0.45$. For $\hat{\kappa} > 10$, the factor in $\hat{\kappa}$ in (6.4.4) is negligible and we can display the calculations in a usual analysis of variance table, viz.,

Source	D.Fr.	SS	MS = SS/D.Fr.	F
Between Samples	$q - 1$	$\Sigma R_i - R$	$(\Sigma R_i - R)/(q - 1) = \text{I}$	I/II
Within Samples	$n - q$	$n - \Sigma R_i$	$(n - \Sigma R_i)/(n - q) = \text{II}$	
Total	$n - 1$	$n - R$		

Of course, the last column of this analysis of variance table can be modified to incorporate the correction factor in (6.4.4).

Let us now take $0 < \kappa < 1$ and $q > 2$, i.e. $\bar{R} < 0.45$. Consider the likelihood ratio test for this problem. Using the approximations (6.3.23), we find that the likelihood criterion is

$$- 2 \log_e \lambda \doteq \frac{2}{n} \{ (\Sigma R_i)^2 - R^2 \} = U \quad \text{say.} \tag{6.4.5}$$

We note that the approximations (6.3.23) amounts to neglecting κ^3 and the lower order terms. For large n, U is distributed as a chi-square variable with $q - 1$ d. of fr. when H_0 is true. To improve this approximation, we use from (4.7.8) and (4.9.21)

$$E(R_i) = n_i \rho + \frac{1}{2\kappa} + o\left(\frac{1}{n_i}\right), \quad \kappa > 0, \quad E(R_i^2) = n_i + n_i(n_i - 1)\rho^2, \quad \rho = A(\kappa)$$

in $E(U)$ to obtain

$$E(U) \doteq (q - 1) \left\{ \frac{2A(\kappa)}{\kappa} + \frac{q}{2n\kappa^2} \right\}.$$

Using $A(\kappa)/\kappa \doteq \frac{1}{2}(1 - \frac{1}{8}\kappa^2) + o(\kappa^{-3})$, we may take

$$cU \simeq \chi_{q-1}^2, c^{-1} = 1 - \frac{1}{8}\kappa^2 + \frac{q}{2n\kappa^2}. \tag{6.4.6}$$

This approximation is found to be satisfactory for moderately small values of n provided κ is not near 0 or 1. In practice, we replace κ by its m.l.e. as in (6.4.4) and we reject H_0 for large values of cU.

We can obtain confidence intervals for the simple contrasts $(\mu_{0,i} - \mu_{0,j})$ (mod 2π) by the method of Section 6.3.1c.

For large κ, J. S. Rao and Sengupta (1970) investigate the problem of choice of sample size in attaining a desired precision in estimating the mean direction. They also consider the problem of optimum allocation of resources under this model.

Example 6.11. Table 6.3 gives wind directions in degrees at Gorleston, England, at 11 hr–12 hr on Sundays in 1968 classified according to the four

TABLE 6.3. Wind directions in degrees at Gorleston on Sundays in 1968 according to the four seasons

Season	Wind directions in degrees
Winter	50, 120, 190, 210, 220, 250, 260, 290, 290, 320, 320, 340,
Spring	0, 20, 40, 60, 160, 170, 200, 220, 270, 290, 340, 350
Summer	10, 10, 20, 20, 30, 30, 40, 150, 150, 150, 170, 190, 290
Autumn	30, 70, 110, 170, 180, 190, 240, 250, 260, 260, 290, 350

seasons. For this data, $q = 4$, $n_1 = n_2 = n_4 = 12$, $n_3 = 13$, $n = 49$. Three readings were missing because it was 'calm' on three of the Sundays. Does the data indicate that the wind directions for the four seasons are significantly different?

TABLE 6.4. Calculations of various statistics for the wind direction data in Table 6.3

Season	C_i	S_i	R_i	$\hat{\mu}_{0,i}$	$\hat{\kappa}_i$
Winter	0·1661	−5·1158	5·1185	272°	0·95
Spring	1·8420	−1·0737	2·1321	330°	0·37
Summer	2·1214	3·2344	3·5705	57°	0·63
Autumn	−1·9661	−2·5093	3·4534	232°	0·56
Combined sample	2·1634	−5·4644	5·8771	292°	0·24

We assume that the concentration parameters are equal (see Example 6.12). Table 6.4 gives the values of the relevant statistics for this data. Since $\hat{\kappa} = 0·24$, we use (6.4.6). In fact, all the $\hat{\kappa}_i$ are less than 1. We have $c = 0·6110$, $\Sigma R_i = 14·2745$, and $R = 5·8771$ giving $cU = 4·22$. Now, the 5% value of χ_3^2 is 7·81. Hence, the wind directions for the four seasons are not significantly different.

6.4.2. Test for the Homogeneity of Concentration Parameters

Consider the composite hypothesis

$$H_0 : \kappa_1 = ... = \kappa_q = \kappa, \qquad (6.4.7)$$

where $\mu_{0,1}, ..., \mu_{0,q}$ and κ are not specified. Following Section 6.3.2, we divide our test procedure into three parts.

Case I. $\bar{R} < 0·45$. After using the $\sin^{-1}$ transformation g_1, given by (6.3.29), to $\tilde{R}_i = 2\bar{R}_i$, we obtain $g_1(\tilde{R}_i)$. Under H_0, the $g_1(\tilde{R}_i)$ are approximately distributed as independent $N\{g_1(\kappa), \sigma_i\}$ where

$$\sigma_i^2 = 3/4(n_i - 4) = 1/w_i, \quad \text{say.} \qquad (6.4.8)$$

The best unbiased estimate of $\beta = g_1(\kappa)$ is obtained by minimizing

$$\Sigma w_i \{g_1(\tilde{R}_i) - \beta\}^2 \qquad (6.4.9)$$

with respect to β. On equating the derivative of (6.4.9) with respect to β to zero, the best estimate of $g_1(\kappa)$ is found to be

$$\hat{g}_1(\kappa) = \Sigma w_i g_1(\tilde{R}_i)/\Sigma w_i. \qquad (6.4.10)$$

On substituting it in (6.4.9), we obtain our criterion as

$$U_1 = \Sigma w_i g_1^2(\tilde{R}_i) - \{\Sigma w_i g_1(\tilde{R}_i)\}^2/\Sigma w_i \simeq \chi^2_{q-1}. \qquad (6.4.11)$$

Example 6.12 illustrates this procedure.

Case II. $0{\cdot}45 \leqslant \bar{R} \leqslant 0{\cdot}70$. On using precisely the same treatment as in Case I to g_2, the $\sinh^{-1}$ transformation defined by (6.3.34), we find that the appropriate criterion is

$$U_2 = \Sigma w_i g_2^2(\bar{R}_i) - \{\Sigma w_i g_2(\bar{R}_i)\}^2/\Sigma w_i \simeq \chi^2_{q-1}, \qquad (6.4.12)$$

where now

$$w_i^{-1} = 0{\cdot}7979/(n_i - 3).$$

Case III. $\bar{R} > 0{\cdot}70$. For this case, under H_0 we have that $2\kappa(n_i - R_i)$ is approximately distributed as $\chi^2_{n_i-1}$ which implies that this quantity behaves like the normal theory sample variance. Hence, we can use Bartlett's test for this situation, viz.,

$$U_3 = [v \log \{(n - \Sigma R_i)/v\} - \Sigma v_i \log \{(n_i - R_i)/v_i\}]/(1 + d) \simeq \chi^2_{q-1}, \quad (6.4.13)$$

where $v_i = n_i - 1$, $v = n - q$ and $d = (\Sigma v_i^{-1} - v^{-1})/\{3(q - 1)\}$.

Example 6.12. Test the homogeneity of the concentration parameters for the wind direction data in Example 6.11.

TABLE 6.5. Calculations for testing homogeneity of the κ's for the wind direction data in Table 6.3

n	$a\tilde{R}$	g_1	w	wg_1	wg_1^2
12	0·5223	0·5495	10·6667	5·8614	3·2208
12	0·2176	0·2194	10·6667	2·3403	0·5135
13	0·3643	0·3729	12·0000	4·4748	1·6687
12	0·3253	0·3317	10·6667	3·5381	1·1736
Total			44·0001	16·2146	6·5766

Since $\bar{R} = 0{\cdot}199$, we use the U_1-test. Table 6.5 shows the relevant calculations where $a\tilde{R} = 1{\cdot}2247\bar{R}$, $w = 4(n - 4)/3$. Using the totals in the last three columns in (6.4.11), we get

$$U = 6{\cdot}5766 - (16{\cdot}2146)^2/44{\cdot}0001 = 0{\cdot}6013.$$

The 5% value of χ_3^2 is 7·81 so the concentration parameters for the wind directions, according to the seasons, may be regarded as homogeneous.

In passing, we note from (6.3.23) that the likelihood ratio statistic for testing the null hypothesis $\mu_{0,1} = \ldots = \mu_{0,q}$ $\kappa_1 = \ldots = \kappa_q$ against the general alternative leads for small κ's to

$$- 2 \log_e \lambda = 2(\Sigma R_i^2/n_i - R^2/n). \tag{6.4.14}$$

6.5. A REGRESSION MODEL

As in Section 5.5, assume that $\theta_i, i = 1 \ldots n$, are independently distributed as $M(\mu_0 + \beta t_i, \kappa)$ $i = 1, \ldots, n$. Let us consider the problem of testing

$$H_0 : \beta = 0, \qquad H_1 : \beta \neq 0.$$

Suppose that $\mu_0{}^*$ and $(\hat{\mu}_0, \beta)$ are the maximum likelihood estimates of the parameters under H_0 and H_1 obtained from Section 5.5. Let us write

$$S_0 = n - \Sigma \cos (\theta_i - \mu_0 - \beta t_i).$$

By the result (b) of Section 4.9.3, $2\kappa S_0$ has a χ^2 distribution with n d. of fr. if κ is large. Let $S_{0,0}$ and $S_{0,1}$ be the values of S_0 under H_0 and H_1 respectively. Now, for large κ, $2\kappa S_0$ is equivalent to

$$\kappa \sum_{i=1}^{n} (\theta_i - \mu_0 - \beta t_i)^2.$$

It therefore follows that

$$2\kappa S_{0,1} \simeq \chi^2_{n-2}, \qquad 2\kappa(S_{0,1} - S_{0,0}) \simeq \chi_1{}^2. \tag{6.5.1}$$

Further, we may assume that these are independently distributed. Consequently, for testing H_0 against H_1, we may use the following F-statistic.

$$F_{1,n-2} = (S_{0,1} - S_{0,0})(n - 2)/S_{0,1}. \tag{6.5.2}$$

This problem can be extended to the multiple regression model (see Gould, 1969).

6.6. TESTS FOR MULTI-MODAL AND AXIAL DATA

6.6.1. Multi-modal Data

We now consider samples drawn from the multi-modal von Mises-type distribution with p.d.f.

$$\{2\pi I_0(\kappa)\}^{-1} \exp [(\kappa \cos l (\theta - \mu_0)], \quad 0 < \mu_0 \leqslant 2\pi/l, \quad 0 < \theta \leqslant 2\pi. \tag{6.6.1}$$

Let us assume that the value of l is known e.g. from the inherent nature of the particular experiment under study. In view of the distribution theory of Section 4.5.5, we see immediately that all the tests developed in Sections 6.2–6.4 for the von Mises case are all valid for this case on replacing $\bar{x}_0$ and R by $m_l{}^0$ and R_l respectively, where

$$R_l \cos m_l{}^0 = \Sigma \cos l\theta_i = C_l, \qquad R_l \sin m_l{}^0 = \Sigma \sin l\theta_i = S_l. \qquad (6.6.2)$$

(The notation R_l should not be confused with R_i used in the multi-sample case.) Hence, we transform the observations from (6.6.1) to θ' by

$$\theta' = (l\theta)(\mathrm{mod}\ 2\pi) \qquad (6.6.3)$$

and treat $\theta_1{}', ..., \theta_n{}'$ as observations from $M(\mu_0{}', \kappa)$ where

$$\mu_0{}' = l\mu_0\ (\mathrm{mod}\ 2\pi). \qquad (6.6.4)$$

The concentration parameter κ in (6.6.1) should be adjusted by (3.6.7) if its value is to be judged relative to the value of κ for the von Mises distribution. Further, if (ϕ_1, ϕ_2) is a $(1 - \alpha)$-confidence interval for $\mu_0{}'$, the corresponding $(1 - \alpha)$-confidence interval for μ_0 is simply $(\phi_1/l, \phi_2/l)$. We illustrate this procedure in Example 6.13.

If in the bimodal case, it is suspected that the two modes are not of the same strength, we can transform the data to $(0, \pi)$ by

$$\theta^* = \theta(\mathrm{mod}\ \pi), \qquad (6.6.5)$$

and double the angles and then proceed as above. This procedure is justified because of the following result of Section 3.6. Let ξ be the random variable corresponding to the mixture of two von Mises distributions given by (3.6.1). This is a reasonable model if the two modes are not of the same strength. Let θ be the random variable corresponding to the p.d.f. (6.6.1) with $l = 2$. Now, by Section 3.6, the distributions of $\theta^* = \theta$ (mod π) and $\tilde{\theta} = \xi$ (mod π) can be made to approximate each other closely.

Example 6.13. In a pigeon homing experiment, 13 birds were released singly in the Toggenburg Valley under subalpine conditions. Their vanishing angles were (Wagner's data cited in Batschelet, 1971)

$$20°, 135°, 145°, 165°, 170°, 200°, 300°, 325°, 335°, 350°, 350°, 350°, 355°.$$

The birds did not adjust to their home direction but appeared to fly in the direction of the axis of the valley. Is there any evidence to show that they prefer flying in an axis rather than flying in random directions?

Let us test the null hypothesis of uniformity. We shall apply the Rayleigh test given in Section 6.2.1b using $\bar{R}_2 = R_2/n$ in place of $\bar{R}$. From Appendix 2.5, the 5% and 1% values of $\bar{R}$ (i.e. of $\bar{R}_2$) for $n = 13$ are 0·475 and 0·580 respectively. After doubling the observed angles and arranging them in ascending order, the data reduces to

$$2\theta: 40, 60, 240, 270, 290, 290, 310, 330, 340, 340, 340, 340, 350.$$

We find that $C_2 = 7\cdot7024$, $S_2 = -5\cdot0442$, $m_2{}^0 = 326\cdot8°$, $\bar{R}_2 = 0\cdot7082$. Hence, we reject the null hypothesis at the 1% level of significance. Therefore, there is strong evidence to suggest that the birds prefer flying in an axis.

We now obtain a 95% confidence interval for μ_0. From Appendix 2.7a, for $\bar{R} = 0\cdot71$, $\delta = 31°$ if $n = 12$ and $\delta = 28°$ if $n = 14$. Consequently, $\delta = 29\cdot5°$ for $n = 13$. A 95% confidence interval for the mean direction $\mu_0{}'$ corresponding to the doubled angles is $326\cdot8° \pm 29\cdot5°$. Hence on halving this interval, the corresponding 95% confidence interval for μ_0 is $(149\cdot2°, 177\cdot6°)$. Of course, the estimate $m_1{}^0/2 = 163\cdot4°$ of μ_0 is its mid-point.

6.6.2. Axial Data

Let the data be concentrated on $(0, 2\pi/l)$ and let the population p.d.f. be

$$l/\{2\pi I_0(\kappa)\} \exp\left[\kappa \cos l\,(\theta - \mu_0)\right], \qquad 0 < \mu_0 < 2\pi/l, \quad 0 < \theta \leqslant 2\pi/l.$$

On using the transformation $\theta' = l\theta$, it reduces to the von Mises distribution. Hence, we can regard $\theta_1{}', \ldots, \theta_n{}'$ as a sample from a von Mises population and proceed to use the test procedures of Sections 6.2–6.4 as done for the multi-modal case. We give two examples to illustrate some of the procedures.

Example 6.14. From a geological formation known as the "Upper Whitcliffian", a random sample of rock sepcimens from a locality gave the following values of the "strike" (Dr. A. I. Rees, Southampton University).

$$14°, 15°, 23°, 54°, 55°, 73°, 77°, 83°, 113°, 116°.$$

The strikes are the dip-directions reduced to $(0, \pi)$ by (6.6.5) and are thought to represent the directions of depositing water currents (the paleo-currents). Does the data indicate that the directions are uniformly distributed?

We have

$$n = 10, \quad C_2 = -2\cdot2159, \quad S_2 = 3\cdot3118, \quad \bar{R}_2 = 0\cdot3985.$$

From Appendix 2.5, the 5% value of $\bar{R}_2$ (i.e. of $\bar{R}$) is 0·540. Hence, we accept the hypothesis of uniformity.

It should be noted that experimenters may present the above data in the form

$$14°, 15°, 23°, 54°, 55°, 244°, 247°, 277°, 283°, 287°.$$

This, of course, does not imply that the data is bimodal and it should be reduced to $(0, \pi)$ by $\min (\theta, 360° - \theta)$ before using a test.

Example 6.15. In a geological study, the following samples of sizes 8 and 10 are observed at two sites.

Site 1: 74°, 78°, 80°, 88°, 89°, 92°, 93°, 113°, .
Site 2: 37°, 90°, 93°, 104°, 105°, 109°, 111°, 116°, 121°, 124°.

The measurements are the axes of maximum susceptibility in magnetization of the Fransciscan rocks from the Diablo Range in California (Hamilton and Rees, 1965). Is the difference between the mean directions significant?
After doubling the angles, we find for the first sample,

$$C_2^{(1)} = -7{\cdot}3850, \qquad S_2^{(1)} = 0{\cdot}4897, \qquad \bar{R}_2^{(1)} = 0{\cdot}9252$$

while for the second sample,

$$C_2^{(2)} = -6{\cdot}4587, \qquad S_2^{(2)} = -3{\cdot}9956 \quad \text{and} \quad \bar{R}_2^{(2)} = 0{\cdot}7595.$$

The sample mean directions after halving the mean directions for the doubled angles are 88·1° and 105·8° respectively. For the combined sample, we have

$$C_2 = -13{\cdot}8437, \qquad S_2 = -3{\cdot}5059, \qquad \bar{R}_2 = 0{\cdot}7934.$$

We now test the equality of the concentration parameters using Section 6.3.2c. Noting that our $\bar{R}_2^{(1)}$, $\bar{R}_2^{(2)}$ and $\bar{R}_2$ correspond to $\bar{R}_1$, $\bar{R}_2$ and $\bar{R}$ respectively in Section 6.3, we have in the notation of Section 6.3, $R_1 = 7{\cdot}40$, $R_2 = 7{\cdot}59$, $R = 14{\cdot}28$, $\bar{R} = 0{\cdot}79$. Since $\bar{R} > 0{\cdot}70$, the F-test given by (6.3.39) is appropriate. We find that its reciprocal is

$$F_{9,7} = 7 \times (10 - 7{\cdot}59)/9 \times (8 - 7{\cdot}40) = 3{\cdot}12.$$

The 2·5% value of $F_{9,7}$ is 4·83. Hence we accept the hypothesis of equality of the concentration parameters.
Next, we test equality of the mean directions. Since $\bar{R} > 0{\cdot}70$, we use (6.3.13). From Appendix 2.3, for $\bar{R} = 0{\cdot}79$, $\hat{\kappa} = 2{\cdot}75$. Hence, from (6.3.13),

$$F_{1,16} = \left(1 + \frac{3}{8 \times 2{\cdot}75}\right) \times 16 \times (7{\cdot}40 + 7{\cdot}59 - 14{\cdot}28)/(18 - 7{\cdot}40 - 7{\cdot}59)$$

$$= 3{\cdot}48.$$

The 5% value of $F_{1,16}$ is 4·49. Hence, there is no significant difference between the mean directions.

7

NON-PARAMETRIC TESTS

7.1. INTRODUCTION AND BASIC RESULTS

In this chapter, we give some appropriate analogues of important non-parametric tests on the line when the underlying populations are continuous. It will be assumed that the reader is familiar with the basic non-parametric tests on the line. Since there is no unique way of ordering a sample on the circle, the circular analogues are taken to be invariant under rotations. We have already obtained a maximal invariant under rotations in Section 6.2.1c which will be discussed further in Section 7.1.1. We also consider tests for samples from multimodal and axial populations. It should be noted that the tests of goodness of fit on the circle are frequently used to test the hypothesis of uniformity.

7.1.1. The Maximal Invariant

Let $\theta_1, \theta_2, ..., \theta_n$ be a random sample from a continuous circular population with p.d.f. $f(\theta)$. Suppose that $\theta_{(1)}, ..., \theta_{(n)}$ are the statistics obtained by arranging $\theta_1, ..., \theta_n$ in ascending order. We call these order statistics the *linear* order statistics of $\theta_1, ..., \theta_n$. Suppose that a statistic $t(\theta_1, \theta_2, ..., \theta_n)$ is invariant under rotations. By choosing θ_n as the zero direction, we have

$$t(\theta_1, \theta_2, ..., \theta_n) = t(\theta_1{}^*, ..., \theta_{n-1}^*, 0), \qquad (7.1.1)$$

where

$$\theta_i{}^* = (\theta_i - \theta_n)(\text{mod } 2\pi), \qquad i = 1, ..., n-1. \qquad (7.1.2)$$

171

Hence, we may regard t as a statistic based on $\theta_1, ..., \theta_{n-1}$. The likelihood function of $\theta_1{}^*, ..., \theta_{n-1}^*$ is

$$\int_0^{2\pi} f(\theta) \prod_{i=1}^{n-1} f(\theta_i{}^* + \theta)\, d\theta, \qquad 0 < \theta_i{}^* \leqslant 2\pi, \quad i = 1, ..., n-1. \quad (7.1.3)$$

Since $\theta_1{}^*, ..., \theta_{n-1}^*$ are interchangeable, the distribution of their linear order statistics $\theta_{(1)}^*, ..., \theta_{(n-1)}^*$ is given by

$$(n-1)! \int_0^{2\pi} f(\theta) \prod_{i=1}^{n-1} f(\theta_{(i)}^* + \theta)\, d\theta, \quad 0 < \theta_{(1)}^* < ... < \theta_{(n-1)}^* < 2\pi. \quad (7.1.4)$$

If $f(\theta)$ corresponds to the uniform variable on $(0, 2\pi)$, the p.d.f. of $\theta_1{}^*, ..., \theta_{n-1}^*$ is

$$(n-1)! \, (2\pi)^{-(n-1)}, \qquad 0 < \theta_i{}^* \leqslant 2\pi. \quad (7.1.5)$$

Hence, a sample of size n from the uniform circular population can be regarded as a sample of size $n - 1$ from the uniform distribution on the line over the interval $(0, 2\pi)$.

Let $\theta_{(1)}, ..., \theta_{(n)}$ be the linear order statistics of $\theta_1, ..., \theta_n$. The sample spacings

$$T_i = \theta_{(i)} - \theta_{(i-1)}, \qquad i = 1, ..., n-1, \quad T_n = 2\pi - (\theta_{(n)} - \theta_{(1)}), \quad (7.1.6)$$

are the successive arc-lengths between the observations. If the underlying distribution is uniform, then from the preceding discussion, the p.d.f. (degenerate) of $T_1, ..., T_n$ is

$$(n-1)! \, (2\pi)^{-(n-1)}, \qquad 0 < T_i \leqslant 2\pi, \quad \sum_{i=1}^{n} T_i = 2\pi. \quad (7.1.7)$$

Hence, these spacings have the same distribution as the spacings of a sample of size $n - 1$ from the uniform distribution on the line over $(0, 2\pi)$. Further, from (7.1.4), the random variables

$$\theta_{(i)}^* = \theta_{(i)} - \theta_{(1)}, \qquad i = 2, ..., n, \quad (7.1.8)$$

can be regarded as the order statistics of a sample of size $n - 1$ from the uniform distribution on the line over $(0, 2\pi)$, i.e. the $\theta_{(i)}^*$ are the *uniform order statistics*.

7.1.2. Empirical Distribution Function

After taking a *fixed* zero direction, we define the empirical d.f. $S_n(\theta)$ as on the line. Define $\theta_{(0)} = 0$, $\theta_{(n+1)} = 2\pi$. We have

$$S_n(\theta) = i/n, \quad \text{if} \quad \theta_{(i)} \leqslant \theta < \theta_{(i+1)}, \qquad i = 0, 1, ..., n. \quad (7.1.9)$$

The domain of this d.f. can be extended by following the approach of Section 3.1. The results for the empirical d.f. on the line are obviously valid. In particular, $S_n(\theta)$ is a binomial variate with the parameter p as $F(\theta)$ and the number of trials as n. We have

$$E\{S_n(\theta)\} = F(\theta), \quad \text{var}\,\{S_n(\theta)\} = F(\theta)\{1 - F(\theta)\}/n. \qquad (7.1.10)$$

Consequently, $S_n(\theta)$ is a consistent estimate of $F(\theta)$. Further, by the Glivenko–Cantelli theorem $S_n(\theta)$ converges uniformly to $F(\theta)$. However, $S_n(\theta)$ and $F(\theta)$ depend on the origin.

We note that the probability integral transformation

$$U = F(\theta) \qquad (7.1.11)$$

implies that U is distributed uniformly on $(0, 1)$ provided that F is continuous.

7.2. TESTS OF GOODNESS OF FIT AND TESTS OF UNIFORMITY

We wish to test

$$H_0 : F = F_0 \quad \text{against} \quad H_1 : F \neq F_0. \qquad (7.2.1)$$

For a given F_0, the above problem can be reduced to testing uniformity on applying the transformation (7.1.11). Since the transformed null hypothesis

$$F_0(\theta) = \theta/(2\pi), \qquad 0 < \theta \leqslant 2\pi \qquad (7.2.2)$$

is itself of interest, we will confine our attention to this case for some of the tests. The chi-square test of goodness of fit is well-known and will not be discussed here.

7.2.1. A Kolmogorov-type Test (Kuiper's Test)

As in the linear case, define the deviations

$$D_n{}^+ = \sup_\theta \{S_n(\theta) - F(\theta)\}, \qquad D_n{}^- = \sup_\theta \{F(\theta) - S_n(\theta)\}, \qquad (7.2.3)$$

where $S_n(\theta)$ is the empirical d.f. given by (7.1.9). Both statistics $D_n{}^+$ and $D_n{}^-$ depend on the choice of the zero direction. This led Kuiper (1960) to define a new statistic

$$V_n = D_n{}^+ + D_n{}^- \qquad (7.2.4)$$

which, as we shall see below, is invariant under rotations. The null hypothesis is rejected for large values of V_n. On using the probability integral transformation, the distribution-free property of V_n under H_0 follows easily. We shall deduce this property from an alternative representation of V_n given below.

7.2.1a. An Alternative Representation of V_n

We have

$$D_n^+ = \max_{0 \le i \le n} \ \sup_{\theta_{(i)} \le \theta < \theta_{(i+1)}} \ \{i/n - F(\theta)\}$$

$$= \max_{0 \le i \le n} \ \{i/n - \inf_{\theta_{(i)} \le \theta < \theta_{(i+1)}} F(\theta)\}$$

so that

$$D_n^+ = \max_{0 \le i \le n} (i/n - U_i), \tag{7.2.5}$$

where

$$U_0 = 0, \quad U_i = F(\theta_{(i)}), \quad i = 1, ..., n. \tag{7.2.6}$$

Similarly,

$$D_n^- = \max_{0 \le i \le n} \{U_i - (i - 1)/n\}. \tag{7.2.7}$$

On substituting (7.2.5) and (7.2.7) in (7.2.4), we obtain the following equivalent representation of V_n.

$$V_n = \max_{0 \le i \le n} \{i/n - U_i\} + \max_{0 \le i \le n} \{U_i - (i - 1)/n\}, \tag{7.2.8}$$

where the U_i are defined by (7.2.6). Under H_0, $U_1, ..., U_n$ are the uniform order statistics. Hence, from (7.2.8), it follows that V_n is completely distribution-free.

7.2.1b. An Invariance Property

We now show that V_n does not depend on the zero direction. Let us consider the representation of V_n given by (7.2.8). Replace the interval $(0, 1)$ by the modulo 1 so that $2\pi U_1, ..., 2\pi U_n$ are angles in ascending order and $U_0 = 0$ corresponds to the zero direction. Let the new zero direction be $\theta = c$ and let $2\pi U_j'$, $j = 1, ..., n$, be the new angles in ascending order. For a fixed c and a given sample, there exists an integer k such that $U_k < c < U_{k+1}$. The equalities are omitted since we are dealing with samples from continuous populations. Hence,

$$U_j' = U_{k+j} - c, \qquad \text{for} \quad j = 1, ..., n - k,$$
$$= U_{k+j-n} + 1 - c, \quad \text{for} \quad j = n - k + 1, ..., n.$$

Consequently, for $i = k + j$, we have

$$j/n - U_j' = \{(i - k)/n\} - (U_i - c)$$

whereas for $i = k + j - n$, we have

$$j/n - U_j' = \{(i - k + n)/n\} - (U_i + 1 - c).$$

Therefore, we find that

$$j/n - U_j' = i/n - U_i + c - k/n, \quad i = (k + j)\,(\mathrm{mod}\,n), \quad j = 1, ..., n. \quad (7.2.9)$$

We note that the integer k so defined is a random variable but is constant for a given sample and a fixed c. Further, if $a_0, a_1, ..., a_n$ are any n numbers and d is a constant, we obviously have

$$\max_{0 \le i \le n} (a_i + d) = d + \max_{0 \le i \le n} (a_i). \qquad (7.2.10)$$

On substituting for $i/n - U_i$ from (7.2.9) into the V_n defined by (7.2.8), we find after using (7.2.10) that V_n does not depend on k and c. Hence, the result is proved.

7.2.1c. The Null Distribution of V_n

To obtain the null distribution of V_n, it is convenient to consider another statistic K_n of Brunk (1962) which is related to V_n. Let

$$C_n^+ = \max_{0 \le i \le n} \{i/(n + 1) - U_i\}, \qquad C_n^- = \max_{0 \le i \le n} \{U_i - i/(n + 1)\}. \quad (7.2.11)$$

These are based on distances between the uniform order statistics and their expected values. Define

$$K_n = C_n^+ + C_n^-. \qquad (7.2.12)$$

Relation Between V_n and K_n. Following Stephens (1969g), we show that

$$\Pr\{K_n < z\} = \Pr\{V_{n+1} < z + (n + 1)^{-1}\}. \qquad (7.2.13)$$

Let $U_1', ..., U_{n+1}'$ be the uniform order statistics for a sample of size $n + 1$. Since V_{n+1} is invariant under rotations, we may take U_1' as the new origin by transforming the variables to

$$U_0^* = U_1' = 0, \qquad U_1^* = U_2' - U_1', ..., U_n^* = U_{n+1}' - U_1'.$$

Therefore, from (7.2.8), we have

$$V_{n+1} = \max_{0 \le i \le n} \{i/(n + 1) - U_i^*\} + \max_{0 \le i \le n} \{U_i^* - (i - 1)/(n + 1)\}.$$

Using (7.2.10), the above expression reduces to

$$V_{n+1} = \max_{0 \leq i \leq n} \{i/(n+1) - U_i^*\} + \max_{0 \leq i \leq n} \{U_i^* - i/(n+1)\} + 1/(n+1). \quad (7.2.14)$$

From (7.1.8), $U_1^*, \ldots, U_n^*$ are uniform order statistics. Consequently, by (7.2.12) and (7.2.14), we have

$$V_{n+1} = K_n + 1/(n+1)$$

which immediately leads to (7.2.13).

It should be noted that K_n is not invariant under rotations.

The Null Distribution of K_n. We now show on following Brunk (1962) that

$$\Pr\{K_n \leq t/(n+1)\} = (n+1)p_n(t), \quad (7.2.15)$$

where

$$p_n(t) = \Pr\{(j-t)/(n+1) \leq U_j < j/(n+1),$$
$$j = 1, \ldots, n, \quad 0 < U_1 < \ldots < U_n < 1\} \quad (7.2.16)$$

which is the probability that the n-points $(U_j, j/(n+1))$ lie between the lines $y = x$ and $y = x + t/(n+1)$.

Let us take $U_0 = 0$ and $U_{n+1} = 1$. It is clear from (7.2.12) that

$$K_n = \max_{0 \leq i \leq j \leq n+1} |\{i/(n+1) - U_i\} - \{j/(n+1) - U_j\}|. \quad (7.2.17)$$

Let us define

$$X_i = \{i/(n+1) - U_i\} - \{(i-1)/(n+1) - U_{i-1}\}, \quad i = 1, \ldots, n+1, \quad (7.2.18)$$

$$S_j = X_1 + \ldots + X_j = j/(n+1) - U_j, \quad j = 0, 1, \ldots, n+1. \quad (7.2.19)$$

We have $S_0 = 0$ and $S_{n+1} = 0$. To obtain the probability of the event

$$E: K_n \leq t/(n+1),$$

we note the following points.

(i) The random variables $X_1, \ldots, X_{n+1}$ are cyclically permutable, i.e. the distribution of $(X_2, X_3, \ldots, X_{n+1}, X_1)$ is the same as the distribution of $(X_1, X_2, \ldots, X_{n+1})$ and so on. (ii) We have $\Pr(S_i = S_j) = 0$ for $i, j = 1, \ldots, n$. (iii) From (7.2.17) and (7.2.19), we have

$$K_n = \max_{0 \leq i \leq j \leq n+1} |S_i - S_j|. \quad (7.2.20)$$

Further, $S_{n+1} = 0$ so that the event E is cyclically permutable with respect to $X_1, ..., X_{n+1}$.

Now, consider the event A_q that exactly q of the points (j, S_j), $j = 1, ..., n$ lie above the straight line from $(0,0)$ to $(n + 1, S_{n+1})$ where $q = 0, 1, ..., n$. On taking the points (i)–(iii) into account, we find that the $n + 1$ events $A_q \cap E$, $q = 0, 1, ..., n$ are mutually exclusive and equivalent. Further, E is the union of these $n + 1$ events. Hence,

$$\Pr (E) = (n + 1) \Pr (A_n \cap E). \tag{7.2.21}$$

This result is a particular case of a general result of Andersen (1953, Theorem 3) for interchangeable variables. A shorter proof of this general result follows from Spitzer (1956, Theorem 1).

It remains to establish that

$$\Pr (A_n \cap E) = p_n(t). \tag{7.2.22}$$

Since $S_{n+1} = 0$, the event A_n implies that all the points (j, S_j) are above the x-axis, i.e. $S_j > 0$, $j = 1, ..., n$. From (7.2.20), the event $A_n \cap E$ is equivalent to $S_j > 0$ and $S_j \leqslant t/(n + 1)$ for $j = 1, ..., n$ where S_j is given by (7.2.19). Hence, the result follows.

Brunk (1962) has given an iterative procedure for evaluating the probabilities $p_n(t)$.

The Null Distribution of V_n. On using the null distribution of K_n, we can obtain the null distribution of V_n from (7.2.15). In particular, from (7.2.13) and (7.2.15), we deduce that

$$F(z) = \Pr (V_n < z) = n! \int_{2/n-z}^{1/n} \int_{3/n-z}^{2/n} \cdots \int_{1-z}^{(n-1)/n} du_1 \cdots du_{n-1}, \tag{7.2.23}$$

where $0 < u_1 < ... < u_{n-1} < 1$. By tedious induction, we can now deduce the following explicit expressions due to Stephens (1965a).

(i) If $1/n \leqslant z \leqslant 2/n$, $n \geqslant 2$, $F(z) = n!(z - 1/n)^{n-1}$.

This result can be obtained directly from (7.2.23) since the ranges of integration of $u_1, ..., u_{n-1}$ do not overlap.

(ii) Let $z \geqslant \frac{1}{2}$ if n is even and let $z \geqslant (n - 1)/2n$ if n is odd. Then, we have

$$F(z) = 1 - \sum_{j=0}^{m} \binom{n}{j} (1 - y_j)^{n-j-1} y_j^{j-3} T_j,$$

where m is the integral part of $n(1 - z)$, $y_j = z + j/n$ and

$$T_j = y_j^3 n - y_j^2 j(3 - 2/n) + y_j j(j-1)\{(3 - 2/n)/n\} - j(j-1)(j-2)/n^2.$$

Stephens (1965a) has obtained the upper percentage points of V_n by using result (ii) for small values of n; for large n, the following asymptotic result of Kuiper (1960) has been used.

$$\Pr\left(n^{\frac{1}{2}} V_n \leqslant z\right) = 1 - 2 \sum_{m=1}^{\infty} \left(4m^2 z^2 - 1\right) e^{-2m^2 z^2}$$

$$+ \left(8z/3n^{\frac{1}{2}}\right) \sum_{m=1}^{\infty} m^2 \left(4m^2 z^2 - 3\right) e^{-2m^2 z^2} + O(n^{-1}). \qquad (7.2.24)$$

Appendix 2.10 gives the upper percentage points for the distribution of

$$V_n' = n^{\frac{1}{2}} V_n.$$

based on the tables of Stephens (1965a). Stephens (1970) shows that if $n \geqslant 8$, we can also use

$$V_n^* = \left(n^{\frac{1}{2}} + 0 \cdot 155 + 0 \cdot 24 n^{-\frac{1}{2}}\right) V_n.$$

The upper percentage points of V_n^* for all n are given in Table 7.1. These values are reproduced with the kind permission of the author and the editor of the *J. Roy. Stat. Soc.* Maag and Dicaire (1971) give another approximation.

TABLE 7.1.   Upper Percentage Points of V^*.

α	0·10	0·05	0·025	0·01
V^*	1·620	1·747	1·862	2·001

Example 7.1. Test the hypothesis of uniformity for the bird migration data of Example 6.2. by using Kuiper's test. (The data is also shown in Table 7.2).

Under the hypothesis of uniformity, $F(\theta) = \theta/2\pi$, Hence if $\theta_{(1)}, \ldots, \theta_{(n)}$ are the order statistics for the data, we have $U_i = \theta_{(i)}/2\pi$. Further, we can write V_n from (7.2.8) as

$$V_n = \max_{1 \leqslant i \leqslant n} \left(U_i - i/n\right) - \min_{1 \leqslant i \leqslant n} \left(U_i - i/n\right) + 1/n.$$

Table 7.2 shows the necessary calculations. The underlined entries denote the maximum and minimum values of $(U_i - i/n)$. We therefore have

$$V_n = 0 \cdot 053 - (-0 \cdot 294) + 0 \cdot 1 = 0 \cdot 447.$$

Table 7.2. Calculations required for an application of Kuiper's V_n-test to the bird migration data of Example 6.2.

i	1	2	3	4	5	6	7	8	9	10
$\theta_{(i)}$	55°	60	65	95	100	110	260	275	285	295
$U_i = \theta_{(i)}/360$	·153	·167	·181	·264	·278	·306	·722	·764	·792	·819
i/n	·1	·2	·3	·4	·5	·6	·7	·8	·9	1·0
$U_i - i/n$	·053	−·033	−·119	−·136	−·222	−·294	·022	−·036	−·108	−·181

Consequently $V_n' = n^{\frac{1}{2}} V_n = (10)^{\frac{1}{2}} \times 0.447 = 1.41$. From Appendix 2.10 the 5% value of V_n' is 1.63. Hence, we accept the hypothesis of uniformity. The conclusion is the same as in Example 6.2.

The values of D_n^+ and D_n^- can be obtained from

$$D_n^+ = - \min_{1 \leqslant i \leqslant n} (U_i - i/n), \quad D_n^- = \max_{1 \leqslant i \leqslant n} (U_i - i/n) + 1/n.$$

For this example, $D_n^+ = 0.294$ and $D_n^- = 0.153$. We can also use a graphical method to obtain D_n^+ and D_n^- and consequently V_n. We plot the graph of $S_n(\theta)$ and $F(\theta)$ for the data (see Fig. 7.1). The graph of $F(\theta) = \theta/2\pi$ is a straight line. Now, D_n^+ will be the maximum vertical distance of the step function $S_n(\theta)$ from the line when the distance is measured above the line while D_n^- is the maximum distance measured below the line. It is then found that $D_n^+ = 0.29$ and $D_n^- = 0.15$. The values, however, cannot be obtained with the same accuracy as before.

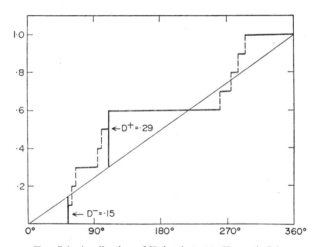

FIG. 7.1. Application of Kuiper's test to Example 7.1.

7.2.2. A Cramér–von Mises Type Test (Watson's U^2 test)

Watson (1961) proposed the statistic

$$U^2 = n \int_0^{2\pi} \{S_n(\theta) - F(\theta) - \mu\}^2 \, dF(\theta), \qquad (7.2.25)$$

where

$$\mu = \int_0^{2\pi} \{S_n(\xi) - F(\xi)\} \, dF(\xi) = \frac{1}{2} - \frac{1}{n} \sum_{i=1}^{n} F(\theta_{(i)}). \qquad (7.2.26)$$

The Cramér–von Mises statistic W^2 is measured about the origin rather than μ, and we may therefore interpret U^2 as a type of variance. On using the probability integral transformation (7.1.11), we know that the Cramér–von Mises statistic W^2 can be expressed as

$$W^2 = \sum_{i=1}^{n} [U_i - \{(2i-1)/(2n)\}]^2 + 1/(12n), \qquad (7.2.27)$$

where the U_i are the uniform order statistics defined by (7.2.6). Let $\overline{U} = (U_1 + \dots + U_n)/n$. Similarly, from (7.2.25) and (7.2.26), we obtain

$$U^2 = \sum_{i=1}^{n} [U_i - \overline{U} - \{(2i-1)/(2n)\} + \tfrac{1}{2}]^2 + 1/(12n). \qquad (7.2.28)$$

From (7.2.28), it follows that the statistic U^2 is completely distribution-free.

7.2.2a. *Properties of U^2*

We show that U^2 is invariant under rotations. Let us consider U^2 given by (7.2.28). Suppose that $\theta = c$ is the new zero direction. On using the notation of Section 7.2.1b, we find from (7.2.9) that

$$j/n - U_j' - \overline{U}' = i/n - U_i - \overline{U},$$

where $\overline{U}'$ is the mean of $U_1', \dots, U_n'$. Hence, the result follows from (7.2.28).

We now give another interesting property of U^2 which is also due to Watson (1961). Using (7.2.9) in (7.2.27), W^2 with c as the starting point is given by

$$W^2(c) = \sum_{i=1}^{n} [U_i - \{(2i-1)/(2n)\} - c + k/n]^2 + 1/(12n).$$

After equating the derivative of $W^2(c)$ with respect to c, to zero, we obtain with the help of (7.2.28)

$$U^2 = \min_c W^2(c). \qquad (7.2.29)$$

7.2.2b. *The Null Distribution of U^2*

On using the form (7.2.28) of U^2, Stephens (1963b, 1964a) has obtained the exact null distribution of U^2 for $n = 1, 2, 3, 4$ and discussed a general geometrical approach for $n > 4$. For large n, Watson (1961) has shown that

$$\lim_{n \to \infty} \Pr(U^2 > u) = 2 \sum_{m=1}^{\infty} (-1)^{m-1} e^{-2m^2\pi^2 u}. \qquad (7.2.30)$$

For a proof, see Section 7.2.5c. He has also shown that the limiting distributions of V_n^2/π^2 and U^2 are the same.

Using the binomial distribution of $S_n(\theta)$ (see Section 7.1.2) and following the usual method of obtaining $E(W^2)$ and var (W^2), we find that

$$E(U^2) = 1/12, \quad \text{var } (U^2) = (n - 1)/360n. \qquad (7.2.31)$$

Stephens (1963b) has also given the third and fourth moments of U^2 and has used these first four moments to obtain the approximate percentage points of U^2. However, Stephens (1970) has shown that the percentage points of the modified statistic

$$U^{*2} = (U^2 - 0 \cdot 1/n + 0 \cdot 1/n^2)(1 \cdot 0 + 0 \cdot 8/n) \qquad (7.2.32)$$

given in Table 7.3 are adequate for $n \geqslant 8$. These values are reproduced with the kind permission of the author and the editor of the *J. Roy. Stat. Soc.*

TABLE 7.3.   Percentage Points of U^{*2}

α	0·10	0·05	0·025	0·01
U^{*2}	0·152	0·187	0·221	0·267

Pearson, E. S. and Stephens (1962) and Tiku (1965) have discussed other approximations.

Example 7.2. Test the hypothesis of uniformity for the bird migration data of Example 6.2 by using Watson's test. (The data is also shown in Table 7.2).

We can rewrite U^2 given by (7.2.28) as

$$U^2 = \sum_{i=1}^{n} U_i^2 - n\bar{U}^2 - \frac{2}{n} \sum_{i=1}^{n} iU_i + (n + 1)\,\bar{U} + \frac{n}{12}.$$

The values of the U_i for the data are shown in Table 7.2. It is found that

$$\Sigma U_i^2 = 2 \cdot 7277, \qquad \Sigma iU_i = 31 \cdot 7960, \qquad \bar{U} = 0 \cdot 4446.$$

Consequently, $U^2 = 0 \cdot 1157$ and $U^{*2} = 0 \cdot 115$. The 5% value of U^{*2} from Table 7.3 is 0·187. Hence, we again accept the hypothesis of uniformity.

7.2.3. Hodges–Ajne's Test

Let us regard $\theta_1, \ldots, \theta_n$ as n points on a circle. We draw a straight line l through the centre of the circle and count the number of points on each side of this straight line. By rotating the line l about the centre, we find the minimum possible number of sample points on one side of this line. Let this number be m. Since small values of m will indicate a departure from uniformity, we can take m as our test statistic.

This test as a bivariate sign test was proposed by Hodges (1955). For the circular case, it was later studied independently by Ajne (1968) who used the maximum number '$n - m$' on one side of the line as his test statistic. This interrelation between the two tests was pointed out by Bhattacharyya and Johnson (1969).

7.2.3a. *A Representation of m*

We now obtain a formal representation for m. Let θ_i be obtained from the transformation $\theta_i{}^* = \theta_i \bmod \pi$, $0 < \theta_i \leqslant 2\pi$, $i = 1, ..., n$. Suppose that $\theta_{(i)}^*$, $i = 1, ..., n$ are the corresponding ordered values. Define

$$z_i = 1 \quad \text{if} \quad \theta_{(i)}^* = \theta_j \quad \text{for some} \quad j$$
$$ = -1 \quad \text{if} \quad \theta_{(i)}^* = \theta_j - \pi \quad \text{for some } j. \tag{7.2.33}$$

The vector $\mathbf{Z} = (z_1, ..., z_n)$ indicates which of the observations lie above or below the zero direction. Rotation of the line l will lead to $2n$ values of $\mathbf{Z}$. All these values can be obtained from the initial value of $\mathbf{Z}$ by successively using the operator

$$\zeta(\mathbf{Z}) = (z_2, z_3, ..., z_n, -z_1)$$

$2n$ times. Let K_r, $r = 1, 2, ..., 2n$ be the successive numbers of -1's in these $2n$ values of $\mathbf{Z}$, i.e. K_1 denotes the total number of -1's in the initial value of $\mathbf{Z}$, K_2 the number in $\zeta(\mathbf{Z})$ and so on. We have

$$m = \min (K_1, ..., K_{2n}), \qquad 0 \leqslant m \leqslant [\tfrac{1}{2}n], \tag{7.2.34}$$

and

$$K_{i+1} = K_i + z_i, \qquad K_i = n - K_{n+i}, \qquad i = 1, ..., n. \tag{7.2.35}$$

Hence,

$$K_1 = \tfrac{1}{2}(n - S_1), \qquad K_{i+1} = S_i + K_1, \qquad i = 1, ..., n-1, \tag{7.2.36}$$

$$K_{n+1} = n - K_1 = K_1 + S_n, \tag{7.2.37}$$

where

$$S_i = z_1 + ... + z_i, \qquad S_0 = 0. \tag{7.2.38}$$

We can therefore express m in terms of the S_i with the help of (7.2.35) and (7.2.36) as

$$m = \tfrac{1}{2}n - \max \left\{ -\tfrac{1}{2}S_n + \max_{0 \leqslant i \leqslant n} S_i, \tfrac{1}{2}S_n - \min_{0 \leqslant i \leqslant n} S \right\}. \tag{7.2.39}$$

7.2.3b. *The Null Distribution of m*

Suppose that E is the event $m > t$. We have

$$\Pr(m \leqslant t) = 1 - \Pr(E). \tag{7.2.40}$$

From (7.2.35), m is the minimum value of $(K_i, n - K_i)$ for $i = 1, ..., n$ so that the event E is equivalent to

$$E : t < K_i < n - t, \qquad i = 1, ..., n.$$

Further, on using (7.2.36) and (7.2.37), the event reduces to

$$E : t < S_i + K_1 < n - t, \qquad i = 1, ..., n - 1;$$
$$t < K_1 < n - t, \quad K_1 + S_n = n - K_1, \quad S_0 = 0. \tag{7.2.41}$$

Under H_0, $\Pr(z_i = \pm 1) = 1/2$ and S_i is the sum of i independent and identically distributed random variables. Let

$$p_n(i, j, c) = \Pr[0 < S_j < c, \quad j = 1, ..., n-1; \ S_n = j | S_0 = i] \tag{7.2.42}$$

be the probability of arriving at the point j in a one-dimensional random walk starting at the point $S_0 = i$, proceeding by n independent and equally likely steps of ± 1 and not passing through the points 0 and c. Putting $U_j = S_j + K_1 - t$ and $K_1 = i$ in the event E given by (7.2.41), it is found that the event E is equivalent to

$$E : 0 < U_j < n - 2t, \qquad U_n = n - i - t, \qquad U_0 = i - t, \qquad t < i < n - t.$$

Hence we have

$$\Pr(E) = \sum_{i=t+1}^{n-t-1} p_n(i - t, n - i - t, n - 2t). \tag{7.2.43}$$

Now, let us consider the solution of the above random walk problem. Let c and i be kept fixed. From (7.2.42), it can easily be seen that

$$p_{n+1}(i, j, c) = \{p_n(i, j - 1, c) + p_n(i, j + 1, c)\}/2, \qquad 0 < j < c,$$
$$p_n(i, 0, c) = p_n(i, c, c) = 0, \quad p_0(i, j, c) = 1 \quad \text{if} \quad i = j, \quad = 0 \quad \text{if} \quad i \neq j.$$

These relations uniquely determine the function p_n. It is easy to verify that the following function satisfies all the above relations.

$$p_n(i, j, c) = 2^{-n} \sum_{k=-\infty}^{\infty} \left\{ \binom{n}{(n + j - i + 2kc)/2} - \binom{n}{(n + j + i + 2kc)/2} \right\}.$$
$$\tag{7.2.44}$$

Using (7.2.44) in (7.2.43), we have

$$\Pr(m > t) = 2^{-n}(T_1 - T_2),\tag{7.2.45}$$

where

$$T_1 = \sum_{i=t+1}^{n-t-1} \sum_{k=-\infty}^{\infty} V(i, k), \qquad T_2 = (n - 2t - 1) \sum_{k=-\infty}^{\infty} V(t, k)$$

with

$$V(i, k) = \binom{n}{i + k(n - 2t)}.\tag{7.2.46}$$

It can be shown after some reduction that

$$T_1 = \sum_{r=0}^{n} \binom{n}{r} - 2(n - 2t) \sum_{k=0}^{\infty} V(t, -k) + T_2.$$

On substituting T_1 into (7.2.45), we finally have

$$\Pr(m \leqslant t) = 2^{-n+1}(n - 2t) \sum_{k=0}^{r} V(t, -k),\tag{7.2.47}$$

where $0 \leqslant m \leqslant [n/2]$, $r = [t/(n - 2t)]$ and V is given by (7.2.46). For $t < n/3$, we have $n - 2t > n/3$ implying $r < 1$. Hence for this case, (7.2.47) reduces to

$$\Pr(m \leqslant t) = 2^{-n+1}(n - 2t) \binom{n}{t}, \qquad t < n/3.\tag{7.2.48}$$

The null distribution derived above follows the method of Daniels (1954) who has obtained this distribution in connection with another test. The relation between his test and the m-test was established by Hill (1960). The method of Ajne (1968) is very much similar. Joffe and Klotz (1962) and Klotz (1959) provide other forms of (7.2.47). Klotz (1959) tabulates the complete distribution for n up to 30 and a tail area for n from 31 to 50. The formula (7.2.48) was obtained by Hodges (1955) who has given a tail area for $n = 50$. This formula gives a tail area which does not fall below the 5% level until $n = 72$. For large n, it can be shown (Daniels, 1954; Ajne, 1968) that

$$\Pr(m^* \leqslant t) \sim 4t(2\pi)^{-\frac{1}{2}} \sum_{k=0}^{\infty} \exp\{-\tfrac{1}{2}(2k + 1)^2 t^2\},$$

where $m^* = (n - 2m)/n^{\frac{1}{2}}$. The 5% and 1% values of m^* are 3·023 and 3·562 respectively. Appendix 2.11 gives some critical values of the test. The hypothesis of uniformity should be rejected for small values of m.

Example 7.3. Test the hypothesis of uniformity for the following data of Example 1.1 obtained on spinning a roulette wheel.

$$43°, 45°, 52°, 61°, 75°, 88°, 88°, 279°, 357°.$$

Since all the observations are on one side of the y-axis, we have $m = 0$. This fact is clear from Figs. 1.1 and 1.2. Using Appendix 2.11, we reject the null hypothesis of uniformity. Alternatively, we can obtain m as follows. We have

$$\theta_i^* : 43°, 45°, 52°, 61°, 75°, 88°, 88°, 99°, 177°.$$

Hence $\mathbf{Z} = (1, 1, 1, 1, 1, 1, 1, -1, -1)$. After using the operator ζ on $\mathbf{Z}$ it is also found that $m = 0$.

Example 7.4. Test the hypothesis of uniformity for the bird migration data in Example 6.8.

By drawing a circular plot, as in Fig. 1.1, for this data, we find that $m = 1$. Using Appendix 2.11, we reject the null hypothesis. For $n = 15$, the 5% value of m is 2. In fact, all the angles lie below the line l making the angle $\theta = 110°$ with the x-axis except the observation $345°$. However, if we try to obtain $\mathbf{Z}$, we are faced with the problem of resolving a tie. The tie arises since the observation $345°$ reduced modulo $180°$ corresponds to another observation, viz. $165°$.

7.2.3c. *Grouped Data*

For grouped data, we can regard the frequencies as being concentrated at the mid-points of the angular intervals and rotate the line l to find the number m. That is, if $N(\theta)$ is the total number of frequencies on the semi-circle $(\theta, \pi + \theta)$, we have

$$m = \min_{0 \leqslant \theta \leqslant 2\pi} N(\theta).$$

We now consider a special case of practical interest. Suppose there are $r = 2k$ class-intervals of equal lengths with frequencies f_i, $i = 1, ..., r$. Write $f_{i+r} = f_i$. It is clear that

$$m = \min_j (A_j), \qquad A_j = \sum_{i=1}^{k} f_{i+j}, \qquad j = 0, 1, ..., r. \qquad (7.2.49)$$

Let

$$B = \max_j |A_j - A_{j+k}|. \qquad (7.2.50)$$

We show that

$$B = n - 2m.$$

Since $A_j + A_{j+k} = n$, the right hand side of (7.2.50) is equivalent to $\max_j (n - 2A_j, 2A_j - n)$ which is seen to be equal to $n - 2m$ because $m = \min A_j$ and $n - m = \max A_j$.

In fact, David and Newell (1965) have proposed the criterion $m^* = B/n^{\frac{1}{2}}$ to test for possible periodic effects in cyclic data. The statistic gives an overall comparison of totals over two halves of the cycle when the line of demarcation between the two halves is arbitrary. Under the hypothesis of uniformity, B will be small.

Example 7.5. Test the hypothesis of uniformity for the leukemia data in Table 6.2 against the alternative that there may be a six-monthly periodic effect.

On forming the totals of frequencies of six successive months, we find that

$$A_j: 247, 258, 275, 283, 285, 281, 259, 248, 231, 223, 221, 225.$$

The last six entries follows on subtracting the first six entries from 506. Hence, $m = 221$. We have $n = 506$ and $m^* = (n - 2m)/n^{\frac{1}{2}} = 2\cdot85$. The 5% value of m given previously cannot be used since grouping of the data implies that we are sampling from a discrete population. From David and Newell (1965), the 5% and 1% values of m^* are $2\cdot53$ and $3\cdot09$ respectively. Hence we reject the null hypothesis at the 5% level of significance. It may be recalled that we have dealt with this data under more specific alternatives in Example 6.3.

7.2.3d. *An Optimum Property*

Ajne (1968) has shown that the m-test is the best invariant test for testing the hypothesis of uniformity against alternatives of the form

$$\left.\begin{array}{ll} f(\theta) = p/\pi, & \text{if } \alpha < \theta < \pi + \alpha, \\ \quad\quad = q/\pi, & \text{if } \alpha + \pi < \theta < 2\pi + \alpha, \end{array}\right\} \quad (7.2.51)$$

where $p + q = 1$ but it is assumed that p and q differ considerably, i.e. $p \to 1$. The power of the test can be obtained from (7.2.43) and (7.2.44) after replacing the factor 2^{-n} in (7.2.44) by $p^i q^{n-i}$. We shall discuss in Section 7.2.5 an optimum test when p and q are nearly the same.

7.2.4. Spacing Tests

We now give two tests which are based on the sample arc-lengths $T_1, ..., T_n$ defined by (7.1.6).

7.2.4a. *The Range Test*

In Section 2.6.4, we have already defined the circular sample range w as the length of the smallest arc which contains all the observations, i.e.

$$w = 2\pi - T, \qquad T = \max_{1 \leqslant i \leqslant n} T_i. \tag{7.2.52}$$

Since small values of w indicate clustering of the observations, the hypothesis of uniformity is rejected for small values of w. Obviously, w is invariant under rotations.

We now obtain the d.f. $F(r)$ of the circular range under the hypothesis of uniformity. The event $w \leqslant r$ holds if and only if at least one of the n arc-lengths T_i exceed $r' = 2\pi - r$. Let E_i be the event that $T_i > r'$. The p.d.f. of $T_1, ..., T_n$ given by (7.1.7) is symmetrical in $T_1, ..., T_n$ so that by the generalized theorem of total probability

$$\begin{aligned}
F(r) &= \Pr\left(\bigcup_{i=1}^{n} E_i \right) \\
&= n \Pr(E_1) - \binom{n}{2} \Pr(E_1 E_2) + ... + (-1)^{s-1} \binom{n}{s} P(E_1 ... E_s),
\end{aligned} \tag{7.2.53}$$

where s is the integral part of $2\pi/r'$. We now evaluate the probability of the event $E_1 E_2 ... E_k$, $k = 1, 2, ..., s$. From (7.1.7), the p.d.f. of $T_1, ..., T_k$ is

$$\begin{aligned}
g(T_1, ..., T_k) &= (n-1)!(2\pi)^{-n+1} \int_0^{2\pi - T_1} ... \int_0^{2\pi - T_1 - ... - T_{n-2}} dT_{n-1} ... dT_{k+1} \\
&= [(n-1)!/\{(n-k-1)!(2\pi)^{n-1}\}] (2\pi - T_1 - ... - T_k)^{n-k-1}.
\end{aligned}$$

On using the preceding result in

$$\Pr(E_1 ... E_k) = \int_{r'}^{2\pi} ... \int_{r'}^{2\pi - T_1 - ... - T_{k-1}} g(T_1, ..., T_k) \, dT_k ... dT_1,$$

we obtain

$$\Pr(E_1 ... E_k) = \{1 - (kr'/2\pi)\}^{n-1}.$$

Consequently, (7.2.53) reduces to

$$F(r) = \sum_{k=1}^{\infty} (-1)^{k-1} \binom{n}{k} [1 - k\{(2\pi - r)/2\pi\}]^{n-1}, \tag{7.2.54}$$

where the series continues as long as $1 - k\{(2\pi - r)/2\pi\}$ is positive. This result has already appeared in various contexts (see H. A. David, 1970), Section 5.4) and was first obtained by Fisher (1929). In this context, it was given by Laubscher and Rudolph (1968) and J. S. Rao (1969). Laubscher and Rudolph (1968) have shown that

$$E(w) = (2\pi/n)(Z + n - 1),$$

$$\text{var}(w) = (2\pi/n)^2 [Z^2 - \{2/(n + 1)\} \sum_{i=1}^{n} (n - i) Z_i/i],$$

where

$$Z_i = (-1)^i \binom{n}{i} (1 - i/n)/i, \quad Z = \sum_{i=1}^{n-1} Z_i.$$

Appendix 2.12 gives some percentage points of the distribution of the circular range w.

Example 7.6. Test the hypothesis of uniformity for the roulette data in Example 7.3.

From Example 2.12, we have $w = 169°$. From Appendix 2.12, the 5% value of w for $n = 9$ is 88·1°. Hence, we reject the hypothesis of uniformity.

7.2.4b. *A Test of Equal Spacings*

Under the hypothesis of uniformity, the expected length of T_i is constant and is equal to $2\pi/n$. Hence, we can take our criterion as

$$L = \tfrac{1}{2} \sum_{i=1}^{n} |T_i - (2\pi/n)|. \tag{7.2.55}$$

Large values of L indicates clustering of the observations. This test in the above context was introduced by J. S. Rao (1969) who noted that for the linear case, it was suggested by Kendall (1946a) and studied by Sherman (1950). Its null distribution follows from Sherman (1950) and Darling (1953) and the former reference also gives the first two moments of L.

Some critical values for the test are given in Appendix 2.13. The hypothesis of uniformity is rejected for large values of L. Sherman (1950) has shown that, for large n, the statistic

$$n^{\frac{1}{2}}(L - 2\pi/e)/\{2\pi(2e^{-1} - 5e^{-2})^{\frac{1}{2}}\}$$

is distributed as $N(0, 1)$ where e = 2·7183.

Example 7.7. Test the hypothesis of uniformity for the bird-migration data in Example 6.13 using the L-test.

The successive values of the T_i are

$$115°, 10°, 20°, 5°, 30°, 100°, 25°, 10°, 15°, 0°, 0°, 5°, 25°.$$

We have $n = 13$ and $360°/n = 27\cdot7°$ so that $L = 162°$. Since the 5% value of L from Appendix 2·13 is $167\cdot8°$, we accept the hypothesis of uniformity.

7.2.5. Beran's Class of Tests of Uniformity and Ajne's A_n-test

We now discuss an important class of tests of uniformity developed by Beran (1968, 1969a) which includes the Rayleigh test (Section 6.2.1b), Ajne's A_n-test (defined below) and Watson's U^2 test. Let $\theta_1, ..., \theta_n$ be a random sample from a continuous population. Let $f(\theta)$ be any p.d.f. on the circle. The statistic

$$B_n = 2\pi \int_0^{2\pi} \left[\left\{ \sum_{i=1}^{n} f(\theta + \theta_i) \right\} - n(2\pi)^{-1} \right]^2 d\theta \qquad (7.2.56)$$

provides a criterion for testing uniformity. The null hypothesis is rejected for large values of B_n since $B_n = 0$ if $f(\theta)$ is uniformly distributed.

7.2.5a. *An Alternative Form of B_n with some Special Cases*

We now derive another form of (7.2.56) which is more useful in studying its special cases.

From the inversion formula (4.2.7), the Fourier expansion of $f(\theta)$ is

$$f(\theta) = (2\pi)^{-1} \left\{ 1 + 2 \sum_{p=1}^{\infty} (\alpha_p \cos p\theta + \beta_p \sin p\theta) \right\}. \qquad (7.2.57)$$

Let

$$C_p = \sum_{i=1}^{n} \cos p\theta_i, \qquad S_p = \sum_{i=1}^{n} \sin p\theta_i.$$

Using (7.2.57), we have

$$\sum_{i=1}^{n} f(\theta + \theta_i) - n/2\pi = \sum_{p=1}^{\infty} (\alpha_p C_p + \beta_p S_p) \cos p\theta$$

$$+ \sum_{p=1}^{\infty} (\beta_p C_p - \alpha_p S_p) \sin p\theta.$$

On substituting this value into (7.2.56), we obtain either after squaring the resulting series and integrating term by term or by using the Parseval formula (4.2.30),

$$B_n = 2 \sum_{p=1}^{\infty} \rho_p^2 (C_p^2 + S_p^2), \qquad \rho_p^2 = \alpha_p^2 + \beta_p^2, \qquad (7.2.58)$$

which can be rewritten as

$$B_n = \sum_{i=1}^{n} \sum_{j=1}^{n} h(\theta_i - \theta_j), \tag{7.2.59}$$

where

$$h(\theta) = 2 \sum_{p=1}^{\infty} \rho_p^2 \cos p\theta. \tag{7.2.60}$$

We now consider some special cases.

(1) We show that Watson's U_n^2 is a special case of B_n. Consider the p.d.f.

$$f(\theta) = \theta/2\pi^2, \qquad 0 < \theta \leqslant 2\pi. \tag{7.2.61}$$

We have

$$\alpha_p = 0, \qquad \beta_p = 1/\pi p, \qquad \rho_p = 1/\pi p \tag{7.2.62}$$

so that (7.2.60) reduces to

$$h(\theta) = (2/\pi^2) \sum_{p=1}^{\infty} p^{-2} \cos p\theta = 2\{\tfrac{1}{6} - U + U^2\}, \qquad 0 < U < 1, \tag{7.2.63}$$

where $U = \theta/2\pi$. On substituting (7.2.63) into (7.2.59) and writing $U_i = \theta_i/2\pi$, we find that B_n given by (7.2.59) reduces to

$$B_n = 4n\left\{ n^{-1} \sum_{i<j} (U_i - U_j)^2 - n^{-1} \sum_{i<j} |U_i - U_j| + n/12 \right\}.$$

After simplification of B_n and use of (7.2.28), we obtain

$$U_n^2 = B_n/4n. \tag{7.2.64}$$

(2) *Ajne's A_n Test.* Let $N(\theta)$ be the number of observations in the semi-circle θ to $\theta + \pi$. Following Ajne (1968), define

$$A_n = \int_0^{2\pi} \{N(\theta) - n/2\}^2 \, d\theta. \tag{7.2.65}$$

It can easily be seen to be a particular case of (7.2.56). The null hypothesis is rejected for large values of A_n. Using $f(\theta)$ given by (7.2.51) with $p = P$, $q = Q$, we obtain as before

$$\rho_{2p}=0, \quad \rho_{2p+1}=2|1 - 2P|/\pi(2p+1), \quad h(\theta) \propto \{\tfrac{1}{2}\pi - |\theta|\}, \quad -\pi < \theta \leqslant \pi. \tag{7.2.66}$$

Substitution of $h(\theta)$ in (7.2.59) leads to the following computational formula

$$A_n = n\pi/4 - (2/n) \sum_{j=2}^{n} \sum_{i=1}^{j=1} \min \{\theta_{(j)} - \theta_{(i)}, 2\pi - \theta_{(j)} + \theta_{(i)}\}. \qquad (7.2.67)$$

This is related to the circular mean difference given by (2.6.10).

Watson (1967a) has obtained its asymptotic null distribution and Stephens (1969b) has given the percentage points of A_n by the Pearson-curve-approximation. We will discuss its optimal property in Section 7.2.5b.

(3) By taking

$$f(\theta) = (1 + \cos \theta)/2\pi, \qquad 0 < \theta \leqslant 2\pi, \qquad (7.2.68)$$

we easily see from (7.2.56) and (7.2.59) that B_n reduces to

$$R^2 = (\Sigma \cos \theta_i)^2 + (\Sigma \sin \theta_i)^2 = \sum_i \sum_j \cos (\theta_i - \theta_j), \qquad (7.2.69)$$

which is the Rayleigh test-statistic.

Watson (1967b) has considered another interesting special case where $f(\theta + \theta_i)$ is replaced by a consistent estimator of the true density generating the observations.

7.2.5b. An Optimum Property of B_n

Consider alternatives of the form

$$g(\theta; k) = \{1 + k[f(\theta + \mu_0) - (2\pi)^{-1}]\}/(2\pi), \quad 0 < \theta \leqslant 2\pi, \quad 0 < k < 1, \qquad (7.2.70)$$

where μ_0 is an unknown location parameter. Following Beran (1968), we show that for testing $k = 0$ (uniformity) against these alternatives, the test B_n is a locally (in the sense that k is small) best invariant test under rotations.

We have shown in Section 6.2.1c that the best invariant critical region (BICR) is given by (6.2.19). On substituting (7.2.70) in (6.2.59), we easily see that it does not depend on μ_0 and consequently, the BICR is defined by

$$I = \int_0^{2\pi} \prod_{i=1}^{n} [1 + k\{f(\theta + \theta_i) - (2\pi)^{-1}\}]d\theta > K. \qquad (7.2.71)$$

We expand the integrand in a power series in k and use the fact that $f(\theta + \theta_i)$ is a p.d.f. to obtain

$$I = 1 + k^2 \int_0^{2\pi} \sum_{i \neq j} b_i b_j \, d\theta + O(k^3), \quad b_i = f(\theta + \theta_i) - (2\pi)^{-1}.$$

Hence, we have

$$I = 1 + k^2 B_n - k^2 \sum_{i=1}^{n} \int_0^{2\pi} b_i^2 \, d\theta + O(k^3). \qquad (7.2.72)$$

On transforming the variable θ to $\theta + \theta_i$ in the last term in (7.2.72), it is found that this term does not depend on θ_i. Hence, on using (7.2.72) in (7.2.71), (7.2.71) reduces to $B_n > K$ and therefore, the assertion is proved.

We can now deduce the optimal property for various special cases. For example, the A_n-test is a locally BICR for the alternatives (7.2.51) when p and q are nearly the same, i.e. $p/q \to 1$. We have already noted in Section 7.2.3d that Hodges–Ajne's test is a BICR for $p \to 1$, $q \to 0$ when p and q are markedly different. Further, Watson's U^2 test is a locally BICR for the alternatives (7.2.70) with $f(\theta)$ given by (7.2.61). For the Rayleigh test, we already know a much more general result from Section 6.2.1c, i.e. the test is uniformly BICR for the von Mises distribution.

7.2.5c. *The Asymptotic Null Distribution of B_n and Other Results*

Under the hypothesis of uniformity, we find by the central limit theorem (cf. Case II in Section 4.9.2) that $2(C_p^2 + S_p^2)/n$ is distributed as a chi-square with two d. of fr. Further, on an application of the lemma in Section 4.9.2, it is seen that $C_1, C_2, ..., S_1, S_2, ...$ are independently distributed for large n so that the asymptotic c.f. of B_n/n from (7.2.58) is

$$\prod_{p=1}^{\infty} (1 - 2\rho_p^2 \, it)^{-1}.$$

The proof is heuristic since we have assumed that the results used above hold for infinitely many variables. When the non-vanishing ρ_p^2 are all distinct, the c.f. may be inverted and it is found by a partial fraction expansion of the c.f. that

$$\lim_{n \to \infty} \Pr(B_n/n > x) = \sum_{p=1}^{\infty} a_p \exp(-x/2\rho_p^2), \qquad (7.2.73)$$

where $a_p = \prod_{k \neq p} \{1 - (\rho_k/\rho_p)^2\}^{-1}$. These results are due to Beran (1969a). Hence, the asymptotic null distribution of various special cases can be derived. In particular, a proof of the asymptotic null distribution of U^2 given by (7.2.30) follows.

We now consider the consistency property of the B_n-test (Beran, 1969a). Let $G(\theta)$ be the d.f. under the alternative hypothesis. From (7.2.59), we have by the strong law of large numbers

$$B_n/n^2 \rightarrow E(B_n/n^2) = \int_0^{2\pi} \int_0^{2\pi} h(x - y)\,dG(x)\,dG(y) = \sum_{p=1}^{\infty} \rho_p{}^2 \rho_p{}^{*2}, \quad (7.2.74)$$

where $\rho_p{}^*$ is the value of ρ_p corresponding to the distribution with d.f. $G(\theta)$. Hence, the test B_n is consistent if there exists at least one p for which both ρ_p and $\rho_p{}^*$ do not vanish. Since, $\rho_p{}^* \neq 0$ for some p for nonuniform cases, by (7.2.62), $U_n{}^2$ is a consistent test for uniformity against all possible alternatives. On the other hand, in view of (7.2.66), this is not true for the A_n-test. However, in particular, it is consistent against all alternatives with symmetric unimodal densities.

Beran (1969a) has also obtained the asymptotic distribution of B_n under general alternatives and derived the Bahadur efficiency of B_n.

7.2.6. Relative Performances of Various Tests of Uniformity

By Monte Carlo trials, Stephens (1969b) has compared the power of Kuiper's V_n, Watson's U^2 and Ajne's A_n tests. For alternatives given by (7.2.51), the A_n test is the best invariant test but it is found to be only very slightly more powerful than V_n or U^2. In fact, their powers are almost the same. This led Stephens (1969b) to further investigate their powers for the alternatives

$$f(x) = k(2^r x)^{k-1}, \qquad\qquad 0 \leqslant x < 2^{-r},$$
$$= k\{2(1 - 2^{r-1}x)\}^{k-1}, \quad 2^{-r} \leqslant x < 2^{1-r},$$

where $k \geqslant 0$, $r = 1, 2, 3$, the density is repeated with period 2^{1-r} to cover the whole range $0 < x < 1$ and $\theta = 2\pi x$. For $r = 1, 2, 3$ it produces one, two and four peaked distributions. It is found that (i) for the unimodal alternatives, all the three tests are equally powerful, (ii) for the bimodal alternatives, V_n and U^2 have the same power but both are much more powerful than A_n while (iii) for the four peaked alternatives, V_n is more powerful than U^2 which in turn is more powerful than A_n. The difference between the power of V_n and U^2 is less marked for moderately large samples. This study suggests that Kuiper's test may be preferred for small samples.

J. S. Rao (1969) has obtained the Bahadur asymptotic efficiency (AE) of various tests when the alternative is a von Mises population with small κ. He has found that the Rayleigh test, Watson's U^2 test and Ajne's A_n test have the same AE. Further, the AE of Kuiper's test is the same as the AE of Hodges–Ajne's m-test. The ARE of the equal spacings test L relative to all these tests is found to be zero. Further, the ARE of V_n relative to the Rayleigh test is found to be $8/\pi^2$, i.e. 81%. However, these comparisons are local in nature and do not seem to provide a reliable criterion of their relative powers (Beran, 1969a; J. S. Rao 1969). J. S. Rao (1969) has shown by Monte Carlo trials that for small samples, the power of the L-test relative to the Rayleigh test for von Mises alternatives is tolerable for large κ.

Hence, at least for small sample sizes, Kuiper's test is preferable. Hodges–Ajne's test and the range test provide two quick methods of assessing uniformity. The role of the equal spacings test seems to lie between these two cases.

7.3. TESTS OF SYMMETRY

To test the hypothesis that the zero direction is the axis of symmetry against the alternative of a displaced axis, we can use the usual tests of symmetry on the line. We describe briefly two standard procedures adapted for the circular case. (i) The sign test rejects the null hypothesis if the number of observations on the upper semi-circle, n', is either too large or too small. (ii) We can also use the one-sample Wilcoxon test as follows. Let $\theta_{(1)}, \ldots, \theta_{(n)}$ be the ordered observations. Suppose that s of these observations lie in the upper semi-circle and

$$\theta_i^* = \theta_{(i)} - \pi, \qquad i = s + 1, \ldots, n.$$

Let $r_1, \ldots, r_s$ be the ranks of these s observations in the sequence $\{\theta_{(1)}, \ldots, \theta_{(s)}, \theta_{s+1}, \ldots, \theta_n^*\}$. We reject the null hypothesis if the sum $r_1 + \ldots + r_s$ is either too large or too small.

Their parameter competitor has been given in Section 6.2.2b and is based on the statistic $R|C$. Schach (1969a) has shown that the ARE of the Wilcoxon test relative to the *best* test for the von Mises population is $6/\pi^2$ as $\kappa \to 0$ and $3/\pi$ as $\kappa \to \infty$. For the sign test, the ARE is $8/\pi^2$ as $\kappa \to 0$ and $2/\pi$ as $\kappa \to \infty$. Further, in each case, the ARE is monotonically bounded by the values of the ARE for $\kappa \to 0$ and $\kappa \to \infty$. As we would expect, for $\kappa \to \infty$ the ARE's of both non-parametric tests coincide with the corresponding ARE's for detecting shifts of a normal distribution. These comparisons indicate that for small κ and large n, the sign test may be preferred to the Wilcoxon test.

Example 7.8. Test the hypothesis of symmetry about $\theta = 149°$ for the following pigeon-homing data (in degrees) of Example 6.6 by applying the sign test.

85, 135, 135, 140, 145, 150, 150, 150, 160, 185, 200, 210, 220, 225, 270.

We find that the number of observations in the interval (149°, 329°) is 10. Since the probability of $n' \geqslant 11$ for $n = 15$ is 0·118 (see, for example, Siegel, 1956, p. 250), we accept the null hypothesis, i.e. the population circular median may be taken as 149°.

7.4. TWO-SAMPLE TESTS

7.4.1. A Maximal Invariant

Let $\theta_{11}, \ldots, \theta_{1n_1}$ and $\theta_{21}, \ldots, \theta_{2n_2}$ be two independent random samples from continuous population having d.f.'s $F_1(\theta)$ and $F_2(\theta)$ respectively. Let $n = n_1 + n_2$. We wish to test

$$H_0 : F_1(\theta) = F_2(\theta) \quad \text{against} \quad H_1 : F_1(\theta) \neq F_2(\theta). \qquad (7.4.1)$$

These hypotheses are invariant under rotations and we look for the test statistics which satisfy this invariance property. Suppose that $r_1, \ldots, r_m$ are the *linear ranks* of the first sample in the combined sample, i.e. the ranks of the first sample in the combined sample obtained on going round the circle in the anti-clockwise direction with starting point $\theta = 0$. If we start from any other point on the circle, the new ranks $r_1', \ldots, r_{n_1}'$ of the first sample in the anti-clockwise direction are easily seen to be of the form

$$r_i' = (r_i + h) \,(\text{mod } n), \qquad i = 1, \ldots, n_1, \qquad (7.4.2)$$

where h is a positive integer and we take $r_i' = n$ if $r_i' = 0$. Further, if we rank the observations in the clockwise direction, we will have

$$r_i' = (-r_i + h) \,(\text{mod } n) \quad \text{for} \quad i = 1, \ldots, n_1. \qquad (7.4.3)$$

Let $t(r_1, \ldots, r_{n_1})$ be a statistic based on these ranks. The statistic t will be invariant under rotations if and only if

$$t(r_1, \ldots, r_{n_1}) = t(r_1', \ldots, r_{n_1}').$$

We may call $(r_1, \ldots, r_{n_1})$ a *circular ordering* when all possible orderings defined by (7.4.2) and (7.4.3) are considered equivalent. That is, $r_1, \ldots, r_{n_1}$ are the ranks of the first sample starting from any reference point and any direction (clockwise or anti-clockwise). In this case, there is a unique *arrangement* of the combined sample on the circle and this arrangement is a maximal invariant under rotations. Consequently, any rank test invariant under rotations is distribution-free. Further, irrespective of the underlying hypothesis, there are exactly $\binom{n}{n_1}/s$ distinct allocations of the two samples where s is the number of distinct $(r_1', ..., r_{n_1}')$ in (7.4.2) and (7.4.3) for $h = 0, 1, ..., n - 1$. The integer s is of the form $n\delta/l$ where l is a divisor of n, and δ is either 1 or 2. For example, when $n = 8$, we have $s = 4, 8, 16$ respectively for the circular orderings $(1, 5)$, $(1, 3)$, $(1, 3, 4)$.

7.4.2. The Uniform-scores Test

7.4.2a. *The Test*

Let us again regard the observations in the two-samples as points on the circle of unit radius and let $r_1, ..., r_{n_1}$ be the linear ranks of the first sample in the combined sample. We alter the spaces between successive points in such a way that all the spaces are of length $2\pi/n$ (see Fig. 7.2). That is, we replace the angular observations in the combined sample by the *uniform scores* $2\pi k/n$, $k = 1, ..., n$ on the circle and the n_1 observations in the first sample by

$$\beta_i = 2\pi r_i/n, \qquad i = 1, ..., n_1. \qquad (7.4.4)$$

For the data in Fig. 7.2, the ranks r_i are 6, 7, 8, 9, 10, 12, 13, 14, 15. The test-statistic should be based on the length of the resultants as in the von Mises

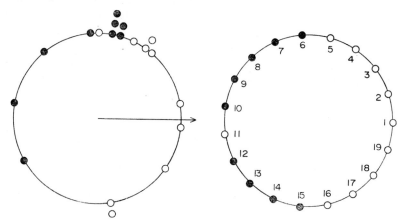

FIG. 7.2. Generation of equidistant sample points and the combined ranks for the two samples in Example 7.10.

theory (Section 6.3). Let R_1 and R_2 be the length of resultants of the first and second samples respectively and let R be the resultant of the combined sample. Since,

$$\sum_{k=1}^{n} \cos 2\pi k/n = \sum_{k=1}^{n} \sin 2\pi k/n = 0,$$

we have $R = 0$ and $R_1 = R_2$. Consequently, the test can be based simply on R_1 where

$$R_1^2 = \left(\sum_{i=1}^{n_1} \cos \beta_i\right)^2 + \left(\sum_{i=1}^{n_1} \sin \beta_i\right)^2 = C_1^2 + S_1^2, \qquad (7.4.5)$$

and the β_i are defined by (7.4.4). The quantity R_1 will be a maximum if all the points of the first sample are separated away from the points of the second sample. Hence, we reject H_0 for large values of R_1.

In fact, we have seen in Section 6.3.1b that every similar test for testing equality of the mean directions in the von Mises case should be based on R_1 and R_2 given R. Using these uniform scores, we are again led to the test statistic R_1. Another motivation to the test will be given in Section 7.4.5.

To prove the invariance of the test under rotations, we rewrite (7.5.5) as

$$R_1^2 = n_1 + \sum_{i=1}^{n_1} \sum_{j=1}^{n_1} \cos 2\pi (r_i - r_j)/n,$$

which depends only upon differences in ranks so that on using (7.4.2) and (7.4.3), the result follows.

This test was proposed by Wheeler and Watson (1964) following a suggestion of Hodges, J. L. Jr. The test is a particular case of a test for the bivariate location problem given independently by Mardia (1967, 1968). The relation between these two tests was shown in Mardia (1969b). Hodges–Ajne's test is another example where the relationship between tests for the bivariate and the circular cases has been exploited.

7.4.2b. Moments of R_1

We obtain the first two moments of R_1 under H_0. Let z_k be 1 if the kth order statistics of the combined sample is an observation from the first sample and let z_k be 0 otherwise, $k = 1, ..., n$. We have

$$C_1 = \Sigma \cos \beta_i = \Sigma z_k \cos (2\pi k/n), \quad S_1 = \Sigma \sin \beta_i = \Sigma z_k \sin (2\pi k/n). \quad (7.4.6)$$

By the usual argument, we have

$$E(z_k) = n_1/n, \quad \text{var} (z_k) = n_1 n_2/n^2, \quad \text{cov} (z_k, z_l) = -n_1 n_2/\{n^2(n-1)\}.$$

Further,

$$\sum_{k=1}^{n} \{\cos (2\pi sk/n)\}^r$$

$$= \sum_{k=1}^{n} \{\sin (2\pi sk/n)\}^r = 2^{-r} n \binom{r}{\frac{1}{2}r} \quad \text{if} \quad r \text{ is even}, \qquad (7.4.7)$$

and is zero if r is odd, s being an integer. On using these results, we find that $E(C_1)$ and $E(S_1)$ are zero. Obtaining the values of var (C_1) and var (S_1), we find that

$$E(R_1{}^2) = (n_1 n_2)/(n - 1). \qquad (7.4.8)$$

Similarly, after some algebra

$$\text{var } (R_1{}^2) = n n_1 n_2 (n_1 - 1)(n_2 - 1)/\{(n - 1)^2 (n - 2)\}. \qquad (7.4.9)$$

These moments can also be obtained by using the moments of the sample mean from a finite population (Sukhatme, 1953, pp. 188–192).

The maximum value of R_1 will occur when the first n_1 points belong to the first sample, i.e. $\beta_i = 2\pi i/n$, $i = 1, ..., n_1$. On substituting this value of β_i into (7.5.5), the maximum value of R_1 is found to be

$$\{\sin (n_1 \pi/n)/\sin (\pi/n)\}^2.$$

7.4.2c. *Its Null Distribution and Power*

Appendix 2.14 gives some selected critical values for the test statistic $B = R_1{}^2$. For $n > 20$, we can use the result (Mardia, 1967, 1969a) that

$$R^* = 2(n - 1) R_1{}^2/n_1 n_2 \qquad (7.4.10)$$

is approximately distributed as χ^2 with two d. of fr. In fact, it can be shown that R^* is asymptotically distributed as χ^2 with two d. of fr. under H_0 (Mardia, 1967). This result is expected since as $n, n_1, n_2 \to \infty$, we have from (7.4.8) and (7.4.9),

$$E(R^*) \to 2, \qquad \text{var } (R^*) \to 4.$$

For $\alpha < 0\!\cdot\!025$, greater accuracy can be achieved by using the approximation (Mardia, 1967) that $R^*/(n - 1 - R^*)$ is distributed as F with d and $(n - 3)d$ d. of fr.'s where

$$d = 1 + [\{n(n + 1) - 6n_1 n_2\}/n(n_1 - 1)(n_2 - 1)].$$

This approximation is obtained by fitting a beta distribution to the null distribution of B with the help of the first two moments.

The asymptotic power of this test is given in Mardia (1969b) and Schach (1969b). The test is consistent against those alternatives (F_1, F_2) where F_1 and F_2 are unimodal (Mardia, 1969b). For the shift-type of alternatives, it is shown in Mardia (1969b) and Schach (1969b) that the ARE of this test relative to its competitor tends to 1 when the underlying population is von Mises and κ tends to zero.

Example 7.9. In an experiment on pigeon homing, similar to that described in Example 6.9, it was predicted from sun-azimuth compass theory that the angles in the experimental group should deviate about 90° in the anti-clockwise direction relative to the angles of the birds in the control group. The vanishing angles of the birds for this experiment with $n_1 = 12$ and $n_2 = 14$ are given below in degrees (Schmidt–Koenig's data cited in Watson, 1962).

Control group (θ_{i1}): 50, 290, 300, 300, 305, 320, 330, 330, 335, 340, 340, 355

Experimental group (θ_{i2}): 70, 155, 190, 195, 215, 235, 235, 240, 255, 260, 290, 300, 300, 300.

Let us first test the null hypothesis that the two samples are drawn from the same population. We break up the ties in the combined sample by replacing the observations 290, 300, 300 of the control group to 285, 295, 295 so that all ties between samples are broken in favour of H_0. Since the test is invariant under all rotations, we rank the observations by taking the first angle in the combined sample as 50° and proceed in the clockwise direction. The ranks r_i for the control group thus obtained are shown in Table 7.4. It also gives the angles $2\pi r_i/n$ and their sines and cosines. However, it is convenient to use the tabulated values of the sines and cosines for these regular angles; some sources of such tables are Abrahamowitz and Stegun (1965, p. 202, $n \leqslant 26$, 10 d.p.), Kendall (1946b, pp. 67–76, $n \leqslant 100$, 4 d.p.),

TABLE 7.4. Calculations required for an application of the uniform scores test to the bird migration data of Example 7.9.

Rank r_i	$\beta_i = 360r_i/26$	$\cos \beta_i$	$\sin \beta_i$
1	13° 51′	0·9709	0·2394
2	27° 42′	0·8854	0·4648
3	41° 32′	0·7486	0·6631
4	55° 23′	0·5681	0·8230
5	69° 14′	0·3546	0·9350
6	83° 5′	0·1204	0·9927
7	96° 55′	−0·1204	0·9927
8	110° 46′	−0·3546	0·9350
9	124° 37′	−0·5681	0·8230
13	180°	−1·0000	0·0000
14	193° 51′	−0·9709	−0·2394
16	221° 32′	−0·7486	−0·6631
Total		$C_1 = -0·1146$	$S_1 = 5·9662$

Pollak and Egan (1949, $n \leqslant 100$, 8 d.p.). Using the values of C_1 and S_1 from Table 7.4 in (7.4.5) and (7.4.10), we find that

$$R^* = 10 \cdot 60.$$

The 1% value of $\chi_2{}^2$ is 9·21. Hence, we reject H_0 strongly.

We now take the angles $\theta_2 + 90°$ instead of the angles θ_2 in the second sample before performing the test, since the shift in the location parameter is expected to be 90°. Breaking up the ties by randomization, we find that the data supports the theory. For this example, the conclusion remains the same irrespective of how the ties are broken.

We now give an example where $n < 20$.

Example 7.10. Test the hypothesis of equality of the two populations for the following pigeon homing data (in degrees) of Example 6.9. (Figure 7.2 shows the data and the combined ranks.)

Sample 1: 75, 75, 80, 80, 80, 95, 130, 170, 210

Sample 2: 10, 50, 55, 55, 65, 90, 285, 285, 325, 355.

On taking the r_i as 1, 2, 3, 4, 5, 7, 8, 9, 10, we have as above

$$n_1 = 9, \quad n_2 = 10, \quad C_1 = -1 \cdot 0849, \quad S_1 = 4 \cdot 9537, \quad R_1{}^2 = 25 \cdot 72.$$

From Appendix 2.14, the 1% value of $R_1{}^2$ is 21·07. Hence, we reject the null hypothesis strongly.

7.4.3. Watson's Two-sample U^2 test

We have discussed the one-sample U^2 test of Watson (1961) in Section 7.2.2. He also introduced its two-sample analogue as (Watson, 1962):

$$U^2_{n_1,n_2} = (n_1 n_2/n) \int_0^{2\pi} \left[S_{n_1}(\theta) - S_{n_2}(\theta) - \int_0^{2\pi} \{S_{n_1}(\xi) - S_{n_2}(\xi)\} \, \mathrm{d}S^*(\xi) \right]^2 \mathrm{d}S^*(\theta),$$
$$(7.4.11)$$

where $S_{n_1}(\theta)$ and $S_{n_2}(\theta)$ are the empirical d.f.'s of the two samples and $S^*(\theta)$ is the d.f. of the combined sample given by

$$S^*(\theta) = \{n_1 S_{n_1}(\theta) + n_2 S_{n_2}(\theta)\}/n.$$

We reject H_0 for large values of $U^2_{n_1,n_2}$. The statistic $U^2_{n_1,n_2}$ is, of course, a Cramér–von Mises type statistic for the two-sample case.

Let the combined sample be ordered. Suppose that a_i is the number of observations from the first sample among the first i order statistics of the combined sample and b_i is the number of observations from the second sample, i.e. $a_i + b_i = i$. We have from (7.4.11),

$$U^2_{n_1,n_2} = n_1 n_2 n^{-2} \sum_{k=1}^{n} (d_k - \bar{d})^2,$$ (7.4.12)

where

$$d_k = (b_k/n_2) - (a_k/n_1), \qquad \bar{d} = \Sigma d_k/n.$$

Since $U^2_{n_1,n_2}$ depends only on the relative ranks of the two samples, it is invariant under rotations.

Following Burr (1964), we now express (7.4.12) in terms of the linear rank $r_1, ..., r_{n_1}$ of the first sample. This alternative form is more useful for calculations. Let s_i observations of the second sample precede the ith observation of the first sample in the combined sample. Therefore, $s_i = r_i - i$ and

$$d_1 = 1/n_2, ..., d_{r_1} = r_1/n_2, \qquad d_{r_1+1} = (r_1 + 1)/n_2 - 1/n_1, ...,$$

$$d_{r_2} = r_2/n_2 - 1/n_1, \qquad d_{r_2+1} = r_2/n_2 - 2/n_1, ..., d_n = n_2/n_2 - n_1/n_1.$$

Hence, from (7.4.12), we obtain

$$U^2_{n_1,n_2} = (nn_2)^{-1} \sum_{i=1}^{n_1} [(r_i - \bar{r}) - \{n(2i - 1) - n_1\}/2n_1]^2 + (n + n_1)/12nn_1.$$ (7.4.13)

By following the same procedure as for the Cramér von–Mises statistic, we have from (7.4.11) under H_0

$$E(U^2) = (n + 1)/12n, \qquad \text{var}(U^2) = (n_1 - 1)(n_2 - 1)(n + 1)/360nn_1n_2.$$

Stephens (1965b) has obtained the first four moments of $U^2_{n_1,n_2}$ and has fitted a Pearson curve to its null distribution. Watson (1962) has shown that, under H_0, its asymptotic distribution under H_0 is the same as that of the one-sample Watson U^2-statistic. Burr (1964) has given the exact tail area of U^2 for $n \leqslant 17$ and some selected critical values for the test are given in Appendix 2.15. For $n > 17$ and n_1/n_2 not near zero, $n_1 < n_2$, we can use the values of $U^2_{\infty,\infty}$ given in Appendix 2.15. For $n > 17$, the percentage points from the Pearson curve approximation are given in Stephens (1965b).

Beran (1969b) has shown that the test is consistent against all alternatives. However, no small sample comparisons with other tests are yet available.

Example 7.11. For the bird migration data in Example 7.9, test the hypothesis that the two samples are from the same population.

Using the ranks r_i for the first sample given in Table 7.4, we find from (7.4.13) that $U^2_{12,14} = 0.3204$. From Appendix 2.15, the 1% value of $U^2_{\infty,\infty}$

is 0·268. Hence H_0 is again rejected. We can also perform the test after adding 90° to the experimental group and it is again found that the same conclusion is reached as in Example 7.9.

7.4.4. The Run Test

Let us plot the two samples on a circle. As in the linear case, a run is an uninterrupted sequence of points belonging to one of the samples. Let

r = the total number of runs in the two samples on the circle.   (7.4.14)

The hypothesis H_0 is rejected if r is small since a small number of runs indicates a separation of the two samples. We always have an even number of runs on the circle—the number of runs being the same for each sample.

Barton and David (1958) and David and Barton (1962, pp. 94–95, 132–136) have given a method of enumerating the null distribution of runs. Asano (1965) has tabulated the distribution of runs for $n \leqslant 40$ and Appendix 2.16 gives some selected critical values for the test obtained from these tables. For $n \geqslant 40$, we can use the result that

$$[r + 1 - \{(2n_1 n_2 + n)/n\}]/\{2n_1 n_2(2n_1 n_2 - n)/n^2(n - 1)\}^{\frac{1}{2}} \quad (7.4.15)$$

is approximately distributed as $N(0, 1)$.

The normal approximation (7.4.15) is obtained as follows by using a relation between the runs on the line and on the circle. Let n_1 and n_2 be prime numbers. For the two-sample case, let P_l and P_c be the probabilities of r runs on the line and on the circle respectively. The fact that there are r runs on the circle implies that there are r or $r + 1$ runs on the line, depending on the cut-point. Hence, under our assumption, we have

$$P_c(r) = P_l(r) + P_l(r + 1) \quad (7.4.16)$$

which implies that

$$P_c(r \leqslant h) = P_l(r \leqslant h + 1). \quad (7.4.17)$$

Hence, the lower tail of the null distribution for the circular case can be obtained from the corresponding linear case. In fact, (7.4.17) provides an adequate approximation to the lower tail even when n_1 and n_2 are not prime. The approximation (7.4.15) now follows by using the well-known normal approximation to the distribution of runs for the linear case.

This test provides a quick method of testing the equality of two populations but we should expect it to be less powerful than the tests discussed earlier. Its consistency properties are the same as in the linear case (J. S. Rao, 1969).

Example 7.12. For the pigeon-homing data of Example 7.10, test the hypothesis of equality of the two populations.

We order the combined sample starting from the observation 75°. If we write '0' for an observation from the first sample and '1' for an observation from the second sample, the combined sample reduces to

$$00000100000111111111$$

(For obvious reasons, the cut-point is selected so that it is a starting point of a new run.) Hence $r = 4$. We have $n_1 = 9$ and $n_2 = 10$. From Appendix 2.16, the 5% value of r is 6 and the 1% value is 4. Hence, the null hypothesis is again rejected.

7.4.5. Some Other Two-sample Tests

Kuiper (1960) introduced the following two-sample analogue of his one-sample test V_n.

$$V_{n_1, n_2} = \sup_{\theta} \{S_{n_1}(\theta) - S_{n_2}(\theta)\} - \inf_{\theta} \{S_{n_1}(\theta) - S_{n_2}(\theta)\}, \qquad (7.4.18)$$

where S_{n_1} and S_{n_2} are the empirical d.f.'s of the two samples.

Kuiper (1960) has shown that its asymptotic null distribution is the same as that of V_n. Steck (1969) has given a method of evaluating its null distribution but the cirtical points are not yet available. For an example and further details, the reader is referred to Batschelet (1965, p. 35). Abrahamson (1967) has compared the asymptotic relative behaviours of the Kolmogorov–Smirnov test with Kuiper's tests for the linear case.

Beran (1969b) has given a two-sample analogue of Ajne's A_n test (see Section 7.4.6). Batschelet (1965, p. 37) has proposed a test based on the minimum value of the various rank-sums of the first sample obtained by rotating the combined sample. Rothman (1971) gives tests of independence for bivariate samples.

7.4.6. Derivations of Two-sample Tests from Tests of Uniformity

The similarity between the tests of uniformity and the two-sample tests of equality of circular populations discussed above is very striking. For example, the formulae for Watson's U^2 and $U^2_{n_1, n_2}$ given by (7.2.28) and (7.4.13) respectively are similar. Indeed, if we are given a test of uniformity, we can construct a corresponding two-sample test as follows (Beran, 1969b). Let $r_1, ..., r_{n_1}$ be the linear rank of the first sample and let us alter all the spaces between the n points in the combined sample to $2\pi/n$. We have thus transformed the observations in the first sample to

$$\beta_i = 2\pi r_i/n, \qquad i = 1, ..., n_1. \qquad (7.4.19)$$

Under the null hypothesis of equality of the two populations, the angles β_i will be uniformly distributed relative to the angles in the second sample. But if the null hypothesis is not true, the angles β_i will be markedly separated from the second sample. Hence, we can apply the given test of uniformity to the angles β_i. In fact, we have already followed this procedure in deriving the uniform scores test (Section 7.4.2a).

Schach's Class of Two-sample Tests

Following Beran (1969b), we now apply the above procedure to the class B_n of tests of uniformity given in Section 7.2.5. On replacing θ_i by β_i in (7.2.59), we obtain the corresponding two-sample statistic

$$B_n{}^* = \sum_{i=1}^{n_1} \sum_{j=1}^{n_1} h\{2\pi(r_i - r_j)/n\}, \tag{7.4.20}$$

where the function $h(\theta)$ is defined by (7.2.60). An alternative form of $B_n{}^*$ can be obtained from (7.2.56). Schach (1967) considered a general statistic $B_n{}^*$ where $h(\theta)$ can also depend on n.

On using the special forms of $h(\theta)$ given in Section 7.2.5a, for some important tests of uniformity, we can now obtain the corresponding two-sample tests. For example, on substituting $\theta_i = \beta_i$ in the Rayleigh test-statistic R^2 given by (7.2.69), we obtain the uniform scores test-statistic $R_1{}^2$ given by (7.4.5). Using $U_i = r_i/n_1$ in Watson's U^2 statistic given by (7.2.28), we find that U^2 reduces to a linear function of $U^2_{n_1,n_2}$ where $U^2_{n_1,n_2}$ is given by (7.4.13). From Ajne's A_n statistic (7.2.67), we obtain the corresponding two-sample statistic

$$A_n{}^* = n_1\pi/4 - (4\pi/n_1) \sum_{i>j} d(r_i/n, r_j/n), \tag{7.4.21}$$

where

$$d(x, y) = \min (|x - y|, 1 - |x - y|). \tag{7.4.22}$$

We should expect from the above correspondence that the asymptotic null distributions of B_n and $B_n{}^*$ will be the same. In fact, the asymptotic null distribution of a statistic more general than B_n is similar to that of $B_n{}^*$ (Schach, 1967, 1969b). In particular,

$$(n - 1)B_n{}^*/n_1 n_2 \tag{7.4.23}$$

has the same asymptotic null distribution as B_n provided that

$$0 < \lambda < 1, \qquad \lambda = \lim_{n\to\infty} n_1/n.$$

Beran (1969b) has proved this result by a simpler argument.

Consistency of the B_n*-test. Let $S_1(\theta)$ and $S^*(\theta)$ be the empirical d.f.'s of the first sample and the combined sample respectively. As in the linear case, the empirical d.f. of the transformed observations of the first sample after ranking and spacing out the combined sample is $S_1\{S^{*-1}(\theta)\}$ which for large n tends to the d.f.

$$G(\theta) = F_1\{H^{-1}(\theta)\}, \tag{7.4.24}$$

where

$$H = \lambda F_1 + (1 - \lambda)F_2.$$

If $F_1 \equiv F_2$ then $G(\theta) = \theta$. Hence, if B_n generates a test of uniformity against the alternative $G(\theta)$, B_n^* gives a two-sample test consistent against alternatives (F_1, F_2) where $F_1 \neq F_2$. Therefore, from the consistency properties of B_n given in Section 7.2.5c, we dedcue that the U_{n_1,n_2}^2 test is consistent against all alternatives (F_1, F_2) whereas the A_n^*-test is consistent at least against those alternatives (F_1, F_2) for which $G(\theta)$ corresponds to a unimodal symmetric density.

By the same argument, it follows that the uniform scores test is consistent only for the alternatives for which the density of G is unimodal (Beran, 1969b). By varying λ, Mardia (1969b) has shown by a different method that the test is consistent when F_1 and F_2 correspond to unimodal densities.

It is expected that the B_n^*-test will perform favourably against the alternatives of Section 7.2.5a since for these alternatives the B_n-test is a locally best invariant test.

7.5. MULTI-SAMPLE TESTS

The q-sample Uniform Scores Test. Let $\theta_{ij}, j = 1, ..., n_i$, $i = 1, ..., q$ be q independent random samples of sizes $n_1, ..., n_q$ from continuous d.f.'s. Let $n = \Sigma n_i$. We wish to test equality of the q-populations against the translation type of alternatives. Let the n angles be ranked in a single sequence and let $r_{ij}, j = 1, ..., n_i$ be the ranks of the angles in the ith sample. We replace the n angles by the uniform scores

$$\beta_{ij} = 2\pi r_{ij}/n, \qquad j = 1, ..., n_i, \quad i = 1, ..., q.$$

We can now obtain a suitable criterion by using these angles in the test-statistic for the multi-sample problem for the von Mises populations. For small κ, we may choose between (6.4.5) and (6.4.14.) The later statistic has the advantage that its asymptotic null distribution is a standard distribution.

TABLE 7.5. Calculations required for an application of the W-test to the wind direction data of Table 6.3.

Seasons	Ranks r_{ij}	C_i	S_i
Winter	12, 16, 27, 29, 30, 33, 37, 40, 41, 44, 45, 46	0·1133	−4·7425
Spring	1, 4, 10, 13, 20, 22, 28, 31, 38, 43, 47, 48	1·5282	0·1947
Summer	2, 3, 5, 6, 8, 9, 11, 17, 18, 19, 21, 25, 42	1·2155	6·4761
Autumn	7, 14, 15, 23, 24, 26, 32, 34, 35, 36, 39, 49	−2·8570	−1·9283

(Although the statistic is sensitive to shifts of scale). Hence, from (6.4.14), a suitable criterion is

$$W = 2 \sum_{i=1}^{q} (C_i^2 + S_i^2)/n_i, \qquad (7.5.1)$$

where
$$C_i = \sum_{j=1}^{n_1} \cos (2\pi r_{ij}/n), \qquad S_i = \sum_{j=1}^{n_1} \sin (2\pi r_{ij}/n).$$

The null hypothesis is rejected for large values of W. Appendix 2.17 gives some critical values for the test when $q = 3$. For other values of n and q, we can use the fact that W is distributed as χ^2 with $2(q - 1)$ d. of fr. (Mardia, 1970). For $q = 2$, W reduces to $2nR_1^2/n_1n_2$.

The invariance of W under rotation follows on observing that W depends only on the rank differences $r_{ij} - r_{ij'}$ which do not change under transformations of the type (7.4.2) and (7.4.3).

Mardia (1972) has shown that the Bahadur efficiency of the W-test relative to its parametric competitor (6.4.14) tends to 1 as $\kappa \to 0$, i.e. uniformity.

Example 7.13. Test equality of the populations for the wind direction data of Example 6.11. (The data is given in Table 6.3.)

Table 7.5 shows the ranks r_{ij} for the data obtained with $\theta = 0$ as the starting point. The ties were broken by a process of randomization. On using the totals C_i and S_i from Table 7.5 in (7.5.1), it is found that $W = 12.81$. We have here $q = 4$ and $n = 49$. The 5% and 1% values of χ_6^2 are 12.59 and 16.81 respectively. Hence, we reject the null hypothesis at the 5% level. This is a borderline case since $\Pr (\chi_6^2 > 12.59) = 0.46$. The conclusion is not the same as in Example 6.11 and this difference in behaviour of the two tests could be due to the influence of the ties on the W-test. However, in general, the W-test not only detects changes of location but also shifts of scale.

Maag (1966) has given a multi-sample analogue of Watson's U_{n_1,n_2}^2 test and has also dealt with its asymptotic null distribution. Its critical values for small samples are not yet available. The run test can easily be extended to the multi-sample case. Its critical values for $q = 3$ and 4 can be obtained on using the enumeration of the null distribution of runs given by Barton and David (1958).

7.6. TESTS FOR MULTIMODAL AND AXIAL DATA

The tests discussed in earlier sections are basically for unimodal populations on $(0, 2\pi)$. We now indicate how these tests can be adapted for multimodal and axial cases.

7.6.1. The Multimodal Case

7.6.1a. *One-sample Tests*

Let $\theta_1, ..., \theta_n$ be a random sample from a l-modal distribution on $(0, 2\pi)$. We transform the observations θ_i to θ_i' by using

$$\theta_i' = (l\theta_i) \,(\text{mod } 2\pi), \qquad i = 1, ..., n, \qquad (7.6.1)$$

and then apply the one-sample tests given in Sections 7.2, 7.3, 7.4 to the θ_i'.

For the von Mises case, this procedure has already been used in Section 6.6.1 with some justification. It is also intuitively appropriate if the underlying population has a symmetric density with l equi-distant modes. In fact, Beran (1969b) has shown that Ajne's A_n test so adapted is a locally best invariant test against symmetric l modal densities.

Example 7.14. By using the equal spacings test, test the hypothesis of uniformity for the data of Example 6.13 under the (realistic) assumption that the population is bimodal.

The values of $\theta_i' = 2\theta_i \text{ mod } 360°$ in degrees are

$$\theta_i' : 40, 60, 240, 270, 290, 290, 310, 330, 340, 340, 340, 340, 350$$

and so the successive arc-lengths T_i are

$$20, 180, 30, 20, 0, 20, 20, 10, 0, 0, 0, 10, 50.$$

Further, $360°/n = 27\cdot7°$. Consequently, it is found from (7.2.55) that $L = 176\cdot9°$. From Appendix 2.13, the 5% and 1% values for $n = 13$ are $167\cdot8°$ and $185\cdot8°$ respectively. Hence, the null hypothesis is rejected as in Example 6.13.

7.6.1b. *Two-sample Tests*

Let the two-samples be drawn from l-modal populations. We first consider an analogue of the uniform scores test R_1^2 for this situation. Let $r_1, ..., r_{n_1}$ be the linear ranks of the first sample. Following the derivation of the R_1^2 test, we substitute the angles $\beta_i = 2\pi r_i / n$ into the two-sample test-statistic for the l-modal von Mises density given in Section 6.6.1. Consequently, the test statistic for this situation is given by

$$R_l^2 = (\Sigma \cos l\beta_i)^2 + (\Sigma \sin l\beta_i)^2. \qquad (7.6.2)$$

The null hypothesis is rejected for large values of R_l^2. Appendix 7.18 gives some selected critical values for the test. Since the sine and cosine sums given by (7.4.7) do not depend on the integer s, the statistics R_1^2 and R_l^2 have exactly the same moments. Hence, from (7.4.10), the null distribution of the statistic $2(n - 1)R_i^2/n_1 n_2$ can be approximated by the chi-square distribution with 2 d. of fr. Further, as in the unimodal case, the test is consistent against alternatives with symmetric l-modal densities.

The above procedure for the multimodal case amounts to replacing the angles β_i by $l\beta_i$ in the unimodal case. Hence, on replacing β_{ij} by $l\beta_{ij}$ in the test statistic W for the multi-sample case leads to the appropriate statistics for the l-modal case. This test has been studied by Mardia and Spurr (1972). The procedure also implies that the ranks r_i in the unimodal two-sample test are replaced by $(lr_i) \bmod n$. This fact when utilized in the A_n^*-statistic given by (7.4.21) leads to the multi-modal two-sample A_n^*-test (Beran, 1969b). The run test can also be applied to the transformed angles $\theta_{ij}' = (l\theta_{ij})$ mod 2π where the θ_{ij} are the given observations. Critical values given previously for the run test in Appendix 2.16 can be used.

Example 7.15. Two random samples were drawn from a record of hourly wind directions in June and July 1968 for Gorleston (England), and the following values were obtained.

$$\text{June: } 10°, 20°, 30°, 90°, 90°, 170°, 220°, 330°$$
$$\text{July: } 50°, 100°, 150°, 220°, 320°, 350°, 350°,$$

If it is known from earlier records that the hourly readings over a month have a bimodal distribution, test whether the two samples can be regarded as drawn from the same population.

The ties were broken up by a process of randomization and the ranks r_i of the first sample with starting point $\theta = 10°$ were found to be 1, 2, 3, 5, 6, 9, 11, 13. We have $l = 2$ and $n = 15$. The ranks $r_i' = (2r_i) \bmod n$ are 2, 3, 4, 6, 7, 10, 11, 12. Let $\beta_i' = 2\pi r_i'/n$. We have from (7.6.2)

$$R_2^2 = (\Sigma \cos \beta_i')^2 + (\Sigma \sin \beta_i')^2.$$

It is found that

$$\Sigma \cos \beta_i' = -1\cdot2090, \qquad \Sigma \sin \beta_i' = 0\cdot6728, \qquad R_2^2 = 1\cdot91.$$

For $n = 15$ and $n_1 = 7$, from Appendix 7.18, the 5% value of R_2^2 is 11·57. Hence, the null hypothesis is accepted.

7.6.2. The Axial Case

Let $\theta_1, ..., \theta_n$ be observations from a unimodal population on $(0, 2\pi/l)$. The transformed observations

$$\theta_i' = l\theta_i, \qquad i = 1, ,... n \qquad (7.6.3)$$

belong to a unimodal population on $(0, 2\pi)$ so that we can apply the test procedures of Sections 7.2–7.5 to the θ_i'.

It can easily be seen that this transformation is not required for the tests which depend only on the relative positions of the observations and not on their spacings. This result applies to all the two-sample and multi-sample tests we have considered. It also applies to Kuiper's test and Watson's U^2 test. Mardia and Spurr (1972) have studied the uniform scores test for this situation. For the range test and the equal spacings test, this result does not hold but it can be used after multiplying the values of the test statistic by l.

Example 7.16. Test equality of the two populations for the geological data of Example 6.15.

The ranks of the first sample with starting point $\theta = 74°$ are $1, 2, 3, 4, 5, 7, 9, 14$. On carrying out similar calculations to those done in Example 7.9, we find that

$$C_1 = 0\cdot6133, \qquad S_1 = 3\cdot4784, \qquad R_1{}^2 = 12\cdot48$$

From Appendix 2.14, the 5% value of $R_1{}^2$ for $n_1 = 8$, $n_2 = 10$ is $13\cdot82$. Hence, at the 5% level of significance, the null hypothesis is accepted as in Example 6.15.

8

DISTRIBUTIONS ON SPHERES

8.1. SPHERICAL DATA

There are various practical situations where the observations are directions in three dimensions, e.g. the direction of the paleocurrent since its velocity is not known, the direction of the normal to a bedding surface towards the course of more recent deposition etc. For various other examples, see Sections 1.5.1, 1.5.6, 1.5.8 and 1.5.9. Directional data in three dimensions also appear where the original observations have magnitude as well as directions but from the nature of the experiments, only the directions may be relevant. For example, in vector cardiograms the orientation of the electric field vector summarizing the electrical activity of the heart are relevant for comparisons but not the magnitude. Since over the course of ventricular contraction, the path of the vector is a closed curve.

The directions of three dimensional observations can be specified as follows. Let $P(x, y, z)$ be the Cartesian co-ordinates of an observation in three dimensions and let O be the origin. The direction of the vector **OP** (starting at O with its arrowhead at P, see Fig. 8.1) is the observed direction and is specified by the direction cosines (l, m, n) of the line OP which are given by

$$l = \cos a, \qquad m = \cos b, \qquad n = \cos c,$$

where a, b and c are the angles the line OP makes with the positive directions of the three co-ordinates axes. We have

$$l^2 + m^2 + n^2 = 1, \tag{8.1.1}$$

and therefore the direction of **OP** is represented by the unit vector (l, m, n).

Let the vector **OP** cut at the point P' the surface of a sphere having unit radius and centre at the origin. We can identify the direction of **OP** with the point P' and, as in the circular case, we shall use interchangeably the directed line OP' to describe the point P' and vice versa.

The directions of observations may not have a sense, for example, the directions of the optic axes of specimens of rocks, the direction of a normal to a plane where its two sides are not distinguished such as in a cleavage plane. Such data can be described as *axial* data. In this case, the observations can be represented either as points on a hemisphere, or on a unit sphere by the entire diameters. We describe these observations as *axes* in contrast to *directions*.

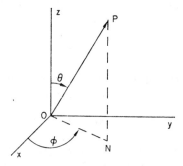

FIG. 8.1. Polar co-ordinates θ (colatitude) and ϕ (latitude) of the vector **OP**.

Polar Co-ordinates. We shall also use the spherical polar co-ordinates $P(\theta, \phi)$ to represent the direction of **OP**. Suppose that θ is the angle between the z-axis and the line OP in the clockwise direction while ϕ is the angle between the x-axis and the line ON in the anticlockwise direction where the point N is the foot of perpendicular P on XOY plane (see Fig. 8.1.). We have

$$l = \sin\theta\cos\phi, \quad m = \sin\theta\sin\phi, \quad n = \cos\theta, \quad 0 < \theta < \pi, \quad 0 < \phi < 2\pi. \quad (8.1.2)$$

The cone angle θ will be described as the colatitude of P while the polar distance ϕ will be described as the latitude of P. The origin O is the pole of the reference and the z-axis is the polar axis. The x-axis is along $\theta = \pi/2$, $\phi = 0$ and the y-axis is along $\theta = \phi = \pi/2$.

Axial data is usually represented on a lower hemisphere so that the point (θ, ϕ) with $\frac{1}{2}\pi < \theta < \pi$, $0 < \phi < 2\pi$ is replaced by the point $(\pi - \theta, \phi \pm \pi)$.

8.2. OTHER SPHERICAL CO-ORDINATE SYSTEMS

8.2.1. Geographical

The pole of the reference ($\theta = 0°$) is usually the north pole, $\theta = 90°$ is the equator and $\theta = 180°$ is the south pole while the polar axis is the northward direction. The angle ϕ is the longitude measured from $0°$ to $360°$ eastwards from $\phi = 0°$. Let θ' be the latitude. We have $\theta' = 90° - \theta$ so that (8.1.2) reduces to

$$l = \cos\phi\,\cos\theta', \quad m = \sin\phi\,\cos\theta', \quad n = \sin\theta'. \qquad (8.2.1)$$

In the northern hemisphere (the upper-half) $\theta = 90° - \theta'$ where θ' is the northern latitude. In the sourthern hemisphere, $\theta = 90° + \theta'$, θ' being the southern latitude. The great circles through the poles are meridians and the prime meridian is $\theta' = 0°$.

8.2.2. Geological

Let A be the azimuth (trend, declination, orientation, azimuth of dip) and let D be the angle of "dip" (inclination, plunge). We have,

$$\theta = D + 90°, \quad \phi = 360° - A, \quad -90° < D < 90°, \quad 0 < A < 360°, \quad (8.2.2)$$

since the azimuth A is the angle between two vertical planes containing the line OP and the line joining P and the magnetic north pole (measured clock-wise from north) while the angle of "dip" D is the angle between the vector $\mathbf{OP}$ and the horizontal plane (taken as positive if the vector lies below the horizontal plane). From (8.1.2) and (8.2.2), we obtain

$$l = \cos D \cos A, \quad m = -\cos D \sin A, \quad n = -\sin D. \qquad (8.2.3)$$

However, if we take x, y, z axes as northwards, eastwards, vertically downwards, A is the angle between $\mathbf{OP}$ and the XOY plane (measured as positive for downward directions) and D is the angle between the x-axis and the projection ON (measured clockwise, north at $0°$ through east $90°$). The direction cosines of $\mathbf{OP}$ are then

$$l' = \cos D \cos A, \quad m' = \cos D \sin A, \quad n' = \sin D. \qquad (8.2.4)$$

This choice eliminates the negative signs appearing in (8.2.3).

The orientation of a given plane with a facing is determined by its strike and dip (to be distinguished from "dip" within quotes defined previously). The strike of a plane is the smaller of two possible angles between the northward direction and the line of intersection of the plane with horizontal plane.

On the other hand, the dip is the diehadral angle between these two planes. It is specified further to the "west" or to the "east". Let x, y, z axes be taken as vertically downwards, northwards and eastwards, respectively. If a plane has strike s and the up-face of the plane dips down to the west by d, the direction cosines of the normal to the up-face of the plane are

$$l'' = -\cos s \sin d, \quad m'' = -\cos d, \quad n'' = \sin s \sin d, \quad -\tfrac{1}{2}\pi < s < \tfrac{1}{2}\pi. \quad (8.2.5)$$

Further, if **OP** is a vector in the plane, its *pitch* is the angle with the strike line having northern sense. The directed line **OP** is completely specified by strike, dip and pitch. This account is due to Watson (1970).

8.3. AZIMUTHAL PROJECTIONS

8.3.1. Observation on a Hemisphere

To obtain a "scatter diagram" in two dimensions of observations on the surface of a sphere, we can use some projection on a plane. Let us first consider the case when the observations are axial so that we can represent them on a hemisphere.

Let (ρ, ψ) be the polar co-ordinates in two dimensions where ρ is the polar distance and ψ is the polar angle. In azimuthal projections of the polar point (θ, ϕ) on a hemisphere, we identify ψ with ϕ and take ρ as a suitable function of θ. We shall assume that the points are on the upper hemisphere so that the points are projected on the tangent plane at the north pole which will be the centre of the projected diagram. We have $0 < \theta < \pi/2$. If the points are on the lower hemisphere, we replace θ by $\pi - \theta$ since the points will be projected on the tangent at the south pole. In this case, we are looking vertically down into the lower hemisphere and so the projections show where the lines through the origin cut the hemisphere.

Polar Projections. There are two methods in common use.

(i) *Lambert's equal area projection.* This projection is defined by

$$\rho = 2|\sin(\theta/2)|, \quad \psi = \phi, \quad 0 < \rho < \sqrt{2}, \quad 0 < \psi < 2\pi. \quad (8.3.1)$$

This projection in structural geology was first used by Schmidt (1925) and after him the plot is known as the Schmidt-net.

(ii) *Stereographic equal-angle projection*. This projection is defined by

$$\rho = |\tan(\theta/2)|, \qquad \psi = \phi, \qquad 0 < \rho < 1, \qquad 0 < \psi < 2\pi. \qquad (8.3.2)$$

The plot is known as the Wulff-net or the stereographic-net.

In interpreting the scatter of the points probabilistically, the Schmidt-net is preferred since it is area-preserving. The density of plotted points in different regions can easily be judged by this projection and is commonly used in geology. For example, a set of points uniformly distributed over the hemisphere will be projected into a set of points uniformly distributed over the circular area.

Equatorial Projections. If there is a cluster of points around the equator of a hemisphere, a rotation is necessary to bring these points in the centre of the projected diagram since otherwise the points will be projected at the perimeter. This can be achieved by taking a pole on the equator. Suppose the pole is at the point $(\tfrac{1}{2}\pi, \tfrac{1}{2}\pi)$. Let (ω, λ) be the new co-ordinates of (θ, ϕ). We have $0 \leqslant \omega, \lambda \leqslant \pi$ and

$$\sin\theta \cos\phi = \sin\omega \sin\lambda, \qquad \sin\theta \sin\phi = \cos\omega, \qquad \cos\theta = \sin\omega \sin\lambda.$$

Consequently, from (8.3.1), the point of projection in this case is

$$\rho = \{2(1 - \sin\omega \cos\lambda)\}^{\frac{1}{2}}, \qquad \phi = \cot^{-1}(\tan\omega \sin\lambda). \qquad (8.3.3)$$

The nets in the first case are called polar while in the second case the nets are called equatorial (the pole being on the equator).

8.3.2. Observations on a Sphere and Rotations

If the observations are on the surface of a sphere, the points of the lower and the upper hemispheres can be projected by the nets described above. The points are usually projected on the same diagram and are distinguished by using two different symbols such as closed and open circles for the lower and the upper hemispherical cases respectively. Further, in the upper hemispherical case, ψ is replaced by $2\pi - \psi$.

It may be desirable to rotate the sphere before using the above projections, e.g. if the points are clustered around the equator or about a preferred direction. Suppose that it is required to project the points on a hemisphere with the pole at (α, β). The new co-ordinates (θ', ϕ') of the point corresponding to (θ, ϕ) with pole at $\theta = 0$ are seen to be

$$l' = (\cos\alpha \cos\beta)\, l + (\cos\alpha \sin\beta)\, m - (\sin\alpha)\, n, \qquad (8.3.4)$$

$$m' = -(\sin\beta)\, l + (\cos\beta)\, m, \qquad (8.3.5)$$

$$n' = (\sin\alpha \cos\beta)\, l + (\sin\alpha \sin\beta)\, m + (\cos\alpha)\, n, \qquad (8.3.6)$$

where (l, m, n) and (l', m', n') are the direction cosines corresponding to (θ, ϕ) and (θ', ϕ') respectively and are defined by (8.1.2). This transformation implies a rotation of the axes where the new pole is (α, β). We can now obtain a projection diagram of the points (θ', ϕ') by following one of the two methods. In fact, by two rotations about orthogonal axes, the projection diagram of the hemisphere with pole at (α, β) can also be obtained from the projection of the hemisphere with pole at $\theta = 0$ (Selby, 1964).

Excellent accounts of the projection diagrams from practical points of view will be found in Turner and Weiss (1963, Chapter 3) and Vistelius (1966). An elegant summary of the mathematical formulation of Lambert's projection is given in Selby (1964). There are various methods of drawing contours of the density (or smoothing the data) but these methods of contouring do not seem to have been investigated statistically. For their descriptions and practical usage, the reader is again referred to Turner and Weiss (1963) and Vistelius (1966).

Example 8.1. Table 8.1 shows 20 cross-bed measurements of azimuth and "dip" from sandstone bodies in the Eocene Cathedral Bluffs Member of the Wasatch Formation in Wyoming (Steinmetz, 1962). Draw a Schmidt-net (polar) for the data.

TABLE 8.1.   Crossbedding measurements from the Wasatch Formation, Eocene, Wyoming (Steinmetz, 1962).

Azimuth (degrees)	Dip (degrees)	$\theta'/2$	ρ	Azimuth (degrees)	Dip (degrees)	$\theta'/2$	ρ
18	13	38·5	1·245	81	12	39	1·259
34	8	41	1·312	267	16	37	1·204
36	5	42·5	1·351	302	6	42	1·338
37	7	41·5	1·325	307	8	41	1·312
40	12	39	1·259	310	8	41	1·312
43	4	43	1·364	321	19	35·5	1·161
58	6	42	1·338	322	24	33	1·089
60	13	38·5	1·245	324	10	40	1·286
70	4	43	1·364	338	10	40	1·286
81	5	42·5	1·351	346	10	40	1·286

On recalling the definitions of the azimuth and "dip" in Section 8.2.2, we see that the data is confined to the lower hemisphere. Hence θ is replaced by $\pi - \theta$ in (8.3.1). However, from (8.2.2), $\theta = 90° + D$ where D is the angle of "dip". From (8.3.1), we thus have $\rho = 2|\sin(\theta'/2)|$ where $\theta' = 90° - D$. The value of $\theta'/2$ and ρ are shown in Table 8.1. Fig. 8.2 shows a Schmidt-net by plotting the polar points (ρ, ψ) where the ψ are taken equal to the azimuth angles A. The point N denotes the north and the angles ψ are measured in the clockwise direction. The plotting is, of course, much simplified by using the standard nets especially produced for this purpose.

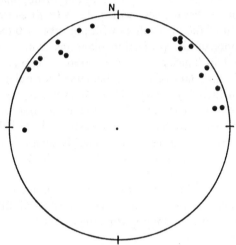

FIG. 8.2. Schmidt-net for the cross-bed data of Table 8.1. (Steinmetz, 1962).

8.4 DESCRIPTIVE MEASURES

8.4.1. Spherical Mean Direction and Variance

Definition. Let (l_i, m_i, n_i), $i = 1, ..., n$ be n observed direction cosines. To define the spherical mean direction, we first note a similiarity between the circular and the spherical cases. Let θ_i, $i = 1, ..., n$ be the circular observations. These observations can be represented by (l_i, m_i) where $l_i = \cos\theta_i$, $n_i = \sin\theta_i$, $i = 1, ..., n$. Now, the circular mean direction is the direction of the resultant of (l_i, m_i), $i = 1, ..., n$, so that we can define analogously the spherical mean direction as the direction of the resultant of (l_i, m_i, n_i), $i = 1, ..., n$. Let $(\bar{l}_0, \bar{m}_0, \bar{n}_0)$ be the direction cosines of the resultant, we have

$$\bar{l}_0 = \sum_{i=1}^{n} l_i/R, \qquad \bar{m}_0 = \sum_{i=1}^{n} m_i/R, \qquad \bar{n}_0 = \sum_{i=1}^{n} n_i/R, \qquad (8.4.1)$$

where R is the length of the resultant given by

$$R = \{(\Sigma l_i)^2 + (\Sigma m_i)^2 + (\Sigma n_i)^2\}^{\frac{1}{2}}. \qquad (8.4.2)$$

We shall denote the x, y and z components of the resultant by R_x, R_y and R_z respectively. We have

$$R_x = \bar{l}_0 R, \qquad R_y = \bar{m}_0 R, \qquad R_z = \bar{n}_0 R. \tag{8.4.3}$$

As in the circular case (Section 2.3), R will be as large as n if the observations are clustered about a direction whereas if the observations are very dispersed such as in the uniform case, R will be small. Hence R is a measure of concentration about the mean direction if it exists. Consequently, we may define the spherical variance as

$$S^* = (n - R)/n, \qquad 0 \leqslant R \leqslant n, \quad 0 < S^* < 1. \tag{8.4.4}$$

We are led to the same measure by using the analogy with the circular case.

Properties. We can now prove various properties of these measures analogous to those in the circular case.

Let $\mathbf{L}_i = (l_i, m_i, n_i)'$, $i = 1, ..., n$. Consider the rotation of axes defined by

$$\mathbf{L}_i^* = \mathbf{A}\mathbf{L}_i,$$

where $\mathbf{A}$ is an orthogonal matrix and $\mathbf{L}_i^*$ is the transformed value of $\mathbf{L}_i$. We can easily see that R is invariant under the rotation and the direction cosines of the new mean direction $\mathbf{L}_0 = (\bar{l}_0, \bar{m}_0, \bar{n}_0)'$ are given by

$$\mathbf{L}_0^* = \mathbf{A}\mathbf{L}_0. \tag{8.4.5}$$

Further, if (α, β) is the new pole under the transformation, the matrix $\mathbf{A}$ is precisely the matrix of coefficients in (8.3.4)–(8.3.6), i.e.

$$\mathbf{A} = \begin{bmatrix} \cos\alpha\cos\beta & \cos\alpha\sin\beta & -\sin\alpha \\ -\sin\beta & \cos\beta & 0 \\ \sin\alpha\cos\beta & \sin\alpha\sin\beta & \cos\alpha \end{bmatrix}. \tag{8.4.6}$$

Hence, on replacing (l, m, n) by $(\bar{l}_0, \bar{m}_0, \bar{n}_0)$ in (8.3.4)–(8.3.6), the new mean direction can be obtained.

We can define the variance about the direction (λ, μ, ν) as

$$S(\lambda, \mu, \nu) = \{n - (\lambda\bar{l}_0 + \mu\bar{m}_0 + \nu\bar{n}_0)\}/n = (n - R\cos\theta')/n, \tag{8.4.7}$$

where θ' is the angle between the resultant and the given direction. It can be seen that $S(\lambda, \mu, \nu)$ has a minimum when (λ, μ, ν) is the sample mean direction. In particular, let the z-axis be the true direction. We can partition the total variation into

$$n - R_z = (n - R) + (R - R_z), \tag{8.4.8}$$

TABLE 8.2.   Measurements (in degrees) from the magnetized lava flows in 1947–48 in Iceland (Hosper's data cited in Fisher, 1953).

Decl. A	Incl. D	Colat. θ	Long. ϕ	$\sin\phi$ I	$\cos\phi$ II	$\sin\theta$ III	l II×III	m I×III	n $\cos\theta$
5·7	73·0	163·0	354·3	−·0993	·9951	·2924	·2910	−·0290	−·9563
27·0	82·1	172·1	333·0	−·4540	·8910	·1374	·1224	−·0624	−·9905
36·9	70·1	160·1	323·1	−·6004	·7997	·3404	·2722	−·2044	−·9403
44·0	51·4	141·4	316·0	−·6947	·7193	·6239	·4488	−·4334	−·7815
50·4	69·3	159·3	309·6	−·7705	·6374	·3535	·2253	−·2724	−·9354
62·0	68·7	158·7	298·0	−·8829	·4695	·3633	·1706	−·3208	−·9317
343·2	66·1	156·1	16·8	·2890	·9573	·4051	·3878	·1171	−·9143
357·6	58·8	148·8	2·4	·0419	·9991	·5180	·5176	·0217	−·8554
359·0	79·5	169·5	1·0	·0175	·9998	·1822	·1822	·0032	−·9833
						Totals	2·6179	−1·1804	−8·2887

and, as in the circular case, we may say that the total variation is decomposed into two components. The first component measures the variation of the observations about the sample mean direction whereas the second component measures the variation of the sample mean direction from the true mean direction.

Calculation of the mean direction and R. If we are given $(l_i, m_i, n_i)\, i = 1, ..., n$, there is no difficulty in obtaining (l_0, m_0, n_0) and R from (8.4.1) and (8.4.2). We need only obtain the sums of the direction cosines $\Sigma l_i, \Sigma m_i$ and Σn_i. However, in practice, we are invariably given the observations in the polar co-ordinates $(\theta_i, \phi_i)\, i = 1, ..., n$ or in similar co-ordinate systems. Example 8.2 gives a procedure for such cases. Let $(\bar{x}_0, \bar{y}_0)$ be the polar co-ordinates of the mean direction $(\bar{l}_0, \bar{m}_0, \bar{n}_0)$. We have

$$\bar{l}_0 = \sin \bar{x}_0 \cos \bar{y}_0, \qquad \bar{m}_0 = \sin \bar{x}_0 \sin \bar{y}_0, \qquad \bar{n}_0 = \cos \bar{x}_0. \qquad (8.4.9)$$

Consequently, $\bar{x}_0$ is given by

$$\bar{x}_0 = \text{arc cos } \bar{n}_0, \qquad 0 < \bar{x}_0 < \pi, \qquad (8.4.10)$$

whereas $\bar{y}_0$ is given by

$$\cos \bar{y}_0 = \bar{l}_0 \, \text{cosec } \bar{x}_0, \qquad \sin \bar{y}_0 = \bar{m}_0 \, \text{cosec } \bar{x}_0, \qquad 0 < \bar{y}_0 < 2\pi. \qquad (8.4.11)$$

For R, we may use any one of the eight combinations $(\pm l_i, \pm m_i, \pm n_i)$. Further, its value remains the same under rotations, i.e. it does not depend on the choice of the pole of reference. The value of $(\bar{x}_0, \bar{y}_0)$ after a rotation can be obtained by using (8.3.4)–(8.3.6) as described above.

Example 8.2. The first two columns of Table 8.2 give declinations (azimuth, A) and inclinations ("dip" D) of nine specimens of remanent magnetization in the Icelandic lava flows of 1947–48. Obtain their mean direction, the resultant length and the spherical variance.
    From (8.2.2), θ and ϕ are given by

$$\theta = 90° + D, \qquad \phi = 2\pi - A. \qquad (8.4.12)$$

The direction cosines l_i, m_i and n_i from (8.1.2) are given by

$$l_i = \sin \theta_i \cos \phi_i, \qquad m_i = \sin \theta_i \sin \phi_i, \qquad n_i = \cos \theta_i.$$

Table 8.2 obtains the values of $(l_i, m_i, n_i), i = 1, ..., 9$. The entries in the last column for $\cos \theta$ can be obtained simultaneously with the entries in Column III for $\sin \theta$. From Table 8.2, we have

$$\Sigma l_i = -2 \cdot 6179, \qquad \Sigma m_i = -1 \cdot 1804, \qquad \Sigma n_i = -8 \cdot 2887.$$

Hence, $R^2 = 76 \cdot 9485$, $R = 8 \cdot 7720$, $S^* = 0 \cdot 0253$. The small value of S is consistent with the data (see also Example 9.1). The direction cosines of the mean direction from (8.4.1) are

$$\bar{l}_0 = 0 \cdot 2984, \qquad \bar{m}_0 = -0 \cdot 1346, \qquad \bar{n}_0 = -0 \cdot 9449. \qquad (8.4.13)$$

Consequently, from (8.4.10), we have $\bar{x}_0 = 160 \cdot 9°$. On substituting this value of $\bar{x}_0$ into (8.4.11), we find that $\bar{y}_0 = 335 \cdot 7°$. Finally, on substituting the values of $\bar{x}_0$ and $\bar{y}_0$ into (8.4.12), the mean direction of declinations and "dips" is found to be $(22 \cdot 3°, 70 \cdot 9°)$.

8.4.2. Forms of Distributions and The Moment of Inertia

It is useful to gain some insight into the configuration of sample points on the sphere such as whether the distribution is uniform, unimodal, bimodal etc. This problem can be studied roughly by considering various projections of the sample points but much more effectively by considering the moment of inertia of the sample points. Before discussing this method, we first describe various forms of distributions which occur in practice.

8.4.2a. *Forms of Spherical Distributions*

The uniform distribution. The distribution is uniform if the points are uniformly distributed on the sphere. In this case, there is no preferred direction.

Unimodal distributions. In this case, the directions have a modal direction, e.g. when the points are clustered about the north pole. If there is rotational symmetry about the modal direction, we call the distribution a *unipolar distribution*, e.g. when the mass is distributed on the sphere in the form of a spinning top (see Fig. 8.3a).

Bimodal distributions. There are two modal directions in this case. If the distribution is rotationally symmetric about the axis joining the two modes

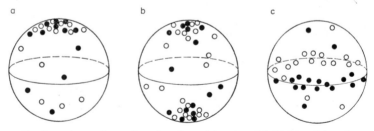

FIG. 8.3. Configurations of sample points from (a) unimodal (b) bimodal and (c) girdle distributions. (An open circle denotes a point on the other side).

as well as about the axis joining the two anti-modes, the distribution will be described as *bipolar*, e.g. when the mass is distributed on the sphere in the form of a rugby ball. Bipolar distributions also arise in the axial case when the points are clustered at the ends of an axis, e.g. when the points are concentrated around the north and south poles (see Fig. 8.3b).

Girdle distributions. If an axial distribution has its maximum in a plane around a great circle rather than at the end points of an axis, the distribution is called a *girdle distribution*, e.g. when the mass is distributed in form of an elliptic pattern (as a girdle) around a great circle. If there is a rotational symmetry about the axis perpendicular to the girdle-plane, the distribution is called a *symmetric girdle distribution*, e.g. when the mass is concentrated in a circular pattern around the equator (see Fig. 8.3c).

8.4.2b. *The Moment of Inertia*

Let $(x_i, y_i, z_i), i = 1, ..., n$ be n points of unit mass and suppose that $\mathbf{u} = (u, v, w)'$ is a fixed direction. The moment of inertia of these n points about the direction $\mathbf{u}$ is the sum of the squares of the perpendicular distances of the points (x_i, y_i, z_i) from the direction $\mathbf{u}$ and is given by

$$\Sigma(x_i^2 + y_i^2 + z_i^2) - \Sigma(x_i u + y_i v + z_i w)^2.$$

Hence, the moment of inertia of the directions $(l_i, m_i, n_i), i = 1, ..., n$ about $\mathbf{u}$ is

$$M = \mathbf{u}' \mathbf{B} \mathbf{u}, \tag{8.4.14}$$

where

$$\mathbf{B} = n\mathbf{I} - \mathbf{T} \tag{8.4.15}$$

and $\mathbf{T} = (t_{ij})$ is the 3×3 matrix of the sums of squares and products of (l_i, m_i, n_i), i.e.

$$\mathbf{T} = \begin{bmatrix} \Sigma l_i^2 & \Sigma l_i m_i & \Sigma l_i n_i \\ \Sigma l_i m_i & \Sigma m_i^2 & \Sigma m_i n_i \\ \Sigma l_i n_i & \Sigma m_i n_i & \Sigma n_i^2 \end{bmatrix}. \tag{8.4.16}$$

Let β_1, β_2 and β_3 be the eigen values of $\mathbf{B}$ in *descending* order and let $\mathbf{b}_1, \mathbf{b}_2$ and $\mathbf{b}_3$ be the corresponding eigen vectors. We remind ourselves of the following points.

   (i) If all the β_i are distinct, the eigen vectors $\mathbf{b}_1, \mathbf{b}_2$ and $\mathbf{b}_3$ can be regarded as the direction cosines of a set of three co-ordinate axes. If two or more roots are equal, the directions of the axes are not unique and may be chosen in an infinity of orthogonal positions.

(ii) We have

$$\beta_i = \mathbf{b}_i' \mathbf{B} \mathbf{b}_i \qquad (8.4.17)$$

so that β_i is the moment of inertia of the points about $\mathbf{b}_i$. That is, β_i is the sum of the squares of the perpendiculars of the points from $\mathbf{b}_i$. Since $\mathbf{u}' \mathbf{u} = 1$, it can be shown that β_1 is the maximum possible value of M whereas β_3 is the minimum possible value of M. Further, we have

$$\beta_i \geqslant 0, \qquad \beta_1 + \beta_2 + \beta_3 = 2n. \qquad (8.4.18)$$

The last result follows on noting that the trace of $\mathbf{B}$ is equal to the sum of the β_i.

(iii) Since the perpendicular distance of the point (l_i, m_i, n_i) on the sphere to $\mathbf{u}$ is the same as the perpendicular distance of the diametrically opposite point $(-l_i, -m_i, -n_i)$ to $\mathbf{u}$, the moment of inertia does not distinguish between the directional and the axial data. However, the value of the length of the resultant R can be used to distinguish between these two cases, e.g. R will be large for the unimodal case.

We are now able to detect the form of the distribution of the points (l_i, m_i, n_i) using the nature of β_1, β_2 and β_3.

Case I. β_1 large. From (8.4.18), it follows that β_2 and β_3 are small. Using the moment of inertia interpretation of the eigen values given in (ii), we may say that the sum of the squares of the perpendiculars of the points is large from $\mathbf{b}_1$ but small from $\mathbf{b}_2$ and $\mathbf{b}_3$. From (i), the eigen vectors can be regarded as three co-ordinate axes and therefore most of the observations must be concentrated in the plane containing $\mathbf{b}_2$ and $\mathbf{b}_3$ whose normal is $\mathbf{b}_1$. Hence, large values of β_1 imply a girdle distribution.

Case II. β_1 and β_2 large. In this case, β_3 will be small. By the same argument as in Case I, most of the observations will be concentrated on the sphere around the end points of the diameter $\mathbf{b}_3$. Consequently, from (iii), the distribution is unimodal for large R; otherwise the distribution is bimodal.

Case III. $\beta_2 \doteq \beta_3$. From (i) and (ii), the moment of inertia will be almost constant about any diameter of the circle containing $\mathbf{b}_2$ and $\mathbf{b}_3$. Hence, there will be approximate rotational symmetry about $\mathbf{b}_1$. Further, if β_1 is large then the distribution will be a symmetrical girdle distribution with rotational symmetry about $\mathbf{b}_1$. The case for $\beta_1 \doteq \beta_2$ can similarly be dealt with.

Case IV. $\beta_1 \doteq \beta_2 \doteq \beta_3$. From (ii), the moment of inertia will be almost the same whatever is $\mathbf{u}$. Hence, in this case, the distribution is uniform. In virtue of (iii), it implies that the axes have no preferred orientation.

For statistical purposes, it is much more convenient to work on $\mathbf{T}$ rather than $\mathbf{B}$. Let τ_1, τ_2 and τ_3 be the eigen values of $\mathbf{T}$ in *ascending* order and let $\mathbf{t}_1$, $\mathbf{t}_2$ and $\mathbf{t}_3$ be the corresponding eigen vectors. Using (8.4.15), it follows that

$$\tau_i = n - \beta_i, \qquad \mathbf{t}_i = \mathbf{b}_i, \qquad \tau_1 + \tau_2 + \tau_3 = n, \qquad \tau_i \geqslant 0. \qquad (8.4.19)$$

Hence, the above results apply to $\mathbf{T}$ after replacing (i) $\mathbf{b}_i$ by $\mathbf{t}_i$ and (ii) large β_i by small τ_i and vice versa. Table 8.3 summarizes these results for $\mathbf{T}$.

TABLE 8.3.   The classification of spherical distributions according to the nature of the eigen values of $\mathbf{T}$.

Nature of the eigen values	Type of the distribution	Other features
$\tau_1 \doteq \tau_2 \doteq \tau_3$	Uniform	Axes having no orientation
τ_3 large, τ_1, τ_2 small		
(i) $\tau_1 \neq \tau_2$	Unimodal if R is large Bimodal otherwise	Concentration at one end of $\mathbf{t}_3$ Concentration at both ends of $\mathbf{t}_3$
(ii) $\tau_1 \doteq \tau_2$	Unimodal if R is large Bipolar otherwise	Rotational symmetry about $\mathbf{t}_3$
τ_1 small, τ_2, τ_3 large		
(i) $\tau_2 \neq \tau_3$	Girdle	Girdle-plane spanned by $\mathbf{t}_2$, $\mathbf{t}_3$
(ii) $\tau_2 \doteq \tau_3$	Symmetric girdle	Rotational symmetry about $\mathbf{t}_1$

In practice, we calculate τ_1, τ_2, τ_3 and R from the points (l_i, m_i, n_i) and then use Table 8.3 to obtain the form of the distribution. Example 8.3 illustrates this method.

The above discussion is also applicable to the circular case. In this case, the eigen values of $\mathbf{T}$ lead to (i) uniformity or (ii) unimodality or bimodality depending on R.

These results are mainly due to Bingham (1964) and have appeared in studying the statistical inference problems for Bingham's distribution (see Sections 8.5.5b, 9.2, 9.7). The above intuitive interpretation of the moment of inertia as a general diagonistic tool is due to Watson (1966, 1970). In fact, the matrix $\mathbf{T}$ with some interpretation first appeared in Watson (1960).

The analogy of the above treatment with the multivariate principle component is striking. In fact, Loudon (1964) has used the multivariate analysis approach. We may deduce the above results by imagining the mass concentrated on the ellipsoid with the ith principal axes along $\mathbf{b}_i$ and the length of the semi-axes $\beta_i^{-\frac{1}{2}}$, $i = 1, 2, 3$.

Example 8.3. From 30 measurements of direction on the *c*-axis of calcite grains from the Taconic mountains of New York (Bingham, 1964), it is found that the matrix **T** is

$$\begin{bmatrix} 14\cdot1181 & 0\cdot0136 & 2\cdot5596 \\ 0\cdot0136 & 10\cdot5879 & 1\cdot7179 \\ 2\cdot5596 & 1\cdot7179 & 5\cdot2938 \end{bmatrix}.$$

What is the nature of the distribution?

We find that the eigen values and the eigen vectors are

$$\tau_1 = \ 4\cdot1764, \quad \mathbf{t}_1' = (-0\cdot2411, \quad -0\cdot2507, \quad 0\cdot9376),$$
$$\tau_2 = 10\cdot9639, \quad \mathbf{t}_2' = (-0\cdot1760, \quad 0\cdot9613, \quad 0\cdot2118),$$
$$\tau_3 = 14\cdot8595, \quad \mathbf{t}_3' = (0\cdot9544, \quad 0\cdot1140, \quad 0\cdot2759).$$

(Techniques to obtain these quantities can be found in books on multivariate analysis (see Kendall, 1957, pp. 19–25) and the computer programs for this purpose are commonly provided in packages.) Hence, the two largest roots are relatively close and are separated from the smallest root τ_1. Consequently, from Table 8.3, we may say that the distribution is a symmetric girdle distribution with rotational symmetry about $\mathbf{t}_1$. This point will be pursued further in Example 9.13.

8.5. MODELS

8.5.1. Introduction

Let colatitude θ and latitude ϕ be random variables on the surface of a unit sphere. We will mainly be concerned with continuous random variables whose p.d.f. can be reduced to the following form (by a rotation or otherwise).

$$g(\theta, \phi) = f(\theta)/(2\pi), \quad 0 < \theta < \pi, \quad 0 < \phi < 2\pi, \quad (8.5.1)$$

i.e. θ and ϕ are independently distributed, ϕ is uniformly distributed on $(0, 2\pi)$ and θ has the p.d.f. $f(\theta)$. Since the variables are continuous, the half *z*-axis represented by $\theta = 0$ $(\theta = \pi)$ has zero probability.

Let $\mathbf{L}' = (l, m, n)$ be the vector of the direction cosines corresponding to θ, ϕ, i.e.

$$l = \sin\theta \cos\phi, \quad m = \sin\theta \sin\phi, \quad n = \cos\theta. \quad (8.5.2)$$

Let $g_1(l, m, n)$ be the p.d.f. (singular) of (l, m, n). The Jacobian of the transformation of (l, m, n) to (θ, ϕ) is $\sin \theta$ so that

$$g_1(l, m, n)dS = g_1(\sin \theta \cos \phi, \sin \theta \sin \phi, \cos \theta) \sin \theta \, d\theta \, d\phi, \qquad (8.5.3)$$

where dS is the surface element on the sphere. Following Section 8.4.1, it is appropriate to define the population mean direction (λ, μ, ν) as

$$\lambda = E(l)/\rho, \qquad \mu = E(m)/\rho, \qquad \nu = E(n)/\rho, \qquad (8.5.4)$$

where

$$\rho = \{E(l)^2 + E(m)^2 + E(n)^2\}^{\frac{1}{2}} \qquad (8.5.5)$$

is the population resultant length. For the random variable (θ, ϕ) distributed as (8.5.1), it can be seen that the mean direction is the z-axis. Let us define the rth moment of $\cos \theta$ for this case as

$$\lambda_r = E(\cos^r \theta). \qquad (8.5.6)$$

We have $\rho = |\lambda_1|$.

8.5.2. Uniform Distribution

If the directions are uniformly distributed on the surface of a sphere, we have from (8.5.3)

$$g(\theta, \phi) = c \sin \theta \, d\theta \, d\phi, \qquad 0 < \theta < \pi, \quad 0 < \phi < 2\pi.$$

A random variable having uniform distribution is called *isotropic* but if the distribution has a preferred direction, the random variable is called *anisotropic*.

It is easily seen that $c = 1/(4\pi)$ and

$$f(\theta) = \tfrac{1}{2} \sin \theta, \qquad 0 < \theta < \pi. \qquad (8.5.7)$$

Consequently, the random variable $\cos \theta$ is uniformly distributed on $(-1, 1)$. We have

$$\lambda_1 = 0, \qquad \lambda_2 = 1/3, \qquad \lambda_r = \{1 + (-1)^r\}/2(r + 1). \qquad (8.5.8)$$

Irving and Ward (1964) consider the distribution of ψ defined by the transformation

$$\tan \psi = \sigma \sin \theta/(1 + \sigma \cos \theta), \qquad \sigma > 0.$$

The distribution provides a model of the geomagnetic field.

8.5.3. The Brownian Motion Distribution

The Brownian motion distribution on the surface of a sphere is of the form (Perrin, 1928)

$$f(\theta, \phi) = (4\pi)^{-1} \sum_{k=0}^{\infty} (2k + 1) P_k(\cos\theta) e^{-\frac{1}{2}k(k+1)\sigma^2} \sin\theta, \qquad (8.5.9)$$

where P_k is the Legendre polynomial of order k. The point θ measures the angular displacement of the pole in a random walk (the steps being infinitesimal). Roberts and Ursell (1960) have examined a general problem more recently which also simplifies the proof for this limiting case. They have shown that the distribution can be closely approximated by a Fisher distribution (see, Section 8.5.4). A similar investigation on the circle has already been discussed in Section 3.4.9g.

8.5.4. The Fisher Distribution

8.5.4a. *Definition*

Let us consider an extension of the von Mises distribution. Suppose that the circular random variable θ is distributed as $M(\mu_0, \kappa)$. Let us write

$$l = \cos\theta, \qquad m = \sin\theta, \qquad \lambda = \cos\mu_0, \qquad \mu = \sin\mu_0.$$

The p.d.f. of θ reduces to

$$c \exp\{\kappa(l\lambda + m\mu)\}, \qquad \kappa > 0.$$

Its extension to the spherical case is obviously

$$g_1(l, m, n) = c \exp\{\kappa(l\lambda + m\mu + n\nu)\}, \qquad \kappa > 0, \qquad (8.5.10)$$

where the density is defined on the surface of the sphere with unit radius and centre at the origin (the normalizing constant c is derived below at (8.5.12)), and (λ, μ, ν) is expected to be the vector of the direction cosines of the mean direction (shown below). We shall call it the Fisher distribution and denote it by $F\{(\lambda, \mu, \nu), \kappa\}$. If (λ, μ, ν) is the polar axis, we shall simply denote it by $F\{0, \kappa\}$.

    The distribution is unimodal with mode at (λ, μ, ν) and antimode at $(-\lambda, -\mu, -\nu)$. Further, the distribution is unipolar since it is rotationally symmetric about the modal direction.

    Let (μ_0, ν_0) be the polar co-ordinates of the mean direction so that (λ, μ, ν) and (α, β) are related by (8.5.2), i.e.

$$\lambda = \sin\mu_0 \cos\nu_0, \qquad \mu = \sin\mu_0 \sin\nu_0, \qquad \nu = \cos\mu_0.$$

From (8.5.3), we find that the p.d.f. of (θ, ϕ) is given by

$$g_\kappa(\theta, \phi) = c \exp[\kappa\{\cos \mu_0 \cos \theta + \sin \mu_0 \sin \theta \cos(\phi - v_0)\}] \sin \theta, \quad (8.5.11)$$

where $0 < \theta < \pi$, $0 < \phi < 2\pi$ and $\kappa \geq 0$. For $\kappa = 0$, the density reduces to the uniform density (8.5.7). If the pole is at $\mu_0 = v_0 = 0$, we have

$$g(\theta, \phi) = c \, e^{\kappa \cos \theta} \sin \theta, \qquad 0 < \theta < \pi, \quad 0 < \phi < 2\pi, \quad \kappa > 0. \quad (8.5.12)$$

It follows from Section 8.5.1 that the z-axis is the mean direction for (8.5.12). From (8.5.12), we have

$$c = c(\kappa)/2\pi, \qquad c(\kappa) = \kappa/(2 \sinh \kappa). \quad (8.5.13)$$

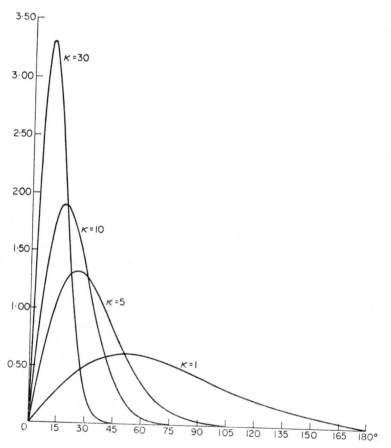

FIG. 8.4. Density of θ for the Fisher distribution for $\kappa = 1, 5, 10, 30$.

The p.d.f. of θ is given by

$$f_\kappa(\theta) = c(\kappa)\, e^{\kappa \cos\theta} \sin\theta, \qquad 0 < \theta < \pi, \qquad \kappa > 0, \qquad (8.5.14)$$

and the p.d.f. of ϕ is, of course,

$$h(\phi) = 1/2\pi, \qquad 0 < \phi < 2\pi. \qquad (8.5.15)$$

Fig. 8.4 shows the density (8.5.14) for some selected values of κ which indicates that the probability mass concentrates about $\theta = 0$ as κ increases.

The shape of the density (8.5.12) can be visualized by imagining the mass to be distributed on the unit sphere. The distribution is rotationally symmetric about the polar axis having a maximum at the north pole $\theta = 0$ and a minimum at the south pole. The mass can roughly be imagined as distributed on the sphere in the shape of a top with the spinning axis as the polar axis and the spinning head towards the north pole. It can roughly be generated by rotating the polar diagram (Fig. 3.3) for the von Mises distribution about the mean direction. The ratio of the distances between the north pole to the top's head and the south pole to the top's base is $e^{2\kappa}$. Hence, the concentration of the mass is much less on the base. For large κ, the mass is concentrated on a small portion of the sphere around the north pole and for $\kappa = 0$, the mass is uniformly distributed. Consequently, we may describe κ as the concentration parameter.

8.5.4b. *History and Characterizations*

The distribution was studied by Fisher (1953) to investigate certain statistical problems in paleomagnetism. Arnold (1941) considered this distribution much earlier who gave a maximum likelihood characterization of this distribution together with the point estimates but the significant advances towards its statistical applications were only made by Fisher (1953) and this fact has led to its present name. In fact, the distribution first appeared in statistical mechanics dating to 1905 in the following context (Langevin, 1905). Let us consider a statistical assemblage of weakly interacting dipoles of moments m which are subject to an external electric field. From the Maxwell–Boltzmann distribution, the p.d.f. of the dipoles with energy U is

$$A \exp(-U/kT), \qquad (8.5.16)$$

where k is the Boltzmann's constant and T is the absolute temperature. If H is the strength of the field and θ is the angle between the dipole and the field, we have

$$U = -mH \cos\theta. \qquad (8.5.17)$$

On using (8.5.17) in (8.5.16), we find that θ has a Fisher distribution. The distribution also appears as an approximate solution to a problem associated with paths and chains of random segments in three dimensions (Kuhn and Grün, 1942).

The Fisher distribution can be characterized by the same two methods which were used for the von Mises distribution in Section 3.4.9f. Let $f(\theta, \phi; \mu_0, v_0)$ be a p.d.f. of (θ, ϕ) with the mean direction at (μ_0, v_0). Let (θ_i, ϕ_i) $i = 1, \ldots, n$ be a random sample of size n from this population and let $z_i = \log f(\theta_i, \phi_i; \mu_0, v_0)$. It can be shown that the maximum likelihood equations

$$\sum_{i=1}^{n} \partial z_i / \partial \mu_0 = 0, \quad \sum_{i=1}^{n} \partial z_i / \partial v_0 = 0$$

for μ_0 and v_0 are equivalent to

$$\sin \mu_0 \, \Sigma \cos \theta_i - \cos \mu_0 \, \Sigma \sin \theta_i \cos (\phi_i - v_0) = 0, \quad \Sigma \sin \theta_i \sin (\phi_i - v_0) = 0$$

(8.5.18)

if and only if the p.d.f. corresponds to a Fisher distribution. This result is due to Arnold (1941) and it is proved by Breitenberger by a simple method. Rao (1965, pp. 141–2) has given the maximum entropy characterization of the Fisher distribution.

8.5.4c. Other Properties

(i) We have from (8.5.14) and (8.5.15)

$$\Pr (\theta_1 < \theta < \theta_2) = (e^{\kappa \cos \theta_1} - e^{\kappa \cos \theta_2})/(e^{\kappa} - e^{-\kappa}),$$

(8.5.19)

and

$$\Pr (\phi_1 < \phi < \phi_2) = (\phi_2 - \phi_1)/2\pi.$$

(8.5.20)

In fact, if $\Pr (\theta > \delta) = \alpha$ then we have

$$\delta = \arccos [-1 + \kappa^{-1} \log \{1 + \alpha(e^{2\kappa} - 1)\}].$$

(8.5.21)

Appendix 3.1 gives some percentage points of θ which will be useful in certain inference problems (Section 9.3.2). We can interpret δ as the semi-vertical angle of a $(1 - \alpha) 100\%$ confidence cone for the observed direction with the true mean direction as its axis. Appendix 3.1 shows that δ decreases as κ increases. If χ_α^2 is the upper α percent point of a chi-square variable with 2 d. of fr., it is found that for moderately large κ,

$$\delta = \chi_\alpha/\sqrt{(\kappa - \tfrac{1}{2})}$$

provides an adequate approximation to (8.5.21). It is based on (8.5.26) that $\kappa\theta^2$ is distributed as χ_2^2 when κ is large. Indeed, for large κ, $e^{-\kappa}$ is negligible and so (8.5.19) gives

$$\Pr(\theta > \delta) = \exp\{-\kappa(1 - \cos\delta)\}. \qquad (8.5.22)$$

There is no difficulty in drawing a random pair (θ_0, ϕ_0) from $F\{0, \kappa\}$. For a random value "α" of the uniform variable on $(0, 1)$, we can obtain $\theta_0 = \delta$ from (8.5.21). A random value ϕ_0 can easily be obtained since ϕ itself is uniformly distributed on $(0, 2\pi)$.

(ii) From (8.5.14), we easily find that the resultant length is

$$\lambda_1 = E(\cos\theta) = \coth\kappa - 1/\kappa = B(\kappa), \text{ say.} \qquad (8.5.23)$$

Similarly, if λ_r is the rth power moment of $\cos\theta$, we have

$$\lambda_r = I_{r+\frac{1}{2}}(\kappa)/I_{\frac{1}{2}}(\kappa), \qquad \lambda_{r+1} = \lambda_{r-1} - \{(2r+1)/\kappa\}\lambda_r, \qquad (8.5.24)$$

where $I_r(\cdot)$ is the Bessel function of the rth order. The function $B(\kappa)$ given by (8.5.23) will be used frequently.

For the Brownian motion distribution, it can be shown that

$$\lambda_1 = \exp(-\tfrac{1}{2}\sigma^2). \qquad (8.5.25)$$

On identifying (8.5.23) to (8.5.25), Roberts and Ursell (1960) have shown that the two distributions can be made to approximate each other very closely. Hence, the methodology for the Fisher distribution will be approximately applicable to the Brownian motion distribution.

(iii) For large κ, we show that

$$\kappa\theta^2 \simeq \chi_2^2. \qquad (8.5.26)$$

We have

$$\cos\theta \doteq 1 - \tfrac{1}{2}\theta^2, \qquad \sin\theta \doteq \theta, \qquad 2\sinh\kappa \doteq e^\kappa,$$

so that (8.5.14) reduces to

$$f(\theta) = \kappa\theta e^{-\frac{1}{2}\kappa\theta^2}.$$

Hence the result follows. We also have

$$2\kappa(1 - \cos\theta) \simeq \chi_2^2. \qquad (8.5.27)$$

(iv) Let x, y and z be independently distributed as $N(0, \kappa^{-\frac{1}{2}})$, $N(0, \kappa^{-\frac{1}{2}})$ and $N(\kappa^{-\frac{1}{2}}, \kappa^{-\frac{1}{2}})$ respectively. On using the polar transformation,

$$x = r\sin\theta\cos\phi, \qquad y = r\sin\theta\sin\phi, \qquad z = r\cos\theta \qquad (8.5.28$$

we find that the joint distribution of θ and ϕ given $r = 1$ is given by (8.5.12). Downs (1966) and Downs and Gould (1967) have investigated this relationship much further.

(v) Let (l, m, n) be distributed as $F\{(\lambda, \mu, \nu), \kappa\}$. Following Downs (1966), we show that the subvector (l, m) constrainted to have unit length has the von Mises distribution $M(\mu_0', \kappa')$ where

$$\kappa' \cos \mu_0' = \kappa\lambda, \qquad \kappa' \sin \mu_0' = \kappa\mu. \tag{8.5.29}$$

That is,

$$\kappa' = \kappa(\lambda^2 + \mu^2)^{\frac{1}{2}}, \qquad \mu_0' = \arctan (\mu/\lambda).$$

Let (θ, ϕ) be distributed as (8.5.11). On transforming θ and ϕ to

$$r \cos \theta' = \sin \theta \cos \phi, \qquad r \sin \theta' = \sin \theta \sin \phi,$$

the joint p.d.f. of r and θ' is found to be

$$\text{const. } \psi(r) \exp \{r\kappa' \cos (\theta' - \mu_0')\}, \tag{8.5.30}$$

where the function $\psi(r)$ does not depend on θ while parameters κ' and μ_0' are defined by

$$\kappa' \cos \mu_0' = \kappa \sin \alpha \cos \beta, \quad \kappa' \sin \mu_0' = \kappa \sin \alpha \sin \beta, \quad \alpha = \mu_0, \quad \beta = \nu_0.$$

On using the relations between (λ, μ, ν) and (α, β), we see that the last expression is equivalent to (8.5.29). Further, the conditional distribution of θ' given $r = 1$ from (8.5.30) is $M(\mu_0', \kappa')$. Hence, the result follows. The same method can be used to show that the subvector (m, n) as well as (l, n) constrainted to have unit length is distributed as a von Mises distribution.

8.5.5. Axial Distributions

We now consider distributions concentrated on a hemisphere. It is convenient to represent these distributions on the whole sphere by assigning the same probability to the diametrically opposite point. Hence, these distributions can be considered as axial distributions. It may be noted that if $g_1(l, m, n)$ denotes the p.d.f. of an axial distribution then it possesses antipodal symmetry, i.e.

$$g_1(-l, -m, -n) = g_1(l, m, n).$$

8.5.5a. Dimroth–Watson's Distribution

Consider a distribution with p.d.f.

$$f_1(l, m, n) = \{b(\kappa)/2\pi\} \exp \{-\kappa(l\lambda + m\mu + n\nu)^2\}, \quad -\infty < \kappa < \infty, \tag{8.5.31}$$

where $b(\kappa)$ is the normalizing constant and is obtained below. We first assume that $\kappa > 0$. It is rotationally symmetric about (λ, μ, ν) and is highly concentrated around the great circle contained in the plane orthogonal to (λ, μ, ν). Hence, the distribution is a symmetric girdle distribution. On taking (λ, μ, ν) as the z-axis, the p.d.f. given by (8.5.31) in polar co-ordinates is

$$f_2(\theta, \phi) = \{b(\kappa)/2\pi\}\, e^{-\kappa \cos^2\theta} \sin\theta, \quad 0 < \theta < \pi,\ 0 < \phi < 2\pi,\ \kappa > 0. \quad (8.5.32)$$

From (8.5.32), we can easily show that

$$b(\kappa) = 1 \Big/ \Big(2\int_0^1 e^{-\kappa t^2}\, dt\Big). \quad (8.5.33)$$

The density of (θ, ϕ) on the surface of a sphere is clearly seen to have a maximum about the great circle $\theta = \frac{1}{2}\pi$, i.e. the density is concentrated around the equator. The shape of the density on the surface of a unit sphere will be similar to an ellipsoid having its section circular in the x–y plane. As κ increases, the distribution becomes more concentrated about the equator and we may therefore regard κ as a concentration parameter. The distribution was studied and introduced independently by Dimroth (1962, 1963) and Watson (1965).

For $\kappa < 0$, (8.5.31) and (8.5.32) still represent a density. We rewrite (8.5.22) as

$$f(\theta, \phi) = \{b(-\kappa')/2\pi\}\, e^{\kappa' \cos^2\theta} \sin\theta, \quad 0 < \theta < \pi, \quad 0 < \phi < 2\pi, \quad \kappa' > 0. \quad (8.5.34)$$

The density has maximum values at the poles $\theta = 0, \pi$ and is rotationally symmetric about the z-axis. Consequently, it represents a bipolar distribution.

8.5.5b. *Bingham's Distribution*

Let $\mathbf{L} = (l, m, n)'$ represent the random variable associated with the conditional distribution of a trivariate normal vector with zero mean and arbitrary covariance matrix given that the length of the vector is unity. It is found that the p.d.f. of $\mathbf{L}$ is of the form

$$f(\mathbf{L}; \boldsymbol\mu, \boldsymbol\kappa) = \{4\pi d(\boldsymbol\kappa)\}^{-1} \exp\{\kappa_1(\mathbf{L}'\boldsymbol\mu_1)^2 + \kappa_2(\mathbf{L}'\boldsymbol\mu_2)^2 + \kappa_3(\mathbf{L}'\boldsymbol\mu_3)^2\}, \quad (8.5.35)$$

where $\boldsymbol\kappa = \mathrm{diag}\,(\kappa_1, \kappa_2, \kappa_3)$ is a matrix of constants, $\boldsymbol\mu_1, \boldsymbol\mu_2, \boldsymbol\mu_3$ are three orthogonal (normalized) vectors, $\boldsymbol\mu = (\boldsymbol\mu_1, \boldsymbol\mu_2, \boldsymbol\mu_3)$, and $d(\boldsymbol\kappa)$ is a constant which depends only on κ_1, κ_2 and κ_3. This distribution is called Bingham's distribution (Bingham, 1964). We shall show that the distribution contains various important forms.

Normalizing Constant. Let us select μ_1, μ_2, μ_3 as three co-ordinate axes so that $\mu = I$. Suppose that (θ, ϕ) are the new polar co-ordinates of the vector $L = (l, m, n)'$. From (8.1.2) and (8.5.35), the p.d.f. of (θ, ϕ) is given by

$$g(\theta, \phi; \kappa) = \{4\pi d(\kappa)\}^{-1} \left[\exp\{(\kappa_1 \cos^2 \phi + \kappa_2 \sin^2 \phi) \sin^2 \theta + \kappa_3 \cos^2 \theta\}\right] \sin \theta,$$

$$(8.5.36)$$

where $0 < \theta < \pi$ and $0 < \phi < 2\pi$. We have

$$d(\kappa) = (4\pi)^{-1} \int_0^\pi \int_0^{2\pi} \exp\{\kappa_1 \cos^2 \phi \sin^2 \theta\}$$

$$\times \exp\{\kappa_2 \sin^2 \phi \sin^2 \theta\} \exp\{\kappa_3 \cos^2 \theta\} \sin \theta \, d\theta \, d\phi.$$

On expanding the exponentials and changing the order of integration, the above expression reduces to

$$d(\kappa) = (4\pi)^{-1} \sum_{i,j,k=0}^{\infty} \frac{\kappa_1{}^i \kappa_2{}^j \kappa_3{}^k}{i! \, j! \, k!}$$

$$\times \int_0^\pi \int_0^{2\pi} (\sin\theta)^{2i+2j+1} (\cos\theta)^{2k} (\cos\phi)^{2i} (\sin\phi)^{2j} \, d\theta \, d\phi.$$

Hence, we find that

$$d(\kappa) = (2\pi)^{-1} \sum_{i,j,k=0}^{\infty} \frac{\Gamma(i + \tfrac{1}{2}) \Gamma(j + \tfrac{1}{2}) \Gamma(k + \tfrac{1}{2})}{\Gamma(i + j + k + \tfrac{3}{2})} \frac{\kappa_1{}^i \kappa_2{}^j \kappa_3{}^k}{i! \, j! \, k!} \qquad (8.5.37)$$

It can further be shown that

$$d(\kappa) = {}_1F_1(\tfrac{1}{2}; \tfrac{3}{2}; \kappa),$$

where ${}_1F_1$ is a confluent hypergeometric function with matrix argument κ as defined by Herz (1955).

Degeneracy. We have

$$(L'\mu_1)^2 + (L'\mu_2)^2 + (L'\mu_3)^2 = 1$$

so that (8.5.35) can be written for any κ as

$$\{4\pi d(\kappa)\}^{-1} \exp\{(\kappa_1 - \kappa)(L'\mu_1)^2 + (\kappa_2 - \kappa)(L'\mu_2)^2 + (\kappa_3 - \kappa)(L'\mu_3)^2\}.$$

$$(8.5.38)$$

Hence the sum of the parameters κ_j is arbitrary and therefore one of the κ_j may be taken as zero. We shall take $\kappa_3 = 0$.

Particular Cases. On considering (8.5.35) and (8.5.36), the following results can be deduced. (i) For $\kappa_1 = \kappa_2 = \kappa_3$, the distribution reduces to the uniform distribution. (ii) For $\kappa_2 = \kappa_3 \,(=0)$, (8.5.36) reduces to Dimroth–Watson's distribution given by (8.5.31). Hence, the distribution is symmetric girdle distribution for $\kappa_1 < 0$ while the distribution is bipolar for $\kappa_1 > 0$. (iii) For $\kappa_1 \gg \kappa_2, \kappa_3 = 0$, the distribution is an asymmetrical axial distribution while for $\kappa_1 \ll \kappa_2 \leqslant 0, \kappa_3 = 0$, it is an asymmetrical girdle distribution. Hence for this distribution all the three principal axes of the moment of inertia have significance.

For $\kappa_1 = \kappa, \kappa_2 = \kappa_3 = 0$, we have from (8.5.31) and (8.5.36)

$$d(\mathbf{\kappa}) = 1/2b(-\kappa).$$

Hence, using (8.5.37), the integral in $b(\kappa)$ can be expressed in terms of the standard confluent hypergeometric series.

The density (8.5.31) appeared in Breitenberger (1963) in studying the characterization of distributions which minimize the moments of inertia. Bingham (1964) investigated this distribution extensively for statistical applications.

8.5.5c. *Other Axial Distributions*

Arnold (1941) and Selby (1964) have investigated girdle distributions of the form

$$c_1 \exp\left(-\kappa|\cos\theta|\right) dS, \qquad c_2 \exp\left(\kappa \sin\theta\right) dS$$

where dS is the surface element of the sphere. Stephens (1969f) has considered a mixture of two Fisher distributions. The maximum likelihood estimates for these distributions are complicated and these distributions do not seem to possess any natural characterization.

8.6. DISTRIBUTION THEORY

We obtain the distributions of the resultant length and of some other statistics for random samples from the uniform and the Fisher distributions. We use a result on the characteristic function of the polar random variables which is analogous to that used in the circular case (see, Sections 4.2.3 and 4.4). In the following discussion, the details are omitted if they are similar to the circular case.

8.6.1. The Characteristic Function and Polar Distributions

Let $\phi(u, v, w)$ be the c.f. of a three dimensional random variable (x, y, z). We assume that ϕ is integrable. By the inversion theorem, the p.d.f. of

(x, y, z) is given by

$$(2\pi)^{-3} \iiint \exp\{-i(ux + vy + wz)\} \phi(u, v, w) \, du \, dv \, dw, \qquad (8.6.1)$$

where the integration is taken over $-\infty < u, v, w < \infty$. Let us transform the variables (u, v, w) to (ρ, α, β) by

$$u = \rho \sin \alpha \cos \beta, \qquad v = \rho \sin \alpha \sin \beta, \qquad w = \rho \cos \alpha.$$

Then the p.d.f. of the polar random variables r, θ and ϕ defined by

$$x = r \sin \theta \cos \phi, \qquad y = r \sin \theta \sin \phi, \qquad z = r \cos \theta$$

is found from (8.6.1) to be

$$g(r, \theta, \phi) = (2\pi)^{-3} r^2 \sin \theta \int_0^\infty \int_0^\pi \int_0^{2\pi} \exp[-i\rho \, r\{\cos \alpha \cos \theta$$

$$+ \sin \alpha \sin \theta \cos (\phi - \beta)\}] \phi(u, v, w) \rho^2 \sin \alpha \, d\rho \, d\alpha \, d\beta. \qquad (8.6.2)$$

To obtain the p.d.f. of r, we first integrate (8.6.2) over θ and ϕ and then transform (θ, ϕ) to (θ^*, ϕ^*) by the orthogonal transformation

$$\mathbf{L}^* = \mathbf{AL}, \qquad (8.6.3)$$

where $\mathbf{A}$ is given by (8.4.6), $\mathbf{L} = (l, m, n)'$,

$$l = \sin \theta \cos \phi, \qquad m = \sin \theta \sin \phi, \qquad n = \cos \theta,$$

and $\mathbf{L}^*$ is the vector of the direction cosines corresponding to (θ^*, ϕ^*). The transformation (8.6.3) amounts to shifting the pole of reference to (α, β). On evaluating the resulting integral with respect to θ^* and ϕ^*, we find that the p.d.f. of r simplifies to

$$g(r) = 2(2\pi)^{-2} r \int_0^\infty \int_0^\pi \int_0^{2\pi} \rho \sin (\rho r) \phi(u, v, w) \sin \alpha \, d\rho \, d\alpha \, d\beta, \qquad (8.6.4)$$

where

$$\phi(u, v, w) = E\{\exp[i\rho r\{\cos \alpha \cos \theta + \sin \alpha \sin \theta \cos (\phi - \beta)\}]\}. \qquad (8.6.5)$$

We can now obtain the p.d.f. of the length of the resultant for a random sample. The method is illustrated by considering an important case. Let $(\theta_i, \phi_i) \, i = 1, ..., n$ be a random sample from a population with p.d.f. of the form (see Section 8.5.1)

$$g(\theta, \phi) = f(\theta)/(2\pi), \qquad 0 < \theta < \pi, \quad 0 < \phi < 2\pi.$$

The c.f. given by (8.6.5) is valid for singular distributions with $r = 1$. For this case, after integrating over ϕ, it is found that

$$\phi(u, v, w) = \int_0^\pi \exp\{i\rho \cos\alpha \cos\theta\}$$
$$\times J_0(\rho \sin\alpha \sin\theta) f(\theta)\, d\theta = \psi(\rho, \alpha), \text{ say,} \quad (8.6.6)$$

which does not depend on β. Let (l_i, m_i, n_i) be the direction cosines corresponding to (θ_i, ϕ_i), $i = 1, \ldots, n$. The joint c.f. of $(\Sigma l_i, \Sigma m_i, \Sigma n_i)$ is

$$\psi^n(\rho, \alpha). \quad (8.6.7)$$

On assuming that the distribution of R is continuous, we find from (8.6.4) that the p.d.f. of R is given by

$$2(2\pi)^{-1} R \int_0^\infty \int_0^\pi \rho(\sin \rho R)\, \psi^n(\rho, \alpha) \sin\alpha\, d\rho\, d\alpha. \quad (8.6.8)$$

Analogous results for the circular case are given in Section 4.2.3.

8.6.2. Isotropic Case

8.6.2a. *The Distribution of R*

Let (θ_i, ϕ_i), $i = 1, \ldots, n$ be a random sample from the uniform distribution with p.d.f.

$$g(\theta, \phi) = (4\pi)^{-1} \sin\theta, \quad 0 < \theta < \pi, \quad 0 < \phi < 2\pi. \quad (8.6.9)$$

From (8.6.6), we can obtain the c.f. $\phi(u, v, w)$ but in this case it is simpler to use (8.6.5) directly. For $r = 1$, we have form (8.6.5) and (8.6.9),

$$\phi(u, v, w) = (4\pi)^{-1} \int_0^\pi \int_0^{2\pi} \exp[i\rho\{\cos\alpha \cos\theta$$
$$+ \sin\alpha \sin\theta \cos(\phi - \beta)\}] \sin\theta\, d\theta\, d\phi.$$

On transforming (θ, ϕ) to (θ^*, ϕ^*) by the orthogonal transformation (8.6.3), we obtain

$$\phi(u, v, w) = (4\pi)^{-1} \int_0^\pi \int_0^{2\pi} e^{i\rho \cos\theta} \sin\theta\, d\theta\, d\phi = (\sin\rho)/\rho.$$

Hence the joint c.f. of $(\Sigma l_i, \Sigma m_i, \Sigma n_i)$ is

$$\{(\sin\rho)/\rho\}^n. \quad (8.6.10)$$

Consequently, the p.d.f. of R from (8.6.4) is

$$h_n(R) = (2/\pi) R \int_0^\infty \rho(\sin \rho R)\{(\sin \rho)/\rho\}^n \, d\rho. \tag{8.6.11}$$

Let us now consider the case when the length of the ith observed vector is preassigned to be β_i rather than unity. Using the same argument as above the p.d.f. of R is found to be

$$h_n^*(R; \beta_1, ..., \beta_n) = (2/\pi) R \int_0^\infty \rho(\sin \rho R) \prod_{i=1}^n \{(\sin \rho\beta_i)/\rho\beta_i\} \, d\rho. \tag{8.6.12}$$

We now simplify (8.6.12). Let $U_1, ..., U_n$ be n independently and uniformly distributed variables. Suppose that the range of the ith variable is $(-\beta_i, \beta_i)$, $i = 1, ..., n$. By the c.f. method, the distribution of $x = \Sigma U_i$ is easily seen to be

$$b(x) = \pi^{-1} \int_0^\infty \cos tx \prod_{i=1}^n \{(\sin t\beta_i)/t\beta_i\} \, dt. \tag{8.6.13}$$

From (8.6.12) and (8.6.13), we obtain the relation

$$h_n^*(R; \beta_1, ..., \beta_n) = -2R\{db(R)/dR\}. \tag{8.6.14}$$

Hence, to simplify the function h^* in (8.6.12), it is necessary to obtain the distribution of x.

To transform the range of U_i to $(0, \beta_i)$, we consider the variables

$$U_i' = (\beta_i - U_i)/2, \quad 0 < U_i' < \beta_i, \quad i = 1, ..., n.$$

Suppose that

$$y = \Sigma U_i' = \{(\Sigma\beta_i) - x\}/2. \tag{8.6.15}$$

By the method of induction, it can be seen that the p.d.f. of y is

$$a(y) = \left\{(n-1)! \prod_{i=1}^n \beta_i\right\}^{-1} \sum_{r=0}^n (-1)^r \Sigma^* \left(y - \sum_{i=1}^r \beta_{k_i}\right)_+^{n-1} \tag{8.6.16}$$

where $(k_1, ..., k_r)$ is one of the $\binom{n}{r}$ combinations of $(1, ..., n)$, Σ^* is extended over all possible combinations, and

$$(y)_+ = 0 \quad \text{if} \quad y < 0, \quad (y)_+ = y \quad \text{if} \quad y > 0.$$

On using the transformation (8.6.15), we obtain the p.d.f. $b(x)$ from (8.6.16) and on substituting this $b(x)$ into (8.6.14), it is found that

$$h_n^*(R; \beta_1, \ldots, \beta_n) = 2^{-n+1} R \left\{ (n-2)! \prod_{i=1}^{n} \beta_i \right\}^{-1}$$

$$\times \sum_{r=0}^{n} (-1)^r \Sigma^* \left(\sum_{i=1}^{n} \beta_i - R - 2 \sum_{i=1}^{r} \beta_{k_i} \right)_+^{n-2}. \quad (8.6.17)$$

In particular, for $\beta_1 = \ldots = \beta_n = 1$, the p.d.f. of R is given by

$$h_n(R) = 2^{-n+1} R \, \Phi_n(R), \quad (8.6.18)$$

where

$$\Phi_{n,m}(R) = (1/m!) \sum_{r=0}^{n} (-1)^r \binom{n}{r} (n - R - 2r)_+^m, \quad \Phi_{n,n-2}(R) \equiv \Phi_n(R). \quad (8.6.19)$$

For $n = 2$ and $n = 3$, (8.6.18) simplifies to

$$h_2(R) = R/2, \quad 0 < R < 2, \quad (8.6.20)$$

$$h_3(R) = R(3 - R)/4, \quad 1 < R < 3; \quad = R^2/2, \quad 0 < R < 1. \quad (8.6.21)$$

Another version of (8.6.17) can be obtained by putting $U_i' = (U_i - \beta_i)/2$ in (8.6.15).

Rayleigh (1919) derived the p.d.f. of R given by (8.6.11) for the unit length case. For the equal length case $\beta_1 = \ldots = \beta_n$, Quenouille (1947) derived the series from (8.6.18) by an induction method. Fisher (1953) independently derived the form (8.6.18). Feller (1966, pp. 31–2) has given a simple proof of (8.6.18) but the method is applicable only to the uniform case (see Section 8.6.2b). An excellent account of Rayleigh's solution and other general approaches for the random walk problem is given by Chandrasekhar (1943). Vincez and Bruckshaw (1960) obtained a recurrence relation for the equal length case and gave an expanded version of (8.6.18) for $n = 3$ upto $n = 8$. Some of these particular forms were first obtained by Rayleigh (1919) and Chandrasekhar (1943). The general case (8.6.17) has not been investigated before. An alternative method for deriving the distribution of the sum of uniform variables (8.6.16) is given in Gray and Odell (1966) who also give references to various other proofs of (8.6.16). A test of uniformity based on R was first explicity formulated by Watson (1956b) and will be discussed in Section 9.3.1. The moments of R and its limiting distribution will be given in Section 8.7.

8.6.2b. *Distributions of R_x, R_y and R_z*

Let (l_i, m_i, n_i) be the ith vector of the direction cosines corresponding to (θ_i, ϕ_i), $i = 1, ..., n$ and let $(\bar{x}_0, \bar{y}_0)$ be the polar co-ordinates of the direction of the resultant. We have

$$R_x = \Sigma l_i = R \sin \bar{x}_0 \cos \bar{y}_0, \quad R_y = \Sigma m_i = R \sin \bar{x}_0 \sin \bar{y}_0, \quad R_z = \Sigma n_i = R \cos \bar{x}_0.$$
$$(8.6.22)$$

Using the joint c.f. of (R_x, R_y, R_z) given by (8.6.10), we see from (8.6.2) and (8.6.18) that the joint p.d.f. of R, $\bar{x}_0$ and $\bar{y}_0$ is

$$h_0(R, \bar{x}_0, \bar{y}_0) = (4\pi)^{-1} h_n(R) \sin \bar{x}_0, \quad R > 0, \; 0 < \bar{x}_0 < \pi, \; 0 < \bar{y}_0 < 2\pi. \quad (8.6.23)$$

On transforming the variables $R, \bar{x}_0, \bar{y}_0$ to R_x, R_y, R_z by using (8.6.22), we find that the joint p.d.f. of the three components is given by

$$h_0(R_x, R_y, R_z) = (4\pi)^{-1} h_n(R)/R^2. \quad (8.6.24)$$

From (8.6.23), we find that R, $\bar{x}_0$ and $\bar{y}_0$ are independently distributed and $\bar{x}_0$ and $\bar{y}_0$ are uniformly distributed on the surface of a unit sphere. Further,

$$c = \cos \bar{x}_0 \quad (8.6.25)$$

is uniformly distributed on $(-1, 1)$ so that the joint p.d.f. of R and c is simply

$$f(R, c) = h_n(R)/2, \quad R > 0, \quad -1 < c < 1. \quad (8.6.26)$$

We now obtain the marginal distribution of R_z. We have

$$R_z = \Sigma \cos \theta_i = Rc. \quad (8.6.27)$$

Since the $\cos \theta_i$ are independently and uniformly distributed on $(-1, 1)$ (see Section (8.5.2), the density fn. of R_z from (8.6.17) is given by

$$f(R_z) = 2^{-n} \Phi_{n,n-1}(R_z), \quad |R_z| < n, \quad (8.6.28)$$

where $\Phi(\cdot)$ is defined at (8.6.19). Conversely, we can use (8.6.26)–(8.6.28) to obtain the distribution of R. This method is due to Feller (1966, pp. 31–2).

8.6.3. The Fisher Distribution

8.6.3a. *Single Sample Case*

We now obtain the joint distribution of $(R, \bar{x}_0, \bar{y}_0)$ for samples from the Fisher distribution. Suppose that (l_i, m_i, n_i), $i = 1, ..., n$ is a random sample from $F\{(\mu, \lambda, \nu), \kappa\}$. Without any loss of generality, assume that $(\mu, \lambda, \nu) = (0, 0, 1)$ so that the p.d.f. corresponding to $F\{0, \kappa\}$ is given by

$$f_\kappa(l, m, n) = 2c(\kappa)\, e^{\kappa \cos \theta} f_0(l, m, n), \qquad (8.6.29)$$

where $f_0(l, m, n)$ is the p.d.f. of (l, m, n) under uniformity, i.e. when $\kappa = 0$. On writing the likelihood function of (l_i, m_i, n_i), $i = 1, \ldots, n$ and integrating it over constant values of (R_x, R_y, R_z), we obtain

$$h_\kappa(R_x, R_y, R_z) = \{2c(\kappa)\}^n\, e^{\kappa R_z}\, h_0(R_x, R_y, R_z), \qquad (8.6.30)$$

where h_0 is given by (8.6.24). A similar argument was adopted to obtain the distribution of (C, S) in the circular case (see Section 4.5.2). Using the polar transformation (8.6.22), we find that the joint p.d.f. of $(R, \bar{x}_0, \bar{y}_0)$ is

$$g_\kappa(R, \bar{x}_0, \bar{y}_0) = (4\pi)^{-1} \{2c(\kappa)\}^n\, h_n(R)\, e^{\kappa R \cos \bar{x}_0} \sin \bar{x}_0, \qquad (8.6.31)$$

where $R > 0$, $0 < \bar{x}_0 < \pi$, $0 < \bar{y}_0 < 2\pi$, $\kappa > 0$ and $h_n(R)$ is the p.d.f. of R for the uniform case given by (8.6.18). After integrating with respect to $\bar{x}_0$ and $\bar{y}_0$, we find that the p.d.f. of R is given by

$$h_n^{(\kappa)}(R) = \tfrac{1}{2}\{2c(\kappa)\}^n\, h_n(R)/c(\kappa R), \qquad R > 0, \quad \kappa > 0, \qquad (8.6.32)$$

where $c(\kappa)$ is equal to $\{\kappa/2 \sinh \kappa\}$. This result is due to Fisher (1953). Further, from (8.6.31) and (8.6.32), we see that the conditional p.d.f. of $(\bar{x}_0, \bar{y}_0)$ given R is

$$f(\bar{x}_0, \bar{y}_0 | R) = \{c(\kappa R)/2\pi\}\, e^{\kappa R \cos \bar{x}_0} \sin \bar{x}_0, \qquad (8.6.33)$$

which is precisely the distribution corresponding to $F\{0, \kappa R\}$. If the underlying population is $F\{(\lambda, \mu, \nu), \kappa\}$, the distribution of R remains the same but the mean direction $(\bar{x}_0, \bar{y}_0)$ given R is distributed as $F\{(\lambda, \mu, \nu), \kappa R\}$.

We can also prove (8.6.31) by obtaining the c.f. (8.6.6) and then using (8.6.2) as was done for the uniform case. However, this method involves certain complicated results on Bessel functions.

By the same argument as above, we find from (8.6.30) and (8.6.28) that the p.d.f. of R_z is given by

$$\{c(\kappa)\}^n\, e^{\kappa R_z}\, \Phi_{n, n-1}(R_z), \qquad |R_z| < n. \qquad (8.6.34)$$

On transforming $\bar{x}_0$ in (8.6.31) to R_z by $R_z = R \cos \bar{x}_0$, we find after integrating over $\bar{y}_0$ that the joint p.d.f. of R and R_z is given by

$$\{c(\kappa)\}^n\, e^{\kappa R_z}\, \Phi_n(R), \qquad (8.6.35)$$

where $\Phi_n(\cdot)$ is defined at (8.6.19). On using (8.6.34), we find that the p.d.f. of R given R_z is simply

$$f(R|R_z, \kappa) = \Phi_n(R)/\Phi_{n,n-1}(R_z), \qquad |R_z| < R < n, \qquad (8.6.36)$$

which does not involve κ. The result is due to Watson and Williams (1956). Let $1 - S(R_z, \kappa)$ be the d.f. of R_z. Stephens (1967) has shown that

$$\mathrm{Pr}\,(R > R_0) = S(R_0, \kappa) + S(R_0, -\kappa) + 2\{c(\kappa)\}^n (\sinh \kappa R_0)\, \phi_{n,n-1}(R_0)/\kappa.$$

This result is useful in obtaining numerically the d.f. of R from the d.f. of R_z.

8.6.3b. Multi-sample Case

Let $(l_{ij}, m_{ij}, n_{ij}), j = 1, ..., n_i, i = 1, ..., q$ be q independent random samples from $F\{(\mu, \lambda, \nu), \kappa\}$. Let

$$R^2 = (\Sigma R_{x,i})^2 + (\Sigma R_{y,i})^2 + (\Sigma R_{z,i})^2, \quad R_i^2 = R_{x,i}^2 + R_{y,i}^2 + R_{z,i}^2, \quad i = 1, ..., q,$$

where

$$R_{x,i} = \Sigma l_{ij}, \qquad R_{y,i} = \Sigma m_{ij}, \qquad R_{z,i} = \Sigma n_{ij}.$$

Let us first consider the uniform case. The p.d.f. of R given $\mathbf{R}^* = (R_1, ..., R_q)'$ from (8.6.17) is precisely $h_q^*(R; \mathbf{R}^*)$. Let c be the cosine of the angle between the combined resultant and (μ, λ, ν). As in (8.6.26), the p.d.f. of (R, c) given $\mathbf{R}^*$ is $h_q^*(R; \mathbf{R}^*)/2$. However, the joint p.d.f. of $\mathbf{R}^*$ is

$$\prod_{i=1}^{q} h_{n_i}(R_i).$$

Hence, the joint p.d.f. of $(R, c, R_1, ..., R_q)$ is

$$f_0(R, c, \mathbf{R}^*) = \tfrac{1}{2} h_q^*(R; \mathbf{R}^*) \prod_{i=1}^{q} h_{n_i}(R_i), \qquad (8.6.37)$$

where $h^*(\cdot)$ is given by (8.6.17). By using the same argument which was used in obtaining (8.6.30), it is found that

$$f_\kappa(R, c, \mathbf{R}^*) = \{2c(\kappa)\}^n e^{\kappa R c} f_0(R, c, \mathbf{R}^*), \qquad (8.6.38)$$

where $0 < R^2 < \Sigma R_i^2$, $-1 < c < 1$, $\kappa > 0$. Thus, on substituting (8.6.37) in (8.6.38), the distribution of $(R, c, \mathbf{R}^*)$ is known. After integrating (8.6.38) over c and dividing the resulting expression by the p.d.f. of R given at (8.6.32), we find that the conditional distribution of $\mathbf{R}^*$ given R reduces to

$$f_\kappa(R_1, \ldots, R_q | R) = \{\Pi\Phi_{n_i}(R_i)\}/\{\Phi_n(R)(q-2)!\}$$

$$\times \sum_{r=0}^{q}(-1)^r \Sigma^* \left(\sum_{i=1}^{q} R_i - R - 2\sum_{j=1}^{r} R_{k_j}\right)_+^{q-2}, \quad (8.6.39)$$

which does not involve κ. For the notation Σ^* and Φ, see (8.6.16) and (8.6.19).

For the two-sample case, it reduces to

$$f_\kappa(R_1, R_2 | R) = \Phi_{n_1}(R_1)\,\Phi_{n_2}(R_2)/\Phi_n(R), \quad (8.6.40)$$

where

$$0 \leqslant R_1 \leqslant n_1, \quad 0 \leqslant R_2 \leqslant n_2, \quad 0 \leqslant R \leqslant n, \quad |R_1 - R_2| \leqslant R \leqslant R_1 + R_2.$$
$$(8.6.41)$$

This particular case is due to Fisher (1953). Other attempts to obtain (8.6.39) were unsuccessful and the result is new. Indeed, a conjecture of Watson and Williams (1956) was shown to be false by Stephens (1967).

8.7. MOMENTS AND LIMITING DISTRIBUTIONS

We shall assume that θ and ϕ are independently distributed and that ϕ is uniformly distributed on $(0, 2\pi)$. We can obtain the moments of (R_x, R_y, R_z) by following the method usually used for the multivariate case. Its asymptotic normality follows by the central limit theorem provided that the population resultant length ρ defined by (8.5.5) is positive.

The raw moments of R^2 can be obtained as follows. We have

$$E(R^2) = E\{\Sigma(l_i^2 + m_i^2 + n_i^2) + \Sigma(l_il_j + m_im_j + n_in_j)\}.$$

Since

$$l_i^2 + m_i^2 + n_i^2 = 1, \quad E(l_i) = E(m_i) = 0, \quad E(n_i) = E(\cos\theta),$$

the above expression reduces to

$$E(R^2) = n + n(n-1)\lambda_1^2 = n + n(n-1)\rho^2 \quad (8.7.1)$$

The method can similarly be used to obtain the higher moments of R^2.

8.7.1. The Uniform Case

From (8.5.6) $\lambda_1 = 0$ so that (8.7.1) gives

$$E(R^2) = n. \tag{8.7.2}$$

By following the method described above and using (8.5.8), we find that

$$\text{var}\,(R^2) = 2n(n-1)/3. \tag{8.7.3}$$

Haldane (1960) has given the first five cumulants of R^2. The method of Johnson (1966) for obtaining the moments of R^2 is simple and this paper also contains a survey of the related work. Another method which uses the polar c.f. of R (8.6.10) is given by Lord (1954).

Let us now consider the asymptotic distribution of R. The vector (l, m, n) has zero mean vector and covariance matrix $(1/3)\mathbf{I}$ since

$$E(l) = 0, \qquad E(l^2) = \lambda_2 = 1/3, \qquad E(lm) = 0;$$

the other moments follow by symmetry. Hence, (R_x, R_y, R_z) is distributed asymptotically as $N(0, (n/3)\mathbf{I})$ and therefore

$$3R^2/n \simeq \chi_3^2. \tag{8.7.4}$$

This result was first proved by Rayleigh (1919). Johnson (1966) and Stephens (1967) have approximated the distribution of R by a beta curve and Pearson curves respectively.

8.7.2. The Fisher Distribution

(a) Let (l, m, n) be distributed as $F\{0, \kappa\}$. From (8.5.23), we have

$$E(R_z) = nB(\kappa) = n(\coth \kappa - \kappa^{-1}). \tag{8.7.5}$$

If κ_r is the rth cumulant of R_z, we have as for the von Mises case (Section 4.8) that

$$\kappa_{r+1} = n(\mathrm{d}\kappa_r/\mathrm{d}\kappa), \qquad r \neq 0.$$

Hence, on using (8.7.5), we obtain

$$\text{var}\,(R_z) = n(\kappa^{-2} - \text{cosech}^2\,\kappa) = nB'(\kappa). \tag{8.7.6}$$

By the central limit theorem, R_z is asymptotically normal with mean and variance (8.7.5) and (8.7.6) provided that $\kappa > 0$.

From (8.7.1) and (8.7.5), we have

$$E(R^2) = n + n(n-1)\,B^2(\kappa). \tag{8.7.7}$$

Let μ_s be the sth raw moment of R. We find on following the technique for the von Mises case in Section 4.7.2 that

$$\mu_{2s} = \mu_{2s-2}'' + 2p_1\,\mu_{2s-2}' + (p_1^2 + p_2)\,\mu_{2s-2}, \qquad (8.7.8)$$

where μ', μ'' are the derivatives of μ with respect to κ and

$$p_1 = nB(\kappa) + \kappa^{-1}, \qquad p_2 = p_1'. \qquad (8.7.9)$$

For $s = 2$, we deduce that

$$E(R^4) = p_4 + 4p_1 p_3 + 6p_1^2 p_2 + 3p_2^2 + p_1^4,$$

where $p_r(\kappa)$ is the rth derivative of $\log \kappa - n \log c(\kappa)$. Stephens (1967) has also given higher order moments of R^2 using a different recurrence relation.

An application of the lemma of Section 4.9 shows that

$$(R - p_1)\,p_2^{-\frac{1}{2}} \simeq N(0, 1), \qquad (8.7.10)$$

where p_1 and p_2 are given by (8.7.9), i.e.

$$E(R) \doteq nB(\kappa) + \kappa^{-1}, \qquad \mathrm{var}\,(R) \doteq nB'(\kappa) - \kappa^{-2}. \qquad (8.7.11)$$

(b) We now give some approximations for large κ. From (8.5.27), it immediately follows that

$$2\kappa(n - R_z) \simeq \chi_{2n}^2. \qquad (8.7.12)$$

We show now that

$$2\kappa(R - R_z) \simeq \chi_2^2. \qquad (8.7.13)$$

For large κ and small θ, the joint distribution of $w = \kappa\theta^2$ and ϕ is

$$(4\pi)^{-1}\,e^{-\frac{1}{2}w}\,dw\,d\phi. \qquad (8.7.14)$$

We have $l^2 + m^2 \doteq \theta^2$, $\tan\phi = l/m$ so that from (8.7.14), l and m are independently distributed as $N(0, 1/\kappa^{\frac{1}{2}})$. Consequently, R_x and R_y are independent $N(0, (n/\kappa)^{\frac{1}{2}})$ and

$$(R_x^2 + R_y^2)\,\kappa/n \simeq \chi_2^2, \qquad \text{i.e.} \quad (R^2 - R_z^2)\,\kappa/n \simeq \chi_2^2.$$

Finally, for large κ, $R \doteq R_z \doteq n$ so that (8.7.13) follows. An alternative derivation can be found in Section 9.3.2a.

From (8.7.12) and (8.7.13), we deduce that

$$2\kappa(n - R) \simeq \chi_{2n-2}^2. \qquad (8.7.15)$$

Further, (8.7.14) and (8.7.15) will be independently distributed for large κ. Hence, the two components (8.7.14) and (8.7.15) of (8.7.12) behave in the same way as the components in the usual analysis of variance decomposition. These results are due to Watson (1956a). Stephens (1967) has shown that these approximations are tolerable for κ as low as 3 and are accurate for $\kappa \geqslant 5$.

The approximation (8.7.15) can, however, be improved. By comparing the exact upper tail area of R with the modified approximation

$$2\gamma(n - R) \simeq \chi^2_{2n-2}, \qquad \gamma^{-1} = \kappa^{-1} - \tfrac{1}{5}\kappa^{-3} \qquad (8.7.16)$$

it is found that this approximation is quite satisfactory for $\kappa \geqslant 1 \cdot 5$ and can be tolerated for $\kappa \geqslant 1$. The motivations employed for the circular case to obtain γ in (4.9.31) do not work here. For example, using (8.7.5) in

$$E\{2\gamma(n - R_z)\} = 2n$$

we find that $\gamma^{-1} = \kappa^{-1}$ plus a term which approaches zero faster than any power of κ^{-1}. The approximation (8.7.16) is obtained by studying the behaviour of the residuals after fitting the old chi-square approximation (8.7.15) to the distribution of R.

(c) *Approximation in the multi-sample case.* On following the notation of Section 8.6.3b, we have for large κ from (8.7.15)

$$2\kappa(n - R) \simeq \chi^2_{2n-2}, \qquad 2\kappa(n_j - R_j) \simeq \chi^2_{2n_j-2}, \qquad j = 1, ..., q, \quad (8.7.17)$$

which imply that

$$2\kappa\left(n - \sum_{j=1}^{q} R_j\right) \simeq \chi^2_{2n-2q}, \qquad 2\kappa\left(\sum_{j=1}^{q} R_j - R\right) \simeq \chi^2_{2q-2}. \quad (8.7.18)$$

Further, the statistics in (8.7.18) may be taken as independently distributed. This result is due to Watson (1956a). We also have

$$2\gamma\left(n - \sum_{j=1}^{q} R_j\right) \simeq \chi^2_{2n-2q}, \qquad (8.7.19)$$

where γ is given by (8.7.16).

8.8. A DISTRIBUTION ON A HYPERSPHERE

Striking similarities between various results for the von Mises and Fisher distributions are not incidental. In fact, the two distributions are particular cases of a distribution on the surface of a p-dimensional hypersphere having p.d.f. of the $p - 1$ polar angles $\theta_1, ..., \theta_{p-1}$ (defining a point on the hypersphere) as

$$c\ ^{\kappa\cos\theta_1}\sin^{p-2}\theta_1 ... \sin\theta_{p-2}, \qquad (8.8.1)$$

where $0 < \theta_j < \pi$, $j = 1, ..., p - 2$; $0 < \theta_{p-1} < 2\pi$, $\kappa > 0$,

$$c^{-1} = (2\pi)^{\frac{1}{2}p} I_{\frac{1}{2}p-1}(\kappa)/\kappa^{\frac{1}{2}p-1}, \tag{8.8.2}$$

and $I_p(\cdot)$ is the modified Bessel function of order p. For $p = 2$, it reduces to the von Mises distribution while for $p = 3$, it reduces to the Fisher distribution.

This distribution was introduced by Watson and Williams (1956) and their paper contains an excellent treatment of the distribution. Stephens (1962c) has also studied its properties. Papers by Downs (1966) and Downs and Gould (1967) deal mainly with the characterization problems. For $\kappa = 0$, Watson G. N. (1948, p. 421) considered the problem of random flights in p-dimensions.

9

INFERENCE PROBLEMS
ON THE SPHERE

9.1. INTRODUCTION

In Section 9.2, we deal with estimation problems for the Fisher, Dimroth–Watson and Bingham distributions. Subsequent sections deal mainly with hypothesis testing for samples from the Fisher distribution. Most of the testing problems are similar to those for the circular case and their methods of derivation are almost identical. Consequently, various details are omitted and, for further clarification, Chapter 6 should be referred to for the corresponding problem. Tests of coplanarity only arise for the spherical case and are discussed at greater length.

As one would expect, all the procedures depend on the sample mean direction or the length of the resultant or on both. Example 8.2 shows the calculations necessary to obtain these quantities. As in the circular case, each procedure is illustrated with the help of a suitable example.

In contrast to the circular case, non-parametric techniques are almost non-existent on the sphere. This is not surprising since in the multivariate case, there are only a few non-parametric tests of any practical value.

9.2. POINT ESTIMATION

9.2.1. The Fisher Distribution

Suppose that (l_i, m_i, n_i) $i = 1, \ldots, n$ is a random sample from $F\{(\lambda, \mu, v), \kappa\}$, i.e. the Fisher distribution having p.d.f.

$$(\kappa/4\pi \sinh \kappa) \, e^{\kappa(\lambda l + \mu m + v n)}, \qquad \kappa > 0. \tag{9.2.1}$$

As before, we shall write

$$R_x = \Sigma l_i, \quad R_y = \Sigma m_i, \quad R_z = \Sigma n_i, \quad R = (R_x{}^2 + R_y{}^2 + R_z{}^2)^{\frac{1}{2}}, \quad \bar{R} = R/n. \tag{9.2.2}$$

It can easily be seen that R_x, R_y and R_z are jointly complete sufficient statistics for κ and (λ, μ, ν).

9.2.1a. *Maximum Likelihood Estimates*

From (9.2.1), the logarithm of the likelihood function is

$$\text{const.} + n \log \kappa - n \log \sinh \kappa + \kappa(\lambda R_x + \mu R_y + \nu R_z), \tag{9.2.3}$$

where $\lambda^2 + \mu^2 + \nu^2 = 1$. On using the method of Lagrange multipliers, we find that the maximum likelihood estimates (m.l.e.'s) of λ, μ and ν are given by

$$\hat{\lambda}/R_x = \hat{\mu}/R_y = \hat{\nu}/R_z = 1/R. \tag{9.2.4}$$

Therefore, from (8.4.1), the sample mean direction is the m.l.e. of (λ, μ, ν). Further, on differentiating (9.2.3) with respect to κ, we find after using (9.2.4) that the m.l.e. of κ is given by

$$\coth \hat{\kappa} - (1/\hat{\kappa}) = \bar{R}, \quad \text{i.e.} \quad B(\hat{\kappa}) = \bar{R}, \quad 0 < \bar{R} < 1. \tag{9.2.5}$$

Selected values of the inverse function B^{-1} are given in Appendix 3.2. For $\bar{R} < 0.05$ we find that

$$\hat{\kappa} = 3\bar{R} \tag{9.2.6}$$

whereas for $\bar{R} > 0.9$,

$$1 - (1/\hat{\kappa}) = \bar{R}, \quad \text{i.e.} \quad \hat{\kappa} = n/(n - R). \tag{9.2.7}$$

Using (9.2.1), we obtain

$$I = nE(-\partial^2 \log f/\partial\kappa^2) = n(\kappa^{-2} - \operatorname{cosech}^2 \kappa)$$

so that for large n,

$$\text{var}(\hat{\kappa}) \doteq 1/I. \tag{9.2.8}$$

Consequently, we have

$$\text{var}(\hat{\kappa}) \doteq \kappa^2/n \text{ if } \kappa \text{ is large;} \quad \doteq 3/n \text{ if } \kappa \text{ is small.} \tag{9.2.9}$$

An unbiased estimate of κ when κ is large can be obtained as follows. From (8.7.15), we have

$$2\kappa(n - R) \simeq \chi^2_{2n-2}.$$

Now, $E(1/\chi_f^2) = 1/(f-2)$, so that

$$\kappa^* = (n-2)/(n-R) \qquad (9.2.10)$$

is an unbiased estimate of κ. Fisher (1953) has shown from a fiducial distribution of κ that when κ is large, it can be estimated by $(n-1)/(n-R)$. The estimate (9.2.10) is preferable for large values of $\bar{R}$, e.g. $\bar{R} = 0.95$.

We now consider three other estimation problems.

(i)　Suppose that the true mean direction (λ, μ, ν) is known. On taking it as the z-axis, the m.l.e. of κ is found to be a solution of

$$B(\hat{\kappa}_0) = R_z/n. \qquad (9.2.11)$$

The solution $\hat{\kappa}_0$ can be obtained on following the procedure for solving (9.2.5) for $\hat{\kappa}$. From (8.5.23), we immediately see that $B(\hat{\kappa}_0)$ is an unbiased estimate of κ. Its asymptotic variance is precisely (9.2.8).

(ii)　Suppose that the true pole is unknown but the axis is given. An estimate can be obtained by using the distribution of R_z (see Fisher, 1953). This case will be discussed further in Section 9.2.2 with the help of Dimroth–Watson's model.

(iii)　Suppose that we are interested in estimating the parameters μ_0' and κ' of the von Mises distribution when the Fisher distribution is projected onto the x–y plane and restricted to the unit circle (see Section 8.5.4c). From (8.5.29), the maximum likelihood estimates of κ' and μ_0' are

$$\hat{\kappa}' = \hat{\kappa}(\hat{\lambda}^2 + \hat{\mu}^2)^{\frac{1}{2}}, \qquad \cos\hat{\mu}_0' = \hat{\kappa}\hat{\lambda}/\hat{\kappa}', \qquad \sin\hat{\mu}_0' = \hat{\kappa}\hat{\mu}/\hat{\kappa}', \qquad (9.2.12)$$

where $\hat{\lambda}$, $\hat{\mu}$ and $\hat{\kappa}$ are given by (9.2.4) and (9.2.5). Downs and Liebman (1969) have given an application of this result.

Gould (1969) has studied a regression model on the sphere similar to that in Section 5.5 when the errors have the Fisher distribution. However, the estimates are much more complicated.

Example 9.1. Obtain the maximum likelihood estimates of (λ, μ, ν) and κ for the Icelandic lava flow data of Example 8.2.

Since $(\hat{\lambda}, \hat{\mu}, \hat{\nu})$ is precisely the sample mean direction, we have from (8.4.13)

$$\hat{\lambda} = 0.2984, \qquad \hat{\mu} = -0.1346, \qquad \hat{\nu} = -0.9449.$$

Further, $n = 9$ and $R = 8.7720$ so that $\bar{R} = 0.9747$. From Appendix 3.2, the m.l.e. of κ is 39.53. Since κ is large, we can obtain an unbiased estimate of κ from (9.2.10). This is found to be 30.75. Both values indicate a high degree of concentration. We will invariably use (9.2.5) because we are estimating κ without *a priori* knowledge of whether it is large or small.

9.2.1b. *Fitting of the Distribution*

Let (θ_i, ϕ_i) $i = 1, \ldots, n$ be the given observations. By using the method of Example 8.2, we can calculate the sample mean direction and the resultant length. The m.l.e. of $\hat{\kappa}$ can be obtained as in Example 9.1. Let $(\bar{x}_0, \bar{y}_0)$ be the polar co-ordinates of the sample mean direction. We can shift the pole to $(\bar{x}_0, \bar{y}_0)$ by the transformations (8.3.4)–(8.3.6) with $\alpha = \bar{x}_0$ and $\beta = \bar{y}_0$. The new direction cosines (l_i', m_i', n_i') can be converted into the polar co-ordinates $(\hat{\theta}_i, \hat{\phi}_i)$ by using the relations

$$\theta = \arccos n, \quad \cos \phi = l \operatorname{cosec} \theta, \quad \sin \phi = m \operatorname{cosec} \theta.$$

These new polar observations $(\hat{\theta}_i, \hat{\phi}_i)$ have the polar axis as the sample mean direction. If the underlying population has a Fisher distribution, $\hat{\theta}$ and $\hat{\phi}$ will be independently distributed. The observed frequencies in $\hat{\theta}_1 < \hat{\theta} < \hat{\theta}_2$ and $\hat{\phi}_1 < \hat{\phi} < \hat{\phi}_2$ can be obtained from (8.5.19) and (8.5.20). We can test the goodness of fit by using the chi-square statistic. In fitting the distribution of θ, four d. of fr. are lost since $\mu^2 + \nu^2 + \lambda^2 = 1$. However, in fitting the distribution of ϕ, only three d. of fr. are lost since the expected frequencies do not depend on κ. Although $\hat{\phi}$ depends on $(\hat{\lambda}, \hat{\mu}, \hat{\nu})$ since it is measured in the plane whose normal has the direction cosines $(\hat{\lambda}, \hat{\mu}, \hat{\nu})$. However, it is more efficient if the distribution given by (8.5.11) is fitted directly. In this case, only 4 d. of fr. are lost but the joint d.f. of θ and ϕ given by (8.5.11) is not easy to handle.

Example 9.2. Fit the Fisher distribution to the directions $(\hat{\theta}_i, \hat{\phi}_i)$ shown in Table 9.1 (as observed frequencies) for 70 specimens from the Diabaig Group of the Torridonian Sandstones (Watson and Irving, 1957).

TABLE 9.1.   Measurements of directions in degrees from the Diabaig Group of the Torridonian Sandstone (upper entry) and the corresponding expected frequencies from the Fisher distribution (lower entry). (Watson and Irving, 1957).

$\hat{\theta}$	0–	3·5–	6·5–	9·5–	12·5–	>15·5	Total
Observed	5	13	15	16	11	10	70
Expected	7	13·8	16·4	13·9	9·5	9·4	70

$\hat{\phi}$	1–	45–	90–	135–	180–	225–	270–	315–	Total
Observed	10	6	8	12	4	9	11	10	70
Expected	8·75	8·75	8·75	8·75	8·75	8·75	8·75	8·75	70

It is found that $\hat{\kappa} = 55\cdot2$. Since κ is large we may neglect $e^{-\kappa}$ in (8.5.19) and obtain the expected frequencies of $\theta_1 < \theta < \theta_2$ from

$$n\,e^{-\kappa}(e^{\kappa\cos\theta_1} - e^{\kappa\cos\theta_2}). \qquad (9.2.13)$$

The expected frequencies calculated by the above method are also shown in Table 9.1. The observed value of the chi-square statistic for fitting the distribution of θ is $1\cdot5$ and the 5% value of χ_5^2 is $11\cdot07$. Further, the observed value of the chi-square statistic for fitting the distribution of ϕ is $2\cdot3$ and the 5% value of χ_2^2 is $5\cdot99$. Hence, the fit is satisfactory.

9.2.2. Dimroth–Watson's Distribution

Let us assume that (l_i, m_i, n_i) $i = 1, ..., n$ is a random sample from the distribution with p.d.f.

$$\{b(\kappa)/2\pi\} \exp\{-\kappa(l\lambda + m\mu + nv)^2\}, \qquad \kappa > 0,$$

where

$$b(\kappa) = 1\bigg/\bigg(2\int_0^1 e^{-\kappa t^2}\,dt\bigg).$$

The logarithm of the likelihood function is

$$\text{const.} - n\log\bigg\{\int_0^1 e^{-\kappa t^2}\,dt\bigg\} - \kappa\sum_{i=1}^n (l_i\lambda + m_i\mu + n_iv)^2. \qquad (9.2.14)$$

Let $\mathbf{u} = (\lambda, \mu, v)'$ and let $\mathbf{T}$ be the matrix of the sum of squares and products of (l_i, m_i, n_i) given by (8.4.16). Further, let

$$\cos\theta_i = l_i\lambda + m_i\mu + n_iv. \qquad (9.2.15)$$

From (9.2.14), the maximum likelihood equations for estimating $\mathbf{u}$ and κ are

$$\mathbf{T}\hat{\mathbf{u}} = \tau\hat{\mathbf{u}}, \qquad D(\hat{\kappa}) = (\Sigma\cos^2\hat{\theta}_i)/n \qquad (9.2.16)$$

where $\tau(\lambda^2 + \mu^2 + v^2 - 1)$ is added to (9.2.14), τ is a Lagrange multiplier and

$$D(\kappa) = \int_0^1 t^2 e^{-\kappa t^2}\,dt\bigg/\int_0^1 e^{-\kappa t^2}\,dt. \qquad (9.2.17)$$

Hence, $\hat{\tau}$ is an eigen value of $\mathbf{T}$. Now, the likelihood function given by (9.2.14) is maximum with respect to $\hat{\mathbf{u}}$ when

$$\hat{\tau} = \hat{\mathbf{u}}'\mathbf{T}\hat{\mathbf{u}} = \Sigma\cos^2\hat{\theta}_i \qquad (9.2.18)$$

is minimum. Hence, $\hat{\tau}$ is the least root of $\mathbf{T}$, Let τ_1, τ_2 and τ_3 be the eigen values of $\mathbf{T}$ in ascending order with corresponding eigen vectors $\mathbf{t}_1, \mathbf{t}_2, \mathbf{t}_3$. From (9.2.16), the m.l.e. of $\mathbf{u}$ and κ are therefore given by

$$\hat{\mathbf{u}} = \mathbf{t}_1, \qquad D(\hat{\kappa}) = \bar{\tau}_1, \qquad (9.2.19)$$

where $\bar{\tau}_1 = \tau/n$. In fact, we have intuitively arrived at similar estimates in Section 8.4.2 for the girdle case.

Appendix 3.3 gives selected values of the function D^{-1}. It can be shown that $0 < D(\kappa) < \frac{1}{3}$. We have for small κ and large κ respectively that

$$D(\kappa) \doteq \tfrac{1}{3}(1 - \tfrac{4}{15}\kappa), \qquad D(\kappa) \doteq (2\kappa)^{-1}. \qquad (9.2.20)$$

These approximations are adequate for $\kappa < 0.2$ and $\kappa > 10$ respectively. For $\kappa < 0$, Dimroth–Watson's distribution is bipolar. Let $\kappa' = -\kappa$. Following the above method, it can easily be seen that

$$\hat{\mathbf{u}} = \mathbf{t}_3, \qquad D(-\hat{\kappa}') = \bar{\tau}_3, \qquad (9.2.21)$$

where $\bar{\tau}_3 = \tau_3/n$. The function D^{-1} is tabulated in Appendix 3.4 for some values of κ'. For small κ', (9.2.20) holds, whereas for large κ',

$$D(-\kappa') = 1 - (1/\kappa'). \qquad (9.2.22)$$

Example 9.3. Obtain the maximum likelihood estimates of the mean vector and the concentration parameter for the calcite grains data of Example 8.3.

From Example 8.3, we have $\tau_1 = 4\cdot1764$. From Section 8.4.2b, the underlying distribution is a girdle distribution. Now $\tau_1/n = 0\cdot1392$ so that from Appendix 9.3, $\hat{\kappa} = 3\cdot33$. The vector $\mathbf{t}_1$ given in Example 8.3 is, of course, the maximum likelihood estimate of the mean direction.

9.2.3. Bingham's Distribution

Let $\mathbf{L}_1, ..., \mathbf{L}_n$ be a random sample from Bingham's distribution with p.d.f.

See also section 8.5.5b.

$$\{4\pi\, d(\mathbf{\kappa})\}^{-1} \exp\left\{ \sum_{j=1}^{3} \kappa_j(\mathbf{\mu}_j'\mathbf{L})^2 \right\}, \qquad (9.2.23)$$

where $\mathbf{\mu} = (\mathbf{\mu}_1, \mathbf{\mu}_2, \mathbf{\mu}_3)$ is an orthogonal matrix and $\mathbf{\kappa} = \operatorname{diag}(\kappa_1, \kappa_2, \kappa_3)$ is a matrix of constants. We have

$$\sum_{j=1}^{3} \kappa_j(\mathbf{\mu}_j'\mathbf{L})^2 = \operatorname{tr}(\mathbf{\kappa}\,\mathbf{\mu}'\mathbf{L}\mathbf{L}'\mathbf{\mu})$$

so that

$$\sum_{i=1}^{n}\sum_{j=1}^{3}\kappa_j(\mu_j' \, L_i)^2 = \sum_{i=1}^{n} \text{tr} \, (\kappa \, \mu' \, L_i L_i' \, \mu) = \text{tr} \, (\kappa \, \mu' \, T\mu), \qquad (9.2.24)$$

where

$$T = \sum_{i=1}^{n} L_i L_i' \qquad (9.2.25)$$

is again the matrix of the sum of squares and products. On using (9.2.24), we find that the logarithm of the likelihood function is

$$- n \log 4\pi - n \log d(\kappa) + \text{tr} \, (\kappa\mu' \, T\mu).$$

This has to be maximized subject to the condition

$$\mu'\mu = I. \qquad (9.2.26)$$

Let Λ be a symmetric matrix of Lagrange multipliers. The problem then reduces to maximizing

$$- n \log 4\pi - n \log d(\kappa) + \text{tr} \, (\kappa\mu' \, T\mu) + \text{tr} \, \{\Lambda(I - \mu'\mu)\}. \qquad (9.2.27)$$

On equating the derivatives of (9.2.27) with respect to μ and κ to zero, we find that the m.l.e.'s are solutions of

$$\kappa\mu' \, T = \Lambda\mu' \qquad (9.2.28)$$

and

$$\partial \log d(\kappa)/\partial\kappa_i = \frac{1}{n}\mu_i' \, T\mu_i, \qquad i = 1, 2, 3. \qquad (9.2.29)$$

Let us assume that the κ's are distinct. Using (9.2.26), we can write (9.2.28) as

$$\kappa\mu' \, T\mu = \Lambda.$$

Now $\mu'T\mu$ and Λ are both symmetric matrices so that if the κ's are distinct, Λ must be a diagonal matrix, i.e.

$$\kappa_i T\mu_i = \lambda_{ii}\mu_i, \qquad (9.2.30)$$

where λ_{ii} is the ith diagonal element of Λ. We can assume that $\kappa_i \neq 0$ and therefore from (9.2.30), it follows that (9.2.27) is maximized if μ_i is an eigen vector of T. Hence, if t_1, t_2 and t_3 are the eigen vectors of T, the m.l.e. of μ_i is

$$\hat{\mu}_i = t_i. \qquad (9.2.31)$$

Further, let τ_1, τ_2, τ_3 be the eigen values of $\mathbf{T}$ so that

$$\mathbf{t}_i' \, \mathbf{T} \mathbf{t}_i = \tau_i. \tag{9.2.32}$$

Using (9.2.31) and (9.2.32) in (9.2.29), we see that the m.l.e. $\hat{\boldsymbol{\kappa}}$ of $\boldsymbol{\kappa}$ is given by

$$\partial \log \mathrm{d}(\hat{\boldsymbol{\kappa}})/\partial \hat{\kappa}_i = \bar{\tau}_i, \qquad i = 1, 2, 3, \tag{9.2.33}$$

where $\bar{\tau}_i = \tau_i/n$. Since the κ_i are estimable only to an additive constant because of the degeneracy established in Section 8.5.5b, we assume that $\kappa_3 = 0$. The two equations (9.2.32) for $i = 1, 2$ can be solved by using Tables or nomograms given in Bingham (1964). An approximation is given in Example 9.13 with a numerical illustration.

By considering the likelihood function for given $\boldsymbol{\kappa}$, it can be shown that $\kappa_1 < \kappa_2 < \kappa_3$ implies that the m.l.e.'s $\hat{\boldsymbol{\mu}}_i = \mathbf{t}_i$ $i = 1, 2, 3$ are such that $\tau_1 < \tau_2 < \tau_3$. Similarly, if $\kappa_1 = \kappa_2 \leqslant \kappa_3$, we have Dimroth–Watson's distribution and Section 9.2.2 implies that $\tau_1 = \tau_2 \leqslant \tau_3$. In general, the τ_i behave in the same way as the κ_i. This is expected since on identifying the particular cases of Bingham's distribution discussed in Section 8.5.5b with those in Table 8.3, we find that all the results of Table 8.3 hold on replacing the κ_i by the τ_i. For example, using the uniform case, we deduce that $\kappa_1 = \kappa_2 = \kappa_3$ implies $\tau_1 \doteq \tau_2 \doteq \tau_3 \doteq n/3$ and vice versa.

We note from (8.4.19) that $\bar{\tau}_1 + \bar{\tau}_2 + \bar{\tau}_3 = 1$, $\bar{\tau}_i \geqslant 0$.

9.3. SINGLE SAMPLE TESTS

We shall assume throughout that (l_i, m_i, n_i), $i = 1, \ldots, n$ is a random sample of size n from the Fisher distribution with p.d.f.

$$\{c(\kappa)/2\pi\} \exp \{\kappa(\lambda l + \mu m + \nu n)\}, \qquad \kappa > 0. \tag{9.3.1}$$

where

$$c(\kappa) = \kappa/2 \sinh \kappa.$$

9.3.1. A Test of Uniformity (The Rayleigh Test)

Consider testing the hypothesis

$$H_0 : \kappa = 0 \quad \text{against} \quad H_1 : \kappa \neq 0, \tag{9.3.2}$$

where the true mean direction (λ, μ, ν) is unknown. It can be shown as was done for the circular case (Section 6.2.1b) that the likelihood ratio test leads to the critical region

$$R > K. \tag{9.3.3}$$

This test is due to Rayleigh (1919) and was first explicitly formulated by Watson (1956b).

Following Watson (1967b) and Beran (1968), we show that this test is the UMP invariant test under rotations. Let us take (λ, μ, ν) as the z-axis and let (θ_i, ϕ_i) be the polar co-ordinates corresponding to (l_i, m_i, n_i), $i = 1, ..., n$. We shift the pole to (θ_n, ϕ_n) by using the orthogonal transformations (8.3.4)–(8.3.6). The new observations (θ_i', ϕ_i'), $i = 1, ..., n-1$ corresponding to (θ_i, ϕ_i), $i = 1, ..., n-1$ define a maximal invariant under rotations. On following the same steps as used in Section 6.2.1c, it is found from the Neyman–Pearson lemma that the most powerful invariant test is given by

$$\{c(\kappa)/2\pi\}^n \int \prod_{i=1}^{n} \exp \{\kappa(xl_i + ym_i + zn_i)\} \, dS(x, y, z) > K,$$

where the integral is taken over the surface of the unit sphere $x^2 + y^2 + z^2 = 1$, and $S(x, y, z)$ is the surface element. This expression reduces to

$$\{c(\kappa)/2\pi\}^n \int \exp \{\kappa R(x\bar{l}_0 + y\bar{m}_0 + z\bar{n}_0)\} \, dS(x, y, z) > K, \qquad (9.3.4)$$

where $\bar{l}_0$, $\bar{m}_0$ and $\bar{n}_0$ are the direction cosines of the sample mean direction. After using the fact that the total integral of (9.2.1) is unity, the last expression reduces to

$$c(\kappa R) > K$$

which implies that (9.3.3) is the UMP invariant test.

The p.d.f's of R under H_0 and H_1 have been derived already in Chapter 8 (see (8.6.18) and (8.6.32)). Appendix 3.5 gives some selected critical values for the test. For large n, we have from Section 8.7.1 that $3R^2/n$ is distributed as χ^2 with 3 d. of fr.

$$3_n R^2$$

Example 9.4. Bernoulli (1734) raised the question—could the close coincidence of the orbit planes of the seven planets (then known) have arisen by chance? Consider this problem for nine planets (Watson, 1970). Each orbit determines one directed line, viz. the normals to the orbital plane of the planet given a sense of direction by the right hand rule as described below. Its direction cosines can be obtained as follows. Let i be the inclination of the orbital plane to the ecliptic (the apparent path described by the sun about the earth). Further let Ω be the angle between a fixed line in the ecliptic (the line joining the sun to the earth at the time of the vernal equinox which is about 21st March) and the line joining the sun and the ascending node of the planet (the point where the orbit of the planet rises to the positive side of the ecliptic). The positive side of the ecliptic is taken as the direction of the right hand thumb when the fingers point in the direction of the earth's orbit. The data is shown in Table 9.2. Is the data uniformly distributed?

TABLE 9.2. Orbits of the nine planets (Watson, 1970).

Planet	i	Ω	Planet	i	Ω
Mercury	7° 0'	47° 08'	Saturn	2° 30'	112° 47'
Venus	3° 23'	75° 47'	Uranus	0° 46'	73° 29'
Earth	0°	0°	Neptune	1° 47'	130° 41'
Mars	1° 51'	48° 47'	Pluto	17° 10'	109° 0'
Jupiter	1° 19'	99° 26'			

The direction cosines are given by

$$(\sin \Omega \sin i, \; -\cos \Omega \sin i, \; \cos i).$$

It is found by following the method of Example 8.2 that $R^2 = 50\cdot85$ so that $\bar{R} = 0\cdot79$. From Appendix 3.5, the 5% and 1% values of $\bar{R}$ for $n = 9$ are 0·529 and 0·624 respectively. Hence, the null hypothesis is strongly rejected.

9.3.2. Tests for the Mean Direction

9.3.2a. *Concentration Parameter Known*

Consider the problem of testing

$$H_0 : (\lambda, \mu, v) = (0, 0, 1) \quad \text{against} \quad H_1 : (\lambda, \mu, v) = (\lambda', \mu', v'), \quad (9.3.5)$$

where κ is known and is non-zero. Let λ be the likelihood ratio statistic for this problem. It is found that the critical region is

$$-2 \log_e \lambda = 2\kappa(R - R_z) > K. \quad (9.3.6)$$

For $\kappa > 3$ (by (8.7.13)) or for large n, the statistic $2\kappa(R - R_z)$ is distributed as chi-square with two d. of fr. when H_0 is true. For large n, this provides an alternative proof of (8.7.13). For small κ, the percentage points of $R - R_z$ are not available but it is possible to use the following test for all κ.

On applying the Fisher ancillary principle, it is found with the help of (8.6.31) that a test can be based on the statistic $\bar{x}_0|R$, which, under H_0, is distributed as

$$f(\bar{x}_0|R, \kappa') = \{c(\kappa')/2\pi\} \exp(\kappa' \cos \bar{x}_0) \sin \bar{x}_0, \quad 0 < \bar{x}_0 < \pi, \quad (9.3.7)$$

where $\kappa' = \kappa R$. The null hypothesis H_0 is rejected for large values of $\bar{x}_0$. Appendix 3.1 gives some selected critical values.

9.3.2b. *Concentration Parameter Unknown*

Consider now the problem (9.3.5) when κ is unknown and the hypothesis of uniformity is ruled out. Under H_0, we can easily see that R_z is a complete sufficient estimate for κ so that any similar tests will be conditional upon R_z. Therefore, to obtain the BCR for this problem, we apply the Neyman–Pearson lemma where κ and R_z are regarded as constants. It is then found that the BCR is

$$\lambda' R_x + \mu' R_y > K \quad (9.3.8)$$

which is equivalent to

$$R \sin \bar{x}_0 \cos(\bar{y}_0 - v_0') > K,$$

where (μ_0', v_0') and $(\bar{x}_0, \bar{y}_0)$ are the polar co-ordinates of (λ', μ', v') and the sample mean direction respectively. Hence, there is no UMP similar test for this problem.

Watson and William's Test. From (8.6.36), the distribution of R given R_z does not depend on κ so that we may use $R|R_z$ as a test statistic. The hypothesis H_0 is rejected for large values of R.

This test was proposed by Watson and Williams (1956). Stephens (1962b) has given nomograms for $\alpha = 0.1$, 0.05, 0.01 and the nomograms for $\alpha = 0.05$, 0.01 are reproduced in Appendices 3.6a and 3.6b. For $n > 8$, we can also use the following procedure to obtain R_α where

$$\Pr(R > R_\alpha|R_z) = \alpha. \quad (9.3.9)$$

(i) If $0 < R_z < \tfrac{1}{4}n$, we use

$$R_\alpha = \{R_z^2 + (n/3)\chi_2^2(\alpha)\}^{\frac{1}{2}}, \quad (9.3.10)$$

where $\chi_2^2(\alpha)$ is the upper $100\alpha\%$ of χ_2^2.

(ii) If $\tfrac{1}{4}n \leqslant R_z \leqslant 3n/5$, we use

$$R_\alpha = \tfrac{1}{2}(R_{\alpha,1} + R_{\alpha,2}),$$

where $R_{\alpha,1}$ denotes the R_α defined by (9.3.10) and $R_{\alpha,2}$ is obtained from

$$F_{2,2n-2}(\alpha) = (R_\alpha - R_z)(n-1)/(n-R_\alpha), \qquad (9.3.11)$$

where $F_{2,2n-2}(\alpha)$ is the upper $100\alpha\%$ point of $F_{2,2n-2}$.

(iii) For $R_z > 3n/5$, we use $R_\alpha = R_{\alpha,2}$ defined by (9.3.11).

The proof of results (9.3.10) and (9.3.11) follows from Section 8.7 by the same argument as was used in the circular case (Section 6.2.2b). The derivation of (9.3.11) from the analysis of variance decomposition of $n - R$ should be noted. The approximation (9.3.11) is due to Watson (1956a).

The test can also be carried out by using the following confidence cone for the population mean direction (as done in the circular case).

A Confidence Cone for the Mean Direction. Let R_α be given by (9.3.9). Let us consider a graph of (R_α, R_z) for a fixed α, e.g. the nomograms in Appendices 3.6a and 3.6b. Suppose that R_0 is the observed value of R. For $R = R_0$, we can obtain the corresponding value of R_z, say $R_{z,\alpha}$ from the graph, i.e. $R_{z,\alpha}$ satisfies the equation

$$\Pr(R > R_0 | R_{z,\alpha}) = \alpha.$$

Let δ be defined by

$$R_{z,\alpha} = R_0 \cos \delta, \qquad \delta = \arccos(R_{z,\alpha}/R_0). \qquad (9.3.12)$$

Now, $R_z = R \cos \bar{x}_0$ where $\bar{x}_0$ is the angle between the true mean direction and the sample mean direction. Consequently, the probability that the true mean direction lies within a cone with vertex at $(0,0,0)$, axis as the sample mean direction and semi-vertical angle δ is $1 - \alpha$. This confidence zone may be described as a $100(1-\alpha)\%$ confidence cone for the true mean direction (see Fig. 9.1).

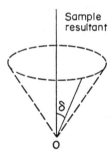

FIG. 9.1. Confidence cone for the true mean direction.

We can now construct 95% and 99% confidence cones from Appendices 3.6a and 3.6b. For $n > 30$ and all values of κ, δ can also be obtained by the following approximation. Let $\hat{\kappa}$ be the m.l.e. of κ obtained from (9.2.5). Suppose that θ is distributed as $F\{0, \kappa'\}$ where $\kappa' = \hat{\kappa}R$, then δ is defined by

$$\Pr(\theta > \delta) = \alpha. \tag{9.3.13}$$

The idea behind this approximation is self-evident. Appendix 3.1 gives the solution of (9.3.13) for given κ'. Further, if κ' is large we have from (8.5.22)

$$\delta = \arccos\{1 + (\kappa')^{-1}\log_e \alpha\}. \tag{9.3.14}$$

If κ is also large, from (9.2.7) we have $\hat{\kappa} = n/(n - R)$ so that on using $(\kappa')^{-1} = (n - R)/nR$ in (9.3.14), δ can be obtained. This approximation is closely related to the approximation $\hat{\kappa} = (n - 1)/(n - R)$ of Fisher (1953) who obtained it by a fiducial argument. The F-approximation (9.3.11) can also be used for large κ. That is,

$$\delta \doteq \arccos[1 - \{(n - R)\,F_{2,2n-2}(\alpha)/(n - 1)R\}].$$

Example 9.5. In an early Quaternary zone of lava flows from Western Iceland (mean geographical coordinates 64·6° N.L., 22·0° W.L.), it was found for 45 readings (Hosper's data cited in Fisher, 1953) that the sums of the observed direction cosines were

$$-11\cdot6127, \qquad -37\cdot2193, \qquad +0\cdot6710,$$

with the co-ordinate axes as northward, eastward and downward, respectively. The simple dipole field appropriate to the geographical latitude is found to have the direction cosines

$$N : 0\cdot2334, \qquad E : 0, \qquad Down : 0\cdot9724.$$

Does the direction of magnetization differ from the *reversed* dipole field? (For further geological significance of this problem, see Hosper, 1955).

We take the co-ordinate axes x, y and z as northward, eastward and downward respectively. For this example, there is no need to change the co-ordinates to the usual reference system given by (8.2.3). We have

$$R_x = -11\cdot6127, \qquad R_y = -37\cdot2193, \qquad R_z = 0\cdot6710.$$

Consequently, $R = 38\cdot9946$. The direction cosines of the sample mean direction are

$$(\bar{l}_0, \bar{m}_0, \bar{n}_0) = (-0\cdot2978, +0\cdot0172, -0\cdot9545).$$

Under H_0, we may take the true mean direction as the reversed dipole field, i.e.

$$(\lambda, \mu, \nu) = (-0\cdot2334, 0, -0\cdot9724).$$

We have

$$\cos \bar{x}_0 = l_0 \lambda + m_0 \mu + n_0 \nu = 0.9977$$

so that $\bar{x}_0 = 3.9°$. Since $\bar{R}$ is large, we use $\hat{\kappa} = n/(n - R)$ and obtain $\hat{\kappa} = 7.3$. Further, $\kappa' = R\hat{\kappa} = 284.66$. From (9.3.14), the 5% value of $\bar{x}_0$ is 8.3°. Hence, the null hypothesis is accepted.

Alternatively, under H_0, we have $R_z' = Rc = 38.9034$. The observed value of

$$F_{2, 2n-2} = (R - R_z')(n - 1)/(n - R) = 0.67$$

whereas the 5% value of $F_{2, 88}$ is 3.10. Hence, the null hypothesis is again accepted.

Example 9.6. For recent lava flows in a locality, it is found that $R = 6.25$ for $n = 16$. If the angle between the sample mean direction and the reversed dipole field is 12.5°, can we regard the true direction as the reversed dipole field?

From Appendix 3.6a, the 5% value of R for $R_z = 6.25 \times \cos 12.5° = 6.10$ is found to be 8.1. Hence, the null hypothesis is accepted. In fact, for $R = 6.25$, Appendix 3.6a gives $R_z = 2.8$ so that for the 95% confidence cone for the mean direction as defined above, we have $\delta = \cos^{-1}(2.8/6.25) = 63°$.

9.3.3. A Test for Concentration Parameter

Suppose that we wish to test $\kappa = \kappa_0$ when the true mean direction is unknown. The statistic R is maximal invariant under rotations. On using the p.d.f. of R given by (8.6.32), it can be seen that the UMP invariant test is given by

$$R \geqslant K. \tag{9.3.15}$$

Appendix 3.7 gives some selected critical values of R. For $\kappa \geqslant 1.5$, we can use the approximation

$$2\gamma_0(n - R) \simeq \chi^2_{2n-2}, \gamma_0^{-1} = \kappa_0^{-1} - \tfrac{1}{5}\kappa_0^{-3} \tag{9.3.16}$$

obtained at (8.7.16).

9.4. TWO-SAMPLE TESTS

Suppose that $(l_{ij}, m_{ij}, n_{ij}), j = 1, \ldots, n_i, i = 1, 2$ are two independent random samples of sizes n_1 and n_2 respectively from $F\{(\lambda_i, \mu_i, \nu_i), \kappa_i\}, i = 1, 2$. Let R_1 and R_2 be the lengths of the resultants of the first and second samples, i.e.

$$R_i = (R_{x,i}^2 + R_{y,i}^2 + R_{z,i}^2)^{\frac{1}{2}}, \tag{9.4.1}$$

where

$$R_{x,i} = \sum_{j=1}^{n_i} l_{ij}, \quad R_{y,i} = \sum_{j=1}^{n_i} m_{ij}, \quad R_{z,i} = \sum_{j=1}^{n_i} n_{ij}, \quad i = 1, 2.$$

Further, let R be the length of the resultant of the combined sample so that

$$R = (R_x^2 + R_y^2 + R_z^2)^{\frac{1}{2}}, \tag{9.4.2}$$

where

$$R_x = \Sigma R_{x,i}, \quad R_y = \Sigma R_{y,i}, \quad R_z = \Sigma R_{z,i}.$$

9.4.1. A Test for Mean Directions (Watson–Williams' Test)

We assume that $\kappa_1 = \kappa_2 = \kappa$ where κ is unknown. We wish to test

$$H_0 : (\lambda_1, \mu_1, \nu_1) = (\lambda_2, \mu_2, \nu_2) \tag{9.4.3}$$

against the alternative of unequal mean directions. We have shown in Section 8.6.3b that the conditional distribution of R_1, R_2 given R does not depend on κ when H_0 is true. Consequently, as in the circular case, we can take our criterion as $R_1 + R_2$ (Watson and Williams, 1956). The critical region is then given by

$$R_1 + R_2 > K, \tag{9.4.4}$$

where

$$\Pr(R_1 + R_2 > K|R) = \alpha. \tag{9.4.5}$$

holds under H_0.

We can easily write down an expression for the null distribution of $R_1 + R_2$ given R from (8.6.40) which gives the joint distribution of (R_1, R_2) given R. However, it does not simplify further.

A Test Procedure. Let $n_1 < n_2$ and $r = n_1/n$, $0 < r < \frac{1}{2}$. Calculate $\bar{R}' = (R_1 + R_2)/n$. For $r = \frac{1}{2}$ and $r = \frac{1}{3}$, Appendices 3.8a and 3.8b give the 1% and 5% critical values for the test based on $\bar{R}'$ when the value of $\bar{R}$ is given.

(i) Let $0 < \bar{R} < 0.35$. For $\frac{1}{3} < r < \frac{1}{2}$, Appendices 3.8a and 3.8b should be used to obtain the values of $\bar{R}'$ for $r = \frac{1}{3}$ and $r = \frac{1}{2}$ respectively. The required critical value of $\bar{R}'$ is then obtained by linear interpolation. For $0 < r < \frac{1}{3}$ and $\bar{R} < 0.35$, linear extrapolation can be used if r is not too small.

(ii) Let $0.35 \leqslant \bar{R} \leqslant 0.70$. For any moderate values of r, not near zero, Appendix 3.8a alone can be used.

(iii) Let $\bar{R} > 0.70$. We can use the F-approximation from (8.7.18) given by

$$F_{2,2n-2} = (n-1)(R_1 + R_2 - R)/(n - R). \tag{9.4.6}$$

Example 9.7. Table 9.3 shows the directions of needle-shaped crystals in two exposures from the Yukspor Mountain, Kola peninsula (Vistelius, 1966, p. 92). Do the two sections of the crystals have the same orientation?

TABLE 9.3.   Directions of crystals in two exposures from the Yukspor Mountain Kola peninsula (Vistelius, 1966)

Exposure I		Exposure II	
Azimuth	Dip	Azimuth	Dip
18°	26°	5°	4°
34	22	31	10
64	10	145	20
265	6	279	10
314	8	309	8
334	6	325	20
340	24	342	8
342	20	344	10
345	14	350	12
355	8	359	18

We have here $n_1 = n_2 = 10$. On following the procedure of Example 8.2, we obtain

$$R_{x,1} = -7·226, \quad R_{y,1} = -1·397, \quad R_{z,1} = 2·466,$$
$$R_{x,2} = -6·418, \quad R_{y,2} = -1·912, \quad R_{z,2} = 2·071.$$

Consequently, from (9.4.1)

$$R_1 = 7·76, \quad R_2 = 7·01, \quad \bar{R}' = 0·738,$$

and

$$R = \{(-13·644)^2 + (-3·309)^2 + (4·537)^2\}^{\frac{1}{2}} = 14·75.$$

Hence, $\bar{R} = 0·74$. Using these values in (9.4.6), we find that the observed value of F is 0·07. The 5% value of $F_{2,38}$ is 3·24 and therefore the null hypothesis is accepted. The hypothesis of equality of concentration parameters will be tested in Example 9.9.

9.4.2. A Test for Concentration Parameters

Let us consider the problem of testing

$$H_0 : \kappa_1 = \kappa_2 \quad \text{against} \quad H_1 : \kappa_1 \neq \kappa_2, \quad (9.4.7)$$

where the mean directions $(\lambda_i, \mu_i, \nu_i), i = 1, 2$ are not specified. Since R_1 and R_2 are invariant under rotations, it is desirable to consider test statistics which are functions of R_1 and R_2. As in the circular case, we derive a similar test by developing approximations to the distribution of the length of the resultant R.

9.4.2a. *Approximations to the Distribution of R*

We have seen in Section 8.7.2 that for $\kappa > 3$, the distribution of R can be approximated by

$$2\kappa(n - R) \simeq \chi^2_{2n-2}. \tag{9.4.8}$$

We now derive approximations for $0 < \kappa < 1\cdot5$ and $1\cdot5 \leqslant \kappa \leqslant 3$. For large n, we have from (8.7.11) that $\bar{R}$ is distributed normally with

$$E(\bar{R}) \doteq \rho, \qquad \text{var}\,(\bar{R}) \doteq (1 - 2\kappa^{-1}\rho - \rho^2)/n, \tag{9.4.9}$$

where

$$\rho = B(\kappa) = \coth \kappa - \kappa^{-1}. \tag{9.4.10}$$

Case I. $0 < \kappa < 1\cdot5$. Using the approximation

$$\coth \kappa = \kappa^{-1} + \tfrac{1}{3}\kappa - \frac{\kappa^3}{45},$$

it is found for small κ that

$$\tilde{R} = 3\bar{R} \simeq N(\kappa, (3\{1 - a^2\kappa^2\}/n)^{\frac{1}{2}}), \tag{9.4.11}$$

where $a = 1/\sqrt{5}$ By following the same method as used in the circular case (Section 6.3.2b) to obtain a variance-stabilizing transformation, it is found for the statistic

$$g_1(\tilde{R}) = \sin^{-1}(a\tilde{R}), \qquad a = 1/\sqrt{5}, \qquad \tilde{R} = 3\bar{R} \tag{9.4.12}$$

that

$$E\{g_1(\tilde{R})\} \doteq \sin^{-1}(a\kappa), \qquad \text{var}\,\{g_1(\tilde{R})\} \doteq 3/5n. \tag{9.4.13}$$

On comparing the exact upper tail area of $\bar{R}$ with the above approximation and then modifying the variance, it is found that the approximation having the modified variance

$$\text{var}\,\{g_1(\tilde{R})\} = 3/\{5(n - 5)\}, \tag{9.4.14}$$

is quite satisfactory for n as low as 8.

Case II. $1\cdot5 \leqslant \kappa \leqslant 3$. Using (9.4.9), the transformation is given by

$$g_2(\kappa) = cn^{\frac{1}{2}}\int \{1 - 2\kappa^{-1}\rho - \rho^2\}^{-\frac{1}{2}}\,d\rho. \tag{9.4.15}$$

To express the integrand in terms of only ρ, we follow a procedure similar to that used in the circular case (Case II, $1 \leqslant \kappa \leqslant 2$). We have in the neighbourhood of $\kappa = 2$.

$$\kappa^{-1} \doteq \tfrac{1}{2}(1 - \tfrac{1}{4}\kappa^*), \qquad \kappa^* = \{\rho - B(2)\}/B'(2).$$

On substituting the resulting value of κ^{-1} in terms of ρ in (9.4.15), we find that the transformation is of the form

$$\sinh^{-1}\{(\rho - E)/D\}. \tag{9.4.16}$$

This approximation was found to be inadequate and could not be substantially improved even after making various modifications. However, after fitting a normal curve to the upper-tail of

$$g_2(\bar{R}) = \sin^{-1}\{(\bar{R} + c_1)/c_2\} \tag{9.4.17}$$

with $\kappa = 2$ and

$$E\{g_2(\bar{R})\} = \sin^{-1}\{(\rho + c_1)/c_2\}, \qquad \mathrm{var}\,\{g_2(\bar{R})\} = c_3^2/(n - 4), \tag{9.4.18}$$

it is found that

$$c_1 = 0\cdot17595, \qquad c_2 = 1\cdot02903, \qquad c_3 = 0\cdot62734. \tag{9.4.19}$$

On comparing the exact tail area with this normal approximation over the range $1\cdot5 \leqslant \kappa \leqslant 3$, the new approximation was found to be adequate for n as low as 8.

9.4.2b. *A Two-sample Test*

We can now construct a two-sample test for testing equality of concentration parameters. Let κ be the common value of κ_1 and κ_2 under H_0. The boundary values of κ for the above approximations are $\kappa = 1\cdot5$ and $\kappa = 3$ which correspond to $\bar{R} = 0\cdot44$ and $\bar{R} = 0\cdot67$ respectively.

Case I. $\bar{R} < 0\cdot44$. Under H_0, the statistic

$$U_1 = (5/3)^{\frac{1}{2}}\{g_1(\tilde{R}_1) - g_1(\tilde{R}_2)\}/\{(n_1 - 5)^{-1} + (n_2 - 5)^{-1}\}^{\frac{1}{2}} \simeq N(0, 1), \tag{9.4.20}$$

where $g_1(\cdot)$ is defined by (9.4.12), $\tilde{R}_i = 3\bar{R}_i$, and $\bar{R}_i = R_i/n_i$. This result is an immediate consequence of (9.4.12) and (9.4.14).

Case II. $0\cdot44 \leqslant \bar{R} \leqslant 0\cdot67$. From (9.4.17) and (9.4.18), under H_0, the statistic

$$U_2 = \{g_2(\bar{R}_1) - g_2(\bar{R}_2)\}/c_3\{(n_1 - 4)^{-1} + (n_2 - 4)^{-1}\}^{\frac{1}{2}} \simeq N(0, 1), \tag{9.4.21}$$

The function $g_2(\cdot)$ is defined by (9.4.17) and c_1, c_2 and c_3 are given by (9.4.19).

Case III $\bar{R} \geqslant 0.67$. From (9.4.8), under H_0, we have

$$\{(n_1 - R_1)(n_2 - 1)/(n_2 - R_2)(n_1 - 1)\} \simeq F_{2(n_1 - 1),\, 2(n_2 - 1)}. \qquad (9.4.22)$$

The null hypothesis is rejected for large values of F.

We can correct (9.4.20) and (9.4.21) for bias when $n_1 \neq n_2$ as was done in the circular case. However, in general, such a correction is not necessary unless n_1 and n_2 are widely different.

Example 9.8. For two sets of 20 cross-bedding measurements from sandstone bodies in the Wastach Formation, Eocene, Wyoming (Steinmetz, 1962), it is found that

$$R_{x,1} = 12.318, \quad R_{y,1} = 2.226, \quad R_{z,1} = 3.458$$
$$R_{x,2} = 0.736, \quad R_{y,2} = -5.433, \quad R_{z,2} = 5.538.$$

Test the hypothesis of equality of concentration parameters.

We find that

$$R_x = 13.054, \ R_y = -3.207, \ R_z = 8.996, \ R = 16.1751.$$

Hence $\bar{R} = 0.404$ which is less than 0.44. Consequently, we use the test statistic U_1 given by (9.4.20). Now,

$$a = 0.44721, \quad (5/3)^{\frac{1}{2}} = 1.29099, \quad \bar{R}_1 = 0.6493, \quad \bar{R}_2 = 0.3896.$$

Consequently,

$$g_1(\tilde{R}_1) = 1.05745, \quad g_2(\tilde{R}_2) = 0.55000.$$

The observed value of U_1 is therefore 1.79. Since the 5% value of U_1 is 1.96, the null hypothesis is accepted.

Example 9.9. Test the hypothesis of equality of concentration parameters for the crystal direction data of Example 9.7.

From Example 9.7, $n_1 = n_2 = 10$, $R_1 = 7.76$, $R_2 = 7.01$, $\bar{R} = 0.74$ and we therefore use the F-statistic given by (9.4.22). The 2.5% value of $F_{18,18}$ is 2.63 which has to be compared with the observed value $2.99/2.24 = 1.33$. Hence, the null hypothesis is accepted.

9.5. MULTI-SAMPLE TESTS

We shall use a straightforward extension of the notation of the two-sample case for the multi-sample situation. Let (l_{ij}, m_{ij}, n_{ij}), $j = 1, ..., n_i$, $i = 1, ..., q$

be q independent random samples of sizes n_i drawn from $F\{(\lambda_i, \mu_i, \nu_i), \kappa_i\}$, $i = 1, ..., q$. Let $n = \Sigma n_i$. Suppose that R_i is the length of the resultant of the ith sample and R is the length of the resultant of the combined sample.

9.5.1. One-way Classification

Let us assume that $\kappa_1 = ... = \kappa_q = \kappa$ where κ is unknown. We wish to test

$$H_0 : (\lambda_i, \mu_i, \nu_i) = (\lambda, \mu, \nu), \qquad i = 1, ..., q, \qquad (9.5.1)$$

against the alternative that at least one of the equalities is not satisfied. By Section 8.6.3b, the test defined by

$$R_1 + ... + R_q|R > K$$

is a similar test. However, its percentage points are not yet available except for the two-sample case which has already been considered. As in the circular case, we shall consider some alternative procedures which are at least equivalent to the above test for large n or large κ.

Case I. $\bar{R} \geqslant 0.32$. Let us assume that $\kappa \geqslant 1$. By considering the likelihood ratio test for (9.5.1) with known κ, we obtain

$$2\kappa(\Sigma R_i - R) \simeq \chi^2_{2q-2}. \qquad (9.5.2)$$

On using this result as well as the modified chi-square approximation given at (8.7.19), we find that under H_0 that

$$(1 - 1/5\hat{\kappa}^2)\{(n - q)(\Sigma R_i - R)/(n - \Sigma R_i)(q - 1)\} \simeq F_{2q-2, 2n-2q}, \qquad (9.5.3)$$

where $\hat{\kappa}$ is the m.l.e. of κ which depends only on $\bar{R}$ and is defined by (9.2.5). This approximation is found to be adequate for $\hat{\kappa} \geqslant 1$. The correction term in $\hat{\kappa}$ can be omitted if $\bar{R} \geqslant 0.67$. The relevant calculations can be displayed in an analysis of variance table as was done in the circular case in Section 6.4.1. Example 9.10 illustrates this procedure.

Case II. $\bar{R} < 0.32$. We follow the same method as was used in the circular case for small values of κ. For the problem of testing the hypothesis (9.5.1), the likelihood ratio principle gives

$$\log_e \lambda = n \log_e c(\hat{\kappa}) - n \log_e c(\kappa^*) + \hat{\kappa}R - \kappa^*\Sigma R_i, \qquad (9.5.4)$$

where $\hat{\kappa}$ and κ^* are the m.l.e.'s of κ under H_0 and H_1 respectively and are given by

$$B(\hat{\kappa}) = \bar{R}, \qquad B(\kappa^*) = \Sigma R_i/n. \qquad (9.5.5)$$

For small values of κ, we have from (9.2.6)

$$c(\kappa) \doteq \tfrac{1}{2}\left(1 - \frac{\kappa^2}{6}\right), \qquad B(\kappa) \doteq \tfrac{1}{3}\kappa, \tag{9.5.6}$$

which when used in (9.5.4) gives

$$U = -2\log_e \lambda = \frac{3}{n}\{(\Sigma R_i)^2 - R^2\}. \tag{9.5.7}$$

For large n, U is distributed as a chi-square variable with $(2q - 2)$ d. of fr. when H_0 is true. To improve this approximation, we calculate $E(U)$. From (8.7.11),

$$E(R_i) = n_i\rho + \kappa^{-1} + O\left(\frac{1}{n_i}\right), \qquad E(R_i^2) = n_i + n_i(n_i - 1)\rho^2, \qquad \rho = B(\kappa),$$

so that

$$E(U) \doteq 3(q - 1)\{(2\rho/\kappa) + (q/n\kappa^2)\}.$$

Now, $\rho/\kappa \doteq \tfrac{1}{3}(1 - \tfrac{1}{15}\kappa^2)$, and therefore we may take

$$cU \simeq \chi^2_{2q-2}, \qquad c^{-1} = 1 - \tfrac{1}{15}\kappa^2 + \frac{3q}{2n\kappa^2}. \tag{9.5.8}$$

This new approximation is found to be satisfactory for small values of n provided that κ is not very near 0 or 1. In practice, we replace κ by its m.l.e. $\hat{\kappa}$ given by (9.5.5) and reject H_0 when cU is large.

    Watson and Irving (1957) have investigated the problem of selecting the sample size necessary to attain a desired precision in estimating the mean direction when κ is large. (See also Irving, 1964, pp. 63–68).

Example 9.10. For measurements from three sites in the Torridonian Sandstone Series, the following components along a set of three axes were obtained (E. Irving's data analysed in Watson 1956a).

> Sample 1 ($n_1 = 10$):   6·3702,   −2·6931,   1·0124
> Sample 2 ($n_2 = 11$):   7·1335,   −1·6893,   3·7011
> Sample 3 ($n_3 = 15$):   11·9296,   −2·3687,   0·8782

Are there any significant differences between the mean directions?

    We assume that the three samples come from populations with the same concentration parameter (see Example 9.11). It is found from (9.4.1) that

$$n = 36, \quad R_1 = 6\cdot990, \quad R_2 = 8\cdot212, \quad R_3 = 12\cdot194, \quad R = 26\cdot902.$$

Since $\bar{R} = 0.747$, we can use the F-test given by (9.5.3) without using the correction factor involving $\hat{\kappa}$. Further calculations are displayed in the following analysis of variance table.

Source	D.Fr.	SS	MS	F
Between sites	4	0·494	0·1233	0·95
Within sites	66	8·604	0·1304	
Total	70	9·098		

The 5% value of $F_{4,66}$ is 2·52. Hence, we accept the null hypothesis, i.e. there are no significant differences between the mean directions for the three sites.

9.5.2. A Test for the Homogeneity of Concentration Parameters

Following the circular multi-sample case of Section 6.4.2, the two-sample test for equality of concentration parameters of Section 9.4.2b. can easily be extended to the multi-sample situation. The results are as follows.

Case I. $\bar{R} < 0.44$. Under H_0, we have

$$U_1 = \Sigma w_i g_1{}^2(\tilde{R}_i) - [\{\Sigma w_i g_1(\tilde{R}_i)\}^2/\Sigma w_i] \simeq \chi^2_{q-1}, \qquad (9.5.9)$$

where

$$w_i{}^{-1} = 3/5(n_i - 5), \qquad \tilde{R}_i = 3\bar{R}_i, \qquad g_1(\tilde{R}_i) = \sin^{-1}(\tilde{R}_i/\sqrt{5}).$$

Case II. $0.44 \leqslant \bar{R} \leqslant 0.67$. Under H_0, it is found that

$$U_2 = \Sigma w_i g_2{}^2(\bar{R}_i) - [\{\Sigma w_i g_2(\bar{R}_i)\}^2/\Sigma w_i] \simeq \chi^2_{q-1}, \qquad (9.5.10)$$

where now

$$w_i{}^{-1} = 0.39356/(n - 4), \qquad g_2(\bar{R}_i) = \sin^{-1}\{(\bar{R}_i + 0.17595)/1.02903\}.$$

Case III. $\bar{R} \geqslant 0.67$. Under H_0, we have

$$U_3 = [v \log_e \{(n - \Sigma R_i)/v\} - \Sigma v_i \log_e \{(n_i - R_i)/v_i\}]/(1 + d) \simeq \chi^2_{2q-2}, \qquad (9.5.11)$$

where

$$v_i = 2(n_i - 1), \quad v = 2(n - q) \quad \text{and} \quad d = (\Sigma v_i{}^{-1} - v^{-1}))\{3(q - 1)\}.$$

Example 9.11. Test the homogeneity of concentration parameters for the Torridonian Sandstone Series data of Example 9.10.

From Example 9.10, we have $\bar{R} > 0.67$. Hence, we use the test statistic U_3. Further,

$$v_1 = 18, \quad n_1 - R_1 = 3.010, \quad v_2 = 20, \quad n_2 - R_2 = 2.788,$$
$$v_3 = 28, \quad n_3 - R_3 = 2.806, \quad v = 66, \quad n - \Sigma R_i = 8.604.$$

Using these values, it is found that

$$v \log_e \{(n - \Sigma R_i)/v\} = -134.4514, \quad \Sigma v_i \log_e \{(n_i - R_i)/v_i\} = -136.0186.$$

Further, $d = 0.03153$ and $q = 3$. Hence, $U_3 = 1.52$. The 5% value of χ_4^2 is 9.49, and therefore the null hypothesis is accepted, i.e. the three samples may be regarded as drawn from populations with the same concentration parameter.

9.6. A TEST FOR COPLANARITY

Following Watson (1960), we shall now give a test for coplanarity when q independent random samples are drawn from $F\{(\lambda_i, \mu_i, v_i), \kappa_i\}, i = 1, ..., q$. In the first two sections, we assume that $\kappa_1 = ... = \kappa_q = \kappa$ and κ is large.

The notation of the preceding section will be used and, in addition, we suppose that $(\bar{l}_{0i}, \bar{m}_{0i}, \bar{n}_{0i}) i = 1, ..., q$ are the direction cosines of the q-sample mean directions. That is, if (R_{xi}, R_{yi}, R_{zi}) are the components of the ith sample resultant, we have

$$\bar{l}_{0i} = R_{xi}/R_i, \quad \bar{m}_{0i} = R_{yi}/R_i, \quad \bar{n}_{0i} = R_{zi}/R_i, \quad (9.6.1)$$

where

$$R_{xi} = \sum_j l_{ij}, \quad R_{yi} = \sum_j m_{ij}, \quad R_{zi} = \sum_j n_{ij}. \quad (9.6.2)$$

9.6.1. Prescribed Normal

Let the null hypothesis be that the population mean directions lie in a plane whose normal has the direction cosines (u, v, w) which are initially assumed to be known. Our problem is to test

$$H_0 : u\lambda_i + v\mu_i + wv_i = 0 \quad \text{against} \quad H_1 : (\lambda_i, \mu_i, v_i) \quad \text{unspecified}, \quad (9.6.3)$$

where $i = 1, ..., q, \lambda_i^2 + \mu_i^2 + v_i^2 = 1$ and κ is unspecified. Under H_0, the logarithm of the likelihood function is proportional to

$$L(H_0) = n \log c(\kappa) + \kappa \Sigma R_i (\bar{l}_{0i} \lambda_i + \bar{m}_{0i} \mu_i + \bar{n}_{0i} v_i) + \Sigma a_i (u\lambda_i + v\mu_i + wv_i)$$
$$+ \Sigma b_i (\lambda_i^2 + \mu_i^2 + v_i^2 - 1), \quad (9.6.4)$$

where the a_i, b_i are Lagrange multipliers. On differentiating (9.6.4) with respect to λ_i, μ_i and ν_i respectively, we find that the maximum likelihood equations for these parameters are

$$\kappa R_i \bar{l}_{0i} + ua_i + 2\lambda_i b_i = 0, \qquad (9.6.5)$$

$$\kappa R_i \bar{m}_{0i} + va_i + 2\mu_i b_i = 0, \qquad (9.6.6)$$

$$\kappa R_i \bar{n}_{0i} + wa_i + 2\nu_i b_i = 0. \qquad (9.6.7)$$

On multiplying the first equation by u, the second by v and the third by w, we obtain, after adding them together,

$$a_i = -\kappa R_i d_i, \qquad d_i = \bar{l}_{0i} u + \bar{m}_{0i} v + \bar{n}_{0i} w. \qquad (9.6.8)$$

Hence, from (9.6.5)–(9.6.7), the m.l.e.'s of λ_i, μ_i and ν_i are given by

$$\lambda_i/(\bar{l}_{0i} - ud_i) = \mu_i/(\bar{m}_{0i} - vd_i) = \nu_i/(\bar{n}_{0i} - wd_i) = 1/(1 - d_i)^{\frac{1}{2}}. \qquad (9.6.9)$$

On using these in (9.6.4), we find that

$$\max L(H_0) = n \log c(\hat{\kappa}) + \hat{\kappa} S, \qquad (9.6.10)$$

where

$$S = \sum_{i=1}^{q} R_i (1 - d_i^2)^{\frac{1}{2}}, \qquad B(\hat{\kappa}) = S/n \qquad (9.6.11)$$

and the d_i are given by (9.6.8). Let us assume that n and κ are large so that from (9.2.7)

$$c(\kappa) = \kappa/e^{\kappa}, \qquad B(\kappa) = 1 - 1/\kappa.$$

Consequently, (9.6.10) reduces to

$$\max L(H_0) = n(\log \hat{\kappa} - 1), \qquad \hat{\kappa} = n/(n - S). \qquad (9.6.12)$$

Similarly, under H_1, it is found for large n and κ that

$$\max L(H_1) = n(\log \kappa^* - 1), \qquad (9.6.13)$$

where

$$\kappa^* = n/S_0, \qquad S_0 = n - \Sigma R_i. \qquad (9.6.14)$$

From (9.6.12) and (9.6.13), we thus have

$$-2 \log_e \lambda \doteq 2n \log \left[1 + \sum_{i=1}^{q} R_i \{1 - (1 - d_i^2)^{\frac{1}{2}}\}/S_0 \right].$$

On assuming that all the n_i are large and using $(1 - d_i^2)^{\frac{1}{2}} \doteq 1 - \frac{1}{2}d_i^2$ together with (9.6.3), the last expression reduces to

$$-2\log_e \lambda \doteq n(\mathbf{u}'\mathbf{Vu})/(n - \Sigma R_i) \simeq \chi_q^2, \qquad (9.6.15)$$

where $\mathbf{u}' = (u, v, w)$ and $\mathbf{V}$ is a symmetric matrix given by

$$\mathbf{V} = \begin{bmatrix} \Sigma R_i \bar{l}_{0i}^2, & \Sigma R_i \bar{l}_{0i}\bar{m}_{0i}, & \Sigma R_i \bar{l}_{0i}\bar{n}_{0i} \\ & \Sigma R_i \bar{m}_{0i}^2, & \Sigma R_i \bar{m}_{0i}\bar{n}_{0i} \\ & & \Sigma R_i \bar{n}_{0i}^2 \end{bmatrix}. \qquad (9.6.16)$$

Finally, on using the analysis of variance analogy, we may use the statistic

$$(\mathbf{u}'\mathbf{Vu})(n - q)/\{(n - \Sigma R_i)q\} \simeq F_{q,2n-2q} \qquad (9.6.17)$$

to test (9.6.3). We would expect the F-approximation to be adequate for moderately large values of κ.

9.6.2. Unspecified Normal

In practice, we are usually interested in testing the hypothesis (9.6.3) when $\mathbf{u}$ is unknown. On following the same procedure as above, we find that we are again led to (9.6.17) except that the term $\mathbf{u}'\mathbf{Vu}$ in the numerator of (9.6.17) now becomes

$$\min \mathbf{u}'\mathbf{Vu}$$

which is of course equal to v_1 which is the smallest eigen value of $\mathbf{V}$. Further, the eigen vector corresponding to v_1 is the m.l.e. of the normal to the best fitting plane. The test criterion (9.6.17) reduces to

$$v_1(n - q)/\{(q - 2)(n - \Sigma R_i)\} \simeq F_{q-2,2n-2q}. \qquad (9.6.18)$$

Since $\mathbf{u}'\mathbf{Vu} - v_1$ measures deviations from the prescribed normal $\mathbf{u}$, we can now test the hypothesis (9.6.3) by using

$$\tfrac{1}{2}(n - q)\{\mathbf{u}'\mathbf{Vu} - v_1\}/(n - \Sigma R_i) \simeq F_{2,2n-2q}. \qquad (9.6.19)$$

Let v_1, v_2, v_3 be the eigen values of $\mathbf{V}$. By using the eigen vectors of $\mathbf{V}$ as our co-ordinate axes, (9.6.19) reduces to

$$\tfrac{1}{2}(n - q)(v_1 u^2 + v_2 v^2 + v_3 w^2 - v_1)/(n - \Sigma R_i) \simeq F_{2,2n-2q}. \qquad (9.6.20)$$

Consequently, if

$$\Pr\{F_{2,2n-2q} > F_0\} = \gamma,$$

then a $(1 - \gamma)100\%$ confidence cone around the normal to the common plane in terms of spherical polar co-ordinates (α, β) is given by

$$(v_1 \cos^2 \beta + v_2 \sin^2 \beta) \sin^2 \alpha + v_3 \cos^2 \alpha \leqslant t \qquad (9.6.21)$$

where

$$t = v_1 + \{2F_0(n - \Sigma R_i)/(n - q)\}.$$

The axis of this cone is the eigen vector corresponding to v_1.

We can gather some information about the semi-angle α of this cone as follows. From the uniformity of β, we have $E(\cos^2 \beta) = E(\sin^2 \beta) = \frac{1}{2}$ so that the average value $\bar{\alpha}$ of α is given by

$$(v_1 + v_2) \sin^2 \bar{\alpha} + 2v_3 \cos^2 \bar{\alpha} = 2t. \qquad (9.6.22)$$

Confining the range of β to $(0, \pi)$, we find that $\alpha_{\max}$ occurs when $\beta = 0$ and $\alpha_{\min}$ occurs when $\beta = \pi/2$.

9.6.3. Non-homogeneous Case

So far it has been assumed that all the κ_i are equal. We can, however remove this restriction from the above procedure. Let $\mathbf{W}$ be the matrix obtained on replacing R_i by $R_i(n_i - 1)/(n_i - R_i)$ in $\mathbf{V}$. Let w_1 be the least eigen value of $\mathbf{W}$. It is found that

$$\text{Deviations from coplanarity} = w_1 \simeq \chi^2_{q-2} \qquad (9.6.23)$$

and

$$\text{Deviations from prescribed normal } \mathbf{u} = \mathbf{u'Wu} - w_1 \simeq \chi_2^2. \qquad (9.6.24)$$

Example 9.12. By certain geophysical considerations, it is to be expected that the following samples taken from three populations are coplanar (Watson, 1960 dealing with some data of K.M. Creer)

	size	l_0	m_0	n_0	R
Sample 1	35	-0.0698	-0.9589	-0.2750	33.172
Sample 2	9	-0.8572	0.2575	-0.4460	8.567
Sample 3	6	-0.5469	-0.7302	-0.4095	5.786

Does the data support the prediction (A sign in sample 2 of Watson (1960) has been corrected).

By Appendix 3.2, $\hat{\kappa}_1 = 19.1$, $\hat{\kappa}_2 = 20.8$, $\hat{\kappa}_3 = 28.0$ which are fairly large. On using the test given by (9.5.11), it is found that the samples may be regarded as drawn from populations having the same concentration parameter κ. The matrix $\mathbf{V}$ is found to be

$$\mathbf{V} = \begin{bmatrix} 8\cdot187167, & 2\cdot639875, & 5\cdot207803 \\ & 34\cdot154391, & 9\cdot493608 \\ & & 5\cdot183002 \end{bmatrix}.$$

Its eigen values are

$$v_1 = 0\cdot02682, \qquad v_2 = 9\cdot9497, \qquad v_3 = 37\cdot5481.$$

The corresponding eigen vectors are

$$(-0\cdot4802, -0\cdot2004, 0\cdot8540), \quad (0\cdot8663, -0\cdot2615, 0\cdot4257),$$
$$(0\cdot1380, 0\cdot9442, 0\cdot2992).$$

From (9.6.18), we obtain

$$F_{1,94} = 47 \times 0\cdot02682/2\cdot475 = 0\cdot509.$$

The 5% value of $F_{1,94}$ is 3·95 and therefore the hypothesis of coplanarity of the three populations is accepted.

From (9.6.21), a 95% confidence cone around the normal to this plane is given by

$$(9\cdot9497\cos^2\beta + 37\cdot5481\sin^2\beta)\sin^2\alpha + 0\cdot02682\cos^2\alpha \leqslant 0\cdot103. \quad (9.6.25)$$

The average semi-angle $\bar{\alpha}$ of the cone satisfies

$$23\cdot7489\sin^2\bar{\alpha} + 0\cdot02682\cos^2\bar{\alpha} = 0\cdot103.$$

It is found that $\bar{\alpha} = 3°15'$. On putting $\beta = 0$ and $\beta = \pi/2$ in (9.6.25), we find that $\alpha_{\max} = 5°$ and $\alpha_{\min} = 2°35'$. Hence, the axis of the cone has the direction cosines $(-0\cdot4802, -0\cdot2004, 0\cdot8540)$ and the semi-angle of the cone varies between $2°35'$ and $5°$, with the average value $\bar{\alpha}$ of $3°15'$.

9.7. TESTS FOR AXIAL DATA

Suppose that $\mathbf{L}_1, ..., \mathbf{L}_n$ is a random sample of size n from Bingham's distribution with p.d.f.

$$\{4\pi d(\kappa)\}^{-1}\exp\left\{\sum_{j=1}^3 \kappa_j(\mathbf{\mu}_j'\mathbf{L})^2\right\}, \qquad (9.7.1)$$

where $\mu = (\mu_1, \mu_2, \mu_3)$ is an orthogonal matrix. Let $\kappa_1 \leqslant \kappa_2 \leqslant \kappa_3$. We are interested in the following problems

(i) To test the hypothesis of uniformity:

$$H_{0,u} : \kappa_1 = \kappa_2 = \kappa_3. \qquad (9.7.2)$$

(ii) If $H_{0,u}$ is rejected, to test the hypothesis of rotational symmetry about an axis, i.e. to test the equality of two of the κ's. There are two cases, the girdle case for which

$$H_{0,g} : \kappa_2 = \kappa_3 \qquad (9.7.3)$$

and the bipolar case for which

$$H_{0,b} : \kappa_1 = \kappa_2. \qquad (9.7.4)$$

(iii) If $H_{0,g}$ is accepted, to test some special hypotheses for the girdle case, e.g. testing whether a prescribed axis is the axis of symmetry.

(iv) If $H_{0,b}$ is accepted, to test some special hypotheses for the bipolar case.

Let $\mathbf{T}$ be the matrix of the sum of squares and products given by (9.2.25). Suppose that τ_1, τ_2 and τ_3 are its eigen values in ascending order and let $\mathbf{t}_1$, $\mathbf{t}_2$ and $\mathbf{t}_3$ be the corresponding eigen vectors.

9.7.1. A Test of Uniformity

In this case, we know from Section 9.2.3 that $\tau_1 \doteq \tau_2 \doteq \tau_3 \doteq n/3$ so that a test-statistic for uniformity should depend on the differences $\tau_i - n/3$. Using the m.l.e.'s of κ and μ given in Section 9.2.3, we can obtain the likelihood ratio statistic λ_u for this problem. For large n, it can be shown that $-2 \log_e \lambda_u$ reduces to

$$S_u = (15/2n) \sum_{i=1}^{3} (\tau_i - \tfrac{1}{3}n)^2. \qquad (9.7.5)$$

It follows from a property of the likelihood ratio tests that S_u is asymptotically distributed as χ_5^2 under the null hypothesis. The hypothesis of uniformity is rejected for large values of S_u. The d. of fr. associated with the chi-square is five since (a) $\kappa_1 = \kappa_2 = \kappa_3$ implies two restrictions under $H_{0,u}$ and (b) the specification of the orthogonal matrix μ implies fixing three axes, i.e. three Eulerian angles. For example, the new axes OX', OY' and OZ' can be specified by using the three angles defined as follows. Specify OX' by the colatitude and latitude of a point on OX' while specifying OY' in the plane normal to

OX' by the angle which OY' makes with one of the old axes. The axis OZ' is then fixed.

The above result is due to Bingham (1964). The null distribution of S_u for small samples is not known.

9.7.2. Tests of Rotational Symmetry

Consider the girdle case. Using the results of Sections 9.2.2 and 9.2.3, it can be shown (Bingham, 1964) that if λ_g is the likelihood ratio statistic for this problem then for large n, $-2\log_e \lambda_g$ reduces to

$$S_g = \tfrac{1}{2}(\hat{\kappa}_3 - \hat{\kappa}_2)(\tau_3 - \tau_2), \tag{9.7.6}$$

where $\hat{\kappa}_3$ and $\hat{\kappa}_2$ satisfy (9.2.33).

Under $H_{0,g}$, the statistic S_g is asymptotically distributed as χ_2^2. The d. of fr. associated with the chi-square is two since (i) $\kappa_1 = \kappa_2$ and (ii) μ_1 and μ_2 are indeterminate so that any pair of vectors orthogonal to μ_3 will determine μ_1 and μ_2. In terms of the previous discussion, the angle which OY' makes with one of the old axes is now specified. The null hypothesis $H_{0,g}$ is rejected for large values of S_g.

For the bipolar case, it is similarly found that

$$S_b = \tfrac{1}{2}(\hat{\kappa}_2 - \hat{\kappa}_1)(\tau_2 - \tau_1) \tag{9.7.7}$$

is asymptotically distributed as χ_2^2 when $H_{0,b}$ is true. The null hypothesis is rejected for large values of S_b. The estimates $\hat{\kappa}_1$ and $\hat{\kappa}_2$ satisfy Eqn. (9.2.33).

For large samples, it is expected that if $H_{0,u}$ is rejected then both of the hypotheses $H_{0,g}$ and $H_{0,b}$ cannot be accepted.

Example 9.13. For the calcite grains data of Example 8.3, test the hypothesis of uniformity. If the hypothesis of uniformity is rejected, test the hypothesis of rotational symmetry.

From Example 8.3, $n = 30$ and the eigen values of $\mathbf{T}$ are

$$\tau_1 = 4\cdot1764, \qquad \tau_2 = 10\cdot9639, \qquad \tau_3 = 14\cdot8595. \tag{9.7.8}$$

On substituting these values into S_u, it is found that $S_u = 14\cdot61$. The 5% and 1% values of χ_5^2 are $11\cdot07$ and $15\cdot09$ respectively. Hence, the hypothesis of uniformity is rejected at the 5% level of significance.

We now test the hypothesis of rotational symmetry. It is seen either from Tables in Bingham (1964) or by numerical evaluation that

$$\hat{\kappa}_1 = -3\cdot62, \qquad \hat{\kappa}_2 = -0\cdot68, \qquad \hat{\kappa}_3 = 0. \tag{9.7.9}$$

On substituting (9.7.8) and (9.7.9) into (9.7.6) and (9.7.7), we obtain

$$S_g = 1 \cdot 32, \qquad S_b = 9 \cdot 98.$$

The 5% and 1% values of χ_2^2 are 5·99 and 9·21 respectively so that the hypothesis of a girdle distribution is accepted. This conclusion was foreseen in Example 8.3 on intuitive grounds. The hypothesis of a bipolar distribution is rejected which is consistent with our previous conclusions.

Numerical evaluation of $\hat{\kappa}_1$ and $\hat{\kappa}_2$ defined by (9.2.33) is tedious. However, the following approximation* can be used when the τ_i's indicate that the distribution is nearly rotationally symmetric, i.e. either bipolar or symmetric girdle. In the bipolar case, define

$$d = \bar{\tau}_2 - \bar{\tau}_1, \quad s = \bar{\tau}_2 + \bar{\tau}_1, \quad D(-\hat{\kappa}') = \bar{\tau}_3, \quad \hat{\kappa}_0 = -\hat{\kappa}',$$

where $\hat{\kappa}'$ can be obtained from Appendix 3.4. In the girdle case, define

$$d = \bar{\tau}_3 - \bar{\tau}_2, \quad s = \bar{\tau}_3 + \bar{\tau}_2, \quad D(\hat{\kappa}) = \bar{\tau}_1, \quad \hat{\kappa}_0 = \hat{\kappa}, \qquad (9.7.10)$$

where $\hat{\kappa}$ can be obtained from Appendix 3.3. Then approximately

$$\left. \begin{array}{l} \text{(bipolar case)} \ \hat{\kappa}_1 = \hat{\kappa}_0 - \delta, \quad \hat{\kappa}_2 = \hat{\kappa}_0 + \delta, \quad \hat{\kappa}_3 = 0, \\ \text{(girdle case)} \ \ \hat{\kappa}_1 = -\hat{\kappa}_0 - \delta, \quad \hat{\kappa}_2 = -2\delta, \quad \hat{\kappa}_3 = 0, \end{array} \right\} \qquad (9.7.11)$$

where

$$\delta = 2d\hat{\kappa}_0 / \{s(\hat{\kappa}_0 - 1\cdot5) + 1\},$$

Since Example 8.3 suggests that the calcite grain distribution is approximately girdle in form, we obtain from (9.7.10) and (9.7.8) that

$$d = 0 \cdot 1299, \quad s = 0 \cdot 8608, \quad D(\hat{\kappa}_0) = 0 \cdot 1392, \quad \hat{\kappa}_0 = 3 \cdot 33.$$

Consequently, it is found from (9.7.11) that

$$\delta = 0 \cdot 336, \quad \hat{\kappa}_1 \doteq -3 \cdot 67, \quad \hat{\kappa}_2 = -0 \cdot 67, \quad \hat{\kappa}_3 = 0.$$

These values of the κ's are very close to the exact values given by (9.7.9). Using these values in (9.7.6) and (9.7.7), we find that

$$S_g \doteq 1 \cdot 31, \quad S_b \doteq 10 \cdot 18$$

so that the conclusions remain the same.

9.7.3. The Girdle Case

Let us now assume that the hypothesis of a girdle distribution is accepted. Using the notation of Sections 8.5.5a and 8.5.5b, we may rewrite (9.7.1) in this case as

$$\{b(\kappa)/2\pi\} \exp\{-\kappa(\mathbf{L}'\,\boldsymbol{\mu})^2\}, \qquad \kappa > 0, \qquad (9.7.12)$$

* This result was communicated to me by Dr. C. Bingham.

where μ is now a vector. On selecting μ as the z-axis, the p.d.f. of θ is

$$c\,e^{-\kappa\cos^2\theta}\sin\theta, \qquad 0 < \theta < \pi, \quad \kappa > 0.$$

Hence, for large κ, we have

$$2\kappa\cos^2\theta \simeq \chi_1^2. \tag{9.7.13}$$

A Test of a Prescribed Axis. We now give a method for testing

$$H_0 : \mu = \mu_0, \tag{9.7.14}$$

where μ_0 is the vector of direction cosines of the prescribed axis. We assume that κ is large but unknown. Let (θ_i, ϕ_i), $i = 1, \ldots, n$ be n observations from this population. From (9.7.13), we have

$$2\kappa\sum_{i=1}^{n}\cos^2\theta_i \simeq \chi_n^2. \tag{9.7.15}$$

Further, let $(\hat{\theta}_i, \hat{\phi}_i)$ be the new observations when the z-axis is the direction of $\hat{\mu}$ estimated by the method of Section 9.2.2. We have

$$2\kappa\sum_{i=1}^{n}\cos^2\hat{\theta}_i \simeq \chi_{n-2}^2 \tag{9.7.16}$$

since for $\hat{\mu}' = (\hat{\mu}, \hat{v}, \hat{\lambda})$, $\hat{\mu}^2 + \hat{v}^2 + \hat{\lambda}^2 = 1$, and therefore only two angles are estimated. Further,

$$\Sigma\cos^2\theta_i = \Sigma(L_i'\mu)^2 = \mu'T\mu, \quad \Sigma\cos^2\hat{\theta}_i = \min_{\mu}\Sigma(L_i'\mu)^2 = \tau_1$$

which, as in (9.6.23), represent deviations from the true and the fitted axes respectively. Consequently, we have the analysis of variance decomposition

$$\mu'T\mu = \tau_1 + (\mu'T\mu - \tau_1). \tag{9.7.17}$$

Hence, the test statistic is

$$(n-2)(\mu_0'T\mu_0 - \tau_1)/2\tau_1 \simeq F_{2,n-2}.$$

We can now obtain a $(1-\gamma)100\%$ cone for μ as was done in Section 9.6.2. Let

$$\Pr(F_{2,n-2} > F_0) = \gamma$$

and

$$\hat{\mu}'t = \cos\alpha, \qquad \hat{\mu}'t_2 = \sin\alpha\cos\beta, \qquad \hat{\mu}'t_3 = \sin\alpha\sin\beta.$$

It is found that the cone is given by

$$\tau_1 \cos^2 \alpha + (\tau_2 \cos^2 \beta + \tau_3 \sin^2 \beta) \sin^2 \alpha \leqslant a,$$

where

$$a = \tau_1(n - 2 + 2F_0)/(n - 2).$$

The axis of this cone is $\mathbf{t}_1$. It is almost circular since for the girdle case $\tau_2 \doteq \tau_3$.

A Test of Equality of Two Populations. Suppose that $\mathbf{L}_{ij}$ $i = 1, ..., n_j, j = 1, 2$ are observations from (9.7.12) with different $\boldsymbol{\mu}$'s ($\boldsymbol{\mu}_1$ and $\boldsymbol{\mu}_2$, say) but the same κ. We have the identity,

$$\min \{\Sigma(\mathbf{L}_{i1}'\boldsymbol{\mu})^2 + \Sigma(\mathbf{L}_{i2}'\boldsymbol{\mu})^2\} \equiv \min \Sigma(\mathbf{L}_{i1}'\boldsymbol{\mu}_1)^2 + \min \Sigma(\mathbf{L}_{i2}'\boldsymbol{\mu}_2)^2 + A,$$

where A is the residual term. By analogy with the analysis of variance, the quantities on the right hand side are independently distributed as $(1/2\kappa)\chi^2_{n_1-2}$, $(1/2\kappa)\chi^2_{n_2-2}$ and $(1/2\kappa)\chi_2^2$ respectively if κ is large. Let τ_{11}, τ_{21} and τ_1^* be the smallest eigen values of the matrices

$$\mathbf{T}_1 = \Sigma\mathbf{L}_{i1}\mathbf{L}_{i2}', \qquad \mathbf{T}_2 = \Sigma\mathbf{L}_{i2}\mathbf{L}_{i2}' \qquad \text{and} \qquad \mathbf{T}_1 + \mathbf{T}_2 \qquad (9.7.18)$$

respectively. Let $n = n_1 + n_2$. Hence, to test equality of two axes, we use the statistic

$$(\tau_1^* - \tau_{11} - \tau_{21})(n - 4)/2(\tau_{11} + \tau_{21}) \simeq F_{2,n-4}. \qquad (9.7.19)$$

These results are due to Watson (1965). We can also obtain these results by using the likelihood ratio principle and these methods can be used to obtain further tests. The above approximations are adequate for $\kappa > 5$. The percentage points of $\Sigma \cos^2 \theta_i$ under uniformity are given by Stephens (1965c) but these can only be used to test the hypothesis of uniformity against the hypothesis of a girdle distribution; Anderson and Stephens (1971) give percentage points of τ_1 and τ_3, for unknown mean direction.

9.7.4. The Bipolar Case

Let us now suppose that the hypothesis of a bipolar distribution is accepted. In this case, the p.d.f. (9.7.1) can be written as

$$\{b(-\kappa)/2\pi\} \exp \{\kappa(\mathbf{L}'\boldsymbol{\mu})^2\}, \qquad \kappa > 0, \qquad (9.7.20)$$

and the p.d.f. of θ with $\boldsymbol{\mu}$ as the z-axis is

$$c \, e^{\kappa \cos^2 \theta} \sin \theta. \qquad 0 < \theta < \pi.$$

For large κ, we have

$$2\kappa(1 - \cos^2 \theta) \simeq \chi_1^2. \qquad (9.7.21)$$

Hence, on replacing $2\kappa \cos^2 \theta_i$ by $2\kappa(1 - \cos^2 \theta_i)$ in the above tests for the girdle case, we can obtain the corresponding tests for the bipolar case. For example,

$$2\kappa(n - \Sigma \cos^2 \theta_i) = 2\kappa(n - \mathbf{\mu}'\mathbf{T}\mathbf{\mu}) \simeq \chi_n^2,$$

and

$$2\kappa(n - \max \Sigma \cos^2 \theta_i) = 2\kappa(n - \tau_3) \simeq \chi_{n-2}^2.$$

Thus, to test $\mathbf{\mu} = \mathbf{\mu}_0$, the test statistic is

$$(n - 2)(\tau_3 - \mathbf{\mu}_0' \mathbf{T}\mathbf{\mu}_0)/2\tau_3 \simeq F_{2,n-2}. \qquad (9.7.22)$$

Further, the $(1 - \gamma)100\%$ cone for $\mathbf{\mu}$ with axis $\mathbf{t}_3$ is

$$(\tau_1 \cos^2 \beta + \tau_2 \sin^2 \beta) \sin^2 \alpha + \tau_3 \cos^2 \alpha \geqslant b$$

where $b = \tau_3(n - 2 - 2F_0)/(n - 2)$ and (α, β) are the polar co-ordinates of $\mathbf{\mu}$ when the eigen vectors $\mathbf{t}_1$, $\mathbf{t}_2$ and $\mathbf{t}_3$ are the x, y and z-axes respectively. Again, we have $\tau_1 \doteq \tau_2$ so that the cone is approximately circular.

Let τ_{13}, τ_{23} and τ_3^* be the maximum eigen values of $\mathbf{T}_1$, $\mathbf{T}_2$ and $\mathbf{T}_1 + \mathbf{T}_2$ respectively where $\mathbf{T}_1$ and $\mathbf{T}_2$ are defined by (9.0.18). To test equality of two axes, the test-statistic is

$$(\tau_{13} + \tau_{23} - \tau_3^*)(n - 4)/2(n - \tau_{13} - \tau_{23}) \simeq F_{2,n-4}. \qquad (9.7.23)$$

Similarly, other tests can be constructed.

9.8. A REVIEW OF SOME OTHER TESTS AND TOPICS

9.8.1. Robustness Studies

Watson (1967b) has studied the robustness of the size of the mean direction tests and the dispersion (concentration parameter) tests for the Fisher distribution. The p.d.f. of the Fisher distribution can be expressed as

$$f_1(\theta, \phi) = f(\theta) g(\phi), \qquad 0 < \theta < \pi, \quad 0 < \phi < 2\pi, \qquad (9.8.1)$$

where $\kappa(1 - \cos \theta)$ is distributed as the negative exponential on $(0, 2\kappa)$ and ϕ is uniformly distributed on $(0, 2\pi)$.

The tests may be influenced by changes in f and g. There are two important types of departure from the Fisher distribution. (i) *The Skewness Case* where g is varied but f corresponds to the Fisher distribution and (ii) the *Kurtosis Case* where g is uniform but f is varied. The robustness study for the first case will give some idea of the effect of asymmetry while for the second case, it will show the effect of varying the mass on the sphere in the form of a spinning top.

We now describe the robustness studies of Watson (1967b) for these two cases. In the first case, $g(\phi)$ was taken to be linear (piecewise) in ϕ from $\alpha + \beta$ at $\phi = 0$ to α at $\phi = \pi/2$, to $\alpha + \beta$ at $\phi = \pi$, to α at $\phi = 3\pi/2$, to $\alpha + \beta$ at $\phi = 2\pi$. For the total probability to be unity, $\pi(2\alpha + \beta) = 1$. For $\beta = 0$, the distribution is uniform. It was found for this case that there was no effect on the mean direction tests but there was a slight effect on the dispersion tests. In the second case, $\kappa(1 - \cos\theta)$ was taken as (a) Cauchy on $(0, 2\kappa)$ and (b) a standard normal. It was found that the mean direction tests were robust but not the dispersion tests. This conclusion is analogous to the well known result for the normal theory tests.

9.8.2. A Non-parametric Test of Uniformity

The spherical generalization of Ajne's statistic A_n (7.2.67) is defined by Beran (1968) as

$$A_n = \tfrac{1}{4}n - \pi^{-n} \sum_{i<j} \Psi_{ij}, \qquad (9.8.2)$$

where Ψ_{ij} is the smaller of the two angles between the directions represented by (θ_i, ϕ_i) and (θ_j, ϕ_j). For sufficiently large x, Beran (1968) has shown that

$$\Pr(16A_n > x) = 1 \cdot 65 \Pr(\chi_3^2 > x) \qquad (9.8.3)$$

provides a good approximation for $n > 20$. The test is locally most powerful invariant against the alternatives with p.d.f. $f(\theta, \phi)$ on the sphere defined by

$$f(\theta, \phi) = p/(2\pi), \quad \text{if} \quad (\theta, \phi) \text{ is a point on a hemisphere with}$$
$$\text{unknown pole } (\alpha, \beta), \quad 0 < p < 1,$$

$$= (1 - p)/(2\pi), \quad \text{otherwise.}$$

9.8.3. A Test for Serial Correlation

Let $\mathbf{L}_1, ..., \mathbf{L}_n$ be n observed directions which are not necessarily random. This occurs when there is a serial correlation between the successive directions, e.g. in paleomagnetic studies of superimposed strata, successive

(NRM) directions from adjacent horizons may be correlated. Watson and Beran (1967) have proposed the statistic

$$U = \sum_{i=1}^{n-1} \mathbf{L}_i' \, \mathbf{L}_{i+1}, \qquad (9.8.4)$$

for testing the null hypothesis of randomness against the hypothesis of a serial correlation. The null hypothesis is rejected for large values of U. The null distribution of U is not known for samples from the Fisher distribution. However, its permutation distribution over $n!$ permutations of $(\mathbf{L}_1, ..., \mathbf{L}_n)$ has been studied by Watson and Beran (1967). For large n, it is found that U is distributed normally. Let $b_{ij} = \mathbf{L}_i' \, \mathbf{L}_j$. The permutation moments are

$$E(U) = (2/n) \, \Sigma b_{ij}, \qquad (9.8.5)$$

$$E(U^2) = \frac{1}{n} \Sigma b_{ij}^2 + \frac{2}{n(n-1)} \Sigma b_{ij} b_{jk} + \frac{1}{n(n-1)} \Sigma b_{ij} b_{kl}, \qquad (9.8.6)$$

where the sums are taken over unequal subscripts. These moments do not simplify very much, and, in practice, it is better to calculate the moments directly from the permutation distribution of U.

9.8.4. Further References

We have not considered the problem of computer programming for the tests. This problem is not difficult and some programs will be found in Andrews and Shimizu (1966), Fox (1967) and Jones (1967).

Mackenzie (1957) has studied the problem of inference for the orthogonal matrix $\mathbf{R}$ when the observed directions $\mathbf{L}_i$ are distributed as $F\{\mathbf{R}\mathbf{b}_i, \kappa w_i\}$ and the directions $\mathbf{b}_i$ and the weights w_i are known but κ and $\mathbf{R}$ are unknown. This problem arises in crystallography when the standard orientation $\mathbf{b}_i$ in a crystal has undergone an unknown rotation $\mathbf{R}$. Other regression problems are considered by Creer (1962) and Gould (1969) (see Section 9.2.1). The reader is referred to Watson (1970) for some other problems arising in geology such as the estimation of the second order tensor. Box (1954) and Scheffé (1970) have obtained confidence cones for the axis and the direction respectively of the mean vector under the assumption of multivariate normality, i.e. when the observations have magnitude as well as direction.

In our treatment, we have used only the classical approach to statistical inference. Fisher (1953) and Fraser (1968, pp. 224–25) have used the Fiducial Structural approaches; Fraser (1968, pp. 202–12) has also investigated the circular case. The inference problems (especially for the circular case) have been studied by Garner (1968) from the Bayesian view-point.

APPENDICES

APPENDIX 1

Bessel functions

We list below some important formulae involving Bessel functions. Most of these formulae are proved in the main text and in brackets, we cite the location of each proof.

1. The *modified Bessel function* of the *first* kind and the pth order is defined by

$$I_p(\kappa) = \sum_{r=0}^{\infty} \{\Gamma(p + r + 1)\Gamma(r + 1)\}^{-1}(\tfrac{1}{2}\kappa)^{2r+p}.$$

2. $I_0(\kappa) = \dfrac{1}{2\pi} \displaystyle\int_0^{2\pi} e^{\kappa \cos\theta} \, d\theta = \dfrac{1}{\pi} \displaystyle\int_0^{\pi} e^{\kappa \cos\theta} \, d\theta.$ (Section 3.4.9a)

3. $I_p(\kappa) = \dfrac{1}{2\pi} \displaystyle\int_0^{2\pi} \cos p\theta \, e^{\kappa \cos\theta} \, d\theta.$ (Section 3.4.9d)

4. $I_2(\kappa) = I_0(\kappa) - \dfrac{2}{\kappa} I_1(\kappa).$ (Equation 3.4.53)

5. $I_0'(\kappa) = I_1(\kappa).$ (Equation 5.4.5)

6. $\dfrac{d}{d\kappa} \{\kappa I_1(\kappa)\} = \kappa I_0(\kappa).$ (Equation 3.4.52)

7. $I_1'(\kappa) = I_0(\kappa) - \{I_1(\kappa)/\kappa\} = \tfrac{1}{2}\{I_0(\kappa) + I_2(\kappa)\}.$ (Equation 4.7.10, 6.2.12)

8. For large κ, with $m = 4p^2$,

$$I_p(\kappa) \sim (2\pi\kappa)^{-\frac{1}{2}} e^{\kappa}\{1 - \frac{(m-1)}{8\kappa} + \frac{(m-1)(m-9)}{2!(8\kappa)^2}$$

$$- \frac{(m-1)(m-9)(m-16)}{3!(8\kappa)^3} + ...\}.$$

287

9. Let $A(\kappa) = I_1(\kappa)/I_0(\kappa)$.

For large κ,

$$A(\kappa) = 1 - \frac{1}{2\kappa} - \frac{1}{8\kappa^2} - \frac{1}{8\kappa^3} + 0(\kappa^{-3}). \qquad \text{(Equation 3.4.50)}$$

For small κ,

$$A(\kappa) = \tfrac{1}{2}\kappa \left\{ 1 - \frac{1}{8}\kappa^2 + \frac{1}{48}\kappa^4 + 0(\kappa^6) \right\}. \qquad \text{(Equation 3.4.48)}$$

10. $A'(\kappa) = 1 - A^2(\kappa) - \{A(\kappa)/\kappa\}.$ \qquad (Section 6.2.1a)

11. $I_0\{(\kappa_1{}^2 + \kappa_2{}^2 + 2\kappa_1\kappa_2 \cos\theta)^{\frac{1}{2}}\}$

$$= I_0(\kappa_1)I_0(\kappa_2) + 2 \sum_{p=1}^{\infty} I_p(\kappa_1)I_p(\kappa_2) \cos p\theta. \qquad \text{(Equation 3.4.68)}$$

12. The *standard Bessel function* of the pth order is given by

$$J_p(\kappa) = \sum_{r=0}^{\infty} (-1)^r \{\Gamma(p + r + 1)\Gamma(r + 1)\}^{-1}(\tfrac{1}{2}\kappa)^{2r+p}.$$

13. $J_p(\kappa)_{\downarrow} = e^{\frac{1}{2}p\pi i} I_p(e^{-\frac{1}{2}\pi i}\kappa).$ \qquad (Equation 4.2.17)

14. $J_0\{(b^2 - a^2)^{\frac{1}{2}}\} = \dfrac{1}{2\pi} \displaystyle\int_0^{2\pi} \exp\{a\cos\theta + ib\sin\theta\}\, d\theta.$ \qquad (Equation 4.5.9)

15. $\displaystyle\int_0^{\infty} \int_0^{\infty} v(R)J_0(uR)J_0(ur)uR\, du\, dR = v(r).$ \qquad (Equation 4.2.23)

APPENDIX 2

Tables and Charts for the Circular Case

The tables and charts in this appendix are presented in the same order in which they were first cited in the text. Their abridged titles are given in the Contents.

APPENDIX 2.1. The distribution function* $F(\alpha) = \Pr(0° < \theta < \alpha)$ of the von Mises distribution on the linear interval $(0°, 360°)$ with symmetry about $\mu_0 = 180°$. The lower tail area $\Pr(-180° < \theta < -180° + \alpha) = G(\alpha; 0, \kappa)$ is $F(\alpha)$ if θ is on $(-180°, 180°)$ and $\mu_0 = 0°$.

$F(\alpha)$

α (degrees)	$\kappa = 0$	$\kappa = \cdot2$	$\kappa = \cdot4$	$\kappa = \cdot6$	$\kappa = \cdot8$	$\kappa = 1\cdot0$	$\kappa = 1\cdot2$	$\kappa = 1\cdot4$	$\kappa = 1\cdot6$	$\kappa = 1\cdot8$
0	0·00000	0·00000	0·00000	0·00000	0·00000	0·00000	0·00000	0·00000	0·00000	0·00000
5	·01389	·01126	·00895	·00699	·00536	·00404	·00301	·00221	·00161	·00116
10	·02778	·02254	·01793	·01400	·01074	·00811	·00604	·00444	·00323	·00233
15	·04167	·03385	·02697	·02108	·01620	·01225	·00913	·00672	·00490	·00353
20	·05556	·04522	·03608	·02826	·02175	·01647	·01230	·00907	·00662	·00479
25	·06944	·05665	·04531	·03557	·02744	·02083	·01559	·01153	·00843	·00611
30	·08333	·06816	·05467	·04304	·03329	·02535	·01903	·01411	·01035	·00753
35	·09722	·07978	·06420	·05071	·03936	·03007	·02266	·01686	·01241	·00906
40	·11111	·09152	·07392	·05861	·04567	·03504	·02650	·01981	·01465	·01073
45	·12500	·10338	·08386	·06679	·05228	·04029	·03062	·02299	·01709	·01259
50	·13889	·11540	·09405	·07527	·05921	·04587	·03505	·02647	·01978	·01466
55	·15278	·12757	·10452	·08409	·06653	·05184	·03985	·03028	·02278	·01699
60	·16667	·13992	·11529	·09331	·07428	·05825	·04509	·03450	·02614	·01965
65	·18056	·15246	·12639	·10295	·08251	·06517	·05082	·03919	·02994	·02270
70	·19444	·16520	·13784	·11306	·09128	·07265	·05711	·04442	·03425	·02620
75	·20833	·17815	·14968	·12368	·10064	·08078	·06407	·05030	·03915	·03027
80	·22222	·19132	·16192	·13485	·11066	·08962	·07176	·05690	·04477	·03501
85	·23611	·20471	·17460	·14662	·12139	·09925	·08028	·06436	·05122	·04053
90	·25000	·21834	·18772	·15901	·13289	·10975	·08974	·07277	·05863	·04699
95	·26389	·23222	·20130	·17206	·14522	·12122	·10025	·08228	·06714	·05455
100	·27778	·24633	·21537	·18582	·15844	·13372	·11191	·09302	·07693	·06339
105	·29167	·26069	·22992	·20030	·17260	·14734	·12483	·10514	·08816	·07370
110	·30556	·27529	·24498	·21554	·18774	·16217	·13913	·11876	·10101	·08571
115	·31944	·29014	·26054	·23154	·20392	·17825	·15491	·13405	·11566	·09962

	$\kappa = 2.0$	$\kappa = 2.2$	$\kappa = 2.4$	$\kappa = 2.6$	$\kappa = 2.8$	$\kappa = 3.0$	$\kappa = 3.2$	$\kappa = 3.4$	$\kappa = 3.6$	$\kappa = 3.8$
120	·33333	·30522	·27659	·24832	·22114	·19566	·17226	·15112	·13228	·11565
125	·34722	·32053	·29314	·26587	·23944	·21444	·19125	·17009	·15103	·13402
130	·36111	·33606	·31017	·28420	·25882	·23460	·21194	·19106	·17206	·15491
135	·37500	·35180	·32766	·30327	·27926	·25616	·23435	·21408	·19545	·17847
140	·38889	·36774	·34559	·32306	·30073	·27909	·25849	·23918	·22127	·20479
145	·40278	·38385	·36392	·34353	·32319	·30334	·28431	·26633	·24951	·23390
150	·41667	·40013	·38263	·36463	·34656	·32883	·31172	·29544	·28010	·26575
155	·43056	·41655	·40166	·38628	·37077	·35546	·34060	·32638	·31290	·30020
160	·44444	·43309	·42098	·40841	·39570	·38309	·37079	·35897	·34769	·33701
165	·45833	·44973	·44053	·43095	·42122	·41155	·40208	·39294	·38418	·37585
170	·47222	·46644	·46025	·45379	·44722	·44066	·43423	·42800	·42201	·41630
175	·48611	·48321	·48009	·47684	·47353	·47022	·46696	·46381	·46077	·45786
180	·50000	·50000	·50000	·50000	·50000	·50000	·50000	·50000	·50000	·50000

	$\kappa = 2.0$	$\kappa = 2.2$	$\kappa = 2.4$	$\kappa = 2.6$	$\kappa = 2.8$	$\kappa = 3.0$	$\kappa = 3.2$	$\kappa = 3.4$	$\kappa = 3.6$	$\kappa = 3.8$
0	0·00000	0·00000	0·00000	0·00000	0·00000	0·00000	0·00000	0·00000	0·00000	0·00000
5	·00083	·00059	·00041	·00029	·00020	·00014	·00010	·00007	·00005	·00003
10	·00167	·00118	·00084	·00059	·00041	·00029	·00020	·00014	·00010	·00007
15	·00253	·00180	·00127	·00090	·00063	·00044	·00031	·00021	·00015	·00010
20	·00344	·00245	·00174	·00123	·00086	·00060	·00042	·00029	·00020	·00014
25	·00440	·00314	·00223	·00158	·00111	·00078	·00055	·00038	·00027	·00019
30	·00543	·00389	·00278	·00197	·00139	·00098	·00069	·00048	·00034	·00024
35	·00656	·00472	·00338	·00241	·00171	·00121	·00085	·00060	·00042	·00029
40	·00781	·00564	·00406	·00290	·00207	·00147	·00104	·00074	·00052	·00037
45	·00920	·00669	·00483	·00348	·00249	·00178	·00127	·00090	·00064	·00046
50	·01078	·00788	·00574	·00416	·00300	·00216	·00155	·00111	·00079	·00057
55	·01259	·00927	·00679	·00496	·00361	·00262	·00190	·00137	·00099	·00071

* Reproduced from Batschelet (1965) by the kind permission of the author and the publisher, Amer. Inst. Biol. Sciences.

APPENDIX 2.1. (*continued*)

$F(\alpha)$

α (degrees)	$\kappa = 2\cdot0$	$\kappa = 2\cdot2$	$\kappa = 2\cdot4$	$\kappa = 2\cdot6$	$\kappa = 2\cdot8$	$\kappa = 3\cdot0$	$\kappa = 3\cdot2$	$\kappa = 3\cdot4$	$\kappa = 3\cdot6$	$\kappa = 3\cdot8$
60	0·01467	0·01089	0·00805	0·00593	0·00435	0·00319	0·00233	0·00170	0·00124	0·00090
65	·01709	·01281	·00956	·00711	·00527	·00390	·00288	·00213	·00157	·00116
70	·01993	·01509	·01138	·00856	·00642	·00481	·00360	·00269	·00201	·00150
75	·02328	·01782	·01360	·01035	·00786	·00596	·00452	·00343	·00260	·00197
80	·02723	·02111	·01631	·01258	·00969	·00746	·00573	·00441	·00339	·00261
85	·03193	·02508	·01965	·01537	·01201	·00938	·00733	·00573	·00448	·00350
90	·03752	·02988	·02376	·01887	·01498	·01189	·00944	·00750	·00596	·00475
95	·04418	·03571	·02882	·02325	·01876	·01514	·01223	·00988	·00800	·00648
100	·05210	·04276	·03506	·02875	·02359	·01936	·01591	·01308	·01077	·00888
105	·06150	·05127	·04273	·03563	·02972	·02482	·02075	·01737	·01456	·01222
110	·07263	·06152	·05212	·04419	·03749	·03185	·02710	·02308	·01968	·01681
115	·08574	·07379	·06355	·05477	·04727	·04084	·03534	·03062	·02657	·02308
120	·10109	·08840	·07736	·06777	·05946	·05223	·04595	·04048	·03571	·03154
125	·11895	·10564	·09391	·08360	·07452	·06652	·05946	·05323	·04771	·04282
130	·13954	·12581	·11356	·10264	·09290	·08421	·07644	·06947	·06322	·05760
135	·16308	·14917	·13662	·12530	·11507	·10583	·09746	·08986	·08294	·07665
140	·18970	·17592	·16335	·15188	·14141	·13183	·12305	·11499	·10756	·10071
145	·21948	·20618	·19393	·18264	·17222	·16259	·15367	·14538	·13767	·13048
150	·25239	·23996	·22841	·21766	·20766	·19832	·18959	·18140	·17371	·16647
155	·28829	·27713	·26668	·25688	·24769	·23903	·23088	·22317	·21586	·20893
160	·32694	·31744	·30848	·30004	·29206	·28450	·27732	·27050	·26399	·25776
165	·36795	·36047	·35339	·34667	·34029	·33421	·32841	·32287	·31755	·31244
170	·41087	·40570	·40079	·39612	·39166	·38740	·38332	·37941	·37563	·37200
175	·45509	·45246	·44994	·44755	·44526	·44306	·44095	·43893	·43697	·43508
180	·50000	·50000	·50000	·50000	·50000	·50000	·50000	·50000	·50000	·50000

	$\kappa = 4 \cdot 0$	$\kappa = 4 \cdot 2$	$\kappa = 4 \cdot 4$	$\kappa = 4 \cdot 6$	$\kappa = 4 \cdot 8$	$\kappa = 5 \cdot 0$	$\kappa = 5 \cdot 2$	$\kappa = 5 \cdot 4$	$\kappa = 5 \cdot 6$	$\kappa = 5 \cdot 8$
0	0·00000	0·00000	0·00000	0·00000	0·00000	0·00000	0·00000	0·00000	0·00000	0·00000
5	·00002	·00002	·00001	·00001	·00001	·00000	·00000	·00000	·00000	·00000
10	·00005	·00003	·00002	·00001	·00001	·00001	·00000	·00000	·00000	·00000
15	·00007	·00005	·00003	·00002	·00002	·00001	·00001	·00001	·00000	·00000
20	·00010	·00007	·00005	·00003	·00002	·00002	·00001	·00001	·00000	·00000
25	·00013	·00009	·00006	·00004	·00003	·00002	·00001	·00001	·00001	·00000
30	·00016	·00011	·00008	·00005	·00004	·00003	·00002	·00001	·00001	·00001
35	·00021	·00014	·00010	·00007	·00005	·00003	·00002	·00002	·00001	·00001
40	·00026	·00018	·00013	·00009	·00006	·00004	·00003	·00002	·00001	·00001
45	·00032	·00023	·00016	·00011	·00008	·00006	·00004	·00003	·00002	·00001
50	·00040	·00029	·00021	·00015	·00010	·00007	·00005	·00004	·00003	·00002
55	·00051	·00037	·00027	·00019	·00014	·00010	·00007	·00005	·00004	·00003
60	·00066	·00048	·00035	·00025	·00018	·00013	·00010	·00007	·00005	·00004
65	·00085	·00063	·00046	·00034	·00025	·00018	·00014	·00010	·00007	·00005
70	·00112	·00084	·00062	·00047	·00035	·00026	·00019	·00015	·00011	·00008
75	·00149	·00113	·00086	·00065	·00049	·00037	·00028	·00022	·00016	·00013
80	·00201	·00155	·00119	·00092	·00071	·00055	·00042	·00033	·00025	·00020
85	·00274	·00215	·00168	·00132	·00104	·00082	·00064	·00051	·00040	·00031
90	·00378	·00301	·00240	·00192	·00154	·00123	·00098	·00079	·00063	·00051
95	·00525	·00426	·00346	·00282	·00229	·00187	·00152	·00124	·00102	·00083
100	·00733	·00606	·00501	·00415	·00344	·00286	·00237	·00197	·00164	·00137
105	·01027	·00864	·00727	·00613	·00517	·00437	·00370	·00313	·00265	·00224
110	·01437	·01231	·01055	·00905	·00777	·00668	·00575	·00495	·00426	·00367
115	·02008	·01748	·01524	·01330	·01162	·01016	·00889	·00778	·00682	·00597
120	·02789	·02470	·02189	·01941	·01724	·01531	·01362	·01212	·01079	·00961
125	·03847	·03460	·03114	·02806	·02530	·02284	·02062	·01863	·01685	·01524
130	·05253	·04795	·04382	·04007	·03667	·03358	·03077	·02821	·02588	·02375
135	·07089	·06563	·06081	·05638	·05232	·04857	·04512	·04194	·03900	·03628
140	·09438	·08852	·08309	·07804	·07334	·06897	·06488	·06107	·05751	·05418
145	·12377	·11748	·11159	·10605	·10084	·09594	·09132	·08695	·08283	·07893

APPENDIX 2.1. (*continued*)

α (degrees)	$F(\alpha)$									
	κ = 4·0	κ = 4·2	κ = 4·4	κ = 4·6	κ = 4·8	κ = 5·0	κ = 5·2	κ = 5·4	κ = 5·6	κ = 5·8
150	0·15964	0·15319	0·14708	0·14129	0·13578	0·13055	0·12558	0·12083	0·11631	0·11199
155	·20234	·19606	·19006	·18433	·17884	·17358	·16853	·16368	·15902	·15453
160	·25180	·24608	·24059	·23530	·23020	·22528	·22053	·21593	·21148	·20716
165	·30752	·30277	·29818	·29374	·28944	·28527	·28122	·27728	·27344	·26971
170	·36848	·36508	·36177	·35857	·35545	·35241	·34944	·34655	·34372	·34096
175	·43324	·43146	·42973	·42805	·42641	·42481	·42324	·42171	·42021	·41873
180	·50000	·50000	·50000	·50000	·50000	·50000	·50000	·50000	·50000	·50000

α (degrees)	κ = 6·0	κ = 6·2	κ = 6·4	κ = 6·6	κ = 6·8	κ = 7·0	κ = 7·2	κ = 7·4	κ = 7·6	κ = 7·8
30	0·00000	0·00000	0·00000	0·00000	0·00000	0·00000	0·00000	0·00000	0·00000	0·00000
35	·00001	·00000	·00000	·00000	·00000	·00000	·00000	·00000	·00000	·00000
40	·00001	·00001	·00000	·00000	·00000	·00000	·00000	·00000	·00000	·00000
45	·00001	·00001	·00000	·00000	·00000	·00000	·00000	·00000	·00000	·00000
50	·00001	·00001	·00001	·00000	·00000	·00000	·00000	·00000	·00000	·00000
55	·00002	·00001	·00001	·00001	·00000	·00000	·00000	·00000	·00000	·00000
60	·00003	·00002	·00001	·00001	·00001	·00001	·00000	·00000	·00000	·00000
65	·00004	·00003	·00002	·00002	·00001	·00001	·00001	·00000	·00000	·00000
70	·00006	·00005	·00003	·00003	·00002	·00001	·00001	·00001	·00001	·00000
75	·00010	·00007	·00006	·00004	·00003	·00002	·00002	·00001	·00001	·00001
80	·00015	·00012	·00009	·00007	·00006	·00004	·00003	·00003	·00002	·00002
85	·00025	·00020	·00015	·00012	·00010	·00008	·00006	·00005	·00004	·00003

90	0·00041	0·00033	0·00026	0·00021	0·00017	0·00014	0·00011	0·00009	0·00007	0·00006
95	·00068	·00056	·00046	·00037	·00031	·00025	·00021	·00017	·00014	·00011
100	·00114	·00095	·00079	·00066	·00055	·00046	·00038	·00032	·00027	·00023
105	·00190	·00161	·00137	·00116	·00099	·00084	·00071	·00061	·00052	·00044
110	·00317	·00274	·00236	·00204	·00176	·00153	·00132	·00114	·00099	·00086
115	·00524	·00460	·00404	·00355	·00312	·00274	·00241	·00212	·00187	·00164
120	·00857	·00764	·00681	·00608	·00543	·00485	·00434	·00388	·00346	·00310
125	·01379	·01249	·01131	·01025	·00929	·00843	·00765	·00694	·00630	·00572
130	·02181	·02003	·01841	·01693	·01556	·01432	·01318	·01213	·01117	·01029
135	·03377	·03144	·02928	·02728	·02543	·02371	·02211	·02063	·01925	·01796
140	·05106	·04814	·04540	·04283	·04041	·03815	·03602	·03402	·03213	·03036
145	·07525	·07175	·06844	·06530	·06233	·05950	·05681	·05426	·05184	·04953
150	·10787	·10392	·10015	·09654	·09308	·08976	·08658	·08353	·08061	·07780
155	·15020	·14604	·14202	·13814	·13440	·13078	·12728	·12390	·12063	·11746
160	·20298	·19893	·19499	·19116	·18744	·18382	·18029	·17686	·17352	·17027
165	·26606	·26251	·25904	·25566	·25235	·24911	·24594	·24285	·23981	·23684
170	·33826	·33561	·33302	·33047	·32798	·32553	·32312	·32076	·31844	·31616
175	·41729	·41588	·41449	·41312	·41178	·41045	·40915	·40787	·40661	·40537
180	·50000	·50000	·50000	·50000	·50000	·50000	·50000	·50000	·50000	·50000

APPENDIX 2.1. (continued)

α (degrees)	κ = 8·0	κ = 8·2	κ = 8·4	κ = 8·6	κ = 8·8	κ = 9·0	κ = 9·2	κ = 9·4	κ = 9·6	κ = 9·8	κ = 10·0
					$F(\alpha)$						
70	0·00000	0·00000	0·00000	0·00000	0·00000	0·00000	0·00000	0·00000	0·00000	0·00000	0·00000
75	·00001	·00000	·00000	·00000	·00000	·00000	·00000	·00000	·00000	·00000	·00000
80	·00001	·00001	·00001	·00001	·00000	·00000	·00000	·00000	·00000	·00000	·00000
85	·00002	·00002	·00002	·00001	·00001	·00001	·00001	·00000	·00000	·00000	·00000
90	·00005	·00004	·00003	·00003	·00002	·00002	·00001	·00001	·00001	·00001	·00001
95	·00009	·00008	·00006	·00005	·00004	·00004	·00003	·00002	·00002	·00002	·00001
100	·00019	·00016	·00013	·00011	·00009	·00008	·00007	·00005	·00005	·00004	·00003
105	·00038	·00032	·00027	·00023	·00020	·00017	·00014	·00012	·00011	·00009	·00008
110	·00074	·00064	·00056	·00048	·00042	·00036	·00032	·00027	·00024	·00021	·00018
115	·00145	·00127	·00112	·00099	·00087	·00077	·00068	·00060	·00053	·00047	·00041
120	·00277	·00248	·00222	·00199	·00178	·00160	·00143	·00128	·00115	·00103	·00092
125	·00519	·00472	·00429	·00390	·00354	·00322	·00293	·00266	·00242	·00221	·00201
130	·00948	·00873	·00805	·00742	·00684	·00631	·00582	·00537	·00495	·00457	·00422
135	·01677	·01566	·01462	·01366	·01276	·01193	·01115	·01042	·00974	·00911	·00852
140	·02869	·02712	·02564	·02425	·02293	·02169	·02052	·01942	·01838	·01740	·01647
145	·04733	·04524	·04325	·04136	·03955	·03783	·03619	·03463	·03314	·03171	·03036
150	·07510	·07251	·07001	·06762	·06531	·06310	·06096	·05891	·05693	·05503	·05319
155	·11440	·11143	·10855	·10576	·10305	·10043	·09789	·09542	·09302	·09069	·08843
160	·16710	·16400	·16099	·15804	·15517	·15236	·14962	·14694	·14433	·14177	·13927
165	·23393	·23107	·22827	·22552	·22283	·22019	·21759	·21504	·21253	·21007	·20765
170	·31391	·31170	·30952	·30738	·30527	·30319	·30115	·29913	·29714	·29517	·29323
175	·40414	·40293	·40174	·40056	·39940	·39825	·39712	·39600	·39489	·39380	·39271
180	·50000	·50000	·50000	·50000	·50000	·50000	·50000	·50000	·50000	·50000	·50000

APPENDIX 2.2. The length of the resultant $\rho = A(\kappa)$ for the von Mises distribution*. Replace κ by $\hat{\kappa}$, ρ by $\bar{R}$ for estimation.

κ	ρ	κ	ρ	κ	ρ
0·0	0·00000	3·5	0·84110	7·0	0·92553
0·1	·04994	3·6	·84616	7·1	·92663
0·2	·09950	3·7	·85091	7·2	·92770
0·3	·14834	3·8	·85537	7·3	·92874
0·4	·19610	3·9	·85956	7·4	·92975
0·5	·24250	4·0	·86352	7·5	·93072
0·6	·28726	4·1	·86726	7·6	·93168
0·7	·33018	4·2	·87079	7·7	·93260
0·8	·37108	4·3	·87414	7·8	·93350
0·9	·40984	4·4	·87732	7·9	·93438
1·0	·44639	4·5	·88033	8·0	·93524
1·1	·48070	4·6	·88320	8·1	·93607
1·2	·51278	4·7	·88593	8·2	·93688
1·3	·54267	4·8	·88853	8·3	·93767
1·4	·57042	4·9	·89101	8·4	·93844
1·5	·59613	5·0	·89338	8·5	·93919
1·6	·61990	5·1	·89565	8·6	·93993
1·7	·64183	5·2	·89782	8·7	·94064
1·8	·66204	5·3	·89990	8·8	·94134
1·9	·68065	5·4	·90190	8·9	·94202
2·0	·69777	5·5	·90382	9·0	·94269
2·1	·71353	5·6	·90566	9·2	·94398
2·2	·72803	5·7	·90743	9·4	·94521
2·3	·74138	5·8	·90913	9·6	·94639
2·4	·75367	5·9	·91078	9·8	·94752
2·5	·76500	6·0	·91236	10	·94860
2·6	·77545	6·1	·91389	12	·95730
2·7	·78511	6·2	·91536	15	·96607
2·8	·79404	6·3	·91678	20	·97467
2·9	·80231	6·4	·91816	24	·97937
3·0	·80999	6·5	·91949	30	·98319
3·1	·81711	6·6	·92078	40	·98739
3·2	·82375	6·7	·92202	60	·99163
3·3	·82993	6·8	·92323	120	·99582
3·4	·83570	6·9	·92440	∞	1·00000

* Based on Table C of Batschelet (1965), by the kind permission of the author and the publisher, Amer. Inst. Biol. Sciences.

APPENDIX 2

APPENDIX 2.3. The maximum likelihood estimate $\hat{\kappa}$ for given $\bar{R}$ in the von Mises case*. For the solution $\kappa = A^{-1}(\rho)$, replace $\hat{\kappa}$ by κ, $\bar{R}$ by ρ.

$\bar{R}$	$\hat{\kappa}$	$\bar{R}$	$\hat{\kappa}$	$\bar{R}$	$\hat{\kappa}$
0·00	0·00000	0·35	0·74783	0·70	2·01363
·01	·02000	·36	·77241	·71	2·07685
·02	·04001	·37	·79730	·72	2·14359
·03	·06003	·38	·82253	·73	2·21425
·04	·08006	·39	·84812	·74	2·28930
·05	·10013	·40	·87408	·75	2·36930
·06	·12022	·41	·90043	·76	2·45490
·07	·14034	·42	·92720	·77	2·54686
·08	·16051	·43	·95440	·78	2·64613
·09	·18073	·44	·98207	·79	2·75382
·10	·20101	·45	1·01022	·80	2·87129
·11	·22134	·46	1·03889	·81	3·00020
·12	·24175	·47	1·06810	·82	3·14262
·13	·26223	·48	1·09788	·83	3·30114
·14	·28279	·49	1·12828	·84	3·47901
·15	·30344	·50	1·15932	·85	3·68041
·16	·32419	·51	1·19105	·86	3·91072
·17	·34503	·52	1·22350	·87	4·17703
·18	·36599	·53	1·25672	·88	4·48876
·19	·38707	·54	1·29077	·89	4·85871
·20	·40828	·55	1·32570	·90	5·3047
·21	·42962	·56	1·36156	·91	5·8522
·22	·45110	·57	1·39842	·92	6·5394
·23	·47273	·58	1·43635	·93	7·4257
·24	·49453	·59	1·47543	·94	8·6104
·25	·51649	·60	1·51574	·95	10·2716
·26	·53863	·61	1·55738	·96	12·7661
·27	·56097	·62	1·60044	·97	16·9266
·28	·58350	·63	1·64506	·98	25·2522
·29	·60625	·64	1·69134	·99	50·2421
·30	·62922	·65	1·73945	1·00	∞
·31	·65242	·66	1·78953		
·32	·67587	·67	1·84177		
·33	·69958	·68	1·89637		
·34	·72356	·69	1·95357		

* Based on Table B of Batschelet (1965) with the kind permission of the author and the publisher, Amer. Inst. Biol. Sciences, and on Table 2 of Gumbel et al. (1953) with the kind permission of the authors and the editor of J. Amer. Statist. Ass.

APPENDIX 2.4. Critical values* of the test statistic $\bar{C}$ for testing uniformity when the mean direction is known. $\Pr(\bar{C} \geqslant \bar{C}_0) = \alpha$.

n $\alpha \rightarrow$	0·10	0·05	0·025	0·01
5	0·413	0·522	0·611	0·709
6	·376	·476	·560	·652
7	·347	·441	·519	·607
8	·324	·412	·486	·569
9	·305	·388	·459	·538
10	·289	·368	·436	·512
11	·275	·351	·416	·489
12	·264	·336	·398	·468
13	·253	·323	·383	·451
14	·244	·311	·369	·435
15	·235	·301	·357	·420
16	·228	·291	·345	·407
17	·221	·282	·335	·395
18	·215	·274	·326	·384
19	·209	·267	·317	·374
20	·204	·260	·309	·365
21	·199	·254	·302	·356
22	·194	·248	·295	·348
23	·190	·243	·288	·341
24	·186	·238	·282	·334
25	·182	·233	·277	·327
30	·17	·21	·25	·30
35	·15	·20	·23	·28
40	·14	·18	·22	·26
45	·14	·17	·21	·25
50	·13	·16	·20	·23
$(2n)^{\frac{1}{2}}\,\bar{C} \simeq N(0, 1)$	1·282	1·645	1·960	2·326

* Based on Table 3 of Stephens (1969d) with the kind permission of the author and the editor of *J. Amer. Statist. Ass.*

APPENDIX 2.5. Critical values* of the Rayleigh test of uniformity with the test-statistics $\bar{R}$. $\Pr(\bar{R} \geqslant \bar{R}_0) = \alpha$.

n $\alpha \rightarrow$	0·10	0·05	0·025	0·01	0·001
5	0·677	0·754	0·816	0·879	0·991
6	·618	·690	·753	·825	·940
7	·572	·642	·702	·771	·891
8	·535	·602	·660	·725	·847
9	·504	·569	·624	·687	·808
10	·478	·540	·594	·655	·775
11	·456	·516	·567	·627	·743
12	·437	·494	·544	·602	·716
13	·420	·475	·524	·580	·692
14	·405	·458	·505	·560	·669
15	·391	·443	·489	·542	·649
16	·379	·429	·474	·525	·630
17	·367	·417	·460	·510	·613
18	·357	·405	·447	·496	·597
19	·348	·394	·436	·484	·583
20	·339	·385	·425	·472	·569
21	·331	·375	·415	·461	·556
22	·323	·367	·405	·451	·544
23	·316	·359	·397	·441	·533
24	·309	·351	·389	·432	·522
25	·303	·344	·381	·423	·512
30	·277	·315	·348	·387	·470
35	·256	·292	·323	·359	·436
40	·240	·273	·302	·336	·409
45	·226	·257	·285	·318	·386
50	·214	·244	·270	·301	·367
100	·15	·17	·19	·21	·26
$2n\bar{R}^2 \simeq \chi_2^2$	4·605	5·991	7·378	9·210	13·816

* Based on Table 2 of Stephens (1969d) with the kind permission of the author and the editor of *J. Amer. Statist. Ass.* and on Batschelet (1971) with the kind permission of the author and the publisher, Amer. Inst. Biol. Sciences and Dr. W. T. Keeton, New York Univ.

APPENDIX 2.6. Percentage Points (in degrees) of the von Mises distribution with θ on the linear interval $(-180°, 180°)$ and $\mu_0 = 0°$. The lower tail area $\Pr(-180° < \theta < -180° + \delta)$ is $\frac{1}{2}\alpha$. $\Pr(-180° + \delta < \theta < 180° - \delta) = 1 - \alpha$. For θ on $(0°, 360°)$ and $\mu_0 = 0°$, $\Pr(180° < \theta < 180° + \delta) = \frac{1}{2}\alpha$.

κ $\alpha\to$	0.001	0.01	0.05	0.1	κ $\alpha\to$	0.001	0.01	0.05	0.1
0.0	0.1	0.6	2.9	5.7	4.6	71.1	102.4	123.4	133.2
0.1	0.2	2.0	10.0	19.9	4.7	73.2	103.5	124.1	133.8
0.2	0.2	2.2	11.1	22.1	4.8	75.2	104.6	124.8	134.3
0.3	0.2	2.5	12.4	24.6	4.9	77.1	105.6	125.5	134.9
0.4	0.3	2.8	13.9	27.5	5.0	78.8	106.6	126.2	135.4
0.5	0.3	3.2	15.7	30.8	5.2	82.0	108.4	127.4	136.4
0.6	0.4	3.6	17.7	34.5	5.4	84.9	110.1	128.5	137.3
0.7	0.4	4.1	20.1	38.7	5.6	87.5	111.7	129.6	138.2
0.8	0.5	4.7	22.9	43.3	5.8	89.8	113.2	130.6	139.0
0.9	0.5	5.4	26.0	48.3	6.0	92.0	114.5	131.5	139.7
1.0	0.6	6.2	29.6	53.5	6.2	94.0	115.8	132.4	140.5
1.1	0.7	7.2	33.6	58.9	6.4	95.8	117.0	133.3	141.1
1.2	0.8	8.3	38.1	64.3	6.6	97.6	118.2	134.1	141.8
1.3	1.0	9.6	42.9	69.6	6.8	99.2	119.2	134.8	142.4
1.4	1.1	11.2	47.9	74.8	7.0	100.7	120.3	135.5	143.0
1.5	1.3	13.1	53.1	79.6	7.2	102.1	121.2	136.2	143.6
1.6	1.6	15.3	58.4	84.1	7.4	103.5	122.2	136.9	144.1
1.7	1.8	17.9	63.5	88.3	7.6	104.7	123.0	137.5	144.6
1.8	2.2	20.8	68.4	92.1	7.8	105.9	123.9	138.1	145.1
1.9	2.6	24.2	73.0	95.6	8.0	107.1	124.7	138.7	145.6
2.0	3.0	28.0	77.3	98.8	8.2	108.2	125.5	139.2	146.0
2.1	3.6	32.1	81.3	101.7	8.4	109.2	126.2	139.8	146.5
2.2	4.3	36.6	84.9	104.3	8.6	110.2	126.9	140.3	146.9
2.3	5.1	41.2	88.3	106.7	8.8	111.2	127.6	140.8	147.3
2.4	6.0	46.0	91.3	109.0	9.0	112.1	128.2	141.2	147.7
2.5	7.2	50.7	94.1	111.0	9.2	113.0	128.9	141.7	148.0
2.6	8.5	55.2	96.7	112.9	9.4	113.8	129.0	142.1	148.4
2.7	10.1	59.6	99.1	114.6	9.6	114.7	130.1	142.6	148.8
2.8	12.1	63.6	101.3	116.2	9.8	115.4	130.6	143.0	149.1
2.9	14.3	67.4	103.3	117.7	10.0	116.2	131.2	143.4	149.4
3.0	16.9	70.9	105.1	119.1	10.5	118.0	132.5	144.3	150.2
3.1	19.9	74.2	106.9	120.4	11.0	119.6	133.7	145.2	150.9
3.2	23.2	77.1	108.5	121.6	11.5	121.1	134.8	146.0	151.6
3.3	26.9	79.9	110.0	122.8	12.0	122.5	135.8	146.7	152.2
3.4	30.8	82.4	111.4	123.8	12.5	123.8	136.8	147.5	152.8
3.5	34.9	84.8	112.7	124.9	13.0	125.0	137.7	148.1	153.4
3.6	39.1	86.9	114.0	125.8	14	127.2	139.3	149.3	154.4
3.7	43.2	89.0	115.2	126.7	15	129.2	140.8	150.4	155.3
3.8	47.1	90.8	116.3	127.6	20	136.5	146.3	154.5	158.7
3.9	50.9	92.6	117.3	128.4	30	144.9	152.7	159.3	162.7
4.0	54.5	94.3	118.3	129.2	40	149.7	156.4	162.1	165.0
4.1	57.8	95.8	119.3	129.9	50	153.0	159.0	164.0	166.6
4.2	60.9	97.3	120.2	130.7	100	161.1	165.2	168.7	170.6
4.3	63.7	98.7	121.0	131.3	N_α	3.291	2.576	1.960	1.645
4.4	66.3	100.0	121.9	132.0					
4.5	68.8	101.2	122.7	132.6					

$$\delta = 180° - 57.296° \, N_\alpha \kappa^{-\frac{1}{2}}$$

APPENDIX 2.7.   Confidence intervals for μ_0.

APPENDIX 2.7a.   Batschelet chart* for obtaining a 95% confidence interval for the mean direction μ_0. $\Pr(-\delta < \mu_0 < \delta) = 0.95$.

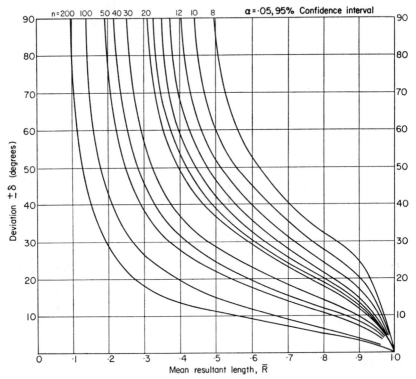

* Reproduced from Batschelet (1971) with the kind permission of the author and the publisher, Amer. Inst. Biol. Sciences.

APPENDIX 2.7b.   Batschelet chart* for obtaining a 99% confidence interval for the mean direction μ_0. $\Pr(-\delta < \mu_0 < \delta) = 0.99$.

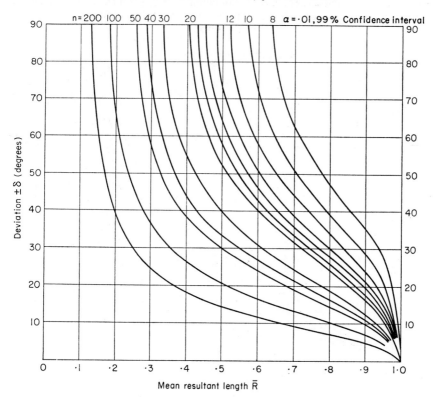

* Reproduced from Batschelet (1971) with the kind permission of the author and the publisher, Amer. Inst. Biol. Sciences.

APPENDIX 2.8. Confidence intervals for κ.

APPENDIX 2.8a. Batschelet chart* for obtaining a 90% confidence interval for the concentration parameter κ. For the upper curves $\alpha = 0.95$ and for the lower curves $\alpha = 0.05$.

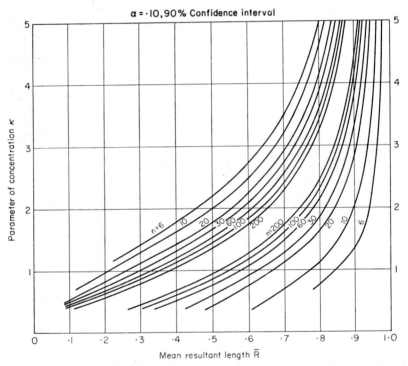

* Reproduced from Batschelet (1971) with the kind permission of the author and the publisher, Amer. Inst. Biol. Sciences.

APPENDIX 2.8b.   Batschelet chart* for obtaining a 98% confidence interval for the concentration parameter κ. For the upper curves $\alpha = 0.99$ and for the lower curves $\alpha = 0.01$.

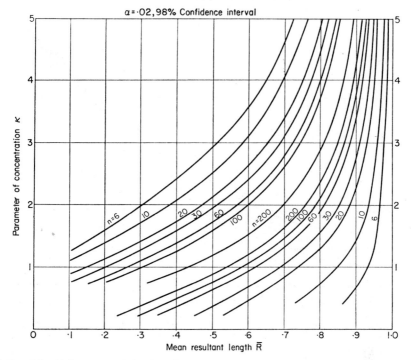

$a = .02$, 98% Confidence interval

Parameter of concentration κ

Mean resultant length $\bar{R}$

* Reproduced from Batschelet (1971) with the kind permission of the author and the publisher, Amer. Inst. Biol. Sciences.

APPENDIX 2.9.   Critical values for Watson and William's two-sample test.

APPENDIX 2.9a.   Chart for obtaining the 5% critical values for the two-sample test with the test-statistic $\bar{R}' = (R_1 + R_2)/n$ when $\bar{R}$ for the combined sample is given. $\alpha = 0.05$, $n_1 = n_2$, $r = \frac{1}{2}$.

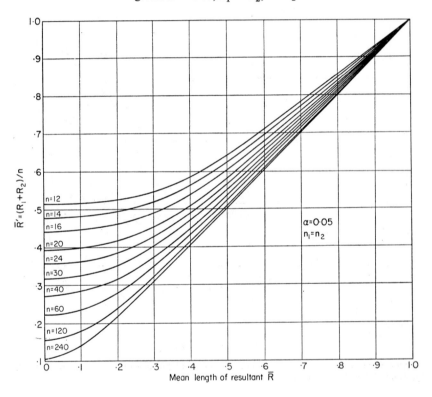

APPENDIX 2.9b. Chart for obtaining the 5% critical values for the two-sample test with the test-statistic $\bar{R}' = (R_1 + R_2)/n$ when $\bar{R}$ for the combined sample is given. $\alpha = 0.05$, $n_2 = 2n_1$, $r = \frac{1}{3}$.

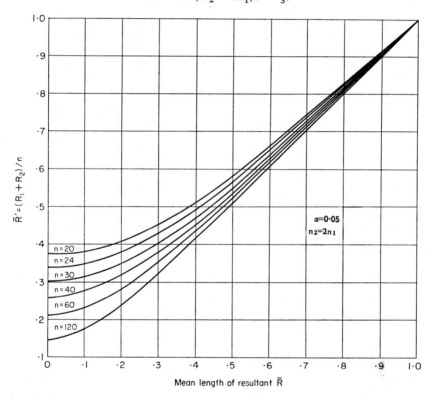

Mean length of resultant $\bar{R}$

APPENDIX 2.10. Critical values* for Kuiper's test with the test-statistic $V_n' = n^{\frac{1}{2}}V_n$. $\Pr(V_n' \geq V_{n,0}') = \alpha$.

n $\alpha \to$	0·10	0·05	0·01	0·005
5	1·46	1·57	1·76	1·84
6	1·47	1·58	1·79	1·87
7	1·48	1·60	1·81	1·89
8	1·49	1·61	1·83	1·91
9	1·50	1·62	1·84	1·93
10	1·51	1·63	1·85	1·94
11	1·51	1·63	1·86	1·95
12	1·52	1·64	1·87	1·96
13	1·52	1·64	1·88	1·96
14	1·53	1·65	1·88	1·97
15	1·53	1·65	1·89	1·98
16	1·53	1·66	1·89	1·98
17	1·54	1·66	1·90	1·99
18	1·54	1·66	1·90	1·99
19	1·54	1·66	1·90	2·00
20	1·55	1·67	1·91	2·00
25	1·55	1·67	1·92	2·01
30	1·56	1·68	1·93	2·02
40	1·57	1·69	1·94	2·03
50	1·58	1·70	1·95	2·04
100	1·59	1·72	1·97	2·06
∞	1·62	1·75	2·00	2·10

* Based on Table 1 of M. A. Stephens in *Biometrika*, Vol. 52, pp. 309–21, 1965. Reproduced with the kind permission of the author and the editor.

APPENDIX 2.11. Critical values* for Hodges–Ajne's test with the test-statistic m. $\Pr(m \leqslant m_0)$ is closest to the nominal level α.

n	$\alpha \rightarrow$ 0·10	0·05	0·025	0·01
9	0	0	0	0
10	1	0	0	0
11	1	0	0	0
12	1	1	0	0
13	1	1	1	0
14	2	1	1	0
15	2	2	1	1
16	2	2	1	1
17	3	2	2	1
18	3	3	2	2
19	3	3	2	2
20	4	3	3	2
21	4	4	3	2
22	5	4	3	3
23	5	4	4	3
24	5	5	4	3
25	6	5	4	4
30	7	7	6	5
35	9	9	8	7
40	11	10	10	9
50	15	14	13	12

* Compiled from Hodges (1955) with the kind permission of the author and the editor of *Ann. Math. Statist.*

APPENDIX 2.12.   Critical values* of the circular range w in degrees. $\Pr(w < w_0) = \alpha$.

n $\alpha \rightarrow$	0·005	0·01	0·05	0·10
4	38·8	48·9	83·6	105·3
5	64·0	76·1	113·8	135·4
6	87·2	100·2	138·2	158·7
7	107·6	120·8	158·0	177·3
8	125·5	138·5	174·4	192·5
9	141·1	153·8	188·1	205·1
10	154·7	167·1	199·8	215·8
11	166·8	178·7	209·9	225·0
12	177·4	189·0	218·7	233·0
13	187·0	198·1	226·5	240·0
14	195·5	206·2	233·4	246·2
15	203·2	213·5	239·5	251·7
16	210·2	220·1	245·1	256·7
17	216·6	226·2	250·1	261·2
18	222·4	231·6	254·7	265·3
19	227·7	236·7	258·8	269·1
20	232·7	241·3	262·7	272·5
21	237·2	245·6	266·2	275·6
22	241·4	249·5	269·4	278·6
23	245·4	253·2	272·5	281·3
24	249·0	256·7	275·3	283·8
25	252·5	259·9	277·9	286·1
26	255·7	262·9	280·4	288·3
27	258·7	265·7	282·7	290·4
28	261·5	268·3	284·8	292·3
29	264·2	270·8	286·9	294·1
30	266·7	273·2	288·8	295·9

* Reproduced from Laubscher and Rudolph (1968) with the kind permission of the authors.

APPENDIX 2.13.   Critical values* for the test of equal spacings with the test-statistic
L in degrees. $\Pr(L \geqslant L_0) = \alpha$.

n	$\alpha \rightarrow$	0·01	0·05	0·10
4		221·0	186·5	171·7
5		212·0	183·6	168·8
6		206·0	180·7	166·3
7		202·7	177·8	164·9
8		198·4	175·7	163·4
9		195·1	173·5	162·4
10		192·2	172·1	161·3
11		189·7	170·3	160·2
12		187·6	169·2	159·2
13		185·8	167·8	158·4
14		184·0	166·7	157·7
15		182·2	165·6	157·0
16		180·7	164·9	156·6
17		179·6	164·2	155·9
18		178·2	163·1	155·2
19		177·1	162·4	154·8
20		176·0	161·6	154·4
25		171·9	158·9	152·7
30		168·8	156·7	151·4
35		166·4	155·0	150·3
40		164·4	153·6	149·5
45		162·7	152·4	148·7
50		161·2	151·4	148·1
100		152·8	146·8	143·7
200		146·8	142·6	140·4

* Reproduced from J. S. Rao (1969) with the kind permission of the author.

APPENDIX 2.14. Critical values* for the two-sample uniform scores test with the test-statistic $R_1{}^2$. $\Pr(R_1{}^2 \geqslant R_{1,0}^2)$ is closest to the nominal level α.

n	n_1	$\alpha \rightarrow$ 0·001	0·01	0·05	0·10
8	4				6·83
9	3				6·41
	4			8·29	4·88
10	3				6·85
	4			9·47	6·24
	5			10·47	6·85
11	3			7·20	5·23
	4			10·42	7·43
	5		12·34	8·74	6·60
12	3			7·46	5·73
	4		11·20	8·46	7·46
	5		13·93	10·46	7·46
	6		14·93	11·20	7·46
13	3			7·68	6·15
	4		11·83	9·35	7·03
	5		15·26	10·15	7·39
	6		17·31	10·42	8·04
14	3			7·85	6·49
	4		12·34	9·30	7·60
	5		16·39	10·30	7·85
	6	19·20	15·59	12·21	7·94
	7	20·20	16·39	11·65	8·85
15	3			7·99	6·78
	4		12·78	8·74	7·91
	5	17·35	14·52	10·36	7·91
	6	20·92	17·48	11·61	9·12
	7	22·88	16·14	11·57	9·06
16	3			8·11	5·83
	4		13·14	9·44	7·38
	5	18·16	15·55	10·44	9·03
	6	22·43	16·98	11·54	9·11
	7	25·27	18·16	12·66	9·78

APPENDIX 2.14. (*continued*)

n	n_1	$\alpha \rightarrow$	0·001	0·01	0·05	0·10
17	3			8·21	7·23	6·14
	4		13·44	11·76	9·74	7·64
	5		18·86	16·44	11·03	8·76
	6		23·73	17·76	12·21	9·41
	7		27·40	17·98	12·63	10·11
	8		29·37	19·11	13·36	10·15
18	2					3·88
	3			8·29	7·41	6·41
	4		13·70	12·17	9·94	8·06
	5		19·46	16·05	11·45	8·76
	6		24·87	17·40	12·25	9·94
	7		29·28	19·46	13·41	10·29
	8		28·40	20·11	13·82	10·60
	9		29·28	20·23	13·99	11·04
19	2					3·89
	3			8·36	7·56	6·48
	4		13·93	12·52	9·69	7·54
	5		19·98	15·88	11·29	8·96
	6		25·87	18·19	12·57	9·87
	7		27·71	19·34	13·54	10·55
	8		31·04	21·12	14·29	11·12
	9		29·46	21·07	14·58	11·37
20	2					3·90
	3			8·42	7·70	6·70
	4		14·12	12·83	9·87	7·80
	5		20·43	16·29	11·49	9·08
	6		26·75	18·64	12·93	9·98
	7		29·36	20·43	14·05	11·03
	8		30·08	21·77	14·77	11·47
	9		32·44	22·99	15·45	11·97
	10		33·26	22·67	15·39	12·19
	$R^* = \chi_2^2$		13·816	9·210	5·991	4·605

* Reproduced from Mardia (1967, 1969a) with the kind permission of the editor of *J. Roy. Statist. Soc.*

APPENDIX 2.15. Critical values* for Watson's two-sample test with the test-statistic $U^2_{n_1,n_2}$. $Pr(U^2_{1,n_2} \geqslant U^2_{n_1,n_2,0})$ is closest to the nominal level α.

n	n_1	$\alpha \to$ 0·001	0·01	0·05	0·10
9	4			0·204	
10	4			·217	
	5			·225	
11	4		0·169	·227	
	5		·242	·182	
12	4		·236	·181	0·163
	5		·257	·200	·171
	6		·264	·206	·171
13	4		·244	·192	·175
	5		·269	·189	·165
	6		·282	·190	·154
14	4		·250	·186	·157
	5	0·280	·229	·191	·159
	6	·298	·246	·186	·161
	7	·304	·251	·199	·158
15	4		·256	·195	·156
	5	·289	·241	·177	·161
	6	·311	·262	·188	·156
	7	·322	·239	·182	·156
16	4	·260	·217	·182	·156
	5	·297	·251	·188	·156
	6	·323	·248	·190	·156
	7	·339	·245	·182	·156
	8	·344	·250	·184	·156
17	4	·265	·224	·185	·154
	5	·304	·239	·186	·155
	6	·333	·253	·185	·157
	7	·353	·247	·185	·155
	8	·363	·248	·186	·155
$U^2_{\infty,\infty}$		·385	·268	·187	·152

* Compiled from Burr (1964) with the kind permission of the author and the editor of *Ann. Math. Statist.*

APPENDIX 2.16.   Critical values* of the total number of runs r. $\Pr(r \geqslant r_0)$ is closest to the nominal level α.

$\alpha = 0.05$

$n_1 \rightarrow$ n_2	3	4	5	6	7	8	9	10	11	12	13	14	15	16	17	18	19	20
4		2																
5		2	2															
6	2	2	2	2														
7	2	2	2	2	4	4												
8	2	2	2	4	4	4												
9	2	2	2	4	4	4	4											
10	2	2	4	4	4	4	6	6										
11	2	2	4	4	4	6	6	6	6									
12	2	2	4	4	4	6	6	6	6	8								
13	2	2	4	4	4	6	6	6	8	8	8							
14	2	2	4	4	6	6	6	8	8	8	8	8						
15	2	2	4	4	6	6	6	8	8	8	8	10	10					
16	2	2	4	4	6	6	6	8	8	8	10	10	10	10				
17	2	4	4	4	6	6	8	8	8	10	10	10	10	12	12			
18	2	4	4	6	6	6	8	8	8	10	10	10	12	12	12	12		
19	2	4	4	6	6	6	8	8	8	10	10	10	12	12	12	12	14	
20	2	4	4	6	6	8	8	8	10	10	10	12	12	12	12	14	14	14

$\alpha = 0.01$

n_2	3	4	5	6	7	8	9	10	11	12	13	14	15	16	17	18	19	20
5			2															
6		2	2	2														
7		2	2	2	2														
8		2	2	2	2	2												
9		2	2	2	2	2	4											
10	2	2	2	2	2	4	4	4										
11	2	2	2	2	4	4	4	4	4									
12	2	2	2	2	4	4	4	4	6	6								
13	2	2	2	2	4	4	4	6	6	6	6							
14	2	2	2	4	4	4	4	6	6	6	6	8						
15	2	2	2	4	4	4	6	6	6	6	8	8	8					
16	2	2	2	4	4	4	6	6	6	6	8	8	8	8				
17	2	2	2	4	4	4	6	6	6	8	8	8	8	10	10			
18	2	2	2	4	4	6	6	6	6	8	8	8	10	10	10	10		
19	2	2	2	4	4	6	6	6	8	8	8	8	10	10	10	10	12	
20	2	2	4	4	4	6	6	6	8	8	10	10	10	10	10	12	12	12

* Compiled from Asano (1965) with the kind permission of the author and the editor of *Ann. Inst. Statist. Math.*

APPENDIX 2.17. Critical values* for the q-sample uniform scores test with the test-statistic W. $\Pr(W \geqslant W_0)$ is closest to the nominal level α.

n_1	n_2	n_3 $\alpha \rightarrow$	0·01	0·05	0·10
3	3	3	12·82	9·45	9·06
4	3	2	11·95	9·06	8·02
4	3	3	10·89	9·40	7·97
4	4	1		10·29	8·59
4	4	2	10·47	9·05	8·05
4	4	3	11·53	9·36	8·21
4	4	4	12·20	9·60	8·23
5	2	2	10·38	8·48	7·85
5	3	1		9·59	7·90
5	3	2	12·38	9·14	7·65
5	3	3	11·78	9·22	7·85
5	4	1	10·92	9·31	6·97
5	4	2	11·48	9·00	7·72
5	4	3	11·50	9·30	8·05
5	4	4	11·82	9·52	8·19
5	5	1	11·87	8·99	7·14
5	5	2	11·14	8·79	7·68
5	5	3	11·87	9·25	7·99
5	5	4	12·00	9·46	8·20
	χ_4^2		13·277	9·488	7·779

* Reproduced from Mardia (1970) with the kind permission of the editor of *J. Roy. Statist. Soc.*

APPENDIX 2.18. Critical values* for the bimodal two-sample uniform scores test with the test-statistic R_2^2. $\Pr(R_2^2 \geq R_{2,0}^2)$ is closest to the nominal level α.

n	n_1	$\alpha \to$ 0·001	0·01	0·05	0·1
8	4			8·00	4·00
9	3				6·41
	4			8·29	4·86
10	3				6·24
	4			10·47	6·85
	5				9·47
11	3				7·20
	4			10·42	7·43
	5		12·34	8·74	6·60
12	3				7·78
	4		12·00	9·00	7·00
	5		13·00	9·00	7·00
	6		16·00	12·00	9·00
13	3			7·68	6·15
	4		11·83	9·35	7·03
	5		15·26	10·15	7·39
	6		17·21	10·42	8·04
14	3				7·49
	4		12·99	10·54	6·22
	5		15·59	10·10	9·49
	6	20·20	16·39	11·65	8·00
	7		19·20	12·34	9·30
15	3			7·99	6·38
	4		12·78	8·74	7·91
	5	17·35	14·52	10·36	7·91
	6	20·92	17·48	11·61	9·12
	7	22·88	16·14	11·57	9·06
16	3			7·83	5·83
	4		13·66	10·24	7·41
	5	17·49	14·66	11·83	9·00
	6	23·31	17·07	11·66	10·24
	7	24·31	18·66	12·66	9·83
	8	27·32	19·90	12·00	10·24
17	3		8·21	7·23	6·14
	4		13·44	9·74	7·64
	5	18·86	16·45	11·03	8·76
	6	23·72	17·76	12·21	9·41
	7	27·40	17·98	12·63	10·11
	8	29·37	19·11	13·36	10·15

* Reproduced from Mardia and Spurr (1972) with the kind permission of Mr. B. D. Spurr.

APPENDIX 3

Tables and Charts for the Spherical Case

The tables and charts in this appendix are presented in the same order in which they were first cited in the text. Their abridged titles are given in the Contents.

APPENDIX 3.1. Percentage points of colatitude θ in the Fisher distribution. $\Pr(\delta < \theta < \pi) = \alpha$. δ is the semi-vertical angle of a $(1 - \alpha)$ 100% confidence cone with the true direction as its axis.

κ	$\alpha \rightarrow$	0·001	0·01	0·05	0·10
0·0		176·4	168·5	154·2	143·1
0·1		176·2	167·9	152·9	141·4
0·2		176·0	167·3	151·5	139·5
0·3		175·8	166·6	150·0	137·4
0·4		175·5	165·8	148·4	135·3
0·5		175·3	165·0	146·6	133·1
0·6		175·0	164·1	144·8	130·7
0·7		174·6	163·1	142·8	128·3
0·8		174·3	162·1	140·8	125·7
0·9		173·9	161·0	138·6	123·1
1·0		173·5	159·7	136·3	120·4
1·1		173·1	158·4	133·9	117·7
1·2		172·6	157·0	131·4	114·9
1·3		172·1	155·5	128·9	112·2
1·4		171·5	153·8	126·2	109·4
1·5		170·9	152·1	123·6	106·8
1·6		170·2	150·2	120·9	104·1
1·7		169·5	148·3	118·3	101·5
1·8		168·7	146·2	115·6	99·0
1·9		167·8	144·0	113·0	96·6
2·0		166·9	141·8	110·4	94·3
2·1		165·9	139·4	107·9	92·1
2·2		164·8	137·0	105·4	89·9
2·3		163·6	134·6	103·1	87·9
2·4		162·3	132·1	100·8	86·0
2·5		160·9	129·6	98·6	84·1
2·6		159·4	127·1	96·5	82·4
2·7		157·9	124·7	94·5	80·7
2·8		156·2	122·2	92·6	79·1
2·9		154·4	119·8	90·8	77·6
3·0		152·5	117·5	89·0	76·1
3·1		150·6	115·2	87·4	74·7
3·2		148·5	113·0	85·8	73·4
3·3		146·4	110·9	84·3	72·2
3·4		144·3	108·9	82·8	71·0
3·5		142·1	106·9	81·4	69·9
3·6		139·8	105·0	80·1	68·8
3·7		137·6	103·2	78·8	67·7
3·8		135·3	101·5	77·6	66·7
3·9		133·1	99·8	76·5	65·8
4·0		130·9	98·2	75·4	64·8
4·1		128·7	96·7	74·3	64·0
4·2		126·6	95·2	73·3	63·1
4·3		124·6	93·8	72·3	62·3

APPENDIX 3.1 (*continued*)

κ	$\alpha\rightarrow$	0·001	0·01	0·05	0·10
4·4		122·6	92·5	71·3	61·5
4·5		120·6	91·2	70·4	60·8
4·6		118·7	89·9	69·6	60·0
4·7		116·9	88·7	68·7	59·3
4·8		115·2	87·6	67·9	58·6
4·9		113·5	86·5	67·1	58·0
5·0		111·9	85·4	66·4	57·3
5·2		108·8	83·4	64·9	56·1
5·4		106·0	81·5	63·6	55·0
5·6		103·4	79·8	62·3	53·9
5·8		100·9	78·1	61·1	52·9
6·0		98·6	76·6	60·0	52·0
6·2		96·5	75·1	58·9	51·1
6·4		94·5	73·7	57·9	50·2
6·6		92·7	72·4	56·9	49·4
6·8		90·9	71·2	56·0	48·6
7·0		89·2	70·0	55·1	47·9
7·2		87·7	68·9	54·3	47·1
7·4		86·2	67·8	53·5	46·5
7·6		84·8	66·8	52·7	45·8
7·8		83·4	65·8	52·0	45·2
8·0		82·2	64·9	51·3	44·6
8·2		80·9	64·0	50·6	44·0
8·4		79·8	63·1	50·0	43·5
8·6		78·7	62·3	49·3	42·9
8·8		77·6	61·5	48·7	42·4
9·0		76·6	60·8	48·2	41·9
9·2		75·6	60·0	47·6	41·4
9·4		74·6	59·3	47·1	41·0
9·6		73·7	58·6	46·5	40·5
9·8		72·8	58·0	46·0	40·1
10·0		72·0	57·4	45·5	39·7
10·5		70·0	55·8	44·4	38·7
11·0		68·2	54·5	43·3	37·8
11·5		66·5	53·2	42·3	36·9
12·0		64·9	52·0	41·4	36·1
12·5		63·4	50·8	40·5	35·3
13·0		62·1	49·8	39·7	34·6
14·0		59·6	47·9	38·2	33·3
15·0		57·4	46·1	36·8	32·2
20·0		49·1	39·7	31·8	27·8
30·0		39·7	32·2	25·8	22·6
40·0		34·2	27·8	22·3	19·5
50·0		30·5	24·8	19·9	17·5
100·0		21·3	17·4	14·0	12·3
$\delta = a\kappa^{-\frac{1}{2}}$,	$a\rightarrow$212·9		173·9	140·2	123·0

APPENDIX 3.2. The maximum likelihood estimate $\hat{\kappa}$ for given $\bar{R}$ in the Fisher case. For the solution $\kappa = B^{-1}(\rho)$, replace $\hat{\kappa}$ by κ, $\bar{R}$ by ρ.

$\bar{R}$	$\hat{\kappa}$	$\bar{R}$	$\hat{\kappa}$	$\bar{R}$	$\hat{\kappa}$
0·00	0·00000	0·35	1·13739	0·70	3·30354
·01	·03000	·36	1·17584	·71	3·42314
·02	·06001	·37	1·21490	·72	3·55051
·03	·09005	·38	1·25459	·73	3·68655
·04	·12012	·39	1·29497	·74	3·83232
·05	·15023	·40	1·33605	·75	3·98905
·06	·18039	·41	1·37789	·76	4·15819
·07	·21062	·42	1·42053	·77	4·34143
·08	·24093	·43	1·46401	·78	4·54076
·09	·27132	·44	1·50839	·79	4·75857
·10	·30182	·45	1·55372	·80	4·99772
·11	·33242	·46	1·60005	·81	5·26167
·12	·36315	·47	1·64745	·82	5·55463
·13	·39402	·48	1·69599	·83	5·88181
·14	·42503	·49	1·74573	·84	6·24971
·15	·45621	·50	1·79676	·85	6·66652
·16	·48756	·51	1·84915	·86	7·14279
·17	·51909	·52	1·90300	·87	7·69228
·18	·55083	·53	1·95842	·88	8·33333
·19	·58278	·54	2·01550	·89	9·09091
·20	·61497	·55	2·07437	·90	10·00000
·21	·64740	·56	2·13515	·91	11·11111
·22	·68009	·57	2·19799	·92	12·50000
·23	·71306	·58	2·26304	·93	14·28571
·24	·74632	·59	2·33049	·94	16·66667
·25	·77990	·60	2·40050	·95	20·00000
·26	·81381	·61	2·47331	·96	25·00000
·27	·84806	·62	2·54914	·97	33·33333
·28	·88269	·63	2·62825	·98	50·00000
·29	·91771	·64	2·71093	·99	100·00000
·30	·95315	·65	2·79751	1·00	∞
·31	·98902	·66	2·88836		
·32	1·02536	·67	2·98389		
·33	1·06218	·68	3·08456		
·34	1·09951	·69	3·19091		

APPENDIX 3.3. The maximum likelihood estimate $\hat{\kappa}$ for given $\bar{\tau}_1 = \tau_1/n$ for Dimroth–Watson's distribution. (The girdle case.) For the solution $\kappa = D^{-1}(\rho)$, replace $\hat{\kappa}$ by κ, $\bar{\tau}_1$ by ρ.

$\bar{\tau}_1$	$\hat{\kappa}$	$\bar{\tau}_1$	$\hat{\kappa}$	$\bar{\tau}_1$	$\hat{\kappa}$
0·000	∞	0·115	4·1959	0·230	1·3571
·005	100	·120	3·9925	·235	1·2786
·010	50·00	·125	3·8024	·240	1·2018
·015	33·33	·130	3·6242	·245	1·1268
·020	25·00	·135	3·4565	·250	1·0534
·025	20·00	·140	3·2982	·255	0·9815
·030	16·67	·145	3·1483	·260	0·9110
·035	14·29	·150	3·0061	·265	0·8419
·040	12·25	·155	2·8703	·270	0·7741
·045	11·11	·160	2·7411	·275	0·7075
·050	9·9923	·165	2·6174	·280	0·6420
·055	9·0874	·170	2·4988	·285	0·5775
·060	8·3268	·175	2·3850	·290	0·5141
·065	7·6812	·180	2·2754	·295	0·4517
·070	7·1255	·185	2·1699	·300	0·3902
·075	6·6413	·190	2·0680	·305	0·3295
·080	6·2148	·195	1·9695	·310	0·2697
·085	5·8355	·200	1·8742	·315	0·2106
·090	5·4952	·205	1·7818	·320	0·1523
·095	5·1875	·210	1·6921	·325	0·0946
·100	4·9075	·215	1·6050	·330	0·0375
·105	4·6510	·220	1·5202	·333	0·0037
·110	4·4147	·225	1·4376		

324   APPENDIX 3

APPENDIX 3.4. The maximum likelihood estimate $\hat{\kappa}'$ for given $\bar{\tau}_3 = \tau_3/n$ for Dimroth–Watson's distribution. (The bipolar case.) For the solution $-\kappa' = D^{-1}(\rho)$, replace $\hat{\kappa}'$ by κ', $\bar{\tau}_3$ by ρ.

$\bar{\tau}_3$	$\hat{\kappa}'$	$\bar{\tau}_3$	$\hat{\kappa}'$	$\bar{\tau}_3$	$\hat{\kappa}'$
0·34	0·0745	0·57	2·3921	0·80	5·7970
·35	0·1843	·58	2·4962	·81	6·0630
·36	0·2922	·59	2·6019	·82	6·3544
·37	0·3983	·60	2·7092	·83	6·6762
·38	0·5028	·61	2·8185	·84	7·0346
·39	0·6059	·62	2·9299	·85	7·4379
·40	0·7077	·63	3·0437	·86	7·8969
·41	0·8086	·64	3·1602	·87	8·4256
·42	0·9085	·65	3·2796	·88	9·0433
·43	1·0076	·66	3·4022	·89	9·7758
·44	1·1061	·67	3·5285	·90	10·6594
·45	1·2042	·68	3·6588	·91	11·7460
·46	1·3019	·69	3·7636	·92	13·1124
·47	1·3994	·70	3·9335	·93	14·8782
·48	1·4969	·71	4·0789	·94	17·2418
·49	1·5944	·72	4·2305	·95	20·5597
·50	1·6920	·73	4·3892	·96	25·5458
·51	1·7900	·74	4·5558	·97	33·8664
·52	1·8884	·75	4·7314	·98	50·5213
·53	1·9874	·76	4·9173	·99	100·5103
·54	2·0872	·77	5·1148	1·00	∞
·55	2·1877	·78	5·3257		
·56	2·2893	·79	5·5523		

APPENDIX 3.5. Critical values* for the Rayleigh test of uniformity with the test statistic $\bar{R}$. $\Pr(\bar{R} \geqslant \bar{R}_0) = \alpha$.

n	$\alpha\rightarrow$	0·10	0·05	0·02	0·01
5		0·637	0·700	0·765	0·805
6		·583	·642	·707	·747
7		·541	·597	·659	·698
8		·506	·560	·619	·658
9		·478	·529	·586	·624
10		·454	·503	·558	·594
11		·433	·480	·533	·568
12		·415	·460	·512	·546
13		·398	·442	·492	·526
14		·384	·427	·475	·507
15		·371	·413	·460	·491
16		·359	·400	·446	·476
17		·349	·388	·443	·463
18		·339	·377	·421	·450
19		·330	·367	·410	·438
20		·322	·358	·399	·428
21		·314	·350	·390	·418
22		·307	·342	·382	·408
23		·300	·334	·374	·400
24		·294	·328	·366	·392
25		·288	·321	·359	·384
30		·26	·29	·33	·36
35		·24	·27	·31	·33
40		·23	·26	·29	·31
45		·22	·24	·27	·29
50		·20	·23	·26	·28
100		·14	·16	·18	·19
$3n\bar{R}^2 = \chi_3^2$		6·251	7·815	9·837	11·345

* Based on Table 1 of Stephens (1964b) with the kind permission of the author and the editor of *J. Amer. Statist. Ass.*

APPENDIX 3.6. Critical values of R for testing a prescribed direction.

APPENDIX 3.6a. Stephens charts* for the critical values R_0 of R for $\alpha = 0.05$.

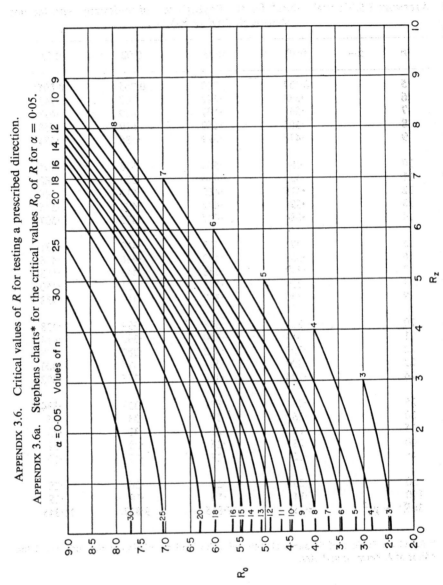

* Rv M. A. Stephens in Biometrika, Vol. 49, pp. 547–552, 1962. Reproduced with the kind permission of the author and the editor.

APPENDIX 3.6b. Stephens charts* for the critical values R_0 of R for $\alpha = 0.01$.

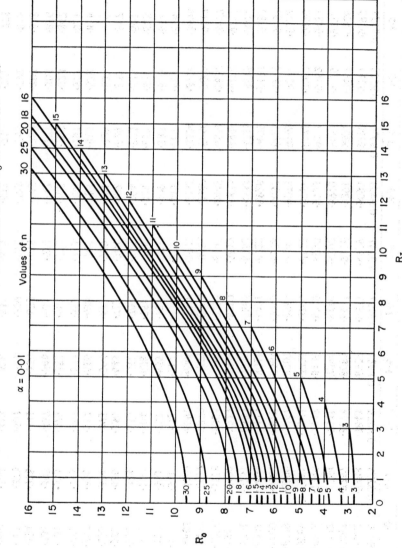

$\alpha = 0.01$

Values of n

* By M. A. Stephens in *Biometrika*, Vol. 49, pp. 547–552, 1962. Reproduced with the kind permission of the author and the editor.

APPENDIX 3.7. Critical values* of $\bar{R}$ for testing a prescribed concentration parameter. $\Pr(\bar{R} > \bar{R}_0) = \alpha$. $\alpha = 0\cdot01$ (upper entry) and $\alpha = 0\cdot05$ (lower entry).

n $\kappa\rightarrow$	0·0	0·5	1·0	1·5	2·0	2·5	3·0	3·5	4·0	4·5	5·0
5	0·8046	0·8275	0·8668	0·8982	0·9197	0·9347	0·9453	0·9530	0·9588	0·9634	0·9670
	·7002	·7288	·7843	·8327	·8675	·8919	·9093	·9220	·9317	·9393	·9454
6	·7467	·7767	·8278	·8683	·8963	·9156	·9291	·9391	·9467	·9526	·9574
	·6422	·6764	·7241	·7994	·8410	·8702	·8910	·9063	·9179	·9270	·9343
7	·6986	·7346	·7949	·8426	·8760	·8990	·9153	·9271	·9362	·9433	·9490
	·5969	·6355	·7084	·7725	·8194	·8525	·8761	·8935	·9067	·9170	·9253
8	·6579	·6990	·7667	·8207	·8585	·8847	·9033	·9169	·9271	·9352	·9417
	·5600	·6024	·6813	·7504	·8015	·8378	·8637	·8829	·8974	·9087	·9179
9	·6236	·6691	·7425	·8016	·8431	·8722	·8928	·9079	·9193	·9282	·9353
	·5291	·5751	·6587	·7320	·7865	·8253	·8533	·8736	·8895	·9017	·9115
10	·5940	·6432	·7217	·7849	·8299	·8612	·8835	·8999	·9124	·9221	·9298
	·5028	·5518	·6396	·7163	·7735	·8147	·8443	·8661	·8827	·8957	·9061
12	·5457	·6012	·6872	·7572	·8075	·8428	·8680	·8866	·9007	·9117	·9205
	·4603	·5147	·6090	·6909	·7526	·7972	·8295	·8534	·8716	·8858	·8972
16	·476	·541	·638	·717	·774	·815	·845	·867	·883	·896	·906
	·400	·463	·567	·655	·723	·773	·809	·835	·856	·872	·884
20	·428	·500	·604	·688	·751	·796	·828	·852	·871	·885	·897
	·358	·428	·538	·631	·703	·755	·794	·823	·845	·862	·876
30	·355	·436	·550	·643	·713	·764	·802	·829	·850	·867	·880
	·295	·374	·493	·594	·671	·729	·771	·803	·827	·846	·862
40	·307	·398	·517	·616	·690	·745	·785	·815	·838	·856	·870
	·255	·343	·467	·572	·653	·713	·758	·791	·817	·837	·853
60	·251	·353	·479	·583	·663	·722	·765	·798	·823	·842	·858
	·208	·307	·437	·546	·631	·694	·742	·777	·805	·826	·844
100	·194	·308	·441	·550	·635	·698	·745	·780	·807	·828	·845
	·161	·272	·407	·521	·609	·676	·725	·763	·792	·815	·834
∞	·000	·164	·313	·438	·537	·613	·672	·716	·751	·778	·800

* From M. A. Stephens in *Biometrika*, Vol. 54, pp. 211–223, 1967. Reproduced with the kind permission of the author and the editor.

APPENDIX 3.8. Critical values for Watson–Williams' two-sample test.

APPENDIX 3.8a. (Equal samples). Critical values* for the two-sample test with the test-statistic $\bar{R}' = (R_1 + R_2)/n$ when $\bar{R}$ for the combined sample is given. $\Pr(\bar{R}' > \bar{R}_0) = \alpha$. $\alpha = 0.01$ (upper entry), $\alpha = 0.05$ (lower entry). $n_1 = n_2 = n/2$, $r = 1/2$.

n	$\bar{R} \rightarrow$ 0.05	0.10	0.15	0.20	0.25	0.30	0.35	0.40	0.45	0.50	0.55	0.60	0.65	0.70
12	0·571	0·573	0·557	0·583	0·592	0·605	0·622	0·642	0·666	0·692	0·720	0·749	0·780	0·811
	·482	·486	·492	·501	·514	·531	·552	·577	·606	·637	·670	·704	·741	·778
16	·493	·496	·502	·511	·524	·542	·563	·589	·617	·648	·680	·714	·749	·784
	·415	·419	·427	·440	·457	·478	·505	·535	·568	·603	·640	·679	·718	·758
20	·440	·444	·452	·464	·480	·500	·525	·555	·586	·620	·655	·692	·730	·768
	·369	·375	·385	·400	·420	·466	·475	·509	·545	·583	·622	·663	·704	·746
24	·401	·407	·416	·429	·448	·471	·499	·531	·565	·610	·639	·677	·716	·757
	·337	·343	·355	·372	·395	·423	·455	·491	·529	·569	·601	·652	·695	·738
30	·359	·365	·376	·392	·414	·441	·474	·507	·544	·581	·621	·662	·703	·746
	·300	·308	·322	·341	·368	·400	·435	·473	·514	·555	·598	·642	·686	·731
40	·311	·319	·332	·352	·378	·409	·444	·481	·521	·562	·604	·647	·691	·734
	·260	·270	·286	·310	·340	·376	·414	·455	·492	·542	·586	·631	·677	·723
60	·255	·265	·282	·307	·339	·375	·414	·455	·498	·542	·586	·632	·677	·723
	·213	·225	·247	·276	·312	·351	·393	·437	·482	·528	·574	·621	·668	·715
120	·182	·197	·223	·258	·297	·339	·383	·428	·474	·521	·568	·616	·664	·711
	·153	·171	·201	·239	·281	·326	·372	·419	·466	·514	·562	·610	·659	·708
240	·133	·155	·189	·230	·274	·320	·367	·415	·463	·511	·559	·608	·657	·706
	·113	·139	·177	·220	·267	·314	·363	·410	·458	·507	·556	·605	·654	·704
∞	0·05	0·10	0·15	0·20	0·25	0·30	0·35	0·40	0·45	0·50	0·55	0·60	0·65	0·70

* From M. A. Stephens in *Biometrika*, Vol. 56, pp. 169–181, 1969. Reproduced with the kind permission of the author and the editor.

APPENDIX 3.8b. (Unequal samples.) Critical values* for the two-sample test with the test-statistic $\bar{R}' = (R_1 + R_2)/n$ when $\bar{R}$ for the combined sample is given. $\Pr(\bar{R}' > \bar{R}_0') = \alpha$. $\alpha = 0.01$ (upper entry) and $\alpha = 0.05$ (lower entry), $n_1 = \frac{1}{2}n_2 = n/3, r = 1/3$.

n $\bar{R}\to$	0·10	0·15	0·20	0·25	0·30	0·35
20	0·420	0·436	0·454	0·474	0·497	0·525
	·355	·371	·392	·414	·444	·475
24	·385	·403	·422	·445	·469	·499
	·325	·345	·366	·392	·422	·455
30	·350	·366	·387	·412	·441	·472
	·296	·314	·338	·367	·399	·435
40	·307	·325	·350	·378	·409	·444
	·261	·281	·309	·340	·376	·414
60	·257	·278	·307	·339	·375	·414
	·220	·244	·275	·312	·351	·393
120	·195	·223	·258	·297	·339	·383
	·169	·201	·239	·281	·326	·372
∞	0·10	0·15	0·20	0·25	0·30	0·35

* From M. A. Stephens in *Biometrika*, Vol. 56, pp. 169–181, 1969. Reproduced with the kind permission of the author and the editor.

BIBLIOGRAPHY AND AUTHOR INDEX

Pages on which authors are cited are given in brackets following each entry.

Abrahamson, I. G. (1967). Exact Bahadur efficiencies for the Kolmogorov–Smirnov and Kuiper one- and two-sample statistics. *Ann. Math. Statist.* **38**, 1475–90. [204]

Abramowitz, M. and Stegun, I. A. (1965). "Handbook of Mathematical Functions". Dover, New York. [63, 123, 200]

Ajne, B. (1968). A simple test for uniformity of a circular distribution. *Biometrika* **55**, 343–54. [136, 183, 185, 187, 191]

Andersen, E. S. (1953). On the fluctuations of sums of random variables. *Math. Scand.* **1**, 263–85. [177]

Anderson, T. W. and Stephens, M. A. (1971). Tests for randomness of directions against equatorial and bimodal alternatives. *Tech. Report No. 5.* Dept. of Statist., Stanford Univ. [280]

Andrews, J. T. and Shimizu, K. (1966). Three dimensional vector technique for analyzing till fabrics: Discussion and Fortran program. *Geog. Bull.* **8**, 151–65. [283]

Arnold, K. J. (1941). "On Spherical Probability Distributions". Ph. D. thesis. Massachusetts Institute of Technology. [70, 230, 231, 236]

Asano, C. (1965). Runs test for a circular distribution and a table of probabilities. *Ann. Inst. Statist. Math.* **17**, 331–46. [203, 315]

Barton, D. E. and David, F. N. (1958). Runs in a ring. *Biometrika* **45**, 572–8. [203, 208]

Batschelet, E. (1965). "Statistical Methods for the Analysis of Problems in Animal Orientation and Certain Biological Rhythms". Amer. Inst. Biol. Sciences, Washington. [60, 61, 64, 76, 204, 291, 296, 297, 298]

Batschelet, E. (1971). Recent statistical methods for orientation data. "Animal Orientation, Symposium 1970 on Wallops Island". Amer. Inst. Biol. Sciences, Washington. [151, 168, 300, 302, 303, 304, 305]

Beckmann, P. (1959). The probability distribution of the vector sum of n unit vectors with arbitrary phase distributions. *Acta Technica* **4**, 323–35. [15]

Bellman, R. A. (1961). "A Brief Introduction to Theta Functions". Holt, Rinehart and Winston, New York. [55]

Benford, F. (1938). The law of anomalous numbers. *Proc. Amer. Phil. Soc.* **78**, 551–72. [92, 93]

Beran, R. J. (1968). Testing for uniformity on a compact homogeneous space. *J. Appl. Prob.* **5**, 177–95. [190, 192, 257, 282]

Beran, R. J. (1969a). Asymptotic theory of a class of tests for uniformity of a circular distribution. *Ann. Math. Statist.* **40**, 1196–206. [190, 193, 194, 195]

Beran, R. J. (1969b). The derivation of nonparametric two-sample tests for uniformity of a circular distribution. *Biometrika* **56**, 561–70. [202, 204, 205, 206, 209, 210]

Bernoulli, D. (1734). *Récherches physiques et astronomiques, sur le problème proposé pour la seconde fois par l'Académie Royale des Sciences des Paris.* Récuiel des pièces qui ont remporté le prix de l'Académie Royale des Sciences, Tome III, 95–134. [16, 257]

Bhattacharyya, G.K. and Johnson, R. A. (1969). On Hodges's bivariate sign test and a test for uniformity of a circular distribution. *Biometrika* 56, 446–9. [137, 183]

Bingham, C. (1964). "Distributions on the Sphere and on the Projective Plane". Ph.D. thesis. Yale University. [225, 226, 234, 236, 256, 277]

Bingham, M. S. (1971). Stochastic processes with independent increments taking values in an abelian group. *Proc. Lond. Math. Soc.* 22, 507–30. [56]

Bishop, B. V. (1947). The frequency of thunderstorms at Kew observatory. *Met. Mag.* 76, 108–111. [8]

Boneva, L. I., Kendall, D. G. and Stefanov, I. (1971). Spline transformations: Three new diagnostic aids for the statistical data-analyst. *J. Roy. Statist. Soc.* B33, 1–70. [130]

Box, G. E. P. (1954). Discussion in the "Symposium on Interval Estimation". *J. Roy. Statist. Soc.* B16, 211–2. [283]

Breitenberger, E. (1963). Analogues of the normal distribution on the circle and the sphere. *Biometrika* 50, 81–8. [236]

Brunk, H. D. (1962). On the range of the difference between hypothetical distribution function and Pyke's modified empirical distribution function. *Ann. Math. Statist.* 33, 525–32. [175, 176, 177]

Burr, E. J. (1964). Small-sample distributions of the two-sample Cramér-von Mises W^2 and Watson's U^2. *Ann. Math. Statist.* 35, 1091–8. [202, 314]

Chandrasekhar, S. (1943). Stochastic problems in physics and astronomy. *Rev. Mod. Phys.* 15, 1–89. [240]

Creer, K. M. (1962). The dispersion of the geomagnetic field due to secular variation and its determination for remote times from paleomagnetic data. *J. Geophys. Res.* 67, 3461–76. [283]

Curray, J. R. (1956). The analysis of two-dimensional orientation data. *J. Geol.* 64, 117–31. [7, 13]

Daniels, H. E. (1954). A distribution-free test for regression parameters. *Ann. Math. Statist.* 25, 499–513. [185]

Darling, D. A. (1953). On a class of problems related to the random division of an interval. *Ann. Math. Statist.* 24, 239–53. [189]

David, F. N. and Barton, D. E. (1962). "Combinatorial Chance". Griffin, London. [203]

David, F. N., Kendall, M. G. and Barton, D. E. (1966). "Symmetric Functions and Allied Tables". Cambridge Univ. Press. [107]

David, H. A. (1970). "Order Statistics". Wiley, New York. [188]

David, H. A. and Newell, D. J. (1965). The identification of annual peak periods for a disease. *Biometrics* 21, 645–50. [136, 187]

Dimroth, E. (1962). Untersuchungen zum Mechanismus von Blastesis und syntexis in Phylliten and Hornfelsen des südwestlichen Fichtelgebirges I. Die statistische Auswertung einfacher Gürteldiagramme. *Tscherm. Min. Petr. Mitt.* 8, 248–74. [234]

Dimroth, E. (1963). Fortschritte der Gefügestatistik. *N. Jb. Min. Mh.* 13, 186–92. [234]

Downs, T. D. (1966). Some relationships among the von Mises distributions of different dimensions. *Biometrika* 53, 269–72. [66, 233, 248]

Downs, T. D. and Gould, A. L. (1967). Some relationships between the normal and von Mises distributions. *Biometrika* **54**, 684–7. [233, 248]

Downs, T. D. and Liebman, J. (1969). Statistical methods for vectorcardiographic directions. *IEEE Trans. Bio-med. Engr.* **16**, 87–94. [16, 251]

Dovretzky, A. and Wolfowitz, J. (1951). Sums of random integers reduced modulo *m. Duke Math. J.* **18**, 501–7. [91]

Durand, D. and Greenwood, J. A. (1957). Random unit vectors II: Usefulness of Grame–Charlier and related series in approximating distributions. *Ann. Math. Statist.* **28**, 978–85. [95, 109, 133]

Dyck, H. D. and Mattice, W. A. (1941). A study of excessive rainfalls. *Monthly Weather Rev.* **69**, 293–302. [8]

Edwards, J. H. (1961). The recognition and estimation of cyclic trends. *Ann. Hum. Genet. Lond.* **25**, 83–6. [136]

Feller, W. (1966). "An Introduction to Probability Theory and its Applications". Vol. 2, Wiley, New York. [92, 240, 241]

Findlater, J., Harrower, T. N. S. and Howkins, G. A. (1966). "Surface and 900 mb Wind Relationships". H.M.S. Publ., Met. Office, London. [12]

Fisher, R. A. (1929). Tests of significance in harmonic analysis. *Proc. Roy. Soc. Lond.* **A125**, 54–9. [188]

Fisher, R. A. (1953). Dispersion on a sphere. *Proc. Roy. Soc. Lond.* **A217**, 295–305. [220, 230, 240, 242, 244, 251, 261, 283]

Fisher, R. A. (1959). "Statistical Methods and Scientific Inference". 2nd edn., Oliver and Boyd. Edinburgh. [61, 138]

Fox, W. T. (1967). Fortran IV program for vector trend analyses of directional data. *Computer Science Contribution 11*, Kansas Univ. [283]

Fraser, D. A. S. (1968). "The Structure of Inference". Wiley, New York. [283]

Garner, J. B. (1968). Analysis of the distribution of directions in two dimensions. *Res. Report No. 48.* Dept. of Prob. & Statist., Sheffield Univ. [283]

Gilroy, J. F. (1965). "Corrections for Grouping for Circular Distributions". Ph.D thesis, Michigan Univ. [79]

Gould, A. L. (1969). A regression technique for angular variates. *Biometrics* **25**, 683–700. [16, 127, 128, 167, 251, 283]

Gray, H. L. and Odell, P. L. (1966). On sums and products of rectangular variates. *Biometrika,* **53**, 615–9. [240]

Greenwood, J. A. (1959a). Corrections to trigonometric moments for grouping. *Tech. Report No.* 1.11. Statist. Lab. Iowa State College. [79]

Greenwood, J. A. (1959b). "Distribution Theory of some Angular Variates". Ph.D. thesis. Harvard Univ. [121]

Greenwood, J. A. and Durand, D. (1955). The distribution of length and components of the sum of *n* random unit vectors. *Ann. Math. Statist.* **26**, 233–46. [95, 97, 98, 135, 154]

Gumbel, E. J., Greenwood, J. A. and Durand, D. (1953). The circular normal distribution: theory and tables. *J. Amer. Statist. Ass.* **48**, 131–52. [64, 298]

Gumbel, E. J. (1954). Applications of the circular normal distribution. *J. Amer. Statist. Ass.* **49**, 267–97. [15, 16, 125]

De Hass-Lorentz, G. L. (1913). "Die Brownsche Bewegung und einige verwandte Erscheinungen". Frieder, Vieweg und Sohn, Brunswick. [56]

Haldane, J. B. S. (1960). The addition of random vectors. *Sankhyā,* **22**, 213–20. [108, 245]

Hamilton, N. and Rees, A. I. (1965). The anisotropy of magnetic susceptibility of the Francisan Rocks of the Dablo range, Central California. *Res. Report.* Marine Physical Lab., Scripps Inst. of Oceanography, Univ. of California San Diego. [170]

Herglotz, G. (1911). Ueber Potenzreihen mit positivem, reellen Teil im Einheitskreis. *Ber. Kgl. Sächs. Ges. Wiss. Leipzig, Math. Phys. K1.* **63**, 501–11. [86]

Herz, C. S. (1955). Bessel functions of matrix argument. *Ann. Math.,* **61**, 474–523. [235]

Hill, B. M. (1960). A relationship between Hodges' bivariate sign test and a non-parametric test of Daniels. *Ann. Math. Statist.* **31**, 1190–2. [185]

Hodges, J. L., Jr. (1955). A bivariate sign test. *Ann. Math. Statist.* **26**, 523–7. [183, 185, 309]

Hogg, R. V. and Craig, A. T. (1965). "Introduction to Mathematical Statistics". 2nd edn. Macmillan. New York. [126]

Hospers, J. (1955). Rock magnetism and polar wandering. *J. Geol.* **63**, 59–74. [261]

Hoyt, R. S. (1947). Probability functions for the modulus and angle of the normal complex variable. *Bell Syst. Tech. J.,* **26**, 318–59. [112]

Hurwitz, A. (1903). Ueber die Fourierschen Konstanten integrierbarer Funktionen. *Math. Ann.* **57**, 425–446; **59**, 553. [86]

Irving, E. (1964). "Paleomagnetism and its Applications to Geological and Geophysical Problems". Wiley, New York. [269]

Irving, E. and Ward, M. A. (1964). A statistical model of the geomagnetic field. *Geofis. Pura. Appl.* **57**, 47–52. [227]

Jaffe, L. (1956). Effect of polarized light on polarity of fucus. *Science* **123**, 1081–2. [14]

Jeffreys, H. (1948). "Theory of Probability". 2nd ed. Oxford Univ. Press. [51]

Jensen, H. (1959). Daily determinations of the microseismic direction in Copenhagen during the IGY 1958. *Meddr. Danm. Geod. Inst.* No. 38. [15]

Joffe, A. and Klotz, J. (1962). Null distribution and Bahadur efficiency of the Hodges bivariate sign test. *Ann. Math. Statist.* **33**, 803–7. [185]

Johnson, N. L. (1966). Paths and chains of random straight-line segments. *Technometrics* **8**, 303–17. [96, 108, 245]

Jones, T. A. (1967). Estimation and testing procedures for circular normally distributed data. *Tech. Report No.* 3. Dept. of Geol., Northwestern Univ. [283]

Jones, T. A. and James, W. R. (1969). Analysis of bimodal orientation data. *Math. Geol.* **1**, 129–35. [128]

Kac, M. and Van Kampen, E. R. (1939). Circular equidistributions and statistical independence. *Amer. J. Math.* **61**, 677–82. [69]

Kendall, M. G. (1946a). Discussion on "The statistical study of infectious diseases". by Greenwood, M. *J. Roy. Statist. Soc.* **109**, 103–5. [189]

Kendall, M. G. (1946b). "Contributions to the Study of Oscillatory Time-series". Univ. Press, Cambridge. [200]

Kendall, M. G. (1957). "A Course in Multivariate Analysis". Griffin, London. [226]

Kendall, M. G. and Stuart, A. (1967). "The Advanced Theory of Statistics". Vol. 2 (2nd edn.) Griffin, London. [138, 142, 153]

Kendall, M. G. and Stuart, A. (1969). "The Advanced Theory of Statistics". Vol. 1 (3rd edn.) Griffin, London. [77, 78]

Klotz, J. (1959). Null distribution of the Hodges bivariate sign test. *Ann. Math. Statist.* **30**, 1029–33. [185]

Klotz, J. (1964). Small sample power of the bivariate sign tests of Blumen and Hodges. *Ann. Math. Statist.* **35**, 1576–82. [53]

Kluyver, J. C. (1906). A local probability theorem. *Ned. Akad. Wet. Proc.* **A8**, 341–50. [96]

Krumbein, W. C. (1939). Preferred orientation of pebbles in sedimentary deposits. *J. Geol.* **47**, 673–706. [10, 70]

Kuhn, W. and Grün, F. (1942). Beziehungen zwischen elastischen Konstanten and Dchnugs doppelbrechung hochelastischer Stoffe. *Kolloid. Zeit.*, **101**, 248–71. [231]

Kuiper, N. H. (1960). Tests concerning random points on a circle. *Ned. Akad. Wet. Proc.* **A63**, 38–47. [173, 178, 204]

Langevin, P. (1905). Magnetisme et theorie des électrons. *Ann. de Chim. et de Phys.*, **5**, 70–127. [230]

Laubscher, N. F. and Rudolph, G. J. (1968). A distribution arising from random points on the circumference of a circle. *Res. Report No.* 268. C.S.I.R., Pretoria. [189, 310]

Lee, J. H. A. (1963). (Correspondence) *Brit. Med. J.* **10**, 623. [11]

Lehmann, E. L. (1959). "Testing Statistical Hypotheses". Wiley, New York. [136, 142, 144, 149, 150]

Lévy, P. (1939). L'addition des variable aléatoires définies sur une circonférence. *Bull. Soc. Math. France* **67**, 1–41. [55, 56, 57, 91]

Lord, R. D. (1948). A problem on random vectors. *Phil. Mag.* (7), **39**, 66–71. [99]

Lord, R. D. (1954). The use of the Hankel transform in statistics. I, General theory and examples. *Biometrika* **41**, 44–55. [84, 245]

Loudon, T. V. (1964). Computer analysis of orientation data in structural geology. *Tech. Report No.* 13. Northwestern Univ. [13, 225]

Lukacs, E. (1970). "Characteristic Functions". 2nd edn. Griffin, London. [57, 87, 88]

Maag, U. R. (1966). A k-sample analogue of Watson's U^2 statistic. *Biometrika* **53**, 579–83. [208]

Maag, U. R. and Dicaire, G. (1971). On Kolmogorov–Smirnov type one-sample statistics. *Biometrika* **58**, 653–6. [178]

Mackenzie, J. K. (1957). The estimation of an orientation relationship. *Acta. Cryst. Canb.* **10**, 61–2. [283]

Mardia, K. V. (1967). A non-parametric test for the bivariate two-sample location problem. *J. Roy. Statist. Soc.* **B29**, 320–42. [198, 199, 313]

Mardia, K. V. (1968). Small sample power of a non-parametric test for the bivariate two-sample location problem in the normal case. *J. Roy. Statist. Soc.*, **B30**, 83–92. [198]

Mardia, K. V. (1969a). On the null distribution of a non-parametric test for the bivariate two-sample problem. *J. Roy. Statist. Soc.*, **B31**, 98–102. [199, 313]

Mardia, K. V. (1969b). On Wheeler and Watson's two-sample test on a circle. *Sanhkyā* **A31**, 177–90. [198, 199, 206]

Mardia, K. V. (1970). A bivariate non-parametric c-sample test. *J. Roy. Statist. Soc.* **B32**, 74–87. [208, 316]

Mardia, K. V. (1971). Discussion on "Spline transformations". by Boneva, L. I., Kendall, D. G. and Stefanov, I. *J. Roy. Statist. Soc.*, **B33**, 50–1. [57]

Mardia, K. V. (1972). A multisample uniform scores test on a circle and its parametric competitor. *J. Roy. Statist. Soc.* **B34**, Part 1. [112, 208]

Mardia, K. V. and Spurr, B. D. (1972). Multi-sample tests for multi-modal and axial circular populations. Unpublished. [210, 211, 317]

Markov, A. A. (1912). "Wahrscheinlichkeitsrechnung". Taubner, Leipzig. [96]

Marshall, A. W. and Olkin, I. (1961). Game theoratic proof that Chebyshev inequalities are sharp. *Pac. J. Math.* **11**, 1421–9. [46]

Matthews, G. V. T. (1961). "Nonsense" orientation in mallard *anas platyrhynchos* and its relation to experiments on bird navigation. *Ibis* **103a**, 211–30. [3]

Milne-Thomson, L. M. (1933). "The Calculus of Finite Differences". Macmillan, London. [77]

Parthasarathy, K. R. (1967). "Probability Measures on Metric Spaces". Academic Press, New York. [91]

Pearson, E. S. (1963). Comparison of tests for randomness of points on a line. *Biometrika* **50**, 315–23. [182]

Pearson, E. S. and Stephens, M. A. (1962). The goodness-of-fit tests based on $W_N{}^2$ and $U_N{}^2$. *Biometrika* **49**, 397–402. [96]

Pearson, K. (1905). The problem of the random walk. *Nature* **72**, 294, 342. [96]

Pearson, K. (1906). "A Mathematical Theory of Random Migration". Draper's company research memoirs. Biometric Series, III, No. 15. [95, 96, 135]

Perrin, F. (1928). Etude mathématique du mouvement brownien de rotation. *Annls Scient. Ec. Norm. Sup. Paris,* **45**, 1–51. [228]

Pincus, H. J. (1953). The analysis of aggregates of orientation data in the earth sciences. *J. Geol.* **61**, 482–509. [13]

Pinkham. R. S. (1961). On the distribution of first significant digits. *Ann. Math. Statist.* **32**, 1223–30. [92]

Poincaré, H. (1912). Chance. Monist **22**, 31–52. [91]

Pollak, L. W. and Egan, U. N. (1949). All term guide for harmonic analysis and synthesis using 3 to 24, 26, 28, 30, 34, 36, 38, 42, 44, 46, 52, 60, 68, 76, 84 and 92 equidistant values. *Geophy. Publications,* Vol. **2**, Stationary Office, Dublin. [201]

Pólya, G. (1919). Zur Statistik der sphaerischen Verteilung der Fixsterne. *Ast. Nachr.* **208**, 175–80. [17]

Pólya, G. (1930). Sur quelques points de la théorie des probabilitiés. *Ann. Inst.H. Poincaré* **1**, 117–61. [66]

Quenouille, M. H. (1947). On the problem of random flights. *Proc. Camb. Phil. Soc.* **43**, 581–2. [240]

Rao, C. R. (1965). "Linear Statistical Inference and its Applications". Wiley, New York. [65, 66, 159, 231]

Rao, J. S. (1969). "Some Contributions to the Analysis of Circular Data". Ph. D. thesis. Indian Stat. Inst., Calcutta. [103, 189, 194, 195, 203, 311]

Rao, J. S. and Sengupta, S. (1970). An optimum hierarchical sampling procedure for cross-bedding data, *J. Geol.* **78**, 533–44. [164]

Rayleigh, Lord. (1880). On the resultant of a large number of vibrations of the same pitch and or arbitrary phase. *Phil. Mag.* **10**, 73–8. [96]

Rayleigh, Lord. (1905). The problem of the random walk. *Nature* **72**, 318. [96]

Rayleigh, Lord. (1919). On the problem of random vibrations, and of random flights in one, two, or three dimensions. *Phil. Mag.* (6), **37**, 321–47. [15, 96, 240, 245, 257]

Roberts, P. H. and Ursell, H. D. (1960). Random walk on a sphere and on a Riemannian manifold. *Phil. Trans. Roy. Soc.* **A252**, 317–56. [228, 232]

Ross, H. E., Crickmar, S. D., Sills, N. V. and Owen, E. P. (1969). Orientation to the vertical in free divers. *Aerospace Med.* **40**, 728–32. [16]

Rothman, E. D. (1971). Tests of coordinate independence for a bivariate sample on a torus. *Ann. Math. Statist.* **42**, 1962–9. [204]

Schach, S. (1967). Nonparametric tests of location for circular distributions. *Tech. Report No. 95*. Dept. of Statist., Minnesota Univ. [205]

Schach, S. (1969a). Nonparametric symmetry tests for circular distributions. *Biometrika* **54**, 571–7. [195]

Schach, S. (1969b). On a class of nonparametric two-sample tests for circular distributions. *Ann. Math. Statist.* **40**, 1791–800. [199, 205]

Scheffé, H. (1970). Multiple testing versus multiple estimation. Improper confidence sets. Estimation of directions and ratios. *Ann. Math. Statist.* **41**, 1–29. [283]

Schmidt, W. (1925). Gefügestastik. *Tscherm. Min. Petr. Mitt.* **38**, 392–423. [215]

Schmidt-Koenig, K. (1958). Experimentelle Einflussnahme auf die 24-Stunden-Periodik bei Brieftauben und deren Auswirkungen unter besonderer Berücksichtigung des Heimfindevermögens. *Z. Tierpsychol.* **15**, 301–31. [156]

Schmidt-Koenig, K. (1963). On the role of the loft, the distance and site of release in pigeon homing (the "cross-loft experiment"). *Biol. Bull.* **125**, 154–64. [135, 146]

Schmidt–Koenig, K. (1965). Current problems in bird orientation, 217–78. "Advances in the Study of Behaviour". Lehrman, D. S. *et al.* eds. Academic Press, New York. [14, 123, 124]

Schuler, M. and Gebelin, H. (1955). "Five Place Tables of Elliptical Functions based on Jacobi's Parameter *q*". Springer, Berlin. [56]

Selby, B. (1964). Girdle distributions on a sphere. *Biometrika* **51**, 381–92. [217, 236]

Sengupta, S. and Rao, J. S. (1966). Statistical analysis of crossbedding azimuths from the Kamthi formation around Bheemaram, Pranhita-Godavari valley. *Sankhyā* **B28**, 165–74. [10]

Sherman, B. (1950). A random variable related to the spacing of sample value. *Ann. Math. Statist.* **21**, 339–51. [189]

Shohat, J. A. and Tamarkin, J. D. (1943). "The Problem of Moments". *Math. Surveys. No.* **1**, Amer. Math. Soc. [86]

Siegel, S. (1956). "Nonparametric Statistics for the Behavioural Science". McGraw-Hill, New York. [196]

Spitzer, F. (1956). A combinatorial lemma and its application to probability theory. *Amer. Math. Soc. Trans.* **82**, 323–31. [177]

Steck, G. P. (1969). The Smirnov two-sample tests as rank tests. *Ann. Math. Statist.* **40**, 1449–66. [204]

Steinmetz, R. (1962). Analysis of vectorial data. *Jour. Sed. Petr.* **32**, 801–12. [217, 218, 267]

Stephens, M. A. (1962a). Exact and approximate tests for directions I. *Biometrika* **49**, 463–77. [95, 146]

Stephens, M. A. (1962b). Exact and approximate tests for directions II. *Biometrika* **49**, 547–52. [259, 326, 327]

Stephens, M. A. (1962c). "The Statistics of Directions". Ph.D. thesis. Univ. of Toronto. [248]

Stephens, M. A. (1963a). Random walk on a circle. *Biometrika* **50**, 385–90. [56, 66, 67]

Stephens, M. A. (1963b). The distribution of the goodness-of-fit statistic U_N^2. I. *Biometrika* **50**, 303–13. [181, 182]

Stephens, M. A. (1964a). The distribution of the goodness-of-fit statistic U_N^2. II. *Biometrika* **51**, 393–7. [181]

Stephens, M. A. (1964b). The testing of unit vectors for randomness. *J. Amer. Statist. Ass.* **59**, 160–7. [324]

Stephens, M. A. (1965a). The goodness-of-fit statistic V_N: distribution and significance points. *Biometrika* **52**, 309–21. [177, 178]

Stephens, M. A. (1965b). Significance points for the two-sample statistic $U^2_{M,N}$. *Biometrika* **52**, 661–3. [202]

Stephens, M. A. (1965c). Appendix to "Equatorial distributions on a sphere", by Watson, G. S. *Biometrika* **52**, 200–1. [280]

Stephens, M. A. (1967). Tests for the dispersion and the modal vector of a distribution on a sphere. *Biometrika* **54**, 211–23. [243, 244, 245, 246, 247, 328, 329]

Stephens, M. A. (1969a). Tests for the von Mises distribution. *Biometrika* **56**, 149–60. [108, 109, 115, 149, 151]

Stephens, M. A. (1969b). A goodness-of-fit statistic for the circle, with some comparisons. *Biometrika* **56**, 161–8. [192, 194]

Stephens, M. A. (1969c). Multi-sample tests for the Fisher distribution for directions. *Biometrika* **56**, 169–81. [328, 329]

Stephens, M. A. (1969d). Tests for randomness of directions against two circular alternatives. *J. Amer. Statist. Ass.* **64**, 280–9. [96, 108, 109, 299, 300]

Stephens, M. A. (1969e). Multi-sample tests for the von Mises distribution. Unpublished. [155, 163]

Stephens, M. A. (1969f). Techniques for directional data. *Tech. Report* No. 150. Dept. of Statist., Stanford Univ. [11, 129, 236]

Stephens, M. A. (1969g). Results from the relation between two statistics of the Kolmogorov–Smirnov type. *Ann. Math. Statist.* **40**, 1833–7. [175]

Stephens, M. A. (1970). Use of the Kolmogorov–Smirnov, Cramér–von Mises and related statistics without extensive tables. *J. Roy. Statist. Soc.* **B32**, 115–22. [178, 182]

Sukhatme, P. V. (1953). "Sampling Theory of Surveys with Applications". Iowa State College Press, Ames. [199]

Tiku, M. L. (1965). Chi-square approximations for the distributions of goodness-of-fit statistics $U_N{}^2$ and $W_N{}^2$. *Biometrika* **52**, 630–3. [182]

Titchmarsh, E. C. (1958). "The Theory of Functions". 2nd edn., Oxford Univ. Press. [42, 43, 82, 87]

Tucker, G. B. (1960). Upper winds over the world. Part III. *Geophy. Memoirs* No. 105. H.M.S. Publ., Met Office, London. [13]

Turner, E. J. and Weiss, L. E. (1963). "Structural Analysis of Metamorphic Tectonites". McGraw-Hill, New York. [217]

Upton, G. J. G. (1970). "Significance Tests for Directional Data". Ph.D. thesis. Birmingham Univ. [147]

Vincez, S. A. and Bruckshaw, J. M. (1960). Note on the probability distribution of a small number of vectors. *Proc. Camb. Phil. Soc.* **56**, 21–6. [240]

Vistelius, A. B. (1966). "Structural Diagrams". Pergamon, London. [217, 264]

Von Mises, R. (1918). Über die "Ganzzahligkeit" der Atomgewicht und verwandte Fragen. *Physikal. Z.* **19**, 490–500. [15, 58, 59, 60, 61, 64, 65, 133, 136]

Waterman, T. H. (1963). The analysis of spatial orientation. *Ergeb. Biol.* **26**, 98–117. [14]

Watson, G. N. (1948). "A Treatise on the Theory of Bessel Functions". 2nd edn. Cambridge Univ. Press. [84, 248]

Watson, G. S. (1956a). Analysis of dispersion on a sphere. *Monthly Notices Roy. Astr. Soc., Geophys. Suppl.* **7**, 153–9. [247, 260, 269]

Watson, G. S. (1956b). A test for randomness of directions. *Monthly Notices Roy. Astr. Soc., Geophys. Suppl.* **7**, 160–1. [240, 257]

Watson, G. S. (1960). More significance tests on the sphere. *Biometrika* **47**, 87–91. [225, 271, 274]

Watson, G. S. (1961). Goodness-of-fit tests on a circle. *Biometrika* **48**, 109–14. [180, 181, 201]

Watson, G. S. (1962). Goodness-of-fit tests on a circle, II. *Biometrika* **49**, 57–63. [200, 201, 202]

Watson, G. S. (1965). Equatorial distributions on a sphere. *Biometrika* **52**, 193–201. [234, 280]

Watson, G. S. (1966). The statistics of orientation data. *J. Geol.* **74**, 786–97. [225]

Watson, G. S. (1967a). Another test for the uniformity of a circular distribution. *Biometrika* **54**, 675–7. [192]

Watson, G. S. (1967b). Some problems in the statistics of directions. *Bull. of the 36th Session Int. Statist. Inst.*, Sydney, Australia. [192, 257, 281, 282]

Watson, G. S. (1970). Orientation statistics in the earth sciences. *Bull. Geol. Inst., Univ. Uppsala* **2**, 73–89. [13, 17, 215, 225, 257, 258, 283]

Watson, G. S. and Beran, R. J. (1967). Testing a sequence of unit vectors for serial correlation. *J. Geophys. Res.* **72**, 5655–9. [283]

Watson, G. S. and Irving, E. (1957). Statistical methods in rock magnetism. *Monthly Notices Roy. Astr. Soc., Geophys. Suppl.* **7**, 289–300. [252, 269]

Watson, G. S. and Williams, E. J. (1956). On the construction of significance tests on the circle and the sphere. *Biometrika* **43**, 344–52. [103, 115, 131, 146, 147, 148, 153, 243, 244, 248, 259, 263]

Wheeler, S. and Watson, G. S. (1964). A distribution-free two-sample test on a circle. *Biometrika* **51**, 256–7. [198]

Winter, A. (1933). On the stable distribution laws. *Amer. J. Maths* **55**, 335–9. [56]

Winter, A. (1947). On the shape of the angular case of Cauchy's distribution curves. *Ann. Math. Statist.* **18**, 589–93. [57]

Zernkie, F. (1928). Wahrscheinlichkeitsrechnung und mathematische Statistik. *In* "Handbuch der Physik". **3**, 419–92. [56]

Zygmund, A. (1959). "Trigonometric Series". Vol. **1**, Cambridge Univ. Press. [42]

SUBJECT INDEX

A

Ajne's A_n-test, 191
  BICR, 193
  consistency, 193
  multimodal case, 209
    BICR, 209
  null distribution, 193
  relation with Beran's class, 191
Ajne's m-test, 182
  See Hodges–Ajne's test
Ajne's two-sample test, 205
  consistency, 206
  multimodal case, 210
Analysis of variance,
  circle, 147, 163
  sphere, 260, 268
  identity, circle, 24, 147
    sphere, 219, 274, 279–281
Angular data, see data
Angular data on $(0, 2\pi/l)$, 7
  mean direction and variance, 26, 28
  (axial for $l = 2$, circular for $l = 1$)
Angular distributions on $(0, 2\pi/l)$, 69
  mean direction, 70
  variance, 70
  (axial for $l = 2$, circular for $l = 1$)
  See distribution
Angular observations, 1
  See data
Angular parameter, 118
Angular tests, see axial tests
Angular unbiased estimate, 118, 120
Anisotropic distribution, 227
Antimode, 10
Antipodal symmetry, circular, 72
  spherical, 233
Arc lengths, 34, 172
  distribution for the uniform case, 172

Astronomy, 16
  Bernoulli's problem, 257
  co-ordinates, 257
Asymptotic distributions, a general
  lemma, 111
  See under specific statistic
Asymptotic relative efficiency (ARE):
  Kuiper's two-sample test, 204
  tests of symmetry, 195
  tests of uniformity, 194–195
  uniform scores test, 208
Atomic weights data, 133
Average grouping correction to
  moments, 79
  See correction
Axes = observations in axial data, 213
Axial data, circular, 1
  fitting von Mises type axial distribu-
    tion, 124
  mean direction, 70
    calculation, 26, 28
  variance, 70
    calculation, 26, 28
Axial data, spherical, 213
Axial distribution on circle, 69
  See von Mises type axial distribution
Axial distribution on sphere, 233–236
  See Bingham, Dimroth–Watson
    distributions
Axial symmetry = antipodal symmetry,
  72, 233
Axial tests, parametric, see von Mises-
  type, angular and axial, Bing-
  ham, Dimroth–Watson distributions
  non-parametric, 210, 211
    circular tests adapted, 210
    Example, 211
Azimuth, 214

340

INDEX OF NOTATION

A notation is followed by a brief indication of its meaning and then by the number of the page where its definition appears in the text. Population and sample characteristics are distinguished by using Greek and Roman letters respectively.

Greek

α: first cosine moment, 44

$\alpha_p, \bar{\alpha}_p$: pth raw and central cosine moments, 44

β: first sine moment, 44

$\beta_p, \bar{\beta}_p$: pth raw and central sine moments, 44

$\gamma_1{}^0, \gamma_2{}^0$: skewness and kurtosis, 74

δ: deviation from the true mean direction

θ: circular random variable

$\theta_1, \ldots, \theta_n$: random sample, 19

$\theta_{(1)}, \ldots, \theta_{(n)}$: linear order statistics, 171

θ^*: random variable on $(0, 2\pi/l)$

κ: concentration parameter, 61

λ: likelihood ratio statistic, $\max L_0/\max L_1$, L likelihood

μ_0: mean direction, 45

$\mu_p{}', \mu_p$: pth raw and central trigonometric moment, 44

$\mu_p{}^0$: direction of the pth resultant, 44

ξ_0: circular median, 28

ρ: resultant length, 45

ρ_p: length of the pth resultant, 44

σ_0: circular standard deviation, 74

$\phi_n(R^2)$: p.d.f. of R^2 under uniformity, 94

ϕ_p: circular characteristic function, 41

$\bar{\psi}(\rho, \Phi)$: polar characteristic function, 83

SPHERE

Roman

$B(\kappa)$: $\coth \kappa - \kappa^{-1}$, 245

$c(\kappa)$: normalizing constant in the Fisher p.d.f. of θ, 229

$F\{(\lambda, \mu, \nu), \kappa\}$: Fisher distribution with mean direction (λ, μ, ν) and concentration parameter κ, 228

$h_n(R)$: density of R under uniformity, 240

$L' = (l, m, n)$: random vector of direction cosines, 212

$(\bar{l}_0, \bar{m}_0, \bar{n}_0)$: direction cosines of the mean direction, 218

(l_i, m_i, n_i): ith observation on (l, m, n)

R: the resultant length, 218

R_x, R_y, R_z: x, y, z, components of the resultant, 219

S^*: spherical variance, 219

T: matrix of sums of squares and products of the (l_i, m_i, n_i), 212

t_1, t_2, t_3: eigen vectors of T

$(\bar{x}_0, \bar{y}_0)$: spherical polar co-ordinates of the mean direction, 221

Greek

δ: deviation from the true mean direction

(θ, ϕ): spherical polar co-ordinates, colatitude and latitude, 213

(θ_i, ϕ_i): ith observation on (θ, ϕ)

κ: concentration parameter, 234

(λ, μ, ν): direction cosines of the mean direction, 227

λ_r: rth power cosine moment of θ, 227

(μ_0, ν_0): spherical co-ordinates of the mean direction, 228

ρ: the resultant length of θ, 227

$(\rho, \bar{\psi})$: polar distance and polar angle, 215

τ_1, τ_2, τ_3: eigen values of T

$\bar{\tau}_i$: τ_i divided by the sample size